Contents

3 Devices for Display and Interaction

4 Future Interfaces

5 Applications and Tools

6 Online Communities

7 Foundations for Interaction

8 The Business/Academia/Research/Government Axis

9 Invited Authors

Frontiers of Human-Centered Computing, Online Communities and Virtual Environments

Springer
London
Berlin
Heidelberg
New York
Barcelona
Hong Kong
Milan
Paris
Singapore
Tokyo

Rae Earnshaw, Richard Guedj,
Andries van Dam and John Vince (Eds)

Frontiers of Human-Centered Computing, Online Communities and Virtual Environments

 Springer

Rae A. Earnshaw
Department of Electronic Imaging and Media Communications,
University of Bradford, Bradford BD7 1DP

Richard A. Guedj
Institut National des Télécommunications, France

Andries van Dam
Department of Computer Science, Watson Center for Information
Technology, Brown University, Providence, RI 02912, USA

John A. Vince
School of Media Arts and Communication, Bournemouth University,
Poole BH12 5BB

ISBN 1-85233-238-7 Springer-Verlag London Berlin Heidelberg

British Library Cataloguing in Publication Data
Frontiers of human-centred computing, online communities
    and virtual environments
    1.Human-computer interaction 2.Computer networks 3. Virtual
    reality
    I.Earnshaw, R. A. (Rae A.)
    004'.019

ISBN 1852332387

Library of Congress Cataloging-in-Publication Data
A catalog record for this book is available from the Library of Congress

Typesetting: Ian Kingston Editorial Services, Nottingham, UK
Printed and bound at the Athenæum Press Ltd., Gateshead, Tyne and Wear
34/3830-543210 Printed on acid-free paper SPIN 10747874

List of Contributors

Kozo Akiyoshi
Monolith Co Ltd
1-7-3 Azabu-juban
Minato-ku
Tokyo
106-0045 Japan
Email:
kozo@monolith-prime.co.jp

Nobuo Akiyoshi
Monolith Co Ltd
1-7-3 Azabu-juban
Minato-ku
Tokyo
106-0045 Japan
Email:
nobu@monolith-prime.co.jp

Daniel Andler
University of Paris X
Nanterre
France
Email:
andler@poly.polytechnique.fr

Josephine Anstey
Electronic Visualization
Laboratory (EVL)
University of Illinois at Chicago
851 S. Morgan St.
Room 1120
Chicago
IL 60607-7053
USA
Email:
jranstey@acsu.buffalo.edu

David Arnold
School of Information Systems
University of East Anglia
Norwich NR4 7TJ
UK
Email:
arnold@sys.uea.ac.uk

Niels Ole Bernsen
Natural Interactive Systems
Laboratory
Odense University
Science Park 10
5230 Odense M
Denmark
Email:
nob@nis.sdu.dk

Jehan Bing
Computer Human Interaction
Center (CHIC!)
SRI International
333 Ravenswood Avenue
Menlo Park
CA 94025
USA
Email:
jehan.bing@sri.com
Home page:
http://www.chic.sri.com/

Mike Bogucki
Electronic Visualization
Laboratory (EVL)
University of Illinois at Chicago
851 S. Morgan St.
Room 1120
Chicago
IL 60607-7053
USA
Email:
mbogucki@evl.uic.edu

Judith R. Brown
The University of Iowa
Iowa City
Iowa 52242
USA
Email:
judy-brown@uiowa.edu

Maxine Brown
Electronic Visualization
Laboratory (EVL)
University of Illinois at Chicago
851 S. Morgan St.
Room 1120
Chicago
IL 60607-7053
USA
Email:
maxine@evl.uic.edu

Christoph Busch
Fraunhofer Institute for
Computer Graphics (IGD)
Rundeturmtr. 6
D-64283 Darmstadt
Germany
Email:
busch@igd.fhg.de

Adam Cheyer
Computer Human Interaction
Center (CHIC!)
SRI International
333 Ravenswood Avenue
Menlo Park
CA 94025
USA
Email:
adam.cheyer@sri.com
Home page:
http://www.chic.sri.com/

Greg Dawe
Electronic Visualization
Laboratory (EVL)
University of Illinois at Chicago
851 S. Morgan St.
Room 1120
Chicago
IL 60607-7053
USA
Email:
dawe@evl.uic.edu

Tom DeFanti
Electronic Visualization
Laboratory (EVL)
University of Illinois at Chicago
851 S. Morgan St.
Room 1120
Chicago
IL 60607-7053
USA
Email:
tom@uic.edu

Rae Earnshaw
Dept of Electronic Imaging and
Media Communications
University of Bradford
Bradford BD7 1DP
UK
Email:
R.A.Earnshaw@bradford.ac.uk

José L. Encarnação
Fraunhofer Institute for
Computer Graphics (Fraunhofer-
IGD)
Rundeturmstr. 6
D-64283 Darmstadt
Germany
Email:
jle@igd.fhg.de
Home page:
http://www.igd.fhg.de/

Steven Feiner
Department of Computer Science
Columbia University
New York
USA
Email:
feiner@cs.columbia.edu

Thomas A. Furness
Human Interface Technology
Laboratory
University of Washington
Seattle
WA 98195
USA
Email:
tfurness@u.washington.edu
Home page:
http://www.hitl.washington.edu/

Richard A.Guedj
Institut National des
Telecommunications
France

and

University of Bradford
Bradford
BD7 1DP
UK
Email:
R.Guedj@bradford.ac.uk
Richard.Guedj@wanadoo.fr

Véronique Havelange
Université de Technologie de
Compiègne
Département Technologie et
Sciences de l'Homme
Centre Pierre Guillaumat
BP 60319
60206 Compiègne Cedex
France
Email:
veronique.havelange@utc.fr
havelang@ext.jussieu.fr

Bertram Herzog
University of Michigan
Ann Arbor
MI 48109
USA
Email:
bherzog@crcg.edu

and

Fraunhofer CRCG
321 South Main Street
Providence
RI 02903
USA
Email:
bherzog@crcg.edu
Home page:
http://www.crcg.edu/company/
staff/bherzog.php3

Thomas S. Huang
Beckman Institute for Advanced
Science and Technology
University of Illinois at Urbana-
Champaign
405 N. Mathew Ave.
Urbana
IL 61801
USA
Email:
huang@ifp.uiuc.edu

Mikael Jern
Advanced Visual Systems
15 Blokken
DK 3460
Birkeroed
Denmark
E-mail:
mikael@avs.dk

Andy Johnson
Electronic Visualization
Laboratory (EVL)
University of Illinois at Chicago
851 S. Morgan St.
Room 1120
Chicago
IL 60607-7053
USA
Email:
aej@evl.uic.edu

Luc Julia
Computer Human Interaction
Center (CHIC!)
SRI International
333 Ravenswood Avenue
Menlo Park
CA 94025
USA
Email:
luc.julia@sri.com
Home page:
http://www.chic.sri.com/

Simon Julier
ITT Systems and Sciences/
Advanced Information
Technology Division
Naval Research Laboratory
Washington
DC 20375-5337
USA
Email
julier@ait.nrl.navy.mil

Thomas Kirste
Fraunhofer-Institute for
Computer Graphics
Joachim-Jungius Str. 11
D-18059 Rostock
Germany
Email:
kirste@rostock.igd.fhg.de

Charles Koelbel
Advanced Computational
Research
National Science Foundation
4201 Wilson Boulevard
Arlington
VA 22230
USA
Email:
ckoelbel@nsf.gov

Tosiyasu L. Kunii
Faculty of Computer and
Information Sciences
Hosei University
3-7-2 Kajino-co
Koganei City
Tokyo 184-8584
Japan
Email:
kunii@k.hosei.ac.jp
Home page:
http://www.kunii.com

and

Monolith Co., Ltd
1-7-3 Azabu-juban
Minato-ku
Tokyo
106-0045 Japan
Email:
tosi@monolith-prime.co.jp

David Leevers
VERS Associates
Cranbrook House
37 Beacon Way
Rickmansworth WD3 2PF
UK
Email:
David.Leevers@VERS.co.uk
Home page:
http://www.vers.co.uk/
dleevers.htm

Sakaki Morishita
Monolith Co Ltd
1-7-3 Azabu-juban
Minato-ku
Tokyo
106-0045 Japan
Email:
sakaki@monolith-prime.co.jp

S. P. Mudur
National Centre for Software
Technology
Juhu
Mumbai 400 049
India
Email:
mudur@saathi.ncst.ernet.in

William Newman
Xerox Research Centre Europe
61 Regent Street
Cambridge CB2 1AB
UK
Email:
wnewman@xrce.xerox.com

Dave Pape
Electronic Visualization
Laboratory (EVL)
University of Illinois at Chicago
851 S. Morgan St.
Room 1120
Chicago
IL 60607-7053
USA
Email:
pape@evl.uic.edu

Jenny Preece
Information Systems
Department
University of Maryland
Baltimore County
1001 Hilltop Circle
Baltimore
MD 21250
USA
Email:
Preece@umbc.edu
Home page:
http://www.ifsm.umbc.edu/
~preece/

Lawrence Rosenblum
Advanced Information
Technology Division
Naval Research Laboratory
Washington
DC 20375-5337
USA
Email:
rosenblu@ait.nrl.navy.mil

Dan Sandin
Electronic Visualization
Laboratory (EVL)
University of Illinois at Chicago
851 S. Morgan St.
Room 1120
Chicago
IL 60607-7053
USA
Email:
dan@evl.uic.edu

Jürgen Schönhut
Fraunhofer-IGD
Rundeturmstr. 6
D-64283 Darmstadt
Germany
Email:
juergen.schoenhut@igd.fhg.de

Ben Shneiderman
Department of Computer Science
Human-Computer Interaction
Laboratory
Institute for Advanced Computer
Studies & Institute for Systems
Research
University of Maryland
College Park
MD 20742
USA
Email:
ben@cs.umd.edu

Bernard Stiegler
Institur National de L'Audivisuel
94366 Bry-sur-Marne cedex
France
Email:
Stiegler.bernard@wanadoo.fr

Daniel Thalmann
Computer Graphics Lab
EPFL
CH 1015 Lausanne
Switzerland
Email:
thalmann@lig.di.epfl.ch
Home page:
http://ligwww.epfl.ch/

John C. Thomas
IBM T. J. Watson Research
PO Box 704
Yorktown Heights
New York 10598
Email:
jcthomas@us.ibm.com

Matthew Turk
Microsoft Research
One Microsoft Way
Redmond
WA 98052
USA
Email:
mturk@microsoft.com

Andries van Dam
Watson Center for Information
Technology
Brown University
Providence
RI 02912
USA
Email:
avd@cs.brown.edu

John A. Vince
School of Media Arts and
Communication
Talbot Campus
Fern Barrow
Poole BH12 5BB
UK
Email:
jvince@bournemouth.ac.uk

Turner Whitted
Microsoft Research
One Microsoft Way
Redmond
WA 98052
USA
Email:
jtw@microsoft.com

Turner Whitted
Microsoft Research
One Microsoft Way
Redmond
WA 98052
USA

Email:
jtw@microsoft.com

Introduction

Rae Earnshaw and John A. Vince

1 Introduction

The US President's Information Technology Advisory Committee (PITAC) recently advised the US Senate of the strategic importance of investing in IT for the 21st century, particularly in the areas of software, human–computer interaction, scalable information infrastructure, high-end computing and socioeconomic issues [1].

Research frontiers of human–computer interaction include the desire that interaction be more centered around human needs and capabilities, and that the human environment be considered in virtual environments and in other contextual information-processing activities. The overall goal is to make users more effective in their information or communication tasks by reducing learning times, speeding performance, lowering error rates, facilitating retention and increasing subjective satisfaction. Improved designs can dramatically increase effectiveness for users, who range from novices to experts and who have diverse cultures with varying educational backgrounds. Their lives could be made more satisfying, their work safer, their learning easier and their health better. Research areas that need to be addressed include:

- High-level content descriptions and their access, such as metadata and MPEG7
- Reducing cognitive load and providing more scope for creativity
- Cross-disciplinary interaction and how to make it work
- Handling interaction in specific social contexts and with cultural differences
- Dealing with universality and the problems of the differently-abled
- Interaction styles and their implications
- Consistency of cognition models across information appliances
- Paradigms for emerging new kinds of interaction; beyond WIMP interfaces: multimodal and perceptual user interfaces
- Challenges for virtual environment technology and interfaces
- Usability issues and measuring the effectiveness of symbiosis
- Design and evaluation of online communities for intranet and Internet

- Scaling online communities to support millions of people
- Universal access, social and ethical issues

2 Joint European and US Initiatives

A recent joint European Commission/National Science Foundation Workshop was set up to examine these research issues in more detail. This joint Workshop was set up under the auspices of the Joint European Commission/National Science Foundation Strategy Group, which had its first meeting, in Budapest, on 3–4 September 1998. The meeting derived from a joint collaboration agreement between the EC and NSF in August 1998, signed by Dr George Metakides (Director, Information Technologies, EC) and Professor Juris Hartmanis (Director, CISE, NSF). The collaboration aims to facilitate the joint development of knowledge and applications in key emerging science and technology areas of mutual interest. Successful cooperation holds the promise of more cost-effective investment of research funds in the USA and the European Union.

National initiatives in the USA and many European countries are recognizing the benefits to scientific research in supporting larger groupings, often with interdisciplinary teams of researchers. It is possible to achieve results with a national grouping that it is not possible to achieve on the same time-scale with an institutional one. This model has also been used for a number of years by the European Commission to facilitate research and development in European countries, and to accomplish faster technology transfer to European industry by corporate participation in projects. These initiatives have recently been extended to include non-European partners on a self-funded basis. Collaborative links have also been established with Japan. It is clear that with the increasing globalization of research and development there is a need for companies to develop products that are viable in world markets. Thus what is being proposed by the EC and NSF is a logical extension of existing paradigms for securing significant progress in key research areas.

It was felt desirable to arrange a series of research Workshops to enable early identification of key research challenges and opportunities in information technology. It was intended that each Workshop should bring together eminent scientists and technologists in the USA and Europe in the area being addressed, and that the themes would emanate from the research community.

At the meeting of the Joint EC/NSF Strategy Group on 3–4 September, a number of possible themes were identified. These included "human-centered computing and virtual environments", "large-scale scientific databases" and "intelligent implants". Scientists on this Strategy Group included: Prof. Andy van Dam (Brown University, USA), Prof. Paul Messina (California Institute of Technology, USA), Prof. Rae Earnshaw (University of Bradford, UK), Prof. Giorgio Baccarani (University of Bologna, Italy), Prof. Rolf Eckmiller (University of Bonn, German) and Prof. Gilles Kahn (Inria, France).

It was agreed that the first joint research Workshop should concentrate on the themes of human-centered computing and virtual environments. Human centered computing is perceived as an area of strategic importance because of the move towards greater decentralization and decomposition in the location and provision of computation. The area of virtual environments is an area where increased collaboration should facilitate more rapid progress in solving some of the more intractable problems in building effective applications. It is intended that further Workshops should follow this one, either on separate topics or on specific issues arising out of this first Workshop.

The results and recommendations from the Workshop are intended to inform the process of collaboration between the EC and the NSF on the development of mechanisms to support international level collaborative research and to identify optimal areas in which cooperation could take place. These results are also being circulated to the community for discussion and comment. This present summary is one such dissemination of the information. More detailed summaries will be made available in further documents and articles, and this book contains the material considered at the Workshop.

3 Research Recommendations

3.1 Virtual Environments and Human-Centered Computing

Although virtual environments and human-centered computing are rather different areas, it proved to be very useful to have researchers joining together to consider the issues on the lines of continuum between the two areas. Virtual environments face challenges, especially in the areas of display technology, interaction methodologies, update rates and collaboration between users in different geographic locations. A mobile augmented reality environment is challenged by portability issues, devices, interfaces and communications. It is difficult to make computing human-centered with standardized technology such as keyboards and mice, impedance mismatches, and the current shift towards ubiquity. As a result of this ubiquity, the computation is incorporated in mobile devices or embedded in the infrastructure or the environment, rather than in a particular desktop device with which the user can interact. There are challenges in steering technological innovation towards meeting human needs, in ensuring that the results of empirical research are useful to designers and in orienting the system developer to think more in terms of the human user. Output devices can range between the two extremes of light-emitting polymers for coating wallpaper (for large-scale, wall-sized displays) and small-scale retinal displays, where the image is focused directly on the retina.

3.2 Diversity of Technology and Users

The current diversity of the field, such as in displays, is both a challenge and an opportunity. Current developments in technology and content generation, and the rapid rise of new uses and applications, require diverse kinds of interdisciplinary

expertise in order to exploit the technology effectively. There is a diversity of technology (hardware, software and networking), a diversity of users (especially in
areas where technology has not yet made significant inroads) and an increasing gap
between what users know and what they need to know to use current systems effectively. All this bears testimony to tools and systems being technology-driven rather
than user-driven. Much more attention needs to be given to end-to-end design and
integrating the needs of the user from the very beginning. Critical parameters in the
design and evaluation process need to be much more firmly identified, quantified
and rigorously upheld. Research is needed in this area.

3.3 Research Integration

The wide range of expertise available at the Workshop enabled us to recognize the
challenge of diversity and seek to address it. It was agreed that the breadth of the
field is not being taken into account by current research. The experts in converging
areas are not working together, and research programs are not getting the right
kind of interdisciplinary expertise, or support, to give added-value integration.
Indeed, the need for a greater degree of integration and greater attention to
scalability pervaded many of the research issues highlighted at the Workshop.

3.4 Multiple Disciplines

One important area of future work is the behavior of individuals and communities
in their relationship to each other and to the world. There is a long history of educational, psychological, social psychological and sociological studies, but methodological innovations are needed to capture and understand the complex nature of
individual and group behaviors that occur while using technology. Analytic and
descriptive studies can provide useful insights, but there is a strong need for more
prescriptive outcomes that can guide designers of new technologies. Guidelines are
available for basic user interface design, and these need to be extended to accommodate new technologies. In addition, validated metrics, user surveys, task taxono-
mies, ethnographic methods of observation, participatory design methods,
usability testing strategies, expert review techniques and software development
methodologies would all help produce more orderly development processes for
new technologies. Social impact statements prepared in advance of implementations could facilitate broad discussions of critical technologies and thereby minimize the number and severity of unanticipated side effects.

Understanding community relationships becomes even more critical when it is a
community of users interacting in a shared world or information space, such as on
the World Wide Web. The interface needs to be appropriate to the task to be
performed, the social behavior of the user (or groups of users), and the maintenance of relationships. Research programs should be developed in this area.

Strong encouragement should be given for universities to support multi
disciplinary activities and to reform traditional computer science departments so

that they include a human-centered approach throughout their research and educational programs. A specific suggestion for moving the center of gravity in this direction would be to fund graduate fellowships in human-centered systems.

3.5 Pure and Applied Research

The resistance to a full recognition of the value of interdisciplinary research was felt to reside in both funding bodies and academia. Academia prefers promotion criteria that emphasize "pure" science, with elegant solutions being derived for somewhat arbitrary intellectual problems; funding bodies promote research areas recommended by scientific peer groups in the same tradition. This roadblock to interdisciplinary research must be overcome. Currently academia is losing many valuable people to industry simply because industry is paying them to do the kind of exciting and meaningful research they are unable to do in academia and get tenure. There is a lack of synchronization between academia, the changing nature of the world and the research needed to shed light on important current issues.

Much stronger promotion of evaluation and empirical testing of systems in the context of work is needed. This evaluation and testing should be both controlled and ethnographic, in the laboratory and in the field. The needs, requirements and behavior of the users, as well as the range of problems they need to solve, should be considered. Progress in VR, online communities, universal usability and other user-centered areas will be dramatically increased if the funders insist on some form of assessment.

3.6 Key Application Drivers

Problems to be solved can be key drivers in the domain. These represent in some sense "pull" requirements from the user that need to be considered alongside the more normal "push" technology from the vendors. The Working Group that considered the agenda for collaboration between industry, academia and government proposed the "Content" age as the key driver for 2010. Content is needed for human media technology, augmented reality, digital story telling, interactive broadcasting and multimedia workspaces. Indeed, the whole nature of the human–computer interface may move away from one operating on a model of sequential task definition and processing. The new human–computer interface could operate on a model of behavior, context, cultural background, information awareness and imagination, namely "storytelling" at the interface, thus drawing on its own values of context and history.

A working model and methodology is needed for the Content Age. The technology should be user-centered and mobile with new types of interaction technology and information display. Three key application domains have requirements for this technology:

- Health and continuing medical education (both doctors and patients)
- Environment
- Cultural heritage

It is proposed that a follow-up Workshop should be organized on this theme with content experts, perceptualization experts and representatives of potential funding sources from governments and industry. The objective would be to stimulate and integrate government and academic research agendas in this area.

3.7 The Networked Community

Current developments in online communities present a major strategic opportunity for the information technology (IT) community. This is another key application driver. Although the nature of these new communities is not well understood, because of their rapid growth, they have the potential for changing the world, especially in the developing countries.

As the community moves towards the "million person interface" what will the needs and requirements of the community be, and how should they be supported? How can multi-cultural and multilingual requirements be handled and represented? These are complex and difficult challenges, and there is an opportunity to make a significant impact on the world stage.

Universality need not imply a loss of functionality for particular domains and applications, nor should it be seen necessarily as "lowest common denominator" IT. However, the global nature of the online communities phenomenon does present a major strategic opportunity for governments to collaborate on research in this area – thus benefitting from the pooling of expertise from different cultures, backgrounds, and countries.

3.8 A Taxonomy of Human-Centered Systems

An initial taxonomy for human-centered computing in the context of virtual environments was produced. This provides a framework for an understanding of multi-channel input and output, the skills of the user, the particular technology selected for a task and the task to be performed (whether simple or complex). A foreground and background task model is proposed, and it highlights two key issues for the future:

- How to get foreground and background to assist each other
- How to increase the effective contribution of the background (i.e. to make the computer more aware of the user's context, needs and requirements at any point in time).

4 Additional Activity in Europe, Acknowledgements, Bibliography

The Issues highlighted and uncovered at the Workshop are exciting and challenging. They are also complex and require much research. However, the benefits can be substantial. We have proposed areas where future research is needed, and we also made specific recommendations on follow up actions to this Workshop.

The following information is a brief summary of the current priorities of the funding agencies in Europe.

Framework 5

The European Commission's Framework 5 program in 1999 (http://www.cordis.lu/fp5/) has initiated a number of Key Actions as follows:

Key Action 1: Systems and services for the citizen

Key Action 2: New methods of work and e-commerce

Key Action 3: Multimedia content and tools

Key Action 4: Essential technologies and infrastructures

One of the main foci is enhancing the user-friendliness of the Information Society by means of the following:

- improving the accessibility, relevance and quality of public services, especially for the disabled and elderly
- empowering citizens as employees, entrepreneurs and customers
- facilitating creativity and access to learning
- helping to develop a multilingual and multi-cultural society
- ensuring universally available access and the intuitiveness of next generation interfaces
- encouraging design-for-all

A second focus is on integration and convergence across information processing, communication and media. This is reflected in Key Action 1 in its support of new models of public service provision, in Key Action 2 in the context of new workplace tools and commerce systems, in Key Action 3 in linking interactive publishing with cultural heritage, and in Key Action 4 in convergent infrastructure technology developments.

A third focus is on the globalization of cooperation in research and technology development.

UK Foresight Program

The UK government's Foresight program is seeking to identify opportunities in markets and technologies that will enhance the nation's prosperity and quality of life. The panel on Information Communications and Media has produced a Forward Look paper that seeks to identify the technologies required to support the future Information Society.

Further information is at http://www.foresight.gov.uk/.

UK EPSRC

The UK's Engineering and Physical Sciences Research Council has initiated a program of Interdisciplinary Research Collaborations to link together information technology and other appropriate research disciplines, with a strong involvement of users. This is primarily due to the issues expected in this area in the future. A large increase in variety, numbers and usage of mobile information artefacts in a global information space will result in problems to do with interfacing to different kinds of appliance, and the creation of virtual environments and multimedia applications.

Acknowledgments

We express our thanks and appreciation to the European Commission and the National Science Foundation for co-sponsoring the Workshop. We are also grateful to the following organizations for support and assistance: Brown University, University of Bradford, Fraunhofer IGD, INT, and the British Computer Society.

This introduction was brought together by amalgamating the reports of the Working Groups at the Workshop, and we would like to fully acknowledge the contributions of all the participants.

References

[1] http://www.ccic.gov/.
[2] An NSF Workshop produced a special issue of *Behaviour & Information Technology*, 12(2), March–April 1993.
[3] A useful Canadian policy document that thoughtfully deals with Universal Access: http://www.fis.utoronto.ca/research/iprp/ua/.
[4] A SIGGRAPH agenda document that deals with graphics and user interfaces: http://www.siggraph.org/othercom/whitepaperGII.html and http://www.siggraph.org/pub-policy/.
[5] *Virtual Reality: Scientific and Technological Challenges*, National Research Council Report, 1995: http://www.nap.edu/.
[6] An NSF Workshop on "Human Centred Systems", 17–19 February 1997. This has many useful position papers and recommendations from four working groups: http://www.ifp.uiuc.edu/nsfhcs/.
[7] *More than Screen Deep – Toward Every-Citizen Interfaces to the Nation's Infrastructure*, National Research Council Report, 1997: http://www.nap.edu/readingroom/books/screen/index.html.
[8] *Modeling and Simulation: Linking Entertainment and Defense*, National Research Council Report, 1997: http://www.nap.edu/readingroom/books/modeling/.
[9] The Unpredictable Certainty: White Papers, in *Internetwork Infrastructure Requirements for Virtual Environments*, National Academy Press, 1998, pp 110–122; http://www.nap.edu/books/0309060362/html/110.html.
[10] The following document is a recent publication outlining a basic taxonomy of approaches to VR with special consideration to their affordances to support collaborative work, both same-place and remote: http://www.siggraph.org/publications/newsletter/v32n4/contributions/buxton2.html.

[11] Funding a Revolution: Government Support for Computing Research, in *Virtual Reality Comes of Age*, National Academy Press, 1999, pp. 226–249; http://www.nap.edu/books/0309062780/html/226.html.

[12] *The PITAC Report*, a recent and influential US Presidential Information Technology Advisory Council Report: http://www.ccic.gov/ac/report/.

[13] J Preece (2000) *Online Communities: Supporting Sociability and Designing Usability*, John Wiley & Sons, Chichester.

Virtual Environments

1

Virtual Environments: a Review

John A. Vince

Abstract

This chapter examines how the flight simulation industry prepared the way for today's VE systems, and examines why their design still presents such a technological challenge. Several critical issues facing VE systems are identified (technology, breadth of applications, geometry, system complexity, interaction modalities, physical simulation and system cost), which are discussed briefly with appropriate examples. Although no solutions are proposed to what, in some cases, are apparently insurmountable problems, topics of future research are identified to progress the design of future VEs.

1.1 Introduction

Ivan Sutherland's landmark paper "The Ultimate Display" (Sutherland, 1965) described how, one day, the computer would provide a window into virtual worlds. In 1968 Sutherland built a head-mounted display (HMD) that presented to the user left and right views of a computer-generated 3D scene, such that the user's head movements caused corresponding spatial changes in the images. In just over a decade, Evans & Sutherland Corporation were manufacturing image generators (IGs) that created real-time images of virtual landscapes for use in flight simulators. Figure 1.1 shows an image from an E&S IG, and reveals the high level of realism found in a contemporary military flight simulator.

Prior to IGs, scale model boards of generic airports were used as an image source, in conjunction with a servo-controlled video camera (Vince, 1995). These physical models had many drawbacks: they were very large (10 m × 3 m), they were static, they required large levels of illumination, they could not support weather effects, they depicted a limited geographical region, they were unique structures, and each airport required a discrete model. With the advent of computer-generated imagery (CGI) it became possible to simulate large areas of 3D terrain, at a virtual level, that supported dynamic objects, weather effects, time of day/year illumination and collision detection.

Figure 1.1 Real-time textured scene from an E&S IG. (Image courtesy of Evans & Sutherland Computer Corporation, Salt Lake City, Utah, USA.)

Although virtual environments (VEs) resolved many problems associated with model boards, they introduced a new set of problems, such as dynamic level-of-detail, photo-realism, latency, low-polygon modeling, shadows, 3D trees and software tools for converting real-world terrain into surface topology.

For two decades the flight simulation industry has successfully pioneered the use of VEs in both military and commercial simulators, and created an industry that integrates several state-of-the art technologies. Figure 1.2 shows a Boeing 737-800 simulator manufactured by Thomson Training & Simulation. Its immersive nature hides the complexity of the underlying technology, which includes a motion platform, force feedback controls, instrumentation, collimated panoramic display, real-time IG, 3D surround sound, weather models, touch-activated training environment, and simulated radar and navigation systems.

In the late 1980s virtual reality systems surfaced as an emerging technology and their designers rediscovered many of the issues already known to the flight simulation community. And because these VR systems employed general-purpose computers and low-cost displays, problems of latency, field of view, scene complexity, immersion etc. were aggravated to such a degree that few industries were convinced that there was a long-term future for these systems.

Head-mounted displays were a constant problem and introduced serious issues of hygiene, nausea, ergonomics, cost, efficiency, immersion etc. Furthermore, over

Figure 1.2 A Boeing 737-800 simulator. (Image courtesy of Thomson Training & Simulation Ltd.)

the past decade the unique importance of a first-person view has given way to the advantages of screen-based displays offered by CAVEs, panoramic screens, virtual tables and domes. Today, VR is no longer dominated by the need for a single person to be immersed within a VE. There is a need for systems where several people can simultaneously visualize and interact with complex 3D databases – hence the success of screen-based systems that cater for groups of individuals (Figure 1.3).

Although HMDs still play a useful role in VEs, there is a consensus that a VE system can embrace any computer graphics system supporting real-time interaction, which implies that VEs can range from real-time computer games consoles to hemispherical multi-channel dome displays.

Historically, CGI has been applied across a wide range of application areas that include animation, computer games, simulation, CAD, image processing, visualization, graphics, medical imaging etc. Due to this wide range of applications, many strategies have been adopted to meet their specific individual needs. For instance, computer animation software has evolved such that unique tools are available to model and animate 3D objects (Vince, 1992). Computer game algorithms have also been developed to support real-time animation of textured low-polygon models. A totally separate range of software tools exists to support the visualization of complex datasets (Brown *et al.*, 1995). Similarly, VEs have been applied across a wide range of application areas and their designers have encountered a corresponding range of issues that have no apparent simple solution. For example, a VE system used to visualize industrial CAD databases cannot be used to support a laparoscopic surgical simulator, and the modeling tools used in flight simulation have little relevance to Internet-based VEs. In CAD and flight simulation

Figure 1.3 Screen-based VE system. (Image courtesy of Trimension Ltd.)

applications, for example, geometry is rigid and sometimes articulated, while in medical applications the surface geometry is flexible and may have to respond to a gravitational field and support complex, dynamic modification. Furthermore, the GUI tools vary dramatically from one application to another.

The Internet has also introduced another application for VEs: online 3D VEs, where a user downloads 3D geometry and interacts with it locally. VRML (Virtual Reality Modeling Language) has been developed to support this application, which has introduced another layer of system definition to add to the growing complexity.

1.2 The Critical Issues

There are several critical issues facing designers of VE systems: technology, breadth of applications, geometry, system complexity, interaction modalities, physical simulation and system cost.

1.2.1 Technology

Generally, VEs comprise a range of sophisticated technologies that include digital processors, audio processors, parallel-processing architectures, 3D tracking, haptic feedback mechanisms, displays and human–machine interfaces. These are by no means trivial technologies, and what is most confusing to any potential buyer is that the technologies are developing at such a pace that a specific VR configuration may only be commercially viable for about two years.

The increase in processor speeds shows no sign of leveling off. Today, twin-processor PCs easily outperform graphic workstations that one or two years ago cost many times the price of a modern PC. And over the next few years, micropro-cessor manufacturing processes will advance to such an extent that even real-time ray tracing will become a reality. Furthermore, multiprocessing architectures will make it easier to support the parallel activities of rendering, interaction, simula-tion, display, collision detection and audio.

Tracking the user's head and hand created many of the latency problems associated with early VR systems. System latency was responsible for unworkable interfaces and nausea, and was why VE systems were shunned by industry. Today, latency times have improved, although there is still room for further improvement. But another associated problem is update rate. The flight simulation industry has always maintained that real time meant real time – i.e. video rate. If a display system was refreshed at 50 Hz, the update rate should at least equal this. Unfortu-nately, the update rate of VE systems varies from 1 Hz upwards, which is distracting to the point of being unusable. No doubt this will improve with processor perfor-mance, but one can anticipate that as processor performance increases, so too will model complexity, which could effectively cancel any apparent advantage. This has a parallel in computer animation, where the rendering time for a single image has remained relatively constant for 15 years, in spite of all the technological advances that have occurred.

Fortunately, no single solution is required for real-time tracking. A variety of solu-tions are needed to resolve the individual needs of specific applications. Mechan-ical devices, which are simple, accurate and virtually latency free, are very effective in medical applications, such as surgical simulators. But where a user's head and hand have to be monitored over a large volume of space, magnetic or optical systems provide a solution. However, both technologies are far from perfect.

Haptic feedback interfaces are currently a luxury for any VE system, and can only be afforded by applications, such as flight simulation, where they play a vital role in the user interface. Figure 1.4 shows an internal view of a simulator cockpit where the flight controls return realistic forces to the pilots. It would be unthinkable for a full flight simulator to operate without such an interface, as flight control forces communicate important cues concerning the status of flight surfaces and the landing gear. The technology behind this interface is accurate, robust and expen-sive, and remains unique to this sector.

At the other end of the training spectrum, such as a low-cost surgical simulator (Figure 1.5), force feedback is still a prerequisite, but problems of size, accuracy and cost raise a totally new set of technological issues.

Display technology has developed considerably over the past decade, and today VE systems can incorporate HMDs, shutter glasses, CRTs, screens, BOOMs, virtual tables, CAVEs and domes. Figure 1.6 shows typical examples.

Such a wide range of technologies creates a corresponding range of display issues, such as size, level of immersion, field of view, flicker, resolution, collimation, stereopsis and cost.

Figure 1.4 Internal view of a flight simulator showing the central flight controls fitted with haptic feedback. (Image courtesy

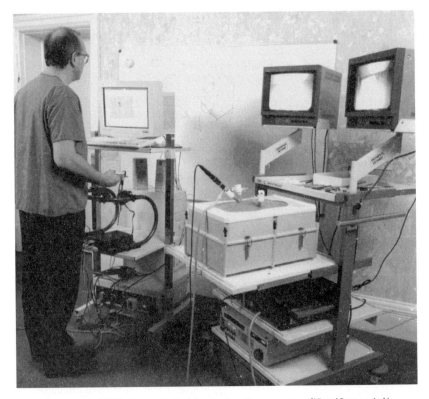

Figure 1.5 The MIST keyhole surgical training simulator. (Image courtesy of Virtual Presence Ltd.)

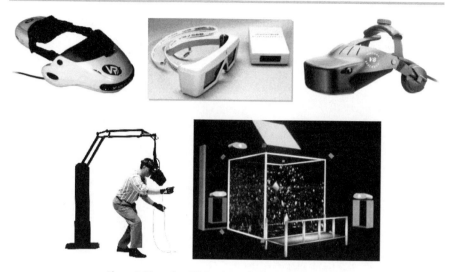

Figure 1.6 Examples of HMDs, shutter glasses, BOOM and a CAVE.

1.2.2 Interaction Modalities

Early VR systems incorporated a tracked glove for user interaction, but the 3D mouse quickly became a preferred interaction device. Nevertheless, in spite of the success of the 3D mouse, glove-based systems are still required to support accurate interactions with a database. Furthermore, as new applications have emerged for VE systems, especially in the area of servicing mechanical structures, it has become evident that the user's hand is insufficient to represent the user within the VE. The user's arm, or, in some cases, the complete body, is required to simulate accurately issues of physical access and the ability to withdraw components without interfering with other objects.

One solution to this problem has been to place a virtual mannequin within the VE, under the direct control of the user (Figures 1.7 and 1.8). Collision detection can then be monitored between the entire mannequin and the database.

When this type of investigation is undertaken using an HMD the user requires access to an efficient tool-set for controlling the mannequin. Currently, such interfaces are very limited and require considerable experience to achieve any reasonable level of efficiency.

We have considerable experience in the design and use of screen-based GUIs such as the one shown in Figure 1.9, but we are only beginning to appreciate the complexity of interfacing a human operator with a real-time VE. This, perhaps, presents one of the greatest challenges for designers of VEs.

Figure 1.7 Transom Jack being used to assess user access to a confined space. (Image courtesy Transom Corporation.)

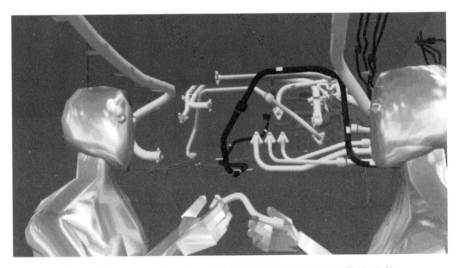

Figure 1.8 Two mannequins passing a database component. (Image courtesy Division Ltd.)

1.2.3 Geometry

VEs are used to visualize and interact with virtually every dataset that has a computer representation, which includes polygons, surface patches, NURBS, particles, voxels, implicit objects, height fields etc. Very often, though, such data have to be converted into a polygonal form due to the constraints imposed by the VE

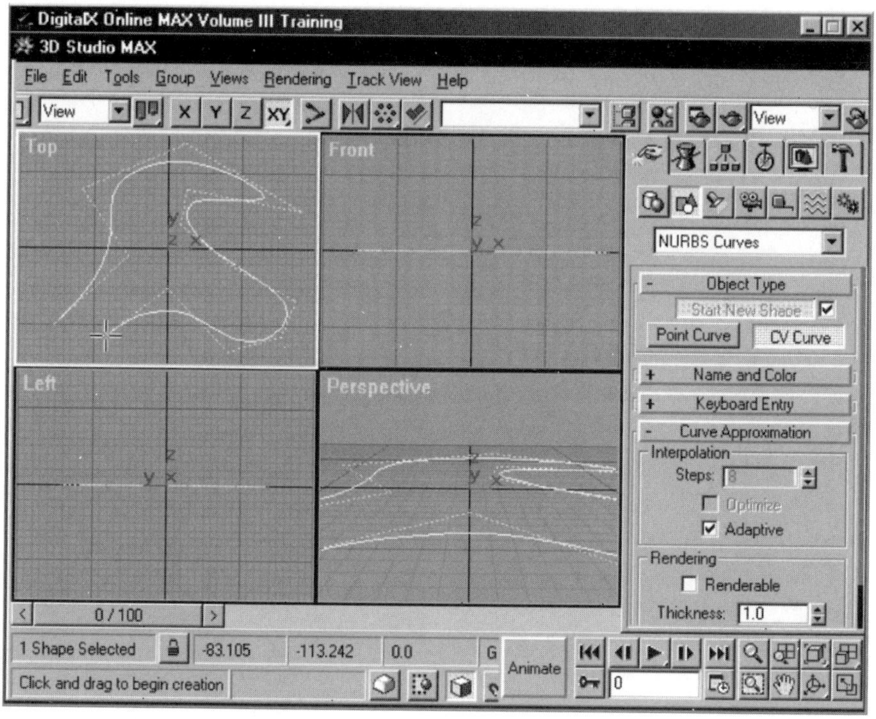

Figure 1.9 The GUI for modeling NURBS in 3D Studio MAX. (Image courtesy DigitalX.)

rendering environment – a process which introduces erroneous geometric anomalies. Furthermore, real-world geometric databases are often highly complex and can easily exceed the rendering capacity of any real-time IG. Dynamic level of detail – where a database is modeled at various levels of detail – is a strategy that enables large databases to be rendered in real time. But this is a task that has been introduced by the shortcomings of today's technology, and hopefully will eventually disappear.

1.2.4 Physical Simulation

A major challenge for any real-time system is simulating real-world behaviors such as multiple object collisions, gravitational and electromagnetic fields, physical constraints, soft objects, liquids, gases, deformations etc., most of which are readily simulated using conventional computer animation techniques (Vince, 1992). Simple behaviors such as collisions and some deformations are features of existing VEs (Vince, 1995), and considerable programming effort is needed to support the real-time animation of articulated structures.

Figure 1.10 shows a CAD model of an excavator, which has been enhanced with extra information that allows the cabin controls to activate the excavator within its normal working envelope. This is an excellent example of how CAD benefits from

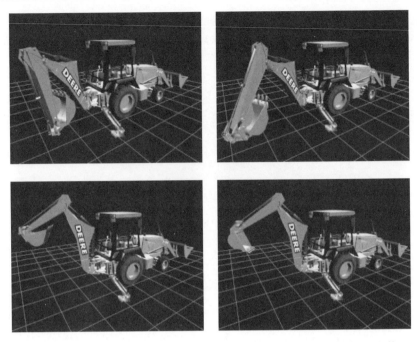

Figure 1.10 Four views of an excavator simulating a digging manoeuvre. (Image courtesy Division Ltd.)

the features offered by a VE system, and in fact identifies a major application for VEs. Eventually, CAD will subsume VE processes as a natural part of the computer-aided design methodology.

1.2.5 System Complexity

Many of the technologies associated with VEs are individually complex. But a VE requires them to operate in unison, with the levels of accuracy and efficiency that industry expects from any other technology. Integrating these technologies has been a major challenge to the relatively small companies pioneering the design of VE systems, and it is no surprise that it has taken so long to develop viable systems. We still have not reached a point where industry can purchase an off-the-shelf VE system that can be interfaced easily with other computer-based processes. It still requires painstaking configuration and technical support to keep the simplest simple operating. This is not unreasonable, given the circumstances surrounding the history of VE systems.

1.2.6 Applications

As mentioned above, the range of applications for VEs is extremely broad, and covers everything from a simple Internet system to large screen-based display

Figure 1.11 Caister Murdoch gas compression platform using Cadcentre's Review Reality System. (Image courtesy of Conoco/Brown & Root.)

systems for visualizing CAD models of offshore platforms (Figure 1.11). This breadth of applications is another major challenge for designers of VE systems, for although hardware can be configured to support different applications, software is application-specific, and requires an in-depth knowledge of the subject area. Take, for example, the problem of configuring a computer animation system. Five years ago, it was almost impossible to find such a system that did not include an SGI workstation and work within a Unix environment. Today, with the arrival of high-performance PCs and the Windows NT operating system, alternative configurations are available, where software has been suitably redesigned. This relatively simple transition has taken a lot of time for an industry that understands its own subject area.

Compare this with the problems facing the designers of VE systems, whose task is to develop software tools for a technology that is not only changing in front of them, but which spans such a wide range of applications. It is daunting, if not impossible. A VE should provide a software environment where system features can be interfaced to a wide variety of application software packages. This in itself is no trivial process, and must also engage the companies supplying the individual application software.

1.2.7 System Cost

Early VR systems were no more than toys, but to the detriment of the VR industry they were masqueraded as solutions to real industrial problems. Today, there are still few real users of VE systems in the world – and those that do exist are employed as simple display systems for exploring relatively simple visualization problems.

Most small companies cannot afford to integrate incomplete technologies into commercial processes driven by small profit margins and global markets, which is why VE systems have been widely ignored by this sector. Fortunately, though, larger corporations can afford to include VEs into R&D programmes, and, where possible, have introduced the technology into experimental commercial scenarios. In particular, the automotive and offshore platform industries are investigating how VEs can play a viable role in their design processes.

1.3 The Future of VEs

The flight simulation industry has successfully exploited VEs for many years, and has reacted to the changes in technology with great care. Improvements in processor speed resulted in a corresponding increase in database complexity and scene realism. But previous customers could not be left behind using multi-million dollar systems designed to last for ten years or more, which were becoming increasingly obsolete with every passing year. Upgrade paths were designed to provide them with cost-effective ways of keeping abreast with technological developments and system enhancements.

The only way this could operate was within a sector that could absorb the high costs of simulators and their maintenance. But what really made it possible was the legal requirement for pilots to be assessed every six months. The aviation industry had no choice but to make VEs work.

One cannot ignore the fact that it has taken three decades to perfect CAD systems to such a point that even the smallest component is worth designing and manufacturing with computer-based systems. And it is unreasonable to expect the advantages promised by VEs to be realized in just a few years. Furthermore, a VE cannot exist as an isolated technology – it requires careful interfacing to existing CAD systems to provide a seamless design environment. The long-term benefits are enormous, and industry can look forward to a design scenario where the following will be the norm:

- visualizing prototype engineering concepts
- assessing servicing and maintenance strategies
- simulating the interaction of assemblies
- simulating the dynamic properties of articulated structures
- simulating and visualizing stress analysis
- distributed product development management
- simulating manufacturing processes
- collaborative engineering on large AEC projects
- machining and pressing simulation
- concurrent engineering
- training personnel
- evaluating ergonomic issues

Today, however, there are real applications for VE systems and include the support and visualization of large CAD databases, automotive concept cars, maintenance issues of jet engines, large architectural projects, and simulators for training and familiarizing personnel with complex interiors such as aircraft, submarines, and space stations. These are all large commercial sectors that can reap the benefits of realistic 3D visualization. Eventually, VEs will replace the need to build physical mock-ups of engineering projects designed using CAD. But this is still some way in the future.

1.4 Conclusion

Ivan Sutherland's original concept of creating 3D virtual worlds within a computer is already thirty years old, and we have only just completed the 'proof of concept' stage with an exciting vision of the future. The next stage, which has already begun, requires the CAD sector to extend their systems to incorporate the necessary interfaces to VE systems. This is no mean task, but one that has to be borne by the CAD sector.

Fortunately, many of the features listed above as potential advantages of future VE systems already exist, albeit as discrete processes. But a VE provides the opportunity to integrate the processes of design (CAD), manufacture (CAM), stress analysis (FEA), simulation (CFD) and interactive visualization (VE) into one environment.

Industrial use of VEs is just one application, but represents a sector that can quickly realize the obvious benefits. Other sectors, such as medicine, education, military, entertainment and service-based industries, must be prepared to develop systems that satisfy their unique requirements. There are bound to be problems that span several sectors, which will be resolved by the adoption of mutually acceptable standards.

A continuous program of research is vital to develop new interfaces, new ways of representing large geometric databases, new display technologies, new interactive modes, new ways of visualizing complex datasets and new algorithms for simulating physical behaviors, and to understand how the emerging disciplines of AI, parallel processing and the Internet can be successfully exploited.

References

Brown, JR, Earnshaw, RA, Jern, M and Vince, JA (1995) *Visualization: Using Computer Graphics to Explore Data and Present Information*, John Wiley & Sons, New York.
Sutherland, IE (1965) The ultimate display. *Proceedings of the IFIP Congress*, 2, 506–508.
Vince, JA (1992) *3D Computer Animation*, Addison-Wesley, Wokingham.
Vince, JA (1995) *Virtual Reality Systems*, Addison-Wesley, Wokingham.

About the Author

Professor John Vince is Head of Computer Animation at the National Centre for Computer Animation, Bournemouth University, UK. Prior to taking up this academic post in 1995, he was Chief Scientist at

Thomson Training & Simulation, manufacturers of commercial and military flight simulators. Prior to this appointment, he spent 16 years at Middlesex University working in computer graphics. He has written and co-edited 20 books on computer graphics, computer animation, virtual reality and digital media. He is a co-founder of the Virtual Reality Society and an Editor-in-Chief of the *Virtual Reality Journal*.

2

The Role of Virtual Humans in Virtual Environment Technology and Interfaces

Daniel Thalmann

Abstract

The purpose of this chapter is to show the importance of virtual humans in Virtual Reality and to identify the main problems to solve to create believable virtual humans.

2.1 Introduction

The ultimate reason for developing realistic-looking virtual humans is to be able to use them in virtually any scene that re-creates the real world. However, a virtual scene – beautiful though it may be – is not complete without people virtual people, that is. Scenes involving virtual humans imply many complex problems we have been solving for several years [1]. With the new developments of digital and interactive television [2] and multimedia products, there is also a need for systems that provide designers with the capability for embedding real-time simulated humans in games, multimedia titles and film animations. In fact, there are many current and potential applications of human activities that may be part of a VR system involving virtual humans:

- simulation-based learning and training (transportation, civil engineering etc.)
- simulation of ergonomic work environments
- virtual patients for surgery, plastic surgery
- orthopedy and prostheses and rehabilitation
- plastic surgery
- virtual psychotherapies
- architectural simulation with people, buildings, landscapes, lights etc.

Figure 2.1 Virtual humans.

- computer games involving people and "Virtual Worlds" for Lunaparks/casinos
- game and sport simulation
- interactive drama titles in which the user can interact with simulated characters and hence be involved in a scenario rather than simply watching it.

Mainly, however, telepresence is the future of multimedia systems and will allow participants to share professional and private experiences, meetings, games and parties. Virtual humans (Figure 2.1) have a key role to play in these shared Virtual Environments and true interaction with them is a great challenge. Although a lot of research has been going on in the field of Networked Virtual Environments, most of the existing systems still use simple embodiments for the representation of participants in the environments. More complex virtual human embodiment increases the natural interaction within the environment. The users' more natural perception of each other (and of autonomous actors) increases their sense of being together, and thus the overall sense of shared presence in the environment.

However, the modeling of virtual humans is an immense challenge as it requires us to solve many problems in various areas. Table 2.1 shows the various aspects of research in Virtual Human Technology. Each aspect will be detailed and the problems to solve will be identified.

2.2 Face and Body Representation

Human modeling is the first step in creating virtual humans. For heads, although it is possible to create them using an interactive sculpting tool, the best way is to reconstruct them from reality. Three methods have been used for this:

1. Reconstruction from 2D photos [3]
2. Reconstruction from a video sequence [4]
3. Construction based on laser technology

Table 2.1 Aspects of research in virtual humans

Face and body representation

Avatar functions

Motion control

High-level behavior

Interaction with objects

Intercommunication

Interaction with user

Collaborative Virtual Environments

Crowds

Rendering

Standards

Applications

These methods could also be used for body modeling, but the main problem is still body deformations, which has been addressed by many researchers but is still not 100% solved.

Four methods of dealing with facial expressions in Networked VEs are possible: video-texturing of the face, model-based coding of facial expressions, lip movement synthesis from speech, and predefined expressions or animations. Believable facial emotions are still very hard to obtain.

Main problem to solve: realistic body and face construction and deformations

2.3 Avatar Functions

The avatar representation fulfills several important functions:

1. the visual embodiment of the user
2. means of interaction with the world
3. means of sensing various attributes of the world

It becomes even more important in multi-user Networked Virtual Environments [5], as participants' representations are used for communication. Avatar representation in NVEs has crucial functions in addition to those of single-user virtual environments [6,7]:

1. perception (to see if anyone is around)
2. localization (to see where the other person is)
3. identification (to recognize the person)
4. visualization of the other's interest focus (to see where the person's attention is directed)
5. visualization of the other's actions (to see what the other person is doing and what is meant through gestures)

6. social representation of self through decoration of the avatar (to know what the other participant's task or status is)

Using articulated models for avatar representation fulfills these functionalities with realism, as it provides the direct relationship between how we control our avatar in the virtual world and how our avatar moves relative to this control, allowing the user to use his or her real-world experience. We chose to use complex virtual human models, aiming for a high level of realism, but articulated "cartoon-like" characters could also be well suited to express ideas and feelings through the non-verbal channel in a more symbolic or metaphoric way.

Main problem to solve: easy way of directing an avatar

2.4 Motion Control

The main goal of computer animation is to synthesize the desired motion effect, which is a mixing of natural phenomena, perception and imagination. The animator designs the object's dynamic behavior with a mental representation of causality. The animator imagines how it moves, gets out of shape or reacts when it is pushed, pressed, pulled or twisted. So the animation system has to provide the user with motion control tools able to translate the user's wishes from his or her own language.

In the context of virtual humans, a Motion Control Method (MCM) specifies how the virtual human is animated and may be characterized according to the type of information it privileged in animating this virtual human. For example, in a keyframe system for an articulated body, the privileged information to be manipulated is the angle. In a forward dynamics-based system, the privileged information is a set of forces and torques; of course, in solving the dynamic equations, joint angles are also obtained in this system, but we consider these to be derived information. In fact, any MCM will eventually have to deal with geometric information (typically joint angles), but only geometric MCMs explicitly privilege this information at the level of animation control.

Many MCMs have been proposed: motion capture, keyframe, inverse kinematics, dynamics, walking models, grasping models etc. However, no method is perfect and only a combination or blend of methods can provide good and flexible results.

Main problem to solve: flexible reuse, combination and parameterization of existing movements

2.5 High-Level Behavior

Autonomous virtual humans should be able to have a behavior, which means they must have a manner of conducting themselves. Typically, the virtual human should perceive the objects and the other virtual humans in the environment through virtual sensors [8]: visual, tactile and auditory sensors. Based on the perceived information, the actor's behavioral mechanism will determine the actions that it will perform. An actor may simply evolve in its environment or it may interact with this environment or even communicate with other actors. In this latter case, we will consider the actor as an interactive perceptive actor.

Virtual vision [9,10] is a main information channel between the environment and the virtual actor. The virtual human perceives its environment from a small window in which the environment is rendered from its point of view. As it can access the depth values of the pixels, the color of the pixels and its own position, it can locate visible objects in its 3D environment. To recreate a virtual audition, as a first step we must model a sound environment in which the virtual human can directly access positional and semantic sound source information for an audible sound event. Virtual tactile sensors may be based on spherical multisensors attached to the articulated figure. A sensor is activated for any collision with other objects. These sensors could be integrated in a general methodology for automatic grasping.

A high-level behavior in general uses sensorial input and special knowledge. A way of modeling behaviors is to use an automaton approach. Each actor has an internal state which can change at each time step according to the currently active automaton and its sensorial input. Abstraction mechanisms to simulate intelligent behaviors have been discussed in the AI (Artificial Intelligence) and AA (Autonomous Agents) literature. Several methods have been introduced to model learning processes, perceptions, actions, behaviors etc. in order to build more intelligent and autonomous virtual agents.

Main problem to solve: development of very complex believable behaviors.

2.6 Interaction with Objects

The need to model interactions between an object and a virtual human agent (hereafter just referred to as an agent), appears in most applications of computer animation and simulation. Such applications encompass several domains, such as virtual autonomous agents living and working in virtual environments, human factors analysis, training, education, virtual prototyping and simulation-based design. A good overview of such areas is presented by Badler [11]. An example of an application using agent–object interactions is presented by Johnson *et al.* [12], whose purpose is to train equipment usage in a populated virtual environment.

Commonly, simulation systems perform agent–object interactions for specific tasks. Such an approach is simple and direct, but most of the time the core of the system needs to be updated whenever one needs to consider another class of objects.

To overcome such difficulties, a natural approach is to include, within the object description, more useful information than just the object's intrinsic properties. Some proposed systems already use this kind of approach. In particular, object-specific reasoning [13] creates a relational table to inform object purpose and, for each object-graspable site, the appropriate hand shape and grasp approach

Figure 2.2 Interaction with objects.

direction. This set of information may be sufficient to perform a grasping task (eg Figure 2.2), but more information is needed to perform different types of interaction.

Another interesting method is to model general agent–object interactions based on objects containing interaction information of various kinds: intrinsic object properties, information on how to interact with it, object behaviors, and also expected agent behaviors. The smart object approach, introduced by Kallmann and Thalmann [14], [15] extends the idea of having a database of interaction information. For each object modeled, we include the functionality of its moving parts and detailed commands describing each desired interaction by means of a dedicated script language. A feature modeling approach [16] is used to include all the desired information in objects. A graphical interface program permits the user to specify different features in the object interactively and to save them as a script file.

Main problem to solve: make the virtual human learn how to interact with objects

2.7 Intercommunication

Behaviors may also be dependent on the emotional state of the actor. Non-verbal communication is concerned with postures and their indications on what people are feeling. Postures are the means to communicate and are defined by a specific position of the arms and legs and angles of the body (Figure 2.3). This non-verbal communication is essential to drive the interaction between people with or without contact.

What gives real substance to face-to-face interaction in real life, beyond speech, is the bodily activity of the interlocutors, the way they express their feelings or

Figure 2.3 Intercommunication.

thoughts through the use of their body, facial expressions, tone of voice etc. Some psychological researchers have concluded that more than 65% of the information exchanged during a face-to-face interaction is expressed through non-verbal means [17]. A VR system that has the ambition to approach the fullness of real-world social interactions and to offer its participants the possibility of achieving high-quality and realistic interpersonal communication must address this point; and only realistic embodiment makes non-verbal communication possible.

2.8 Interaction with the User

Real people are of course easily aware of the actions of the virtual humans through VR tools like head-mounted displays, but one major problem to solve is to make the virtual actors conscious of the behavior of the real people. Virtual actors should sense the participants through their virtual sensors. Such a perceptive actor would be independent of each VR representation and could in the same manner communicate with participants and other perceptive actors. Perceptive actors and participants may easily be independent. For virtual audition, we encounter the same problem as in virtual vision. The real-time constraints in VR demand fast reaction to sound signals and fast recognition of the semantic it carries. For interaction between virtual humans and real ones, gesture recognition will be a key issue. As an example, Boulic *et al.* [18] produced a fight between a real person and an autonomous actor. The motion of the real person is captured using a flock of birds. The gestures are recognized by the system and the information is transmitted to the virtual actor who is able to react to the gestures and decide which attitude to do.

Main problem to solve: development of a complete real-time vision-based recognition

2.9 Specific Problems of Networked Virtual Environments

Inserting virtual humans in the NVE is a complex task [5]. The main issues are:

1. Selecting a scalable architecture to combine these two complex systems
2. Modeling the virtual human with a believable appearance for interactive manipulation
3. Animating it with a minimal number of sensors to have maximal behavioral realism
4. Investigating different methods of decreasing the networking requirements for exchanging complex virtual human information

In particular, controlling the virtual human with limited input information is one of the main problems. For example, a person using a mouse will need extra input techniques or tools to exploit the functionalities of his or her embodiment. In this chapter, we survey the tools that help a user with desktop VR configuration. We do not consider full tracking of the body using magnetic trackers, although this approach can be combined with limited tracking of the participant's arms.

Main problems to solve: controlling a realistic virtual human with limited input information, minimizing the information to be transmitted.

2.10 Crowds

An accepted definition of a crowd (Figure 2.4) is of a large group of individuals in the same physical environment, sharing a common goal (eg people going to a rock concert or a football match). The individuals in a crowd may act in a different way than when they are alone or in a small group [19].

Figure 2.4 Crowds.

Although sociologists are often interested in crowd effects arising from social conflicts or social problems [20] the normal behavior of a crowd can also be studied when no changes are expected.

There are, however, some other group effects relevant to our work which are worth mentioning. Polarization occurs within a crowd when two or more groups adopt divergent attitudes, opinions or behavior, and they may argue or fight even if they do not know each other. In some situations the crowd, or a group within it, may seek an adversary. The sharing effect is the result of influences by the acts of others at the individual level. "Adding" is the name given to the same effect when applied to the group. Domination happens when one or more leaders in a crowd influence the others.

Our goal [21] is to simulate the behavior of a collection of groups of autonomous virtual humans in a crowd. Each group has its general behavior [22] specified by the user, but the individual behaviors are created by a random process through the group behavior. This means that there is a trend shared by all individuals in the same group because they have a pre-specified general behavior.

Main problem to solve: define collective behaviors while keeping individualities

2.11 Rendering

Rendering and animating in real-time a multitude of articulated characters presents a real challenge and few hardware systems are up to the task. Up to now little research has been conducted to tackle the issue of real-time rendering of numerous virtual humans. However, due to the growing interest in collaborative virtual environments the demand for numerous realistic avatars is becoming stronger.

There exist various techniques to speed up the rendering of a geometrical scene. They roughly fall into three categories: culling, geometric level of detail and image-based rendering, which encompasses the concept of image caching. They all have in common the idea of reducing the complexity of the scene while retaining its visual characteristics.

Geometric level of detail (LOD) attempts to reduce the number of rendered polygons by using several representations of decreasing complexity of an object. At each frame the appropriate model or resolution is selected. Typically the selection criterion is the distance to the viewer, although the object motion is also taken into account (motion LOD) in some cases. The major hindrance to using LOD is related to the problem of multi-resolution modeling, that is to say the automatic generation from a 3D object of simpler, coarser 3D representations that bear as strong a resemblance as possible to the original object.

Because 3D chips were not affordable, or did not even exist, in the 1980s, video game characters, human-like or not, were then represented with 2D sprites. A sprite can be thought of as a block of pixels and a mask. The pixels give the color information of the final 2D image, while the mask corresponds to a binary transparency channel. Using sprites, a human figure could easily be integrated into the decor. As more computing power became available in the 1990s, the video game industry

Figure 2.5 Use of impostors.

shifted towards 3D. However, the notion of sprites can also be used in the context of 3D rendering. This has been successfully demonstrated with billboards, which are basically 3D sprites, used for rendering very complex objects like trees or plants. In our opinion, image-based rendering can also be used in the case of virtual humans by relying on the intrinsic temporal coherence of the animation. Current graphics systems rarely take advantage of temporal coherence during animation, yet changes from frame to frame in a static scene are typically very small, which can obviously be exploited [23]. This still holds true for moving objects, such as virtual humans, providing the motion remains slow in comparison with the graphics frame rate. Aubel and Thalmann [24] propose an approach to accelerated rendering of moving, articulated characters, which could easily be extended to any moving and/or self-deforming object. The method is based on impostors (Figure 2.5), a combination of traditional level-of-detail techniques and image-based rendering, and relies on the principle of temporal coherence. It does not require special hardware (except texture mapping and Z-buffering capabilities, which are commonplace on high-end workstations nowadays) though fast texture paging and frame buffer texturing are desirable for optimal performance.

Main problems to solve: introduction of LOD for animation, integration with impostor technology

2.12 Standards

Currently, a number of standardization efforts are continuing to solve different aspects of representing virtual humans in NVEs. Among them, the most significant efforts are MPEG-4 Face and Body Animation (FBA) [25] and VRML 2.0 Humanoid Animation (H-Anim) [26] specifications. The VRML 2.0 H-Anim group attempts to define a standard humanoid that can be exchanged between different users, or programs. The MPEG-4 FBA group aims at streaming virtual human bodies and faces with very low bit rates (less than 10 kbit/s for the whole body).

Main problem to solve: defining standards for high-level behaviors of autonomous virtual humans

2.13 Areas of Application

We may identify several areas [27] where autonomous virtual humans are essential:

Virtual people for Inhabited Virtual Environments. Their role is very important in virtual environments with many people, such as virtual airports or even virtual cities. In the next few years we will see a lot of humanoids or virtual humans in many applications. These virtual humans will be more and more autonomous. They will also tend to become intelligent.

Virtual substitutes. A virtual substitute is an intelligent computer-generated agent able to act instead of the real person and on behalf of this person on the network. The virtual substitute has the voice of the real person and his or her appearance. He or she will appear on the screen of the workstation/TV, communicate with people, and have predefined behaviors planned by the owner to answer to the requests of the people.

Virtual medical assistance. Nowadays it seems very difficult to imagine an effective solution for chronic care without including the remote care of patients at home by a kind of virtual medical doctor. The modeling of virtual patients with corresponding medical images is also a key issue and a basis for telesurgery.

2.14 Conclusions and Recommendations

Telepresence is the future of multimedia systems and will allow participants to share professional and private experiences, meetings, games and parties. The concepts of Distributed Virtual Environments are a key technology to implement this telepresence. The use of humanoids within the shared environment is an essential supporting tool for presence. Real-time realistic 3D avatars will be essential in the future, but we will need interactive perceptive actors to populate the virtual worlds. The ultimate objective in creating realistic and believable virtual actors is to build intelligent autonomous virtual humans with adaptation, perception and memory. These actors should be able to act freely and emotionally. Ideally, they should be conscious and unpredictable. But how far are we from such a ideal situation? Our interactive perceptive actors are able to perceive the virtual world and the people living in this world and in the real world. They may act based on their perception in an autonomous manner. Their intelligence is constrained and limited to the results obtained in the development of new methods of artificial intelligence. However, representation in the form of virtual actors is a way of visually evaluating progress. In the future, we may expect to meet intelligent actors able to learn or understand a few situations.

References

[1] N Magnenat Thalmann and D Thalmann (1991) Complex models for animating synthetic actors, *IEEE Computer Graphics and Applications*, 11(5), 32–44.

[2]   N Magnenat Thalmann and Thalmann D. (1995) Digital actors for interactive television, *Proc. IEEE, Special Issue on Digital Television*, Part 2, 1022–1031.

[3]   WS Lee and N Magnenat-Thalmann (1998) Head modeling from pictures and morphing in 3D with image metamorphosis based on triangulation, in *Modelling and Motion Capture Techniques for Virtual Environments*, Berlin, Springer-Verlag.

[4]   P Fua, R Plankers and D Thalmann (1999) From synthesis to analysis: fitting human animation models to image data, *Proc. CGI '99*, IEEE Computer Society Press.

[5]   TK Capin, IS Panzic, N Magnenat-Thalmann and D Thalmann (1999) *Avatars in Networked Virtual Environments*, Chichester, John Wiley & Sons.

[6]   TK Capin, IS Panzic, N Magnenat-Thalmann and D Thalmann (1997) Virtual human representation and communication in VLNET networked virtual environment, *IEEE Computer Graphics and Applications*, March.

[7]   SD Benford *et al.* (1997) Embodiments, avatars, clones and agents for multi-user, multi-sensory virtual worlds, in *Multimedia Systems*, Berlin, Springer-Verlag.

[8]   D Thalmann (1995) Virtual sensors: a key tool for the artificial life of virtual actors, in *Proc. Pacific Graphics '95*, Seoul, Korea, August, pp. 22–40.

[9]   O Renault, N Magnenat Thalmann and D Thalmann (1990) A vision-based approach to behavioural animation, *The Journal of Visualization and Computer Animation*, 1(1), 18–21.

[10] X Tu and D Terzopoulos (1994) Artificial fishes: physics, locomotion, perception, behavior, in *Proc. SIGGRAPH '94, Computer Graphics*, pp. 42–48.

[11] NN Badler (1997) Virtual humans for animation, ergonomics, and simulation, in *IEEE Workshop on Non-Rigid and Articulated Motion*, Puerto Rico, June.

[12] WL Johnson and J Rickel (1997) Steve: an animated pedagogical agent for procedural training in virtual environments, *Sigart Bulletin*, 8(1–4), 16-21.

[13] L Levison (1996) Connecting planning and acting via object-specific reasoning, *PhD Thesis*, Department of Computer & Information Science, University of Pennsylvania.

[14] M Kallmann and D Thalmann (1998) Modeling objects for interaction tasks, in *Proc. Eurographics Workshop on Animation and Simulation*, Berlin, Springer-Verlag.

[15] M Kallmann and D Thalmann (2000) A behavioral interface to simulate agent–object interactions in real-time, in *Proc. Computer Animation '99*, IEEE Computer Society Press (to appear).

[16] JJ Shah and M Mäntylä (1995) *Parametric and Feature-Based CAD/CAM*, Chichester, John Wiley & Sons.

[17] M Argyle (1988) *Bodily Communication*, New York, Methuen.

[18] L Emering, R Boulic and D Thalmann (1998) Interacting with virtual humans through body actions, *IEEE Computer Graphics and Applications*, 18(1), 8–11.

[19] ME Roloff (1981) *Interpersonal Communication – The Social Exchange Approach*. London, Sage.

[20] JS McClelland (1989) *The Crowd and The Mob*, Cambridge, Cambridge University Press.

[21] SR Musse, C Babski, T Capin and D Thalmann (1998) Crowd modelling in collaborative virtual environments, in *ACM VRST '98*, Taiwan.

[22] SR Musse and D Thalmann (1997) A model of human crowd behavior: group inter-relationship and collision detection analysis, in *Proc. Workshop of Computer Animation and Simulation of Eurographics '97*, Budapest, September.

[23] G Schaufler and W Stürzlinger (1996) A three dimensional image cache for virtual reality, in *Proc. Eurographics '96*, pp. C-227–C-234.

[24] A Aubel, R Boulic and D Thalmann (1998) Animated impostors for real-time display of numerous virtual humans, in *Proc. Virtual Worlds '98*, Paris, September.

[25] MPEG-N1902, Text for CD 14496-2 Video, ISO/IEC JTC1/SC29/WG11 N1886, MPEG97/November 1997.

[26] H-Anim, http://ece.uwaterloo.ca/~h-anim/spec.html.

[27] D Thalmann, L Chiariglione, F Fluckiger, EH Mamdani, M Morganti, J Ostermann, J Sesena, L Stenger and A Stienstra (1997) *Report on Panel 6: From Multimedia to Telepresence, Expert groups in Visionary Research in Advanced Communications*, ACTS, European Commission.

3

Perceptual User Interfaces

Matthew Turk

Abstract

For some time, graphical user interfaces (GUIs) have been the dominant platform for human–computer interaction. The GUI-based style of interaction has made computers simpler and easier to use, especially for office productivity applications where computers are used as tools to accomplish specific tasks. However, as the way we use computers changes and computing becomes more pervasive and ubiquitous, GUIs will not easily support the range of interactions necessary to meet users' needs. In order to accommodate a wider range of scenarios, tasks, users and preferences, we need to move toward interfaces that are natural, intuitive, adaptive and unobtrusive. The aim of a new focus in HCI, called Perceptual User Interfaces (PUIs), is to make human–computer interaction more like how people interact with each other and with the world. This chapter describes the emerging PUI field and then reports on three PUI-motivated projects: computer vision-based techniques to visually perceive relevant information about the user.

3.1 Introduction

Recent research in the sociology and psychology of how people interact with technology indicates that interactions with computers and other communication technologies are fundamentally social and natural [1]. That is, people bring to their interactions with technology attitudes and behaviors similar to those which they exhibit in their interactions with one another. Current computer interfaces, however, are primarily functional rather than social, used mainly for office productivity applications such as word processing. Meanwhile, the world is becoming more and more "wired" – computers are on their way to being everywhere, mediating our everyday activities, our access to information and our social interactions [2,3]. Rather than being used as isolated tools for a small number of tasks, computers will soon become part of the fabric of everyday life.

Table 3.1 shows the progression of major paradigms in human–computer interaction (HCI). Historically, there was initially no significant abstraction between users (at that time only programmers) and machines – people "interacted" with computers by flipping switches or feeding a stack of punch cards for input, and

Table 3.1 The evolution of user interfaces

Era	Paradigm	Implementation
1950s	None	Switches, wires, punched cards
1970s	Typewriter	Command-line interface
1980s	Desktop	GUI/WIMP
2000s	*Natural interaction*	*PUI (multimodal input and output)*

reading LEDs or getting a hard copy printout for output. Later, interaction was focused on a typewriter metaphor – command line interfaces became commonplace as interactive systems became available. For the past 10 or 15 years, the desktop metaphor has dominated the landscape – almost all interaction with computers is done through WIMP-based graphical interfaces (using windows, icons, menus and pointing devices).

In recent years, people have been discussing post-WIMP [4] interfaces and interaction techniques, including such pursuits as desktop 3D graphics, multimodal interfaces, tangible interfaces, virtual reality and augmented reality. These arise from a need to support natural, flexible, efficient and powerfully expressive interaction techniques that are easy to learn and use [5]. In addition, as computing becomes more pervasive, we will need to support a plethora of form factors, from workstations to handheld devices to wearable computers to invisible ubiquitous systems. The GUI style of interaction, especially with its reliance on the keyboard and mouse, will not scale to fit future HCI needs.

The thesis of this chapter is that the next major paradigm of HCI, the overarching abstraction between people and technology, should be the model of human–human interaction. *Perceptual user interfaces*, which seek to take advantage of both human and machine perceptual capabilities, must be developed to integrate in a meaningful way such relevant technologies as speech, vision, natural language, haptics and reasoning, while seeking to understand more deeply the expectations, limitations and possibilities of human perception and the semantic nature of human interactions.

3.2 Social Interaction with Technology

In their book *The Media Equation*, Reeves and Nass [1] argue that people tend to equate media and real life. That is, in fact, the "media equation": *media = real life*. They performed a number of studies testing a broad range of social and natural experiences, with media taking the place of real people and places, and found that "individuals' interactions with computers, television, and new media are *fundamentally social and natural*, just like interactions in real life" [1, p. 5]. For example, people are polite to computers and display emotional reactions to technology.

These findings are not limited to a particular type of media nor to a particular type of person. Such interactions are not conscious – although people can bypass the media equation, it requires effort to do so and it is difficult to sustain. This makes sense, given the fact that, during millennia of human existence anything that appeared to be social was in fact a person. The social responses that evolved in this environment provide a powerful, built-in assumption that can explain social responses to technology – even when people know the responses are inappropriate.

This raises the issue of (although does not explicitly argue for) anthropomorphic interfaces, which are designed to appear intelligent by, for example, introducing a human-like voice or face in the user interface (e.g. [6]). Schneiderman [7–9] argues against anthropomorphic interfaces, emphasizing the importance of direct, comprehensible and predictable interfaces which give users a feeling of accomplishment and responsibility. In this view, adaptive, intelligent and anthropomorphic interfaces are shallow and deceptive, and they preclude a clear mental model of what is possible and what will happen in response to user actions. Instead, users want a sense of direct control and predictability, with interfaces that support direct manipulation.

Wexelblat [10] questions this point of view and reports on a preliminary study that fails to support the anti-anthropomorphic argument. The experiment involved users performing tasks presented to them with different interfaces: a "standard" interface and an anthropomorphic interface. In general, the debate on anthropomorphic interfaces has engendered a great deal of (sometimes heated) discussion in recent years among interface designers and researchers. (As Wexelblat writes, "Don't anthropomorphize computers; they hate that!".)

This debate may be somewhat of a red herring. When a computer is seen as a *tool* – e.g. a device used to produce a spreadsheet for data analysis – the anti-anthropomorphic argument appears convincing. Users would not want a humanoid spreadsheet interface to be unpredictable when entering values or calculating sums, for example, or when moving cells to a different column. However, when computers are viewed as *media* or *collaborators* rather than as tools, anthropomorphic qualities may be quite appropriate. Tools and tasks that are expected to be predictable should be so – but as we move away from office productivity applications to more pervasive use of computers, it may well be that the requirements of predictability and direct manipulation are too limiting.

Nass and Reeves write about their initial intuitions [1, p. 6]:

> What seems most obvious is that media are *tools*, pieces of hardware, not players in social life. Like all other tools, it seems that media simply help people accomplish tasks, learn new information, or entertain themselves. People don't have social relationships with tools.

However, their experiments subsequently convinced them that these intuitions were wrong, and that people do not predominately view media as tools.

The growing convergence of computers and communications is a well-discussed trend [11,12]. As we move towards an infrastructure of computers mediating human tasks and human communications and away from the singular model of the computer as a tool, the anti-anthropomorphic argument becomes less relevant. The question becomes, how can we move beyond the current "glorified typewriter" model of human–computer interaction, based on commands and responses, to a more natural and expressive model of interaction with technology?

3.3 The Role of User Interfaces

The role of a user interface is to translate between application and user semantics. In other words, to translate user semantics to applications semantics using some combination of input modes, and to translate application semantics to user semantics using some combination of output modes. When people communication with one another, we have a rich set of modes to use – e.g. speech (including prosody), gesture, touch, non-speech sounds and facial expression. Input modes and output modes are not necessarily distinct, mutually exclusive, and sequential; in real conversations they are tightly coupled. We interrupt one another, nod and shake our heads, look bored, say "uh-huh", and use other backchannels of communication.

To build interfaces that support understanding the semantics of the interaction, we must:

- model user semantics
- model application semantics
- model the context
- understand the constraints imposed by the technology
- understand the constraints imposed by models of human interaction

We also constantly deal with ambiguity in human–human interactions, resolving the ambiguity by either considering the context of the interaction or by active resolution (moving one's head to see better, asking "What?", or "Did you mean him or me?"). Alternatively, current human–computer interfaces try to eliminate ambiguity. To effectively model the semantics of the interaction we must support ambiguity at a deep level and not require a premature resolution of ambiguities.

Understanding and communicating semantics is not just an issue of knowledge representation, but also of interaction techniques. The use of a keyboard, mouse and monitor in the GUI paradigm limits the interaction to a particular set of actions – typing, pointing, clicking etc. This in turn limits the semantic expression of the interface.

The ideal user interface is one that imposes little or no effort or cognitive load on the user, so that the user's intent is communicated to the system without an explicit translation on the user's part into the application semantics and a mapping to the system interaction techniques. As the nature of computing changes from the predominantly desktop office productivity scenario toward more ubiquitous computing environments, with a plethora of form factors and reasons to interact with technology, the need increases for a paradigm of human–computer interaction that is less constraining, more compelling to the non-technical elite, and more natural and expressive than current GUI-based interaction. An understanding of interaction semantics and the ability to deal with ambiguity are vital to meet these criteria. This may help pave the way for the next major paradigm of how people interact with technology – perceptual interfaces modeled after natural human interaction.

3.4 Perceptual User Interfaces

The most natural human interaction techniques are those we use with other people and with the world around us – that is, those that take advantage of our natural sensing and perception capabilities, along with social skills and conventions that we acquire at an early age. We would like to leverage these natural abilities, as well as our tendency to interact with technology in a social manner, to model human–computer interaction after human–human interaction. Such *perceptual user interfaces* [13,14], or PUIs, will take advantage of both human and machine capabilities to sense, perceive and reason. Perceptual user interfaces may be defined as:

> Highly interactive, multimodal interfaces modeled after natural human-to-human interaction, with the goal of enabling people to interact with technology in a similar fashion to how they interact with each other and with the physical world.

The perceptual nature of these interfaces must be bidirectional – i.e. both taking advantage of machine perception of its environment (especially hearing, seeing and modeling people who are interacting with it) and leveraging human perceptual capabilities to communicate with people most effectively (through, for example, images, video and sound). When there is sensing involved, it should be transparent and unobtrusive – users should not be required to don awkward or limiting devices in order to communicate. Such systems will serve to reduce the dependence on proximity that is required by keyboard and mouse systems. They will enable people to transfer their natural social skills to their interactions with technology, reducing the cognitive load and training requirements of the user. Such interfaces will extend to a wider range of users and tasks than traditional GUI systems, since a semantic representation of the interaction can be rendered appropriately by each device or environment. Perceptual interfaces will also leverage the human ability to do and perceive multiple things at once, something that current interfaces do not do well.

Perceptual user interfaces should take advantage of human perceptual capabilities in order to present information and context in meaningful and natural ways. So we need to further understand human vision, auditory perception, conversational conventions, haptic capabilities etc. Similarly, PUIs should take advantage of advances in computer vision, speech and sound recognition, machine learning, and natural language understanding to understand and disambiguate natural human communication mechanisms.

These are not simple tasks, but progress is being made in all these areas in various research laboratories worldwide. A major emphasis in the growing PUI community [13,14] is on integrating these various sub-disciplines at an early stage. For example, the QuickSet system at OGI [15] is an architecture for multimodal integration, and is used for integrating speech and (pen) gesture as users create and control military simulations. Another system for integrating speech and (visual) gesture is described in [16], applied to parsing video of a weather report. Another example of tight integration between modalities is in the budding "speechreading" community [17,18]. These systems attempt to use both visual and auditory information to understand human speech – which is also what people do, especially in noisy environments.

One main reason that GUIs became so popular is that they were introduced as application-independent *platforms*. Because of this, developers could build applications on top of a consistent event-based architecture, using a common toolkit of widgets with a consistent look and feel. This model provided users with a relatively consistent mental model of interaction with applications. Can PUIs provide a similar platform for development? Are there perceptual and social equivalents to atomic GUI events such as mouse clicks and keyboard events? (For example, an event that a person entered the scene, or a user is looking at the monitor or nodding his head.) These and other questions need to be addressed more thoroughly by the nascent PUI community before this new paradigm can have a chance to dislodge the GUI paradigm.

The next section describes a few projects in our lab which emphasize one aspect of perceptual interfaces – using computer vision techniques to visually perceive relevant aspects of the user.

3.5 Vision-Based Interfaces

Present-day computers are essentially deaf, dumb and blind. Several people have pointed out that the bathrooms in most airports are smarter than any computer one can buy, since the bathroom "knows" when a person is using the sink or toilet. Computers, on the other hand, tend to ask us questions when we're not there (and wait 16 hours for an answer) and decide to do irrelevant (but CPU-intensive) work when we're frantically working on an overdue document.

Vision is clearly an important element of human–human communication. Although we can communicate without it, people still tend to spend endless hours traveling in order to meet face to face. Why? Because there is a richness of communication that cannot be matched using only voice or text. Body language such as facial expressions, silent nods and other gestures add personality, trust and important information in human-to-human dialog. We expect that it could do the same in human–computer interaction.

Vision-based interfaces (VBI) are a subfield of perceptual user interfaces which concentrates on developing visual awareness of people. VBI seeks to answer questions such as:

- Is anyone there?
- Where are they?
- Who are they?
- What are the subject's movements?
- What are the subject's facial expressions?
- Are the subject's lips moving?
- What gestures is the subject making?

These questions can be answered by implementing computer vision algorithms to locate and identify individuals, track human body motions, model the head and face, track facial features, interpret human motion and actions. (For a taxonomy and discussion of movement, action and activity, see [19].)

VBI (and, in general, PUIs) can be categorized into two aspects: *control* and *awareness*. Control is explicit communication to the system – e.g. put *that* object *there*. Awareness, picking up information about the subject without an explicit attempt to communicate, gives *context* to an application (or to a PUI). The system may or may not change its behavior based on this information. For example, a system may decide to stop all unnecessary background processes when it sees me enter the room – not because of an explicit command that I issue, but because of a change in its context. Current computer interfaces have little or no concept of awareness. While many research efforts emphasize VBI for control, it is likely that VBI for awareness will be more useful in the long run.

The remainder of this section describes VBI projects to quickly track a user's head and use this for both awareness and control (Section 3.5.1), recognize a set of gestures in order to control virtual instruments (Section 3.5.2), and track the subject's body using an articulated kinematic model (Section 3.5.3).

3.5.1 Fast Simple Head Tracking

In this section we present a simple but fast technique to track a user sitting at a workstation, locate his head, and use this information for subsequent gesture and pose analysis (see [20] for more details). The technique is appropriate when there is a static background and a single user – a common scenario.

First a representation of the background is acquired by capturing several frames and calculating the color mean and covariance matrix at every pixel. Then, as live video proceeds, incoming images are compared with the background model and pixels that are significantly different from the background are labeled as "foreground", as in Figure 3.1b. In the next step, a flexible "drape" is lowered from the top of the image until it smoothly rests on the foreground pixels. The "draping" simulates a row of point masses, connected to each neighbor by a spring – gravity pulls the drape down, and foreground pixels collectively push the drape up (see Figure 3.1e). A reasonable amount of noise and holes in the segmented image is

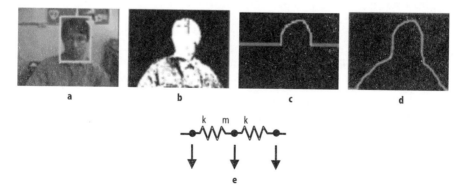

Figure 3.1 a Live video (with head location). **b** Foreground segmentation. **c** Early "draping" iteration. **d** Final "drape". **e** Draping simulates a point mass in each column, connected to its neighbors by springs.

acceptable, since the drape is insensitive to isolated noise. After several iterations, the drape rests on the foreground pixels, providing a simple (but fast) outline of the user, as in Figure 3.1d.

Once the user outline ("drape") settles, it is used to locate the user's head – Figure 3.1a shows the head location superimposed on the live video. All this is done at frame rate in software on a standard low-end PC. The head location can then be used for further processing. For example, we detect the "yes" and "no" gestures (nodding and shaking the head) by looking for alternating horizontal or vertical patterns of coarse optical flow within the head box. Another use of the head position is to match head subimages with a stored set, taken while looking in different directions. This is used to drive a game of Tic-Tac-Toe (Noughts and Crosses), where the head direction controls the positioning of the user's X.

Finally, the shape of the drape (Figure 3.1d) is used to distinguish between a small number of poses, based on the outline of the user. Although limited to the user outline, this can be used for several purposes – for example, to recognize that there is a user sitting in front of the machine, or to play a simple visual game such as Simon Says.

3.5.2 Appearance-Based Gesture Recognition

Recognizing visual gestures may be useful for explicit control at a distance, adding context to a conversation, and monitoring human activity. We have developed a real-time, view-based gesture recognition system, in software, on a standard PC, with the goal of enabling an interactive environment for children [21]. The initial prototype system reacts to the user's gestures by making sounds (e.g. playing virtual bongo drums) and displaying animations (e.g. a bird flapping its wings along with the user).

The algorithm first calculates dense optical flow by minimizing the sum of absolute differences (SAD) to calculate disparity. Assuming the background is relatively static, we can limit the optical flow computation time by only computing the flow for pixels that appear to move. So we first do simple three-frame motion detection, then calculate flow at the locations of significant motion. Once the flow is calculated, it is segmented by a clustering algorithm into 2D elliptical "motion blobs." See Figure 3.2 for an example of the segmented flow and the calculated flow blobs. Since we are primarily interested in the few dominant motions, these blobs (and their associated statistics) are sufficient for subsequent recognition.

After calculating the flow blobs, we use a rule-based technique to identify an action. The action rules use the following information about the motion blobs: the number of blobs, the direction and magnitude of motion within the blobs, the relative motion between blobs, the relative size of the blobs, and the relative positions of the blobs. Six actions – waving, clapping, jumping, drumming, flapping and marching – are currently recognized. Once the motion is recognized, the system estimates relevant parameters (e.g. the tempo of hand waving) until the action ceases. Figure 3.3 shows two frames from a sequence of a child playing the "virtual cymbals."

Figure 3.2 a Original image. **b** Flow vectors and calculated flow blobs.

Figure 3.3 A user playing the virtual cymbals, with flow blobs overlaid.

Informal user testing of this system is promising. Participants found it to be fun, intuitive and compelling. The immediate feedback of the musical sounds and animated characters that respond to recognized gestures is engaging, especially for children. An interesting anecdote is that the child shown in Figure 3.3, after playing with this system in the lab, went home and immediately tried to do the same thing with his parents' computer.

3.5.3 Full Body Tracking

To interpret human activity, we need to track and model the body as a 3D articulated structure. We have developed a system [22] which uses disparity maps from a stereo pair of cameras to model and track articulated 3D blobs which represent the major portions of the upper body: torso, lower arms, upper arms and head. Each blob is modeled as a 3D gaussian distribution, shown schematically in Figure 3.4. The pixels of the disparity image are classified into their corresponding blobs, and missing data created by self-occlusions is properly filled in. The model statistics are

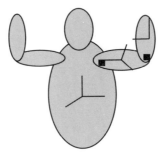

Figure 3.4 Articulated 3D blob body model.

Figure 3.5 Tracking of connected head and torso blobs.

then re-computed, and an extended Kalman filter is used in tracking to enforce the articulation constraints of the human body parts.

After an initialization step in which the user participates with the system to assign blob models to different body parts, the statistical parameters of the blobs are calculated and tracked. In one set of experiments, we used a simple two-part model consisting of head and torso blobs. Two images from a tracking sequence are shown in Figure 3.5.

In another set of experiments, we used a four-part articulated structure consisting of the head, torso, lower arm and upper arm, as shown in Figure 3.6. Detecting and properly handling occlusions is the most difficult challenge for this sort of tracking. The figure shows tracking in the presence of occlusion. Running on a 233 MHz Pentium II system, the unoptimized tracking runs at 10–15 Hz.

3.6 Summary and Critical Issues

People treat media – including computers and technology in general – in ways that suggest a social relationship with the media. Perceptual user interfaces, modeled after human-to-human interaction and interaction with the physical world, may

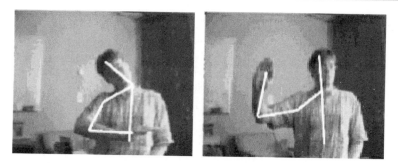

Figure 3.6 Tracking of head, torso, upper arm and lower arm.

enable people to interact with technology in ways that are natural, efficient and easy to learn. A semantic understanding of application and user semantics, which is critical to achieving perceptual interfaces, will enable a single specification of the interface to migrate among a diverse set of users, applications and environments.

Perceptual interfaces do not necessarily imply anthropomorphic interfaces, although the jury is still out as to the utility of interfaces that take on human-like characteristics. It is likely that, as computers are seen less as tools for specific tasks and more as part of our communication and information infrastructure, combining perceptual interfaces with anthropomorphic characteristics will become commonplace.

Although the component areas (such as speech, language and vision) are well researched, the community of researchers devoted to integrating these areas into perceptual interfaces is small – but growing. Some of the critical issues that need to be addressed in the early stages of this pursuit include:

- What are the most relevant and useful perceptual modalities?
- What are the implications for usability testing – how can these systems be sufficiently tested?
- How accurate, robust and integrated must machine perceptual capabilities be to be useful in a perceptual interface?
- What are the compelling tasks ("killer apps") that will demand such interfaces, if any?
- Can (and should) perceptual interfaces be introduced in an evolutionary way in order to build on the current GUI infrastructure, or is this fundamentally a break from current systems and applications?

The research agenda for perceptual user interfaces must include both (1) development of individual components, such as speech recognition and synthesis, visual recognition and tracking, and user modeling, and (2) integration of these components. A deeper semantic understanding and representation of human–computer interaction will have to be developed, along with methods to map from the semantic representation to particular devices and environments. In short, there is much work to be done. But the expected benefits are immense.

Acknowledgments

Thanks to Ross Cutler and Nebojsa Jojij for their contributions to this chapter. Ross is largely responsible for the system described in Section 3.5.2. Nebojsa is primarily responsible for the system described in Section 3.5.3.

References

[1]   B Reeves and C Nass (1996) *The Media Equation: How People Treat Computers, Television, and New Media Like Real People and Places*, Cambridge, Cambridge University Press.

[2]   S Shafer, J Krumm, B Brumitt, B Meyers, M Czerwinski and D Robbins (1998) The new EasyLiving project at Microsoft Research, in *Proc. Joint DARPA/NIST Smart Spaces Workshop*, Gaithersburg, MD, 30–31 July.

[3]   M Weiser (1991) The computer for the twenty-first century, *Scientific American*, September, 94–104.

[4]   A van Dam (1997) Post-WIMP user interfaces, *Communications of the ACM*, 40(2), 63–67.

[5]   S Oviatt and W Wahlster (eds.) (1997) *Human–Computer Interaction* (Special Issue on Multimodal Interfaces), 12(1&2).

[6]   K Waters, J Rehg, M Loughlin, SB Kang and D Terzopoulos (1996) Visual sensing of humans for active public interfaces, *Technical Report CRL 96/5*, DEC Cambridge Research Lab, March.

[7]   B Shneiderman (1997) Direct Manipulation for Comprehensible, Predictable, and Controllable User Interfaces, in *Proceedings of IUI97, 1997 International Conference on Intelligent User Interfaces*, Orlando, FL, 6-9 January, pp. 33–39.

[8]   B Shneiderman (1989) A nonanthropomorphic style guide: overcoming the Humpty Dumpty syndrome, *The Computing Teacher*, 16(7), 5.

[9]   B Shneiderman (1993) Beyond intelligent machines: just do it!, *IEEE Software*, 10(1), 100–103.

[10] A Wexelblat (1998) Don't make that face: a report on anthropomorphizing an interface, in *Intelligent Environments* (ed. M. Coen), AAAI Technical Report SS-98-02, AAAI Press.

[11] J Straubhaar and R LaRose (1997) *Communication Media in the Information Society*. Belmont, CA, Wadsworth.

[12] N Negroponte (1995) *Being Digital*, New York, Vintage Books.

[13] M Turk and Y Takebayashi (eds.) (1997) *Proceedings of the Workshop on Perceptual User Interfaces*, Banff, Canada, October.

[14] M Turk (ed.) (1998) *Proceedings of the Workshop on Perceptual User Interfaces*, San Francisco, CA, November, http://research.microsoft.com/PUIWorkshop/.

[15] P Cohen, M Johnston, D McGee, S Oviatt, J Pittman, I Smith, L Chen and J Clow (1997) QuickSet: multimodal interaction for distributed applications, in *Proceedings of the Fifth Annual International Multimodal Conference*, New York, ACM Press.

[16] I Poddar, Y Sethi, E Ozyildiz and R Sharma (1998) Toward natural speech/gesture HCI: a case study of weather narration, *Proc. PUI'98 Workshop*, November.

[17] D Stork and M Hennecke (eds.) (1996) *Speechreading by Humans and Machines: Models, Systems, and Applications*, Berlin, Springer-Verlag.

[18] C Benoît and R Campbell (eds.) (1997) *Proceedings of the Workshop on Audio-Visual Speech Processing*, Rhodes, Greece, September.

[19] A Bobick (1997) Movement, activity, and action: the role of knowledge in the perception of motion, in *Royal Society Workshop on Knowledge-based Vision in Man and Machine*, London, February.

[20] M Turk (1996) Visual interaction with lifelike characters, in *Proc. Second IEEE Conference on Face and Gesture Recognition*, Killington, VT, October.

[21] R Cutler and M Turk (1998) View-based interpretation of real-time optical flow for gesture recognition, in *Proc. Third IEEE Conference on Face and Gesture Recognition*, Nara, Japan, April.

[22] N Jojic, M Turk and T Huang (1999) Tracking articulated objects in stereo image sequences, in *Proc. II Workshop on Detection, Estimation, Classification, and Imaging, Sante Fe, NM, 21 25 February.*

About the Author

Matthew Turk is a founding member of the Vision Technology Group at Microsoft Research in Redmond, Washington. He worked on vision for mobile robots in the mid-1980s and has been working in various aspects of vision-based interfaces since his PhD work at the MIT Media Laboratory in 1991. His research interests include perceptual user interfaces, gesture recognition, visual tracking and real-time vision.

4

Guidelines for Telepresence and Shared Virtual Environments

Rae Earnshaw

Abstract

This chapter focuses on critical aspects in the design, implementation and successful exploitation of shared virtual environments. These include architecture, devices, standards, networks, interaction, telepresence, modeling and cost/benefit analysis. The emphasis is on real applications with real users.

4.1 Introduction and Background

Shared virtual environments are increasingly being used to bring together local and remote users for the purposes of communication, collaboration, design and modeling in a variety of application domains. What are the minimum technology requirements in input and output devices, network support and interaction speeds that are necessary in order to support effective use of the technology in particular application domains? What are the guidelines of best practice for the users in order to derive optimum benefit from the new ways of working? This is the purpose of this work.

4.2 Objectives of the SID Chain

The Telepresence and Shared Virtual Environments Chain in the European Commission's ACTS Programme addresses the critical aspects in the design, implementation and successful application of shared virtual environments, including architecture, devices, standards, networks, interaction and sharing, telepresence, modeling, and cost/benefit analysis.

The Chain brings together results from a number of European projects concerned with virtual working, collaborative design, shared environments, telerobotics, remote scene reconstruction and distributed video. These networked technologies are already allowing researchers, developers, designers and users to enter a shared space within which work can be done.

The extent to which local and real experiences have been effectively replaced by remote and distant interactions with multiple groups of participants is being quantitatively analyzed. Inclusion of remote participants over networks represents added value to the local group expertise, and this is being studied in several of the projects.

A series of generic guidelines for the use of telepresence and shared virtual environments are being defined, and this chapter presents the initial results.

A framework for shared virtual activities has also been constructed. This enables a range of scenarios to be understood within the comprehensive context of persistent multimedia communications environments. Such environments are becoming increasingly ubiquitous as the power and functionality of networks and processors increases.

This framework is currently known as "the cycle of cognition" or "the cycle of collaboration". The cycle defines the paths between one communication type and another and also the changes that are needed in moving from one form of communication to another. The functional stages in the cycle are: rehearsal, navigation, exploration, discussion, collaboration, persuasion and acceptance. These are generic entities that have to be supported by tele- and virtual communications over a wide range of time-scales and life cycles if the networked part of the everyday environment is to be as ubiquitous and persistent as it needs to be.

A conceptual architecture for future communications technologies and services is being constructed. The relationship of this architecture to current network-based virtual environments and future Web-based virtual worlds is also being investigated.

4.3 Guidelines for the SID Chain

These Guidelines present the results of a number of other projects in the SID Chain who have contributed their results to date. As VPARK is still in progress it is not so easy yet to distill the overall results for virtual entertainment applications. Where preliminary results have been obtained which have relevance for the particular Guideline, these are included. Where further work or investigation is required, this is specified.

The Guidelines have been arranged into a hierarchy starting first with collaborative and social aspects, then individual aspects, and finally the perceptual aspects (including kinesthetic aspects).

Primary contributors to the Social and Collaborative Aspects were VISINET, VPARK, DVP and CICC.

Primary contributors to the Individual Aspects were TAPESTRIES, COVEN and USINATCS.

Primary contributors to the Perception Aspects were VPARK, MAESTRO, TELEBORG and CICC.

These Guidelines are intended for users and implementers in order to indicate the range of applicability of the methodology for the domain of interest, and also the limitations and requirements of the technology for successful exploitation. In addition, there is a specification of the extent to which new types of environments and working procedures resulting from the application of the technology leads to additional benefits for the user.

4.4 Program of Work

The work program consisted of discussion with members of the project teams working on shared virtual environments. A number of plenary meetings and Workshops have been held to focus attention on particular aspects of the domain. The key results from these are presented in more detail in the Appendix to this chapter. These meetings and Workshops are ongoing.

4.5 Social and Collaborative Aspects

Guideline for Collaboration and Networking

Applications considering distribution and exploitation over network links need to consider the following parameters:

- bandwidth
- cost/benefit
- response time required for the application domain
- interoperability of equipment and software, and standards
- synchronization and jitter
- quality of service required by the users (e.g. minimum level, and whether this can be guaranteed)
- the HCI aspects of large groups of users interacting with each other

Certain application domains (e.g. tele-operation, distributed music rehearsal) have time-critical requirements necessitating response times of less than 40 ms. Applications such as architectural design are more dependent on a quality rendition of the 3D model so that the designer has a clear picture of how the design will look from different directions and under different conditions, e.g. visual appearance, lighting model and shading.

There is clear added value from using shared virtual environments over networks. This includes the following aspects:

- Direct interaction of all participants with a shared 3D model (e.g. for design or CSCW).
- Participants are able to see new things that they could previously not see with location-based work.
- Opportunities to try "What if?" scenarios in real time and see the effects directly, thus allowing more design iterations to be accomplished over time, leading to better efficiency for the user and a better quality of result.
- The closer coupling of the users and the application promotes creativity and the reduction of time to perform the overall task.

ATM has current limitations with regard to guaranteed quality of service, due to the design of AAL5. It is clear that experts in the technical aspects of ATM networking need to address this observation and indicate whether a solution can be found.

4.6 Individual Aspects

Guideline for Usability

All applications interfaces should adhere to the following design principles:

- consistency
- provide short cuts for frequent use
- provide information feedback (reinforcement)
- provide user dialogs which always lead to closure
- provide simple and clear error handling
- permit easy reversal of actions
- support user-centered interaction
- reduce the short-term memory load on the user

For an environment to provide a sense of presence the user needs to be "immersed" in some sense in the space containing the information, and be able to interact with it in a reasonably intuitive way. This can be via shutter glasses connected to a stereo display, via a headset and tracking system, or via a walk-in environment such as a CAVE. It has been demonstrated that stereo motion cues add to the sense of presence.

The following issues are where further work is required, and no firm recommendation can be given at the present time. A number of EC projects are working on various aspects of these areas:

- The optimum combination of different types of sensory information to provide the best sense of presence (e.g. stereo, field of view, tactile sensors).
- Quantitative measures for the degree of presence in a virtual environment, and the extent to which (for example) a response time of 150 ms to each sense is as good as 40 ms in one sense.
- The ability to modify the environment
- The control of the sensors

- Being aware of the presence of others in the virtual environment and social interaction with them.
- The speed with which the user believes in the virtual environment from start-up, i.e. how quickly is the sense of presence established?
- Which medium creates the best sense of presence (e.g. motion, 3D sound, realistic rendering, fast interaction)
- Use of alternative technologies (videoconferencing etc).

4.7 Perception Aspects

Guideline for Tele-Operation and Augmented Reality

Successful and safe tele-operation requires a latency (the delay between performing an action and seeing the results of that action) of less than 15 frames/s and a response time of less than 40 ms. Longer delays lead to instabilities in the control loop. Constraints may be needed on the degree and extent of user motion, depending on the application. In addition, simple and easy to follow setup procedures are needed in order to minimize the risk of error on the part of the user.

The CAVALCADE Project (ESPRIT HPCN) is concerned with Collaborative Virtual Construction and Design. According to this project, human performance begins to degrade when latency goes above 100 ms, and that 10 frames per second is the minimum rate for sustaining the illusion of animation in typical interactive applications supporting navigation and 3D object manipulation.

The following issues are where further work is required and no firm recommendation can be given at the present time. A number of EC projects are working on aspects of these areas:

- Determination of registration procedures
- Use of non-invasive tracking devices
- Treatment of images, e.g. generality versus precision of information displayed, and speed of processing required
- Multimodal user interfaces
- Standards for security and safety
- Tracking procedures – multi-sensor visual/inertia/force
- Fusion of real and virtual worlds
- Quality of service

4.8 Recommendations for Standards Bodies

Currently we have no definitive recommendations for Standards Bodies. However, it is important to bring forward recommendations when the work still to be done is completed.

Areas where standards recommendations would be beneficial are:

1. Format for supplying information from one robot to another or to operate an actuator.
2. Standard metrics for evaluating the sense of presence in shared virtual environments.

4.9 Market-Related Issues for the Chains

Key aspects of VR usability studies were to:

- identify key functions of VR application
- assess the relative importance of VR functions to users
- assess how well the VR application enabled these functions

The findings of these usability studies were the following.

- Most important and best enabled VR functions were:
  - being able to understanding the shape of the building
  - being able to move around the spaces
  - being able to view the interior appearance of the building
- Less important functions were:
  - a sense of "being there" (quoted by manufacturers as most important)
  - being able to manipulate objects in the space
- Overall findings were the universally and strongly expressed positive feelings about the potential of all VR applications, in particular regarding the potentials of:
  - computer-supported collaborative work
  - collaborative virtual reality
  - access to supercomputing for rendering

For each of the applications the perceived benefits and potentials were the following.

- Collaborative virtual reality design applications:
  - level of detail about right for urban planning discussions
  - level of detail usable for architect–client discussions about overall shape and design of buildings
  - level of detail insufficient for interior designers and construction specialist subcontractors
  - key benefit enabling and fostering understanding between client and architect/ designer
  - audioconferencing quality could be improved
  - videoconferencing nice but not essential
  - most frequently mentioned improvement: speed of response across network

- Access to supercomputing facilities:
  - most important use: remote rendering of "wire" designs
  - important because small companies cannot afford HPC facilities
  - current usage of remote HPC facilities can reduce rendering time by up to 80%
  - next stage in improving performance needs to be faster computer processing rather than faster networks
- Computer-supported collaborative work:
  - most important functions are multilocation interactive whiteboard and audioconferencing
  - most important benefits include shortening time taken to agree design modifications
  - designers tend to be more interested than architects/constructors in adding videoconferencing to audio
  - improvements required include fast access to shared databases and better audio communication

The impact on user processes and business performance is as follows.

- Relevant factors are:
  - users' business process and business performance
  - the structure of users' businesses
  - users' working relationships with other parties
- Tangible attributes are:
  - overall time savings on projects
  - "time to market" (the length of time it took to get from an initial briefing to a commercially viable product which could be marketed to a customer)
- The major findings to date are as follows:
  - The use of the applications and the technology brought both time and cost savings, particularly in relation to travel.
  - The ability to work interactively also brought time savings. The technology allowed changes to be made immediately, and so eliminated time delays between client instructions and discussion and the supplier being able to carry out that instruction (the traditional pattern of "meeting – work carried out – further meeting").

4.10 Conclusions

4.10.1 Technology Revolution

Rapid developments in broadcasting technology and the creation and dissemination of content are being caused by the following:

- convergence of media, computing and telecommunications
- professional standards on the desktop (creation, production, post-production)

- roll-out of multi-channel digital broadcasting and the increased requirement for quality content and its access
- new media industries for repurposing of traditional content for Web, HDTV, DVD-ROM and interaction

4.10.2 Beyond the Desktop Paradigm

The future of new media requires the following:

- better user interfaces that are multisensory and multimedia
- collaboration and interaction between creators, editors, repurposers and users
- meeting the actual needs of the market-place – what are the killer applications? (Football clubs?)
- conversion of storyboard to media product (film, books, CD-ROM, Web etc.).

Shared virtual environments provide a framework for facilitating multi-user inter-action with 3D worlds and for allowing remote users to interact with local ones. This can be via virtual representation of themselves (avatars) or real representations linked by networks such as the Internet. The latter is now capable of supporting 3D worlds via VRML, Java 3D, MPEG-4, and Chromeffects and Metastreams.

The VISTA project (ESPRIT MPCN) is allowing users on PC clients to interact in real-time with a shared 3D environment via the Internet or Studio LAN as an integral part of interactive television program production.

TAPESTRIES is measuring presence in new broadcast media by performing psychological evaluations of entertainment and multimedia applications. COVEN is comparing user behavior and task performance in the shared virtual world with the same interaction in the real world.

4.10.3 The Future

It is clear that convergence is producing a situation with great potential for the future, but which is also inherently very complex and which is changing the nature of the users (or groups of users) interaction with the information. Some modes are passive (reading and viewing), some are interactive (information search, video games), some are rational and some are emotional. Information is in different forms ranging from high complexity and structure (research papers) to narrative simplicity (e.g. story-telling). New user behaviors and communities will emerge in response to the different kinds of broadcast and online access now becoming available.

A framework is being devised for representing these different kinds of information, their methods of access, and their interfaces to the users and their communities.

4.11 Areas for Future Work

Guidelines have been produced to date in the area of collaboration, usability and teleoperation. These are recommendations for good practice; it is too early for standardization in these areas, simply because of the rate of change of technology and the users.

Work is continuing, in the aggregation of results from telepresence and robotics projects, to produce Version 2 of the Guidelines.

Acknowledgments

This work was done in association with the ACTS TEN-IBC Project VISINET: 3D Visualization over Networks, and the ACTS Project VPARK: A Virtual Amusement Park. Thanks and appreciation are expressed to the members of the project consortia for their contributions in these areas.

References

Further information on the work of the Telepresence and Shared Virtual Environments Chain can be found at http://www.uk.infowin.org/acts/.
Further information on the work of the European Commission ACTS programme (Advanced Communications, Technologies, and Services) may be found at http://www.uk.infowin.org/acts/.
Further information on the work in the area of Interactive Multimedia within ACTS may be found at http://www.uk.infowin.org/acts/analysys/concertation/multimedia/.

Appendix: New Media Workshop, 18 February 1998

Report on the New Media Workshop, 18 February 1998, Royal Crown Hotel, Rue Royale, Brussels

As part of the ACTS Concertation Meeting, 16-18 February 1998, a Workshop was hosted by the European Commission to explore future directions for new media in the areas of technology, content creation, services, applications, and new business areas for European industry. What are the areas that the work program of Framework 5 should seek to address in the area of new media?

The program agenda was as follows and was chaired by Fernando Pereira.

1. Introduction (Eric Badique, EC ACTS Programme)
2. Telepresence and Shared VEs (David Leevers, BICC)
3. Technology for Content Creation (Richard Storey, BBC)
4. The Future of New Media (Rae Earnshaw, University of Bradford)
5. Open Discussion and Conclusions

A.1 Introduction (Eric Badique, EC ACTS Programme)

http://www.at.infowin.org/ACTS/people/badique/

In the area of multimedia services there are currently around 60 projects funded by ACTS. These are concerned with the management and manipulation of multimedia content, interactive distribution and transmission, and the development of services.

Developments in 3D, virtual reality, telepresence, coding, computer vision and technology convergence are all creating a framework for the future that we should capitalize on. In addition, Europe's content assets can be linked into the technology for content – whether animation, games, miniaturization, access, search, control, management or new languages. Entertainment is taking on new forms of context, structure and aesthetics via virtual actors, motion painting and cubist cinema.

The ACTS SIC Chain (Service Integration – Content) aims to bring together the relevant ACTS projects in this area (e.g. 3D acquisition, virtual environments, restoration of film and media, virtual and distributed studios, and museums) and distill out generic guidelines and best practice recommendations. Areas to be covered include:

- content creation
- acquisition and low-level processing
- virtual studios
- MPEG-4 authoring
- content indexing (and retrieval)
- packaging, watermarking and contribution
- quality evaluation

The ACTS SID Chain (Service Integration – Distributed) aims to bring together the relevant ACTS projects in this area (e.g. A/V content elements, networked VR, CSCW, telepresence, shared environments, telerobotics, scene reconstruction and distributed video) and produce generic guidelines and recommendations for best practice. Areas to be covered include:

- collaboration and networking
- usability
- teleoperation and augmented reality
- 3D and multimodal telepresence
- networked VR

As communication environments become more sophisticated, the technology baseline moves up the content chain and they borrow from the content creation toolbox. Thus it is inevitable that the areas of SID and SIC will merge into one where the toolset supports various kinds of advanced program production.

The Information Society Technologies Programme (IST) from 1998–2002 will receive 3.36 billion ECU for funding work in the key action areas:

- Systems and services for the citizen
- Electronic commerce

- Multimedia content and tools
- Essential technologies and infrastructure

Issues for the future will include the following:

- user-friendly interfaces (VR, wearable etc.)
- better content management (dealing with volume, complexity)
- more intelligence (analysis, understanding, synthesis)
- higher levels (hybrid images, objects, 3D)
- integrated technology (interdisciplinarity)
- invisible technology (more room for creativity)
- secure environments (protection of assets)
- new media

A.2 Telepresence and Shared VEs (David Leevers, BICC)

`http://www.uk.infowin.org/ACTS/ANALYSYS/CONCERTATION/`
`CHAINS/SI/HOME/CH_SID/private.htm`

Projects in the SID Chain covered the following generic areas:

- understanding and visualizing remote tasks
- awareness of remote or virtual surroundings
- participation at remote locations
- membership of a dispersed community

These may be regarded as rings of virtuality around the real world. Often these were rings of decreasing sense of presence. Virtual communities needed to be anchored in real locations.

The BT Laboratories' "Shared Spaces" project is currently exploring our relationships with real and virtual space: `http://webster.info.bt.co.uk/ InfoGarden2_5/main.html`.

Generic guidelines have currently been produced for:

- collaboration and networking
- usability
- teleoperation and augmented reality

Closer coupling of users and the model or application has been demonstrated to promote creativity and the reduction of time to perform the particular creation task.

A.3 Technology for Content Creation Chain (Richard Storey, BBC)

Tomorrow's consumers will be:

- computer-literate

- accustomed to interactivity
- accustomed to navigating through 3D environments

Current areas of shortfall in technology are:

- actor-friendly real action capture, body and face
- dialog capture (words, nuance, emotion)
- photorealistic virtual environments (on a domestic PC/TV)
- effective and user-friendly content production, management and trading tools
- stable and bug-free software for consumers
- full-space 3D displays, nausea-free VR displays
- language, gesture, attitude translation?

The future will involve repurposing content for books and remastering content for CD-ROM. Currently 95% of the content is discarded after the TV program has been constructed. The end product is the video. Content creation in 2005 will involve the repurposing of objects as required. This in turn will shift the emphasis from re-manu-facture to re-use, with the consequent need for the cataloging, searching and trading engines currently under development in MPEG-7. Video, CD-ROM and 3D interactive game products will in the future be produced as an integral part of the content creation process. Increasing interactivity on the part of the user/viewer will allow for user selec-tion of the producer's choice or viewer's choice, or will be fully interactive.

A.4 The Future of New Media (Rae Earnshaw, University of Bradford)

http://www.eimc.brad.ac.uk/earnshaw.html

Current user interfaces do not enable the user to be fully creative. The emphasis is on the technology rather than being designed for the content to be accessed. For example, in general, voice or gestures from the user are not utilized. Today we are largely using "new" technology for old things in old ways.

We have recently celebrated the 100th anniversary of the cinema. History illustrates that it took many years for tools to develop that would effectively handle the language the cinema was using (illusion, montage, close-up, reproduction, sound, color, wide screen, digital compositing) and enable the viewer to understand and relate to the story without thinking of the medium being used to present it.

Similarly, multimedia technology needs to get to the point where the user interacts with the content without being aware of the medium being used to present it. Currently multimedia is being used to present traditional materials but allowing rather more interaction (e.g. computer-based training and simulation) than was possible before.

Games are an area where the technology is utilized directly to maximize the user's interaction with the content. Thus content (i.e. potential user sales) is driving the technological development and design.

Content makes the impact and is the product of the creative process. Technology should assist directly in this process and in the mediation to the user.

In the future, content creators should be able to move from storyline to media product via online metadata. Dramatized CNN could generate immediate spin-offs in media other than TV. Advanced interfaces, intelligent agents and speech are all areas where investment of time and effort will improve the quality of our access to, and creation of, tomorrow's content.

A.5 Open Discussion and Conclusions

One way of presenting the relationship between people, content and technology is shown in Figure 4.1 (with two-way interaction between all adjacent vertices). The new media axis is from Technology and through the gap between People and Content.

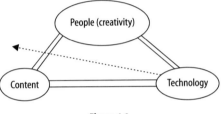

Figure 4.1

In the area of communication, "one-to-one" and "one-to-many" had been covered. However, "many-to-one" has not been covered.

Augmented Reality and Mobile Computing

5

Mobile Augmented Reality: a Complex Human-Centered System

Simon Julier, Steven Feiner and Lawrence Rosenblum

Abstract

A major new thrust in the information sciences will be getting information to a user, in a usable form, regardless of location. A high-end example that involves many aspects of human-centered systems is the use of augmented reality to display information atop the real world without distracting users from their task. This chapter discusses the scientific and technical difficulties for mobile augmented reality by examining a recently initiated research project, the Battlefield Augmented Reality System (BARS). BARS is exploring how important information can be overlaid on what users see, hear, and otherwise experience of the surrounding world as they walk through an urban environment. We argue that the development of such a human-centered system introduces many difficult challenges in a variety of areas, including: accurate wide-area tracking systems; navigation user interface design; information filtering; wireless networking and software architectures; and societal issues for distributed collaboration.

5.1 Introduction

Using sensors, computers and interactive devices to provide information to people in usable form, regardless of location, is one of the upcoming challenges for computer and information science. Currently, for example, automotive systems that utilize the Global Positioning System (GPS) are becoming available to assist the driver with navigation tasks. The driver inputs start and end positions, and the system provides suggested route options and tells the driver when and where to turn. Certain high-end applications must provide visual information without distracting the user from the task at hand. Augmented reality (AR) offers a solution.

Recent developments in computing hardware have finally begun to make wearable mobile AR systems feasible. With this new freedom, it becomes possible for AR systems to be used in a very wide range of applications, including disaster relief,

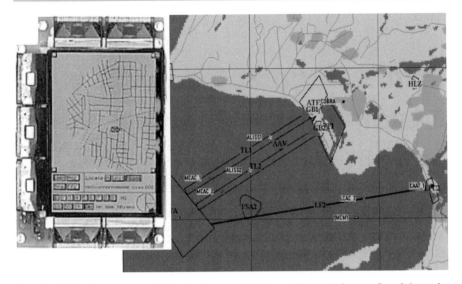

Figure 5.1 Digital and paper maps provide situational awareness to their users, but require that users divert their attention from the task at hand.

management and repair of utilities in a street, and even as an assistant for tourists walking through unfamiliar historical sites. However, working with large environments introduces many new challenges to be concerned with: navigation and wayfinding (users know where they are and how they can get to new desired locations); querying for information about the environment (finding out what they are looking at).

Given its ubiquitous nature, the problem of urban complexity is the subject of intense study within the field of wearable computers and a number of research avenues have been pursued. Within the military context approaches such as digital maps or "rolling compass" displays have been used (Gumm et al., 1998). Although these methods have been demonstrated to be superior to systems based on radioed instructions (Figure 5.1), new and better approaches are being sought. The most promising are those based on Augmented Reality (AR), where the user sees, hears or otherwise experiences the real environment augmented by additional information.

Experimental AR prototypes have been demonstrated in task domains ranging from aircraft manufacturing (Caudell and Mizell, 1992; Caudell, 1994) to image-guided surgery (Fuchs et al., 1998), and from maintenance and repair (Feiner et al., 1993; Hoff et al., 1996) to building construction (Webster et al., 1996). These have provided many insights into how to design and use AR systems. However, mobile AR systems introduce a new set of challenging and largely unstudied research problems. First, since the user potentially operates over a very large area, conventional tracking systems that rely on bounded working volumes or specially prepared are inappropriate. For example, Welch and Bishop (1997) and Koller et al. (1997) have demonstrated room-sized tracking systems which rely on populating the environment with a set of distinctive beacons. Second, as users move through the environment their context can change dramatically, depending on their position and current intent. To explore these and other issues raised by mobile augmented reality, the Naval Research Laboratory and Columbia University has embarked on a research program called the Battlefield Augmented Reality System (BARS).

BARS was motivated by the fact that with the proliferation of urbanization throughout the world, it is expected that many future military operations (such as peace-keeping or hostage rescue) will occur in urban environments. These environments present many challenges. First, urban environments are extremely complicated and inherently three-dimensional. Above street level, the infrastructure of buildings may serve many different purposes (such as hospitals or communication stations) and can harbor many types of risk (such as snipers or instability due to structural damage). These features are often distributed and interleaved over several floors of a multi-floor building. Below street level, there may be a complex network of sewers, tunnels and utility systems. Cities can be confusing (especially if street signs are damaged or missing), and coordinating multiple team members can be difficult. To ensure the safety of both civilian and military personnel, it has long been argued that environmental information must be delivered to the individual user *in situ* in that environment. Despite the specific nature of this application, it touches on many areas of research, including user interface design, software architecture and distributed interaction.

BARS builds from two thrusts. The first is the commercial development of wearable hardware that is finally beginning to make wearable AR systems feasible (Figure 5.2). Wearable computers are becoming small enough and powerful enough to

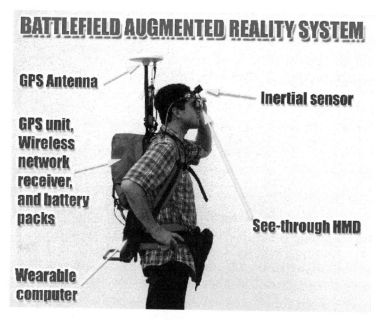

Figure 5.2 Test hardware for the BARS augmented reality system under development at NRL. Both this system and the one shown in Figure 5.3 are built using COTS components. Note the rapid change – the system in Figure 5.3 was developed in 1997, whereas the system above was developed in 1999.

Figure 5.3 The Touring Machine (Feiner *et al.*, 1997), an Augmented Reality walk-through of the Columbia University campus. The insert on the left shows the view through the see-through, head-mounted display. Supplemental information includes the name of the building under view and additional navigation cues and supplemental information.

generate 3D graphics at interactive frame rates. Head-worn displays are on their way to reaching the required resolution, brightness and form factor (Pryor *et al.*, 1998; Spitzer *et al.*, 1998). Many of these components are driven by other commercial considerations (e.g. Sony's Glasstron family of head-worn displays is being developed in large part for entertainment).

The second thrust is the demonstration of a mobile AR testbed called the Touring Machine (Feiner *et al.*, 1997; MacIntyre, 1999). Developed at Columbia University, one of its experimental applications provides information about the environment to a user walking through the Columbia University campus (Figure 5.3). The user's position and orientation are continuously tracked using a real-time kinematic GPS receiver and an inertial tracker. An optical see-through head-worn display allows the user to see overlaid information about surrounding campus buildings. Using a handheld computer, the user can select buildings in the current field of view and acquire information, such as Web pages of the academic department housed in the selected building.

We are extending this work by exploring how AR systems can be used to deliver detailed information about complicated, dynamic and mutable environments. From our experiences with the Touring Machine, we conclude that significant research must be directed towards three main areas: tracking systems, the design of the information displays and the means by which the user interacts with the system.

The structure of this chapter is as follows. In Section 5.2 we outline the problems faced by tracking systems, and describe current solutions and research efforts. Section 5.3 considers user interface design issues. We examine interaction methods in Section 5.4 and present our conclusions in Section 5.5.

5.2 Tracking Systems

To successfully register graphical information with the environment, an AR system must know where the user is located and what the user is looking at. However, the nature of head movements (which can be extremely rapid, with peak angular accelerations of over $200°/s^2$), and the precision that is required (often sub-degree, and ideally sub-pixel level, accuracy) means that tracking is one of the most significant challenges to the development of almost any kind of responsive VR system (Azuma, 1997). See-through AR systems present even greater challenges than their VR counterparts. The fundamental reason is that the visible environment is a function of the user's *actual* position and orientation and is not calculated from any kind of tracking system. However, the graphical displays are generated using a position calculated from a tracking system. Many methods for masking latency or errors in tracking systems cannot be applied. For example, researchers have demonstrated the use of a temporal shift to delay the image of the real world to reduce the effective lag of overlaid material for a video-mixed system (Bajura and Neumann, 1995). However, such an approach would be highly disorienting for a user who had to interact with that world (and impossible in an optical see-through system). Accurate outdoor tracking is significantly more difficult than what is normally addressed by indoor tracking systems: tethered trackers cannot be used and fiducial-based systems are infeasible since the environment may be both unstable and unavailable for the addition of fiducials.

Given these difficulties, it has been acknowledged that any tracking solution must be a hybrid that combines several different tracking technologies (Azuma, 1998). One project that is examining this problem in detail is Geospatial Registration of Information for Dismounted Soldiers (GRIDS) (HRL Laboratories, 1998). Technologies under study include the use of image-based trackers for optical flow and landmark tracking, combined with magnetometers and high-precision inertial systems. To date, GRIDS has primarily focused on the problem of estimating orientation (Azuma *et al.*, 1999; You *et al.*, 1999).

Because the technologies for estimating position and orientation are different, the next two subsections consider the problems of estimating each of these components separately. We conclude with a discussion of estimating both parameters together.

5.2.1 Position

The problem of outdoor position tracking has been greatly mitigated by the development of real-time kinematic GPS systems. Current systems are capable of estimating their own positions with standard deviations of less than 5 cm. However, the urban environment is punishing to this type of technology. The success of a GPS system depends on its ability to observe signals from multiple satellites simultaneously. As the number of visible satellites decreases, the accuracy of the position solution declines. At least four satellites (three, if the altitude is assumed to be a known constant) must be visible for GPS to yield a unique solution. However, the buildings within a city can mask a significant part of the sky and the actual number of satellites depends on the satellite constellation and local building configuration. In simple empirical trials at the Naval Research Laboratory, the number of tracked satellites fell from nine to three when the GPS receiver moved about 10 m from the middle of an open area to the center of a 5 m wide road between three-story research buildings. Buildings create further difficulties through multi-path effects: the signals from a satellite can be reflected from the surroundings and the road, causing multiple copies of the signal, all traversing slightly different routes, to arrive at the receiver at approximately the same time.

Some of these difficulties can be overcome by recent developments in GPS-based tracking technologies. Satellite availability can be increased by using dual–constellation GPS systems. Such systems employ both the US GPS (24 satellites) and Russian GLONASS (currently 17 satellites). Multi-path effects are being addressed in new technologies such as SnapTrack (SnapTrack Inc., 1999). SnapTrack processes measurements from a GPS receiver in conjunction with a local server on cellular telephone network. The local server provides information such as the constellation of satellites currently in view, Doppler offsets and altitude. It provides services such as sequential measurement optimization techniques to mitigate errors caused by multi-path effects and reflections.

Despite these advances, GPS still has a number of limitations. It will not work inside buildings, can be blocked by foliage and is vulnerable to jamming. The additional radio signal used to provide the special differential correction information needed for real-time kinematic GPS have also been problematic since it currently uses frequency spectrum that is also allocated to other uses, including voice transmission. Since FCC regulations mandate that data is a second-class citizen on voice bands, data transmitters must yield to avoid interference with voice. This can result in unpredictable intermittent gaps in the broadcast of differential corrections, during which accuracy plummets. The GPS industry is actively pursuing an initiative to get the FCC to allocate spectrum for RTK systems. While these issues make sole reliance on GPS problematic in production systems, we see GPS as an invaluable research tool.

Although GPS is most popular among researchers, other sensing options are feasible and are being examined. These include the use of rate sensors that integrate position and velocity sensors to estimate the movement of an individual. The Army's Land Warrior system, for example, combines a GPS receiver with a pedometer (Judd, 1997).

5.2.2 Orientation

In some respects, an accurate orientation estimate is more important than an accurate position estimate. The reason is that when targets are viewed at long distance, the errors in registration are dominated by orientation errors. Estimating these states is even harder because orientation is mostly a function of head orientation and, as mentioned earlier, head movements can be extremely violent and unpredictable.

The most feasible solutions are those that fuse an inertial system with some kind of absolute orientation data (Foxlin, 1996) to mitigate gyro drift. The InterSense IS300Pro, for example, fuses a high-frequency inertial loop with gravitometers (to define "vertical") and a magnetic compass. However, a recent analysis of magnetic compasses has shown that they are prone to drift (Azuma *et al.*, 1999) in a natural outdoor environment.

5.2.3 Joint Approaches

Many types of tracking system estimate position and orientation simultaneously. This is an extremely large class and includes magnetic trackers (such as the Polhemus Fastrak), ultrasound- and inertial tracking-based (the InterSense IS600Pro) and vision-based systems (e.g. the fiducial-based system described in Koller *et al.* (1997). Of these types, the latter is potentially the most useful for outdoor AR environments. There is a significant body of work on tracking naturally occurring features in an environment (e.g. [Behringer-99]. Of these different approaches, we believe that a hybrid system of a number of different sensing and tracking technologies will be most able to meet the needs of mobile AR.

We also note that integrating a number of disparate sensor systems together into a hybrid tracking technology introduces a number of challenges to the underlying theoretical foundations of conventional data fusion systems. Although it is rarely appreciated, the successful operation of an algorithm such as the Kalman filter (Welch and Bishop, 1997; Foxlin, 1996) relies on the assumption that the unmodeled disturbances and the errors in the different sensing systems are all independent of one another. However, in practice there are several problems with this assumption. First, most sensing systems perform various kinds of pre-filtering and data manipulation operations. These operations, which are often proprietary, mean that one cannot assume that errors are independent. Second, even if one were able to construct a full model of the operation of each sensor, the resulting system would be of extremely high dimension, and interactive rates (updates on the order of hundreds of Hz) could not be achieved with current computing technologies. Finally, the forces that act on a system (such as a user's actual head motion) are *not* independent.

Given these difficulties, we propose using robust data fusion algorithms such as Covariance Intersection (CI) (Julier and Uhlmann, 1997; Uhlmann *et al.*, 1997). This algorithm is similar to the Kalman filter but does not rely on the independence assumption. Using this algorithm it is possible to manipulate noises that are not independent and break up monolithic sensor fusion architectures into a set of interoperable data fusion systems, each of which runs at its own rate.

5.3 Design of User Displays

The success of any computer-based information system is largely dependent on the quality of its user interface. Otherwise excellent information systems with cumbersome and confusing user interfaces can be of limited use. This is very important for the design of the BARS interface because the urban environment has a very high information density and there is a significant risk of information over-load (Advisory Group for Aerospace Research and Development, 1998). Within a city block, for example, there could be several buildings with dozens of doors and hundreds of windows. Only a small subset of these objects are relevant, but attempting to show all of them to the user would lead to a confusing mess. Almost all guidelines for the design of user interfaces for mobile AR systems are oriented towards the design of heads-up displays for aircraft. Very few studies of the design for wearable systems or AR systems have been made (Billinghurst *et al.*, 1998; (Advisory Group for Aerospace Research and Development, 1998). One important exception was the study of a user interface for the US Army's Land Warrior (LWP) (Gumm *et al.*, 1998).

LWP is exploring how modern computer technology can be used to provide soldiers with personal information processing systems. A wearable computer was developed with an opaque monocular display and a user interface with two options – a digital map and a "rolling compass display". The digital map is a plan view of the environment that contains icons showing the location of the user as well as other objects of interest. The rolling compass display shows a line with bearing marked on it. As the user's head turns, the line "slides" by. Icons are attached to the compass. To test the effectiveness of these interfaces, users underwent a series of test trials in a rural environment (Gumm *et al.*, 1998). It was found that the system improved a number of aspects of performance. However, most soldiers utilized the system for less than 25% of the time. Although Gumm *et al.* did not identify the reasons for this pattern of use, we believe that it illustrates the need to develop good design guidelines for mobile AR systems. We have begun to explore guidelines in related fields to develop a set of hypotheses that will be studied in the BARS project. In particular, we consider the problems of environmental features, displaying routes, coordination information and conclude by discussing the issue of content management.

5.3.1 Environmental Information

The urban environment is extremely rich and densely packed with information. Certain tasks may require naming and highlighting buildings and other structures. When a relatively small number of buildings are to be identified, superimposing labels over the approximate center of the building (Figure 5.1) is relatively simple and does not require a high performance tracking system (Feiner *et al.*, 1997). However, this simple strategy does not work if, for example, some buildings are partially occluded by others. Refinements such as calculating and annotating the visible part of a building must be considered. Furthermore, the methods for anno-tating small-scale features (such as the windows or doors of a building) depend on the accuracy of the tracking system. If tracking accuracy is not accurate enough that a correct feature cannot be uniquely identified, extra cues must be provided. These might include instructions relative to some distinctive feature on the building (e.g. third window in from the left).

5.3.2 Routing

Routing information must show where a user is currently located and the route that must be taken to achieve a particular objective. The question of routing and the utility of different kinds of map display have been extensively analyzed for virtual environments. For example, in Darken and Cevik, 1999) the relative effectiveness of a rotating map and a map with north always pointing up was considered for applications where users had to navigate through a virtual city. The conclusion was that different map displays were better suited for different types of task. In targeted searches, where a user was shown the location of a target of interest, rotating maps were better. This analysis suggests that dynamically updated routing information, expressed as a function of user orientation, is extremely useful. However, no such detailed studies have been carried out for AR systems that are providing continuous navigation cues.

5.3.3 Coordination Information

The BARS system will also present data that can be used to coordinate group activities. For example, users may wish to know the location of colleagues with respect to themselves. As with environmental information, the means of showing this data depends on the number of users and the accuracy of the tracking systems.

5.3.4 Information Filtering

The amount of information that can be shown to a user in a virtual world can be overwhelming. To alleviate this problem, there is a need for an "intelligent" filter that will determine what information is relevant to the user at a particular time. To accomplish this, the aim or goal of the user needs to be defined. For instance, in the BARS system, two goals typical of a reconnaissance mission are (1) go to a particular location; and (2) find out as much as possible about an area. In the first situation, a route between the current and desired locations could be shown, while in the latter situation, important information about selected key objects can be displayed graphically (i.e. whether they are friendly, enemy or unknown). Some information might always be shown, such as known enemy locations and hazards (such as mines). We believe that an intelligent filter will lower the real-time update requirement of the image generator by reducing the information that it needs to display. In addition, users will be shown only what is relevant to them at any particular time.

5.4 User Interactions

Another important research area is to investigate methods for user interaction. Within the BARS project, users are participants with the ability to make queries and send reports that can be distributed to other users and planning systems. There has been a great deal of work dedicated to the study of user interaction paradigms in VR environments (a useful taxonomy can be found in Poupyrev *et al.* (1998)). However, mobile augmented reality systems present fundamentally different challenges because the interaction space is different. For example, one major challenge in VR systems is the process of constructing a user interface to drive how a user's viewpoint will change. A range of approaches including flying, grabbing (Poupyrev *et al.*, 1998) or using a "world in miniature" (Pausch *et al.*, 1995) have been investigated. However, a mobile AR user can only change their position in the environment by physically moving to that new location. As explained in Section 5.3.2, the AR system can only provide prompts or cues to guide the user to the destination. Rather, the main user interactions must allow a user to query objects that can be seen in the environment and to make reports about the state of the environment or about the appearance of a new object. We believe that any successful interaction paradigm must span both 3D and 2D displays.

5.4.1 3D Interaction

Many types of system for 3D interactions employ various types of widgets, menuing systems or button/keyboard operations. However, all of these approaches draw the user's attention away from the environment and towards manipulating physical or virtual input devices. To overcome these limitations, we propose to develop our 3D interaction system using a multimodal input paradigm. This paradigm decomposes user interactions into a combination of several different types of input that occur concurrently. The most widely used methods combine speech with a physical gesture such as pointing or drawing. One of the most successful promising examples of an experimental multimodal input approach is the QuickSet system (Cohen *et al.*, 1997). This research has examined how a combination of speech and 2D gesture can be used to accelerate the setup process for military simulations in 2D and 3D maps (Cohen *et al.*, 1999). Part of the BARS process will be to see whether this 2D approach can be extended to exploit the range of interactions in a full 3D space (Figure 5.4). Two key research areas remain – how is a feature of the environment selected, and how is the action to be specified?

Various types of selection method have been proposed, including virtual hand metaphors for grabbing. However, because the user is constrained to observe objects at the scale of the environment, we believe that virtual pointer metaphors – where the user points at an object rather than grabs it – are the most appropriate for this problem domain. The precise question of which pointer metaphor is most appropriate is an open research problem and is likely to be a function of the task at hand. For example, when selecting pre-existing objects in the environment, selection metaphors such as an aperture (Forsberg *et al.*, 1996), where the selection region is an adjustable cone rather than a line, might be most appropriate. However, when a user enters data about a new object the ray casting metaphor might be more appropriate because it precisely defines the user's line-of-sight. Since a line-of-sight report does not contain sufficient information to uniquely define the position of an object and it must be complemented with other types of information. For example, if the user points at a building and reports that a window

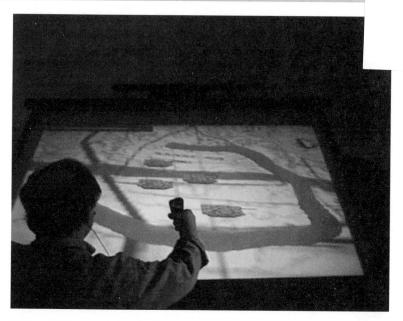

Figure 5.4 NRL and OGI have integrated the QuickSet system with NRL's Dragon VR software to evaluate multimodal interaction for 3D applications. A user is seen laying down 3D digital ink atop a terrain using a Responsive Workbench.

is broken, the system must use the fact that windows occur on the side of a building and the user is pointing at the side of a building.

Once an object or region of the environment has been selected, the type of operation needs to be specified. Within the multimodal paradigm, we propose to use a speech recognizer with a natural language processor.

5.4.2 2D Interaction

Although 3D interactions may be useful for many natural queries with the virtual environment, they are not the only interactions that might be needed. For example, if the user wishes to indicate a 2D path, it may be more effective to do so with a 2D device. Furthermore, the passive feedback of a flat surface to support the user's hand helps prevent fatigue and allows extremely accurate and precise operations to take place.

To address this, the Touring Machine provides both a see-through 3D head-worn display and the opaque 2D display of a handheld computer. The handheld computer's stylus and a finger-controlled trackpad on the back of the handheld display provide input.

The question of when a 2D or a 3D display is most effective is still an open research issue and we expect that a better understanding of the interplay of these different devices and input paradigms will be one useful result of the BARS project.

5.5 Conclusions

This chapter has introduced the problem of building wearable augmented reality systems for users operating in large, unstructured outdoor environments. There are many difficulties associated with moving AR systems from demonstrations within laboratories to systems that work outdoors.

We have also introduced some of the issues that must be solved for the successful application of mobile AR systems to complex outdoor environments. We have provided an overview of some of the key research areas (tracking systems, display designs, user interaction methods, and evaluation).

Acknowledgments

This research is supported by the Office of Naval Research, Arlington, Virginia.

References

Advisory Group for Aerospace Research and Development (1998) Visual effects in the high performance aircraft cockpit, *DTIC Report ADA199306*, AGARD, Neuilly-Sur-Seine.

Azuma, R (1997) A survey of augmented reality, *Presence: Teleoperators and Virtual Environments*, 4(6), 355–385.

Azuma, R (1998) Making augmented reality work outdoors requires hybrid tracking, in *Proceedings of IWARS '98 – the First International Workshop on Wearable Augmented Reality*.

Azuma, R, Hoff, B, Neely, H, III and Sarfaty, R (1999) A motion-stabilized outdoor augmented reality system, in *Proceedings of IEEE VR '99*, Houston, TX, pp. 252–259.

Bajura, M and Neumann, U (1995) Dynamic registration correction in video-based augmented reality systems, *IEEE Computer Graphics and Applications*, 15(5), 52–60.

Behringer, R (1999) Registration for outdoor augmented reality applications using computer vision techniques and hybrid sensors, in *Proceedings IEEE Virtual Reality '99*, Vol. 17, 244–251.

Billinghurst, M, Bowskill, J, Dyer, N and Morphett, J (1998) Spatial information displays on a wearable computer, *IEEE Computer Graphics and Applications*, 18(6), 24–31.

Caudell, TP (1994) Introduction to augmented reality, in *Proceedings of the Conference on Telemanipulator and Telepresence Technologies*, SPIE, Vol. 2351.

Caudell, TP and Mizell, DW (1992) Augmented reality: an application of heads-up display technology to manual manufacturing processes, in *Proceedings of 1992 IEEE Hawaii International Conference on Systems Sciences*, January.

Cohen, P, Johnston, M, McGee, D, Oviatt, S, Pittman, J, Smith, I, Chen, L and Clow, J (1997) QuickSet: Multimodal interaction for distributed applications, in *Proceedings of ACM Multimedia*, New York, ACM.

Cohen, P, McGee, D, Wu, L, Clow, J, King, R, Julier, S and Rosenblum, L (1999) Multimodal Interaction for 2D and 3D Environment, *IEEE Computer Graphics and Applications*, 19(3), 10–13.

Darken, R and Cevik, H (1999) Map usage in virtual environments: orientation issues, in *Proceedings of the 1999 IEEE VR Conference*, March, pp. 133–140.

Feiner, S, MacIntyre, B and Seligmann, D (1993) Knowledge-based augmented reality, *Communications of the ACM*, 36(7), 52–62.

Feiner, S, MacIntyre, B, Höllerer, T and Webster, T (1997) A Touring Machine: prototyping 3D mobile augmented reality systems for exploring the urban environment, in *Proceedings of the International Symposium on Wearable Computers*, Cambridge, MA, October.

Forsberg, A, Herndon, K and Zeleznik, R (1996) Aperture-based selection for immersive virtual environments, in *Proceedings of the ACM Symposium on User Interface and Software Technology (UIST)*, pp. 95–96.

Foxlin, E (1996) Intertial head-tracker sensor fusion by a complementary separate-bias Kalman filter, in *Proceedings of VRAIS '96*, pp. 185–194.

Fuchs, H, Livingston, M, Raskar, R, Colucci, D, Keller, K, State, A, Crawford, J, Rademacher, P, Drake, S and Meyer, A (1998) Augmented reality visualization for laparoscopic surgery, in *Proceedings of the First International Conference on Medical Image Computing and Computer-Assisted Intervention (MICCAI '98)*, October.

Gumm, MM, Marshak, WP, Branscome, TA, Wesler, MMc, Patton, DJ and Mullins, LL (1998) A comparison of soldier performance using current land navigation equipment with information integrated on a helmet-mounted display, *ARL Report ARL-TR-1604, DTIC Report 19980527 081*, April.

Hix, D, Swan, JE, II, Gabard, JL, McGee, M, Durbin, J and King, T (1999) User-centered design and evaluation of a real-time battlefield visualization virtual environment, in *IEEE Virtual Reality '99 Conference*, Houston, TX, pp. 96–103.

Hoff, WA, Lyon, T and Nguyen, K (1996) Computer vision-based registration techniques for augmented reality, in *Proceedings of Intelligent Robots and Control Systems XV, Intelligent Control Systems and Advanced Manufacturing*, SPIE, Vol. 2904, pp. 538–548, November.

HRL Laboratories (1998) *GRIDS: Geospatial Registration of Information for Dismounted Soldiers*, UNC Chapel Hill and Raytheon Systems Company, http://web-ext2.darpa.mil/ETO/wv/98overviews/index.html.

Judd, T (1997) A personal dead reckoning module, in *Proceedings of the ION GPS '97*.

Julier, S and Uhlmann, J (1997) A non-divergent estimation algorithm in the presence of unknown correlations, in *Proceedings of the IEEE American Control Conference*.

Koller, D, Klinker, G, Rose, E, Breen, D, Whitaker, R and Tuceryan, M (1997) Real-time vision-based camera tracking for augmented reality applications, in *Proceedings of the ACM Symposium on Virtual Reality Software and Technology (VRST-97)*, pp. 87–94.

MacIntyre, B (1999) Exploratory programming of distributed augmented environments, *PhD Thesis*, Columbia University, NY.

Pausch, R, Burnette, T, Brockway, D and Weiblen, M (1995) Navigation and locomotion in virtual worlds via flight into hand-held miniatures, *ACM SIGGRAPH '95 Conference Proceedings, Computer Graphics*, July.

Poupyrev, I, Weghorst, S, Billinghurst, M and Ichikawa, T (1998) Egocentric object manipulation in virtual environments: empirical evaluation of interaction techniques, *Computer Graphics Forum [Eurographics Conference Issue]*, 17(3), C-41–C-52, August.

Pryor, H, Furness, T and Viirre, E (1998) The virtual retinal display: a new display technology using scanned laser light, in *Proceedings of Human Factors and Ergonomics Society, 42nd Annual Meeting*, pp. 1570–1574.

SnapTrack Inc. (1999) *An Introduction to SnapTrack Server-Aided GPS Technology*, http://www.snaptrack.com/atwork.html.

Spitzer, M, Rensing, N, Aquilino, P, Olson, M and McClelland, R (1998) Portable human/computer interface mounted in eyewear, in *Helmet and Head-Mounted Displays III, SPIE AeroSense Conference*, Vol. 3362.

Uhlmann, J, Julier, S and Csorba, M (1997) Nondivergent simultaneous map building and localization using covariance intersection, in *Proceedings of the SPIE AeroSense Conference, Navigation and Control Technologies for Unmanned Systems II*.

Webster, A, Feiner, S, MacIntyre, B, Massie, W and Krueger, T (1996) Augmented reality applications in architectural construction, in *Designing Digital Space: An Architect's Guide to Virtual Reality* (ed. D. Bertol), Chichester, John Wiley & Sons, pp. 193–200.

Welch, G and Bishop, G (1997) SCAAT: incremental tracking with incomplete information, *Proceedings of SIGGRAPH '97*.

You, S, Neumann, U and Azuma, R (1999) Hybrid inertial and vision tracking for augmented reality registration, *Proceedings of IEEE VR '99*, Houston TX.

6

Toward Tightly Coupled Human Interfaces

Thomas A. Furness III

As we stand at the portal of the next millennium, I am both excited and terrified about the future. I feel that as a modern civilization we may have become intoxicated by technology, and find ourselves involved in enterprises that push technology and build stuff just because we can do it. At the same time we are confronted with a world that is increasing needful of vision and solutions for global problems relating to the environment, food, crime, terrorism and an aging population. In this information technology milieu, I find myself being an advocate for the human and working to make computing and information technology tools that extend our capabilities, unlock our intelligence and link our minds to solve these pervasive problems.

6.1 Some Assumptions About the Future

It was estimated that in 1995 there were 257.2 million computers in the world (including 96.2 million in the USA, 18.3 million in Japan, 40.3 million in Europe). Collectively, these computers produced a computing capacity of 8 265 419 million instructions per second (mips). By the year 2000, the number of computers relative to 1995 had doubled, with a combined computing capacity of 246 509 000 mips [1]. That's about 41 000 instructions per second for every person who lives upon the earth. Ray Kurzweil [2] predicts that by 2010 we will be able to purchase for $1000 the equivalent information processing capacity of one mouse brain and by 2030 the equivalent computing capacity of one human brain. Continuing this extrapolation, he predicts that by 2060 digital computing (again purchased for $1000) will equal the processing capacity of all the human brains on the earth (and Kurzweil has been pretty good at predicting).

These trends suggest that the following assumptions will be (for all intents and purposes) realized in the coming decades:

- Computing capacity will continue to increase at at least Moore's law rates (i.e. doubling every 18–24 months) [3].
- Dramatic advances will be made in high-resolution digital imaging, compression algorithms and random access mass storage.
- Broadband communications will be available worldwide.
- There will be a rich mix of available wired and wireless communications.
- Reduction in size, cost and power consumption of computational and communications hardware will continue.
- There will be continued advancement in portable power generation and storage.
- AI heuristics will continue to develop, including natural language and learning.
- The world's knowledge resources will be digitized and placed in accessible locations.
- Computers will continue to be connected to people.

My colleagues and I also anticipate an emerging trend toward a "power company" model of networked system architecture, in which "thick" local processing (focused largely on the interface) communicates with "thick" computing and content services through relatively "thin" network devices and servers. A final (and key) assumption is that although humans may be slow relative to the speed and growth of computation, we have an incredible ability to think out of the box and make "cognitive leaps" in solving problems. So humans are not obsolete yet.

Within this context we envision a future in which the boundaries of human thought, communication and creativity are not defined by the design, location and proximity of information technology, but by the human endeavor which these devices support. Tightly coupled human interface technology will produce a symbiotic relationship, supporting and facilitating reflective and experiential thought. Emotional and motivational factors will prove to be as important as cognitive factors in many domains, and natural human behavior will be the predominant mode of interaction. Future media will be personal, flexible, emergent and universal.

6.2 Interface Challenges

While these trends will greatly expand our use of digital media, they will not on their own produce a fundamental shift in the way we conceptualize and interact with media and information technology systems. I feel that the greatest near-term challenge of the information age is that of being able to really use the phenomenal capacity that will be achieved in digital media, computing and networking. How will humans tap and process all that can flow... like drinking from a fire hydrant with our mouths too small?!

Herbert A. Simon, the 1978 Nobel Laureate in Economics and the recognized father of artificial intelligence and cognitive science, stated that:

> What information consumes is rather obvious: it consumes the attention of its recipients. Hence a wealth of information creates a poverty of attention, and a need to

allocate that attention efficiently among the overabundance of information sources that might consume it.

(It should be added parenthetically that the lack of a good interface also consumes many more resources than an intuitive one.)

Even though we have made great progress in developing computing technology, the concomitant development of the interfaces to those media has been lacking. Television is still two-dimensional, telephony is still monophonic and we are still using a highly coded symbol interface (the keyboard) and a small screen to interact with computers. In the last 20 years about the only improvement in the human–computer interface has been the mouse, invented by Douglas Englebart in 1965. The mouse, as a spatial input device, has made a dramatic improvement in working with desktop and windowed screens; but as for the rest, little progress has been made.

This concern about lagging interfaces has been echoed by the United States National Research Council, which recently published a report of its steering committee on computer interfaces titled *More than Screen Deep* [4]. There were three main recommendations of the Committee. The first was the need to break away from 1960s technology and paradigms and develop new approaches for immersing users in computer-mediated interactions. The second recommendation was the need to invest in the research required to provide the component subsystems needed for every-citizen[1] interfaces. The third recommendation was to encourage research on systems-level design and development of human–machine interfaces that support multiperson, multimachine groups as well as individuals.

Computers generally give us a way to create, store, search and process vast amounts of information rapidly in digital domains and then to communicate this information to other computers and/or to people. To fully exploit the potential power of the computer in unlocking and linking minds, I believe that we have to address computation and humans as a symbiotic system.

To achieve this vision of a radically different model of our relationship to information systems we will need to address the following research challenges:

1. What are the most useful and effective methods of integrating the information system interface of the future?
2. What are the most appropriate metrics and methods for determining when we are on the right track?
3. What innovative component appliances will be possible and how will they be used?
4. How will we get bandwidth to the brain and expand human intelligence to make use of the media and information processing appliances of the future?

---

1 In the context of this chapter, the term "every-citizen" includes all ages and physical abilities.

6.3 Some Fundamental Assertions

In an attempt to answer these questions, I propose the following assertions or principles that we should follow in developing better interface appliances:

1. We must exploit the fundamental 3D perceptual organization of the human in order to get *bandwidth into* the brain.
2. We must exploit the fundamental 3D organization of our psychomotor mechanisms to get *bandwidth out of* the brain.
3. We must use multiple sensory and psychomotor modalities to increase the effective bandwidth to and from the brain.
4. We must observe the human unobtrusively and infer intent and emotions, so that we can adapt the information channel to tune the flow of information into and out of the human based upon these measures.
5. We must remember that humans build mental models to predict and conserve bandwidth.
6. We must remember the power of place (e.g. people generally remember "places" better than text).
7. We must put people in "places" in order to put "places" in people.
8. Machines must become more human-like (rather than humans machine-like) in order to advance together.
9. In the future we can expect machines to learn and adapt to humans.
10. We can progress no faster than our tools to measure our progress.

6.4 Matching Machines to Humans

The term *interface* can be described as *what exists between faces*. At the basest level, the role of the human interface is to transfer signals across human and machine boundaries. (One may think of this is where the silicon and carbon meet.) These signals may exist in the form of photons, mechanical vibrations, or electromagnetic and/or chemical signals and may represent discrete events such as key presses and status lights, as well as continuous events such as speech, head/eye movement, visual and acoustic imagery or physiological state. The physical interface is intended to be a means to an end, and not the end itself, and thus it should be transparent to the user in performing a particular task with the medium. Ideally, the interface provides an "impedance match" between human sensory input and machine signal output while simultaneously providing efficient transduction of human intent as reflected in the psychomotor or physiological behavior of the user. The end goal is to create a high bandwidth signal channel between the human cognitive processes and the machine signal manipulation and delivery processes.

To create an ideal interface or "impedance match" between the human and the machine, it is first necessary to understand the saliencies of how humans function. Much can be said on this topic. The reader is encouraged to explore the references at the end of this chapter for further information. To summarize the author's experience in interface design, human capabilities can be boiled down into the following statements:

1. *Humans are 3D spatial beings.* We see, hear and touch in three dimensions. Although providing redundancy, our two eyes and two ears, along with feedback (i.e. proprioceptive cues) from arms, legs etc., allow us to localize ourselves in three-dimensional space. Light rays emitted or reflected from the three-dimensional world reach the retinas of our eyes and are transduced by a two-dimensional receptor field. The brain then uses the signals from both eyes containing vergence, stereographic and accommodative cues to construct three-dimensional understanding. From birth we develop these spatial skills by interacting with the world. Similarly, our ears individually receive and process sound. Depending upon the location of the sound, the brain compares the interaural latencies and sound wavefront (having been manipulated by the pinnae of the outer ear) to create a three-dimensional interpretation of the sound field reaching our ears. If we use interfaces that do not represent signals naturally or in 3D, we have to build new mental models to operate and interpret the signals from these interfaces.

2. *Humans have two visual systems.* Our eyes are amazing. The light-sensitive organ of our eye, the retina, is composed of two receptor types: cones and rods. The cone receptors (of which there are about 7 000 000) are sensitive to color and high spatial detail, and are located primarily in the macula or fovea of the eye. This region only subtends a 2–4° visual angle. The peripheral retina is populated with about 120 000 000 rod receptors, which are not color sensitive but have a shorter time constant, are highly sensitive to movement and can operate at lower light levels. Even though certain portions of the peripheral retina have a greater density of rod receptors than that of the cone receptors in the fovea, these rod receptors are connected together such that they are "ganged" to integrate light. It is interesting that these two receptor fields are processed at different regions of the brain and thereby perform different functions. The foveal region provides the detailed spatial information to our visual cortex so that we can read. This necessitates that we rotate our eyes often by rapid eye movements called saccades in order to read. The function of this region is to provide what we call our *focal vision*, that tells us the "what" of things. Simultaneously, the signals from our peripheral retina are processed in the lateral geniculate and other portions of the brain and do not have as dominant a connectivity to the visual cortex. The function of the peripheral retina is to help us maintain a spatial orientation. It is our peripheral vision or *ambient vision* that tells us the "where" of things. In essence, the ambient visual system tells the focal visual system where to fixate.

    To build a visual interface that takes advantage of the architecture of the human visual system, the display first must be wide field-of-view (e.g. subtend a large enough visual angle to allow the ambient visual system to work in conjunction with the focal visual system), and second, the information needs to be organized so that the spatial or "where" content is in the periphery while the "what" or detail is in the center of vision.

3. *Humans build mental models that create expectations.* William James, the 19th century philosopher/psychologist stated that: "...part of what we perceive comes from the object before us, the other part always comes out of our own head". This is saying that much of what we perceive in the world is a result of prestored spatial models that we have in our heads. We are mental model builders. Pictures spring into our mind as we use language to communicate. Indeed, our state of learning can be attributed to the fidelity of our mental models in allowing us to understand new perceptions and to synthesize new things. The efficiency with which we build mental models is associated with the intuitiveness of the interfaces and environments we inhabit. Highly coded interfaces (such as a computer keyboard) may require that we expend too much mental energy just to learn how to use the interface (the context) rather than concentrating on the content. Such an interface is not transparent and gets in the way of the task we are really trying to perform.

4. *Humans like parallel information input.* People make use of a combination of sensory stimuli to help reduce ambiguity. The sound of a letter dropping in a mailbox tells us a lot about how full the mailbox is. The echoes in a room tell us about the material in the fixtures and floors of a room. We use head movement to improve our directional interpretation of sound. We use touch along with sight to determine the smoothness of a surface. Multiple modalities give us rich combinatorial windows to our environment that we use to define and refine our percept of the environment. It is our way of reducing ambiguity.

5. *Humans work best with 3D motor control.* Generally, people perform motor control functions most efficiently when they are natural and intuitive. For example, using the scaled movement of a mouse in a horizontal two-dimensional plane to position a cursor on a screen in another vertical two-dimensional plane is not naturally intuitive. Learn it we can, and become proficient. Still, this may not be as effective and intuitive as pointing a finger at the screen or better yet, just looking at the item and using eye gaze angle as an input mechanism. Anytime we depart from the natural or intuitive way of manipulating or interacting with the world, we require the user to build new mental models, which creates additional overhead and distracts from the primary task.

6. *Humans are different from each other.* People are all different. We have different shapes, sizes, and physical and cognitive abilities, and even different interests and ways of doing things. Unfortunately, we often build tools and interfaces expecting everyone to be the same. When we have the flexibility of mapping the way we do things into the tools we use, the chances are that we will use them more effectively.

7. *Humans don't like to read instructions.* This is the laughable position in which we now find ourselves, especially in the age of fast food and instant gratification. It is painful to read instructions, and often they are not paid attention to. The best interfaces are those that are natural and intuitive. When instructions are to be given, it is best to use a tutorial, or better yet, context-sensitive on-screen help. Maybe best would be an intelligent agent which watches our progress and mistakes and (politely) makes recommendations.

Table 6.1 Status of current computer interfaces

- Information is still highly coded
- Presentations are not three-dimensional (vision and audition)
- Display fields-of-view too small (i.e. not immersive and don't take advantage of the peripheral retina)
- The user is outside looking in (do not exploit the perceptual organization of the human)
- Inflexible input modalities (such as not using speech and eye gaze)
- Presentations are not transparent (cannot overlay images over the world)
- Interfaces require the user to be "computer-like"
- Interfaces are not intuitive (i.e. they take a while to learn)
- It is difficult to involve multiple participants

6.5 Shortfalls in Current Computer Interfaces to Humans

If we use these characteristics of the human to examine the current incarnation of computer interfaces[2], we find that they fail the impedance matching test dismally and don't take advantage of even the basic criteria of how humans work. I have listed just a few of these in Table 6.1.

In summary, the current state of computer interfaces is poor. There is no match to the capabilities of the human, thereby greatly limiting the linking of digital data streams in and out of the brain.

6.6 Virtual Interfaces – a Better Way?

To overcome the human interface difficulties enumerated above, and to restore our lost vision in the information age, it is clear that a paradigm shift is needed in the way we think about coupling human intelligence to computation processes. The end goal of any coupling mechanism should be to provide bandwidth to the brain through matching the organization and portrayal of digital data streams to sensory, perceptual, cognitive and motor configurations of the human. Since it is difficult to change the configuration of human sensory and psychomotor functions (except through training), it is more advantageous to arrive at a computer interface that is designed from the human out. Indeed, the goal is to "make the computer human-like" rather than our past of making the human computer-like.

Virtual reality is a new human interface that attempts to solve many of these interface problems. Much (and perhaps too much) has been written about virtual reality. It has been called the ultimate computer interface by many [5]. At least in theory, virtual interfaces attempt to couple data streams to the senses ideally, and

---

2 For the sake of discussion, I use the typical computer interface as a flat panel or CRT display that provides a 40 cm diagonal face, an alphanumeric keyboard and a conventional mouse.

afford intuitive and natural interaction with these images. But the central key to the concept of virtual reality is that of sensory immersion within a 3D interactive environment.

6.7 Definitions of the Virtual

The term *virtual reality* originated from the concept within optical physics of virtual images. A *virtual image* is an image that appears to originate from a place in space but does not. It is a projection. In the field of virtual reality, virtual images are extrapolated to include visual, auditory and tactile stimuli which are transmitted to the sensory endorgans such that they appear to originate from within the three-dimensional space surrounding the user. The term *virtual interface* adds the input and output modalities to interacting with virtual images and is defined as: a system of transducers, signal processors, computer hardware and software that create an interactive medium through which (1) information is transmitted to the senses in the form of three-dimensional virtual images; and (2) psychomotor and physiological behavior of the user is monitored and used to manipulate the virtual images. A *virtual world* or *virtual environment* is synonymous with virtual reality and is defined as: the representation of a computer model or database in the form of a system of virtual images which creates an interactive 3D environment which can be experienced and/or manipulated by the user.

The components of a typical virtual interface system are shown in Figure 6.1. Virtual interfaces and the information environments they produce provide new alternatives for communicating between humans and within databases. Instead of directly viewing a physical display screen, the virtual display creates only a small

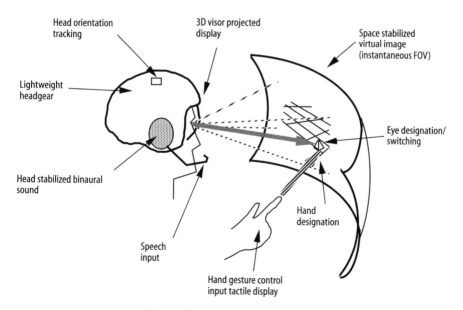

Figure 6.1 Virtual environment display system.

physical image (e.g. nominally one square inch) and projects this image into the eyes by optical lenses and mirrors so that the original image appears to be a large picture suspended in the world. (Note that the virtual retinal display, discussed below, does not use a two-dimensional array of photon emitters, but instead, projects a single photon stream directly on the retina of the eye.)

A personal virtual display system, termed a head-mounted display, usually consists of a small image source (e.g. a miniature cathode-ray tube or liquid crystal array) that is mounted on some headgear, and small optical elements which magnify, collimate and project this image via a mirror combiner into the eyes such that the original image appears at optical infinity. The perceived size of the image is a function of the magnification of the optics and not the physical size of the original image source. With two image sources and projection optics, one for each eye, a binocular virtual display can be created providing a 3D or stereoscopic scene.

With a partially reflective combiner (a mirror that reflects light from the image source into the eyes), the display scene can be superimposed on the normal physical world. The user can also position the image anywhere (i.e. it moves with the head). When combined with a head position sensing system, the information on the display can be stabilized as a function of head movement, thereby creating the effect of viewing a space-stabilized circumambience or "virtual world" which surrounds the user.

An acoustic virtual display can also be created by processing a sound image in the same way that the pinnae of the ear manipulate a sound wavefront. A sound object is first digitized and then convolved with head-related transfer function (HRTF) coefficients which describe the finite impulse response of the ears of a generic head to sounds at particular angles and distances from the head. Monaural digitized sound can thus be transformed to spatially localized binaural sound presented through stereo headphones to the subject. By using the instantaneously measured head position to select from a library of HRTF coefficients, a localized sound which is stable in space can be generated. These sound objects can be used either separately or as an "overlay" of 3D visual objects.

Similarly, a tactile image can be displayed by providing a two-dimensional array of vibration or pressure transducers (termed *tactors*) which are in contact with the skin of the hand or body. Tactors may be actuated as a function of the shape and surface features of a virtual object and the instantaneous position of the head and fingers. Force or inertial feedback can also be provided through a mechanically coupled motor system that senses hand position and provides virtual stops or modulation to hand movement given instantaneous hand position relative to an object.

6.8 Potential Advantages of Virtual Interfaces

Since virtual displays can surround users with three-dimensional stimuli, under ideal conditions of high image resolution and low update latencies users feel a sense of "presence", that we are "inhabiting" a new place instead of looking at a picture. This

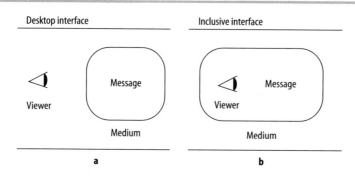

Figure 6.2 In **a**, the viewer is separate from the message; in **b** the viewer and message occupy the same virtual space.

aspect is illustrated by Figure 6.2. Normally, when we look at a display terminal for example, we see an object (i.e. the terminal) embedded in our three-dimensional world through which a separate message is being conveyed. In order to interact effectively within this world, we have to use *three* cognitive models: a model of our immediate environment, a model of the functionality of the medium (the terminal, in this case) and a model of the message and its heuristics as conveyed through this medium.

Conversely, when we are immersed in an inclusive virtual environment, we in effect become a part of the message. The original environment and presentation medium disappear and we are required to draw upon only a single model of the new environment which represents only the message. Then we can interact within this virtual environment using the same natural semantics that we use when interacting with the physical world. These factors empower the virtual interface as a medium with an unprecedented efficiency in communicating computer-generated graphical and pictorial information, making it ideal for a transportation system for our senses, i.e. an electronically mediated presence. This is the best way to substantially increase bandwidth to the brain.

Other advantages of the virtual environment include its flexibility in simultaneously conveying three-dimensional information into several modalities, such as using visual and acoustic representations of an object's location and state in three-space. Multiple modality displays have a greater promise of reducing ambiguity in complex displays and perhaps a more effective way of attracting attention to critical conditions during high workload tasks.

It should be noted here that virtual environments can also serve as a good means of simulating other systems, both physical and virtual (e.g. using a virtual display to simulate another virtual display). We will exploit this aspect extensively in our proposed testbed and experimental activities.

My supposition is that virtual environments can provide a three-dimensional medium through which complex information can be communicated rapidly to humans and between humans. Virtual reality also provides an empirical context for exploring theories of cooperation between human groups and software configurations. In Table 6.2 I summarize these advantages of virtual interfaces. As can be seen from the discussion above, most of the attributes of humans can be matched by virtual interfaces, thereby creating, at least in theory, an ideal interface.

Table 6.2 Potential advantages of virtual interfaces

Multisensory display	Hear, see, touch in a 3D circumambience
Multimodal input	Speech, motion (head, hand, body, eyes), facial expressions and gestures
Presence	Visual and acoustic sensory immersion becomes a 3D place
Transparency	Can superimpose and register virtual images over the real world
Intuitive	Behave naturally rather than symbolically
	Easy to learn
High bandwidth	Between the computer and the brain
	Between brains mediated by the computer
Virtual worlds	Surrogate to real world
	Abstraction of dataspace
Virtual physics	Can manipulate time, scale and physical laws to create a new physics in the virtual world.

6.9 So if VR Is So Good, Why Don't We Have More of It?

This is an easy question to answer: the technology simply does not exist yet and what does exist is too expensive. Most virtual world demonstrations to date have been clunky, in that the quality of the worlds has been limited due to the need to render millions of polygons and texture maps in real time (e.g. 20–30 Hz update rates) while maintaining low latencies in image stabilization (e.g. <16 ms). The headgear and other equipment are often large, heavy and oppressive, and generally get in the way of natural behavior. Furthermore, we may be up against a show-stopper, that of cybersickness: this phenomenon, akin to motion sickness, occurs when there is a sensory conflict between the visual and vestibular cues reaching the brain. The potential for cybersickness, along with the need to improve the VR technology, are slowing progress in adopting virtual interfaces.

But perhaps the single greatest hindrance to the widespread development and adoption of virtual interfaces has been economic. As yet, there are no driving applications for VR, especially ones that would stimulate growth of the industry and encourage risk-taking among hardware and software developers to make the necessary investment. Most VR installations exist at academic, industrial and government research organizations and have not been practical and affordable in the commercial or consumer market-place, except in limited arcade games. Consumer applications especially have been limited by the cost of the VR components and the lack of computer clout to render in real time the enormous number of polygons and texture maps that make the virtual world a satisfactory experience.

6.10 Progress in Virtual Interfaces

In spite of the hindrances to growth and development of virtual interfaces discussed above, VR is inherently appealing and embodies the potential for the impedance matching between computers and humans described above. Because of this potential, progress is also being made on various fronts. But to generate the ideal virtual environment, much work is needed on all modalities, including the transducers and underlying computational hardware and software components. But above all, we need to understand how people really work in virtual environments.

6.10.1 Understanding Humans

The Human Interface Technology Laboratory (HITL) at the University of Washington, along with other academic centers at MIT, University of North Carolina, University of Central Florida, University of Illinois (NCSA), Carnegie Mellon University and other military and industrial concerns, are continuing to work the technology. We have made notable advances in understanding how humans respond to virtual environments. For example, research at the HIT Lab has been aimed at determining the effects of latency and geometric scale on adaptation and readaptation of the vestibulo-ocular reflex and the propensity of users to be affected adversely by these conditions [6]. These efforts have been extended to include methods for overcoming cybersickness and how to measure objectively the sense of presence in a virtual environment [7]. We have obtained overwhelming evidence of the importance of a wide field-of-view in generating a sense of immersion and presence within the computer-generated environment. Indeed, immersion substantially increases our ability to form robust mental models that aid navigation in complex virtual environments. We have also found the importance of using the whole body in navigating within a virtual environment: kinesthetic and proprioceptive feedback reinforce the visual and provide a better mapping of virtual 3D space in the brain, much as in the real world [8].

6.10.2 Acoustic Displays

Digital signal processing has brought spatialized sound into practical realization. The only limitation is the need to increase the fidelity of individualized head-related transfer function so that the fidelity of 3D sound production is the best for each user (otherwise one would be listening through someone else's ears.) So 3D sound is gaining great maturity, but we need a fast way to determine an individual "earprint" [9].

6.10.3 Force Feedback

Bertrand Russell stated: "...it is touch that gives our sense of 'reality'.... Not only our geometry and physics, but our whole conception of what exists outside us, is based upon the sense of touch" [10]. Force feedback and tactile representations are perhaps the least mature virtual interface technology, but some progress is being made in force feedback effectors which sense six degrees of freedom of the hand and provide force modulation based upon the interaction of the position of the force point with a virtual object [11]. To be realistic, a force feedback subsystem needs to update at a 1000 Hz rate. Fast finite element modeling of deformable surfaces such as skin and other tissue will open new areas for surgical simulation involving virtual reality containing force feedback elements. Several studies have shown that realism in virtual environments can be substantially enhanced by incorporating tactile feedback along with visual representation [12,13].

6.10.4 Visual Displays

New advances in the resolution of small image sources such as active matrix LCDs and miniature CRTs have improved somewhat the image quality of virtual displays. Typically, these displays provide SVGA resolution (800 × 600 elements). The trade-off is to create a sufficient number of picture elements so that the virtual scene subtends a large visual angle (to generate a sense of presence) without making each pixel appear too large, thereby sacrificing the detail that can be seen. Generally, the best rule is that the more pixels the better, but magnifying an individual pixel to beyond a subtended visual angle of 3 minutes of arc makes the virtual scene unusable. Ideally, displays would be built that would stimulate the peripheral retina while also coupling detailed color information to the fovea. This would necessitate fields of view of 120° horizontal by 60° vertical, with an ideal pixel density of 4000 × 3000 elements. These performance requirements far exceed the 1000 × 1000 elements that will be available in the near future using matrix element image sources.

6.10.5 Virtual Retinal Display

Perhaps one of the most exciting developments to address the issue of display resolution is the development of the virtual retinal display (VRD) [14,15]. The VRD is truly a breakthrough technology which scans a modulated photon stream directly on the retina of the eye. The VRD eliminates the need for an image-forming source, such as a CRT or matrix element device. Figure 6.3 illustrates the mechanism of the VRD. Photons are generated by low-power gas lasers, lasing diodes or light-emitting diodes with red, green and blue spectra. These photon sources are modulated with a video signal from the computer or other video source. The three modulated color beams are then combined into one beam and focused onto a monofilament fiber which relays the light to the scan head. The scan head contains two mirrors. A resonant mirror oscillates sinusoidally at a frequency of 15–20 kHz and a galvo mirror oscillates in a sawtooth pattern at 60 Hz. The light enters the first mirror and is deflected in the high-speed horizontal direction and then bounces to the second mirror where it is scanned in the vertical direction to create a raster. The light is then bounced off the first mirror again to double the scan angle. The rasterized photon stream is then reflected through spherical optics and a combiner such that it enters the eye through a very narrow crossover point which acts like an exit pupil. When the user positions the entrance pupil of their eye in the exit pupil of the VRD the retina is flooded with the scanned light. The beam forms an instantaneous spot

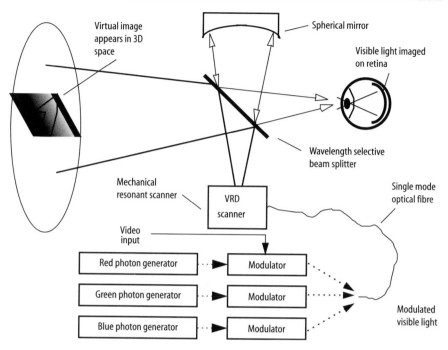

Virtual image appears in 3D space

Spherical mirror

Visible light imaged on retina

Wavelength selective beam splitter

Mechanical resonant scanner

VRD scanner

Single mode optical fibre

Video input

Red photon generator ╌► Modulator

Green photon generator ╌► Modulator

Blue photon generator ╌► Modulator

Modulated visible light

Figure 6.3 Virtual retinal display optical schematic.

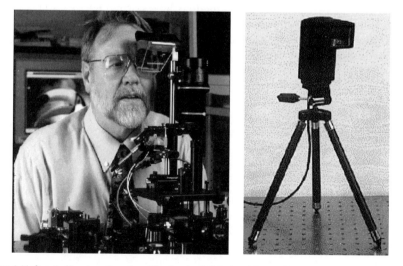

Figure 6.4 Left: optical bench configuration of the virtual retinal display; right: portable monochrome VRD demonstrator.

of approximately 30 mm on the retina at a power level of about 300 nw. Figure 6.4 illustrates a color optical bench version of the VRD with see-through optics, along with a more portable monochrome unit.

Table 6.3 Performance predictions for the virtual retinal display	
● Resolution (goal)	2000 × 1500 elements
● Luminance	>> 10 000 ft lamberts
● Dynamic range	> 3000:1
● Field of view	60°
● Accommodation (static)	−2.0 to +2.0 diopters
● Color	Red, green, blue
● Binocular	
● Weight	~100 g

The VRD is remarkable in that it can create a brilliant, high-resolution wide field-of-view image with very few components. The performance of the display is mainly a function of how fast the photon stream can be modulated. Table 6.3 gives the projected performance parameters for the current VRD development. Multiple beams can substantially increase the overall resolution and field of view. The VRD was invented by the HITL and is licensed to Microvision Inc., a Seattle, Washington, company which is developing commercial version of the VRD.

6.10.6 VR Applications

Applications that are promising now include those settings where visualization of spatial information is important, such as automotive and architectural design and medical visualization – especially when it helps to be inside a computer generated model. The Human Interface Technology Laboratory has been exploring the use of virtual environments for teaching complex scientific and mathematical concepts to children. The results have been profound. We have found that students who typically have been "slow learners" tend to catch up with the "smart" kids [16]. We have also used VR for the treatment of Parkinson's disease [17], phobias (e.g. fear of spiders) [18] and for pain alleviation [19]. We have built and demonstrated distributed virtual worlds, such as the GreenSpace project, wherein we have placed two people in Japan and two people in Seattle into a shared 3D immersive space so that the participants could see, hear and interact with each other in three dimensions [20]. We have built virtual architectural worlds such as Virtual Venice, where we mapped part of the actual city and built a virtual representation which could be use to visualize the prospects of new construction and rehabilitation of old structure.

Other laboratories (e.g. University of North Carolina, NCSA at the University of Illinois, Ford Motor Company) have been using virtual reality for medical imaging, molecular modeling and automotive design. Disney Imagineering has created a virtual world simulating the movie *Aladdin* where participants can fly on a virtual magic carpet and visit a 3D world of fantasy. Applications for virtual worlds truly defy the imagination, going from building real-world-like models to abstractions involving non spatial data sets [21].

6.11 Grand Challenges to Advanced Virtual Interfaces

The sensors and actuator technology community have a great opportunity to contribute to the future of virtual interfaces. Below I have listed some of the areas where innovative solutions are needed to further the utility and performance of virtual interfaces.

6.11.1 Tactile Displays

Even though the skin is the largest organ in the body (approximately 2 m^2), creating a sense of touch within virtual environments is a real challenge. Early work at Wright-Patterson AFB in the Super Cockpit program used a system of pneumatic bladders in a glove to apply pressure to the fingertips, based upon the instantaneous position of the hand relative to a virtual object. Some of the best pioneering work in the field was performed by Margaret Minsky and her colleagues at MIT. Professor Grigore Burdea at Rutgers has also been pioneering methods of providing touch and force feedback [22]. SensAble Technologies Inc. [23] is currently marketing force feedback devices which measure six degrees of freedom and provide force feedback to a stylus. But providing surface simulation to the receptors of the fingers and other parts of the body is difficult. This is an area where microactuators coupled to the skin could make realistic representations of the roughness of surfaces as a function of hand or finger position. Tactors may also be placed on other parts of the body to simulate surfaces.

6.11.2 Smell and Taste

Perhaps the least developed area in virtual interfaces is that of the senses of smell and taste. Certainly chemical sensors have been around for a long time, but the real-time synthesis of fragrances and/or the delivery mechanism to the human is underdeveloped. Morton Heilig made an attempt to build in odor delivery in his invention of the Sensorama in 1963. Using solenoids, wicks and vials of fragrances, users would smell appropriate scents while sitting on a motion platform, viewing a wide field-of-view 3D movie, hearing 3D sound, and feeling the wind in their faces.

The sensors community should continue to build robust detectors and parse the fundamental elements of taste and smell, but also strive to build those delivery mechanisms which can convey remotely the same chemicals or mimetics to the sensory endorgans. It is likely that delivery side of taste and smell will continue to be difficult and may in the short term necessitate a cross-modal representation. The idea here is to use another sensory modality to convey smell or taste, such as a 3D pattern of light and color to represent a particular combination of tastes and 3D sound patterns to represent smell. Since humans are good pattern recognizers, cross-modal patterns might be recognizable after some training. Of course, this training should include the real smell and/or taste which correlates with the sound or visual display of such. But there may be times when it is not desirable to smell or taste the real world, as in the case of hazardous environments or being the king's poison control taster. Still, virtual smell and taste without the stimulation of the olfactory and taste receptors may not be too satisfying.

6.11.3 Photon Generation and Manipulation

Although new display technologies such as the virtual retinal display provide a better coupling of visual images to the retina, there are still many areas for improvement. Even the VRD only covers a fraction (about one sixth) of the total retinal receptor field. New microelectromechanical scanning engines are needed which can steer photon streams at rates up to 30–50 kHz. We also need small solid state devices that can deliver blue and green light and be modulated at bandwidths exceeding 100 MHz.

New technology is also needed to manipulate the light wavefront in order to modulate the apparent distance of each display picture element. Currently, all virtual displays present a field of pixels that appear at the same viewing distance (usually optical infinity). This is like sitting inside a sphere upon which the image projection is being made. But the object of an binocular virtual display is to generate vergence cues (or stereographic cues) between the eyes so that objects will appear at different distances and in three dimensions. This situation creates a conflict between the two sets of cues: the monocular accommodative cues of pixel distance, which is based upon the collimation of the light, versus the binocular vergence cues (between the eyes). A condition may exist wherein the user is viewing an object that has vergence cues of a meter but for which the pixels appear to be originating from optical infinity (i.e. more that 10 meters away). In order to create a true voxel (volume picture element), the accommodative and vergence cues should match. This necessitates the modulation of the light wavefront at video rates to create an appropriate monocular viewing distance that corresponds with the binocular viewing distance. The problem now becomes: how can we cause a wavefront of light to change its collimation at 30 to 100 MHz rates? Depending upon the optical design, it may only be necessary to deflect a surface by a few wavelengths of light to obtain the desired effect.

6.12 Summary

My purpose in writing this chapter is to emphasize the need for better interfaces with computers and to describe potential improvements that virtual interfaces can offer. Virtual interface technology and virtual environments, if developed systematically, may allow us to meld the inductive and rational thinking of the human to the data manipulation power of the computer. Effectively configured, these tools of our age can transport our minds to new places where our vision will yet be extended.

Acknowledgments

The author would like to acknowledge the contributions of Suzanne Weghorst, Joseph King, Maxwell Wells and other staff and students at the Human Interface Technology Laboratory for insights and ideas that are related in this chapter. Research reported herein has been supported in part by the National Science Foundation, Defense Advanced Research Projects Agency, Microvision Inc. and the Virtual Worlds Consortium.

For further information contact: `tfurness@u.washington.edu` or visit the Human Interface Technology Laboratory Web site: `http://www.hitl.washington.edu/`.

References

[1]   *Annual Computer Industry Almanac, 1996.* Computer Industry Almanac, Inc.
[2]   R Kurzweil (1999) *The Age of Spiritual Machines,* New York, Viking.
[3]   `http://www.intel.com/pressroom/archive/speeches/GEM93097.HTM;http://www.intel.com/intel/museum/25anniv/hof/moore.htm`
[4]   National Research Council (1997) *More Than Screen Deep: Toward Every-Citizen Interfaces to the Nation's Information Infrastructure,* National Academy Press.
[5]   I Sutherland (1965) The ultimate display, in *Proceedings of IFIP 65,* Vol. 2, pp. 506–508, 582–583.
[6]   M Draper (1995) Exploring the influence of virtual bodies on spatial awareness, *Master's Thesis,* University of Washington, College of Engineering, `http://www.hitl.washington.edu/publications/draper/`.
[7]   J Prothero (1998) The role of rest frames in vection, presence, motion and sickness, *Dissertation,* University of Washington, College of Engineering. `http://www.hitl.washington.edu/publications/r-98-11/`.
[8]   B Peterson (1998) The influence of whole-body interaction on wayfinding in virtual reality, *Masters Thesis,* University of Washington, `http://www.hitl.washington.edu/publications/r-98-3/`; B Peterson, M Wells, T Furness and E Hunt (1998). The effects of the interface on navigation in virtual environments, In *Proceedings of Human Factors and Ergonomics Society 1998 Annual Meeting,* `http://www.hitl.washington.edu/publications/r-98-5/`.
[9]   J Baldis (1998) Effects of spatial audio on communication during desktop conferencing, *Masters Thesis,* Unversity of Washington.
[10] B Russell (1969) *The ABC of Relativity,* London, George Allen & Unwin.
[11] `http://www.sensable.com/haptics.htm`.
[12] H Hoffman, J Groen, S Rousseau, A Hollander, W Winn, M Wells and T Furness (1996) Tactile augmentation: enhancing presence in virtual reality with tactile feedback from real objects. Paper presented at the meeting of the American Psychological Society, San Francisco, CA.
[13] Y Ikei, K Wakamatsu and S Fukuda (1997) *IEEE Computer Graphics and Applications,* 17(6).
[14] M Tidwell (1995) A virtual retinal display for augmenting ambient visual environments, *Masters Thesis,* University of Washington, `http://www.hitl.washington.edu/publications/tidwell/`.
[15] G Wright (1998) *New Scientist,* 2146, 33–35.
[16] `http://www.hitl.washington.edu/projects/learning_center/vrrv/`
[17] J Prothero (1993) The treatment of akinesia using virtual images, *Masters Thesis,* University of Washington, College of Engineering, `http://www.hitl.washington.edu/publications/prothero/`.
[18] AS Carlin, H Hoffman and S Weghorst (1997) Virtual reality and tactile augmentation in the treatment of spider phobia: a case study, *Behavior Research and Therapy,* 35(2), 153–158. See also `http://www.hitl.washington.edu/research/theraputic/burn.html`.

[19] HG Hoffman, JN Doctor, DR Patterson, S Weghorst and T Furness (1998) VR for burn pain control during wound care. In *Proceedings of Medicine Meets VR 6*, San Diego, CA, IOS Press. See also http://www.hitl.washington.edu/research/therapeutic/exposure.html.
[20] http://www.hitl.washington.edu/research/greenspace/greenspace.html.
[21] http://www.hitl.washington.edu/.
[22] G Burdea (1996) *Force and Touch Feedback for Virtual Reality*, New York, Wiley.
[23] http://www.sensable.com/.

Further Reading

Barfield, W and Furness, T (1995) *Virtual Environments and Advanced Interface Design*, Oxford, Oxford University Press.
http://www.hitl.washington.edu/projects/knowledge_base/guides.html.
http://www.media.mit.edu:80/~marg/haptics-bibliography.html.

7

Situation-Aware Mobile Assistance

Thomas Kirste

Abstract

Ultraportable mobile computers provide electronic assistance for environments and usage situations, where computer support up to now has not been feasible. For the first time, a true physical and cognitive integration of computer support into the everyday business of the real world becomes possible, as envisioned in Mark Weiser's concept of "ubiquitous computing" (Weiser, 1993).

However, although handheld PCs etc. already support a good deal of personal information management and basic access to distributed multimedia information services such as the World Wide Web, they are still surprisingly difficult to use to their full potential. Specifically, lengthy interaction sequences and the inability to find quickly that important piece of information which is embedded somewhere in the machine sometimes make using those devices a very disappointing experience.

In this chapter, we outline a new approach to realizing easy-to-use personal digital assistant systems, based on the concept of Situation Awareness. Using knowledge about task structures, situation dependencies and task contexts, our concept allows a mobile assistant to proactively provide the right information at the right time and the right place, without intruding upon the user's primary task: interacting with reality.

7.1 Introduction

An everyday scene: the network technician is jogging to the office of a user who has complained that her PC simply won't execute the network login scripts at boot time. On the way, somebody else asks him to refill toner for the color laser printer. While troubleshooting the PC, the technician needs to inspect the switchboard rooms: has somebody accidentally removed the connection? And by the way, where is the switchboard documentation? Just then, the boss drops in and demands help in setting up the conference room's multimedia technology: *Now!* While another user complains that his PC still needs fixing.

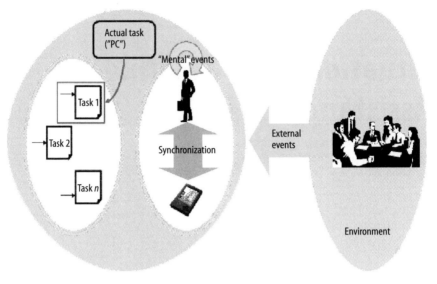

Figure 7.1 Tasks in human–machine context.

Similar scenarios exist for virtually every "multitasking" job, for project managers just as for emergency doctors. Figure 7.1 depicts this situation, where a user has several tasks to manage in parallel. "Context switches" and task progress are caused by external events (observable by a mobile assistant), as well as by (basically non-observable) internal transitions of the user's mental state. Clearly, the mobile assistant should support the user in selecting appropriate tasks based on the current situation, in establishing the new task context ("Er, what did I want to do here?") and in maintaining the internal "stack" of tasks.

In order to support the user in managing such scenarios, an assistant system would be useful that

- keeps track of the user's various activities
- allows the user to add and modify activities as the situation requires
- helps by pulling activities into the foreground in response to events, e.g. by presenting relevant context information
- provides fast access to important information
- supports quick orientation in new situations

Of course, such a system must be available to the user at any time and at any place in order to be a reliable assistant. This requires the use of ultraportable devices, like palm-sized and handheld PCs, personal intelligent communicators, or, *nomen est omen*, personal digital assistants.

While these devices already support a good deal of personal information management and basic access to distributed multimedia information services, such as the

World Wide Web, they are still surprisingly difficult to use to their full potential. Specifically, lengthy interaction sequences and the inability to find quickly that important piece of information which is embedded somewhere in the machine sometimes make using these devices a very disappointing experience.

Creating minimally intrusive user interfaces, good data organization mechanisms and intelligent search agents is one important approach for addressing these problems. But they still do not help users in keeping track of their various activities.

In this chapter we want to discuss an additional strategy that may be used as an orthogonal approach to achieving the above tasks of an assistant system. This approach is based in the concept of *Situation Awareness*.

The work described here is part of the "MoVi"-project, a research group funded by the Deutsche Forschungsgemeinschaft. The focus of MoVi, started in December 1994, is to investigate the aspects of mobile visualization and the interactive use of mobile computers.

7.2 Situation-Aware Mobile Assistance

7.2.1 Mobile Assistance

The notion "assistance" has been introduced in the information technologies in the area of intelligent agents, decision support systems and office automation. Typical assistants are systems supporting the user by allowing the automatization and delegation of routine tasks, such as email filtering or meeting scheduling (Riecken, 1994).

The term "assistant" is also used to denote software systems for critical and monotonous tasks like installation surveillance in buildings or flight monitoring in airports (Willumeit and Kolrepm 1997). Here, the human assigns monitoring tasks to the machine. For a more detailed discussion of today's assistance concepts, the reader is referred to Billings (1997), Endsley (1996), Giesa and Schumann (1997), Sheridan (1996) and Wickens (1997).

The concept of "mobile assistance" is based on the fact that today's mobile devices provide effectively usable computer support for spatially and temporally distributed activities that require interaction with physical reality. Here, the computer support required by a given user in a specific physical environment is determined not only by the user's goals, but also by this environment.

So, in contrast to position and situation-*independent* access to arbitrary information ("anything, anytime, anywhere"), we focus on situation-dependent information presentation. The central goal is to provide the *right* information at the *right* time and place – with minimal interaction.

An optimal assistant provides the required information autonomously and independently, without requiring the user to ask for it explicitly.

7.2.2 Situation Awareness

Ideally, an assistant would simply predict the desires of its "master" using a suitable oracle. This would definitely provide the right information proactively at the right time and the right place.

The question is of course, how to implement such an oracle.

One important fact is that many activities have an internal structure (subtasks, dependencies between subtasks etc.). Furthermore, it is often the case that specific subtasks can only be executed in certain environments. For example, the task of changing switchboard wiring is, obviously, only executable when in front of the switchboard.

So, once the assistant knows the user's activities and specific subtask structures and the dependencies between subtasks and the environment, as well as the current state of the environment, it may be able to predict the most probable activity of the user in the current environment. Instead of having the user manually select the appropriate application, document or functionality, the system does this automatically. Ideally, when the user looks at the personal assistant, it already has the required information on its display.

In other words, by being aware of the user's situation and knowing the situation dependencies of tasks, the mobile assistant can automatically determine the information relevant to the user in this situation. Figure 7.2 summarizes the reasoning behind the fact that situation-aware assistance and mobile computers are two sides of the same coin.

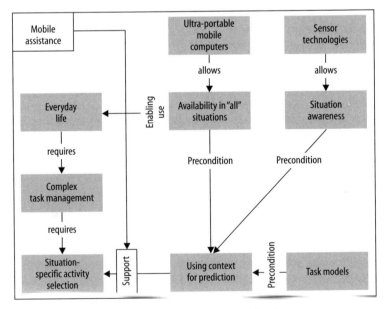

Figure 7.2 Reasoning for situation-aware mobile assistance.

Within the scope of our work, we are developing a framework for *Situation-Aware Mobile Assistance* (SAMoA). In the following, we outline the basic aspects of the SAMoA framework and its use in some of our application prototypes.

7.3 The SAMoA Framework

The SAMoA framework is built around the following concepts:

- **Tasks:** A user might have several tasks to accomplish that are simultaneously active. Each active task consists of a *task definition* and a *task state*. The task definition describes the task's internal structure, the individual subgoals that a user has to reach in order to fulfill the task. The task state describes which goals still have to be fulfilled.

  A critical aspect here is the task definition language. This language must not only be simple and intuitive enough to allow task definition by the end user ("end-user programming"), it also needs to support incremental and *ad hoc* modification and creation of (sub-)tasks by the user in order to account for the unpredictability of real life. Currently, we concentrate on the second requirement – incremental modifiability. Here, a specific derivative of rule-based systems, namely production systems, seems to provide interesting conflict resolution concepts (specificity, recency, refractoriness, rule-ordering) that support the *ad hoc* modification of rule sets even during execution.

  Other task description models, such as the GOMS model (Card *et al.*, 1983) and models developed for task-based user interface design (Browne, 1994; Johnson and Johnson, 1990) are further potential approaches to a task definition language. Common to all task modeling mechanisms is the concept of dividing a complex task recursively into subtasks until *basic activities* are reached. Within SAMoA, this notion has a definite and obvious meaning: a basic activity is a subtask that does not span multiple situations.

- **Situations:** The "situation" is the second important concept in SAMoA. It contains the following aspects:
  - the user's physical environment (objects in proximity etc.), including the user's own position
  - the user's currently active tasks with their respective states
  - user preferences (subjective task priorities, individual preferences for processing orders etc.)

- **Contexts:** There is usually a lot of information, – documents, sketches, contacts, notes etc. – connected to a task, which is not part of the task definition itself but is nevertheless important to the user for fulfilling the task. This collection of information items is called the task's *context*. Although one information item could be contained in more than one context, there is only one context per task.

  When a situation changes, it is useful to switch the context accordingly (i.e. to the task active in the new situation), providing the user with all the information required in the new situation.

- **Dynamic dialog creation:** The goal of the user interface and interaction capabilities in SAMoA is to allow for a seamless integration into established work routine, requiring minimal cognitive overhead for its operation.

  On the other hand, task definitions can be created and modified *ad hoc*. Furthermore, the decision about when to execute which subtask is completely situation-driven. This means that the user interface has to be created dynamically.

  In consequence, we need a user interface concept that allows for:

  – the definition of dedicated dialogs, tailored towards the specific basic activities, and
  – the dynamic configuration of the user interface from these dialogs based on the current situation and the tasks selected by the user for execution.

By exploiting knowledge of the internal structure of a work process and the dependencies between individual process steps and the current physical surroundings, the system is able to tailor its user interface towards the operations required in the current environment.

An important fact about dynamic dialog creation is the flexibility of configuration and context awareness. As SAMoA is designed as an open framework, any particular application can be added to the system by providing application-specific dialog components, application-specific task models, and situation dependencies. Based on these definitions, the dynamic user interface builder creates situation-specific user interfaces as the need arises and thus provides a smooth integration into the workflow.

Figure 7.3 presents a simplified version of the architecture that is used in SAMoA for implementing these concepts. Central components are the task manager, which

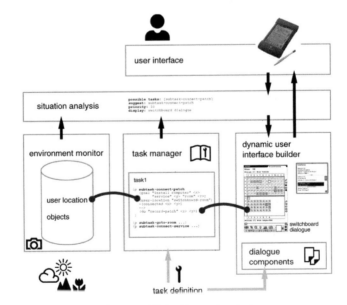

Figure 7.3 SAMoA architecture (overview).

is responsible for maintaining the active tasks and their states, a monitoring unit that provides information about the user's environment, a situation analysis component, which selects subtasks for execution based on the states of environment and active tasks, and the dynamic dialog construction component.

In our prototypes, we use sensor technology such as infrared beacons, radio transponders and GPS for providing the monitoring component with information about the current environment.

7.4 Using SAMoA

For evaluation of the SAMoA concepts we have built prototypes and systems in a number of different application areas, ranging from mobile network administration systems (MONAD – Kirste, 1998) to medical data recording (CliF – Kirste and Lange, 1998). Each of these applications investigates specific aspects of mobile assistance, such as interface design, guidance and orientation functionality. In the following, we outline the use of SAMoA in MONAD.

MONAD is a mobile information system supporting network technicians in setting up and troubleshooting physical network infrastructure, such as switchboards, cable paths and terminal devices (see Figure 7.4). Specifically, it allows the visualization and modification of the state of complex switchboard configurations and cable paths on site.

In the MONAD scenario, the typical task of a technician is to set up a new computer somewhere in the building. This consists of two subtasks:

(a) Install the computer in the room by connecting it to a wall outlet with a suitable interface cable.

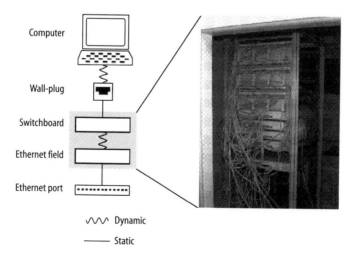

Figure 7.4 Typical network infrastructure.

(b) Connect the required network service to this wall outlet by installing a "patch" between the wall outlet's "back-side" and the service component (e.g. an Ethernet switch) in the switchboard room.

As each subtask covers only one situation, they are already basic activities.

In MONAD, we have used SAMoA as follows:

- Specific dialog components have been developed for the basic activities.
- Task definitions have been established using the OPS5 production system (see Section 7.5).
- A situation monitoring component based on infrared beacons has been developed.

See Figure 7.3 for the interworking of these components. Figure 7.5 shows the basic interaction with the system. On the left is the dialog for instantiating new tasks ("install, remove, configure a terminal device"). On the right is the output of the situation analyzer, suggesting a specific action for a task ("install a terminal device in a room"), together with this basic activity's dialog (displayed in the background).

Figure 7.6 outlines the functionality of infrared beacons. As the user approaches, for example, a switchboard, the situation analyzer is notified of this new situation by the environment monitor sensing the beacon. The analyzer then automatically pops up the corresponding basic activity (in this case, the switchboard manager). In comparison, manual selection of the same dialog requires at least six error-prone interaction steps until the correct room, racks and switchboard fields are selected. This clearly shows the potential of situation-aware assistance.

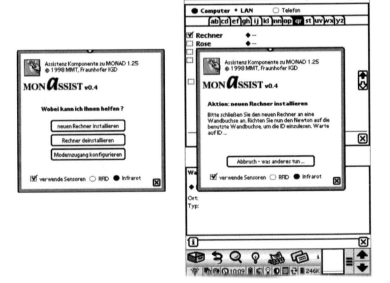

Figure 7.5 Assistance component of MONAD.

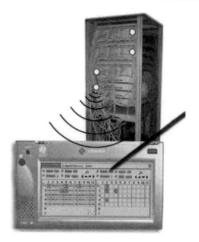

Figure 7.6 Beacon-based environment monitoring.

7.5 Task Modeling

In order to illustrate the specific features that a flexible, situation-aware task management system should provide, this section outlines a (very simple) set of production rules that has been designed for use within MONAD.

The rule set has been developed using the OPS5 production system (Forgy, 1981; Cooper and Wogrin, 1988). Its main purpose is to guide the user through the two subtasks of an installation task.

7.5.1 Why Production Systems?

When looking for a task modeling language to use within SAMoA, we specifically wanted to have a mechanism that would allow the *end-user*[1] *to incrementally* modify task definitions (even for executing tasks) in an *ad hoc* fashion, requiring only *local knowledge*: the user should be able to add tasks and subtasks as the situation requires, without having to know the structure of the tasks already defined in the system. In other words: the system should allow for "training on the job".

These characteristics call for a rule-based system, where rules for specific situations can be added incrementally. Furthermore, there should be the concept of "more general" and "more specific" rules with respect to a situation. This way, the

---

1 Independent of our specific application, there is a generally increasing requirement for supporting end-user programming in the future: "No matter how successfully interface designers are, systems will still need to be customized to the needs of particular users" (Myers *et al.*, 1996).

e *situation* determines which rules match best, not, for example, the time or place of definition in the overall rule set. So, rules can be defined *independently* of each other, requiring no knowledge of other rules. (There are other approaches for prioritizing rules independent of definition time, for example Courteous Logic (Grosof, 1997). Here, the priority of a rule is defined relative to other rules. This approach obviously *does* require non-local knowledge.)

These are characteristics that are quite well met by production systems such as OPS5. In fact, production systems have been used quite successfully in cognitive psychology for modeling human problem-solving behavior, and even as a basis for a general architecture of cognition (Anderson, 1983). So, using the "same" model for representing tasks in the user's mind and in his or her mobile assistant might make such a system easier to use than any other model providing similar expressiveness. However, it remains unclear whether such "cognitive compatibility" indeed helps the user in developing a correct mental model of the system[2] and in using such a system. Therefore the main reasons for choosing production systems remain incremental *ad hoc* modifiability requiring only local knowledge.

7.5.2 Working Memory and Productions

To model the current situation in MONAD, the following working memory elements are introduced (a basic knowledge of the OPS5 formalism is assumed):

```
(svc <s> <r>)
```

Service s has been established for room r by connecting a patch in the switchboard room.

```
(con <d> <r>)
```

Device d has been connected to a wall outlet in room r.

```
(location <l>)
```

The user is at location l.

```
(goal <d> <r> <s>)
```

The user's goal is to set up device d with service s in room r.

Now the set of rules describing the user's tasks can be defined, as follows:

1. If the goal is to set up device d in room r with service s, and the user is in the switchboard room, and the service has not been set up, then suggest setting up the service.

```
(p suggest-connect-service
    (goal <d> <r> <s>)
```

---

2 For example, it is not at all clear whether production systems reflect cognitive reality. It is also not clear (or even doubtful), whether a user's mental model of his or her own cognitive processes reflect this reality...

```
(location patch)
-(svc <s> <r>)
-->
(write "Suggest: Connect service" <s> "to room"
<r>))
```

2. If the goal is to ..., and the user is in room r, and the device has not been connected, connect the device.

```
(p suggest-connect-device-in-room
    (goal <d> <r> <s>)
    (location <r>)
    -(con <d> <r>)
    -->
    (write "Suggest: Connect" <d> " in room " <r>))
```

3. If the goal is ..., and the device is connected, and the service is set up, then the goal has been fulfilled.

```
(p done
    (goal <d> <r> <s>)
    (con <d> <r>)
    (svc <s> <r>)
    -->
    (write "[Setup" <d> <r> <s> "done]")
    (remove 1))
```

4. If the goal is ..., and we have to connect the device, and we are somewhere else, then go to the room where to connect the device.

```
(p suggest-goto-room
    (goal <d> <r> <s>)
    (location <x>)
    -(con <d> <r>)
    -->
    (write "Suggest: Goto" <r>))
```

5. If the goal is ..., and we have to set up the service, and we are not in the patch room, then go to the patch room.

```
(p suggest-goto-patch
    (goal <d> <r> <s>)
    (location <x>)
    -(svc <s> <r>)
    -->
    (write "Suggest: Goto patch"))
```

This set of five rules is already able to handle an arbitrary number of different installation goals. Note that the specific sequence of rules has *no* influence on rule execution. The rules can be defined independently of each other.

7.5.3 *Ad Hoc* Extensions

It is also quite easy to add *new* tasks to the system. Consider for example the fact
that the user would like to be reminded of certain things to do with objects that are
available at specific locations – e.g. buying a newspaper at the cafeteria. This could,
for example, be described by adding the following elements:

```
(remind <a> <o>)
```

The user wants to be remembered to do action a with object o.

```
(at <o> <l>)
Object o can be found at location l.
```

In addition, a new production is introduced:

6.   If the user wants to be reminded of doing action a with object o, and object o is
     at location l, and the user is also at location l, then remind the user.

```
(p loc-remind
    (remind <a> <o>)
    (at <o> <l>)
    (location <l>)
    -->
    (write (crlf) "Remember:" <a> <o>)
    (remove 1))
```

7.5.4 Production System Execution

Now, a typical situation might be defined by the following initial working memory
contents:

```
(at newspaper cafeteria)
(at boss patch)
(remind talk-to boss)
(remind buy newspaper)
(goal pc1 r1 ether)
(goal pc2 r2 atm)
(goal pc3 r1 serial)
(location office)
```

Newspapers can be found in the cafeteria, the user's boss is in the patch room, the
user is in his or her office. The user wants to be reminded to buy a newspaper and to
talk to the boss. Also, the user has three installation tasks.

Running the system might then produce something like the following sequence:

1.   The system suggests going to room R1, where the first device setup for the most
     recent installation task can be done. It observes that the user follows this suggestion.

```
Suggest: Goto R1
Action? goto r1
```

2. It then suggests making the device connection.

```
Suggest: Connect PC3 in room R1
Action? connect pc3 r1
```

3. As there are other tasks with subtasks in this room, it recommends performing these subtasks too, while the user is already there.

```
Suggest: Connect PC1 in room R1
Action? connect pc1 r1
```

4. Then go to the patch room to finish the installation tasks.

```
Suggest: Goto patch
Action? goto patch
```

5. Remind the user to talk to the boss and recommend finishing the first installation task.

```
Remember: TALK-TO BOSS
Suggest: Connect service SERIAL to room R1
Action? service serial r1

[Setup PC3 R1 SERIAL done]
```

6. Recommend finishing the second installation task – and observe that the user decides to do something else.

```
Suggest: Connect service ATM to room R2
Action? goto cafeteria
```

7. Because the user is in the cafeteria, remind the user to buy a newspaper. Then recommend finishing the work.

```
Remember: BUY NEWSPAPER
Suggest: Goto R2
Action? goto r2

Suggest: Connect PC2 in room R2
Action? connect pc2 r2

Suggest: Goto patch
Action? goto patch

Suggest: Connect service ATM to room R2
Action? service atm r2

[Setup PC2 R2 ATM done]

Suggest: Connect service ETHER to room R1
Action? service ether r1

[Setup PC1 R1 ETHER done]
```

```
end -- no production true
```

7.5.5 Observations

This example shows that it is indeed quite straightforward – at least within the scope of such simple scenarios as considered here – to implement task management systems which provide the following features:

- Management of arbitrary parallel tasks.
- Flexible, situation-driven user assistance and context switches.
- Flexible reaction to "unexpected" user actions. (The system provides action recommendations, not commands.)
- Easy handling of related and unrelated tasks.
- Incremental *ad hoc* extension by new tasks.

However, this simple experiment has also shown a number of detailed problems, where modifications of "conventional" production systems are required in order to be useful as a foundation for task-driven situation-aware mobile assistants. These will be outlined in the next section.

7.6 Conclusions and Open Questions

7.6.1 Situation-Aware Mobile Assistance

The idea of using location (and other context data) for retrieving situation-specific information, as well as the idea of using task models for providing situation specific assistance is not new to (mobile) computing (Rhodes, 1997; Maes, 1989).

The new concept we have outlined here is not the idea of creating a mobile assistant for a *specific* activity. We are rather aiming at a *generic, extensible* concept, that allows the mobile system to assist the user in managing the *complete* set of daily activities. In this concept, it is important to provide users with a task modeling language that allows for incremental *ad hoc* modification and creation of tasks, requiring only local knowledge.

The basic concepts of SAMoA have been established and tested in several mobile prototype systems. Situation-Aware Mobile Assistance definitely supports users that need to manage complex, simultaneous tasks in the real world. It helps them to react faster and reduces errors.

While the ultimate goal of a personal assistant that helps a user in *every* aspect of daily life is still some way off (or even unreachable), generic situation-aware mobile assistants that empower the user in several specific application scenarios can be built today.

7.6.2 Specific Open Questions

There are of course numerous aspects of generic situation-aware mobile assistants that need further research – for example, the definition of a suitably general *and* simple to use task definition language, the precise design of contexts and the user interface to the task manager (see also Section 7.5.5). Some of the questions raised by our initial experiments are:

- In OPS5, the most specific rule is the one matching the most specific and most recent working memory elements. If we had indeed used productions as given in Section 7.5.2, the system would *not* have suggested performing a subtask of a *different* goal at step 3 of the execution sequence. It would instead have recommended going to the patch room in order to finish the *current* (i.e. most recent) top-level goal.

In order to create an execution sequence as shown in Section 7.5.4, we had to give the location clauses in the rule heads a higher priority by repeating them, e.g.:

```
(p suggest-connect-device-in-room
   (goal <d> <r> <s>)
   (location <r>) (location <r>)
   -(con <d> <r>)
   --> ...)
```

Using such "tricks" to make the system behavior meet the user's expectations is in no way intuitive. Besides specificity and recency, a production system for SAMoA should therefore also observe measures such as "physical" convenience (adjacency) in its rule prioritization and selection algorithm.

- Rather than suggesting a *single* activity, the system should provide the user with a *list* of possible activities, sorted by applicability to the current situation. The system should always be able to give the user an overview of all currently active tasks, their completion state and other potentially relevant selection criteria.[3]

- While *in principle* supporting *ad hoc* end-user editing, the OPS5 formalism (as well as similar formalisms) is clearly not directly usable by the non-expert. It remains to be investigated which (visual) editors might be used for interacting with the rule base. This might indeed be the most difficult task. However, even if an intuitive general-purpose editor proves to be unrealistic, it may be possible to come up with an extensible editing concept, where task-specific editors are used.

We will try to address some of these questions in the MoVi project.

---

3   It is an interesting question whether such information should perhaps *always* be visible, potentially on a peripheral display, thus giving the user permanent feedback on the state of all his or her activities. However, it is also an interesting question whether the user will always like being notified of all the things that still have to be done...

7.6.3 Correspondences

Finally, the concept of situation-aware mobile assistance spans a broad range of computer science. Even when only focusing on the aspect of situation monitoring and task management, the following research areas are involved:

- *Hardware*: Sensor technology, non-intrusive IO devices.
- *Software*: Context management, rule-based languages.
- *User interface design*: Paradigms for interactive end user programming, task visualization.
- *Cognitive psychology*: "Cognitive compatible" task modeling languages; recommendations and evaluation at all levels of user interface design.

References

Anderson, JR (1983) *The Architecture of Cognition*, Cambridge, MA, Harvard University Press.
Billings, CE (1997) *Aviation Automation: The Search for a Human-Centered Approach*, Mahwah, NJ, Lawrence Erlbaum Associates.
Browne, D (1994) *Structured User Interface Design for Interaction Optimization (STUDIO)*, London, Prentice Hall.
Card, SK, Moran, TP and Newell, A (1983) *The Psychology of Human Computer Interaction*. Hillsdale, NJ, Lawrence Erlbaum Associates.
Cooper, T and Wogrin, N (1988) *Rule-Based Programming With OPS5*, San Mateo, CA, Morgan Kaufmann.
Endsley, MR (1996) Automation and situation awareness. In *Automation and Human Performance: Theory and Application*, (eds. R Parasraman and M Mouloua), Mahwah, NJ, Lawrence Erlbaum Associates.
Forgy, CL (1981) *OPS5 User's Manual*. Technical Report CMU-CS-81-135, Carnegie Mellon University, School of Computer Science, Pittsburgh, PA.
Giesa, H-G and Schumann, J. (1997) Zum Einfluß von Automatisierung und Assistenz in Flugsicherung und Flugführung, in *Wohin führen Unterstützungssysteme? – Entscheidungshilfe und Assistenz in Mensch-Maschine-Systemen. 2* (Hrsg. H-P Willumeit und H Kolrep), Berlin, Berliner Werkstatt Mensch-Maschine-Systeme.
Grosof, BN (1997) Courteous logic programs: prioritized conflict handling for rules, *IBM Research Report RC 20836*, December, http://www.research.ibm.com/iagents/paps/rc20836.ps
Johnson, P and Johnson, H (1990) Designers-identified requirements for tools to support task analysis, in *Proc. Interact '90*, pp. 259–264.
Kirste, T (1998) A mobile information system for the management of networks, in *Proc. 24th IEEE IECON*, Aachen, Germany.
Kirste, T and Lange, M (1998) A mobile system for recording examination data of occlusion and bite function analysis in dentistry, in *Proc. MedInfo '98*, Seoul, Korea.
Maes, P (1989) How to do the right thing, *Technical Report 1180*, MIT.
Myers, B, Hollan, J and Cruz, I (1996) Strategic directions in human computer interaction, *ACM Computing Surveys*, 28(4).
Riecken, D (1994) Intelligent agents, *Communication of the ACM*, 37(7).
Rhodes, BJ (1997) The wearable remembrance agent: a system for augmented memory, *Personal Technologies*, 1(4), 218–224.
Sheridian, TB (1996) Speculations on future relations between humans and automatization, in *Automation and Human Performance: Theory and Application* (eds. R Parasraman and M Mouloua), Mahwah, NJ, Lawrence Erlbaum Associates.
Weiser, M (1993) Some computer science problems in ubiquitous computing, *Communications of the ACM*, 36(12), 75–85.

Wickens, CD, Mavor, AS and McGee, JP (1997) *Flight to the Future, Human Factors in Air Traffic Control*, Washington, DC, National Academy Press.

Willumeit, H-P und Kolrep, H (Hrsg.) (1997) *Wohin führen Unterstützungssysteme? – Entscheidungshilfe und Assistenz in Mensch-Maschine-Systemen. 2*, Berlin, Berliner Werkstatt Mensch-Maschine-Systeme.

About the Author

Thomas Kirste received his diploma in computer science and his PhD from Darmstadt Technical University (TUD) in 1989 and 1995 respectively.

From 1989 to 1993 he worked as a research assistant at the Computer Graphics Center (ZGDV) in Darmstadt. His work concentrated on the area of open and computational hypermedia systems. In 1993, he began his work on Mobile Computing. He was technical manager of the "HyperFunk" project, a prototype mobile hypermedia system developed for DeTeMobil.

In 1994, he joined the Interactive Graphics Systems group of the Department for Computer Science at Darmstadt University (TUD-GRIS). Here, he worked as technical director of the cross-institutional researcher group MoVi, funded by the German Research Society (Deutsche Forschungsgemeinschaft, DFG). The work in MoVi concentrates on basic research on concepts and strategies for the mobile visualization of globally distributed multimedia information services.

Since August 1996, he has headed the R&D department "Mobile Multimedia Technolgies" at the Fraunhofer Institute for Computer Graphics Rostock (IGD Rostock). He is responsible for research and development in the areas of mobile computing, distributed multimedia information systems, and mobile assistance. Also, he continues his work as technical director of the MoVi project.

Thomas Kirste is a member of the ACM.

Devices for Display and Interaction

8

Devices for Display and Interaction

Turner Whitted

Abstract

Devices for interaction – displays, input sensors, and communications mechanisms – are central elements of future computing. However, we tend to think of computing systems in terms of speed and storage and seldom in terms of interactive performance. This will change as computing systems are re-partitioned into components with which we interface more closely and more richly. This review addresses the physical properties of interface devices. It attempts to put real numbers on such variables as bandwidth, range and power consumption, while ignoring cost and size, to better understand just how universal various classes of device can be. Wherever possible it attempts to identify levels of performance which will effect a qualitative change in how computers serve users.

8.1 Introduction

Whether through punch cards, a row of switches, a mouse or a mind reader – all of our interactions with computers pass through a physical device of one sort or another. A user's conception of what a computer is and does is heavily colored by the physical means of interaction. Conversely, a programmer's view of what a human user is and can do is greatly influenced by the mechanics of input and output.

Many of us have long since passed the threshold of one computer per person. We routinely encounter tens or perhaps hundreds of CPUs in the course of daily activity. In an environment so heavily populated by diverse computing devices it is useful to take a physical approach to explaining the possibilities for interaction and attempting to determine what the nature of interaction may be.

Two things are quite clear about this environment. First, the embedded computers which are hidden in our automobiles and appliances and those which are starkly visible on the desktops of our offices and homes have a natural affinity for each other. They wish to talk to each other and we must permit them to. Second, the balance of power between user and computer is shifting to the user. The monolith which we call a personal computer is in the process of being disassembled and reconstructed as a collection of elements which free users from the constraints of the desktop. Performance is then a measure of how effectively a nebulous collection of connected elements serves a user. This isn't exactly what benchmark designers traditionally have in mind.

The internal capacity of computing devices has been reliably predicted by Moore's Law for so long that we actually believe that it is a physical law. On the other hand there is little evidence that human reaction time, memory capacity and visual acuity have advanced since the Stone Age. Furthermore, light moves no faster now than it did at the beginning of the computer age, and the energy density of chemical reactions still has a limit.

In a domain of seemingly limitless performance improvements, there are indeed limits. We interact with our computers through eyes, ears, mouths, and hands, as well as through the overall motion of our bodies. Increasingly we interact over distances, and more and more often we wish to perform these interactions without the benefit of electrical mains and without the tethers of the conventional desktop. We are quickly discovering that Moore's law does not foretell solutions to all of our problems and that the principles of physics and engineering provide better guidance in designing interactive computing systems.

This review discusses the performance of output devices, primarily displays, as well as input and communications devices. After looking backward at the trends in resolution, speed, weight and power consumption for such devices we extrapolate the performance of technology forward, check the sanity of the extrapolation, and attempt to identify significant milestones in the performance of individual components. More importantly, we hope to evaluate plausible combinations of components. In the end we should not expect designs for interactive devices to leap off the page at us. I do hope that this exercise uncovers some principles for linking untethered users to human-centered computing systems.

8.2 Related and Unrelated Work

It is probably easier to describe what this review is not about than to directly state its purpose. This is not a promotional piece for ubiquitous (Weiser, 1992) or invisible (Norman, 1998) computing. It has no discussion of social or privacy issues. It makes no serious attempt to guess at the form of future applications or to predict changes to the way we live. It presents no scenarios to illustrate what life might be like when the air we breathe has intelligence (Stephenson, 1995). I assume that computers will outnumber humans by a large multiple, that a vast network of information and computation will be available to each of us everywhere, and that this atmosphere of computation will benefit us all greatly with no threat to our well-being.

Neither is this an essay on the limits of computation. Such studies have been conducted for many years (Landauer, 1984). There have been extraordinary and surprising results from these efforts, but their practical value as a guide to development has yet to be realized.

Because the era of universal computation is at hand, a practical guide is essential. The analysis in this chapter is narrowly focused. While the laws of physics, thermodynamics and information theory still rule, the analysis here is much more down to earth. Rather than ask "What can a computing system not do?" we ask "What can one expect from ordinary appliances in the near future?".

For the next few years, at least, our computing environment will most likely be constructed of electronic, mechanical and optical components. These components will be connected with and without wires, will be powered with and without mains, and will be highly visible in some cases, e.g. displays, and completely imperceptible in others. Rather than construct a grand unified model of performance for such aggregations, this review takes a more bottom-up approach and examines the properties of each of the components in turn. Programs such as UC Berkeley's InfoPad project for low-power wireless systems, have produced such useful and readily applied design principles (Rabaey *et al.*, 1995).

In the end, though, performance can never be measured apart from applications. As stated above, we cannot know what future applications will evolve. However, there have been numerous demonstrations that hint at the possibilities of such applications. Notable ones involve user location (Want *et al.*, 1992), information exchange (Zimmerman, 1996) and musical performance (Paradiso *et al.*, 1997).

8.3 The Role of Devices in Interaction

To those of us old enough for the question to have meaning, it is interesting to ask "When did computing become interactive?" We would probably all agree that punch cards and paper printouts were never interactive (although I did once get a 5 second turnaround on a batch job). We would just as likely agree that HMDs and 6 DOF input devices support interaction. Somewhere in between is the interface defined by a mouse, keyboard and windowed bitmap display employed by a hundred million users. A comparable number of young users interact with their computers through a game pad and a real-time 3D display. Interestingly, these two dominant interfaces have almost nothing in common. Furthermore, neither has evolved significantly since their inception 30 and 20 years ago respectively.

The most significant recent transformation in computer interfaces is the untethering of users from a fixed desktop. This shift forces an evolution of the interface[1]. Consider some of the questions about input for a wandering user:

---

[1] As an aside, it is worth making a distinction between fixed desktops and mobile desktops. A road warrior reproducing the desktop environment in an airline seat is not the subject of this paper. Furthermore, it isn't entirely clear that a battery-powered personal computer attached to various points of a user's body is more or less tethered than the conventional desktop.

- What functions is a user expecting from an ever-present computing environment?
- What are the explicit inputs that a user expects to convey to the computers?
- What elements of user state define a context for services to the user?
- How is user state conveyed to the computers?
- How are computer responses conveyed to the user?

Note that there are both explicit and implicit inputs to off-the-desktop computers. To gain some appreciation of the burden that explicit inputs impose on a user, I suggest (as an exercise) placing an international telephone call billed to a credit card. For maximum effect the call should be placed by a driver traveling slightly above the legal speed limit on a heavily traveled motorway. A conventional desktop user interface for this example is no more adequate than the meager 12 button keypad. Voice input is most often suggested for such tasks as a way to free up hands and eyes for more important simultaneously occurring tasks. Even better suggestions require that the computer maintain enough information about the user, i.e. user state, to further reduce demands on the user's attention.

Tasks and contexts like this one demand that the user be given substantial assistance by the computers. This seems reasonable if the computers carry a sufficiently rich representation of user state. The most obvious element of user state is identity. In most systems, ranging from our own desktop machines to ATMs, we establish identity by "logging in." It is remarkable that for even the first piece of user state today's systems require explicit user input.

Other elements of user state include location, velocity, history of actions etc. To demand explicit user input to maintain these elements of user state is ludicrous. It is the role of sensors to collect the implicit inputs. Powerful and flexible sensors, cameras for example, scattered throughout the fixed environment can be tied to arbitrarily powerful processors to estimate all of the elements of user state mentioned so far. On the other hand, rather simple low-power sensors placed strategically about the user's person can record "ground truth" user state as long as their power sources hold out. From a hardware standpoint, the latter class of sensor raises the most questions and presents the most challenges.

8.4 Physical Properties

Untethered computation incorporates a user, self-powered appliances which accompany a user, a mains-powered fixed environment, and connections among the elements. Connectivity between the user and anything else is by means of sensors and emitters of various kinds. Other connectivity is electrical or electromagnetic. That's an awfully broad description which has little meaning unless we delve into each component in some detail.

What follows is an inventory of components, a brief discussion of their physical properties and an elementary analysis of the performance that each element can be expected to deliver.

8.4.1 Power

We can assume that devices fall into two categories – fixed with mains power and untethered internally powered. Power management is an issue in both domains. Avoiding meltdown in high-speed fixed circuits is a problem that has been partially solved by shutting down large portions of processors whenever they are idle. For internally powered devices, the issue is more often the refueling interval than heat. This discussion of power management is slanted towards portable internally powered devices.

Like most commodities, power must be viewed in terms of both supply and demand. Designing for low power consumption has been an area of active research for over twenty years. Radical proposals such as reversible computing in which no dissipation occurs (Bennett, 1973) are targeted more towards higher speed that low power. More practical attempts are centered around optimization of systems composed of traditional components for low power consumption.

As an example, the InfoPad project at UC Berkeley provides excellent back-of-the-envelope guidance. From a top-down perspective the expression

$$\text{Power} = C_{\text{eff}} V_{\text{dd}}^2 f$$

where C_{eff} is the effective capacitance switched within a circuit, V_{dd} is the supply voltage and f is the switching frequency describes dissipation in a circuit (Burd *et al.*, 1996). The obvious implication of this expression is that low-power circuits should have very small features and run slowly at low voltages. The trend in all circuits, not just portable ones, is towards lower supply voltages. Making circuits run slowly may not be an option, and may even be counterproductive (Burd *et al.*, 1996), but limiting their duty cycle is common practice.

Taking a typical embedded processor, the ARM9TDMI core, as an example, power consumption is 150 mW at $V_{\text{dd}} = 2.5$ V and $f = 100$ MHz. This corresponds to $C_{\text{eff}} = 240$ pF, a number that is considerably smaller that the actual potential capacitance of a circuit 4 mm on a side[2]. Effective capacitance is best thought of as an expression of the complexity of a circuit that lends itself to simple physical analysis. An alternative expression is in terms of potential device sites. This is a function of total circuit area divided by device area. Whatever expression is chosen, the potential of a circuit to do computation is the product of the circuit complexity times the clock frequency. Of course, the potential to do computation is exactly what we track with Moore's Law. Figure 8.1, from Dally and Poulton (1998), tracks the growth of computational capacity as a combination of fundamental advances in fabrication.

Simply put, feature length and gate delay are shrinking by 13% a year, chips' linear dimensions are growing by 6% a year, and when all effects are combined Moore's Law predicts that capability will grow by five orders of magnitude in the next 20 years. (Capacity is given as number of sites switched per second.) At a constant supply voltage, this would indicate that power consumption will also grow by five

---

2   If the entire surface area of the chip switched at 100 MHz, the dissipation would briefly be about 3.5 kW as the chip evaporated.

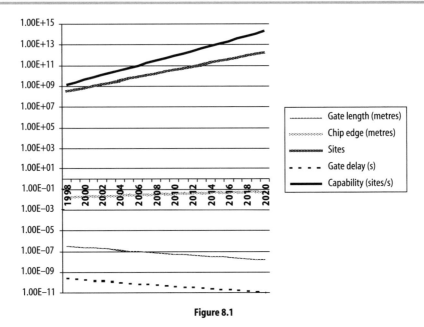

Figure 8.1

orders of magnitude. While it would certainly be interesting to speculate about where all that power will come from and where all that heat will go, at the end of the day this matters very little to designers of portable circuits for interaction. What it *does* mean to us is that circuits will shrink and run faster.

The simple expression for power consumption does not account for the energy spent in interconnections. As we shall see in the next section, this can be considerable. The guiding principle that circuits ought to be partitioned in a manner that minimizes the required speed of interconnections is overwhelmingly important in untethered systems.

From the standpoint of supply, suggested sources of portable power range from the human pulse (Starner, 1996) to microscopic gas turbines. Just as every schoolchild knows that $E = mc^2$ (which, under improbable conditions, provides a nifty 9×10^{16} joules from 1 kg of material) we also know that practical rather then theoretical considerations are the best guide to understanding the near-term potential of power sources. Here are some candidates:

Battery   Relies on chemical reactions, some of which are reversible. Use of batteries assumes that the user is committed to periodically replacing the battery, periodically recharging it or simply discarding the appliance. Energy densities for currently popular batteries are

	kJ/kg	kJ/liter
NiCd	126	288
Lithium	432–864	1044–?
NiMH	252–324	864–1152

To put some perspective on these numbers, a standard CR2025 lithium battery has a capacity of 165 mA/h at 3 V and weighs 2.5 g, corresponding to an energy density of 712 kJ/kg. With a drain of 200 mA, the battery will last for over 30 days.

Capacitor Provides energy from the controlled discharge of a capacitor over time. Of course, the use of capacitors for energy storage implies that the user can reasonably recharge the capacitor frequently. So-called "supercapacitors" in the range of 2–10 farads can be charged to potentials as high as 5 V. Energy densities in the range of 18 kJ/kg do not compare favorably with batteries, but they are tiny devices that can effectively buffer charge harvested from external sources.

Parasitic Extracts energy from motion, stray fields, sunlight etc. Starner estimates that piezo-electric film in the sole of a shoe can harvest 5 W from a walking user (Starner, 1996). Parasitic power harvesting has the additional appeal of being "green" and suitable for environments where consumption of batteries just isn't possible.

Demand and supply go hand in hand for low-power circuits. Seiko produces a quartz watch which consumes on the order of 10^{-6} W. Such tiny demand enables power to be scavenged from ordinary motions of the user. The freedom from ever having to replace batteries represents a qualitative difference in user experience.

8.4.2 Connectivity

When I was trained as an engineer the key to performance was assumed to lie in faster active devices. As active devices have become smaller their speed has increased correspondingly, and the focus of performance prediction has shifted to interconnection.

Wired Interconnection

Wired systems comprise a hierarchy of interconnection, with device-to-device signal paths within an integrated circuit at the bottom level and intercontinental fiber optic cable at the top. (For our purposes optical connections have a lot more in common with electrical wires than they do with propagation paths, so they are lumped together here.)

Over the past 40 years digital busses have been a mainstay of computer systems. Because of their limited speed, they have fallen out of favor in recent years and point-to-point interconnection has become the norm. This discussion treats point-to-point interconnections only. In today's digital systems the rates, ranges, and latencies encountered are roughly as given in Table 8.1.

Today's typical chip-to-chip signaling speeds are lower by an order of magnitude than well-known technology allows, so this table is overly pessimistic in that regard. If we were only concerned with computation, then we could limit most of

Table 8.1			
	Range	Rate/wire	Latency
Device-to-device	< 1 mm	5 GHz	4×10^{-11} s/mm
Chip-to-chip	< 10 cm	100 MHz	Varies
Board-to-board	< 100 cm	100 MHz	Varies
Box-to-box	< 10 m	> 100 MHz	5.5×10^{-9} s/m

our attention to on-chip and chip-to-chip interconnection. As we have seen, however, computation is limited by power dissipation and not by interconnect speed.

On the other hand, interaction is mostly about IO, and external bandwidth is where we should focus our attention. Interactive input doesn't happen very fast. Human users have limited reaction times that limit the number of times that they can push a button in any given time period. As an extreme case, consider tablet input with a 1 kHz sampling rate. With 16 bits of X and Y precision, the input date rate is only 4 kbit/s, a rate that does not stretch performance limits at any level of the wired hierarchy. Output speeds vary considerably, however. Display devices and display processors can easily consume hundreds of Mbit/s of bandwidth at all levels of interconnection.

Wireless Interconnection

Wireless interconnection differs sufficiently from wired interconnection to require its own discussion. For example, wireless transmission paths are rarely guided as they are in the wired case. Signals are not usually transmitted directly, but are instead used to modulate a carrier signal[3]. Normal practice in designing a wireless link is to choose a modulation method and an acceptable bit error rate (BER) and then compute a signal-to-noise ratio (SNR) at the receiver that will achieve this performance. For the sake of this discussion we can gloss over this practice and talk in generalities.

Two fundamental relationships are useful in predicting wireless performance. The first, from (Shannon, 1948):

$$C = W \log_2 \left(1 + \frac{S}{N} \right)$$

gives channel capacity as a function of bandwidth W, signal power S, and noise power N. In this discussion, the primary usefulness of Shannon's capacity theorem is to steer us towards a consideration of bandwidth and SNR. The second expression combines receiver sensitivity and path loss to give

---

3   An exception is the mechanism developed recently by Time Domain, Inc., in which a digital signal is radiated directly from a transmitter to a receiver.

$$\log(SNR) = \log(P_{t}) - \log(kT_{0}) - 10\log(W) - N_{R}$$

$$-20\log\left(\frac{4\pi r_0}{\lambda}\right) - 10n\log\left(\frac{r}{r_0}\right) - \text{fading}$$

This is the standard expression of SNR in terms of

P_{t}	Transmitted power, in dBm, i.e. dB relative to 1 mW.
$-\log(kT_{0})$	Boltzmann's constant times room temperature, approximately – 174 dBm.
W	Receiver bandwidth. Obviously, higher bandwidth requires higher transmitted power to achieve a given SNR.
N_{R}	Receiver noise figure
$-20\log\left(\dfrac{4\pi r_0}{\lambda}\right)$	Reference path loss. The important factor here is the wavelength dependence of path loss. (Antenna gain is ignored.)
n	Attenuation exponent. In free space we expect signal strength to diminish as $1/r^2$, i.e. $n = 2$. In and around buildings and other structures, the loss is much worse, and $n = 4$ provides a better fit to measured loss.
fading	Rather than model the processes which cause fading, most designers just add in a fixed amount of margin to transmitted power, e.g. 20 dB.

As an exercise, one can plug in desired performance numbers and solve for transmitter, receiver and antenna specifications. Figure 8.2 plots the unobstructed range (in meters) of a few specific commercial radios as a function of carrier frequency (the three ISM bands at 915 MHz, 2.4 GHz and 5.8 GHz) and data rate (0–10 Mbit/s).

While a plot like this has little meaning without an indication of transmitted power, antenna gain and other factors, it does give some indication of typical performance with off-the-shelf mobile products. For a typical radio used in portable data networking $P_{t} = 0.1$ W. If P_{t} represented half the total power consumption of a

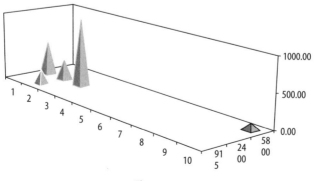

Figure 8.2

portable appliance, then the 2.5 gram battery used as an example above would last only two hours in this appliance. A common efficiency measure for bidirectional data links, especially cellular telephones, is to sense received signal strength from the fixed base station and reduce P_t accordingly. A second measure is to aggressively limit the transmitter duty cycle.

There are also examples of carrier frequencies higher than 5.8 GHz supporting data rates above 100 Mbit/s with high transmitted power and high antenna gains. These are point-to-point, mains-powered, fixed links that have no potential for supporting interactive interfaces.

As an indication of performance trends, the relations given above provide better guidance. The important points are these:

- Higher bandwidths require a higher carrier frequency. This is as much a function of frequency assignment regulations as of signal processing theory.
- Shorter wavelengths require higher transmitted power for a given range.
- Offsetting the higher path loss for shorter wavelengths is their better ability to penetrate buildings, something that is not modeled by the expression above.

With class C amplifiers already achieving 70% efficiency, increases in mobile transmitted power will come only at the expense of battery life. In short, there is no obvious path to both longer range and increased data rates for mobile RF. This fact forces us to consider a hierarchy of wireless links in which the mobile component works over a very limited range (Bennett *et al.*, 1997). The one piece of good news in this is that we can reasonably expect to pack an enormous number of such links into constricted spaces without interference (Shepard, 1996).

8.4.3 Sensors

The use of absolute or relative position measurements is at the heart of traditional direct interaction.

Pens, tablets and touchscreens are common 2D absolute position measurement devices, while mice, thumbwheels and trackballs measure relative position. As mature as desktop interaction may be, there are still improvements to be made (Hinckley and Sinclair, 1999). In the extension of applications to 3D, head tracking, position trackers and 6 DOF manipulators are key elements of immersive computing and have been the subject of much research.

For other everyday appliances the dominant sensors, since the demise of the potentiometer, are buttons and rotary switches. These are simple, cheap, occasionally easy to use, and oh so numerous. We tend not to think of them as sensors, but they are.

All of the devices mentioned above share the trait of demanding attention from the user. In the course of everyday interaction attention is in short supply. Interaction for an untethered user presents a number of problems in interpreting the output of sensors. Even buttons present a challenge when jogging or when flying through turbulent air.

Given the amount of attention required to use even the simplest input device, it seems prudent to use as much passively sensed state as possible to reduce the amount of attention demanded from the mobile user. Accelerometers, for example, are cheap, but we don't yet know how to use large numbers of them in concert. Here we encounter subtle trade-offs between the determinism of explicit inputs and probabilistic nature of implicit inputs. Even so, which of the following statements:

- Given the following indirect clues, a system can conclude with a finite probability that the user is angry, asleep or ill.

versus

- Given the following direct measurements, a system can conclude with a much higher probability that the user is angry, or asleep or ill.

is likely to give more comfort to a user interface developer? I much prefer the latter. There is no substitute for ground truth.

Introducing implicit inputs from simpler sensors is only now starting to receive attention (Picard, 1997). The waveform in Figure 8.3, for example, is the output of a heel-mounted accelerometer with a walking user. The plot gives G force as a function of time in seconds.

Two important elements of user state, i.e. whether the user is walking and how fast, can be determined by looking only at the amplitude and period of the negative spikes. These two pieces of information can be transmitted wirelessly with very little bandwidth and a very low duty cycle. Alternatively, pressure sensors in a smart floor can determine exactly the same information and, given the entire waveform, may uniquely identify the user (Addlesee *et al.*, 1997).

This particular example illustrates a basic dilemma for invisible interface designers: whether to instrument the user or the space. There are pros and cons to each side of the issue and it is a topic which merits debate. The bottom line is that,

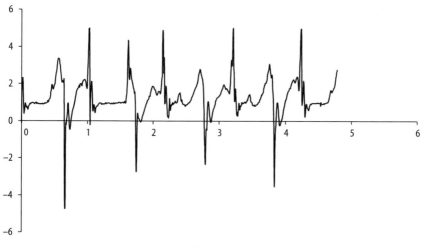

Figure 8.3

other than cameras and microphones, sensors measuring user state will rarely consume much interconnect bandwidth.

8.4.4 Displays

The debate about where to place sensors must be extended to include emitters as well, especially displays. It is technically feasible to build tiny displays which project directly into the eye. However, the emphasis of current development is on large-format displays. There is one overwhelming reason why this makes sense: regardless of how portable a display can be made, the current generation of display processors is power hungry and not totally suitable for portable applications. All of the alternative partitions of display system elements call for a high bandwidth connection somewhere in the chain. This is not feasible with current wireless interconnections.

The properties that we look for in all displays, e.g. resolution, brightness, contrast ratio, gamut, are universal. Only when we distance ourselves from fixed horizontal surfaces capable of supporting heavy objects do we start to think of size and weight. As noted above, this concern applies not only to the display device but also to the accessories which power it and create its signal.

No one display format seems to serve all purposes. The 8.5 × 11 inch (or alternatively the A4) format seems to work well for paper and is strongly advocated by purveyors of documents. The 4:3 aspect ratio viewing surface which computers have inherited from television remains popular, but for no apparent reason. It is available in a broad range of sizes. If ubiquitous display is desired, then the alternative to portability is to cover every available flat surface with light-emitting elements. This presents its own problems, but it seems to be direction in which research efforts are headed. One can well imagine a computing environment in which desktop, wall-mounted, handheld and worn displays all work in concert. It seems safe to assume that no single display technology will suffice for all of them.

Display Technologies

The following observations are largely taken from Starkweather (1998), a wide-ranging overview of the constraints of several common display technologies, and (Whitted, 1998), an exercise in extrapolation of resolution and other graphics throughput numbers.

CRTs   Because of the mechanical strength required to avoid implosion, CRTs become extremely heavy as they grow larger. There seems to be no home for CRTs off the desktop.

CRTs have a single electron gun, a single point of signal injection. The signal rate at this point increases as the square of the linear resolution of the tube. For an 800 × 600 pixel display refreshed at 85 Hz, the pixel clock rate is approximately 50 MHz. At 2048 × 1536 pixels, however, the clock rate increases to nearly 300 MHz. This represents a data rate from the frame buffer of nearly 1 Gbit/s.

Projection

For the time being, projection, front or rear, seems to be the preferred experimental arrangement for large format displays. However, rear projection eats up floor space and front projection has a bit of an obscuration problem. Projection systems do provide a platform for experimentation with large formats without waiting for more convenient large format displays to become practical.

Projection systems generally consist of a light source, a light modulator, a beam deflection system and projection optics. If the modulator is a two-dimensional array, as with micro-mirror assemblies, then no deflection is required. A one-dimensional modulator array such as a grating light valve requires only one axis of deflection. Both of these modulators are MEMS (micro-electromechanical systems) and potentially integrate well with display processor circuitry.

LCDs

Flat displays eliminate much of the physical awkwardness of projection displays. The most successful flat displays, so far, have been LCDs, which remain expensive and do not scale well.

For the short term LCDs seem to be the technology of choice for the desktop. They require little space, flicker is much less of a problem than for CRTs, and new software technologies seem to provide greater effective resolution to LCDs than to CRTs.

For transmission mode active matrix LCDs there are upper limits on the resolution of very small panels because the aperture ratio is limited by the area required for the active device.

For very large panels resolution is limited by the bandwidth of the conducting paths within the panel. The current state of the art is a 200 pixel per inch, 13 × 10 inch panel from IBM with a resolution of 2560 × 2048 pixels.

For current desktop configurations the display processor remains mounted in the same enclosure as the CPU. This means that LCDs, like CRTs, are refreshed through a thin cable[4]. While there is no single standard for digital interfaces to LCDs, most of them utilize serial transmission of data. For extremely high-resolution panels this link is a bottleneck.

Organic LEDs

Organic LEDs emit light from a forward biased junction of dissimilar polymer compounds. They are currently popular for low-resolution numeric indicators, but are well suited for very large displays. Ultimately this technology may become "smart wallpaper".

---

4 Early desktop monitor replacement LCDs were driven from the same analog signals used for CRTs. The analog signals were resampled in the LCD driver electronics. Thankfully, this arrangement is being replaced by all-digital interfaces which eliminate the resampling artifacts and support direct addressing of each LCD subpixel.

Because polymer LEDs emit rather than transmit, no backlight is required. Efficiency is potentially much higher than that of LCDs.

Polymer LED sheets with VGA resolution have been demonstrated. Developers have reportedly fabricated organic active elements to switch the display elements. Other than bandwidth in the matrix of conductors driving the array of emitters, it is not clear what physical constraints limit the performance of these devices.

Electrostatic   These devices are variations of the Gyricon display built by Xerox in the 1970s. Although slow to respond to a driving signal, this class of display tends to hold its pattern of light and dark areas until erased. If they become practical, they may serve as low-power displays for text and other static graphics, i.e. a paper substitute.

This characterization is neither complete nor rigorous. There is a huge amount of variation in individual implementations of each particular technology, the technology is evolving rapidly, and display properties are complex and sometimes subtle.

In any sanity check of display parameters the first question is "How much resolution is enough?". The answer, of course, depends on viewing distance. There are arguments that at normal reading distances, approximately 15 inches, resolutions above 200 pixels per inch are wasted.

We tend to think of display quality as merely a question of resolution. The issue is not nearly that simple. For example, almost all color displays have a patterned surface. Color CRTs may have a triad patterned shadow mask, a slot mask or a striped (Trinitron™) mask. Similarly, LCD panels have a variety of emitter patterns. Each has a unique appearance and a subtle effect on the quality of the displayed image.

Display Processors

In desktop personal computers, the circuit complexity of the graphics generator is approximately the same as that of the host CPU, roughly 8×10^6 in 1999. In the recent past throughput has doubled each year, a rate that exceeds Moore's Law. Figure 8.4 extrapolates this graphics performance increase into the near future[5].

The polygon size trend assumes a depth complexity of one and therefore a constant fill rate. The most important observation is that when polygon size shrinks to less than a pixel many of the traditional techniques of raster graphics make no sense. A few alternative architectures are waiting in the wings, but none is fully developed. The real issue will be communication of intermediate results from one part of the display processor to another, and in the case of large displays, the communication of computed pixels to the display device. In other words, it is the flow of graphical

---

5   Such an increase in performance is probably a transient. In this sense, Figure 8.4 is a cartoon-like exaggeration.

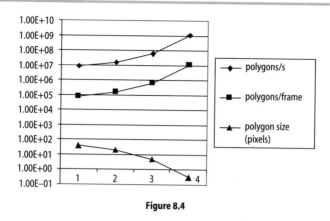

Figure 8.4

data, not its computation that should absorb our attention. For extremely high-resolution displays, this suggests that the pixel processor ought to reside in the display device. There are no architectures waiting in the wings for this case.

8.4.5 Other Emitters

Audio and tactile emitters and sensors are important in interaction, but are beyond the scope of this discussion. It is worth stating that the bandwidth and processing requirements for audio, even spatialized audio, are much less than those for 3D graphics. Consequently the debate about whether to attach the emitting elements to the space or the user may be biased more towards portability in this case.

8.5 Applications

The combination of components rather than any individual component is what really matters to us as designers and users. One way to look at combined performance is to propose an application and calculate the loads which the application places on the interactive elements. One overall fact becomes apparent in such an exercise: one size does not fit all. For example, Table 8.2 gives the generic elements of common applications.

Table 8.2

	Power	Bandwidth	Memory
Tracking	< 0.1 W	< 1 kbit/s	< 100 kbyte
Voice	< 0.5 W	<10 kbit/s	< 0.5 Mbyte
Video	5 W	>100 kbit/s	> 1 Mbyte
3D graphics	10 W	>10 Mbit/s	> 4 Mbyte

At the low end, an appliance for simple tracking clearly does not need the same bandwidth as a video transmission channel. At the high end, partitioning of any application requiring 3D graphics must be done with care. This is worth remembering when defining interconnection strategies.

Here are three applications scenarios that impose substantially different requirements on the interconnections:

Plain old desktop computing (but anywhere, anytime)

Plain old desktop computing generally requires a keyboard and a display. It is conceivable that continuous voice recognition, gesture recognition, wall-mounted displays, derived estimates of user state, and perhaps a credit card scanner can completely support traditional activities such as creation of documents, Web browsing, reading email, and managing finances. It would require no batteries, no wireless bandwidth, and nothing to augment the user's person.

Person-to-person communications

While we may regard voice communications for wandering users to be a solved problem and a prime example of location-aware interaction using wireless interconnection, it isn't so. Today's communication services perpetuate awkward interfaces and provide almost no means of computer mediation or augmentation of conversations. Note that the sensors involved in current implementations are a single microphone, a series of on–off switches, and received signal strength measurements. The bandwidth requirements are currently modest. Augmentation with simple sensors imposes no great increase in bandwidth or power requirements. Any real-time graphical component raises the stakes considerably and the debate about where to locate displays can be conducted largely in the context of this one application.

Interactive video entertainment

Broadcast entertainment is power hungry on the receiving end, but the whole point of broadcast is efficient unidirectional use of bandwidth. Interactive video entertainment, especially with multiple participants, is essentially person-to-person communications with video or graphics. Depending on how elements of the application are partitioned, this can be a real challenge. The ultimate, fully immersive, implementation taxes every technology mentioned so far.

The first and third examples in the list above are everyday desktop applications today. For a mobile user, all of the applications can be cast so that they employ absolutely no technology directly attached to the user. Whether this is desirable, effective or likely is all subject to debate.

Based on the numbers and trends given for the various hardware components, I would argue that sensors embedded in everyday worn appliances can be inexpensively integrated into interactive applications. Whether applications can use them effectively is an unknown. I would also argue that, for the short term, high-performance displays can be more readily attached to fixed environments than to the user directly.

8.6 Going Forward

This review is a standard engineering survey of the sort that has been notoriously misleading in the past. There is nothing wrong with standard engineering practice – it is a good tool for making plans for the future. However, actually planning for the future, as opposed to simply making plans, calls for heeding the unexpected and the unknown. What, then, are likely unexpected developments, the so-called "disruptive technologies"? This is not a silly question. We can ask it in a number of other ways:

- As we extend the performance of any given technology, to which assumptions about the technology is the performance most sensitive?
- For a given computing system built from a given collection of components, which changes in component parameters most affect the performance (and price)?
- What do people want to do that they can't with today's apparatus?
- What might people want to do if it were possible at all? Free?

In the early 1980s AT&T and Knight-Ridder conducted a trial deployment of interactive videotex services. The range of services was selected using the results of a survey in which potential users listed a number of high-minded applications related to information retrieval and education. If interactive games appeared at all on the list they were not prominent. The trial was a failure.

Today, visual services for information retrieval and education, along with games, shopping and any number of other activities are mainstays of (mildly) interactive computing. What has changed? Most apparently, today's interactive users have more display resolution, more memory, more processing speed, more bandwidth and more sites with which to connect. The last item may indeed be the key, but the others are all just physical parameters of the sort discussed in this chapter.

Those of us who are used to these services become frustrated when they are only available at desktops. We have incentives to improve the available technologies, overcome the physical limitations and freely enjoy the activities we believe will be enabled. Without doubt, once we succeed, some radically different activity based on some slightly different technology will become the mainstay instead, and we will all be surprised once again.

References

Addlesee, Michael D., Alan Jones, Finnbar Livesey, and Ferdinando Samaria, "The ORL Active Floor," *IEEE Personal Communications*, vol. 4, no. 5, October 1997, pp 35-41.

Bennett, CH (1973) Logical reversibility of computation, *IBM Journal of Research and Development*, 14, 525–532.

Bennett, F, Clarke, D, Evans, JB, Hopper, A, Jones, A and Leask, D (1997) Piconet – embedded mobile networking, *IEEE Personal Communications*, 4(5), 8–15.

Burd, TD and Brodersen, RW (1996) Processor design for portable systems, *Journal of VLSI Signal Processing*, 13(2/3), 203–221.

Dally, WJ and Poulton, JW (1998) *Digital Systems Engineering*, Cambridge, Cambridge University Press.

Hinckley, K and Sinclair, M (1999) Touch-sensing input devices, in *Proc. ACM CHI'99 Conference on Human Factors in Computing Systems*.

Kymisis, J, Kendall, C, Paradiso, J and and Gershenfeld, N (1998) Parasitic power harvesting in shoes, *Proc. of the Second IEEE International Conference on Wearable Computing, (ISWC)*, IEEE Computer Society Press, pp. 132–139.

Landauer, R. (1984) Fundamental physical limitations of the computational process, in *Computer Culture: The Scientific, Intellectual, and Social Impact of the Computer* (ed. Heinz R. Pagels), Annals of the New York Academy of Sciences, Vol. 426, pp. 161–170.

Lee, TH (1998) *Design Of CMOS Radio-Frequency Integrated Circuits*, Cambridge, Cambridge University Press.

Norman, DA (1984) Worsening the knowledge gap: the mystique of computation builds unnecessary barriers, in *Computer Culture: The Scientific, Intellectual, and Social Impact of the Computer* (ed. Heinz R. Pagels), Annals of the New York Academy of Sciences, Vol. 426, pp. 220–233.

Norman, DA (1998) *The Invisible Computer*, Cambridge, MA, MIT Press.

Paradiso, J, Abler, C, Hsiao, K-Y and Reynolds, M (1997) The magic carpet: physical sensing for immersive environments, in *Proceedings of CHI97*, ACM SIGCHI, March.

Picard, R (1997) *Affective Computing*, Cambridge, MA, MIT Press.

Rabaey, J, Guerra, L and Mehra, R (1995) Design guidance in the power dimension, *ICASSP Proceedings*, May.

Shannon, CE (1948) *The Mathematical Theory of Communication*, Urbana, IL, University of Illinois Press.

Shepard, TJ (1996) A channel access scheme for large dense packet radio networks, *Proceedings of SIGCOMM '96*, August.

Starkweather, G (1998) Display technology: directions & challenges, Internal presentation, Microsoft Research, August.

Starner, T (1996) Human-powered wearable computing, *IBM Systems Journal*, 35(3&4), 618–629.

Stephenson, N (1995) *The Diamond Age*, New York, Bantam Books.

Want, R, Hopper, A, Falcao, V and Gibbons, J (1992) the active badge location system, *ACM Transactions on Information Systems*, 10(1), 91–102.

Want, R, Schilit, BN, Adams, NI, Gold, R, Petersen, K, Goldberg, D, Ellis, JR and Weiser, M. (1995) An Overview of the ParcTab Ubiquitous Computing Experiment. *IEEE Personal Communications*, December, pp. 28–43.

Weiser, M (1992) The Computer for the 21st Century, *Scientific American*.

Whitted, T (1998) Draw on the wall, Capstone talk, *Visualization 98 Conference*, October.

Zimmerman, TG (1996) Personal Area Networks: Near-field intrabody communication, *IBM Systems Journal*, 35(3&4), 609–617.

About the Author

Turner Whitted is a senior researcher in the hardware devices group of Microsoft Research.

9

Technologies for Virtual Reality/Tele-Immersion Applications: Issues of Research in Image Display and Global Networking

Tom DeFanti, Dan Sandin, Maxine Brown, Dave Pape, Josephine Anstey, Mike Bogucki, Greg Dawe, Andy Johnson and Thomas S. Huang

Abstract

The Electronic Visualization Laboratory (EVL) at the University of Illinois at Chicago (UIC) has developed an aggressive program over the past decade to partner with scores of computational scientists and engineers all over the world. The focus of this effort has been to create visualization and virtual reality (VR) devices and applications for collaborative exploration of scientific and engineering data. Since 1995, our research and development activities have incorporated emerging high-bandwidth networks like the vBNS and its international connection point STAR TAP, in an effort now called *tele-immersion*.

As a result of eight years' experience building first- and second-generation projection-based VR devices to support these applications, we wish to describe needed research in *third-generation* VR devices aimed at desktop/office-sized displays. Since no current projection technology is yet configurable with ideal resolution and size, we must first describe the variety of emerging display devices, such as large color plasma displays, LCD projectors, LED panels, Digital Light Valves (DLVs), Grating Light Valves (GLVs) and Digital Micro Mirror Displays (DMDs).

In 1991 we conceived and have since developed the CAVE virtual reality theater, a room-sized, high-resolution, projection-based system that enables users to experience excellent immersion in full 3D imagery. We then developed the ImmersaDesk, a smaller, software-compatible, drafting table-format version of the CAVE that has been deployed to dozens of locations, nationally and internationally, at government institutions, national laboratories, universities and companies.

The hardware now needs to be made smaller, higher resolution and more adaptable to the human and his or her workspace. Middleware that manages connections, bandwidth and latency needs to be integrated with the computer systems driving these hardware devices. Software that increases the quality of human–computer interaction through human output recognition must be brought from specialized lab experiments to routine use, and provided as part of the tele-immersive collaborative experience. This chapter discusses many of the issues at the heart of this research.

9.1 Issues

9.1.1 Background: Projection-Based VR Technologies

The CAVE™ (Figure 9.1a) is a multi-person, room-sized, high-resolution, 3D video and audio environment. Graphics are projected in stereo onto three walls and the floor, and viewed with stereo glasses. As a viewer wearing a location sensor moves within its display boundaries, the correct perspective and stereo projections of the environment are constantly updated, so the image moves with and surrounds the viewer to achieve immersion.

The ImmersaDesk™ (Figure 9.1b) is a drafting table-format version of the CAVE. When folded up, it fits through a standard institutional door, and deploys into a

a   b

c

Figure 9.1 The CAVE™, the ImmersaDesk™ and the Infinity Wall.

$6' \times 8'$ footprint. It requires a single graphics engine of the SGI Onyx or Octane class, one projector, and no architectural modifications to the working space. The ImmersaDesk is software-compatible with the CAVE library.

The Infinity Wall (Figure 9.1c) is derivative of the PowerWall, a research effort of Paul Woodward at the University of Minnesota. The PowerWall achieves very high display resolution through parallelism, building up a single image from an array of display panels projected from the rear onto a single screen. High-speed playback of previously rendered images is possible by attaching extremely fast disk subsystems, accessed in parallel, to an Onyx. The Infinity Wall is a simpler PowerWall that has tracking and stereo; it is CAVE library compatible.

Computational Science and Engineering Research Partners

Since 1986, EVL has partnered with the National Center for Supercomputing Applications (NCSA) at the University of Illinois at Urbana-Champaign and the Mathematics and Computer Science Division at Argonne National Laboratory in ongoing efforts to develop national collaborations at professional conferences – notably ACM SIGGRAPH and ACM/IEEE Supercomputing. These events emphasize high-performance computing and communications, VR, and scientific visualization. The overall purpose is to encourage the development of teams, tools, hardware, system software and human interface models on an accelerated schedule to enable national-scale, multi-site collaborations applied to National Challenge and Grand Challenge problems. As a result of I-WAY, an experimental high-performance network linking dozens of the USA's fastest computers and advanced visualization environments at Supercomputing 95, many successful CAVE collaborations resulted [4,5,16]. Dozens of these scientists continue to work with EVL on various joint research projects, either informally, through grants, or through affiliation in the NSF Partnerships for Advanced Computational Infrastructure (PACI) program (http://alliance.ncsa.uiuc.edu/) A number have CAVEs, Immersa-Desks and similar devices. The CAVE Research Network Users' Society (CAVERNUS) has been in operation for several years, and welcomes members interested in projection-based VR (http://www.ncsa.uiuc.edu/VR/cavernus/).

International STAR TAP Partners

STAR TAP is a persistent infrastructure to facilitate the long-term interconnection and interoperability of advanced international networking in support of applications, performance measuring, and technology evaluations (http://www.startap.net/). STAR TAP, in Chicago, is the Next Generation Internet Exchange (NGIX) point for Next Generation Internet (NGI) (http://www.ngi.gov/) and Internet2 (http://www.internet2.edu/) networks. Several institutions in foreign countries own CAVEs and ImmersaDesks or similar devices and have either obtained STAR TAP connectivity or are applying for it in order to test broadband VR collaborations. Countries currently connected to STAR

TAP include Australia, Canada, Japan, Korea, Taiwan, Singapore, Russia, Norway, Sweden, Denmark, Iceland, Finland, The Netherlands, France and Israel. CERN is also connected.

Tele-immersion

The term *tele-immersion* was first used in October 1996 as the title of a workshop organized by EVL and sponsored by Advanced Network & Services, Inc. to bring together researchers in distributed computing, collaboration, VR, and networking. At this workshop, we paid specific attention to the future needs of applications in the sciences, engineering and education. We define tele-immersion as the union of networked VR and video in the context of significant computing and data mining. EVL's Web site (http://www.evl.uic.edu/) has an extensive tele-immersion bibliography and papers. Tele-immersion has since entered the NGI and Internet2 vocabulary. In the applications section of the Computing Research Association's "Research Challenges for the NGI", *tele-immersion* was one of five key technologies identified as necessary for the future use of the NGI [18]:

> **Tele-immersion.** Tele-immersion will enable users in different locations to collaborate in a shared, virtual, or simulated environment as if they are in the same room. It is the ultimate synthesis of networking and media technologies to enhance collaborative environments. Tele-Immersive applications must combine audio, video, virtual worlds, simulations, and many other complex technologies. They will require huge bandwidth, very fast responses, and guarantees of delivery.

We have connected CAVEs and ImmersaDesks over networks, from ATM-based 622 Mbit and 155 Mbit networks to ISDN. We have implemented video and audio over the networks to enable users to conduct remote teleconferencing and distributed virtual prototyping. At Supercomputing '97, we held a 17-way ImmersaDesk/CAVE tele-immersion experiment with eight ImmersaDesks on the conference exhibit floor and another nine devices connected from as far away as Amsterdam and Tokyo [7]. At Supercomputing '98, 10 countries participated in the iGrid booth, showing many instances of international tele-immersion [23,24] (http://www.startap.net/igrid/).

CAVERN is our acronym for the CAVE Research Network. CAVERN is comprised of dozens of network-connected CAVEs, ImmersaDesks and other VR devices, like Head-Mounted Displays, Responsive Workbenches and BOOMs. CAVERN is managed by the CAVE libraries and CAVERNsoft, a distributed shared memory software package optimized for networked collaboration [12–14].

9.1.2 Issues in Tele-Immersion Development

The ideal tele-immersion system is not hard to imagine. Combine the best computer graphics, audio, computer simulation and imaging. Connect with networking as good as direct memory access. Provide software and hardware to track gaze, gesture, facial expression and body position. Offer it as a built-in feature on all personal computers and video games. Obviously, we are far from achieving ubiquitous tele-immersion.

Consider human voice and audio in general. There is a worldwide network optimized for speech (the telephone system) that supports two-way and multi-way interactions. Computers and other equipment one can purchase in shopping malls can record, edit, playback and duplicate (even net broadcast) audio to perfection. Real-time speech synthesis is close at hand with gigaflop desktop machines. Similarly, mature and optimized systems exist for standard video, recording, editing, playback, global teleconferencing and broadcast, at much higher cost.

No such consumer/corporate demand exists yet for tele-immersion; however, the near-term ubiquity of 3D graphics engines, the expected implosion of telecommunications costs, and the emergence of new display technologies are reasons for timely experimental development of integrated systems. We hope to inspire private sector investment by describing prototypes of fully integrated tele-immersion hardware and software. Many of the barriers are market-based, but several are true technical research issues. Below, we identify and propose to address a set of these research issues.

The tele-immersion system of 2009 would ideally:

- Support one or more flat panels/projectors with ultra-high color resolution (say 5000 × 5000)
- Be stereo capable without special glasses
- Have several built-in micro-cameras and microphones
- Have tether-less, low-latency, high-accuracy tracking
- Network to teraflop computing via multi-gigabit optical switches with low latency
- Have exquisite directional sound capability
- Be available in a range of compatible hardware and software configurations
- Have gaze-directed or gesture-directed variable resolution and quality of rendering
- Incorporate AI-based predictive models to compensate for latency and anticipate user transitions
- Use a range of sophisticated haptic devices to couple to human movement and touch
- Accommodate disabled and fatigued users in the spirit of the Every Citizen Interface to the NII [2]

What we have as parts to integrate into 1999 systems are:

- Heavy, moderately expensive 3-tube projectors as the only straightforward stereo-capable projection devices
- Large projection distances needed for rear projection
- Medium resolution (1280 × 1024 pixel) displays
- Moderately awkward stereo glasses with limited view angle
- Stereo graphics hardware that integrates poorly with non-stereo camera input

- Imprecise electromagnetic tethered tracking with significant latency
- "Best effort" networking with random latency
- Expensive multiprocessor workstations and rendering engines (\$25 000–\$200 000/screen)
- Primitive software models of user interactions within VR and tele-immersive systems
- Very primitive hardware devices for haptic interaction

In addition to the obvious dependency on improvements in display devices, computing hardware, and network integration, the tele-immersion system of 2009 will need to rely on emerging results from the computer science research community, including specifically:

- Data-intensive computing and data mining
- Image-based modeling
- Digital audio/video transmission
- Recording/playback of sessions
- Every citizen interfaces
- Gesture, speech and gaze interaction

9.1.3 Challenges of Tele-Immersion

Tele-immersion has emerged as a high-end driver for the Quality of Service (QoS), bandwidth and reservation efforts envisioned by the NGI and Internet2 leadership. From a networking perspective, tele-immersion is a very challenging technology for several reasons:

- The networks must be in place and tuned to support high-bandwidth applications.
- Low latency, needed for two-way collaboration, is hard to specify and guarantee given current middleware.
- The speed of light in fiber itself is a limiting factor over transcontinental and transoceanic distances.
- Multicast, unicast, reliable and unreliable data transmissions (called "flows") need to be provided for and managed by the networks and the operating systems of supercomputer-class workstations.
- Real-time considerations for video and audio reconstruction ("streaming") are critical to achieving the feel of telepresence, whether synchronous or recorded and played back,
- The computers, too, are bandwidth limited with regard to handling very large data for collaboration.
- Simulation and data mining are open-ended in computational and bandwidth needs – there will never be quite enough computing and bits/second to fully analyze and simulate reality for scientific purposes.

Table 9.1 Tele-immersion data flow types.

Type	Latency	Bandwidth	Reliable	Multicast	Security	Streaming	Dynamic QoS
Control	< 30 ms	64 kbit/s	Yes	No	High	No	Low
Text	< 100 ms	64 kbit/s	Yes	No	Medium	No	Low
Audio	< 30 ms	$N \times 128$ kbit/s	No	Yes	Medium	Yes	Medium
Video	< 100 ms	$N \times 5$ Mbit/s	No	Yes	Low	Yes	Medium
Tracking	< 10 ms	$N \times 128$ kbit/s	No	Yes	Low	Yes	Medium
Database	< 100 ms	> 1 Gbit/s	Yes	Maybe	Medium	No	High
Simulation	< 30 ms	> 1 Gbit/s	Mixed	Maybe	Medium	Maybe	High
Haptic	< 10 ms	> 1 Mbit/s	Mixed	Maybe	Low	Maybe	High
Rendering	< 30 ms	>1 Gbit/s	No	Maybe	Low	Maybe	Medium

Tele-Immersion Flow Types

Progress in all these areas, however, is expected; tele-immersion serves as an integrating technology as pieces of the solution are contributed by the community and computer/networking industry. Table 9.1, developed in discussions with Rick Stevens, director of the Math and Computer Science Division at Argonne National Laboratory, gives our current best *estimations* and *opinions* of the attributes of the nine types of flow simultaneously needed for an *n*-way compute and data-intensive audio, video and haptic (touch) tele-immersive session [35]. The research agenda for the coming years *very much* involves validating this table and creating software intelligence to compensate for the otherwise unachievable.

The columns represent flow-type attributes:

- **Latency** is the sum of all delays in the system, from the speed of light in fiber, to operating system overhead, to tracker settling time and screen refresh.
- **Bandwidth** is the bits/second the system can transmit.
- **Reliable** flows are verified and retransmitted if bad.
- **Multicast** flows go to more than one site at once.
- **Security** involves encryption overhead that may or may not be warranted or legal.
- **Streaming** data is a constant flow of information over time, as with video, audio and tracking.
- **Dynamic QoS** can provide ways to service bursty high-bandwidth needs on request.

The rows indicate the data flow types:

- **Control information** consists of data that is used to manage the tele-immersion session, to authenticate users or processes, to launch processes, to control the display or tracking systems, and to communicate out of band between the world servers and VR systems.
- **Text** provides simple communications capability within collaborative sessions for simple note taking and passing. Text can also command Unix processes driving the environments.

- **Audio** gives ambient auditory cues, allows voice communications among users, and is used to issue commands via voice recognition and speech synthesis. A typical application may use multiple audio streams.
- **Video** can allow teleconferencing or remote monitoring displayed within the virtual world. Synthetic 2D animated bitmaps in video format have application as well.
- **Tracking** is achieved with location and orientation sensors, and captures the position and orientation of the user. Typically this data is streamed to the computer responsible for computing the perspective of the scene. Tele-immersion requires tracking data to be shared among sites. Most VR systems only head and hand track; future systems will have many more sensors to track more complex posture and body motions.
- **Database** is the heart of a tele-immersion application world. The database contains the graphical models of virtual scenes, objects and data, and since the database is used to provide the models that are rendered, it must be maintained in a coherent state across multiple sites. Databases might be as simple as shared VRML files or as complex as multi-terabyte scientific datasets, VR extensions of video serving or even Virtual Director recorded sessions. (Virtual Director is a joint EVL/NCSA development project [29].)
- **Simulation** provides the basis for dynamic behaviors, like responding to the users' actions. Small-scale simulations often run on the computer also generating the VR experience, but frequently the simulation will need a dedicated supercomputer [28]. User input is captured and transmitted to the simulation via the network and the simulation will generate an update, which is then propagated to each user site for local rendering. Typically the data transferred to the simulation is considerably smaller than the data returned by the simulation. For example, if the user is conducting an interactive molecular docking experiment, only tracking data need be sent to the molecular model, indicating the location of the user's hand; however, in response, the simulation will return the updated coordinates of hundreds or thousands of atoms.
- **Haptics** include force and touch sensing/feedback devices and use a variety of sensors and actuators that are "attached" to the hands and/or legs of users. Some systems now generate haptic "images" that augment or replace visual images (e.g. a user feeling the magnetic field around a star simulation or perceiving the texture of an atomic scale surface being imaged by a scanning microscope). Haptics are particularly sensitive to latency and jitter (instantaneous variations in latency).
- **Rendering** is the transformation of geometric information (polygonal or volumetric) into images for display. All VR environments primarily render graphics locally. As networks provide bandwidth adequate for compressed HDTV, however, it will become reasonable and efficient for scenes to be rendered remotely and transmitted to each site in real time.

Note that large peak transfer rates for database, simulation, and rendering are due to the fact that relatively simple actions in the virtual world by a user can cause a considerable demand for synchronization or consistency updates at each participating site. Real-time rendering requirements may imply the need to distribute updates within one frame update interval (1/30–1/60 second) to avoid jerkiness or pauses in the graphics or inconsistencies in the shared world. While intelligent and speculative pre-fetching can often reduce the need for peak bandwidth, the ultimate limit is the nature and complexity of the world model and the expectations of the user.

Lag vs. Network Latency

In tele-immersion systems, an important distinction must be made between the notions of network performance and user-perceived lag in the virtual environment. "Lag" is the term used to describe the perceived sum of all the sources of latency in a system.

Typically, it is thought of as the delay between action in the real world (e.g. as captured by tracking or haptics) and the perceived response of the system to that action. Lag is the critical issue for usability; reducing lag is a major technical challenge. Communications latency is only one component of tele-immersion lag. Effective solutions to reducing lag must attack the component sources of latency at all levels of the system. VR system lag is the result of delays in rendering, display, tracking, simulation, communications and synchronization. There are multiple sources of latency in the communications system alone:

- Transmission latency – the time it takes to send a packet from one node to another
- Bandwidth or transfer latency – the time it takes to move data due to the size of the transfer
- Switching or routing latency – the sum of the delays due to the fact that the network is not composed of just point-to-point links
- Contention – delay caused by competition for limited resources in the network (bandwidth, queues etc.)
- Protocol latency – due to the segmentation and reassembly operations to build data packets and the header processing for protocol stacks.

Most users have difficulty manipulating objects in VR once lag exceeds 200 ms. When the virtual display is coupled with the real world, as in tele-robotics, this limit is approximately 30 ms. Non-network components of the VR system often together exceed 200–300 ms, so there is actually very little room for wide-area communications delay in the lag budget. Research into asynchronous tele-immersion models should improve this situation; however, absolute limits of transmission latency due to time-of-light round trips may ultimately limit the geographical extent of tightly coupled tele-immersion environments.

Quality of Service (QoS)

QoS requirements need the ability to:

- Assign minimum service guarantees and relative priorities to each of many streams

- Specify notification and compensation actions if the QoS dynamics of the network change over time
- Predict the reliability of service guarantees or service estimates

Often the application can make some intelligent use of QoS information provided by the network or middleware software layer by taking corrective or compensatory actions during execution, provided dynamic control interfaces are available. Simplified QoS concepts, such as differentiated services, allow for prioritized traffic without specific service guarantees; this may be a way to provide uncongested bandwidth for tele-immersion and other collaborative users that is scalable.

9.2 Correspondences/Dependencies: Tele-Immersive Device Design Concepts

9.2.1 Motivation for Desktop/Office-Sized VR Display Devices

The VR community needs to conduct research on third-generation VR devices to construct software-compatible, variable-resolution and desktop/office-sized prototypes and products, which evolve over time as technology improves and needs become more demanding; the hardware now needs to be made smaller, higher resolution, and more adaptable to the human and his or her workspace. The recommendation is to procure, evaluate and integrate a variety of emerging display devices, such as large color plasma displays, LCD projectors, LED panels, Digital Light Valves (DLVs), Grating Light Valves (GLVs) and Digital Micro Mirror Displays (DMDs).

To construct the tele-immersive office workspace, one would want affordable wall-sized high-resolution borderless displays with low lag and undiminished image intensity when viewed at an angle. Given that such a display does not exist today, we must rather learn from assembling new VR systems from available components[1]. We must push screen technology development by creating pressure from the computational science and engineering communities with compelling applications projects.

We describe several devices, each of which addresses different major issues in the tele-immersion/VR human–computer interface:

- ImmersaDesk3 Plasma Panel Desktop VR
- Personal Augmented Reality Immersive System (PARIS)

---

1 Several companies, like Panoram (http://www.panoramtech.com/reality-center/wallandesk.html) and VRex (http://www.vrex.com/), offer well-designed, non-tracked displays for the office and showroom. Barco and Fakespace have products similar to the ImmersaDesk. The goal of this chapter is not to suggest competition with the commercial sector, but to investigate and inspire new display and control technologies for the human-centered interface to tele-immersion.

- Personal Penta Panel (P3)
- Totally Active Workspace (TAWS)
- CyberCeiling
- CAVEscope

9.2.2 New Immersive Display Technologies

In the context of building new VR devices, the community needs to investigate the viability, flexibility of operation and breadth of application of the following new display technologies, compared with current three-tube projector systems:

- *Liquid Crystal Display (LCD) projectors and panels.* These are achieving better resolution now (1280 × 1024), but have too high a lag to be used for stereo imaging unless two projectors are used with shutters (http://www.nec.com/, http://www.angleview.com/ and http://www.electrohome.com/).

- *Digital Micro-mirror Displays (DMDs).* These have good resolution (1280 × 1024), and are theoretically fast enough for stereo, but the supplied firmware does not support stereo (http://www.electrohome.com/, http://store.infocus.com/lp420/index.htm, http://www.ti.com/dlp/docs/business/manufacturers/, http://www.ti.com/dlp/docs/business/resources/press/pr94/448asc.htm and http://www.ti.com/dlp/docs/business/manufacturers/ask1.html).

- *Plasma panel displays.* These are low–medium resolution (800 × 480) but probably fast enough to do stereo with the proper driver electronics. These displays have electronics mounted around their edges that make borderless multi-screen configurations a challenge (http://www.nec.com/ and http://www.fujitsu.com/).

- *Light Emitting Diode (LED) displays.* These have low resolution right now (e.g. 208 × 272 and 320 × 192) but are bright and borderless in principle (http://www.lumagraph.com/lumatile.html, http://www.daktronics.com/PAGES/Prostar.HTM and http://www.microweb.com/kwu/fdisplay.html).

- *Digital Light Valve (DLV) displays.* These new desktop projection displays have latency problems for stereo use; they can switch fast enough but do not go to black in the required time. A 2K × 2K resolution version has been built (http://www.almaden.ibm.com/journal/rd/423/melcher.txt).

- *Grating Light Valve (GLV) displays.* Recently demonstrated in prototype form, this laser-driven micro-electromechanical display is capable of HDTV resolution at 96 Hz, very promising for VR. Switching speeds are extremely low, allowing a linear array of deflectable ribbon picture elements to scan out an image [26] (http://www.siliconlight.com/).

9.2.3 ImmersaDesk3

Plasma Panel Desktop Device – a Design Exercise

ImmersaDesks and Responsive Workbenches are large because the available three-tube projection technology has a limit to how small the screen can get (approximately 6' diagonal). Rear projection distances are significant, even when folded with mirrors, and the projector itself is quite large and heavy. Both of these devices are sized for a laboratory, and are too large for a typical faculty office or cubicle. We built a prototype device, called the ImmersaDesk3 (Figure 9.2) to test the plasma panel technology currently available at 640 × 480 resolution for US$10,000.

The ImmersaDesk3 is configured so that a user can position the screen at any angle from horizontal to vertical, forward or back, on the desk. The angle can be measured automatically so that the correct perspective view of the computer-generated images for the tracked user is presented. Cameras can be added to this configuration to make image/gesture recognition, tetherless tracking and tele-immersion experiments possible. Given its configuration flexibility, the ImmersaDesk3 is also amenable to the integration of haptic (tactile input–output) devices.

We built our system around the Fujitsu PDS4201U-H Plasmavision display panel. The Plasmavision has an active display area of 36 × 20 in (in a 16:9 aspect ratio); the entire panel is 41 × 25 × 6 in and weighs 80 pounds.

We mounted the Plasmavision on a modified office desk. To accommodate different applications and for greater flexibility, we wanted to be able to position the screen vertically (perpendicular to the desktop), horizontally (flat on the

Figure 9.2 The ImmersaDesk3, Electronic Visualization Laboratory, University of Illinois at Chicago.

desktop) or at an angle in between. The panel is too heavy for users to shift easily, so we mounted it on hydraulic supports with a hand crank to adjust the angle.

Problems Encountered with Plasmavision Plasma Panel Displays

The Plasmavision outputs a 30 Hz interlaced NTSC resolution image. When this is used for a stereoscopic display, each eye is only seeing a 30 Hz signal and the flicker is very noticeable; prolonged exposure can give many users headaches. Using the NTSC field-interleaved format for stereo yields only 640 × 240 pixel resolution for each eye's image. We also found that the red and green phosphors do not decay quickly enough. When we look at a stereo test pattern, which displays separate red, green and blue color bars for each eye, only the blue bar is sufficiently extinguished; the red and green bars are still visible to the *wrong* eye. In an informal test of 16 users at SIGGRAPH '98, we noted that 25% of them could fuse the full-color images, while 50% could only fuse the images when the red and green channels were disabled, so that the images were just shades of blue; 25% of the users could not fuse the images at all [25].

The Plasmavision is electromagnetically noisy, so much so that it interferes with the accuracy of magnetic tracking systems.

Despite these issues, the Plasmavision had advantages. Application developers were very pleased with the size of the display as well as its brightness and color quality, compared to a video projector. Its size gives a much larger angle of view than a conventional monitor, yet it fits well on a desktop, something a 42" monitor or projection system cannot do.

Current plasma panel technology has severe limitations as a stereo display device for projection-based VR systems. The inability to easily sync the plasma panel to shutter glasses and the red/green phosphor decay problem preclude clear stereo. The low resolution and 30 Hz frame rate also prevent current panels from being serious contenders in this field. Although flat panels can significantly save space, larger display systems would need larger panels or tiled panels. Current plasma panels have borders that prevent seamless tiling.

Nevertheless, the concept of a wide field of view, desktop VR system and space-saving flat panel technology for CAVEs and other large displays is appealing. We look forward to improvements in flat panel technology as it evolves.

9.2.4 Personal Augmented Reality Immersive System (PARIS)

Twenty years ago, Ken Knowlton created a see-through display for Bell Labs using a half-silvered mirror mounted at an angle in front of a telephone operator. The monitor driving the display was positioned above the desk facing down so that its image of a virtual keyboard could be superimposed on an operator's hands working under the mirror. The keycaps on the operator's physical keyboard could be dynamically relabeled to match the task of completing a call as it progressed. Devices that align computer imagery with the user's viewable environment, like

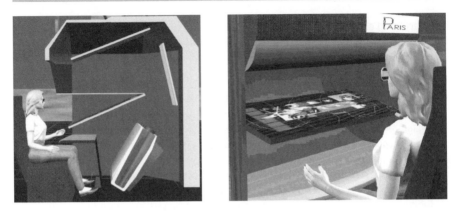

Figure 9.3 Artists renderings of the PARIS system. **a** Cutaway side view. **b** Over-the-shoulder view. (Image courtesy Sam Thongrong, Electronic Visualization Laboratory, University of Illinois at Chicago, 1999.)

Knowlton's, are examples of *augmented reality*, or *see-through VR*. More recently, researchers at the National University of Singapore's Institute of Systems Science built a stereo device of similar plan using a Silicon Graphics monitor, a well-executed configuration for working with small parts in high-resolution VR [15]. Neither of these systems provides tracking, but rather assumes the user to be in a fixed and seated position.

We are currently building a desktop VR device, the Personal Augmented Reality Immersive System (PARIS), a third-generation version of this concept (Figure 9.3). We ensure that a keyboard is integrated, and that suitably positioned cameras can capture facial expressions and head position. Gesture recognition can come from tracking, as well as processed camera input. Audio support can be used for voice recognition and generation as well as for recording and tele-immersion sessions. (See the "Multimodal Human Computer Interfaces" box below.)

Since we are committed to stereo in PARIS, and would like as high a resolution as possible, we cannot initially use a plasma panel display for the reasons belabored in the previous section. Instead, we will use two 1280×1024 LCD projectors with electronic shutters compatible with active glasses to achieve stereo separation[2].

We can also use PARIS to prototype passive (polarized) stereo, since we can polarize the two projector outputs, allowing very inexpensive and lightweight glasses to be incorporated, an important feature for use in museums and schools. If plasma or LED panel displays ever have excellent brightness, stereo speeds and high resolution, these would be preferable devices to adapt.

---

2   LCDs have very high lag, so time-based stereo separation is not possible with a single projector; instead, we propose two projectors with external blinking shutters to separate the left and right eye views. VRex, Inc. markets a line of LCD stereo projectors that use polarization multiplexing with a faceplate over the LCD to separate the left and right eye images. The effective resolution is halved since the displays are spatially multiplexed rather than time multiplexed, but there is evidence that the brain reintegrates the information, lessening the problem.

Multimodal Human Computer Interfaces

Thomas S. Huang

Introduction

As information systems become global, there is increasing interest in making access to computing, communications and information repositories universal. To achieve this goal, it is imperative to explore the use of new modalities (such as vision and speech) in human–computer interfaces (HCI). The Image Laboratory at the Beckman Institute, University of Illinois at Urbana-Champaign, has been collaborating with EVL to develop multimodal human computer interfaces for existing (ImmersaDesk, CAVE) and future (PARIS, etc.) virtual environments [30–34].

Current Research

Current research projects in Multimodal HCI include:

1. Integrating speech and vision-based hand gesture recognition in display controls in virtual environments. Algorithms have been implemented on ImmersaDesks to use the hand to point to a specific object in the display while using voice to ask questions about the object, or to use the hand and voice together to navigate through 3D terrain (the hand is used to steer and the voice is used to stop, go forward, change speed etc.).
2. Real-time algorithms for detecting, recognizing and tracking faces and recognizing (together with tone of voice) emotion.
3. Use of visual lip-reading to help the accuracy of audio speech recognition in noisy environments.
4. We have started to work on the difficult problem of tracking fingers visually, which will be needed for virtual manipulation in the PARIS environment.

Challenging Research Issues

In addition to the visual tracking of the hand/fingers, some of the major research issues for the future are:

1. Visual tracking of humans in less constrained situations. Current work on visual human tracking concentrates on tracking isolated human parts (face, arm/hand, body) and imposes severe constraints, such as front view for faces, long-sleeved shirts for arm/hand, and tight clothing for body. In many future applications, it will be necessary to track the entire human robustly, in real time, and without constraints.
2. Fusion of cues from different modalities. What are good architectures for integrating the information from different modalities to reach decisions?

9.2.5 CyberCeilings, Designed for the Last Unused Projection Surface

In trying to fit large screens and VR into offices, use of overhead space or the ceiling is conceivable, and has distinct advantages in hospital patient settings, assuming the room can be made dark enough. Figure 9.4 indicates some options for ceiling-mounted front projection with a mirror on the floor and a smaller rear projection

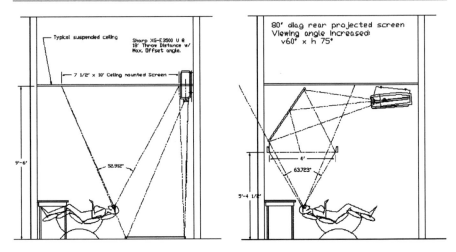

Figure 9.4 Schematic of CyberCeiling. (Image courtesy of Greg Dawe, Electronic Visualization Laboratory, University of Illinois at Chicago, 1999.)

overhead display. Different lensing can alter the projection distances in the former example. The chair shown is a commercially available executive motorized recliner, but could be replaced by a bed in a hospital setting. This configuration has the benefit that the user may not need to be tracked since body position is fixed and head rotation is not accounted for in projected VR environments.

9.2.6 Personal Penta Panel (P3), or Dilbert's Dream

Dilbert's Dream is conceived as an office cubicle whose walls and desk are made from borderless stereo-capable high-resolution panels, not, unfortunately, currently obtainable.

Alternatively, we are proposing a "desktop" cubicle. The Personal Penta Panel (P3; Figure 9.5) is a box made out of 42" diagonal plasma panels. The user places his or her tracked head and hands into the box of screens and is presented with a surround (non-stereo) view. Each panel would have a frame around it, creating seams between screens that would be difficult to eliminate. There are, however, optical methods to relay an image a few inches forward, which could be used to (mostly) eliminate the effects of the frames. Such a device would be useful for all but very close viewing, even in non-stereo, as we wait for the needed technological improvements in panels.

Scott Adams, creator of the *Dilbert* cartoon strip, recently suggested that this kind of device may be harmful to programmers! In his article "Gene fool" in *TIME Magazine* [27], he explains:

> But unlike the sterile boxes of today, every cubicle will be a technology wonderland customized for the occupant. Flat-panel screens on each wall will give the impression you are in a hot air balloon floating over the Alps. Noise-cancellation technology will block out the surrounding sounds while providing a symphony within the cubisphere.

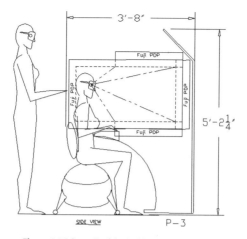

Figure 9.5 Schematic of the P3 (Greg Dawe, EVL, 1998).

The computer will continue its evolution to a full entertainment center, providing a constant supply of first-run movies, live nudity, gambling and video conferencing. The engineer's chair will be soft and warm, conforming to the body and providing simulated motion and vibration to match the entertainment. The cubicle experience will be so much better than life on the outside, engineers won't want to leave. That could be a problem. I heard about an experiment where rats were given the choice between food and cocaine. They chose the cocaine until they starved. The same thing will happen to the engineers. I predict they'll all starve to death inside their cubicle wonderlands. I just hope no one blames me.

9.2.7 Totally Active Work Space (TAWS)

Pending the availability of suitable plasma, LCD or LED panels, we have built screens into a rear-projection desktop structure to simulate the Totally Active Work Space (TAWS; Figure 9.6) – the ultimate Dilbert's Dream or *cubisphere*. TAWS is large enough for two colleagues to share the workspace when need be. EVL has been modifying its LCD shutter glasses to run at 160 Hz, so that four lenses (in two sets of glasses) can operate almost flicker-free at 40 Hz each. This capability, which we call *duo-view*, allows two tracked users of the same display to see the image in correct perspective and size, essential for sharing a workspace. Research into screen materials is needed because the depolarization that comes from looking at screens at very oblique angles creates ghosting that is more of an issue with duo-view than normal stereo.

9.2.8 CAVEscope: Simulating Variable Resolution Displays

All projection-based VR devices trade off wide angle of view for resolution. Human vision is acute only for a very narrow angle, the ~5° of vision falling on the fovea. It

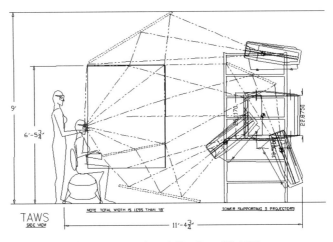

Figure 9.6 TAWS schematic (Greg Dawe, EVL, 1998).

would be desirable, therefore, to have adaptive resolution displays that, given eye tracking, could match human visual acuity in the area of the screen in this 5° angle of view. In stereo, graphics engines currently achieve a resolution of 1280 × 1024 spread across 5 to 10 feet, a *rather less-than-crisp* display. Software techniques can be used to render more detail in the area of interest, but resolution itself cannot improve. The projectors now available are not built to handle the dynamic horizontal scanning fluctuations needed for variable resolution display, and neither are the display engines. CAVEscope (Figure 9.7), however, provides a way to simulate variable resolution in a projection VR setting[3].

We suggest providing a high-resolution (e.g. 1024 × 768 or 1280 × 1024) LCD display that one can move into the area of detailed interest. Such a display would be like a portal into a higher-resolution space. It would be suspended in the projection-based VR space by a counterweighted mechanism, much like an X-ray machine in a dentist's office. One would navigate in the VR space as normal, with low-resolution surround vision, but pull the CAVEscope into place when high-resolution examination is desired. The CAVEscope would be tracked so that it would present the proper perspective projection. Touchscreen technology could also be available for user input. A miniature television camera mounted on the CAVEscope could enable tele-conferencing. Users can see and talk to each other using CAVEscopes, or position their devices for coverage relevant to the task at hand. CAVEscope combines the intuitive navigational capabilities of projection-based VR with the detailed view of the LCD portal, all under user control.

---

3 Some flight simulators have elaborate mechanisms to create high-resolution images at the pilot's center of interest by using a second projector inset at higher resolution. Since VR users have much more freedom than a pilot to move and look around, this technique will not work well since the inset projector, whose image is usually positioned by a moving mirror and has a limited range of motion and focus.

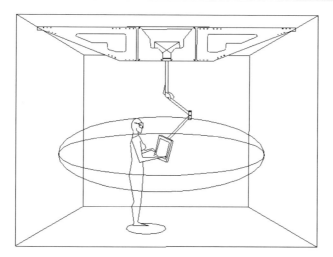

Figure 9.7 CAVEscope schematic (Greg Dawe, EVL, 1998).

CAVEscope should also be usable in an office setting with front projection VR on the office walls and desktop, such as has been proposed by the Advanced Network and Services-sponsored National Tele-Immersion Initiative (`http://www.advanced.org/teleimmersion.html`). Since the wall projections are used mainly for navigation and context, not for detail work, the quality of the projected images could be less than optimal, as long as the CAVEscope image is suitably bright and sharp.

Since LCD panel technology does not permit Crystal Eyes-type stereo (due to high lag) at this point, we will need to work with a mono image, pending the availability of a compatible stereo-capable panel in the future. Taking the stereo glasses on and off is an annoyance.

Tracked handheld panels have been suggested as portals into virtual and augmented reality spaces for some time, although, on videotape, the concept is simulated with chroma keying [17]. Discovering where to look in virtual space is a large part of the problem with narrow-angle-of-view devices like panels held at arm's length, VR binoculars or even head-mounted displays. CAVEscope affords the user both the navigational and wide field of view of projection-based VR with a real-time high-resolution inspection capability. Since CAVEscope has its own rendering engine, the software can be tuned to provide much more detailed rendering in the designated area of interest, which could even be behind or above the user, where there are no projected screens!

In addition, the user can easily enough freeze the motion and build up the display or re-render it with ray tracing, a type of successive refinement not normally usable in VR. We believe these notions will provide enhanced performance in accuracy, resolving power, flexibility of operation, user friendliness and navigation for scientists and engineers using projection-based VR for discovery and observation.

9.3 Questions for the Future

1.   It is appropriate to stipulate that market forces for commodity computing improvement will not be driven by virtual reality or tele-immersion needs for at least a few years. However, it is clear that the designers of future workspaces will use large, high-resolution flat displays given availability at almost any cost. How do we motivate the creation and marketing of these high-resolution panel devices most effectively? How do we convince the panel designers and manufacturers to incorporate features that support stereo?

2.   It is also clear that 3D real-time graphics generation suitable for VR is achievable cheaply from the example set by the Nintendo 64 Silicon Graphics chip set. How do we get such displays boosted in resolution and enable, say, dual-channel output for cheap dual-projector displays, or stereo capability for the appropriate panel displays? How do we encourage manufacturers of micro-electromechanical displays like the GLV and DLV to develop stereo-capable firmware?

3.   Audio is well handled as (one-dimensional) phone calls; video and audio are supported by teleconference (two-dimensional) calls. How do we push the development of operating systems and networks that handle tele-immersion (three-dimensional) calls? Do we develop personal switches and/or routers that have graphics/audio/video boards, or will the personal computer industry develop machines that handle multiple types of network flow?

4.   How do we motivate the development of haptic devices that do not injure users from repetitive use? How do we integrate video and motion detection to have our computers recognize our needs and wants? How do we send haptic inputs and haptic displays over networks?

5.   How do we build systems sufficiently rich in IO to accommodate every citizen, including the elderly? Will we succeed in standardizing/propagating these interfaces before we get too old to enjoy them?

6.   What are the implications of transcontinental and transoceanic distances for tele-immersion.

7.   How do we archive tele-immersive sessions in ways we can play back and/or edit in the near and far future?

Acknowledgments

EVL's virtual reality research, collaborations and outreach programs are made possible by major funding from the National Science Foundation (NSF), awards EIA-9802090, EIA-9871058, EIA-9720351, ANI-9712283 and ACI-9418068, as well as NSF Partnerships for Advanced Computational Infrastructure (PACI) cooperative agreement ACI-9619019 to the National Computational Science Alliance. EVL also receives support from the US Department of Energy Accelerated Strategic Computing Initiative (ASCI) and Pacific Interface on behalf of NTT Optical Network Systems Laboratory in Japan.

The CAVE and ImmersaDesk are trademarks of the Board of Trustees of the University of Illinois.

References

[1] D Cox (1996) Cosmic voyage: scientific visualization for IMAX film (Animator's Sketches), and Cosmic voyage: galaxy formation and interaction (Computer Animation Festival), in *SIGGRAPH '96 Visual Proceedings*, Computer Graphics Annual Conference Series, ACM SIGGRAPH, pp. 129 and 174.

[2] Computer Science and Telecommunications Board, National Research Council (1997) *More Than Screen Deep: Toward Every-Citizen Interfaces to the Nation's Information Infrastructure*, National Academy Press.

[3] M Czernuszenko, D Pape, D Sandin, T DeFanti, GL Dawe and MD Brown (1997) The immersadesk and infinity wall projection-based virtual reality displays, *Computer Graphics, ACM SIGGRAPH*, 31(2), 46–49, http://www.evl.uic.edu/pape/CAVE/idesk/paper/.

[4] TA DeFanti, MD Brown and R Stevens (Guest Editors) (1996) Virtual reality over high-speed networks, *IEEE Computer Graphics & Applications*, 16(4), 14–17, 42–84.

[5] TA DeFanti, I Foster, M Papka, R Stevens and T Kuhfuss (1996) Overview of the I-WAY: wide area visual supercomputing, *International Journal of Supercomputer Applications and High Performance Computing*, 10(2/3), 123–131.

[6] M Ghazisaedy, D Adamczyk, DJ Sandin, RV Kenyon and TA DeFanti (1995) Ultrasonic calibration of a magnetic tracker in a virtual reality space, *Proceedings of the IEEE Virtual Reality Annual International Symposium (VRAIS '95)*, Research Triangle Park, NC, March.

[7] A Johnson, J Leigh and J Costigan (1998) Multiway tele-immersion at Supercomputing '97, *IEEE Computer Graphics and Applications*, July.

[8] R Kenyon and M Afenya (1995) Training in real and virtual environments, *Annals of Biomedical Engineering: Starkfest Conference Proceedings*, 23, 445–455.

[9] C Kesselman, R Stevens, T DeFanti, J Bannister and I Foster (1997) Tele-immersive applications on the next-generation internet (white paper), in *Workshop on Research Directions for the Next Generation Internet*, Computing Research Association, sponsored by the Federal Large Scale Networking Working Group (LSN) of the National Science and Technology Council's Committee on Computing, Information, and Communications R&D Subcommittee, 13–14 May, 1997.

[10] S Latta (1996) Creating computer graphics choreography with Virtual Director, *NCSA Access*, 10(2), 5, http://www.ncsa.uiuc.edu/Pubs/access/96.2/VirtualDir.html.

[11] VD Lehner and TA DeFanti (1997) Distributed virtual reality: supporting remote collaboration in vehicle design, *IEEE Computer Graphics & Applications*, March/April, 13–17.

[12] J Leigh, TA DeFanti, AE Johnson, MD Brown and DJ Sandin (1997) Global tele-immersion: better than being there, in *ICAT '97, 7th Annual International Conference on Artificial Reality and Tele-Existence*, 3-5 December, University of Tokyo, Japan, Virtual Reality Society of Japan, pp. 10–17.

[13] J Leigh, A Johnson and T DeFanti (1997) CAVERN: distributed architecture for supporting scalable persistence and interoperability in collaborative virtual environments, *Virtual Reality: Research, Development and Applications*, 2(2), 217–237.

[14] J Leigh, AE Johnson and TA DeFanti (1997) Issues in the design of a flexible distributed architecture for supporting persistence and interoperability in collaborative virtual environments, in *SC'97 Proceedings*, Sponsored by ACM SIGARCH and IEEE Computer Society, 15–21 November, CD-ROM.

[15] T Poston (1994) The virtual workbench: dextrous virtual reality, in Technical Report TR94-132-0 (eds. G Singh, SK Feiner and D Thalmann), Institute of Systems Science, National University of Singapore, http://www.iss.nus.sg/iss/techreport/.

[16] H Korab and MD Brown (eds.) (1995) Virtual environments and distributed computing, in *SC'95: GII Testbed and HPC Challenge Applications on the I-WAY*, a publication of ACM/IEEE Supercomputing '95, http://www.ncsa.uiuc.edu/General/Training/SC95/GII.HPCC.html.

[17] Sun Microsystems (1995) *Starfire: A Vision of Future Computing* (videotape). (Also in *Tog on Software Design*, Addison-Wesley, Fall 1995.)

[18] JE Smith and FW Weingarten (eds.) (1997) *Research Challenges for the Next Generation Internet*, Computing Research Association, p. 20.

[19] R Stevens, P Woodward, T DeFanti and C Catlett (1997) From the I-WAY to the National Technology Grid, *Communications of the ACM*, 40(11), 51–60.

[20] M Thiébaux (1997) Virtual Director, *MS Thesis*, Electronic Visualization Laboratory, Department of Electrical Engineering and Computer Science, University of Illinois at Chicago, June.

[21] L Petrovich, K Tanaka, D Morse, N Ingle, J Morie, C Stapleton and M Brown (eds.) (1994) Visual proceedings, in *Computer Graphics, Annual Conference Series 1994*, pp. 219–264, http:// www.evl.uic.edu/EVL/VROOM/HTML/OTHER/HomePage.html.

[22] *Virtual Reality at the University of Illinois 5/97* (videotape), Electronic Visualization Laboratory, University of Illinois at Chicago.

[23] M Brown, T DeFanti, M McRobbie, A Verlo, D Plepys, DF McMullen, K Adams, J Leigh, A Johnson, I Foster, C Kesselman, A Schmidt and S Goldstein (1998) The International Grid (iGrid): empowering global research community networking using high performance international Internet services, *INET '99*, San Jose, CA, 22–25 June 1998, San Jose.

[24] DF McMullen, MA McRobbie, K Adams, D Pearson, TA DeFanti, MD Brown, D Plepys, A Verlo and SN Goldstein (1999). The *i*Grid Project: enabling international research and education collaborations through high performance networking, *Internet Workshop '99 (IWS'99)*, Osaka, Japan.

[25] D Pape, J Anstey, M Bogucki, G Dawe, T DeFanti, A Johnson and D Sandin (1999) The ImmersaDesk3 – experiences with a flat panel display for virtual reality, in *Proceedings of the Third International Immersive Projection Technology (IPT) Workshop*, Stuttgart, Germany, 10–11 May 1999.

[26] DM Bloom (1997) The grating light valve: revolutionizing display technology, *SPIE* 3013, 165–171.

[27] S Adams (1998) Gene fool, *TIME Magazine*, 7 December, pp. 216–217.

[28] TM Roy, C Cruz-Neira, TA DeFanti and DJ Sandin (1995) Steering a high performance computing application from a virtual environment, *Presence: Teleoperators and Virtual Environments*, 4(2), 121–129.

[29] D Reed, R Giles and CE Catlett (1997) Distributed data and immersive collaboration, *Communications of the ACM*, November, 39–48.

[30] VI Pavlovic, R Sharma and TS Huang (1997) Visual interpretation of hand gestures for human computer interaction: a review, *IEEE Trans. on Pattern Analysis and Machine Intelligence*, 19(7), 677–695.

[31] AJ Colmenarez, BJ Frey and TS Huang (1999) A probabilistic framework for embedded face and facial expression recognition, in *Proc. IEEE Conference on Computer Vision and Pattern Recognition*, 23-25 June, Fort Collins, CO.

[32] MT Chan, Y Zhang and TS Huang (1998) Real-time lip tracking and bimodal continuous speech recognition, in *Proc. IEEE Workshop on Multimedia Signal Processing*, 7–9 December, Los Angeles, CA.

[33] LS Chen, H Tao, TS Huang, T Miyasato and RN Nakatsu (1998) Emotion recognition from audiovisual information, in *Proc. IEEE Workshop on Multimedia Signal Processing*, 7–9 December, Los Angeles, CA.

[34] VI Pavlovic, BJ Frey and TS Huang (1999) Time-series classification using mixed-state dynamic Bayesian networks, in *Proc. IEEE Conf. on Computer Vision and Pattern Recognition*, 23–25 June, Fort Collins, CO.

[35] R Stevens and TA DeFanti (1999) Tele-immersion and collaborative virtual environments, in *The Grid: Blueprint for a New Computing Infrastructure* (eds. I Foster and C Kesselman), San Mateo, CA, Morgan Kaufmann, pp. 131–158.

About the Author

Thomas A. DeFanti, PhD, is director of the Electronic Visualization Laboratory (EVL), a professor in the department of Electrical Engineering and Computer Science, and director of the Software Technologies Research Center at the University of Illinois at Chicago (UIC). He is also co-associate director of the Grid Division at the National Center for Supercomputing Applications (NCSA) at the University of Illinois at Urbana-Champaign, and a co-PI of the National Computational Science Alliance, one of two recipients of the NSF Partnerships for Advanced Computational Infrastructure (PACI) program. DeFanti has strong working collaborations with other UIC departments, as well as NCSA and the Mathematics and Computer Science division of Argonne National Laboratory. DeFanti is chair of the UCAID/Internet2 Applications Strategy Council and member of the UCAID Board of Trustees.

Current research interests include: high-performance networking, virtual environments, tele-immersion, digital libraries, scientific visualization, new methodologies for informal science and engineering education, paradigms for information display, distributed computing, optimization for scalable computing, sonification, human–computer interfaces, and abstract math visualization.

DeFanti is an internationally recognized expert in computer graphics. Credits include: use of EVL hardware and software for the computer animation produced for the first *Star Wars* movie; early involvement in videogame technology long before videogames became popular; contributor and co-editor of the 1987 National Science Foundation-sponsored report *Visualization in Scientific Computing*; recipient of the 1988 ACM Outstanding Contribution Award; an appointment in 1989 to the Illinois Governor's Science Advisory Board; University Scholar for 1989–1992; appointed an ACM Fellow in 1994; appointed one of several US technical advisors to the G7 GIBN activity in 1995; appointed in 1999 to Mayor Richard M. Daley's Council of Technology Advisors; principal investigator of the STAR TAP initiative to provide a persistent infrastructure to facilitate the long-term interconnection and interoperability of advanced international networking; and, recognition along with EVL co-director Daniel J. Sandin for conceiving the CAVE virtual reality theater in 1991.

He has also been active in the ACM SIGGRAPH organization and in the ACM/IEEE Supercomputing (SC) conferences. Current and past activities include: secretary of SIGGRAPH (1977–1981); co-chair of the SIGGRAPH '79 conference; chair of SIGGRAPH (1981–1985); past chair of SIGGRAPH (1985–1989); editor of the *SIGGRAPH Video Review* video publication, which he founded in 1979; and, member of the SIGGRAPH '92 and SIGGRAPH '94 conference committees. He was information architect of the SC'95 conference, responsible for the I-WAY and GII Testbed activities, and was a member of the SC'97 Program Committee.

Future Interfaces

10

Post-Wimp User Interfaces: the Human Connection

Andries van Dam

Abstract

In this age of (near-)adequate computing power, the power and usability of the user interface is as important to an application's success as its functionality. Most of the code in modern desktop productivity applications resides in the user interface. But despite its centrality, the user interface field is currently in a rut: the WIMP (windows, icons, menus and pointers) GUI based on keyboard and mouse has evolved little since it was pioneered by Xerox PARC in the early 1970s.

Computer and display form factors will change dramatically in the near future and new kinds of interaction devices will soon become routinely available. There will be many different kinds of information appliances, including powerful PDAs that are successors to the Newton (R.I.P.) and Palm Pilot, and wearable computers. On the other end of the size spectrum, there will be large-screen displays produced by large flat panels and new projection technology, including office-based immersive virtual reality environments. And on the input side, we will finally have acceptable speech recognition, force-feedback devices, and non-invasive, vision-based object and people "reconstruction".

Perceptual user-interfaces (PUIs) will use sensors of various types that will sense our state, mood etc., to make computers more aware of and more adaptable to our individual needs. Agent technology, based on improvements in knowledge acquisition and management, will finally make some degree of implicitly specified asynchronous interaction possible. In short, we will be liberated from the tyranny of the desktop computer, with its simple interaction devices and metaphors, and can look forward to user interfaces such as multimodal and perceptual UIs that are dramatically more powerful and better matched to human sensory capabilities than those dependent solely on keyboard and mouse.

The vision of the user experience 5–10 years hence is that of the human interacting with a set of computers in a variety of form factors and environments, working on her behalf as perceptive, responsive partners rather than as tireless but unthinking lackeys executing simple, explicitly specified commands by rote.

Brown University has specialized in post-WIMP UIs that extend the vocabulary of direct manipulation. For example, we pioneered 3D interaction widgets, controlled by mice or interaction devices with three or more degrees of freedom, that are a natural evolution from their two-dimensional WIMP counterparts. They can decrease the cognitive distance between widget and task for many tasks that are intrinsically 3D, such as scientific visualization and MCAD.

More radical post-WIMP UIs are needed for immersive virtual reality (VR) where keyboard and mouse are inappropriate because they were designed for the desktop environment. Immersive VR provides good driving applications for developing post-WIMP 3D UIs based on multimodal interaction that leverages more of our senses by combining the use of gesture, sound (e.g. speech) and haptics for both input and feedback to the user.

For example, we implemented a prototype gesture-based sketching interface for conceptual and mechanical design, a multimodal scientific visualization interface combining gesture and speech, and some simple GUIs that use proof-of-concept 3D modeling and window-manager GUIs based on haptic input and feedback. These are all still first-generation post-WIMP, and we look forward to even more radical departures from today's interfaces.

10.1 Introduction

Unlike the steady, predictable hardware price/performance improvement described by Moore's Law, there has been no such year-to-year progress in user interface design. Instead, the history of user interfaces can be characterized using evolutionary biologist Steven Jay Gould's notion of punctuated equilibrium: long periods of stability interrupted by rapid change. We can identify four separate generations characterized by four distinguishable interface styles, each lasting for many years and optimized to the hardware available at the time. Each style of interface was more "user-friendly" than the previous one; this imprecise term became so generic that I just heard it in a radio advertisement for a local hospital. However, whatever "user-friendly" means, each successive generation of user interface helped create a larger user base.

In the first period, the early 1950s and 1960s, computers were used in batch mode with punched card input and line printer output; there were essentially no user interfaces because there were no interactive users (although some of us were privileged to be able to do console debugging using switches and lights as our "user interface"). The second period in the evolution of interfaces (early 1960s through early 1980s) was the era of timesharing on mainframes and minicomputers using mechanical or "glass" teletypes (alphanumeric displays), when for the first time users could interact with the computer by typing in commands with parameters. Note that this era has persisted even until today, with such operating systems as DOS and Unix with their command line shells and keyboard shortcut-driven editors.

The work of Doug Engelbart, as demonstrated in his landmark 1968 FJCC demo of NLS, provided a transition to the third age of user interfaces spawned at Xerox PARC. While his system was command-line driven, it used multimodal interaction via the mouse, which he invented, and the chording keyboard. He also presaged multiple windows and an early form of tele-collaboration complete with chalk-passing protocols.

During the 1970s, timesharing and manual command lines remained deeply entrenched, but at Xerox PARC [9] the third age of user interfaces dawned. Raster graphics-based networked workstations and "point-and-click" WIMP GUIs (graphical user interfaces based on windows, icons, menus and a pointing device, typically a mouse) are the legacy of Xerox PARC that we are still using today. WIMP GUIs were popularized by the Macintosh in 1984 and later copied by Windows on the PC and Motif on Unix workstations. Applications today have much the same look and feel as the early desktop applications (except for the increased "realism" achieved through the use of drop shadows for buttons and other UI widgets); the main advance lies in the shift from monochrome displays to color and in a large set of software engineering tools for building WIMP interfaces. I find it rather surprising that the third generation of WIMP user interfaces has been so dominant for more than two decades; they are apparently sufficiently good for conventional desktop tasks that the field is stuck comfortably in a rut.

I argue in this chapter that the status quo does not suffice – that the newer forms of computing and computing devices available today necessitate new thinking about fourth-generation UIs, what I have been calling post-WIMP user interfaces. These don't (only) use widgets such as menus, forms or toolbars, but rely on, for example, gesture and speech recognition for operand and operation specification. They started coming out of research labs in the early 1990s but have not yet reached wide-spread deployment. I focus here on the user's side of the interface – interaction devices and techniques. Space does not permit discussion of the equally important computer output or information presentation side of interaction. Information visualization is an important area of study in its own right [3] and deals with such issues as spatial metaphors (e.g. the 3D cityscape vs. the 2D desktop metaphor for organizing information).

10.2 WIMP GUIs

Let's look at the pros and cons of WIMP GUIs to see why a new generation of UIs is needed.

10.2.1 Advantages

In the first few decades of computing we concentrated on the functionality and performance of applications. But during the 1980s, when desktop productivity tools began to be used by millions of people, we recognized that, above some minimal threshold of functionality and performance, the most important predictor of an application's success was its ease of use, both for novices and experienced users. For novices, ease of use is dictated primarily by how easy to learn and remember the interface is, while for power users the concern is less with the learning curve than with the effort required to be highly productive. The same interface is rarely optimal for both classes of users. Indeed, power users today shun WIMP GUIs whenever they can in favor of keyboards.

However user-friendly, an interface is still an intermediary between the user's intent and execution of that intent. As such, it should be considered at best a neces-sary evil because, no matter how fluid, it still imposes a layer of cognitive processing between the user and the computer's execution of the user's intent. The ideal interface is no interface – "I think, therefore the computer gives me what I thought about (and what I should think about)". A more feasible goal to strive for is the computer as perfect butler, *à la* Jeeves, who knows my context, tastes and idiosyncrasies and discreetly does my bidding by anticipating my needs without needing explicit direction. When I do direct this butler I communicate primarily by speaking, gesturing, facial expression and other forms of human communication. In addition, I might still want to make a sketch to indicate a design or a concept or select from a menu of options, or even enter information via a keyboard (still an efficient means of communication). The goal we strive for with today's user interfaces is to minimize the mechanics of manipulation and the cognitive distance between intent and the execution of that intent. To state the obvious, the user wants to focus on the task, not the technology for specifying the task. Thus I see WIMP and post-WIMP GUIs as successive waystations toward a much more powerful and natural interface that will ultimately take decades to develop.

While WIMP GUIs are a long way from a butler-style interface, let me list some measures of their success and importance. They have enabled novice users, even young children who cannot yet read or write, to become comfortable with email, Web surfing and desktop applications. "Point and click", the hallmark of WIMP GUIs, has become part of modern culture. User interface design has become a specialty and user interface designers are highly sought after. In fact, testing in usability labs that "shakes down" the user interface is now a necessary component of the application development process. What WIMP GUIs have made possible is a *de facto* standard for the application interface that, compared with command line interfaces, gives us (relative) ease of learning, ease of use, and ease of transfer of knowledge gained from using one application to another because of consistencies in look and feel. Most users don't read manuals any more because by and large they don't have to.

10.2.2 Drawbacks

Nonetheless, significant problems remain. First, the more complex the application, the non-linearly harder the interface is to learn because of the profusion of widgets and features, each of which is individually easy to learn but in the aggregate creates complexity. Many modern desktop applications are so large that users drown in the functionality and don't want to upgrade to newer releases, preferring to stick with the small subset they know, as described by the classic 90/10 rule.

Second, users spend too much time manipulating the interface, not the application. Expert users are often frustrated by too many layers of "point and click" and screen clutter due to too many widgets, and, as mentioned, prefer keyboard shortcuts.

Third, WIMP GUIs, with their 2D widgets, were designed for and are well suited to 2D applications such as word processing, document layout and spreadsheets. When the information is three-dimensional, the mapping between 3D tasks and 2D control widgets is much less natural. The WIMP interface for 3D applications today typically consists of control panels of 2D buttons and sliders that surround the 3D world (what I call the "TV model") and are used to control 3D cursor and viewpoint manipulation and object editing, thereby introducing significant indirection and "cognitive distance". In general, 3D applications tend to have greater visual complexity than 2D applications, another strain on WIMP GUIs.

Fourth, "mousing" and keyboarding are not suited to all users, either because they don't find it natural or because they develop repetitive stress injuries, not to mention the special needs of users with disabilities.

A deficiency more serious than any of these that affects all users is that, unlike the ideal butler-style interface, WIMP interfaces do not take advantage of speech, hearing and touch. While a large percentage of our neurons lie in the visual cortex and vision is our highest-bandwidth information channel, it is difficult for us to communicate in the physical world without speech, sound and touch as well. As Bill Buxton (Chief Scientist, Alias/Wavefront/SGI) points out, WIMP GUIs based on the keyboard and the mouse are the perfect interface only for creatures with a single eye, one or more single-jointed fingers and no other sensory organs; WIMP GUIs are impedance-mismatched to our full sensorium.

Yet another limitation of WIMP GUIs is that they are designed for a single desktop user who controls objects that have no autonomy and at most react to mouse manipulation. The interaction is one channel at a time, half-duplex; the system responds to each discrete input event and these events can be easily decoded, consisting simply of key presses and mouse selections. The most complicated input is a sequence of mouse positions that represents, for example, the trace of a paintbrush.

10.3 Post-WIMP Interfaces

A post-WIMP interface contains at least one interaction technique not dependent on classical 2D widgets such as menus and icons. Ultimately it will involve all the senses in parallel natural language communication with multiple users. This last extension is especially important as the focus of user interface R&D shifts from the current preoccupation with single users performing tasks with one or more applications on single desktop computers to multiple users – some real, some virtual – interacting simultaneously with multiple computational devices in different form factors.

Consider the following scenario, which is at the opposite extreme from the traditional desktop productivity application, a scenario that we will see increasingly in applications ranging from games to virtual prototyping and training in immersive ("virtual reality") environments.

Multiple non-co-located participants are interacting on a shared task, each having some kind of wide field of view stereo immersive display controlled via head and hand tracking, voice and gesture recognition and the manipulation of a variety of interaction devices with more than the two degrees of freedom provided by a mouse.

The interaction here involves multiple parallel high-bandwidth input and output channels operating full-duplex on continuous (not discrete) signals that are decoded and probabilistically disambiguated in real time.

Figure 10.1 Henry Fuchs's vision of the Office of the Future (University of North Carolina-Chapel Hill) [16]. Remote and local participants seamlessly interact with the part being designed. Projector and camera technology acquire and display the local and remote environments at the geographically distributed sites.

Multimodel interaction, first demonstrated in MIT's "Put That There" demo [2] and the subject of much recent research [7,22], allows parallel channels to provide correlated information. This enables recognition algorithms to reinforce each other by such techniques as OGI's QuickSet "unification" strategy [5]. WIMP interfaces simply cannot handle this much more demanding form of interaction; like the command line interface, they will persist but in restricted contexts that suit their limited scope.

Figure 10.1 shows an illustration of such a scenario envisioned by Henry Fuchs at the University of North Carolina, Chapel Hill. (In such a multi-person, multi-device, communication-rich environment, it may make some sense to use terms such as participant or actor rather than user, a term which focuses on a single user using a single application.)

10.3.1 Components

The most common examples of post-WIMP interaction commercially available today are pen-based gesture recognizers used in handheld PDAs such as the Palm

Pilot and Windows CE devices, and more recently, e-books which are finally bringing Allen Kay's Dynabook vision to market [18]. These devices more or less successfully meld both WIMP and post-WIMP techniques for 2D tasks.

Another instructive example of natural human–computer interaction that uses no WIMP devices or techniques is arcade games, such as driving simulators with a steering wheel and gear shift and golf simulations in which the player swings a real club to hit a real ball, the trajectory of which is then simulated and displayed. What are the components of this type of human–computer interaction? Among others they include 3D interfaces, speech recognition and production interfaces, gestural interfaces, haptic interfaces, and a range of virtual environments, from the semi-immersive Barco BARON, to the small but fully-immersive Cave, to room-sized environments such as are envisioned in Henry Fuchs's Office of the Future.

10.3.2 3D Interfaces

For 3D modeling, 3D widgets are increasingly used that are part of the 3D scene and obviate some of the conventional 2D widgets that would otherwise surround the 3D scene. As an example, in Figure 10.2 the 3D components of the "rake" widget [8] are used to control the rake length, the number of streamlines and their position in a scalar field derived from a numerical simulation of air flow around a Space Shuttle model. Among the now-common 3D widgets are scale/rotation boxes and handles and navigation controllers (used in VRML and other 3D browsers).

Another technique that combines WIMP and post-WIMP to "get the interface out of your face" (as Bill Buxton calls his crusade) is the use of "marking menus", a modern form of multilevel radial menus for which the user can exploit muscle

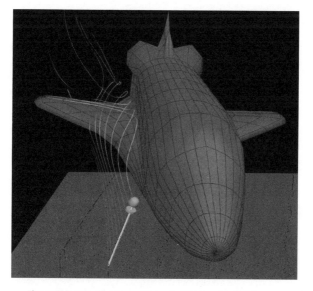

Figure 10.2 A 3D widget is used to manipulate elements of a 3D scene.

memory and perform menu selection gesturally with a mouse or stylus without having the menu actually appear [11]. Buxton is also a proponent of two-handed input in which the non-dominant hand controls coarse movement (e.g. placement of a tool) and the dominant hand fine adjustment (the manipulation of the tool) [10].

10.3.3 Gestural Interfaces

In contrast to visual interfaces based on widgets, considerable attention has recently focused on the use of speech and gesture. The attraction of speech and gesture is that it qualitatively matches natural human interactions and reduces the cognitive effort of experienced users; however, the learning curve for speech and gesture interfaces is typically steeper than with a WIMP interface. Bob Zeleznik and colleagues at Brown University have demonstrated a succession of 3D modeling interfaces that have successively incorporated a range of gesture and speech input. The initial system, Sketch, relied on a small (~20 gestures), purely pen-based gestural vocabulary to support rapid modeling of 3D geometry [25], such as the baseball field, modeled in the matter of a few minutes, shown in Figure 10.3. Later versions of Sketch incorporated bi-manual gestures [24], shown in Figure 10.4, hand-posture gestures with a 6 DOF tracked dataglove and speech recognition.

Users issue commands through simultaneous voice and hand gestures in ErgoSketch [6], the most recent version of Sketch, which was designed for immersive and semi-immersive environments like the Barco BARON and the Cave [4], shown in Figure 10.5.

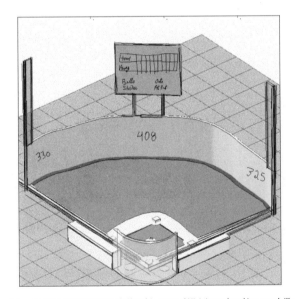

Figure 10.3 A 3D model created in a few minutes with Sketch's gestural UI. It is rendered in a rough illustration style to reinforce the approximate nature of the model.

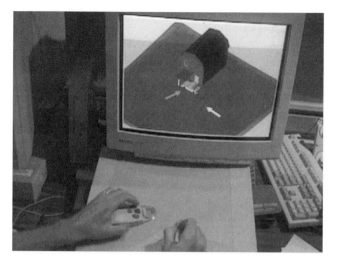

Figure 10.4 An example of two-handed 3D manipulation.

Figure 10.5 A four-wall Cave recently installed at Brown University is a fully immersive work environment that will be used for user interface and tele-immersion research.

10.3.4 Haptic Interfaces

Haptic user interfaces are an even more unexplored area, since haptic hardware has only recently become affordable. As human interaction in the real world is quite dependent on haptics, adding haptics to the user interface may alleviate some human–computer interaction problems and lead to gains in performance, intuition, learnability and enjoyment of the computer interface.

Haptic devices, unlike other interaction devices, can both sense and send information. Thus, most haptic interface designers have two different yet important points to consider: the tactile sense (i.e. feeling by touch) and the kinesthetic sense (the body's sense of where it is). A force-feedback device, such as the PHANToM [19], receives position and gestural information and produces point-force feedback. This enables a user to feel the shape (touch) of a rigid object or push through layers of different resistance (kinesthetics).

Interface Design

The naive approach [13] to incorporating haptics attempts to imitate objects existing in the real world. This, however, does not adequately leverage the potential of a reasonably general force feedback device because it does not include forces whose calculation is not based on a physical model, as well as objects and behavior that are either impossible or prohibitively difficult to physically create.

For example, both the 2D and 3D haptic projects mentioned below make use of "infinitesimal ridges", which feel like ridges on the surface of an object only so long as the user is in contact with the object. These ridges, which can be felt but do not occupy space, provide an interaction widget unique to the haptics-enhanced computer interface.

Another example is the viscosity-driven switch described in [15] where the resistive force varies with the user's velocity in a non-physically based way: there is no force below a certain speed, while at greater speeds a force proportional to the square of the velocity is used. Above a yet higher speed the force drops off to nothing again as the switch is triggered, and does not start again until the user's speed has dropped below a certain threshold.

Projects

Our haptic projects initially cover both 2D and 3D interaction using a 3 DOF force-feedback PHANToM; 2.5D interaction is planned for the future.

First we abstracted certain general qualities involved in haptic interaction from a study of effective real-world and virtual haptic interactions. Some of these qualities were anticipation, follow-through, distinguishing direction and guidance. We then developed techniques that attempted to embody these qualities in novel ways,

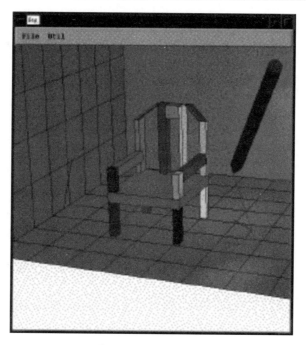

Figure 10.6 Haptic sketching.

including some non-physically based simulation as well as physically based simulations, and in novel applications described in [15].

The 2D project adds force feedback to WIMP user interface elements of the X Window System, thus adding true "feel" to the window system's "look and feel" [14]. Currently we have added haptic interaction to menus, icons and windows, although most of the techniques implemented so far concern window manipulation. Future work will involve adding haptics to a wider range of UI elements and applications as well as doing user studies to determine their impact.

The 3D project involves "3D haptic widgets", which are identifiable pieces of haptic interaction behavior that the user manipulates when creating Sketch-based drawings. Currently this project uses a simple polygonal modeling environment as a testbed – see Figure 10.6.

Widgets

In addition to the infinitesimal ridges and viscosity-driven switches mentioned above, haptic widgets include the haptic virtual pushbuttons presented by a number of researchers [1,13,19], variations of the haptics-enhanced virtual sphere technique described in [1], and virtual notches and dimples made into a surface as alignment aids. As we proceed and extend this work into semi- and fully immersive environments, we expect to develop many more types of widgets.

10.4 The Future

What may we expect in the future? Because of Moore's Law (which shows no signs of letting up for the next decade) and continuing advances in panel display and projector technology, we may expect hugely powerful and ubiquitous computers [23] in many different form factors. Examples include wearable computers (pioneered by such institutions as MIT [12], CMU [20] and Boeing), PDAs and information appliances, whiteboard-sized or even wall-sized displays, and minimally intrusive head-mounted displays for virtual and augmented reality. In augmented reality, the user sees computer-generated information superimposed on real-world images via optical or video merging to provide, for example, annotation or X-ray vision.

Display resolution will have increased well beyond the inadequate 70–100 dpi of today and improved rendering techniques such as Microsoft's ClearType will compound the effect of higher resolution to make online reading less fatiguing and more pleasant. We will finally have what we need even more urgently for post-WIMP interaction: non-invasive, accurate sensors with good spatial and temporal resolution for head, body and eye tracking. These will make possible fast and robust gesture recognition and possibly even non-invasive or minimally invasive biofeedback, especially important to disabled users. Voice recognition based on natural language understanding will be a dominant form of user–computer interaction. Raj Reddy of CMU has described interfaces that will support speech, image and language understanding, all driven by knowledge bases [17].

Haptic display will augment our ability to perceive computer-generated information. Computing power will finally be able to handle large amounts of continuous information from many input channels simultaneously while running real-time simulations of autonomous, reactive objects. And we will learn how to combine the best of user-empowering direct user control via WIMP and post-WIMP interfaces with indirect control provided by certified, trusted agents that can anticipate needs and work offline on our behalf with other such agents distributed over the Net. Needless to say, such agent technology must be based on powerful (as yet non-existent) knowledge bases and inferencing mechanisms. This combination will finally allow us to approach the ideal situation in which user–computer interaction is at least as natural and powerful as human interaction.

10.5 Research Problems

In order to improve the quality of interaction, fundamental changes must be made to the way information flows between the user and computer. However, it is not clear what changes will have the greatest impact. To support the vision of collaborative environments for geographically distributed participants described above, we minimally need better models of human interaction and to develop new techniques that enrich the flow of perceptual information between the user and computer. Yet we expect advances on these two fronts to have their greatest impact only when they become available to a wide range of creative people.

An outline of the most likely research problems is given below. These problems fall into two major categories: hardware and software technology, and modeling human cognition and physiology.

10.5.1 Hardware and Software Issues

IO Devices

Today's input and output devices are not optimal for many tasks. Interaction devices that are far less cumbersome and invasive and have far better temporal and spatial resolution are necessary. For example, advances in wireless technology capable of transmitting signals between IO devices and the computer promise to enable many IO devices to be much more transparent (and therefore usable) in contrast to today's inhibiting tethered IO devices.

Scene Acquisition and Display

Over the past several years there has been progress in vision-based techniques for acquiring scene data that include human participants. Such techniques will allow, for example, remote environments to be brought together, as in Henry Fuchs's vision described above.

However, scene acquisition and display techniques are still in their infancy and require further research in collaboration with the computer vision community. To support the display of acquired scenes, the traditional graphics pipeline must be redesigned to support image-based rendering techniques in addition to polygon-based objects. In addition, techniques for managing hybrid image- and polygonal-based rendered scenes are needed.

Haptics

The relatively new field of haptic interfaces and the demanding nature of the devices used presents its own set of problems. In particular, due to the update rate required to compute the presentation of relatively simple haptic environments with only point force feedback and moderate fidelity, current workstations are just able to keep up. The higher rates necessary for better feedback and more faithful simulation, and particularly for more output channels at the same fidelity, will demand more powerful computers. Further development of the haptic devices themselves will be necessary to be able to present those multiple output channels with reasonable fidelity. For example, there is no current device that would permit sculptors to mold virtual clay using the same techniques that they use in the real world.

Haptic debugging tools form another underdeveloped area, closely akin to the area of multithreaded debugging.

Many current haptic feedback devices have severe ergonomic issues which will need to be addressed, perhaps through more extensive integration of the device with the environment (such as building it into a desk to present the correct working volume if necessary).

An almost completely unexplored field, analogous to the development of graphical user interfaces, is how best to use haptics in user interfaces in a sophisticated fashion.

And finally, all of this will demand more sophisticated and stable underlying haptic libraries to ease the development of higher-level interaction.

Multimodal UI

Most multimodal interaction research has concentrated on the "put that there" metaphor, especially when the modes are hand gestures and speech. One of the main reasons for this stagnation is that multimodal interaction depends on a number of other technologies not specifically related to user interfaces. As an example, consider an application where the user gestures with the hand and simultaneously says, "Take me back to where I was a few minutes ago when the model was here". Processing this style of command requires not only accurate speech and gesture recognition, but also natural language processing, data storage and retrieval, smart object technology, and knowledge-based inferencing systems – all of which have to execute at interactive rates.

Integration

Integrating the technologies described above introduces fundamental systems-level research problems and is a major research and engineering barrier.

10.5.2 Modeling Human Cognition and Physiology

On the human side there are even harder problems that are much less susceptible to engineering solutions than hardware and software problems described above.

Cognitive and Perceptual Problems

We need a far superior understanding of the human side of the human interface. Most interface designers are seriously hampered by not understanding enough about human cognitive and perceptual capabilities and limitations, and their context sensitivity. The lack of an understanding of human physiology has been demonstrated for the last 20 years in the form of RSI disabilities. A corresponding problem for immersive environments is our lack of a model of simulator sickness. With a better model we may be able to direct research to appropriate research areas that promise to minimize or prevent simulator sickness from standing in the way of productive use of immersive environments. For example, we know latency is a principal contributor to simulator sickness, but we have no quantitative model of the relationship. Since simulator sickness can occur even with zero latency [21], we need to model the other causes including characteristics of the individual, the application, and the technology used.

Agent Technology

An agent will provide a degree of autonomy that is not found in today's user interfaces. Barriers to agents fall into three categories: input, inference and response. Some agents will need to perceive the physical traits and gestures through vision algorithms. Others may require parsing of naturally spoken language. Inferring actions based on input and history will build on today's rudimentary mechanisms by increasingly incorporating artificial intelligence techniques. Finally, in order to autonomously respond we will need to improve software component architectures and develop "socially acceptable" strategies for reporting actions to the users.

Social Interaction

Another major issue on the human side is that not only do we not know enough about how humans operate but we are especially poor at understanding how humans interact and collaborate. What are the social protocols that are culturally dependent and extremely context sensitive and how do we get the computer to understand and be a constructive mediator? Increasing, computers will be used for telecollaboration, but the technologists designing such systems know far too little of how people collaborate with each other using existing tools, despite all the CSCW work. As Fred Brooks points out, we don't even know how people do it now. So we need computer science and engineering to be infused by far more knowledge of cognitive/human science and social science, subjects certainly not part of any conventional CS curriculum.

Acknowledgments

Thanks to Andrew Forsberg, Joseph LaViola, Tim Miller, Loring Holden, Bob Zeleznik and Rosemary Simpson for critical reading, writing and helpful suggestions.

References

[1] T Anderson (1997) FLIGHT: a 3D human–computer interface and application development environment, in *Proceedings of the Second PHANToM Users Group Workshop*, December. Published as MIT Artificial Intelligence Laboratory Technical Report AITR-1617 and Research Laboratory for Electronics Technical Report No. 618.

[2]   RA Bolt (1980) Put that there: voice and gesture at the graphics interface, in *Proceedings of SIGGRAPH '80*, ACM Press, pp. 262–270.

[3]   SK Card, JD Mackinlay and B Shneiderman (eds.) (1999) *Readings in Information Visualization: Using Vision to Think*, San Mateo, CA, Morgan Kaufmann.

[4]   EVL has a number of pointers to what Caves are all about and work: http://www.evl.uic.edu/EVL/ and http://www.evl.uic.edu/EVL/VR/.

[5]   PR Cohen, M Johnston, D McGee, S Oviatt, J Pittman, I Smith, L Chen and J Clow (1997) QuickSet: multimodal interaction for distributed applications, in *Proceedings of the Fifth Annual International Multimodal Conference*, Seattle, November, New York, ACM Press.

[6]   AS Forsberg, JJ LaViola and RC Zeleznik (1998) ErgoDesk: a framework for two- and three-dimensional interaction at the ActiveDesk, in *Proceedings of the Second International Immersive Projection Technology Workshop*, Ames, IA, 11-12 May.

[7]   T Funkhouser, I Carlbom, G Elko, G Pingali, M Sondhi and J West (1998) A beam tracing approach to acoustic modeling for interactive virtual environments, in *Proceedings of SIGGRAPH '98*, ACM Press, pp. 21–32.

[8]   KP Herndon and T Meyer (1994) 3D widgets for exploratory scientific visualization, in *Proceedings of UIST '94, ACM SIGGRAPH*, pp. 69–70.

[9]   M Hiltzik (1999) *Dealers of Lightning: XEROX PARC and the Dawn of the Computer Age*, New York, HarperCollins.

[10] P Kabbash, W Buxton and A Sellen (1994) Two-handed input in a compound task, in *Proceedings of CHI '94*, pp. 417–423.

[11] G Kurtenbach and W Buxton (1993) The limits of expert performance using hierarchic marking menus, in *Proceedings of InterCHI '93*, pp. 482–487.

[12] S Mann (1997) Wearable computing: a first step toward personal imaging, *IEEE Computer*, 30(2), 25–32.

[13] TH Massie (1996) Initial haptic explorations with the phantom: virtual touch through pointer interaction, *Master's Thesis*, Massachusetts Institute of Technology.

[14] TS Miller and RC Zeleznik (1998) An insidious haptic invasion: adding force feedback to the X desktop, in *User Interface Software and Technology*, ACM, November.

[15] TS Miller and RC Zeleznik (1999) The design of 3D haptic widgets, in *Proceedings of 1999 Symposium on Interactive 3D Graphics, ACM SIGGRAPH*.

[16] R Raskar, G Welch, M Cutts, A Lake, L Stesin, and H Fuchs (1998) The office of the future: a unified approach to image-based modeling and spatially immersive displays, in *SIGGRAPH '98*, Orlando, FL, 19–24 July.

[17] R Reddy (1996) Turing Award Lecture: To dream the possible dream, *Communications of the ACM* 39(5), 105–112.

[18] RocketBook: http://www.rocket-ebook.com/; http://www.pathfinder.com/@@NMHu9wUAxiklY*CS/fortune/1998/980706/ebo.html

[19] SensAble Technologies, Inc. GHOST™ *Software Developer's Toolkit Programmer's Guide*, http://www.sensable.com/.

[20] A Smailagic and DP Siewiorek (1994) The CMU mobile computers: a new generation of computer systems, in *Proceedings of COMPCON '94*, IEEE Computer Society Press.

[21] RHY So and WT Lo (1999) Cybersickness: an experimental study to isolate the effects of rotational scene oscillations, *Proceedings of Virtual Reality '99 Conference*, 13–17 March, Houston, TX.

[22] B Ullmer, H Ishii and D Glas (1998) mediaBlocks: physical containers, transports, and controls for online media, in *Proceedings of SIGGRAPH '98*, ACM Press, pp. 21–32.

[23] M Weiser (1993) Some computer science problems in ubiquitous computing, *Communications of the ACM*, 36(7), 74–84.

[24] RC Zeleznik, AS Forsberg and PS Strauss (1997) Two-pointer input for 3D interaction, in *Proceedings of 1997 Symposium on Interactive 3D Graphics*, Providence, RI, 27–30 April.

[25] RC Zeleznik, KP Herndon and JF Hughes (1996) Sketch: an interface for sketching 3D scenes, in *Computer Graphics (Proceedings of SIGGRAPH '96)*, ACM Press.

11

Universal Usability: A Research Agenda for Human–Computer Interaction to Empower Every Citizen

Ben Shneiderman

I feel... an ardent desire to see knowledge so disseminated through the mass of mankind that it may... reach even the extremes of society: beggars and kings.

Thomas Jefferson, Reply to American Philosophical Society, 1808

In a fair society, all individuals would have equal opportunity to participate in, or benefit from, the use of computer resources regardless of race, sex, religion, age, disability, national origin or other such similar factors.

ACM Code of Ethics

11.1 Introduction

The goal of universal access to information and communications services is compelling. It has united hardworking Internet technology promoters, telecommunications business leaders and government policy makers. Their positive motivations include innovative visions, corporate opportunities and social goods respectively, although critics see unreasonable zeal for technology, pursuit of high profit margins and regulatory excesses or omissions.

Each sector is working hard to contribute what they see as valuable, while trying to respond to critics. Most technology infrastructure developers seek to accommodate high volumes of use, reliably and rapidly even at peak periods, while ensuring security. Most service providers strive to develop popular communications, e-commerce, healthcare, education and other services, while ensuring profitability. Most government officials struggle to provide safety for consumers, freedom of speech and privacy protection, while supporting voluntary regulation plans.

179

Even if all of these professions succeed in their endeavors and the economies of scale bring low costs, computing researchers will still have much work to do. They will have to deal with the difficult question: *How can information and communications services be made usable for every citizen?* Designing for experienced frequent users is difficult enough, but designing for a broad audience of unskilled users is a far greater challenge. Scaling up from a listserver for 100 software engineers to 100 000 schoolteachers to 100 000 000 registered voters will take inspiration and perspiration.

Designers of older technologies such as postal services, telephones and television have reached the goal of *universal usability*, but computing technology is still too hard to use for many people (Shneiderman, 1998). One survey of 6000 computer users found an average of 5.1 hours per week wasted in trying to use computers. More time is wasted in front of computers than on highways. The frustration and anxiety of users is growing, and the number of non-users is still high. Low-cost hardware, software and networking will bring in many new users, but interface and information design improvements are necessary to achieve higher levels of access.

We can define universal usability as having more than 90% of all households as successful users of information and communications services at least once a week. A 1998 survey of US households shows that 42% have computers and 26% use Internet-based email or other services (NTIA, 1999). The percentage declines in poorer and less well educated areas within the USA and in many countries around the world. Cost is an issue for many, but hardware limitations, the perceived difficulty, and lack of utility discourages others. If we are to meet the goal of universal usability, then we will have to directly address usability design issues.

This chapter presents a research agenda based on three challenges in attaining universal usability for Web-based and other services:

- **Technology variety**: Supporting a broad range of hardware, software and network access
- **User diversity**: Accommodating users with different skills, knowledge, age, gender, handicaps, literacy, culture, income etc.
- **Gaps in user knowledge**: Bridging the gap between what users know and what they need to know

This list may not be complete, but it addresses important issues that need attention. Research devoted to these challenges will have a broad range of benefits for first time, intermittent and frequent users.

The term *universal access* is usually linked to the US Communications Act of 1934 covering telephone, telegraph and radio services. It sought to ensure "adequate facilities at reasonable charges", especially in rural areas, and prevent "discrimination on the basis of race, color, religion, national origin, or sex". The term *universal access* has been applied to computing services, but the greater complexity of computing services means that access is not sufficient to ensure successful usage. Therefore *universal usability* has emerged as an important issue and a topic for computing research. The complexity emerges, in part, from the high degree of interactivity that is necessary for information exploration, commercial applications and creative activities. The Internet is compelling because of its support for interpersonal communications and decentralized initiatives: entrepreneurs can open businesses, journalists can start publications and citizens can organize political movements.

The increased pressure for universal access and usability is a happy byproduct of the growth of the Internet. Since services such as e-commerce, communication, education, healthcare, finance and travel are expanding and users are becoming dependent on them, there is a strong push to ensure that the widest possible audience can participate. Another strong argument for universal usability comes from those who provide access to government information (such as the US Library of Congress's THOMAS system to provide full texts of bills before the Congress) and the movement towards citizen services at federal, state and local levels. These services include tax information and filing, social security benefits, passports, licensing, recreation and parks, and police and fire departments. Another circle of support includes employment agencies, training centers, mental health clinics, parent–teacher associations, public interest groups, community services and charitable organizations. The enormous potential social good from universal usability creates a grand opportunity for the computing profession.

Critics of information technology abound, but often they focus on the creation of an information-poor minority, or worse, Internet apartheid. Although the gap in Internet usage has been declining between men and women, and between old and young, the gap is growing between rich and poor and between well and poorly educated. Less well documented is the continuing separation between cultural and racial groups, and the low rates of usage by disadvantaged users whose unemployment, homelessness, poor health or cognitive limitations raise further barriers (Silver, 1999). Ambitious pursuit of universal access and usability will counter some of their legitimate concerns and help create more effective technologies with more effective support systems for users.

There are other criticisms of information and communications systems that should also be heard by technology promoters. These include concerns about the breakdown of community social systems, alienation of individuals that leads to crime and violence, loss of privacy, expansion of bureaucracies and inadequate attention to potential failures (such as the year 2000 problems or loss of power/data). Open public discussion of these issues by way of participatory design strategies and Social Impact Statements (Shneiderman and Rose, 1997) might reduce negative and unanticipated side effects.

Technology enthusiasts can be proud of what has been accomplished and how many successful Internet users there are, but deeper insights will come from understanding the problems of frustrated unsuccessful users, and of those who have turned away or stayed away. Each step to broaden participation and reach these forgotten users by providing useful and usable services will bring credit to our profession. A necessary first step is to formulate a research agenda.

11.2 Previous Research Agendas

There is growing attention to the computing research issues related to universal access and usability. The thoughtful and focused Rand Corporation report on

Universal Access to Email (Anderson *et al.*, 1995) made it clear that "better under-standing of the capabilities and limitations of current user-computer interfaces is needed". Similarly, when the National Academy of Science/National Research Council convened a panel on *every-citizen interfaces*, they recommended "an aggressive research program, funded by government and private sources, that examines both the human performance side of interfaces and the interface technol-ogies, current and potential" (CSTB, 1997).

During a well-financed but controversial study of 48 Pittsburgh area homes, 133 participants received computers, free network connections, training and assistance with problems. Even in such optimal conditions a central limitation was the diffi-culties that users experienced with the services (Kraut *et al.*, 1996). The researchers wrote "even the easiest-to-use computers and applications pose significant barriers to the use of online services... even with help and our simplified procedure, HomeNet participants had trouble connecting to the Internet".

As attention to the issue of universal access and usability has grown, frameworks for analyzing problems have appeared. Clement and Shade (1999) suggest seven layers of analysis: carriage facilities, devices, software tools, content services, service/access provision, literacy/social facilitation and governance. They see usability as a problem, especially for users with handicaps, and encourage consid-eration of the wide range of users and needs. Universal usability is sometimes tied to meeting the needs of users who are disabled or work in disabling conditions. This is an important direction for research that is likely to benefit all users. The adapt-ability needed for users with diverse physical, visual, auditory or cognitive handi-caps is likely to benefit users with differing preferences, tasks, hardware etc. (Glinert and York, 1992; Newell, 1995; Laux *et al.*, 1996). Plasticity of the interface and presentation independence of the contents both contribute to universal usability.

The forthcoming ACM SIGCHI (Special Interest Group on Computer Human Inter-action, http://www.acm.org/sigchi/) Research Agenda will focus on design of useful, usable and universal user interfaces (Scholtz *et al.*, 1999). SIGCHI has also promoted diversity with its outreach efforts to seniors, children, teachers and inter-national groups. The ACM's SIGCAPH (Special Interest Group on Computers and the Physically Handicapped, http://www.acm.org/sigcaph/) has long promoted accessibility for disabled users and its ASSETS series of conference proceedings (http://www.acm.org/sigcaph/assets/) provide useful guidance. The European conferences on User Interfaces for All (http://www.ics.forth.gr/proj/at-hci/UI4ALL/index.html) also deal with interface design strategies. The Web Accessibility Initiative (http://www.w3.org/WAI/) of the World Wide Web Consortium has a guidelines docu-ment with 14 thoughtful content design items to support disabled users, North Carolina State University's Center for Universal Design lists seven key principles (http://www.design.ncsu.edu/cud/), and the University of Wisconsin's TRACE Center offers links to many resources (http://trace.wisc.edu/world/).

11.3   A Universal Usability Research Agenda

This research agenda focuses on three universal usability challenges to designers: technology variety, user diversity, and gaps in user knowledge. Skeptics caution that forcing designers to accommodate low-end technology, low-ability citizens and low-skilled users will result in a lowest common denominator system that will be less useful to most users. This dark scenario, called dumbing down, is a reasonable fear, but the experience of this author supports a brighter outcome.

I believe that accommodating a broader spectrum of usage situations forces designers to consider a wider range of designs and often leads to innovations that benefit all users. For example, Web browsers, unlike word processors, reformat text to match the width of the window. This accommodates users with small displays (narrower than 640 pixels), and provides a nice benefit for users with larger displays (wider than 1024 pixels), who can view more of a Web page with less scrolling. Accommodating narrower (less than 400 pixels) or wider (more than 1200 pixels) displays presents just the kind of challenge that may push designers to develop new ideas. For example, they could consider reducing font and image sizes for small displays, moving to a multi-column format for large displays, exploring paging strategies (instead of scrolling), and developing overviews.

A second skeptics' caution, called the innovation restriction scenario, is that attempts to accommodate the low end (technology, ability or skill) will constrain innovations for the high end. This is again a reasonable caution, but if designers are aware of this concern the dangers seem avoidable. A basic HTML Web page accommodates low-end users, and sophisticated user interfaces using Java applets or Shockwave plug-ins can be added for users with advanced hardware and software, plus fast network connections. New technologies can often be provided as an add-on or plug-in, rather than a replacement. As the new technology becomes perfected and widely accepted, it may become the new standard. Layered approaches have been successful in the past and they are compelling for accommodating a wide range of users. They are easy to implement when planned in advance, but often difficult to retrofit.

Advocates who promote accommodation of handicapped users often describe the curbcut – a scooped out piece of sidewalk to allow wheelchair users to cross streets. Adding curbcuts after the curbs have been built is expensive, but building them in advance reduces costs because less material is needed. The benefits extend to baby carriage pushers, delivery service workers, cyclists and travelers with roller bags. Other computer-related accommodations that benefit many users are putting the power switch in the front of computers, building adjustable keyboards, and allowing user control over audio volume, screen brightness, and monitor position.

Automobile designers have long understood the benefits of accommodating a wide range of users. They feature adjustable seats, steering wheels, mirrors and lighting levels as standard equipment and offer optional equipment for those who need additional flexibility.

Reaching a broad audience is more than a democratic ideal; it makes good business sense. The case for *network externalities*, the concept that all users benefit from expanded participation (Shapiro and Varian, 1998; Borenstein, 1998), has been made repeatedly. Facilitating access and improving usability expand markets and increase participation of diverse users whose contributions to the community may be valuable to many. Broadening participation is not only an issue of reducing costs for new equipment. As the number of users grows, the capacity to rapidly replace a majority of equipment declines, so strategies that accommodate a wide range of equipment will become even more in demand.

With these concerns in mind, the research agenda for universal usability may provoke many innovations for all users.

11.3.1 Technology Variety: Supporting a Broad Range of Hardware, Software and Network Access

The first challenge is to deal with the pace of technology change and the variety of equipment that users employ. The stabilizing forces of standard hardware, operating systems, network protocols, file formats and user interfaces are undermined by the rapid pace of technological change. The technological innovators delight in novelty and improved features. They see competitive advantage in advanced designs, but these changes disrupt efforts to broaden audiences and markets. Since limiting progress is usually an unsatisfactory solution, an appealing strategy is to make information content, online services, entertainment and user interfaces more malleable or adaptable.

The range of processor speeds in use probably varies by a factor of 1000 or more. Moore's Law, which states that processor speeds double every 18 months, means that after 10 years the speed of the newest processors is 100 times faster. Designers who wish to take advantage of new technologies risk excluding users with older machines. Similar changes for RAM and hard disk space also inhibit current designers who wish to reach a wide audience. Other hardware improvements, such as increased screen size and improved input devices, also threaten to limit access. Research on accommodating varying processor speed, RAM, hard disk, screen size and input devices could help cope with this challenge.

Another hardware-related research topic is software to convert interfaces and information across media or devices. There are already some services for users who wish to get Web page contents read to them over the telephone or for blind users (http://www.conversa.com/), but improvements are needed to speed delivery and extract information appropriately (Thomas et al., 1999). Accommodating assorted input devices by a universal bus would allow third-party developers to create specialized and innovative devices for users with handicaps or special needs (Perry et al., 1997).

Software changes are a second concern. As application programs mature and operating systems evolve, users of current software may find their programs become obsolete because newer versions fail to preserve file format compatibility. Some changes are necessary to support new features, but research would be helpful to identify modular designs that promote evolution while ensuring compatibility and bidirectional file conversion. The Java movement is a step in the right direction, since it proposes to support platform independence, but its struggles indicate the difficulty of the problems.

Network access variety is a third problem. Some users will continue to use slower speed (14.4 kbps) dial-up modems, while others will use 10 Mbps cable modems. This 100-fold speedup requires careful planning to accommodate. Since many Web pages contain large amounts of graphics, providing user control of byte counts would be highly advantageous. Most browsers allow users to inhibit graphics, but more flexible strategies are needed. Users should be able to specify that they want reduced byte count graphics, and invoke procedures on the server to compress the image from 300K to 100K or to 30K. With additional image analysis research, servers should be able to produce a 10K image outline. An alternative is simply a 100 byte textual label, supplied by the author, already a requirement for many Web sites that accommodate blind users.

11.3.2 User Diversity: Accommodating Users with Different Skills, Knowledge, Age, Gender, Handicaps, Literacy, Culture, Income Etc.

A second challenge to broadening participation is the diversity of users (Kobsa and Stephanidis, 1998; Fink *et al.*, in press). Since skill levels with computing vary greatly, many search engines provide a basic and advanced dialog box for query formulation. Since knowledge levels in an application domain vary greatly, some sites provide two or more versions. For example, the National Cancer Institute provides thoughtful information on many forms of cancer for patients and more detailed information for physicians. Since children differ from adults in their needs, NASA provides a K–12 (kindergarten through 12th grade) section of many of their space mission pages. Many other examples of accommodating diverse users by simply creating separate sections of a Web site can be found. Universities often segment their sites for applicants, current students or alumni, but then provide links to shared resources of mutual interest.

Similar segmenting strategies can be employed to accommodate users with poor reading skills or users who require other natural languages. While there are some services to automatically convert Web pages to multiple languages (http://www.altavista.com/, http://www.scn.org/spanish.html) the quality of human translations is much higher. Research on tools to facilitate preparation and updating of Web sites in multiple languages would be helpful. For example, if an e-commerce site maintained multiple language versions of a product catalog, then it would be useful to have a tool that facilitated simultaneous changes to a product price (possibly in different currencies), name (possibly in different character sets) or description (possibly tuned to regional variations). A more difficult problem comes in trying to accommodate users with a wide range of incomes, cultures or religions. Imagine trying to prepare multiple music, food or clothing catalogs that were tuned to local needs by emphasizing highly desired products and eliminating offensive items. E-commerce sites that are successful in these strategies are likely to be more widely used.

Another set of issues deals with the wide range of handicaps or differential capabilities of users. Many systems allow partially sighted users, especially elderly users, to increase the font size or contrast in documents, but they rarely allow users to improve readability in control panels, help messages or dialog boxes. Blind users will be more active users of information and communications services if they can receive documents by speech generation or in Braille, and provide input by voice or their customized interfaces. Physically handicapped users will eagerly use services if they can connect their customized interfaces to standard graphical user interfaces, even though they may work at a much slower pace. Cognitively impaired users with mild learning disabilities, dyslexia, poor memory, and other special needs could also be accommodated with modest design changes to improve layouts, control vocabulary and limit short-term memory demands.

Expert and frequent users also have special needs. Enabling customization that speeds high-volume users, macros to support repeated operations, and inclusion of special-purpose devices could bring many benefits. Research on the needs of high-end users could improve interfaces for all users.

Finally, appropriate services for a broader range of users need to be developed, tested and refined. Corporate knowledge workers are the primary audience for many contemporary software projects, so the interface and information needs of unemployed, homemakers, disabled or migrant workers usually get less attention. This has been an appropriate business decision till now, but as the market broadens and key societal services are provided electronically, the forgotten users must be accommodated. For example, Microsoft Word provides templates for marketing plans and corporate reports, but every-citizen interfaces might help with job applications, babysitting cooperatives or letters to city hall.

The growth of online support communities, medical first-aid guides, neighborhood-improvement councils and parent–teacher associations will be accelerated as improved interface and information designs are developed. Community-oriented plans for preventing drug or alcohol abuse, domestic violence, or crime could also benefit from research on interface and information design. Such research is especially important for government Web sites, since their designers are moving towards providing basic services such as driver registration, business licenses, municipal services, tax filing and eventually voting. Respect for the differing needs of users will do much to attract them to using advanced technologies.

11.3.3 Gaps in User Knowledge: Bridging the Gap Between what Users Know and What They Need To Know

A third challenge is to bridge the gap between what users know and what they need to know. A wide variety of strategies are used in practice and competing theories are promoted by researchers, but their efficacy is poorly studied.

Users approach new software tools with diverse backgrounds. Sometimes they need only a few minutes of orientation to understand the novelties and begin to use new tools successfully. Often users need more time to acquire knowledge about the objects and actions in the application domain and in the user interface. To help these users, designers need clear and validated guidance on effective tutorials for novices, lucid instructions for common tasks, constructive help for intermittent users and compact presentations for experts. Improved designs of user interfaces should emphasize error prevention, but specific, positive tone and constructive error messages, with easy repair strategies, are also important. Other potential aids are easily reversible actions and detailed history keeping for review and consultation with peers and mentors. Systematic logging of usage and observations of users would help greatly. Research on tools to help developers provide, assess and refine such services would be useful.

A more fundamental interface and information design research problem is how to develop improved strategies for evolutionary learning. Proposals for appropriate layered designs, graceful progressive disclosure and comprehensible user-controlled options need to be implemented and tested. Could users begin with an interface that contained only basic features (say 5% of the full system) and become experts at this level within a few minutes? Introductions and tutorials could be finely tuned to meet the needs of users of this narrow set of features. Then how might they explore additional features and add them as needed? Similarly, how can users understand and cope with the many exotic options in modern word processors, email handlers and Web browsers? A good beginning has been made with concepts such as layered implementations and the minimal manual (van der Meij and Carroll, 1995), but scaling up and broader application will require further research.

Finally, the provision of online help by way of email, telephone, video conferencing and shared screens needs further examination and design improvements. There is appealing evidence that online social mechanisms among peers such as newsgroups, listservers and frequently asked question (FAQ) lists are helpful, but there is little research that distinguishes among the best and worst of these. While consumer advocates have studied the time to get responses from telephone helpdesks offered by software providers, there is little insight about how to make these services more effective. Best practices, validated analyses, guidelines and theories could all be improved through extensive research.

11.4 Conclusion

Attaining the benefits of universal access to Web-based and other information, communications, entertainment and government services will require a more intense commitment to lowering costs, coupled with human–computer interaction research and usability engineering. A starting point for research would be a program that addressed at least these universal usability challenges:

- **Technology variety**: Supporting a broad range of hardware, software and network access
- **User diversity**: Accommodating users with different skills, knowledge, age, gender, handicaps, literacy, culture, income etc.

- **Gaps in user knowledge:** Bridging the gap between what users know and what they need to know

America OnLine claims that it is "So easy to use. No wonder it's #1". It recognizes the centrality of usability, and has done well to make its services usable by many. Their success is admirable in reaching a fraction of the potential audience, but much work remains to achieve the goal of universal usability. In planning ahead to a time when vital services will be provided online and when novel social, economic and political programs become possible because of widespread citizen participation, we should consider what research is needed to support our aspirations.

Acknowledgments

Thanks to Alfred Kobsa, Gary Marchionini, Elizabeth Murphy, Jenny Preece, Anne Rose, Andrew Sears, David Silver, Barbara Simons, John Thomas and Bryant York for comments on early versions of this chapter. Thanks also to continuing support from IBM and the US Census Bureau.

References

Anderson, RH, Bikson, T, Law, SA and Mitchell, BM (1995) *Universal Access to E-mail: Feasibility and Societal Implications*, Santa Monica, CA: The Rand Corporation, http://www.rand.org/publications/MR/MR650/.
Bergman, E and Johnson, E (1995) Towards accessible human–computer interaction, in *Advances in Human–Computer Interaction*, Vol. 5 (ed. J Nielsen), Norwood, NJ, Ablex Publishing. Also at http://www.sun.com/tech/access/updt.HCI.advance.html.
Borenstein, N (1998) One planet, one net, many voices, *CPSR Newsletter 16*(1), 1, 5–8.
Clement, A and Shade, LR (1999) *The Access Rainbow: Conceptualizing universal access to the information/communications infrastructure*, University of Toronto.
Computer Science and Telecommunications Board (CSTB) (1997) *More than Screen Deep: Toward an Every-Citizen Interface to the Nation's Information Infrastructure*, National Academy Press, Washington, DC.
Fink, J, Kobsa, A and Nill, A (in press) Adaptable and adaptive information provision for all users, including disabled and elderly people, To appear in *New Review of Hypermedia and Multimedia*. http://zeus.gmd.de/~kobsa/papers/1999-NRMH-kobsa.ps.
Glinert, EP and York, BW (1992) Computers and people with disabilities, *Communications of the ACM* 35(5), 32–35.
Kobsa, A and Stephanidis, C (1998) Adaptable and adaptive information access for all users, including disabled and elderly people, in *Proc. 2nd Workshop on Adaptive Hypertext and Hypermedia, ACM HYPERTEXT'98*, http://wwwis.win.tue.nl/ah98/Kobsa.html.
Kraut, R, Scherlis, W, Mukhopadhyay, T, Manning, J and Kiesler, S (1996) The HomeNet field trial of residential Internet services, *Communications of the ACM* 39(12), 55–63.
Laux, LF, McNally, PR, Paciello, MG and Vanderheiden, GC (1996) Designing the World Wide Web for people with disabilities: a user centered design approach, *Proc. Assets '96 Conference on Assistive Technologies*, ACM, New York, pp. 94–101.
Newell, AF (ed.), (1995) *Extraordinary Human–Computer Interaction: Interfaces for Users with Disabilities*, Cambridge, Cambridge University Press.
NTIA (1999) *Falling Through the Net: Defining the Digital Divide*, National Telecommunications and Information Administration, US Dept. of Commerce, Washington, DC, July 1999, http://www.ntia.doc.gov/ntiahome/digitaldivide/.

Perry, J, Macken, E, Scott, N and McKinley, JL (1997) Disability, inability and cyberspace, in *Human Values and the Design of Technology* (ed. B Friedman), CSLI Publications & Cambridge University Press, pp. 65–89.

Scholtz, J *et al.* (1999) A research agenda for high performance user interfaces: useful, usable, and universal, in *ACM Special Interest Group on Computer Human Interaction (SIGCHI)*, New York.

Shapiro, C and Varian, HR (1999) *Information Rules: A Strategic Guide to the Network Economy*, Boston, MA, Harvard Business School Press.

Shneiderman, B (1998) *Designing the User Interface: Strategies for Effective Human–computer Interaction*, 3rd edn, Reading, MA, Addison-Wesley.

Shneiderman, B and Rose, A (1997) Social impact statements: engaging public participation in information technology design, in *Human Values and the Design of Computer Technology* (ed. B Friedman), CSLI Publications and Cambridge University Press, pp. 117–133.

Silver, D (1999) Margins in the wires: looking for race, gender, and sexuality in the Blacksburg Electronic Village, In *Race in Cyberspace: Politics, Identity, and Cyberspace* (eds. B Kolko, L Nakamura and G Rodman), London, Routledge.

Thomas, JC, Basson, S and Gardner-Bonneau, D (1999) Universal design and assistive technology, in *Human Factors and Voice Interactive Systems* (ed. D Gardner-Bonneau), Boston, Kluwer Academic.

van der Meij, H and Carroll, JM (1995) Principles and heuristics in designing minimalist instruction, *Technical Communication*, 2nd Quarter, 243–261.

12

Virtual Spaces Revive Real World Interaction

Luc Julia, Jehan Bing and Adam Cheyer

Abstract

As virtual spaces become more realistic, researchers are experimenting with new perspectives for interactions with such environments. Based on several prototypes that explore augmented and virtual reality as well as dialogs with lifelike computer characters, we discuss in this chapter future directions for virtual environment interfaces that look back to the "good old ways" of working in the real world: talking, gesturing, moving, drawing and so forth.

12.1 Introduction

In today's computing world, almost all users interact with their computers through the same set of input–output devices – a keyboard, mouse and monitor – and user interface metaphors – a "desktop" on which "folders" and "files" are organized, and "windows" that provide manageable views into larger spaces (documents). However, as Moore's Law makes exponentially greater computational power available to the masses, we expect that new interfaces and paradigms will emerge. What will these be like? It is our hypothesis that for advanced new interfaces to become successful and ubiquitous, they must be made simple and familiar in nature, echoing experiences in real life.

12.2 Augmented Pen and Paper Metaphor

Our first work with extended input peripherals and alternative interface metaphors focused on adapting a user's interaction with a pen and piece of paper to the electronic realm. In the TAPAGE/DERAPAGE applications (Figure 12.1a), a user would conceptualize a complex nested table or flowchart, draw a rough freehand sketch of the concept, and then engage in an interactive dialog with the system until the

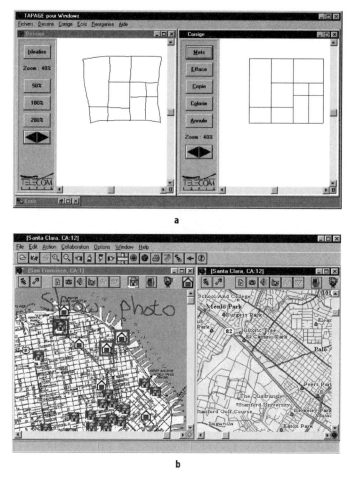

Figure 12.1 TAPAGE and MMap: interactive paper and maps using pen and voice.

desired product was realized [6]. Interactions consist of natural combinations of both pen and speech input – a user can cross out an undesirable line, draw in new additions and reposition lines or objects using commands such as "put this over here". In these applications, we tried to capture the nature of a pen and paper experience, while enhancing the paper's role to become a partner in the process, capable of following high-level instruction and taking an active role in the construction of the document.

A second project focused on applying the metaphor of "smart paper" to the domain of maps, where the goal is to manipulate and reason about information of a geographic nature (Figure 12.1b). Inspired by a simulation experiment described in [7], we developed a working prototype system of a travel planning application, where users could draw, write and speak to the map to call up information about hotels, restaurants and tourist sites [4]. A typical utterance might be: "Find all French restaurants within a mile of this hotel" + <draw arrow towards a hotel>.

The research challenges in constructing such a system are in how to develop a multimodal engine capable of blending incoming modalities in a synergistic fashion, and able to resolve the numerous ambiguities that arise at many levels of processing. One problem of particular interest was that of reference resolution (anaphora). For example, given the utterance "Show photo of *the* hotel", several distinct computational processes may compete to provide information: a natural language agent may volunteer the last hotel talked about, the map process might indicate that the user is looking at only one hotel, and a few seconds later, a gesture recognition process might determine that a user has drawn an arrow or circled a hotel. To better understand these factors, we constructed a set of user experiments based on a novel variant of the Wizard of Oz (WOZ) simulation methodology called the WOZZOW[1] technique. These experiments are run in such a way that we can gather data from a user population, analyze the data and directly adapt our working prototype based on the results, quantifying how much findings actually improve the system [5].

12.3 3D Paper Metaphor?

Through the previous experiments and constructed systems, we were able to develop some sense of how a "smart paper" metaphor could be brought to 2D tasks. However, with 3D becoming more prominent in user interfaces [2], we were thus curious whether the same input techniques (i.e. drawing, writing and speaking) would be effective for 3D situations.

To create an environment in which to pursue this investigation, we began by augmenting our 2D map by a 3D virtual reality (VR) view of the world (Figure 12.2). A user can choose to interact with this system using pen and voice in either a 2D window (map – bird's eye view) or a 3D window, and the two are kept synchronized, with viewports and object information icons updated simultaneously in both.

Although many commands remain primarily the same in both 2D and 3D worlds (e.g. "Bring me to the Hilton"), it is unclear how best to interpret both pen gestures and speech utterances for 3D. For instance, does an arrow to the left indicate that the user wants to turn towards the left, keeping the same position, or rather pan his or her position towards the left, keeping the same orientation? What does the spoken reference "up" mean in the context of complex 3D terrain. Although clearly a 2D paper metaphor does not transparently map onto a 3D environment, we have begin conducting more detailed experiments focusing on pen–voice interactions for 3D models, specifically looking at:

---

1 WOZZOW is a palindrome representing a single experiment with two halves, the WOZ side, which is a standard Wizard of OZ simulation experiment, and the ZOW side, where an expert user receives queries from our WOZ subject, and using a fully automated version of the simulation, tries to produce the desired effect as fast as possible, to make the WOZ subject believe that he or she is using a real system.

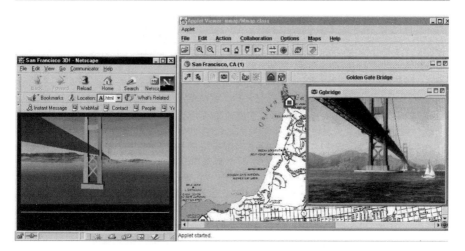

Figure 12.2 Multimodal interactions in synchronized 2D and 3D maps.

- Deictic and gestural reference to features of the terrain: how do people refer to and distinguish between features of a terrain model with words and gesture?
- Discourse structure: how does the structure of the interaction enable more economical communication, and how can a computer system utilize this structure in interpreting spoken and gestural input? How is the discourse structured by the structure of the terrain model and of the task or operation being executed in the terrain?
- Spatial language: how does language carve up space, and what is its relation to more geometric representations of space used in terrain models?

In addition to these experiments, we have been exploring speech recognition in conjunction with other mechanisms for navigation in a 3D virtual world. An initial prototype (Figure 12.3) explores the use of speech to allow higher-level expression of navigational intent for piloting a virtual vehicle (e.g. "Follow this shark"). We believe that this form of interaction will have an impact in the 3D gaming arena, and are planning on investigating these possibilities more closely.

12.4 Augmenting the Real World with a Virtual World

Although pen and voice input seems a potentially promising approach for interacting with 3D environments, we are looking for solutions that provide less intrusive and even more natural interactions. Sensors are now becoming available that allow computer systems to monitor a user's position, orientation, actions and views, and construct a model of the user's experience. Access to such a model will enable computer programs to proactively and continually look to enhance the user's real-world perceptions, without specific intervention from the user. This concept is popularly known as "augmented reality" (AR).

Figure 12.3 Immersion in a virtual world.

To enable exploration of the augmented reality paradigm, we have been constructing an AR application framework, called the Multimodal Augmented Tutoring Environment (MATE). In this framework, multiple processes for providing sensor readings, modality recognition, fusion strategies, viewer displays and information sources can be quickly be integrated into a single flexible application. Our first AR prototype "Travel MATE" (Figure 12.4) makes use of many of the technologies developed in our 2D and 3D tourist applications, but adds GPS and compass sensors. As a user walks or drives around San Francisco, a small laptop computer or PDA simultaneously displays a 3D model of what the user is seeing in the real world, automatically updated based on the user's position and orientation

Figure 12.4 Travel MATE: easy and natural access to touristic information.

[8]. If the user wants to know what a particular building in the distance is, he or she can look at the display, where objects in view are labeled. More detailed multimedia information about these objects can be retrieved on request.

The goal of the Travel MATE application is to provide useful contextual information to the user in an unobtrusive way. We are also working on an "Office MATE" prototype to investigate how AR could enhance the workplace.

12.5 Interacting With a Social Computer

Many interchanges between people involve lively, two-way conversations that make use of spoken dialog. The communication styles between humans and today's computer programs, however, are often much more restricted, with the user directing and the computer passively following orders. We feel that future user interfaces must explore a larger space of interactions with more varied ranges of participation from both sides. In our Travel MATE prototype, we saw an attempt to have a more proactive provision of information from the computer. In our InfoWiz Kiosk application, we look at other interaction styles between human and machine.

The InfoWiz project is centered on the idea of putting an interactive kiosk into the lobby of SRI [3]. People who have a few minutes to spend will be able to learn something about the institute, enjoy themselves and hopefully walk away with a good feeling of having seen something interesting and unusual.

As users approach the kiosk, they are presented with a Web browser containing information about SRI, and an animated cartoon character known as the InfoWiz (Figure 12.5). Instead of using a touchscreen or mouse to navigate through the information, all interactions with the kiosk occur through spoken requests issued into a telephone (a familiar real-world interface). As users browse the InfoSpace, the InfoWiz Wizard can observe their actions, provide supplementary information, answer questions, take users on guided tours and otherwise engage the user in a dialog about what they are seeing and about SRI.

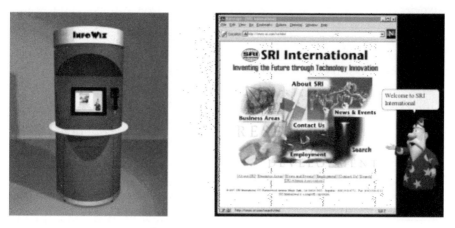

Figure 12.5 InfoWiz, SRI's interactive kiosk.

Research issues in constructing such a system involve how to codify, populate and maintain the InfoWiz's knowledge about the target Web pages; what types of dialog structures will emerge in such a domain; what social cues must the InfoWiz follow when interacting with a user and how do they change across contexts and users; how to maintain the illusion of intelligence given imperfect recognition technologies and inadequate knowledge. These topics must be explored given the challenges of a domain where users will be from a very diverse population (many people visit SRI) and where there is no time to train the users about the system's capabilities – total interaction time with the system is expected to be a few minutes. In addition to our own approach, several good solutions can be found in research such as [1].

12.6 Conclusion and Future Directions

The metaphors we use today to interact with computers were developed primarily in the 1960s and 1970s by researchers from SRI and Xerox. As computers, sensors, bandwidth, display capabilities and software techniques continue to improve at incredible rates, providing computational power only dreamed of during the 1960s and 1970s, opportunities are emerging to transform the paradigms used in human–computer interaction. However, we feel it important to reemphasize that future interfaces can learn a lesson from the longevity of keyboards and desktops – interfaces will be more readily adopted by the population of users if they are simple, natural, intuitive and familiar.

In this chapter, we have discussed some of our research efforts directed at attaining this goal, focusing on techniques for applying the metaphors of "smart paper" to 2D and 3D environments, creating multimodal interfaces for virtual and augmented reality, investigating the use of mixed-initiative spoken language dialog with its implications for social roles between humans and machine. Although much progress has been made in our group and elsewhere, creating "simple" interfaces is still not a simple problem, and much research remains.

As a closing remark, we would like to comment that the speed with which new technologies are emerging is faster now than at any time in our history. It's interesting to note that many of the familiar objects on which today's interface paradigms are based have already been replaced: for instance, although keyboards are everywhere, it is no longer easy to find a typewriter. Will electronic pens and paper eventually replace their real versions? If the world is changing so fast that nothing has time to become familiar before it is replaced by something else, how will our society be able to deal with the pace?

References

[1]   E Andre, T Rist and J Muller (1998) Guiding the User through dynamically generated hypermedia presentations with a life-like character, in *Proceedings of International Conference on Intelligent User Interfaces (IUI-98)*.

[2]   W Ark, C Dryer, T Selker and S Zhai (1998) Representation matters: the effect of 3D objects and a spatial metaphor in a graphical user interface, in *Proceedings of CHI'98*.

[3] A Cheyer and L Julia (1999) InfoWiz: an animated voice interactive information system, in *Proceedings Agents'99, Workshop on Conversational Agents and Natural Language.*

[4] A Cheyer and L Julia (1998) Multimodal Maps: An Agent-based Approach. In book *Multimodal Human–Computer Communication*, Berlin, Springer-Verlag.

[5] A Cheyer, L Julia and JC Martin (1998) A unified framework for constructing multimodal experiments and applications, in *Proceedings of CMC'98.*

[6] L Julia and C Faure (1995) Pattern recognition and beautification for a pen based interface, in *Proceedings of ICDAR'95.*

[7] S Oviatt (1996) Multimodal interfaces for dynamic interactive maps, in *Proceedings of CHI'96.*

[8] http://www.chic.sri.com/projects/MATE.html.

13

An HCI Agenda for the Next Millennium: Emergent Global Intelligence

John C. Thomas

13.1 Overview

> If there is not one among us
> Who contains sufficient wisdom
> Many people together
> May find a clear path.
>
> *Paula Underwood*

In this chapter, I will argue that a worthy agenda for HCI in the next millennium is to develop tools, techniques and technology to enhance collective human intelligence. This idea is not in itself novel. Indeed, Doug Engelbart began his work with exactly this goal in mind and he continues it today (`http://www.boot-strap.org/`). The "mouse" was only one of several inventions as a means to this end. The idea of using technology to enhance collective human wisdom was also the central idea in Vannevar Bush's (1945) landmark paper. Indeed, if we listen with an open mind to the oral history of the Iroquois people (Underwood, 1993), we see that they (among others) have been consciously concerned for thousands of years with developing tools and techniques to enhance collective human intelligence.

The plan of this chapter is to lay out a sequence of independent threads and then attempt to weave them together into a more unified vision of what we might accomplish with modern technology. First, I will give a short overview of the issue. Second, I will attempt to lay out the problem; that is, why enhancing collective intelligence is necessary. Third, I briefly review some of the human capacities and limitations that should help guide our design. Fourth, I examine some existing partial solutions to the problem. Fifth, I try to synthesize these threads into some design considerations. Sixth, I examine some scenarios to determine why and how such a system might fail. Seventh, I lay out a research agenda to move us toward a working system.

McKee (1997), in his excellent manual on writing good stories, claims that conflict, as portrayed in story, exists at three fundamental levels: intrapsychic, interpersonal, and with the wider society or environment. These roughly correspond to three stages in the development of the field of Human–Computer Interaction (HCI). In the first few decades, the emphasis was largely on using cognitive psychology to support individual workers. The last few decades have seen a gradual shift toward an emphasis on supporting the team. In the next decade, we predict that the emphasis will continue to shift toward supporting the entire organization (e.g. intranets), interdependent organizations (e.g. extranets) and ultimately the entire social, i.e. human, experience.

Alexander *et al.* (1977) and Oldenburg (1997) illustrate some of the ways that architectural space can facilitate or inhibit effective social behavior at a variety of levels. Similarly, we believe that a socially oriented and aware computing "field" can be constructed to support or inhibit effective collective action. Popular books are already appearing (e.g. Lipnack and Stamps, 1997) on "how to" build effective virtual teams with little reference to the relevant CSCW and HCI literature. The questions desperately being asked by corporations, governments and the general public about how to use technology in the large to serve human needs are not being answered at the level of scope and generality that our current scientific methodologies provide.

Of course, there are important interactions among the levels of organization. The cognitive difficulties that individuals have that stem from tendencies such as seeking only confirmatory evidence, the fundamental attribution fallacy, focus on the short-term (Ornstein and Ehrlich, 1989), and failure to observe base rates, e.g. produce difficulties at a social level. Of course, poorly designed individual interfaces to technology can also inhibit effective social action. Thus we are certainly not claiming that good HCI design at the individual level will ever become irrelevant to the creation of global intelligence. It is a necessary but not sufficient condition.

While much of CSCW still seems to operate under the implicit assumptions that we need to make teleconferencing as much like face-to-face meetings as possible or that we need to make virtual spaces like real spaces, we are struck with the considerable difficulties that remain in interpersonal communication, even when it is face-to-face. Even small teams and families are often notoriously dysfunctional. Large organizations seldom seem even fractionally as productive as the sum of their parts. Huge amounts of resource are spent worldwide on misunderstandings and miscommunications across various political and organizational boundaries. The costs range from the billions of dollars spent on the mismatch in cognitive models between end-users and helpdesk personnel to the trillions of dollars consumed by armed conflicts.

In *Jihad versus McWorld*, Barber (1995) points out that we are experiencing two seemingly contradictory trends: globalism and retribalization. Jacobs (1992) identifies these trends with two disparate value systems: an older one based on territoriality and a newer one based on commerce. A major challenge for HCI in the next century is to take the next logical step: to address head-on social issues; to provide a space that facilitates creative dialectic and value out of diverse viewpoints and even value systems such as those mentioned above. In order to accomplish this end, we should not draw a sharp boundary around HCI so that it only includes something with an explicit and separate "computer" as a major component. Any tool, technique, policy or procedure as well as any technology, embedded or separate, that helps bring people to the next level of social cooperation should be a legitimate field of inquiry.

Many investigators today, noting the sea of information that we are drowning in, call for more efficient search tools, more comprehensive meta-data, and more effective filtering agents. These are fruitful lines of research and development. We believe that another avenue worth exploring is to turn toward more organic, more integrated, more "primitive" methods of understanding and communicating social information, methods such as "stories".

In contrast to the last few hundred years of increasing emphasis on analysis and trying to dissect factors from each other and content from context, story revels in complex systems; accepts and thrives on conflict; often portrays multiple perspectives; and gives the reader or listener a chance to "live another life". It seems that story may be fundamental to the way we perceive and recall the world (Schank, 1990; Murray, 1997). It may be also fundamental to the world we create for the next century. How can we use the power of story and the story-creation process? Can we create something that transcends the old use of story to help us collectively comprehend the world in greater detail and complexity? Absent electronics or even a written language, the Iroquois used story to teach new generations the wisdom gained through millennia of experience. Can modern technology add anything to this process? Can we provide tools to help synthesize disparate viewpoints into a coherent whole?

It is something of a truism in HCI that the construction of appropriate technological support depends upon the users, their tasks and their contexts as well as the technology available. We might then ask, given limited resources, what tasks, users and contexts of use should HCI focus on for the next millennium? It is suggested that there are three critical interrelated objectives that we might challenge ourselves with in this regard. First, how can we actually design a better worldwide network – not one that hopes at best to mirror the properties of face-to-face communication, but one that transcends face-to-face communication in that it overcomes problems that arise in "normal" human conversation because of our cognitive limitations? In other words, how can we design a system that allows global intelligence to be brought to bear on critical problems.

Second, we need to develop a methodology that can address issues at a scope that is commensurate with the critical problems people face, namely how can technology-social systems be designed to enhance human productivity and enjoyment in the large? How will we be able to measure our progress toward effective global intelligence?

Third, we need to develop new representations that take account of natural human strengths (such as storytelling and comprehending) but that also enable us to achieve the accuracy of analytical thinking. When we think within a representational system, whether it is an analytic framework or a narrative one, we are typically not aware of the limitations introduced by that representation. As Bohm

(1994) says, thought creates our world and then says, "I didn't do it". We need to develop a self-reflective set of representations, rich with annotations about its own limitations, that help global communities develop complex, intelligent adaptive systems.

A more concrete way to state the confluence of these three goals might be: "How do we develop the technological support to let a million people be a million times as smart as one person?". This seems to be a goal that is both challenging and worthy of HCI for the next millennium.

While the goal is, to put it mildly, a "Stretch" goal, it is not discontinuous from current HCI. There is a growing literature in "captology" (Computers As Persuasive Technology; `http://www.captology.org/`), CSCW, organizational learning, and architecture and urban planning that provides some pieces in this rather large puzzle. It is time to start putting them together. Perhaps the UARC and SPARC projects can serve as a model first step. Scientists in the Upper Atmospheric Research community (`http://www.crew.umich.edu/UARC/`) have fundamentally changed the way that they do science as the result of a technological infrastructure designed with some sensitivity to individual and social issues in HCI (Finholt and Olson, 1997). At the University of Colorado, a system has been created for group design that includes a table-top computing environment for construction and a vertical wall-screen space for group reflection (Fischer, 1999).

13.2 The Problem

It has become such a truism that people may have largely become inured to it, but it remains true that the human race faces a number of complex problems of a serious, global nature. Among these are the very real possibility of ecological disaster. For example, global warming could well change ocean currents and produce an Ice Age. Widespread destruction through the use of nuclear weapons remains a possibility. The Earth is running out of arable land and potable water(see `http://www.dieoff.org/` for references and details) though there are organizations trying to conserve vital resources (see, e.g. `http://www.tnc.org/`). There are numerous significant social problems: high rates of poverty, crime and drug use; economic challenges and so forth.

How do we address such problems? Problems of this type require wide-scale cooperation for implementing any potential solution. Yet, any one solution point will probably not be locally optimal for most of the people whose cooperation is needed. There are numerous and complex partially overlapping and contradictory goal-structures for individuals, groups and institutions. One approach might be to support a single very smart individual or small team through knowledge management technology. Perhaps such a person or individual could comprehend such problems in order to find a solution, and then they might be able to convince everyone else to implement their solution. But unless people understand the problem and the proposed solution in fairly great detail, there will be a great deal of understandable skepticism that any proposed solution is especially geared toward the goal structure of the proposers. ("Let's make the rich richer and everyone else will benefit through the wealth trickling down through layers of society. Yeah. Sure.")

It appears that a very different approach will be required to solve such problems and then have the solutions implemented (Thomas, 1996). One such approach is to provide an interactive computational matrix that supports very large-scale groups to find, formulate, solve and commit to implementing solutions to such complex, wicked problems. In order to design such a system, we will first review at a very high level some of the strengths of human knowledge processing that might be exploited and some weaknesses to be compensated.

13.3 Review of Human Capabilities and Limitations

Implicit in many of the writings in Computer-Supported Cooperative Work and Human–Computer Interaction is the notion that a goal of technology should be to allow communication at a distance the same degree of fidelity and the same bandwidth as face-to-face communication. While it may be true that there are some current applications of CSCW that suffer from such limitations today, face-to-face communication is not the ultimate ideal for all situations. Even in face-to-face communications, people misunderstand each other, negotiate from positions instead of needs, avoid looking for the win–win solution, respond on the basis of prejudice and fall prey to their own irrational beliefs. While modern technology may bring with it its own set of problems, the pre-electronic world still had its share of wars and crimes. In addition, because of the structure of natural language and physical reality, face-to-face interaction is effectively limited to either a broadcast mode or a very small group.

Among the human limitations that impinge on our ability to communicate and solve complex problems is a bias toward noticing events that have large scale quick changes. As Ornstein and Ehrlich (1989) point out, the problems that face people today, such as ecological disaster, do not engage us emotionally or sensorially – our attentional mechanisms evolved to deal with falling trees and lunging predators, not slow but systematic destruction of the ecological infrastructure that supports life.

In addition, natural language evolved over many millennia to allow small groups to communicate when those groups shared a common viewpoint and context. Today, we face problems wherein very large numbers of separate contexts and viewpoints are relevant to workable solutions.

Humans have many problems understanding basic statistical properties (Paulos, 1998). Again, failure to take into account base rates, sensitivity to first information, the "Gambler's Fallacy" and other cognitive dysfunctionalities limit people's ability to deal well with complex problems that include probabilistic aspects. Unfortunately, most of the pressing complex problems humanity faces have probabilistic aspects!

Human beings also tend to access problem-solving heuristics and algorithms on the basis of surface features of the problem rather than deep structure. Indeed, it often seems that simple logic eludes people (Wason and Johnson-Laird, 1972). Yet, when these same logic problems are put into a narrative context that people can relate to, they are much more able to make intelligent choices. Schank (1990) suggests that the "depth" of analogy by which a told story reminds one of another story is a sign of intelligence.

People do have some amazing and potentially useful sensory capabilities. For example, people can recognize complex scenes that they have seen before even after brief exposures. They can comprehend speech in the presence of considerable noise and recognize the voices and faces of people they have known when heard or seen in a different context despite years without practice.

People are also capable of making fine relative discriminations in pitch, touch and color in simultaneous presentations. People already have stored in their heads as adults a large amount of knowledge. With practice, people can learn highly complex motor skills. When they do make errors in the performance of these motor skills, the error patterns have some predictability, perhaps allowing the possibility of some degree of automatic correction.

People can also modify behavior on the fly to deal with novelty. For instance, we can "understand" the speech of someone whose vocal tract we've never heard before; we can quickly adapt to a new font or handwriting style. If we have some skilled performance and need to perform the task with a new instrument or with a slight injury, we can adapt to the new situation quickly. People seem to have excellent memory for spatial position and can navigate quickly through two or three dimensions. People also seem quite good at making use of their physical environment in order to aid memory and processing (Norman, 1993).

A natural way for small groups and even larger communities to share knowledge seems to be through the telling of stories. Telling a story often leads to telling another story that is related. By comparing and contrasting elements of stories, groups seem to be able to begin to build up a common and deeper understanding of some situation, culture, person, or artifact. Underwood's work (1993) demonstrates that in some cultures, such as the Iroquois, this process is quite consciously nurtured and that, over time, heuristics for knowledge creation and sharing through stories are themselves embedded in stories.

While people can engage skillfully in natural language behavior in small groups, there is a significant problem in the structure of natural languages that makes it relatively unsuited (in its unaltered state) for highly interactive large-scale use. The problem is that the symbol space and the meaning (or referent) space are not very congruently mapped. While, on the one hand, "I do love my Macintosh computer." and "I do love my Thinkpad computer." are close in symbol space and close in meaning space, the sentences, "I do want to launch all the nuclear bombs." and "I do not want to launch all the nuclear bombs." are close in symbol space but quite different in meaning space (and in pragmatic space).

Formal logic shares this property. Thus, from the statement: "p AND p", one can only deduce "p" or a tautology. But, from "p AND $\sim p$" one can deduce anything. Similarly, a slight change in a programming language completely changes the behavior of a program. When I ran the PDP-8 computer lab on the psychology of aging study, for example, someone had written a program which was intended to collect reaction times. Instead, the actual behavior of the program was to ruin seemingly random parts of the operating system. In this case, the indirect bit had accidentally been set and therefore instead of storing the reaction time, it was using the reaction time as an address.

For this reason, when we attempt to use natural language, mathematics or computer languages as a means for large group collaboration, an inordinate amount of time and energy is spent proofreading, editing and testing. Generally, in fact, a "published" piece of science is seen and reacted to by a moderate to large group of people before it becomes provisionally accepted as "true".

Contrast this behavior, for instance, with what appears to be the highly statistical nature of the brain. The firing behavior of individual neurons in the auditory or visual system at primary levels does not seem to be perfectly correlated with specific events; however, statistically, the behavior does seem predictable and we are able at the organismic level to make fine relative discriminations.

Can we then organize a system of human beings so that the individual human being does not need to be precisely correct but only statistically correct, and do this in a manner which still results in the overall super-organismic behavior being correct?

One path that we might consider exploring would be the design and development of a language in which the symbol space maps well into the referent space. In this way, if a person misspoke slightly or made a typo, there would be no measurable effect on system behavior because the overall meaning would be well preserved. It would be desirable, furthermore, to design the written and spoken language so that basic meaning held up well over distance. In this way, readers and listeners at a great distance could still get the "gist" of what was being communicated though the details would not be present. This would allow the kind of many-layered and textured communication that Tufte (1990) shows in the three-dimensional maps of Paris and Manhattan constructed respectively by Bretez-Turgot and Constantine Anderson. Notice that music, to a much greater degree than spoken language, has this property. As John Seely Brown and others have pointed out, people can use overall visual cues about a familiar genre such as the *Wall Street Journal* to help organize their search and reading behavior. With existing spoken language, however, listening to a host of conversations simultaneously may give us some flavor of the emotional tone and energy in a room, but almost nothing about content. For that to happen, language would have to be designed to accommodate such a purpose rather than for single conversations.

Unfortunately, designing such a language and then getting a significant number of people to learn to speak, hear, read and write it would be a monumental undertaking no more likely of success than Esperanto or the beautifully crafted and phonetic spelling system for English designed by George Bernard Shaw (who left his fortune to promulgate his system, only to have the British courts set aside the will as ridiculous).

On the other hand, existing natural language search technologies such as the Latent Semantic Index (Dumais *et al.*, 1998), are becoming sufficiently accurate, especially with iterative relevance feedback, that we might consider having a powerful enough computer essentially provide such a mapping function, so that, even using natural English in a natural way, we would effectively have the illusion that we received the "essence" of far-away conversations and the "details" of close-in conversations.

13.4 Existing Emergent Solution Elements

It appears that humanity is already embarking on nascent experiments in the general direction of global intelligence systems. Some of these systems are reviewed below.

13.4.1 The Case of the Found Prime Factors and Similar Cases

The search for Mersenne primes (primes of the form $2^n - 1$) has been and is being carried out in a vastly parallel fashion across multiple computational resources by hundreds of investigators worldwide (see http://www.mersenne.org/prime.htm). So far a number of very large primes have been found. (In case it is not intuitively obvious, the largest known as of 31 January 1999 when I wrote the first draft of this chapter was $2^{3021377} - 1$. However, on 1 June 1999, $2^{6972593} - 1$ was discovered, and the search continues.)

In this case, however, a single intelligence was able to "partial out" various discrete non-interacting subparts to various individuals who are all using common software. We can imagine other problems that have similar well-defined structures and are similarly decomposable. Of course, some overhead and organization is required to pull off such an undertaking and it is definitely in the neighborhood of the thesis of this chapter; however, it seems odd to speak of this as a kind of super-intelligence. Yet, we should keep this model in mind for those problems that are luckily completely decomposable.

Science sometimes works in almost this way. Individual anthropologists can focus study on individual tribes; individual medical doctors can publish results on unusual specific patients (e.g. Tueber's HM, who had severe Korsakov's syndrome or Luria's synesthetic mnemonist); individual biologists can focus on particular species or even varieties. After years of study and many false paths, the findings can be published and others can learn the results of these studies at a much reduced cost. This is possible because, to the first approximation, the behavior of individual tribes, individuals and species is decomposable.

13.4.2 The Web

Some ardent supporters of the Web may say that it already provides a "million person interface". Massetti *et al.* (1999) found no evidence that Web use increased the user's idea generation performance. Indeed, although the Web is often portrayed as a place for democracy, extensive empirical studies (e.g. Whittaker *et al.*, 1998) indicate that in actuality, participation is extremely skewed even among those with access. Freeman Dyson (1999) argues that the Internet may be one (along with solar power and genetic engineering) of the three most important revolutionary forces of the next century, but that the full value of the Internet will not be realized unless there is universal access.

Currently, however, many of the mechanisms that have evolved over several centuries for ensuring the accuracy and quality of information in print media are still lacking in the Web. While the capacity to produce animation and grainy video is cheap and therefore widespread, the handling of content is uneven in quality and not very well-organized.

Nonetheless, there are special circumstances, such as the search for primes, in which the Web, even now seems well-suited. I also predicted (Thomas, 1995) that HCI, by the year 2020, would be using distributed Web-based heuristic evaluation. I received the first such request only a few weeks after that chapter was published!

Perhaps a more intriguing and interesting case is the development of the Linux operating system (http://www.linux.org/). Linux was developed under the guidance of Linus Torvalds with the growing assistance of hundreds of developers around the world. How could something so complex be developed in such a distributed fashion essentially by volunteers? How could such a system even run, let alone, by most accounts, prove far superior to comparable systems developed under standard "management control"? Here it is not the case that someone simply partialled out non-interactive pieces and then reassembled them. Does this presage the typical development efforts of the future?

13.4.3 Organizations

Of course, large numbers of people do work together for larger goals. When the subtasks and the resources can each be separated into independent units, productivity can be roughly linear with the number of people. For example, if 10 000 people each have a small plot of arable land, then 10 000 people can basically produce 10 000 times as much as one person. An army of 10 000 door-to-door salespeople with non-overlapping territories can basically sell 10 000 times as much as one such salesperson. This is essentially the same as the problem of finding the prime numbers. Notice also that the non-interactivity of subproblems also has an important *motivational* side-effect. Individual farmers are rewarded and therefore motivated by their individual efforts (unlike the failed experiments of Soviet collective farming). Individual salespeople are generally paid largely on commission. Credit will accrue to those individuals who find the largest primes. This avoids the "tragedy of the commons" problem. Where interactions among subproblems do occur, such linearity may fail, sometimes spectacularly as when lack of any intervening vegetation and other factors produced the Dust Bowl in much of the USA earlier in this century.

We can imagine improving over linearity in some of these situations. If, for instance, the 10 000 salespeople with non-overlapping territories try a number of variations on the sales pitch and keep track of and share results, we could expect 10 000 sales people to sell more than 10 000 times as much as one person through the spread of best practices. In addition, there may be other collective benefits. For example potential customers may move from place to place and help "sell" the product through word of mouth. There is a greater chance of a media-promulgated story about the product if it is being sold by 10 000 people rather than one. Notice that in order to keep the motivational issues in balance, in order to share, salespeople must truly believe that their territories are independent and that contributions to a common knowledge base will be reciprocated. Just as in the case of finding prime factors, it seems odd to use the term "emergent intelligence" applied to this linear increase in productivity that comes about by virtue of the clean decomposability of the problem.

We can imagine further increases above linearity due to specialization. So, for instance, rather than imagining potential customers as an undifferentiated mass, there might be 100 different types of customer who are more willing to buy with specifically geared pitches. Then, if we can arrange to have the "right" salespeople matched with the "right" customers and these salespeople can refine and target their audiences, they can be more than linearly productive. This begins to sound like the rudiments of emergent intelligence.

In the examples above, we have neatly hypothesized discrete territories, a minimum of controlled interaction, and well-structured problems with non-interacting parts. In many real organizations, things are not nearly so cleanly partitioned. In a more typical social or business organization, the environment changes over time, the individuals change over time, and the nature of the task changes over time. Moreover, it is often the case that the subtasks that complex organizations engage in are not independent but highly interdependent. It often seems that the left and right "hands" of an organization are working at cross purposes. For instance, when I managed the Voice Dialing project at NYNEX, one of the computer scientists in the lab ordered the voice dialing service. He was given an installation date. The date came and went but no voice dialing capability appeared. When he called up the Installation and Repair people to find out why his date had not been met, they told him that it was impossible to get voice dialing where he lived; the switch at his Central Office did not have the right system software. So, trying to be a good corporate citizen, he called back the Customer Service Rep who had sold him voice dialing to inform her. But she said, "Yes, you can!". Eventually, the Customer Service Rep and the Installation and Repair person were yelling at each other over the phone.

Whether it is software development, sales efforts, corporate strategy or the weekly update meeting, I think it is fair to say that most of our experience with complex real-world organizations is that they seem far less than linearly productive and intelligent. A typical committee of even 10 people does not seem 10 times as smart as the average committee member. A Senate of 100 people seldom strikes one as 100 times as smart as one Senator. I will return to this issue later. Meantime, are there things known about complex organizations that can inform our design?

A series of empirical studies of highly successful companies seems to indicate some consensus on factors that are correlated with financial success and longevity (Kotter and Heskett, 1992). De Gues (1997) found these common characteristics in large-scale organizations that had survived for more than 100 years:

1. Sensitivity to the environment
2. Cohesion and identity.
3. Tolerance and decentralization; an ability to build constructive relationships with other entities within and outside itself
4. Conservative financing; being able to govern its own growth and evolution effectively

Collins and Porras (1994) infer a number of commonalities in highly successful companies, including experimentation/diversity, building processes and mechanisms to support values, not being satisfied with "good enough", and setting "big hairy audacious goals". For the most part, we are unable to experimentally manipulate organizational variables although a colleague of mine, Bart Burns, used the De Gues principles to run the "People Express" business simulation and managed to raise the stock price from $1 to over $400 in six simulated years. With the increase of business knowledge, modeling savvy and computational power, it may soon be possible to run fairly realistic simulations of complex organizations (Prietula *et al.*, 1998). Meanwhile, we can imagine that the development of "mutual trust" or "social capital" is important in bridging gaps of time and space in allowing reciprocation to take place. If mutual trust is low, for instance, in any effort at having salespeople cooperatively build a database for their mutual benefit, any lag in time between an individual's contribution and reciprocation will tend to produce cynicism and a felt punishment. This in turn will lead to lower levels of participation and less mutual trust. Conversely, high levels of mutual trust lead to higher participation and thus to higher levels of mutual trust. It is not surprising then that Putnam *et al.* (1993) found early "social capital" to be a much better predictor of the later economic vitality of a region in Italy than was the earlier economic vitality of that region.

13.4.4 Using the Community of Communities Principle

Perhaps one of the most compelling stories of large-scale semi-organized social action is the work of Karl-Henrik Robert in Sweden (see http://www.context.org/ICLIB/IC35/Robert.htm).

As a pediatric oncologist, Dr Robert was convinced that increased pollution was contributing to the incidence of several kinds of cancer. Moreover, he became both frustrated and amazed at the apparent contradiction that people were so reluctant to make tiny changes in their behavior to prevent increased pollution, and yet when parents found out their own child had cancer they were willing to make any sacrifice (of course, this is the "tragedy of the commons" again). When he went to conferences on pollution and cancer, experts kept disagreeing on details. Some thought that the levels of chromium in the water were already giving people bladder cancer, while others insisted the concentration would not be sufficient for another two years. In frustration, he began to delve down to a level of shared belief – what it was that the experts did agree on. It took 22 iterations among various experts, but he ended up with a set of four principles that they all agreed on. He also constructed a systems diagram showing the interrelationship of important economic, behavioral and physical variables. He got several major companies in Sweden to agree to the principles leading to a sustainable economy; then got the King of Sweden to order the principles printed up for everyone in the country. Then he used a "community of communities" organization to further promulgate a move toward a sustainable economy. Now in Sweden there are organizations such as "Computer scientists for a sustainable economy", "Church leaders for a sustainable economy" and so on. Each community best knows how to motivate and administer within its own domain.

Essentially, while all the communities agree on the basic principles, they are able to move in parallel in the domains they know best. If they can share best practices of processes and do better than chance at partialing out which contextual factors require modification across domains and which do not, and to the extent that there are few cross-domain negative interactions, they may be able to achieve approximate linearity (or better) in relating effects to effort. Again, precisely to the extent that they are successful because they really are simply applying parallel efforts, it seems odd to call this emergent intelligence, though it may be a good model for effective social or political action. Having a simple system image that everyone can relate to helps not only in that it can guide collective action, but also because, by seeing how compelling the principles are, each individual becomes more trustful that others will also follow the principles. We can also imagine that relying on a community of communities approach further increases mutual trust because primarily and locally you are relying on individuals that you already trust, and you only need trust in the other communities on a longer-term basis.

13.4.5 Rock Concerts, Festivals, Conferences Etc.

There are, of course, a large number of cases where large groups of people congregate and engage in various activities. They have various degrees of structure from a relatively undifferentiated mass of people in an audience watching a few performers to relatively well-structured subdomains. At a rock concert there is certainly a degree of interaction and the communication of mood across the audience. However, it might be stretching the point to hold it up as a model of emergent intelligence.

Nevertheless, I would like to relate an incident that illustrates the possibility for the emergence of some degree of collective intelligence even at a concert. For the last seven or eight years, I have attended Ben and Jerry's Folk Festival in Newport, Rhode Island. What I most enjoy about this outdoor event is that I can dance to the music. One year, we arrived and it poured with rain the entire time. Everyone was huddled, shivering under umbrellas and raingear. After a few hours of this, I thought, "Well, heck with this. I came here to dance!". So, I stripped down to my bathing suit and began dancing to the music. Alone. But I was having a great time – and I was much warmer than I had been huddled down in wet clothes. Several people on stage made reference to my dancing. After a while, a few more people began dancing. By the end of the day, nearly everyone was dancing. The truth was, *especially* in the rain, it was a much more enjoyable way to spend the time. And although a concert is primarily a one-way broadcast event, the idea of dancing spread laterally through the audience. Without any explicit "tournament structure", people throughout the large audience gradually came to adopt the "best" idea for how to enjoy themselves in the pouring rain.

At a complex multi-event festival or conference, intelligent participants can use a variety of printed and social cues to program their behavior so as to benefit more from the conference than a random sampling of venues and events. There is some chance for people to summarize "most notable experiences" for others who did not actually participate. Yet it is hard to imagine that a conference achieves anything like a linear increase in group intelligence. Is either the outcome or the process of a 3000 person CHI conference 1000 times as "intelligent" as a good three-person conversation? (CHI is the Association for Computing Machinery's conference on human factors in computing systems.)

13.4.6 Religion and Custom

One could argue that much of religion and culture is the distillation over time of specific experiences, told and retold through stories that evolve and become more and more significant. Imagine, for example, that over many centuries, people again and again experienced that certain specific instances where deadly plagues were associated with certain dietary practices. Eventually, such stories might well come to take on the quality of "enforced" realities. "You *must not* do such and such". People, through the distillation of many stories, may have come to realize that, basically, murder does not work as a way to solve interpersonal problems. It seems to work at first, but eventually there is revenge and counter-revenge, and it becomes antithetical to the survival of the whole community. Of course, there are many other views on religion and/or custom, but one view is that it is a form of collective intelligence. In Underwood's (1993) *The Walking People*, it is clear that the Iroquois developed very conscious techniques to ensure the essential accuracy of oral history through story – and embedded the explanation of some of these techniques right in the story!

13.4.7 Free Markets

Some might consider the "invisible hand" of the market-place as a kind of global intelligence. Through the individual decisions of many millions of consumers, the money flows to the "right" things more intelligently than it would if it were controlled even by an intelligent and benevolent dictator. Specifically, there might be something to be learned about the million-person interface from the open trading markets. They are highly interactive, highly multidimensional, semi-structured and "liquid".

It is beyond the scope of this chapter to do a detailed critique of unbridled capitalism, but suffice it to say that without any regulations whatsoever, numerous destructive, addictive drugs might be advertised, manufactured, bought and consumed. It is unclear, for example, that thousands of people dying of lung cancer constitutes a manifestation of global emergent intelligence.

13.4.8 Pervasive Computing and Other Interesting Things

There are efforts afoot to embed computing devices more pervasively into the environment; to make architecture itself more "intelligent"; and to provide people with augmented reality devices and active badges to help them understand dynamically their social relations to others. It is now possible to exchange information with another person simply by shaking hands (through small electrical signals conducted over the skin via a Personal Area Network). All of these trends seem to point toward the possibility of larger scale cooperation, but it is not yet clear, at least to me, how to integrate them.

At a recent Institute for the Future meeting, people without musical training were taught small pieces and assembled eventually into a large coordinated improvisational jam session (Smoliar and Baker, 1999). In order to make this work, however, particular processes have to be followed. And, although this is a type of large-scale cooperation, music "composes" well (see Section 13.3) compared with our existing symbol systems for meaning.

Although, as mentioned previously, the typical business meeting often seems much less than linearly productive, there have recently been some promising results with a technique called Dialogue (Bohm, 1990). The word "Dialogue" does not, as most people assume, come for words for "two" and "meaning" but from the Greek words for "through" and "meaning". "Dialogue", then, is not just a genteel alternative word for debate, but connotes an entirely different group process. In a typical group meeting, while one person talks, other people listen briefly, categorize the remarks, determine whether they agree or disagree, and on that basis begin formulating and rehearsing their response carefully, looking for an opportunity to state their case. Of course, the social and political dynamics are much more complex than that, but it is fair to say that the outline above describes many meetings. The best possible outcome one can expect is that the best individual idea is adopted.

In Dialogue, however, the process is different. People share some thought or experience. The others listen. After listening, they reflect for a moment. Then, someone else says something. Together, people try to build "in the center" a more comprehensive systems view of what is relevant to them. Some of the collectively developed knowledge is metaknowledge. "Isn't that interesting. Whenever someone mentions topic X, I immediately assume that they are really talking specifically about Y." "This group seems to have two factions with completely different ideas about our goals." Dialogue seems particularly useful in situations where people are engaged in a complex system but no one person (or even small group) understands the complete system. By "complete system" of course, I'm including the "rules" inside the heads of individuals. This technique has yielded some promising results (Isaacs and Smith, 1994; Isaacs, 1996).

13.5 Design Outline

13.5.1 Organizational Issues

Since we are focusing on problems that exist in a complex and rapidly changing environment, and since we do not already have a long history of working with global intelligence, and since we are working on problems where the voluntary follow-up actions of the participants are necessary in order to bring the proposed solution to fruition, a command and control environment would not seem to be an appropriate model. Rather, a sense and respond model of organizations might work better (Haeckel and Slywotzky, 1999).

Clearly, it will be important to provide some sort of effective feedback to the group at various levels so that it can adapt and improve its performance over time. This proves to be a difficult issue, however. In the types of problem that we are suggesting, it may take a long time before the effectiveness of a solution can be measured and fed back to the group. For several iterations to take place, a very long time-scale would be involved. Furthermore, even if the group were to receive timely feedback, how would the individual learn to modify their behavior? Or, would we assume that individuals would not need to learn and that all the learning would take place at the higher organizational level?

There are two suggested approaches to help meet these challenges. First, theater groups and sports teams do not come together for the first time to produce optimal performance. They practice. Sometimes they practice component skills and sometimes they practice with scrimmages. Similarly, it would make sense to have such a team "practice" on increasingly complex problems in which the "answer", although not obvious, is known.

Second, both the individuals and the team could learn via intrinsic learning. By "intrinsic" learning, I am referring to learning that can occur by comparing the results of a variety of different approaches or representations. So, for instance, in terms of a metaphor in individual learning, a person might work out a mathematical formula and also have a visualization of the approximate answer based on world experience. If the answer from the mathematical formula is totally at odds with his or her intuition, then that is a cue that the formula is either inapplicable or that he or she has made an error.

Similarly, in the case of the million-person interface, individuals (and subgroups) would compare their outputs with those of many others and discrepancies would lead to resolution processes. If the resolution meant that the original output of the individual or group was ultimately wrong, that information can serve as information to "debug" the individual or group process and knowledge that led to the "wrong" answer.

13.5.2 Social Issues

As in the guidelines that Issaes suggest for Dialogue (Isaacs and Smith, 1994), it is important that the participants have some knowledge of the matter at hand, that they care about the results and that they have some legitimate power to do something. Not all topics then are appropriate for this kind of enterprise. Below are some suggested problem areas that might meet these criteria and where multiple viewpoints would be useful contributions, where it is not clear exactly how to pre-structure the problem.

- Deciding how we go about avoiding global ecological disaster
- Deciding what to do about the healthcare problems in the USA
- Deciding what to do about crime
- Deciding whether and how to go about colonizing space
- Deciding what to do about racism, sexism and ageism
- Deciding how to improve the million-person interface
- Deciding what to do about "drugs"

13.5.3 User Interface Design

The key to improving the mapping function among conversations to that which is relevant to the individual user would be providing the system with feedback on the relevance of particular conversations in real time so that the mapping algorithm could be continuously updating and improving itself. Today, this is accomplished in some Web-based systems by having the user take a specific separate step of rating. In the envisioned system, however, the user's attentional mechanisms would be gauged automatically by noting head and eye movements.

13.5.4 Technological Issues

As indicated by the analysis in Section 13.3, the main difficulty in extending natural language conversation, Dialogue and story exchange to the million-person case is that language does not "compose" well. Ten stories might share a lot in meaning space, reflecting the same problem-solving pattern applied even in similar contexts with similar outcomes. The stories might even use many of the same words. But "played" to a human listener simultaneously, the result would largely be cacophony. A listener might attend to one story, or switch among them, but the experience would probably be less educational and less pleasant than simply listening to one story.

13.5.5 Ethical Issues

Is there a way to design the system so that not only is the group more intelligent while functioning, but also so that the individuals involved gain something *qua* individual? In other words, we want to avoid building a system that would have the effect of lessening the individual's capabilities. In a well-run supervisory therapy group, for instance, each of the individual therapists gains expertise from the feedback and suggestions of others, thereby presumably becoming a more effective individual therapist. Similarly, in a well-run creative writing class, individuals improve from the feedback of others. In a tournament structure, people improve by playing their skills off against one another.

13.6 Scenario of Use

In order to visualize what such an interaction space might look like, imagine 100 000 people filing up the University of Michigan stadium (or the University of Colorado or the stadium of your own choosing). The participants are a large subset of the people of Ann Arbor and have come together to deal with the issues of maintaining economic growth and prosperity while also trying to maintain quality of life and ecological sustainability. They have the political power to enact whatever outcome or outcomes result from this large-scale interaction.

Now, we can imagine that they are not in fact at a physical stadium but at a virtual stadium (holding 1 million people) where an intelligent computer switching matrix can rapidly alter the mapping among individuals. In the center of the virtual stadium is a very large, semi-shared multimedia three-dimensional graph structure that illustrates the problem space and solution space that they are exploring and building. Each person feels surrounded by sights, sounds and a tactile environment every bit as exciting as when watching a football game. However, in this case, the people's actions directly influence what is happening "in the field" – not just in a global manner (where, for instance, the loudness of cheering may hearten the team), but also in very specific ways.

A participant, at any given time, might be engaged in conversation, story-sharing, sensori-motor behavior, Dialogue, simulated motion through space, meta-cognition or any combination.

In conversation, the person would be hearing many voices simultaneously aligned by speech technology, perhaps so that multi-sentences could be perceived. In such a multi-sentence, common threads would be heard "as though from everywhere at once". For instance, a person working on healthcare might hear, "The thing I most hate about Medical Doctors is..." omnidirectionally, as though from a huge choir. But the end of the sentence might appear as in many separate locations. Thus, "their snobbishness", "the way they try to control your life", "the expense", "the cost", "their egotism" etc. might seemingly come from different points in space and in individual voices. In this way, a person who at that moment was a listener might get an impression simultaneously of many things:

1. The emotional tone of the group
2. The variety of backgrounds represented
3. The variety of specific concerns
4. The correlation between background and concern

Presumably, some of the many concerns voiced would resonant most closely with the listener's own, either because he or she agreed and had experiences to share that supported that proposition or because the listener strongly disagreed and had experiences to share that would tend to contradict or build a fuller picture.

As the person began replying, it would be natural to turn slightly toward the voice of the person to whom he or she was responding. In effect, this would amplify the projected sound toward that person. Since, presumably, the "intelligent matrix" of computation would be putting like concerns nearby, the reply might be of interest to nearby people in addition to the one the person might be replying to. As the person began talking, the speech recognition engine would begin translating spoken words into an internal representation and dynamically matching the apparent topic of what was being said to the content of other ongoing conversations. In this way, the apparent spatial matrix of the person might be somewhat fluid, extremely fluid or fairly rigid depending on how quickly the tempo of that person's conversational topics changed relative to that of others.

As people began building stories that illustrated some aspect of their own experience with healthcare, we could further imagine the development of clusters of these stories based on "story values" – that is, what happened that was emotionally charged for the person: life/death, health/disease, power/loss of control and so on – as well as more specific substantive categories, such as specific diagnosis, treatment, prognosis outcome.

The experience of users would be something like entering a gigantic agora in which many people were talking about thousands of different things – then, almost magically, they would "find themselves" in a small corner talking to people with very similar concerns. Depending on the users' own behavior (and implied preferences), they might find themselves in heated debate, quiet chat, structured argumentation, story sharing or an open Dialogue.

In Dialogue mode (Section 13.4.8), we could imagine the computer could keep track of the various ideas and viewpoints that were generated, help build a representation of the interrelationship of these ideas and viewpoints, and help arrange Dialogue groups so that those within a group were working on some theme or topic.

We could also imagine a kind of sensori-motor visual interaction for certain kinds of problems in which rich, multilayered representations of data would be presented to people. If a person wished to, they could "zoom in" to a particular region or even a specific data point and hear "the story" behind that data point.

13.7 Scenarios of Non-Use and Misuse

In addition to the above somewhat fanciful scenario of use, it might also be worthwhile to consider some scenarios of possible non-use or misuse. In this way, we can hopefully begin to see further implications for the design of the interface, the context and the process.

13.7.1 Potential Problem: "If You Build It, They Won't Come"

The first hurdle is getting a very large number of people to participate in something that might or might not work. This is a problem, but not an insurmountable one.

People participated, for instance, in "Hands Across America" and actually paid money to do so. Nearly half of the eligible adults vote in national elections. Late each January, many millions of Americans tune in to watch low-fidelity images bounce about on a flat CRT (this is also known as the Super Bowl). If the million-person interface is properly designed and implemented (and advertised) so that the individuals feel that they make a contribution and feel that there is some possibility for really addressing these fundamental problems, I believe that sufficient numbers would participate.

13.7.2 Potential Problem: "If You Build It, They'll Sit on Their Thumbs"

In this scenario, people will sign up and show up, but people won't know what to do and will be reluctant to participate. In the service of preventing this problem, it would be important to teach people some of the component behaviors and set their expectations. In addition, by having a series of smaller successes, people will both learn what to do and gain some confidence in the system technology and in the other participants.

In a variant, people may know what to do, but be too unmotivated to do it. Again, the "tragedy of the commons" problems appears. As Huberman and Loch (1996) point out, the effectiveness of the group interacts with the motivation. As the group becomes more effective, it becomes more worthwhile for people (in their model) to participate. As the group becomes less effective, people may simply do as little as they can get away with. Again, this dilemma points to the importance of practice, but also means that some degree of identifiability of effort needs to be incorporated into the system.

A hopeful note also comes from the research of Axelrod (1984) that shows that a "cooperative strategy with limited retribution" in prisoner's dilemma games "wins out" when played by computer programs or by human teams. As the work of Karl-Henrik Robert shows, there are ways to enhance this effect.

13.7.3 Potential Problem: "If You Build It, They'll Go Numb"

In this scenario, people will attempt to do something, but the stimulation will be so different and disconnected from previous experiences that they will "zone out".

Many people have the experience of being at a cocktail party or conference reception and focusing in on one or two conversations while there are literally hundreds of others in the background. By using a combination of spatial positioning, speaker identity, proximity (correlated with volume), lip reading and meaning continuity, people can follow a conversation fairly well. It would seem that making the background noise more relevant, more synchronized, and making effective distance and positioning under the individual participants' control would net out to an improved experience of coherence.

13.7.4 Potential Problem: "If You Build It, They Won't Sum"

In this scenario, people will find some utility in the system, but the output will be less than the sum of the individual contributions. While it makes sense to try to design such a system based on what we know about good HCI and CSCW as well as naturalistic events involving large numbers of people, ultimately such a system will have to be tried; there will probably be emergent properties that are hard to predict.

13.7.5 Potential Problem: "If You Build It, They'll Grow Dumb"

In this scenario, people will find linear or superlinear utility, but by being in such a rich environment they may suffer some "withdrawal" – that is, become dependent on the environment for thinking. In the theory of aging and the growth of the organism–environment bond proposed by Thomas, a smaller scale version of this actually happens today. As people live, they age, and they are also adapting to their environment and adapting their environment to them. At least some of what we perceive to be the age-related effects of aging, are actually the natural result of increasing interdependence between an adapting, adaptive organism living in an environment over time. People come to rely on their social and technical context. If that context changes radically enough, people cannot be "as intelligent" in terms of measured effective output.

On the other hand, it is a common experience that participating in a group brain-storming meeting or attending a scientific or technical conference is often followed by a subsequent spurt of creative productivity on the part of the individuals. The social facilitation effect does not always seem to end coterminously with actual socialization. Therefore, it is also quite possible that people will leave such a "million-person interaction event" more motivated and intelligent than they other-wise would have been.

13.8 Research Agenda

The following research questions will have to be answered before a million-person interface will be effective.

First, what is the most effective sequencing of various interaction types? Are there new interaction types beyond those that smaller teams use that might emerge from a huge online group? What are the cues of behavior or time that mean it is time to move to another phase of interaction type?

Second, how can multiple conversations best be presented to people to balance the comprehensibility of a single thread and the awareness of multiple threads? How can tens, hundreds, or even thousands of conversations best be summarized ?

Third, how quickly should interest groups and communities be reorganized? Is there a way for people to trust and communicate in a non-disruptive fashion across fast-paced reorganizations?

13.9 Summary of Argument

There are problems that are crucial and time-critical which are not being solved today. The confluence of technological trends in the cost of bandwidth, storage and processing and the increase in knowledge and experience with how to design and use technology for human purposes for individuals, small teams and organizations leads us to believe that developing a million-person interface will be doable in the first few decades of the next millennium.

Acknowledgments

Thanks for interesting dialog on this topic with Donald Norman, Christine Halverson, Shelly Dews, Wendy Kellogg, Rachel Bellamy, Deborah Lawrence, Cynthia Kurtz, Peter Johnson-Lenz, Trudy Johnson-Lenz and Thomas Erickson, as well as with many members of the joint EC/NSF conference in Bonas.

References

Alexander, C, Ishikawa, S, Silverstein, M, Jacobson, M, Fiksdahl-King, I and Angel, S (1977) *A Pattern Language*, New York, Oxford University Press.
Axelrod, R (1984) *The Evolution of Cooperation*, New York, HarperCollins.
Barber, BR (1996) *Jihad vs. McWorld: How the World Is Both Falling Apart and Coming Together*, New York, Ballantine.
Bodker, S (1999) Scenarios in user-centered design – setting the stage for reflection and action, in *Proceedings of the 32nd Hawaii International Conference on System Sciences*, New York, IEEE.
Bohm, D (1994) *Thought as a System*, London, Routledge.
Bohm, D (1990) *On Dialogue*. Ojai, David Bohm Seminars.
Brooks, F (1975) *The Mythical Man-Month: Essays on Software Engineering*, Reading, MA, Addison-Wesley.
Bush, V (1945) As we may think, *The Atlantic Monthly*, July.
Collins, J. C. and Porras, J. I. Built to last: successful habits of visionary companies. New York: Harper/Collins, 1994.
De Gues, A (1997) *The Living Company: Habits for Survival in a Turbulent Business Environment*. Boston, MA, Harvard Business School Press.
Dumais, ST, Platt, J, Hecherman, D and Sahami, M (1998) Inductive learning algorithms and representations for text categorization, in *CIKM 1998*, pp. 148–155.
Dyson, FJ (1999) *The Sun, the Genome, and the Internet: Tools of Scientific Revolution*, New York, Oxford University Press.
Engelbart, D (1962) Augmenting human intellect: a conceptual framework. *AFOSR-3233. SRI Report*.
Finholt, TA and Olson, GM (1997) *From Laboratories to Collaboratories: A New Organizational Form for Scientific Collaboration"*, Ann Arbor, MI, University of Michigan.
Fischer, G (1999) Domain-oriented design environments: supporting individual and social creativity, in *Computational Models of Creative Design IV* (eds. J Gero and ML Maher), Sydney, Key Centre of Design Computing and Cognition, pp. 83–111.
Haeckel, S and Slywotzky, A (1999) *Adaptive Enterprise: Creating and Leading Sense-and-respond Organizations,* Cambridge, MA, Harvard Business School Press.
Huberman, BA and Loch, CH (1996) Collaboration, motivation, and the size of organizations, *Journal of Organizational Computing and Electronic Commerce*, 6, 109–130.
Isaacs, W and Smith, B (1994) Designing a dialogue session, in *The Fifth Discipline Fieldbook* (P Senge, R Ross, B Smith, C Roberts and A Kleiner), New York, Doubleday.

Isaacs, WN (1996) The process and potential of dialogue in social change, *Educational Technology*, Jan/ Feb, 20–30.

Jacobs, J (1992) *Systems of Survival*, New York, Vintage.

Kotter, JP and Heskett, JL (1992) *Corporate Culture and Performance*, New York, The Free Press.

Lipnack, J. and Stamps, J. Virtual teams. New York: Wiley, 1997.

McKee, R (1997) *Story*, New York, HarperCollins.

Massetti, B, White, NH and Spitler, VK (1999) The impact of the World Wide Web on idea generation, in *Proceedings of the 32nd Hawaii International Conference on System Sciences*, New York, IEEE.

Murray, JH (1997) *Hamlet on the Holodeck: the Future of Narrative in Cyberspace*, Cambridge, MA: MIT Press

Nisbett, RE and Wilson, TD (1997) Telling more than we know: verbal reports on mental processes, *Psychological Review*, 84, 231–259.

Norman, DA (1993) *Things That Make Us Smart*, Reading, MA, Addison-Wesley.

Oldenburg, R (1997) *The Great Good Place*, New York, Marlowe.

Ornstein, R and Ehlrich, P (1989) *New World New Mind*. New York, Simon & Schuster.

Paulos, JA (1998) *Once upon a Number: the Hidden Mathematical Logic of Stories*, New York, Basic Books.

Prietula, MJ, Carley, KM and Gasser, L (eds.) *Simulating Organizations*. Menlo Park, CA, AAAI.

Putnam, RD, Leonardi, R and Nanetti, R (1993) *Making Democracy Work: Civic Traditions in Modern Italy*, Princeton, NJ, Princeton University Press.

Schank, RC (1990) *Tell me a story: Narrative and intelligence*, Evanston, Northwestern University.

Smoliar, SW and Baker, JD (1999) Storytelling, jamming and all that jazz: knowledge creation in the world of new media, in *Proceedings of the 32nd Hawaii International Conference on System Sciences*, New York, IEEE.

Thomas, J (1995) Usability engineering in 2020, in *Advances in Human–Computer Interaction* (ed. J Nielsen), Norwood, NJ, Ablex.

Thomas, J (1996) The long term social implications of new information technology, in *New Infotainment Technologies in the Home: Demand Side Perspectives* (eds. R Dholakia, N Mundorf and N Dholakia). Hillsdale, NJ, Lawrence Erlbaum Associates.

Tufte, ER (1990) *Envisioning Information*, Cheshire, CT: Graphics Press.

Turner, M (1996) *The Literary Mind*, New York, Oxford University Press.

Underwood, P (1993) *The Walking People: a Native American Oral History*, San Anselmo, CA, Tribe of Two Press.

Wason, PC and Johnson-Laird, PC (1972) *Psychology of Reasoning: Structure and Content*, Cambridge, MA, Harvard University Press.

Whittaker, S, Terveen, L, Hill, W and Cherny, L (1998) The dynamics of mass interaction, in *Proceedings of CSCW '98*, New York, ACM.

Applications and Tools

14

Application Drivers for Virtual Environment Technology Development

David Arnold

Abstract

There is evidence that the promise of virtual reality has been over-hyped to date and VE applications are being assimilated more slowly than proponents would like, comparable to CAD, and in particular CAAD, in the 1970s. However, research funding, at least in the EU, is being targeted increasingly at predefined exploitation. To attract research funds, visionary but believable "killer apps" are needed against which current technology can be measured. The gap between required and existing technologies can be used to define an implementation path and required research directions. This chapter therefore reviews VE technology and the needs of sustainable cultural heritage projects to define the pressing needs for research progress.

14.1 Introduction

In the early days of computer graphics applications, perhaps 30 years ago, the newish and rapidly emerging discipline, with obvious applications and exploitation potential, benefited from a very favourable climate for attracting research funding. At the same time, some research was built on the objective of achieving particular applications which were often not only well beyond the bounds of the current technology, but also beyond the comprehension of the business sector which the application was intended to serve. Luckily, in those halcyon days the funders were less aggressive about comparing intended research results with what was actually achieved.

In Computer-Aided Architectural Design, for example, a wide range of applications were being predicted – not only relating working drawings to visualizations but through helping the design process, performing structural calculations, checking utilities access and producing bills of quantities etc. In the extreme these applications removed the need for architects completely, starting from site maps and requirements specifications and providing the creative impetus as well!

In reality, architectural practices were only incrementally affected by the onset of technology. It has taken probably 25 years to realize the data processing predictions of the early 1970s, and the creative aspirations seem unlikely to threaten practicing professionals, except in so far as the tools allow the clients more direct interaction with the design process.

To an extent, the same frustratingly slow adoption of technology remains in many potential application areas today, but the parameters have shifted significantly. It is still easy to think of applications (particularly applications using graphics extensively) which are not sustainable with current technology. Market sectors still have difficulty visualizing the ways in which current technology will affect their businesses and still more difficulty in envisaging the pace at which technological potential is moving and creating new business models. Business practice therefore moves somewhat more slowly.

There seems to be an unwritten law that technology will affect application areas at rate proportional to the inverse square of the magnitude of the potential advance! In other words, the more trivial the change, the faster it is adopted, but always rather more slowly than the proponents would like. This has been as true for virtual environment applications as for other areas [1,2]. Those who apply for research funds must continually balance the long-term vision of where the work could lead with the promises of what will be delivered in a single project's time-scale, while still attracting support.

At the same time the 1990s trends of accountability for research funds and applicability of research results will, of course, produce their own range of distortions on the process of conducting research. However, it is clear that keeping funders firmly focused on the potential applicability of research results is an integral part of current wisdom, and this in a sense brings us back to the mindset of the early 1970s. The visionary applications need to be defined to show what we would like to do, but can't. This then allows the specification of a program of research to allow us to achieve the application. The difference from the 1970s is that we need to combine realism with vision and be more precise about how and when we think the goals are achievable.

14.2 Current Adoption of VE Technologies

Carl Machover, in a recent survey of the use of technologies related to graphics [23], reports that VR business is currently turning over about US$1 billion. He has predicted that this will grow by about 20% compound over the subsequent five years to US$2.5 billion by 2003. For 3D graphics he reports almost as much growth (17%), from US$20 billion to US$46 billion in 2003. These levels of activity in the underlying hardware and software systems translate into orders of magnitude more activity in the applications which use the technology, but where is this activity concentrated?

There are a number of recent market surveys on the application areas which are adopting these technologies [2,3]. At a recent event held in Brussels there were verbal reports from a number of European participants in VR projects, although this is only a sample of the level of activity [4]. In addition, industrial sessions at major events have provided examples of the increasing use of VEs, although these are again only snapshots of pockets of activity [5–7].

Almost any area which in the mid-1980s would have been described as a potential application of 3D Computer Graphics is now considered by at least some as a potential VE application. For some application domains (e.g. architecture, automotives and aerospace) developments of VE applications will follow their gradual incorporation of CAD systems over the past 20 years. For these applications it is inevitable that the technologies will affect every aspect of the business eventually, and the questions are more to do with timing and market advantage. These are applications which have developed from the generative computer graphics of the design professional.

In other areas the applications are, or will be, a progression from imaging systems originally developed for remote sensing. The most obvious of these is medicine, where considerable advances have been made in the last decade in the application of different imaging techniques, which now produce a vast range of images. Skillful analysis of these images can be used to automatically reconstruct the 3D world from which the images were taken. Other examples would include simulation of hazardous environments – remote manipulators for undersea work, maintenance in nuclear power stations, remote vehicles for exploring after natural disasters etc.

The applications that will be developed first are those for which the greatest payback can be anticipated, where payback may be measured in either cost or functional terms. For example, engineering design problems where the time to market can be reduced may save on the development costs of the product, but some of that saving may be put into designing a better product and delivering a bigger market share. Similarly, in a less commercially orientated sector (e.g. medicine), there may be a premium placed on results (e.g. more effective diagnosis and treatment) and some additional costs may be acceptable.

For the purposes of this chapter I want to look at the entertainment and virtual heritage areas of application. These are important related sectors of the market, requiring dramatic impact to engender a "Wow" factor. The technology to drive them appears to be ripening for a step change in the applications' potential.

14.2.1 Entertainment

VE-related techniques are used extensively in entertainment. At the low end the videogames industry is continually pushing the bounds of the possible of current chip technology, both by inventing the chipsets needed for this type of computation and by refining the computational process to run as efficiently as possible. Games on the Internet are also pioneering the use of internetworked virtual environments with thousands of simultaneously active users in a shared virtual space, although at present this is not a realistically rendered 3D world. The computer games industry is also the single largest user of motion capture facilities [8].

The top end of videogames includes publicly sited large-screen augmented reality experiences, such as the racing car simulators seen in games arcades all over the place. Recently this industry sector has expanded with the opening in 1998 of DisneyQuest in Orlando, the first of a proposed worldwide chain of themed venues using virtual reality technology and including rides varying from white knuckle experiences to gentle explorations. One particularly imaginative attraction allows the visitors to design their own rollercoaster, which is then programmed onto a motion platform simulator [9].

Another market sector from the games and tourism arena is the motion platform VE ride. For example, Thomson Entertainment is an offshoot of the flight simulator business and now builds motion platforms which are combined with large screen displays. These are then programmed with a filmed ride sequence and the motion programming which simulates the experience. Increasingly the filmed rides are using computer-generated imagery of artificial environments with the latest developments including the use of stereo glasses and 3D film.

At the high end of imagery the film industry is increasingly using virtual sets and image composition to place real actors in unreal and unachievable situations. Most striking perhaps of the recent examples of this has been the widely reported use of virtual sets and virtual actors in the film *Titanic* [10]. In television the use of virtual sets is gaining acceptance, allowing actors or reporters to be recorded independently of the recording of the setting in which they perform [11,12].

In many ways the pressures of the entertainment sector create the developments that other market sectors will use. The games sector pushes the envelope of the achievable in high-volume consumer products (e.g. Nintendo's collaboration with Silicon Graphics to produce the Nintendo 64 chip sets), which in turn influence the PC market and the implementation of graphics accelerator cards. The film industry can devote budgets that others cannot commit to pushing hard at the envelope in high-quality techniques (for example the rendering of special effects; the activity of autonomous agents; the registration of real actors and virtual sets; and the modeling techniques for complex natural environments).

Increasingly projects which use networked games on the Internet as examples of multi-user collaborative environments [13,14] will demonstrate solutions to the demands on technologies supporting these environments in other sectors. Similar experiments have also been, and are continuing to be conducted in shared artistic, cultural and other social interactive environments [15,16].

14.2.2 Virtual Museums and Heritage

This is a huge area of potential application in which any geographic region has Unique Selling Points (USPs), but where the development of content is a monumental task. Europe has particular advantages in having obvious cultural heritage in the form of the volume of historic buildings which are in use today. To offset the costs of implementation, the potential paybacks are, however, equally large both in terms of the enhanced preservation and access to rich cultural heritage and in the potential enhancement of tourist revenues, in many cases in regions of economic deprivation in the modern world and rich history in the past.

Most of the experiments in virtual museums have been more multimedia projects than virtual environments. However, they do have to explore the limits of communications bandwidths and interworking between different technologies. For example, the SICMA project [17] has been examining the problems of connecting the Natural History Museum collections in London with Belgian households, using a mixture of ATM and cable TV technologies. Similarly, the VISEUM project is examining the use of ATM in connecting the National Gallery to locations in Canada [18]. There are other projects supported by the EU in this area [19,20].

There have been a large number of experiments in recreating virtual environments of historic sites. These are intended to offer the opportunity to recreate environments which have been destroyed and to enhance the remaining evidence of these site. They can be used by historians to describe alternative views of past environments, and provide a digital archive that does not suffer from wear when visited by large numbers of virtual tourists. A scan of the Internet will find examples of projects such as the Virtual Stonehenge, Cluny Abbey and the Coliseum in Rome. It is certain that such virtual environments will find increasing use in the promotion of historic sites, both remotely and at the actual site. It is also certain that the areas modeled will increase. For example, the Berlin model quoted early is an attempt to re-create central Berlin in the 19th century [21].

For visitors on site there are also potential applications of augmented reality, since the visitor will be viewing the modern day scene but could have this augmented with reconstructions of past environments. The HIPS project is exploring related problems of mixing the physical space and the information sources related to them in a combined augmented reality application [22]. However, there are clear and obvious problems in viewing augmented reality in an existing physical site, particularly where the circulation routes have changed with time (e.g. demolished staircases or blocked-off doorways).

14.3 Summary of Current Status

So far, experience of VE applications is patchy. There are undoubtedly many application areas where a responsive, networked, interactive, quality, inexpensive, virtual environment would be a considerable asset. Unfortunately, with current technologies the various attributes must be traded off and the resulting application is unlikely to be able to meet the aspirations of its developers. This is not an uncommon situation for technological developments.

The nearest equivalent case would be the introduction of CAD systems in drafting, engineering design, architecture and cartography. The potential was recognized quite early, but it was at least 15 years from the identifiable start of experimental projects before the economics of the implementations reached significant numbers of users. In the case of virtual environments performance is critical to the success of the application. If the virtual environment does not respond fast enough you don't just have a bad application – typically you would have an application that cannot work, since the operator cannot use degraded performance.

Virtual environment applications have now reached the stage where many of the applications can be recognized, but for each of the desirable qualities listed above improvements are needed to turn potential use into commercially viable propositions. One of the lessons of the past is that adoption depends upon having a clear vision of how the potential of the technology can be realized as a sound business proposition. In the next section we will consider business motivations for virtual heritage from a number of perspectives

14.4 Potential Benefits: Why Develop "Virtual Heritage"?

The whole area of virtual heritage will become increasingly important as the time available for leisure increases and as the opportunities for tourism continue to grow. Tourism remains a growth industry, and in many areas where traditional industries have struggled to remain competitive tourism is the only growth industry. Virtual tourism (e.g. visiting sites on the Internet) and other outlets for realistic models (e.g. education and videogames) will add to the commercial viability of virtual heritage.

Motivations for the desirability of the approach are as variable as the vested interests of the participants. However, there are valid reasons for an interest in Virtual Heritage for almost all of those vested interests, from the tourist who wants an enjoyable experience, to the curator interested in preserving the original artifacts and the local politician interest in economic growth or regeneration of an area.

The beauty of the application area is that it brings together exciting technology and unique content. The technology needs to be leading-edge to create the "Wow" factor, while the content is unique to individual sites – there is only one original even if the digital content can be shipped around the world. Thus the virtual tourist attraction is always a digital trailer for the real thing, although the current remains may not match the visual spectacle of the virtual environment, particularly of an entertainment using the virtual environment as a theater setting.

However, VR offers new opportunities for future generations to appreciate the past and the present by allowing:

- Software and data archives as a new medium of preservation
- Controlled access to, and minimum interference with, original historic artifacts
- Education and appreciation of heritage
- New sources of finance for continuing historical research and research into preservation techniques
- Construction of tools that are less labor-intensive and techniques for accomplishing alternative time-variant reconstructions
- Scenarios which stretch current computational techniques and provide impetus to computing research

General appreciation of heritage can also be expected to generate more public support for heritage projects. This roll call of potential benefits potentially disguises the differences that each benefit implies for the work that needs to be undertaken. The objectives of archiving would be to preserve the complete heritage object at whatever level of detail was possible in anticipation that future (as yet unidentified) uses may require access to any part of the original. Education has similar objectives, but is likely to be more selective. At the other end of the spectrum, pure entertainment may require not only selective but also very high-quality sets. At times it seems to require the rewriting of the original facts to support the entertainment value of a storyline. Heritage attractions are unlikely to go this far, but it does seem likely that the sets developed for virtual heritage will disseminate into use for entertainment (e.g. videogames).

14.5 What It Takes

Potentially the VR heritage experience will give virtual visitors the opportunity to feel they are present at significant places and times in the past and to use a variety of senses to experience what it would have felt to be there. They might even have the opportunity to influence the historic outcomes and to investigate the consequences for alternative presents.

But we are not able to do this yet. Why not? What technologies remain to be researched and developed to create such rich, virtual heritage experiences in cost-effective projects? In computer graphics there have already been considerable successes in developing the technology required in three distinct areas:

- Providing visual simulations of modeled environments
- Displaying complex scenes in real time
- Allowing convenient user interaction

However, in all of these areas there is still some way to go.

Building a virtual heritage attraction must involve:

(a) Researching/writing a storyline, including scripts for actors (virtual or real)
(b) Collecting data for the set in digital form
(c) Designing the characters
(d) Scripting the repertoire of allowed audience interactions (which will include consideration of visitor throughput, length of experience etc.)
(e) Implementing the animations
(f) Building physical sets etc. and system integration

Actions (b)–(e) in particular are potential topics for targeted computing research.

To build the basis of commercially successful virtual heritage visitor attractions three components must be brought together – heritage, entertainment value and real-time technology. The heritage component is the content. It consists of the places, people and stories, in suitable digital formats, which are the basis of the entertainment. The important aspect is that the heritage only becomes suitable to exploitation when it is available in suitable digital format. Constructing sufficient volume of content will in itself require substantial developments in technologies in a number of areas:

- for efficient model definition and capture
- for defining the modeling approach so that the environments are in forms suitable for real-time display
- in providing assistance in the reconstruction of those environments from all forms of available historic data, particularly incomplete data

The entertainment aspect requires that the creative arts learn to use new media to best advantage – where best advantage is defined as being entertainment of the largest proportion of potential paying visitors. In this area new technologies are required to support the interactivity so as to intrigue and engage groups of tourists, while ensuring sufficient throughput for commercial return on visitor centers. Development is also required to understand the most appropriate characterization, scripting and direction of virtual humans within the virtual sets in order to stream-line the creation of content.

The technological developments required include support of the first two areas as indicated above, as well as development of the capabilities of current real-time interactive display systems. These latter developments include optimization of models for real-time display and more intelligent distribution of 3D models over networked systems. Solutions in both of these areas will require more intelligent approaches to the ways in which models are defined. In addition, in many cases sites of cultural importance are still in everyday use and digital models of the sites may be designed to accommodate other uses, varying from preservation and plan-ning to utilities servicing and transport system design.

The technology to run the entertainments is applicable to many heritage sites and subjects, so the economic model must be to offset research costs by ensuring they are shared across multiple sites.

Unlike the run-time technology, where development costs may be shared, the content development must involve unique problems and costs for each site or virtual set, since the work depends upon the actual site and the archive material available to describe it. However, there is still considerable opportunity for cost sharing in the development of tools for rapid acquisition of virtual environments.

14.6 Where Virtual Heritage Requires Computing Research

The major computing improvements for exploitable virtual heritage experiences relate to four areas:

(a) Improvements in models and their rendering
(b) Better and faster model acquisition
(c) More natural and effective user interfaces
(d) Multi-user distributed, inter-networked VEs

14.6.1 Improvements in Modeling and Rendering

There are many features of scenes that can be modeled in computer graphics given enough computing power and time. However, the features that can be rendered for real-time interaction are considerably more restricted at present.

In particular, much progress has been made and continues to be made in modeling natural features such as people [24,25], clothing [26], plants [27–29], water [30], wind [31], smoke [32] etc. for the purposes of generating visual simulations. However, all these features continue to be modeled very crudely if the scenes are to be available for real-time interaction. To incorporate such features in VEs requires not only the ability to model the feature, but also the ability to compute the results of the model fast enough. These results and the interaction between the feature and the rest of the scene have to be calculated at a frame rate which is fast enough to give the appearance of smooth motion.

Accurate representations of complex shapes can require very large amounts of data, both for shape and appearance. There are several approaches to achieving comparable descriptions with a low volume of data. Texturing, level of detail control [33] and procedural modeling [34] have all been used, with the objective of cutting down the volume of data to be handled by some part of the pipeline. However, there is still considerable potential for improvement in this area.

Efficient rendering of complex models also requires detailed consideration of the graphics rendering pipeline and tailoring of rendering processes to achieve maximum throughput of frame composition [35]. One aspect of this that requires substantial further development is the ability to assemble complex scenes comprising many characters and other potentially moving objects. Enabling the crowded scenes of infantry battles to be experienced interactively would be far beyond current real-time systems.

While the rendering of visual information has been given great attention and will continue to dominate the computational load in producing VEs, less attention has been paid to the modeling and synchronization of the data streams to other senses. For example, sound has an important role in immersive environments [36].

14.6.2 Better and Faster Model Acquisition

One inhibitor for the rapid adoption of virtual heritage attractions is the cost of data collection. To establish a virtual city is a major undertaking; to reconstruct an historic city requires even more work. Nevertheless, the establishment of a critical mass of content is a prerequisite to growing this market sector. Although adopt brute force and engaging in labor-intensive data capture projects will have its place, particularly initially, what we really need is more efficient ways of acquiring the data. This will involve more research.

Great progress has been made in recent years in the range of techniques for modeling scenes from images of them. Such techniques should be improved to allow further development of the ability to automatically reconstitute an environment from a number of images. These images could either be a related set of still images or, for example, the individual frames of a moving picture sequence [37]. The techniques are probably most widely applied to reconstruction of urban environments [38].

Motion capture has been used for a long time now in recording the movements of real actors and translating their motion to characters in an animated sequence. Improvements in scale, accuracy and reliability continue to be proposed [39], and there is still some way to go (e.g. in capturing the motion of groups, or *in situ* in natural environments). However, it is only recently that digitization of actual people has been extended to recording the appearance of a person fast enough to allow a reasonable prospect of modeling the user in the environment. There is still some way to go, however, to exploit this technology to allow virtual meetings with representations of real people in 3D, fully animated according to the movements of the individual, with synchronization of speech etc. [40].

14.6.3 More Natural User Interfaces

It is widely recognized that the psychology of user interface design can have a radical impact on the success of a computing application [41,42]. Developments in this area will address the broadening of the range of senses which are stimulated with more natural touch, gesture recognition and sound/speech interfaces [43], with haptic (force) feedback [44]. In addition the virtual environment will be brought into more common physical environments with the use of enhanced display technologies (brighter display media capable of being used in normal office lighting levels) [45,46]. There are also unresolved questions in the psychology of using systems large-scale projection systems [47] and head-mounted displays [48].

Haptic feedback will be an important component of many applications and will be used in a variety of ways. Examples include navigational use (force feedback to a joystick, or steering wheel which is used to navigate around a virtual environment), direct manipulation (manipulator arms [49] and specialist tools, such as syringes and remote manipulation of objects [50]), motion platforms (e.g. in vehicle simulators) and tactile feedback (tactile stimulation, possibly using special-purpose clothing both to record body position and provide sensory feedback). Work in this area needs to consider the integration of haptics into the model of the VE held in the graphics store, so that feedback is generated from descriptions of the scene on view. Some additional work on the standardization of the APIs in this area is needed [51].

Part of achieving a more natural feel will be the further development of adaptive interfaces and the use of intelligent agents. These will give "character" to the application [52] and to the HCI, with systems that learn the preferences of the user and are better able to interpret their intentions. Some relevant experiments have been initiated in this area with EU backing [53,54].

On top of the work needed to improve the ease with which an individual may interact with the virtual environment improvements and understanding are needed as to how the interaction should work in a cooperative environment. One possibility is to look to the technology of CSCW and the office of the future to see how well the business model would fit [45,46]. Integral to these considerations are the issues of handling complex virtual environments over the Internet in efficient ways. Significant research has concentrated on incremental update of distributed views of VEs [55–58] and much work continues to be needed if the goal of viewing complex, dynamic interactive environments is to reach the home.

14.7 The Need for Creativity

It would be difficult to over-emphasize the reliance that successful virtual heritage attractions will place on creativity. Perhaps those working in computer graphics will be best able to appreciate the point by considering the leap in entertainment value that short animations such as *Luxor Junior* or *Geri's Game* represent. Although both introduced new technology on the graphics scene, they were and will remain classics for the creative flair, entertainment and storylines that they used.

More explicit and complete visualization is an important aspect of making virtual reality feel "real". Verbal descriptions need only describe the most important elements of a scene – the mind of the listener will complete a rich enough environment from the key elements. As the medium moves to theater and cinema all visible facets of the entertainment area must be described in the appropriate detail, varying from an impression on a flat, painted backdrop to the construction of 3D facades, up to the use of complete buildings, whether real or specially constructed. In fact, even the explicit visual descriptions are often only defined to the level of detail needed, but with pictures there must be *something* at every position in the image.

This emphasis on set-building, on which to tell stories or play out dramas, highlights the importance of clear thinking about why particular work is undertaken. From the entertainment point of view particular buildings and streets will be required for particular dates. As with the fictional American western town which exists purely for filming and only as facades, the virtual set will extend only as far as the storyline requires. From the point of view of archiving and recording, any place and date is a reasonable candidate of interest, although some might be more likely to be sought out.

Virtual environments being used for entertainment with a variety of numbers of participants represent a new medium for the storyteller – and bring with them new challenges. Making the entertainment successful will require its own research. In a recent panel session, attention was drawn to the needs for substantial testing of the effectiveness of VR entertainments, with some using up to 20 rounds of revision and re-trial for audience acceptability [9].

14.8 Conclusions

The climate for bidding successfully for research funding in Europe has been changing continuously over the last 15 years, with a vision of exploitation increasingly seen as the key element of successful bids. In this chapter we have seen how many distinct lines of research from the point of view of the problem can be integrated into a common framework from the point of view of the intended application.

Apart from the general issue of how to present and package research proposals, virtual heritage is also an interesting and potential important topic from the point of view of Europe Inc., because Europe has some notable advantages in potential exploitation of the technologies.

Finally, addressing the requirements for developments in this area will require truly interdisciplinary work addressing creative writing, history, archaeology, psychology and human factors as well as the underpinning technology. These are truly exciting times.

Acknowledgments

This work has been supported in part by the ETHOS project (EC Telematics Applications Programme Project SU1105). I am grateful too for the suggestions and comments from colleagues, in particular to Andy Day.

References

[1]   DB Arnold and AM Day (1999) *Generic Technologies for Virtual Environments*, ETHOS Project (EC Telematics Applications Programme Project SU1105), Deliverable 16(3), February.
[2]   VR for Europe: industrial application of VR, *Report 1786-DOC-97-D-2700-C0017165*, A Study funded by the European Commission DG XIII, Project Officer Patrick Van Hove. Enquiries: pierre.bouchon@syseca.thomson.fr.
[3]   *The Market for Visual Simulation/Virtual Reality*, CyberEdge Information Services, 1st edn, November 1997; 3rd edn, July 2000, http://www.cyberedge.com/.
[4]   *Report on VE in Europe Workshop*, Brussels, 25 June 1998 (more information available from Frampton@cyberwizard.com).
[5]   *Industry Case Studies, Proceedings of 14th Eurographics Workshop on Virtual Environments*, 16–18 June 1998, Stuttgart, Germany.
[6]   C Cruz-Neira (1998) Overview of virtual reality, in *Course 14 "Applied Virtual Reality"*, SIGGRAPH98 Course notes, July.
[7]   *Proceedings of Eurographics98 Conference, Lisbon*, September 2–4, 1998, *Computer Graphics Forum*, 17(3).
[8]   Ultima Online, http://www.owo.com/.
[9]   R Pausch (Moderator) (1998) Location-based entertainment: the next generation, Panel Session at SIGGRAPH 98, in *Conference Abstracts and Applications, SIGGRAPH 98, 25th International Conference on Computer Graphics and Interactive Techniques*, 19–24 July, Orlando, FL, p. 212.
[10] D Loeb and A Bustanoby (1998) *Titanic* and digital character animation, animation sketches, in *Conference Abstracts and Applications, SIGGRAPH 98*, 19–24 July 1998, p. 309.
[11] *Manipulation of Images in Real-Time for the Creation of Artificially Generated Environments*, ACTS Project No. AC044, Start 1 September 1995; Duration 36 months, http://www.itc.co.uk/.
[12] *Virtual Interactive Studio Television Application using Networked Graphical Supercomputers*, FPIV/Esprit Project 22517, Start 1 August 1996; Duration 30 months, http://www.cordis.lu/esprit/src/results/pages/infoind/.

[13] *AMUSEMENT*, FPIV/Esprit Project 25197, Start 1 September 1997; Duration 24 months, http:// www.i3net.org/projects/.

[14] *CO-NEXUS*, FPIV/Esprit Project 25598, Start 1 August 1997; Duration 24 months, http:// www.i3net.org/projects/.

[15] *Electronic Arena*, FPIV/Esprit Project 25379, Start 1 September 1997; Duration 24 months, http:// www.i3net.org/projects/.

[16] *Magic Lounge*, FPIV/Esprit Project 25458, Start 1 July 1997; Duration 24 months, http:// www.i3net.org/projects/.

[17] *Scalable Interactive Continuous Media Server – Design and Application*, ACTS Project No. AC071, Start 1 September 1995; Duration 36 months, http://www.uni-paderborn.de/.

[18] *Virtual Museum International*, ACTS Project No. AC238, Start -1 Sept 1996; Duration 36 months, hellwig@deteberkom.de.

[19] *Museums Over States and Virtual Culture*, FPIV/Other Project TI 1.31, Start 1 January 1997; Duration 12+24 months, http://mosaic.infobyte.it/.

[20] *Promoting Museums through technology-based Article 10 Information Services*, FPIV/Other Project 96.00.29.044.AD, Start 1 January 1997; Duration 24 months, http://www.promise-eu.org/.

[21] I Braun, A Kutzner, B Bohme, U Simmons, A Striepe, C Quintus, A Knoche and L Schafer (1998) Time travels in virtual landscapes, in *Conference Abstracts and Applications, SIGGRAPH 98*, 19–24 July, p. 283.

[22] *HIPS, Human Interaction with Physical Spaces*, FPIV/Esprit Project 25574, Start 1 July 1997; Duration 24 months, http://www.i3net.org/projects/.

[23] Carl Machover Associates, SIGGRAPH98 Press Release.

[24] N Badler, D Metaxas, A Bruderlin, A Goldberg, K Perlin and N Thalmann (1998) Course 28 "Virtual Humans: Behaviors and Physics, Acting and Reacting", *SIGGRAPH98 Course notes*, July.

[25] D Archer (1999) *Modelling Humans, Technical Briefing, ETHOS Project* (EC Telematics Applications Programme Project SU1105), http://www.ethoseurope.org/, February.

[26] D House, D Baraff, B Eberhardt, W Strasser, J Eischen, M Schweppe, N Thalmann and U Thumrugoti. Course 31 "Cloth and Clothing in Computer Graphics", *SIGGRAPH98 Course notes*, July.

[27] O Deussen, P Hanrahan, M Pharr, B Lintermann, R Mech and P Prusinkiewicz (1998) Realistic modeling and rendering of plant ecosystems, in *Proceedings of 25th International Conference on Computer Graphics and Interactive Techniques*, 19–24 July, Orlando, FL, pp. 275–266.

[28] D Terzopoulos, B Blumberg, P Prusinkiewicz, C Reynolds, K Sims and D Thalmann (1998) Course 22 "Artificial Life for Graphics, Animation, Multimedia, and Virtual Reality", *SIGGRAPH98 Course notes*, July.

[29] AMAP/CIRAD Landscape Design Software Information, http://www.cirad.fr/ amap.html.

[30] D Mould and Y-H Yang (1997) Modeling water for computer graphics, *Computers & Graphics*, 21(6), 801–814.

[31] Onyx Computing, *Tree EIAS Storm*, Animating trees in wind, http://www.onyxtree.com/.

[32] HW Jensen and PH Christensen (1998) Efficient simulation of light transport in scenes with participating media using photon maps, in *Proceedings of 25th International Conference on Computer Graphics and Interactive Techniques*, 19–24 July, Orlando, FL, pp. 311–320.

[33] G Taubin, J Rossignac, M Deering, H Hoppe, P Schroder and H-P Seidel (1998) Course 21 "3D Geometry Compression", *SIGGRAPH98 Course notes*, July.

[34] DW Fellner, S Havemann, G Müller (1998) Modeling of and Navigation in Complex 3D Documents, *Computers & Graphics*, 22(6).

[35] H Igehy, G Stoll and P Hanrahan (1998) The design of a parallel graphics interface, in *Proceedings of 25th International Conference on Computer Graphics and Interactive Techniques*, 19–24 July, Orlando, FL, pp. 141–150.

[36] Z Ai and T Frohlich (1998) Molecular dynamics simulation in virtual environments, in *Proceedings of Eurographics98 Conference*, Lisbon, 2–4 September, *Computer Graphics Forum*, 17(3), 267–274.

[37] T Moons, J Vanderkerckhove and L Van Gool (1998) Automatic modelling and 3D construction of urban house roofs from high resolution aerial imagery, in *Computer Vision ECCV 98* (eds. H Burkhardt and B Neumann) (Vol. 1 of the Proceedings of the 5th European Conference on Computer Vision), Freiburg, Germany, June, Berlin, Springer-Verlag, pp. 410–425.

[38] J Cooper (1999) *Modelling Urban Forms, Technical Briefing*, ETHOS Project (EC Telematics Applications Programme Project SU1105), http://www.ethoseurope.org/.

[39] E Foxlin, M Harrington and G Pfeifer (1998) Constellation: a wide range wireless motion tracking system for augmented reality and virtual set applications, in *Proceedings of 25th International Conference on Computer Graphics and Interactive Techniques*, 19–24 July, Orlando, FL, pp. 371–378.

[40] JD Foley (1998) The convergence of graphics and imaging, *Keynote Address at Eurographics98*, Lisbon, 2–4 September 1998, *Computer Graphics Forum*, 17(3) (see *ETHOS Newsletter*, December 1998 for conference report).

[41] J Deisinger, C Cruz-Neira and O Riedel (1997) The effect of different viewing devices for the sense of presence, in *Proceedings of HCI'97*, San Francisco, CA, 24–29 August.

[42] M Wraga, S Bryson, M Kaiser, J Loomis, M Mine, J Schell, R Pausch and D Proffitt (1998) Course 38 "Immersive Environments: Research, Applications, and Magic", *SIGGRAPH98 Course notes*, July.

[43] *SCATIS project (Spatially Coordinated Auditory/Tactile Interactive Scenario)*, FPIII/Esprit Project 6358, Start 1 September 1992; Duration 36 + 3 months, `http://www.cordis.lu/esprit/src/results/pages/infoind/infind9.htm`.

[44] A Courtenay (1999) *Haptic Feedback Devices*, Technical Briefing, ETHOS Project (EC Telematics Applications Programme Project SU1105), `http://www.ethoseurope.org/`.

[45] A van Dam (1998) Frontiers in user–computer interaction, *Keynote Address at Eurographics98*, Lisbon, 2–4 September 1998, *Computer Graphics Forum*, 17(3) (see *ETHOS Newsletter* December 1998 for conference report).

[46] R Raskar, G Welch, M Cutts, A Lake, L Stesin and H Fuchs (1998) The Office of the future: a unified approach to image-based modeling and spatially immersive displays, in *Proceedings of 25th International Conference on Computer Graphics and Interactive Techniques*, 19–24 July, Orlando, FL, pp. 179–188.

[47] R Blach, A Simon and O Riedel (1997) Experiences with user interactions in a CAVE™-like projection environment, in *Proceedings of HCI'97*, San Francisco, CA, 24–29 August.

[48] W Bauer and O Riedel (1996) Ergonomic issues for virtual reality systems: head mounted displays, in *Proceedings of the Virtual Reality World '96*, 13–15 February.

[49] I Poupyrev, S Weghorst, M Billinghurst and T Ichikawa (1998) Egocentric object manipulation in VEs: an empirical evaluation of interaction techniques, in *Proceedings of Eurographics98 Conference*, Lisbon, 2–4 September, *Computer Graphics Forum*, 17(3), 41–52.

[50] JD Mulder (1998) Remote object translation methods for virtual environments, in *Proceedings of 4th Eurographics Workshop on Virtual Environments*, 16–18 June, Stuttgart, p. 10.7.

[51] D Arnold, A Courtenay and D Duce (undated) Haptic device control – does it fit and if so how?. Submitted working paper

[52] *Sid and the Penguins. A demonstration of the IMPROV system*, `http://www.mrl.nyu.edu/` (see also "Characters on the Internet", Panel Session at SIGGRAPH 98, in *Conference Abstracts and Applications, SIGGRAPH 98*, 19–24 July, p. 225.

[53] *COVEN (Collaborative Virtual Environments)*, ACTS Project AC040, Start 1 September 1995; Duration 48 months, `http://chinon-csf.fr/projects/coven/`.

[54] *COMRIS (Co-habited Mixed-Reality Information Spaces)*, FPIV/Esprit Project 25500, Start 1 July 1997; Duration 24 months, `http://www.i3net.org/projects/`.

[55] A Huxor (1998) Grounding and awareness management: two architectural principles for collaborative virtual worlds, in *Proceedings of 14th Eurographics Workshop on Virtual Environments*, 16–18 June, Stuttgart, Germany, p. 8.1.

[56] D Harvey (1999) *Distributed Large VE Models*, Technical Briefing, ETHOS Project (EC Telematics Applications Programme Project SU1105), `http://www.ethoseurope.org/`.

[57] Y Man and D Cohen-Or (1997) Selective pixel transmission for navigating in remote virtual environments, *Proceedings of Eurographics97 Conference*, Budapest, 4–8 September, *Computer Graphics Forum*, 16(3), 201–206.

[58] F Sillion, G Drettakis and B Bodelet (1997) Efficient impostor manipulation for real time visualization of urban scenery, in *Proceedings of Eurographics97 Conference*, Budapest, 4–8 September, *Computer Graphics Forum*, 16(3), 207–218.

15

3D Data Visualization Components on the Web – Results from AVS's Involvement in Several EC Esprit Research Projects

Mikael Jern

Abstract

With the increasing use of electronic documents on the Web, the opportunity to provide interactive data visualization techniques within scientific and engineering reports has become practicable. This evolution of Web-based visualization components allows the author of a report to distribute a Word or Excel document with embedded 3D data visualization viewers.

Answering the call is a new realm of data exploration tools called *Knowledge Management* (KM). This is a process that provides technology to address the challenge of discovering and exploiting information. KM applications are improving the decision-making capabilities of companies by performing spatial and multivariate visual data analysis and providing rapid access to comprehensible information. This chapter examines the visualization tools and issues needed by most businesses – how to turn their data into knowledge and make this knowledge accessible to persons who rely on it. The role of information visualization techniques and the visual user interface in the overall knowledge management process is assessed.

The objective of the EC-funded CONTENTS project is to develop customizable application components for the interactive visual analysis of data within the KM process. The data of interest are large multivariate business-related data sets generated in a distributed and heterogeneous environment.

The visualization components will be based on the emerging industry-standard ActiveX/DCOM archi-tecture, and will be properly "bridged" towards CORBA-based architectures for multi-platform porta-bility and compatibility. CONTENTS will help to improve European awareness of object-oriented component technology in a distributed environment based on the industry standard DCOM.

Industrial partner Unilever will drive the KM project with its pragmatic practical user needs. Industrial partners AVS, AET and Intecs will provide their high-tech competence and experience in data reduction and visualization, image processing and management, multi-platform component design and re-engineering.

The integration of data warehousing, spreadsheet, information visualization, Web and new visual interaction techniques will change and expand the paradigms of current work of humans using computers. Knowledge management will improve visual communication that takes place in all elements of the user interface and provide decreased "time-to-enlightenment".

15.1 Introduction

In industries ranging from financial services to medical imaging, new discovery is being hampered by information overload. Gigabytes of data must be turned into actionable knowledge that transforms complex information into insight. Powerful computer resources, once reserved for a select few, have become available to the desktop user. As a result, these users have gained access to complex databases that are orders of magnitude larger than in the past, but without the accompanying tools that allow them to gain meaningful insights from this wealth of information.

Today's desktops are visually challenged. Tremendous potential exists to increase the types of representations of, and interactions with, data. Typically, business graphics displays and interactive operations are defined by, and frequently limited to, the functionality provided by spreadsheet programs. Spreadsheet functionality, while invaluable, does not provide display types that adequately show data containing a large number of variable interrelationships, or *high data dimensionality*. Furthermore, the *two-way graph interactivity* required for analytical operations such as drill-down and slice-and-dice on warehouse data is not available from standard spreadsheet charting tools designed for data presentation.

Data warehouses and spreadsheets provide a foundation for the information discovery process. By storing large amounts of consolidated data, they provide the fast response times required by analytical applications. Applications built on top of a data warehouse or spreadsheet, in addition to analyzing data, must often shield the user from the underlying data extraction operations.

To present information, analysis results are often displayed using tables, graphs and charts. However, common business graphs, designed to show only one- or two-variable relationships, may be insufficient for representing multivariate information. While graph types such as pie, bar and line graphs can be clustered to provide combined views of several variables, spreadsheet-style graphs may be insufficient for representing complex multivariate information such as that contained in a data warehouse. The static presentational nature of these graphs often means they are not suitable as visual interfaces.

The sheer quantity of data in a data warehouse and spreadsheet presents challenges to effective data utilization. With data repositories easily accumulating many hundreds of gigabytes of data, identifying what data is relevant, and being able to retrieve it an acceptable amount of time, are still formidable challenges.

Visual tools are required that can explore and analyze very large, complex multidimensional data sets both locally and over the Internet. Conventional data exploration tools fall short of this goal. Standard 2D business graphics tools aren't adequate for multivariate data sets, and 3D scientific visualization is too complex for most users. Answering the call is a realm of data exploration tools called *Information Visualization*.

15.2 Challenges

The evolution in information visualization is presenting many technological challenges, but perhaps the greatest challenge is in retaining the intimate involvement and understanding of the end user. The traditional interfaces of mouse, keyboard and screens of text allow us to work *on* the desktop computer, while information visualization truly enables us to work *with* the desktop computer. There are major challenges in providing the perfect information visualization tools that will change and expand the paradigms of current work of humans using computers.

The **first challenge** is *locating and retrieving the relevant data* from a data world which is growing in size, but is also declining in average information content. Our ability, however, to consume information is largely unchanged. Tools will be required to *navigate* efficiently to retrieve specific data, to *explore* data surrounding a topic of general interest, and effortlessly *browse* the wider data world.

The **second challenge** is *understanding the complexity*, i.e. the conversion of appropriate data to relevant information. This can be achieved by maintaining a high level of human involvement and participation in the processing and analysis of data through visual interaction with the data analysis process. Information visualization retains our involvement and understanding, and ensures that we do not generate abstract solutions that are divorced from the original problem. Consider the simple example of regression analysis to fit a straight line. Seeing the points and regression line in the same graph provides an immediate understanding of the process. We can easily spot weaknesses in the interpretation.

The **third challenge** of information visualization techniques is to *find interfaces and display formats* that maximize information content in applications without introducing corresponding levels of application complexity. Visual tools, in addition to representing information, can act to simplify an application's user interface, and by so doing contribute to the application's acceptance on the business desktop.

The **fourth challenge** is in effectively *communicating a vision*, such that it is accurately shared and understood by a wider and less specialist audience. Web-based information visualization tools will provide solutions.

Although advanced data mining techniques are available, they often appear as inaccessible "black box" solutions with a poor user interface and cannot be changed by the users. The **final challenge** is to provide "*open*" and "*customizable*" visualization tools to better integrate the visual user interface with the data mining process. These tools must comply with an industry-standard architecture, such as DCOM/ActiveX or Java.

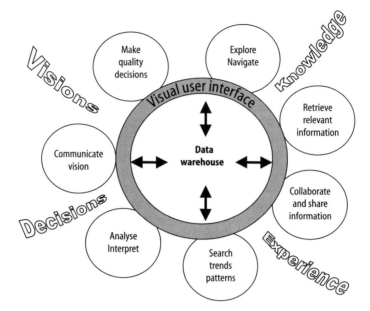

Figure 15.1 Conversion of data to informed decisions and shared knowledge in the overall knowledge management (KM) process provided by a set of tasks (circles).

15.3 The Overall Knowledge Management Process

The important features required from the information visualization tools in a KM process are (see Figure 15.1):

1. Full integration with the data warehouse or spreadsheet process by which data is brought together and stored in a multidimensional data structure.
2. A set of information visualization tasks which may be undertaken by the user.
3. Different categories of users who impose different goals on the process.
4. Visual user interface layer with support for both local and network interaction – "Thin" and "Fat" client scenarios.
5. Web-based component architecture (DCOM/ActiveX or Java).
6. Tight integration between data and visualization supporting "drill-down" features.
7. Customizable and user-friendly solutions instead of inaccessible "black boxes"
8. Sharing of increased knowledge though better "communication" tools.

15.4 Role for Information Visualization in KM

The fundamental purpose of any visualization is to communicate information to users. Visualization sits at the interface between what machines are good at (data information) and what people are good at (knowledge, experience). The overall objective of visual communication that takes place in all phases of a visualization process is to provide decreased "*time-to-enlightenment*".

Information visualization is the glue within the KM process and the user will be able to navigate within this process. The information visualization tasks enables data analysts to quickly analyze large quantities of information (millions of entities), aiding quick understanding of data distributions and rapid detection of patterns. This activity "*explore*" naturally takes place before the detailed specific analysis "*understanding complexity*", which may employ statistical and data mining tools. Finally, information visualization is a powerful tool to "*communicate*" and "*navigate*" through the results of a KM process.

There are three important roles for Information Visualization in the KM process:

- **Explore** (What if?, interaction, drill-down, VUI, integration, open tools)
- **Understanding complexity** (visual tools integrated with analysis process)
- **Communicate and navigate** (descriptive visualization, collaboration, Web)

Visualization components combine the use of industry standard component technology with advanced multidimensional data visualization. More important the visual user interface (VUI) capabilities provide tight integration with the underlying data repository. This integration includes "drill-down" features that enable you to get back to the real, underlying data, while working with the visual tasks. It is important at the outset that a "user interface" is not only a screen design but also a *method of interacting with the data warehouse and its data.*

15.5 Visual Exploration

> Discover relationships without prior knowledge of what is interesting

In this scenario, visualization techniques are used to scan rapidly through the large quantities of data enabling the user to search visually for patterns and relationships. The user will discover relationships without prior knowledge of what is interesting and important information. The aim is to directly engage the user in the KM process using visualization as a discovery tool, and as much as possible bring the user into "direct" association with the data. Visualization will present the data landscape in a natural and intuitive form, making full use of the human capacity to absorb and interact with complex images, far beyond typical directory structures or screens of text and numbers.

Visual exploration tools are:

- Integrated with data storage and data analysis (data warehouse, Excel etc.)
- Fast and interactive but easy to use
- Natural and intuitive visual interface
- Meaningful spatial relationship through 3D geographic visualization
- Multidimensional data analysis, filtering, segmentation, pattern identification

- Programmed to *"look for something interesting"*
- Open and customizable

A concept demonstrator has been developed using the Advanced Visual Systems' OpenViz DCOM/ActiveX components (visualization and visual interaction) and Microsoft's Visual Basic (user interface) to illustrate the use of an interactive visual interface for exploring data in a standard Excel spreadsheet (see Figure 15.6).

15.6 Communication

Discovered knowledge will help the user to make quality decisions

The final role of information visualization in the overall KM process is in effectively communicating a vision such that it is accurately shared and understood by the audience (Figure 15.2). This seemingly easy task can employ an entire marketing department in defining and conveying the features of a service. It is unlikely that the business managers and IT specialists will be able to find a common language for their discussions, but a common expression could be possible in a three-dimensional visual representation.

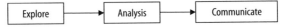
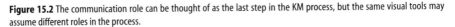

Figure 15.2 The communication role can be thought of as the last step in the KM process, but the same visual tools may assume different roles in the process.

Communication tools support the ability to draw the users focus to the key relationships already discovered and deliver enough information and in the right context for effective decision making. By preparing and presenting the data graphically, the user can uncover properties of the data and quickly and easily detect patterns or deviations from expected results. He or she can get a picture of "what the data is trying to tell him/her", and then perhaps confirm the observations with other statistical analysis.

The KM process allows the user to focus on what is important, but it is critical to have immediate access to the detail data behind the summary data. Detailed data should be available to help provide the rationale for discovered trends.

Communication tools are:

- Delivering the right information in an appropriate context
- 2D and 3D *descriptive* visualization tools
- Open and customizable graphs
- Annotation, layout, axes, color map, text
- Animation supported on any variable
- GIF, TIFF, VRML formats
- Collaborative or Web-based visualization – "Thin" and "Fat" visualization clients

Traditional business graph types such as bar, line, scatter and pie graphs have the advantage of being well known to end-users. The familiarity and acceptance of these graph types is a compelling reason to use them, or variations of them, when they can be satisfactorily applied. By assigning additional variables to aspects of a graph's appearance, many standard business graph types can be extended to support multivariate information.

A bar graph normally displays one variable, which is represented by the height of a bar. A second variable may be represented by the placement of the bar on the base axis. A third variable can be seen as bar color. The graph can be enhanced with a fourth variable by allowing this variable to control the width of each bar. In Figure 15.3a, a bar graph, enhanced to support four variables, is used in combination with a line and area graph to help financial analysts track market trends. The graph is regularly updated with volume of information provided to mutual fund managers.

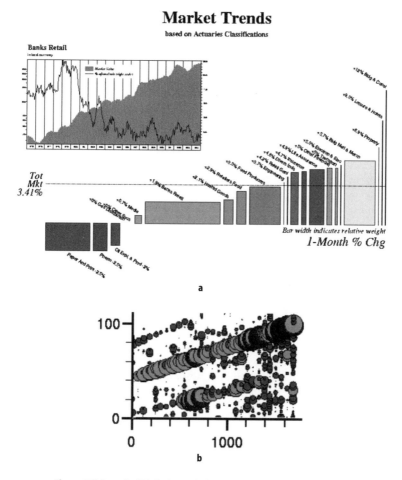

Figure 15.3 Example of 2D display methods representing multidimensional data.

Most business graph types have a number of visual attributes that can be controlled by data variables to increase the multivariate information content of the graph and still retain its familiar and intuitive appearance. Graph types that make use of a 2D-axis system are well suited for multivariate displays, and can also be enhanced to support higher levels of data dimensionality. For example, a scatter graph displays a symbol at points determined by X and Y variables. This graph type can easily be enhanced to represent four variables by letting additional data control the size of each symbol and the color of each symbol. An example of this is shown in Figure 15.3b.

In general, traditional graph types can be enhanced by one or perhaps two additional variables, enabling them to represent relationships in up to four variables. This increases the applicability of the graph for multivariate analysis, although still providing support for only a low level of data dimensionality. While other visual aspects of these graphs could be manipulated to increase this number, the practical limit to this process seems to be about four variables. At this level, familiarity and ease of comprehension are retained. Common business graph types, even with multivariate enhancements, are still limited in their ability to represent multivariate information from data stores containing high levels of data dimensionality. For viewing more complex data relationships, other more advanced visual techniques can be used, such as demonstrated in the Excel glyph visualizer.

15.7 Component-Based Development

A component is a task-specific piece of software that has well-defined interfaces and can be used multiple times in different applications. The published interfaces of a component guarantee that it will behave as specified and can communicate with other components.

Component-Based Development (CBD) offers the creation of plug-and-play applications that overcome differences in platforms and languages. The specification of a problem is broken down into smaller functional units, each of which serves as a component. The component interfaces are designed to conform to agreed-upon specifications so that they can be combined like Lego building blocks in order to develop complex applications.

What makes a component unique is that it can expose its properties, event and methods to any standard Integrated Development Environment (IDE), such as Visual Basic, Delphi or Visual Café. A component can also provide customization features that allow for the modification of its appearance and functionally.

Developing software components for specified tasks encourages reuse of these parts in multiple applications, thus reducing overall application development time. The software industry is also moving existing legacy systems into large components by putting a software "wrapper" around them and designing this wrapper to meet the same interface specifications as all the other components within the same environment.

15.7.1 Why Component-Based Development?

- Avoids *ad hoc* reuse, enforces coherent interface
- Reliable – immutable interfaces
- New services can be added to a component (just add new interfaces)
- Strong infrastructure exists today (DCOM, ActiveX, CORBA, JavaBeans)
- Standard integrated development environments glue components together

Creating software components for specified functions encourages reuse of these parts in multiple applications, thus reducing overall application development time. By assembling applications from components, programmers have the option of creating a "part" from scratch or reusing a part from a library of existing components.

The general concepts of object-oriented design and programming are starting to be well understood by a new generation of programmers. The necessary infrastructure to assemble applications from components is now becoming available. The underlying technologies, however, may not yet be ready for any large-scale production deployment of distributed applications. Networks such as the Internet and corporate intranets have accelerated the trend of moving from large, standalone systems to smaller-grained distributed systems.

15.7.2 What Are Components?

- Latest industry standard for reusable software development
- Two architectures: ActiveX/COM and JavaBeans
- Self-describing objects defined by interfaces that specify properties, methods, and events
- Interface separated from implementation

Component-based development will invariably result in more robust and flexible application software. Testing and bug fixing will only cover limited functionality of a component. This means that once this process is completed, it can be used in any number of projects and will perform without breaking down. Testing and bug fixing for the application to be deployed can then be much less extensive.

15.7.3 What Are Components Good For?

- Inherently distributable
  - Internet/intranet deployable (COM and JavaBeans)
  - Standards for object management
- Easier application deployment
  - Dynamically loaded
  - Versioned/constant interfaces

– Increased quality and reliability
– More easily reusable than class libraries

15.8 Two Component Frameworks

As a consequence, the notion of component-based programs has come to represent the next step in developing new applications that easily plug into the existing infrastructure through well-defined interfaces. Assembling applications or high-level application components from modular components increases the overall reliability and maintainability of an application, because individual components are usually tested, well specified, and designed to have agreed-upon functionality. In addition, component-based development offers increased flexibility for developing applications more quickly. Application components need to be developed to meet the specifications of at least one of the major "request broker architectures". These include CORBA, Microsoft's DCOM (Distributed Common Object Model) and Sun's JavaBeans.

The two predominant component technologies (mostly due to the raw market power of their originators and not due to technological superiority) for application development are JavaBeans and Microsoft's DCOM architecture.

The advantage of the JavaBeans components is their inherent platform independence, which is currently somewhat limited due to the fact that the Java3D standard is not yet available for most platforms. Another issue is that JavaBeans are running in a virtual machine, which may have an impact on performance and functionality. In contrast, the COM-based components feature both full exploitation of the operating system's capabilities and maximum speed, as they are programmed in C++ and then given a COM-compliant interface, which also serves as a data transport layer between different components.

15.9 Developing Visualization Components with ActiveX/DCOM

AVS has developed a framework and infrastructure for developing visualization components supporting both ActiveX/DCOM and JavaBeans component architecture. The product code name is "OpenViz", a component framework designed to move hundreds of person-years of visualization knowledge developed by AVS into a new generation of more accessible and reliable components. This chapter will focus on our experience in developing components for information visualization within the EC project CONTENTS based on the ActiveX/DCOM architecture.

One of the goals of AVS's development efforts has been to keep the applications deployed using the OpenViz technology as small as possible. Therefore the DCOM objects in the OpenViz "atomic" repository are as small and lightweight as possible, and will only expose the minimum number of interfaces necessary to do their job.

There is one major ActiveX control: the Engine or Viewer control itself. This control is the only one that actually appears on the screen (i.e. supports the

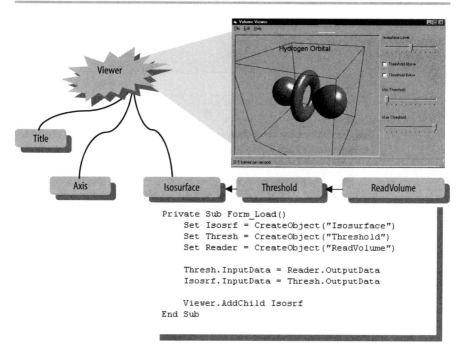

Figure 15.4 An application ActiveX/COM component "Volume Viewer" constructed from low-level "atomic" components and an infrastructure "visualization engine" consisting of a viewer, data model and event mechanism. A developer can assemble a new ActiveX control with a customized set of interfaces by combining Visual Basic's built-in controls (which are, in fact, also are ActiveX controls) with other existing ActiveX controls (in our case, the "atomic" visualization components) and tying them together with a few lines of Visual Basic code.

necessary interfaces). The other objects just provide data for this control and thus can be quite simple DCOM objects (Figure 15.4).

AVS has based the development of OpenViz on Microsoft's ATL (Active Template Library) C++ class library, which is streamlined towards developing DCOM objects. It does not provide application templates or user interface features as the MFC (Microsoft Foundation Classes) class library does; instead it focuses on the encapsulation of the complexity of DCOM into easy-to-use C++ classes. The resulting DCOM objects are generally much smaller than the ones created using MFC or most third-party vendors' technologies. It is also less abstract than MFC, and thus provides you with a lot more control, but requires more understanding about how DCOM works and which interfaces to support for which purpose. The end-user will usually not be required to program DCOM objects at this level.

15.10 "Smart" Documents for Web-Enabled Collaboration

With the increasing use of Microsoft's electronic documents (such as those in Office 97), distributed by Internet and intranet, the opportunity exists to provide

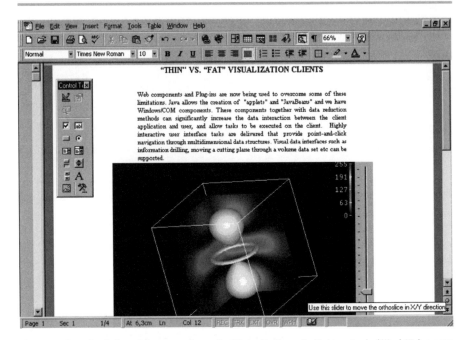

Figure 15.5 Example of a "smart" document – interactive 3D visualization embedded in a standard Word 97 document. "Smart" documents provide revolutionary solutions to any Visual Intelligence process and contribute to the application's acceptance on the business desktop.

easy-to-use advanced interactive 3D visualization techniques within electronic documents on the powerful PC desktop. Open and customizable visualization components allow the author of a report to distribute the relevant electronic information coupled with an embedded data analysis viewer "smartdoc", which allows the recipients to interactively examine the data in the same way as the original analyst. Instead of being a dumb document, the "smartdoc" would be a complete data exploration application through which a reader could, via embedded ActiveX visualization/analysis components, explore the data underlying the report. Instead of being a static summary document the report becomes much more like a very natural interface or portal onto the data.

To embed the new assembled visualization ActiveX component into a Word 97 document (as in Figure 15.5), simply import the ActiveX control into your Word 97 document like any GIF or TIFF file and add interactive 3D visualization to your electronic document. This document can then be transmitted to colleagues over the network. The ActiveX components reside locally on your PC and must only be downloaded and installed once on your local PC. When a "smartdoc" is transferred over the network, it will only refer to the component and thus the total size of the document will remain small (only the text). Any Visual Intelligence project can therefore exchange Word 97 documents with embedded advanced 3D visualization.

15.11 Demonstrator: Excel Visualizer

The "customizable" visualization component in Figure 15.6 is an example of the VUI technique serving as the visual front-end to any Excel application. The user explores various aspects of multidimensional data using a 3D glyph visualization paradigm with value-based filtering and data "drill-down". The selected data to be viewed is automatically transferred from Excel to the embedded visualization component.

The "sphere" is represented by its location in 3D space (x, y, z) described by the first three column values. The fourth column value is size, the fifth is color, and the remaining columns can be viewed after picking the glyph and perform a "drill-down". The "Column Assignment" interface controls which column of data that is interpreted for which visualization attribute.

The user interacts with the data by clicking on any sphere to explore additional information about the multivariate data represented by that sphere, pulling additional annotation information from the Excel data or triggering other references searches through intranet or Internet. This visual user interface technique is "fast and interactive" and an example of "data drill-down", in which interaction with the graphical objects is used to extract more detailed information in order to effect additional investigations. 3D visualization provides an "immersive experience" in which we make full use of the human senses to acquire, process and interpret the data world.

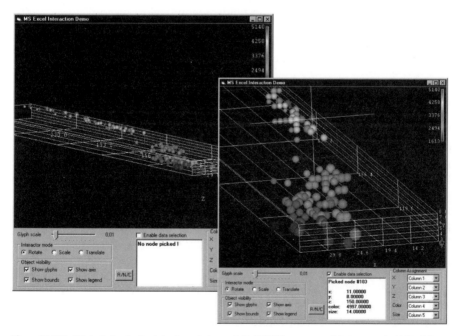

Figure 15.6 The 3D glyph visualization is implemented as an ActiveX DCOM component, fully integrated with Excel. Rows and columns are selected and highlighted in an Excel spreadsheet. Data can easily be selected, viewed, edited, added or deleted. With a simple mouse-click, the user has selected a "sphere" representing data in row 30 of the spreadsheet.

We can conclude that this example response to at least three challenges:

1. Locating and retrieving the relevant data from a data world which is growing in size
2. Understanding the complexity
3. Use industry standard "open" and "customizable" visualization tools

15.12 Conclusion

In this exploding world of abstract data, there is great potential for information visualization to increase the bandwidth between us and an ever-growing and ever-changing world of data. The result will be greatly improved *time-to-insight*.

Traditional software development has moved to a Web component-based approach, building smaller, single-purpose building blocks. Technologies like Sun's Java language with JavaBeans and Microsoft's ActiveX provide an important component of cyberspace – the ability to create an object that behaves similarly in different applications and on different computers. I can create an interactive component on my computer and distribute it to you in cyberspace, and it will still behave in the same way when you use it.

With ActiveX technology, Windows programmers will have a much easier time combining traditional Internet connectivity programs with powerful desktop software packages. For example, with the ActiveX components, projects can exchange "smaller" Office documents over the Internet that refer to these already available and installed components at the client-side.

In the future, a component's location on the network will become as irrelevant to the developer as its source language is today. Developers will expect to be able to compose, distribute, and troubleshoot solutions wherever, whenever. Distributed COM (DCOM) is one way forward.

Over the next couple of years, we will see the Web evolve in giant steps into interactivity and multi-user participation based on the new emerging standards. Visualization will develop into interactive data drilling on the Web providing visualization technology closely integrated with the database. Visualization on the Web will become even more active and dynamic, with JavaBeans and ActiveX components streaming down the Internet to the Web client.

The future trends and improvements in visualization for the Web can be summarized:

- Data structures for accurately modeling complex business and warehouse data.
- Information rich interactive visual representations of highly multivariate data.
- Web-based component architecture (DCOM/ActiveX or Java).
- Tight integration between data and visualization supporting "drill-down" features.
- Customizable and user-friendly solutions instead of inaccessible "black boxes".
- Sharing of increased knowledge though powerful communication tools.

- Descriptive visualization – presentation quality, perception and clarity.
- Multivariate visualization techniques – glyph "iconic" representation.
- "Smart" documents – 3D visualization embedded in Office documents.

Acknowledgments

This chapter was partly supported by the European Community in the ESPRIT Project CONTENTS (EP 29732).

16

Creating a Shared Reality for Research and Education Through Networked Virtual Reality

Judith R. Brown

Abstract

High-speed networks connect researchers around the world and enable new opportunities for more effective collaborations. Coupled with emerging virtual reality technologies and realistic computer graphics, we will be able to meet in a new "shared reality" as we collaborate to solve research problems, design products and educate.

16.1 Area Addressed by This Chapter

This chapter addresses tele-immersive collaboration as an essential research and educational tool. Educational and research collaborations, using enhanced computer graphics, high-performance networks and virtual reality technologies, enable new and exciting opportunities for shared insights. Tele-immersive collaborations provide a new environment for discovery by joining researchers from remote locations in a shared virtual space. Bringing together scientists with cultural differences and diverse perceptions of reality into this shared immersive space allows them to see the same objects and hear the same sounds and to share their own unique views and perceptions, creating a new, shared reality. My vision of this shared reality for research is based on three premises regarding research, learning and collaboration:

1. Visualization is an essential tool for collaboration.
2. Virtual reality, as an interactive technology, is a valuable tool for research.

3.   Enhanced computer graphics and tools for interaction, along with high-performance networks, enable a collaborative environment, a shared reality.

16.1.1 Correspondences (Dependencies, Other Relationships) with Other Areas

Effective tele-immersive collaboration depends on network bandwidth and "quality of service" capabilities, such as low latency and minimal jitter. Therefore, it is dependent upon the development of high-performance networks and the installation of these high-performance networks across the world, into the areas where our colleagues are. Image compression techniques and better user interfaces are also essential.

16.2 Creating a Shared Reality

Building on the experimental work by others and the premises stated above, we are now ready to move from "my reality" and "your reality" to "our reality" [2], where we can observe and explore scientific data and computer-generated models together.

16.2.1 Premise 1: Visualization Is an Essential Tool for Collaboration

The visualization lab is the crossroads between research and education. Although it took a long time after the 1987 report "Visualization in Scientific Computing" [5], finally the importance of the visualization concepts is understood by researchers and by the funding agencies. Researchers and funding agencies now accept visualization as an integral part of the research process. As the computing and networking capabilities increase sufficiently to allow networked collaboration, and the tools become easier to use, this collaborative way of working will be eagerly embraced. There is already widespread cross-disciplinary interest in such activities.

Habanero, developed at National Computational Sciences Alliance (NCSA) aims at enhancing multi-user collaborative work environments by providing a framework for sharing Java objects with colleagues distributed around the Internet. By using Java to avoid platform dependence, the tools that are developed can support low-level workstations, as well as expensive specialized hardware, across the internet. The NCSA Habanero home page is `http://www.ncsa.uiuc.edu/SDG/software/Habanero/`.

Because it is increasingly important for scientists to be able to do their own visualizations, NCSA, in a joint project with Ohio State University and The University of Iowa, is developing Web-based modules for teaching visualization techniques, called VisTutorial. These modules will include techniques for data handling, data representation, rendering and interaction. When completed, VisTutorial will allow scientists who do their computations on remote high-performance computers to also do their visualization remotely. These will be useful on low-end PCs connected to the Internet as well as on high-end networked immersive environments.

Collaboration in medicine through telemedicine activities is increasingly important, with 188 active telemedicine programs worldwide. These activities include distance learning, remote patient care and collaborations among healthcare workers. Some of this activity can use the current Internet. The Virtual Hospital, a digital health sciences library, was started at The University of Iowa in 1992 and provides information, including textbooks, images and animations, for patients, healthcare providers, and students. Many of the textbooks exist only in electronic form. A physician who teaches family practice in North Carolina said that she uses Virtual Hospital every day in her classes and that it has changed the way she teaches medicine.

Remote patient care and other healthcare collaborations require more interactive network capabilities and put greater demands on the network. For example, the standard X-ray transmission time via dial-up modem at 28.8 kbps is 30 minutes. This is reduced to one second if it is sent over a DS3 (45 Mbps) connection. Such remote healthcare capability is especially important in rural areas, where a trauma patient might have to wait three days for a circuit-riding radiologist to read an X-ray. These remote areas are likely to be connected through a state or regional network, or a private network, since security may be an issue. Capabilities being developed under the Internet2 projects described later in this chapter will enable the necessary level of interaction and image transmissions when they are needed.

16.2.2 Premise 2: Virtual Reality, as an Interactive Technology, Is a Valuable Tool for Research

The University of Iowa is making progress with applications on three ImmersaDesks acquired through National Science Foundation funding for educational purposes and environmental research. A year ago, there was very little software for ImmersaDesks, and our programmers had a long learning curve to get started. Now some good tools have been developed and are offered free to the user community. These tools include CAVE5D, a version of the University of Wisconsin's VIS5D software for environmental visualization, and Limbo, from the University of Illinois at Chicago that serves as a template for developing tele-immersive applications, providing avatars, pointers, sound and other tools for working together in a shared immersive environment.

CAVE5D is a modification of the popular VIS5D environmental modeling software from the University of Wisconsin. CAVE5D enables the use of VIS5D on virtual reality equipment, so that scientists can explore the geographic and environmental data by moving around in the virtual space. Both VIS5D and CAVE5D are free and easy to use.

We have local ImmersaDesk applications in higher-dimensional mathematics, geography, chemistry, biochemistry and computational fluid dynamics. Some classes come over to the ImmersaDesk so that the students can experience and share the instructor's discoveries. In other cases, graduate students are sent over to work with us.

One of the key projects being developed with NSF funds is the *ENVISAGE* Project (*Environmental Visualization and Geographic Exploration*). The purpose of ENVISAGE is to allow students to experience a more complete understanding of geographical processes by having them operate in the semi-immersive 3D visualization environment provided by the ImmersaDesk and high-performance networks. Immersion, for analysis of mapped data and model output, enables students to view relationships that would otherwise remain shrouded by the limitations of widely used graphics technologies. Openshaw and Fisher [6], for example, assert the following:

> It is important, therefore, to develop technologies that attempt to understand the data and develop views of the information or database world in which attempts are made by our clumsy spatial analysis tools to find patterns and relationships. Can we look inside spatial databases and walk around in them via virtual reality concepts? Currently we are so blind to many aspects of the data and the data flows being analyzed. We cope by being highly selective and subjective and in the process probably fail to see and find many of the patterns and relationships of potential interest other than those we blindly stumble over by chance!

It is precisely this type of immersive exploratory learning that we are bringing to undergraduate education so that students will be able to more readily grasp basic concepts that have a pronounced visual component. We are currently expanding this project to collaborate with a geographer at Penn State.

A second key project is the *LIVE* project (Laboratory for the Immersive Visualization of the Environment), being developed with NASA funds. Research projects include:

1. An immersive decision support system that will be used to assess the impact on vegetation communities of alternative water management strategies in the Upper Mississippi River Basin.
2. An immersive remote sensing-based visualization capability for Glacier National Park to assess the effects of fire on forested lands.
3. An immersive visualization of ozone and dust generation and transport in East Asia.

(NASA support is provided by COE/97-0104, "Project LIVE: Laboratory for the Immersive Visualization of the Environment".)

16.2.3 Premise 3: Enhanced Computer Graphics and Tools for Interaction, Along with High Performance Networks, Enable a Collaborative Environment, a New Shared Reality

As virtual reality technologies have recently enabled individual scientists to better understand their data by exploring the images of the data, so are these technologies, when networked, allowing them to access remote resources and collaborate with remote colleagues. We have learned a great deal in recent months by participating in tele-immersive applications of others and are now developing our applications.

Networked collaborative learning can begin at a very young age, as shown by the Narrative Immersive Constructionist/Collaborative Environments (NICE) project between the Electronic Visualization Laboratory and the Interactive Computing Environments Laboratory at the University of Illinois at Chicago. In NICE, children can collaborate to plant and cultivate a virtual garden and to create stories from their interactions.

As universities have connected to the very high-performance backbone network service (vBNS), they have looked for high-profile applications to show faculty and administrators the value of these new educational and research networks. Applications that show an ability to link with other universities and explore together in shared virtual space have been popular. As part of the Pennsylvania State University Internet2 Days, we explored a model of the city of Berlin with an additional proposed building designed by a Penn State professor of architecture. Boston University produced a wonderful, whimsical Art World, and we appeared as avatars to play in that world during the Supercomputing 98 conference.

We can now apply what we learned from these experiences to our applications and build new collaborations worldwide. We recently collaborated with the National High Performance Computing Center of Taiwan. They were celebrating the connection of their national high-performance network, TANet, to the vBNS and other national and international high-performance networks at STAR TAP. Because the time for their planned celebration was 3 a.m. our time, they prerecorded our tele-immersive session and showed it on videotape at the celebration. In this collaboration, we investigated together the pressure fields on a high-speed train going through a tunnel, shown in Figures 16.1 and 16.2. We are currently

Figure 16.1 Image of the ImmersaDesk showing the pressure fields on a high-speed train as it goes through a tunnel, the avatar of the remote collaborator and the pointer of the University of Iowa participant. This image illustrates a tele-immersive application between the National Center for High-Performance Computing of Taiwan (NCHC) and Advanced Research Computing Services and Visualization, Information Technology Services, The University of Iowa.

Figure 16.2 Image of the same scene, at the same time, taken at NCHC in Taiwan.

working on computational fluid dynamics applications, including a study of the air flow around two trains as they pass in a tunnel, and developing some user interface tools.

The Internet2 and Next Generation Internet (NGI) projects are enabling this kind of tele-immersion on national and international levels. Internet2 is a project for a faster network with enhanced capabilities. It is currently built on the National Science Foundation vBNS and the University Corporation for Advanced Internet Development (UCAID) Abilene networks. Research is in progress on the enhanced Quality of Service (QoS) capabilities that will enable new research and educational applications. QoS capability means that a network user will be able to receive the network resources (such as high bandwidth, low latency and low jitter) needed by a specific application when it is needed. Current network capabilities at most research institutions are not yet reliable for serious, lengthy tele-immersive collaborations.

An example of a tele-immersive application that doesn't need very high bandwidth, but does need guaranteed low latency, is networked driving simulators. The US National Advanced Driving Simulator (NADS) is located in a rural setting in Iowa, but it has good access to the vBNS. Other universities plan to have projects that link their driving simulators to NADS, and government and industrial partners want to send commands remotely, or connect remote hardware. When remote users send commands, the amount of data sent will be very small, but the reaction to these commands has to be very fast and smooth.

16.3 Critical Issues

There are still some issues with widespread use of these collaborative technologies:

1.   Cost for the high-end
     – Shared immersive technology is expensive

2. Accessibility
   - The tele-immersive equipment requires large spaces
   - The interfaces are not readily accessible by persons with disabilities.
3. Distance
   - Time zone differences make same-time collaborations difficult. In the Taiwan example, we settled on 6 p.m. our time on a Tuesday, 8 a.m. Wednesday in Taiwan.
4. Network performance
   - Complicated graphics and sound require fast networks and low latency. In the Taiwan experiment, the graphics were good, but the six second time lag for the sound was disconcerting. We also need to be able to work seamlessly with more complicated models.
   - QoS capabilities are still under development.

16.4 Questions for the Future

I think the technical problems can be solved. These questions are more concerned with working habits and cultural differences.

1. Can the user interface be adaptable to different disciplinary needs? Can physicists, engineers, chemists, and artists all collaborate in a style familiar to them?
2. Can we deal with cultural differences and be sure that interface designers are aware of words or colors that may be inappropriate in a particular setting or may not translate well?
3. Can we provide alternatives to graphics so that the blind can participate, and alternative interfaces for persons with other disabilities?

References

[1] JR Brown (1998) Computer Graphics Education and Presentation, *Presentation at IGD opening*, Darmstadt, Germany, October.
[2] JR Brown (1998) Reality: yours and mine will become ours, presentation at *International Videoconference: Computer Graphics Pioneers Assess Computer Graphics, SIGGRAPH 98*, Orlando, FL, 23 July.
[3] JR Brown, R Earnshaw, M Jern and J Vince (1995) *Visualization: Using Computer Graphics to Explore Data and Present Information*, Chichester, John Wiley & Sons.
[4] S Cunningham and JR Brown (1997) Computer graphics: from "interactive" to "collaborative", *Interactions*, IV-4, 77–78.
[5] BH McCormick, TA DeFanti and MD Brown (eds.) (1987) Visualization in scientific computing, *Computer Graphics*, 21(6).
[6] S Openshaw and MM Fisher (1995) A framework for research on spatial analysis relevant to geostatistical information systems in Europe. *Geographical Systems*, 2(4), 325–338.

Acknowledgments

This work is supported by the National Science Foundation, Division of Undergraduate Education, under the grant DUE-9750537. The vBNS connection is supported by the National Science Foundation, Division of Advanced Network Infrastructure, grant NR-9613871. All opinions, findings, conclusions and recommendations in any material resulting from this work are those of the principal investigators, and do not necessarily reflect the views of the National Science Foundation.

About the Author

Judith R. Brown is the manager of Advanced Research Computing and Visualization at The University of Iowa. She is also The University of Iowa's Internet2 Project Manager. She has co-authored four books on computer graphics, visualization and user interfaces, and is a frequently invited speaker on topics in computer graphics education, visualization and collaboration. She is a Past Chair of ACM SIGGRAPH, Eurographics Fellow, and honorable member of the Academic Committee of the State Key Lab of CAD & Computer Graphics at Zhejiang University, Hangzhou, China. She was Chair of the SIGGRAPH 30th Year Celebration activities.

Online Communities

17

Online Communities: Usability, Sociabilty, Theory and Methods

Jenny Preece

17.1 Introduction

Internet usage doubles every 52 days. Over 18 million people are AOL subscribers – many of whom are attracted by AOL's emphasis on email, chats, instant messaging and, of course, the Web. Active Worlds, a graphical chat environment, has over a million participants. During the first quarter of 1998, 450 000 messages were posted to 20 000 Usenet groups. The number of people coming online continues to increase as e-commerce, online education, online health, and increasing amounts of information and people with whom to chat entice even more people. Meanwhile, according to Moore's Law computing power doubles every 18 months. For the well educated, with jobs and Internet stock, the future looks bright. However, the gap continues to broaden between low and high income, and between poorly and well-educated people. There are fears that socializing face-to-face will decline leading to an unprecedented number of lonely, psychologically impoverished people. Better access to successful online communities for all citizens could reduce isolation and improve quality of life for all citizens.

Study of online communities is finding a place university agendas and in major laboratories and national funding bodies (Brown *et al.*, 1999b,c). Like other new topics, its status is debatable. At a similar stage in the 1990s, researchers tried to characterize human–computer interaction. At a National Science Foundation workshop, Stu Card identified four stages in the growth of a discipline (Card, 1991; Olson and Olson, 1997). Building and evaluating individual systems, or *point systems*, is the first stage in early development. As more communities develop, research intensifies and *comparative evaluation* studies start to identify dimensions for success. This is the second developmental stage. The third stage is characterized by understanding the *relationships* in online community development more thoroughly, so that *models*, *laws* and *theory* can be articulated, which is an indicator of coming of age.

Current research in online communities deals primarily with individual communities – i.e. stage one. However, critics argue that the basic technology (i.e. email, listservers, bulletin boards, chats etc.) are established technologies, that are used enthusiastically. They question why research is needed. There are four reasons:

- Little is known about the social and technical dynamics of mass communication involving thousands or millions of participants via the Internet.
- People in online communities will come from diverse cultures and vary widely in age, technical and educational experience. Technology with appropriate usability for this broad range of users is needed.
- People have expectations of excellent usability and sociability. At present these expectations are not being met.
- Local, national and international agencies, governments and e-commerce will demand that people go online for certain activities such as voting, paying taxes, licensing, social support, health, all kinds of information, and purchasing of goods. Online communities *must* be well developed so that they are usable by *all* citizens.

Directions[1] for research and development are needed that address usability and sociability problems so that better online communities can be developed. There is a particularly strong need to involve social scientists as well as computer scientists. Successful online communities will result from a blend of good usability and carefully guided social policies that encourage social interaction. Theory and better research methods are also needed to support Internet research and system development.

17.2 Usability and Sociability: a Framework for Online Community Design

There is no formula for a thriving online community. Online communities are new and there is a dearth of experience to guide successful development. Furthermore, online communities evolve and change constantly depending on their membership. What may be important early in the life of a community may not be significant later on. Communities also vary depending on their purpose, participants, policies and the software that supports them. Success is determined by *usability*, *sociability* and the affect of both of these on people's *interactions* in the community. Developers have *little* or *no* control over community members, except in some e-commerce communities where behavior is strongly managed. However, developers

---

1   European Union and National Science Foundation report, 1–4 June 1999, prepared by Christoph Busch, Fraunhofer IGD, Germany; Richard Guedj, INT, France; Wendy Kellogg, IBM T. J. Watson Research Center, USA; David Leevers, VERS Associates, UK; Sudhir Mudur, National Center for Software Technology, India; Jennifer Preece (lead author), University of Maryland Baltimore County, USA; Ben Shneiderman, University of Maryland College Park, USA; John Thomas, IBM T. J. Watson Research Center, USA; Deb Roy, MIT, USA; and Junji Yamaguchi, Independent, Japan.

can do much to set the tone of a community by designing or selecting software with good *usability* and encouraging *sociability*.

Software with good *usability* supports *rapid learning, high skill retention, low error rates* and *high productivity*. It is *consistent, controllable* and *predictable*, making it *pleasant* and *effective* to use. Usability is a key ingredient for the success of *any* software. Good usability supports people's creativity, improves their productivity and makes them feel good. Poor usability leads to frustration and wastes time, energy and money. Norman (1986) describes the transactions between humans and computers in terms of crossing two gulfs. The first is the *gulf of execution* and the second is the *gulf of evaluation*. Meaningful commands, menus and icons, a well-designed navigation system, and comprehensible messages help to reduce the cognitive and physical effort required to bridge these gulfs. Graphical user interfaces (GUIs), based on appropriate visual metaphors, for example, help by enabling users to infer knowledge about the target computer system from their knowledge of the metaphoric system. Three important principles of usability are that systems should be consistent, controllable and predictable (Shneiderman, 1999).

Consistent software uses the same terms and procedures for achieving the same functionality throughout the program. The notion of consistency is far reaching. Sequences of actions should follow the same format. Color, typography and terminology should also be consistent. Users want software that supports but does not take away their sense of *control*, so they can do what they want when they want, and not be constrained by the software. Software that is consistent and controllable is predictable too. *Predictable* software enables users to continually build on their experience so that they develop confidence and skills with experience.

There is a large collection of research, and many books provide guidelines for user interface design (e.g. Nielsen and Mack, 1994; Preece *et al.*, 1994; Shneiderman, 1999; Hackos and Redish, 1998). An increasing number focus specifically on Web design (Lynch and Horton, 1999; Spool *et al.*, 1997). However, although there are excellent books that deal with community development (Schuler, 1996; Figallo, 1998), few pay much attention to usability. However, this will change: as more people gain experience of online communities, there will be cries for better usability (Gaines *et al.*, 1997; Preece, 1999a).

Developers *cannot* control social interaction, but careful, early social planing, coupled with good usability, encourages thriving communities to evolve. *Sociability* focuses on *social interaction*. Communities with good *sociability* have *social policies* that support the community's *purpose* and people's interactions. The policies should be *understandable*, socially *acceptable* and *practicable* (Preece, 2000). Unlike usability, the concept of sociability is not well understood. There are many questions to address. How does a community communicate its purpose? What are the impacts of different personalities and policies (e.g. joining regulations, controlling anti-social behavior, keeping conversations on track etc.)? How should emotion, content and online activity be represented? How can privacy and security be assured? This chapter presents guidelines for sociability. Community population sizes range from millions to under fifty people. There is also huge variation in posting rates (Nonnecke and Preece, 2000). Some people interact frequently, while others may post just once every few months. Some people lurk and never send messages. Perhaps with different software, or a smaller, safer-feeling environment, lurkers might post? Potentially, this large volume of lurkers represents huge revenue for e-commerce. The relationship between usability and sociability is important for online community success. For example, decisions about whether to have registration are sociability considerations. The actual form, interactive procedure, positioning and wording of the policy are usability issues.

Research topics for usability and sociability are discussed in the next two sections (Preece, 1999b). The ideas presented are from a paper submitted to the EC/NSF joint Research Workshop at Bonas, France, in June 1999. Discussion with members of the workshop resulted in a revised version of the paper which was collaboratively published and widely distributed (Brown *et al.*, 1999a,b,c). The ideas were further refined and presented in Preece (1999b). The current version, presented in the next two sections of this chapter, represents yet another iteration.

17.3 Usability

Three areas of central importance for online community development are: design and representation; security and privacy; and scalability.

17.3.1 Design and Representation

Knowledge and theories about culture and social activity in online communities provide a foundation for software design. Research is needed to develop representations to reveal online behavior as it happens, histories of behavior, stored communication and knowledge, the nature of communication (e.g. which topics were discussed), the number of people participating and relationships between participants. In addition, individuals may want to represent themselves in different ways using avatars and other representations.

- *Revealing behavior*
  What is the impact of revealing behavior of individuals and groups in different circumstances? How can online communities support different kinds of behaviors and information, e.g. self-expression, humor, personality, mood, identity, empathy, esthetics and age? What is the impact of different types of representation for community dynamics – e.g. people coming, going and engaging in different behavior? What happens when dealing with different modalities?

- *Interactions between representations and social processes*
  How do representations influence social processes? What kind of new communication processes might arise from use of different representations? Research indicates that socio-emotional processes are different online, particularly in textual environments in which cues from body language and voice tone are absent.

- *Revealing the content and emotion of messages*
  How should different content and emotional states be represented? Words, phrases and emoticons can be available at the press of key, but how useful are they? Avatars can sometimes become animated so that they wave or jump. What

other ways might there be, and what is the effect of enabling people to reveal both content and emotions explicitly? If the collective mood of a group could be established by, for example, a voting system, how could it be expressed and would this encourage better communication? How can users understand the mood and nuances of community when they come online? Similarly, when newcomers join the community what mechanisms would help them to gauge the feelings of the group, depth of conversation etc.?

- *How are large communities represented online?*
Large numbers of people wanting to join online communities present new challenges for designers. What types of features should be provided in software to support large communities, their moderators and administrators? How, for example, do you represent a million people in a community and what should the interface be like?

17.3.2 Security and Privacy

The success of some online communities will be strongly influenced by how secure they are. Personal health and credit card details must be secure. Systems must not only be secure, users must trust the security. Incorporation of strong cryptographic protocols is essential. These protocols realize classical security requirements such as mutual authentication of communication between trading partners, confidentiality of the transaction, and authenticity and integrity of the goods. In addition, the availability and integration of adequate payment protocols are essential to satisfy the needs of commerce. Security is a major technical issue for many online communities. Identifying what security is needed and how to present security procedures to users are usability and sociability concerns.

Two crucial areas require substantial research in the near future in order to develop a powerful electronic market and eliminate lack of trust in online transaction:

- *Conflict between identification vs. privacy or anonymity*
There is a conflict of interest between vendors and content providers in e-commerce systems, which demand identification of their customers using concepts such as globally unique identifiers to realize digital fingerprints (attached to digital goods). In contrast there is the crucial demand for privacy protection raised by consumers that requires non-traceable interactions.
- *Copyright protection*
As content contributed to online systems in commercial and non-commercial instances grows, the question of intellectual property protection gets more and more crucial. Consequently, adequate copyright protection mechanisms must be investigated and developed.

17.3.3 Scalability

Scalability is a research priority with strong technical challenges and implications for usability and sociability. With so many people from across the world wanting to join or develop online communities, research is needed to produce software with high usability and guide sociability in very large communities. How do we guide online crowds and develop social protocols? Research is needed to develop interfaces to support large populations of participants and to develop tools for moderators.

17.4 Sociability

Communities with good sociability have social policies that support the community's purpose and social interaction. Social scientists are needed to provide a deeper understanding of how online communities function. The role of computer scientists will be to translate this knowledge into software that supports social interactions, protects individuals' privacy, provides security and encourages universal access. Important research topics include: community and culture, and ethical issues and universal access.

17.4.1 Community and Culture

We need to understand cultural differences better and how to support diversity online. Communities of all kinds are rich social environments, which cannot be observed through the portholes of individual human–computer interfaces. Many communities have complex life cycles punctuated by temporal events, such as life-cycle phenomena and unanticipated events. So far work in human–computer interaction and virtual environments has not focused on effective online community design and maintenance. Solutions to most of the questions discussed in this section will support better social planning.

- *Understanding differences between communities*
  Research issues include understanding the differences between networked communities, virtual communities and virtual environments – i.e. the full range of the physical and online spectrum of communities. How do the social policies and structures adopted by these different communities compare, differ and relate to each other? What types of governance procedures do they need?
- *Life cycles*
  Physical life has daily cycles that are often upheld by eating rituals, breakfast, lunch, dinner, work, periods of relaxation and sleep. Time zone differences cause severe practical limitations for synchronous communication. Weekly and annual cycles vary from culture to culture and from time zone to time zone. What is the effect of these cycles on international communities? Real communities also have generation cycles – birth, teenage life, marriage, parenting, retirement, old age and death. Perhaps online community developers can take advantage of humans' propensity to structure behaviors around cycles. TV producers appear to understand these cycles well. They can predict maximum viewing times for different sectors of a population. How might software support these life cycles? What role do rituals have offline and how might they translate online? For example, some

communities have experimented with synchronizing snacks to enforce a sense of community. At an appointed time, participants distributed across several locations will have an M&M or cookie and soda break. However, anecdotes from colleagues that have participated in such events suggest that they don't contribute to the sense of community. There is no substitute for being there when it comes to sharing a nice meal or a hug!

- *Interaction dynamics*
  Interaction dynamics are different in four-person peer discussion, a 25-person classroom, a group of 150 friends, and several thousand people meeting for a conference. Each has its own social rituals. In the physical world, participants have different expectations in different social settings. Physical space and the number of people present provide strong cues, which are not available online. The mere act of going to a meeting often conveys a strong message of commitment. The person has risked traveling, and invested time and money in being physically present. Handshaking, hugging and eating are social activities that don't translate well online. Augmenting our senses with wearable computers, empowering creativity with well-designed tools, enabling people to indicate their emotional states etc. could improve the quality of interaction. Access to information, stories and monitored data could be useful to both individuals and communities for developing greater collective intelligence.

17.4.2 Ethical Issues and Universal Access

Designing software that supports good ethics and universal access is a challenge for technical and social scientists. Basic sociological research is needed to develop codes of conduct online and other forms of sociability. However, in order to make the features available to support universal access, challenging computer science issues need solving. Good usability design will be needed to make new functionality usable by the wide range of users for whom it is designed.

Ethical Issues

- *Awareness of the dangers of participating online*
  Many users fail to appreciate the potential dangers of participating online. They are unaware that correspondence is electronically stored and of when they initiate insecure communications or operations. Current software does not give adequate feedback about such operations. Better ways are needed of protecting users by notifying them about unencrypted or encrypted traffic, potential persistent storage in which their privacy is endangered, and acts with possible legal consequences such as digital signatures.
- *Codes of conduct for online communities*
  Protection of individual and group privacy in online communities can be partially realized through improved technology. In addition, policies are needed to ensure that host operators and maintainers are required to follow fundamental privacy rules. Research is also needed to identify successful models of self-governance in

online communities. A better understanding is needed of how cooperation, trust and empathy develop online, how these relationships change over time, and how changes in population size and demography affect them. Contributions from social and political scientists will be needed to develop different models of governance and integrate online policies with pre-existing local, national and international policies.

- *Improved environments*
  Research is needed to understand the impact of digital technology on cultural diversity, environmental issues, conservation of limited resources and changes in people's standard of living. In what ways do online and physical communities interact?

Universal Access

A report entitled "Falling through the digital divide" (National Telecommunications and Information Administration & Commerce, 1999) produced by the US Department of Commerce shows that although the gap between the number of men and women online is diminishing, the gap between rich and poor, and between well-educated and poorly educated, is increasing. Lack of access to computing equipment affects both individuals and nations. To ensure universal access to online communities for people of all ages, cultures, languages, income levels, education, and physical and mental abilities, five broad areas of research are identified. The first, multiple interaction modalities, calls for alternatives to text input and output. The second area suggests research into adaptive interfaces that can be tuned to a wide range of communication abilities and preferences. Third, research is needed into technologies for supporting interaction in any language, opening the door to communities with "around the world access". Fourth, translation technologies are needed for bringing together different language groups.

17.5 Theory and Methods

Many candidate theories exist that are partially relevant to online communities. High-level theories are needed that are directly relevant to online communities. The value of such theories is to:

- *understand* communication in different types of communities
- make *predictions*
- *inform* online community design

Current theories fall into the following three categories:

- one-to-one or small group communication via different media
- social interaction and community networks
- relationship between software design and social behavior

17.5.1 One-to-One and Small Group Communication via Different Media

Social presence theory (Short *et al.*, 1976; Rice, 1987, 1993), *media richness theory* (Daft and Lengel, 1986) and *social contextual cues theory* (Sproull and Kiesler, 1991) differ in detail, but all broadly assert that reduced social cues resulting from low-bandwidth environments encourage impersonal, uninhibited and less social behavior. Communication media differ in how much they can overcome constraints associated with lack of social presence (Rice, 1993). Understanding the relationship between the social presence of different media and the needs of the communication task is vitally important for online community developers.

Common ground theory provides a framework for describing how people develop shared understanding as they communicate through a process of grounding. How grounding occurs varies from situation to situation. Grounding takes one form in face-to-face conversation and another in computer-mediated communication. It is influenced by both the communication medium and the communication task. Clark and Brennan (1993, p. 229) identify *constraints* that a medium may place on common ground, such as co-presence (i.e. perception of sharing same physical environment), visibility (participants can see each other), audibility, co-temporality, reviewability, revisability etc.

Other theories that help to explain human behavior and emotions, such as empathy (Levenson and Ruef, 1992) would also be useful for informing design (Preece, 1998, 1999a). Understanding the development of trust online and providing usability and sociability support has become important in e-commerce. Little work has been done in this area and much more research is needed. Trust is the expectation that arises within a community of regular, honest and cooperative behavior, based on commonly shared norms and part experiences (Fukuyama, 1995, p. x). Trust is also important for any community concerned with knowledge exchange and management (Liebowitz, 1999), particularly if sensitive information is involved.

While these theories help to explain behavior in dyads and small groups, they do not speak of community behavior.

17.5.2 Community Networks

Many theories from sociology, communication studies and psychology can be imported to help explain and predict behavior in online communities. However, a foundational theory is needed that *predicts* online behavior and *guides* usability and sociability design. *Critical mass theory* claims that a critical number of participants are needed to make online participation worthwhile (Markus, 1987, 1990; Morris and Ogan, 1996; Rice, 1994; Ackerman and Starr, 1996). However, it provides no indication of what this magic number might be under certain circumstances for different kinds of communities, so its value to designers is limited.

Social network analysis (Wellman, 1992, 1997; Haythornthwaite, 1996) is a promising theory and set of techniques from sociology. A *social network* is a set of people (or organizations or other social entities) connected by a set of social relations, such as friendship, co-working, or information exchange (Garton *et al.*, 1999, p. 75). Computers support social networks by linking people who are geographically dispersed who could not otherwise relate to each other easily. Analysts seek to describe networks of relations as fully as possible, tease out the prominent patterns in such networks, trace the flow of information (and other resources) through them, and discover what effects these relations and networks have on people and organizations. Analysts look for resources that are exchanged in creating and maintaining social relationships. These relationships can be strong or weak, uni- or bidirectional and occur over long or short periods of time (Garton *et al.*, 1999). A better understanding of how online communities develop and maintain social networks and how they relate to physical communities appears to be a promising avenue for future research.

Successful communities are built on *cooperation*. If community members do not feel a sense of responsibility towards each other they are unlikely to cooperate. Unfortunately, there are often times when behavior that seems perfectly reasonable to an individual and gets the person what they want is damaging to the group. This tension between the group and the individual is known as a *social dilemma* (Kollock, 1998). Social dilemmas form the basis of much research on inter-personal cooperation in psychology, sociology and anthropology. One of the most well-known studies is Axelrod's two-person situation called prisoner's dilemma (Axelrod, 1984), in which three conditions for cooperation are identified.

What is acceptable in any community will depend on the aims of the community, the people who contribute and any rules that have been agreed. The type of community can have a large impact. Professional and scholarly communities focus on communicating ideas and information in a socially acceptable way. They can be controversial. Political communities are concerned with persuasion and debates that can become emotionally charged. Determining the boundaries between acceptable and unacceptable social behavior involves distinguishing between debate about ideas, which is acceptable, and *ad hominem* attacks directed at specific people which should not be tolerated. Support communities have a lower threshold for aggressive behavior, because it can be damaging to people already dealing with problems.

17.5.3 Influence of Software Design on Social Behavior

The last area of theory that would be helpful for online communities involves better understanding of how software design can impact users' perceptions and behavior. Several already existing theories may shed light on this issue. For example, *situated action* explains how people's use of technology is influenced by the environment in which they are situated (Suchman, 1987). *Adaptive structuration* is concerned with the influence of software design on task execution and performance, and how people adapt their behavior to make best use of the technology.

Social informatics is "the interdisciplinary study of the design, uses and consequences of information technologies that takes into account their interaction with institutional and cultural contexts". (Kling, 1999). A key concept in social

informatics research is that the *social context* of information technology development and its consequences for work, organizations and other social relationships.
For example, differences in expertise between users may radically influence their
experiences with technology. Consider, for example, the use of email filters to stop
email from people known to be argumentative in a listserver community. A person
who knows how to use these filters to stop the messages may develop a more favorable impression of the community than a person who receives the messages.

17.6 Methods and Measurement

Methods for designing online communities and investigating and measuring their
effectiveness are starting to be discussed (Jones, 1999; Preece, 2000). The size and
demography of Internet communities are often unknown, making traditional
research approaches, such as sampling, problematic. Community development is
also different from software development (Figallo, 1998; Schuler, 1996). An interactive, *community-centered* approach is needed (Preece, 2000). This method takes
account of sociability as well as usability and emphasizes community solutions as
well as technical solutions. Knowing a community's purpose, the characteristics of
participants and the nature of their communication tasks is an essential part of this
approach.

For research and development (particularly collecting community requirements
and evaluation) surveys, ethnography and data logging are promising methods.
Survey techniques can be delivered through email, Web pages or by paper, making
them highly versatile and economical for researching geographically scattered
populations (Lazar and Preece, 1999). Often combinations of all three approaches
are needed to reach a representative sample of the population. As well as cost
advantages, data can be transferred into a database for immediate analysis and
accessed via statistical programs such as SPSS, SAS or data visualization tools.

Ethnographic techniques have been well developed for CSCW research, but the
distributed nature of many online community populations poses new challenges.
One form of ethnographic research involves interaction logging, which is easy and
unobtrusive (Nonnecke and Preece, 2000; Smith, 1999) but poses ethical questions
for researchers. Metrics describing participant demography, behavior online and
interaction are needed for demographic research and to inform design.

- *Demography of participants:*
  - Number of members/subscribers in the community
  - Number of posters by gender, age, occupation (i.e. demography)
- *Behavior online:*
  - Number of posts per person, connect hours etc.
  - Number of posters over a period of time (e.g. access to Web pages per month)
  - Number of lurkers – but it is hard to get this information.
- *Characteristics of interaction:*
  - Number of posters by category of type of communication

- Length of message
- Number of messages in a thread
- Number of threads
- How much and what type of moderation?

17.7 Summary and Conclusions

Research into online communities will benefit from being multi-disciplinary and involving both social scientists and computer scientists. Software with good usability is important, but software alone will not ensure a successful online community. Sociability is also needed. This chapter has used these categories as a framework for reviewing research needs. In addition, comprehensive theory and new methods for researching online communities are needed.

Usability

Considerable research is needed to develop *representations* to reveal online behavior as it is occurring: histories of behavior, stored communication and knowledge, nature of communication (e.g. which topics were discussed), the number of people participating and relationships between participants. Interfaces and interaction techniques are needed that are usable by a broad range of users for a wide variety of communication tasks. The success of some online communities will be strongly influenced by how *secure* they are. Strong cryptographic protocols are essential.

Scalability is a research priority for online communities. With an increasing number of people from across the world developing and joining online communities, software and social processes are needed to support very large communities.

Sociability

Research is needed by teams of social scientists to answer basic questions about social interaction and mass culture online. How do communities differ and what kind of software is needed to support them? What can we learn from physical communities that will enable us to develop better online communities? For example, how do daily, weekly and yearly cycles translate to online activity? What kinds of behavioral rituals and codes of conduct lead to successful online communities? The results of this research will lead to development of appropriate policies to guide online behavior and will also contribute to better usability design.

Ethical issues and universal access are significant research areas; for example, how to notify users visually about unencrypted or encrypted traffic ensure privacy and encourage appropriate development of trust. Digital technology is affecting cultural diversity, environmental issues, conservation of limited ecological resources and people's standard of living. Research should inform national and international agencies so that they can deploy their resources well. Ways of providing universal access for people of all ages, cultures, languages, income levels, educational, physical and mental abilities should be found.

Theory and Methods

Unifying theories that bring together aspects of sociology, psychology, social psychology, linguistics, communications research and psychotherapy are needed to understand sociability and inform online community development.

Researching, designing, measuring and evaluating online communities requires modification of well-established techniques and creation of new ones. Methods, techniques and tools are needed to measure online activities and to understand how online communities are different from geographical communities. A research agenda that encourages the development of metrics to chart online demography, enriched by ethnographic data, will be particularly fruitful.

A good marriage of usability and sociability informed by strong theory and appropriate research and development methods will produce thriving online communities.

Acknowledgments

This chapter is adapted from Preece (2000) *Online Communities: Supporting Sociability, Designing Usability*, published by John Wiley & Sons. Permission from the publishers should be sought. Parts have also appeared in Brown *et al.* (1999).

References

Ackerman, M, and Starr, B (1996) Social activity indicators for groupware. *IEEE Computer*, 29(6), 37–42.
Axelrod, R (1984) *The Evolution of Cooperation*. New York, Basic Books.
Brown, J, van Dam, A, Earnshaw, R, Encarnacao, J, Guedj, R, Preece, J, Shneiderman, B and Vince, J (1999a) Human-centered computing, online communities and virtual environments, *IEEE Computer Graphics*, 19(6), 70–74.
Brown, J, van Dam, A, Earnshaw, R, Encarnacao, J, Guedj, R, Preece, J, Shneiderman, B and Vince, J (1999b) Human-centered computing, online communities and virtual environments. *ACM SIGCHI Interactions*, 6(5).
Brown, J, van Dam, A, Earnshaw, R, Encarnacao, J, Guedj, R, Preece, J, Shneiderman, B and Vince, J (1999c) Special report on human-centered computing, online communities and virtual environments. *ACM SIGGRAPH Computer Graphics*, 33(3), 42–62.
Card, S (1991) *Presentation on the Theories of HCI at the NSF Workshop on Human Computer Interaction*, Washington, DC, National Science Foundation.
Clark, HH and Brennan, SE (1993) Grounding in communication, in *Groupware and Computer-Supported Cooperative Work* (ed. RM Baecker), San Francisco, CA, Morgan Kaufmann, pp. 222–233.
Daft, RL and Lengel, RH (1986) Organizational information requirements, media richness and structural design, *Management Science*, 32, 554–571.

Figallo, C (1998) *Hosting Web Communities*. New York, John Wiley & Sons.

Fukuyama, F (1995) *Trust*, New York, Free Press Paperbacks, Simon & Schuster.

Gaines, BR, Chen, L-JL and Shaw, MLG (1997) Modeling the Human factors of scholarly communities supported through the Internet and the World Wide Web, *Journal of the American Society of Information Science*, 48(11), 987–1003.

Garton, L, Haythornthwaite, C, and Wellman, B (1999) Studying online social networks, in S Jones (ed.), *Doing Internet Research* (pp. 75–105), London, Sage Publications.

Hackos, J, and Redish, JC (1998) *User Analysis and Task Analysis for Interface Design*, New York, John Wiley & Sons.

Haythornthwaite, C (1996) *Media use in support of communication networks in an academic research environment*, University of Toronto, Toronto.

Jones, SE (1999) *Doing Internet Research. Critical Issues and Methods for Examining the Net*, Thousand Oaks, Sage.

King, S (1994) Analysis of electronic support groups for recovering addicts, *Interpersonal Computing and Technology: An Electronic Journal for the 21st Century (IPCT)*, 2(3), 47–56.

Kling, R (1999) What is social informatics and why does it matter? *D-Lib Magazine*, 5(1).

Kollock, P (1998) Design principles in online communities, *PC Update*, 15, 58–60.

Lazar, J, and Preece, J (1999) Designing and implementing Web-based surveys, *Journal of Computer Information Systems*, xxxix(4), 63–67.

Levenson, RW, and Ruef, AM (1992) Empathy: a physiological substrate, *Journal of Personality and Social Psychology*, 63, 234–246.

Liebowitz, JE (1999) *Knowledge Management Handbook*, Boca Raton, FL, CRC Press.

Lynch, PJ, and Horton, S (1999) *Web Style Guide (Preliminary Version)*, New Haven and London, Yale University Press.

Markus, ML (1987) Toward a critical mass theory of interactive media: universal access, interdependence and diffusion, *Communication Research*, 14, 491–511.

Markus, ML (1990) Toward a critical mass theory of interactive media: universal access, interdependence and diffusion. In *Organizations and Communication Technology* (eds. J Fulk and C Steinfeld), Newbury Park, CA: Sage, pp. 194–218.

Morris, M, and Ogan, C (1996) The Internet as mass medium, *Journal of Communication*, 46(1).

National Telecommunications and Information Administration & Commerce (1999) *Falling Through the Net: Defining the Digital Divide*, Washington, DC.

Nielsen, J and Mack, RL (1994) *Usability Inspection Methods*, New York, John Wiley & Sons.

Nonnecke, B, and Preece, J (2000) Lurker demographics: counting the silent. In press: available from the authors.

Norman, DA (1986) Cognitive engineering, in *User-Centered Systems Design* (eds. D Norman and S Draper), Hillsdale, NJ, Lawrence Erlbaum Associates.

Olson, GM, and Olson, JS (1997) Research on computer supported cooperative work, in *Handbook of Human Computer Interaction*, 2nd edn (eds. M Helander, TK Landauer and P Prabhu), Amsterdam, Elsevier, pp. 1433–1456).

Preece, J (1998) Empathic communities: reaching out across the Web, *Interactions Magazine*, 2(2), 32–43.

Preece, J (1999a) Empathic Communities: balancing emotional and factual communication, *Interacting with Computers*, 12, 63–77.

Preece, J (1999b) *A research agenda for online communities: Understanding behavior, predicting outcomes and informing design*. Bonas, France, EC and NSF Workshop.

Preece, J (2000) *Thriving Online Communities: Usability and Sociability*, Chichester, John Wiley & Sons.

Preece, J, Rogers, Y, Sharp, H, Benyon, D, Holland, S, and Carrey, T (1994) *Human–Computer Interaction*, Wokingham: Addison-Wesley.

Rice, RE (1987) Computer mediated communication and organizational innovations, *Journal of Communication*, 37, 85–108.

Rice, R (1993) Media appropriateness. Using social presence theory to compare traditional and new organizational media, *Human Communication Research*, 19(4), 451–484.

Rice, R (1994) Network analysis and computer-mediated communication systems, in *Advances in Social Network Analysis* (ed. SWJ Galaskiewkz), Newbury Park, CA, Sage, pp. 167–203).

Schuler, D (1996) *New Community Networks: Wired for Change*, Reading, MA, ACM Press and Addison-Wesley.

Shneiderman, B (1999) *Designing the User Interface: Strategies for Effective Human–computer Interaction*, 3rd edn, Reading, MA, Addison-Wesley.

Short, J, Williams, E, and Christie, B (1976) *The Social Psychology of Telecommunications*, London, John Wiley & Sons.

Smith, MA (1999) Invisible crowds in cyberspace: mapping the social structure of the Internet, in *Communities in Cyberspace* (ed. MASP Kollock), London, Routledge, pp. 195–219.

Spool, JM, Scanlon, T, Schroeder, W, Snyder, C, and DeAngelo, T (1997) *Web Site Usability: A Designer's Guide*, North Andover, MA, User Interface Engineering.

Sproull, L, and Kiesler, S (1991) *Connections: New Ways of Working in the Networked Organization*, Cambridge, MA, MIT Press.

Suchman, L (1987) *Plans and Situated Actions: the Problem of Human-machine Communication*, Cambridge: Cambridge University Press.

Wellman, B (1992) Which types of ties and networks give what kinds of social support? *Advances in Group Processes*, 9, 207–235.

Wellman, B (1997) An electronic group is virtually a social network, in *Culture of the Internet* (ed. S Kiesler), Mahwah, NJ, Lawrence Erlbaum Associates, pp. 179–205.

18

Collaboration and Shared Virtual Environments – from Metaphor to Reality

David Leevers

Abstract

This chapter proposes a framework for handling the technologies of networked collaboration. It is suggested that the information appliances and wearable computers that will soon dominate our lives will lead to a major paradigm shift from network-centered to human–centered thinking. By replacing many material goods and travel experiences these "Information Society Technologies" will open the way to global sustainability. They replace the unsustainable consumer product lifestyle of today with an "enhanced reality" that includes tele- and virtual components that can be more fulfilling than the real thing.

The scope of the PC user interface has expanded from self-contained tasks to becoming a persistent portal to the universal information ecosystem. Thus the research issues in HCI are shifting from the ergonomic and perceptual to the longer-term cognitive level. Unfortunately our thoughts are not locked to the PC at this ergonomic level, so future applications will require a much deeper appreciation of the human life cycle.

An earlier example is television. This brought a window on the world into every living room. Even now its fundamental cultural impact is poorly understood. Community values have shifted. Children understand the wider world better than their parents did, but richness of external variety may be acting as a barrier to appreciating the cultural depth of their own community. It is possible that the efforts are advantageous. Believing that all humans share the same fundamental ethical values seems to be preferable to rejecting other cultures as sub-human or even non-human.

Experience in a number of EC research projects on collaborative technology for manufacturing and construction has led to a potential conceptual framework for finding and applying information. This includes a "People and Information Finder" for obtaining the raw material and a "Cycle of Collaboration" or "CyColl" for characterizing the way this material is used individually, competitively and collaboratively (see Figure 18.3).

The CyColl indicates how established user interface metaphors might mature and eventually disappear within the new enhanced reality. The ultimate objective is not longer telepresence at one other place or virtual presence within an information structure. It is to enhance the reality of the local community by adding those aspects of the global community that encourage collaboration, equity, fulfillment and quality of life.

18.1 Networked Collaboration for Industry

About 15 years ago researchers in the UK construction and cable-making company BICC were inspired by Mike Cooley's (1982) book *Architect or Bee* to use early PCs to shift management thinking from process-centered to "human-centered" manufacturing. An early European Community-supported project, DIMUN (1988–91) explored how multimedia communications could help a distributed organization to be as effective as a co-located one. A multimedia communications prototype demonstrated how sales staff in one country, designers in another and shop floor workers in a third could hold meetings in the same virtual environment of video views and shared whiteboard.

This exercise demonstrated that the technology was equally capable of supporting the grapevine of informal communications between peers as the formal channels of communications up and down the hierarchy. Since informal communication is usually difficult and poorly documented, whereas formal messages are well defined and contractual, this new equity of infrastructure implied a dramatic shift of power within the organization. Indeed, 10 years later there are numerous examples of devolution of responsibility that are effective because staff now have all the relevant information at their fingertips.

The organizational structure was also studied. It was shown that only those in the value chain needed the full power of broadband two-way communications. Those in management and strategic functions worked on longer time-scales in which mature judgement was the main critical path. Thus as bandwidth increases the focus of traffic could be expected to shift down the organizational hierarchy faster than was expected. This has been shown over the subsequent 10 years, with astronomic growth of Web access by everyone contrasting with slow growth in the boardroom video conference, and the video game requiring far more processor power than the executive email processor.

The DIMUN multimedia communications interface included a visualization of a Virtual Meeting Room. This was seen as a way of helping users to orient themselves with respect to the various communications channels. Interestingly, the displayed image of a meeting room was hidden by the ubiquitous whiteboard as soon as participants started collaborative work.

Subsequently, the database index, the Web search engine and the multimedia presentation were viewed in metaphoric terms to build the stages of the CyColl. However, this cycle does not always match the way people actually use the different services. As users gain experience, each conscious metaphor sinks down into the subconscious and becomes its own reality. In some cases metaphor reversal takes place. One of the missing scenes from the movie *9 to 5* showed Jane Fonda, on her first day at work, placing the trash can on top of the desk because that is where she had seen it on her home Macintosh.

18.2 Enhanced Reality

Once of the many metaphoric devices that is helping us communicate with computers is the concept of virtual reality, or "almost reality". Unfortunately, VR can get trapped by its own metaphor. Moore's Law can be said to imply that the gap between the virtual and the real halves every 18 months, never actually closing.

A more constructive approach is to combine the best of the real and the best of the virtual to achieve a new "enhanced reality" that can transcend the real. One step along this path is augmented reality, effectively a number of calibration techniques that register the virtual against the real, perhaps via a half-silvered screen. However, registration is not the fundamental issue and an enhanced reality is one in which the social and physical world of our natural surroundings is seamlessly enhanced by other real places and VR visualizations of abstract environments.

18.3 Telepresence and Shared Virtual Environments

In the last four years a group of projects within the EC ACTS (Advanced Communications Technologies and Services) program known as the "Telepresence and Shared Virtual Environments" chain have been exploring the scope for enhancing the real with the telepresent and the virtual. The services explored by these projects can be regarded as the most complex and integrated manifestations of the four key communications modes:

- *One to one* – rapport and fact transfer, supported by the telephone and email
- *One to many* – dissemination, supported by broadcasting technologies
- *Many to one* – information retrieval, supported by data communications
- *Small group* – collaborative, supported by audio and video conferences

Although the delivery mechanisms and the low-level architectures for the four modes are likely to remain an *ad hoc* mixture of copper, glass fiber and radio, there is a true convergence at the user interface, primarily in the Web browser. Before the appearance of the browser the four modes were separate industries, each having its own distinct and part-time interface to the individual; perhaps one hour per day in front of the PC screen, two hours on the telephone, three hours in front of the television set and an occasional one hour video conference session.

Because the Web browser supports the ability to glide seamlessly from one communications mode to another it provides a persistent and ubiquitous interface to remote people and information via all four communication modes. This persistence turns the interface into something more than a link between individual and computer. It becomes a universal "Community-Network Interface", a new social glue linking all of networked humanity.

18.4 ACTS Project CICC

In ACTS project CICC, Collaborative Integrated Communications for Construction, we explored the potential for improving collaboration by using Information and Communications Technologies. Since this was done before many of the applications were robust enough to be used in project-critical situations individual components were explored within a range of trials from a huge construction project to a two-person shared virtual environment. The key trials are outlined below.

18.4.1 Global Virtual Factory: Six Factories

This was the earliest and also the most advanced pilot and implemented most of the stages of the CyColl. It was a self-contained demonstration that suspended disbelief among potential users for the half-hour required to understand the concepts and was used as a framework for the more limited later pilots. The objective was to help staff in six mineral insulated cable plants across four countries to think of their own factory as just part of much larger virtual factory.

The factory demonstration included many components of the People and Information Finder, including home pages, conferences with live video from the shop floor, a virtual reality reference factory and photographic tours of real factories linked to the common artifact of the virtual factory. The major potential benefit was expected to be a fruitful synthesis of the vertical culture of a single factory with the horizontal culture of a global village of networked factories; see Section 18.12.2.

18.4.2 Bluewater Shopping Centre: Over 100 Enterprises

Email and bulletin boards were added to the proven Hummingbird document database that was used by hundreds of participants over the three-year life of the project. These basic facilities prepared the minds of this group for brief demonstrations of many prototype services that were tried out at the site. These included video conferences, desktop video, awareness indicator, photographic walkabouts of the site, a public Web page showing live video from a surveillance camera and a networked screen saver that paged through the latest site photos, giving everyone a strong feeling of identity with the project.

18.4.3 Ove Arup Intranet: 15 Countries

A "People and Information Finder" of home and team pages was set up by one of the CICC partners, Arup Communications. Within a few months 30 groups across 15 countries had copied the approach. This achieved a dramatic but unquantifiable improvement in competitiveness, primarily because it became very much easier to contact other people when preparing bids.

18.4.4 EuroProject People and Information Finder: Client and Consultant

The trial was implemented as a conventional Web site that held all the designs and supporting information about projects such as the Expo98 marina being constructed by the company. It provided an effective link between the headquarters of the EuroProject consultancy in Barcelona and the site in Lisbon. It was innovative in two respects:

- the client had direct access to the design and testing data
- the same Web interface was used to access people, documents, structured information and live video from the site

18.4.5 CICC Team PIF: People and Information Finder

A public Web site which included home pages, video glances and screen glances for members of the CICC team at several locations. These glances could be arranged in groups to form a virtual open plan office or placed across the top of the screen to simulate presence on the other side of a conference table. By reducing the update rate to once every 30 seconds (except when people were actively participating in the meeting) and making the screen window so small that text could not be read the approach was intended to be no more intrusive than being observed while working in an open plan office.

18.4.6 Stanford University Civil Engineering Students: Team Design Exercises

Each design group included four people distributed across the campus and sometimes at another university. They worked together for three months on complete design exercises using NetMeeting and their own specialist collaboration tools. Meetings were logged on video so that much of the ethnographic study could be carried out afterwards.

18.4.7 Augmented Reality: Shared Artefacts

This was a series of demonstrations carried out during the development of registration and tracking software. It was clear that the objective visualization of AR is a powerful tool for lowering communications barriers between the sector and outsiders. As well as providing immediate support to project staff, AR could help neighbors of a new building to fully appreciate its appearance and implications before, during and after construction.

18.4.8 Shared Virtual Environment

The research laboratories of BT and Telefonica were linked by an 8 Mbit/s multimedia communications channel so that it was possible for people at each end to inhabit the same virtual reality office. As indicated elsewhere, this was both the most literal interpretation of a shared virtual environment and perhaps the most disappointing.

Overall, CICC has given us a very clear vision of how the construction community could evolve over the next few years and which collaborative tools are most relevant. In particular, it indicated which aspects of lean manufacturing could be transferred to construction as soon as mobiles and wearable computers provide construction site staff with networking tools comparable to those found on the factory shop floor.

Since the construction sector is effectively a microcosm of virtually all aspect of working life this work is proving a useful starting point for identifying the range of collaboration tools required to enhance reality for the rest of us.

18.5 A Framework for Networked Collaboration

This framework evolved in the light of experience in the industrial projects described above. It includes the following components:

- Four information sources
- People and information finder
- Hyperbola of synchronization
- Cycle of collaboration

Information sources have been classified into four distinct categories: in people's heads, on documents, in structured data and out in the real world. A common browser interface, the "People and Information Finder" (PIF), is used to access all four sources. The PIF includes many different services, primarily Web-based, that are supported by the organization's Knowledge Management function. An Internet portal is effectively a public version of a PIF.

Often we need more than passive information: we need to engage the active support of other people. The process of getting closer and closer to others is described as the "hyperbola of synchronization". This brings out the fact that the exchanges between a pair of people get shorter and faster as they get closer together mentally as well as physically.

This framework is showing considerable promise as a way of relating information processes in the home and workplace (presence) with those that can be transmitted across the network (telepresence), and those that would not be possible without the computer (virtual presence in visualizations of abstract data).

18.5.1 The Four Information Sources

- *Information in people's heads* When this information is emotionally neutral and there is trust a direct question can be asked. However, the more relevant the information is to the task in hand the less likely it is to be neutral. Extracting such information from inside another person's head can then become an enormously ingenious exercise which is highly dependent on the degree of understanding and commitment between the giver and receiver.

- *Information in documents* Both paper and electronic documents are included. These raw facts are usually easier to get hold of than information in the structured database, but may be more difficult to use.

- *Structured database* A database holds and structures a vast amount of information in an accurate and accessible form. However, it can be difficult to link its structure to the subtleties of the real world. Object orientation has improved flexibility and made it easier to reflect these subtleties as they are discovered. This makes it even more necessary for the People and Information Finder to ensure that unstructured and tacit information is adequately represented in the same style as the formal data.

- *Physical reality* Most of the information inside our heads comes from the physical world. After passing through the document and database stages, it often returns to the physical world as new and rearranged objects. This process is particularly clear at the construction site and on the factory shop floor. Augmented reality techniques are a leading-edge approach to linking the implicit information in the construction site with the structured database.

18.5.2 People and Information Finder

The four information sources are reached using a wide range of tools and it is becoming increasingly clear that the quality and compatibility of these tools has a dominant effect on the success of a project. As this is recognized, the new role of Knowledge Manager is expected to become of increasing importance. The PIFs implemented in CICC included the following tools (Figure 18.1):

1. *Home pages* A person's home page includes awareness of their position in the organization and their availability. In its most direct form this includes a small video window and a miniature of the person's PC screen both of which are updated every 30 seconds. Having some idea of what they are doing makes it easier for others to choose the right time to interrupt them, as in an open plan office. Everyone is asked to include pointers to half a dozen organizational "nearest neighbors" on their home page.

2. *Task view* This is the primary common artifact for supporting any collaborative activity. In construction and manufacturing this is usually a fixed image rather than anything dynamic. A top-level consensus task view or project chart is implicit in any group activity. This structure can take many years to discover fully. Making it explicit makes it much easier to bring new team members up to speed. In construction a visualization of the current state of the project is the usual top-level task view.

3. *Augmented reality* The real world is a grossly under-utilized source of information. Far more of this information could be used if it was logically linked with database information. This is the promise of augmented reality. On the one hand it can integrate what should be with what is, on the other, it can annotate the real world via a see-through head-mounted display.

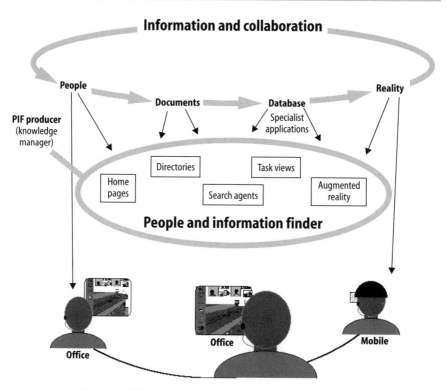

Figure 18.1 Collaboration within the network of trust of a virtual organization.

4. *Directories* These directories are well established both in paper systems and in any filing system. A remarkable step towards universal compatibility has been taken recently in presenting the Web in the same format as local and networked files on the Windows operating system. It will soon be possible to extend this common format to the physical world of the workplace and the mental worlds of colleagues.

5. *Search agents* These are newcomers. Every time someone makes their way through the PIF to reach some nugget of information they leave a record of their pattern of work and recent requirements. The search agent can use this information, together with many other types of analysis, to provide a fast way of getting to information and presenting it in the most convenient form.

18.5.3 The Hyperbola of Synchronization

The hyperbola (Figure 18.2) brings out the way in which the states of mind of a pair of individuals get closer as the messages between them become shorter and more frequent. Early exchanges always take longest: letters, emails and telephone calls

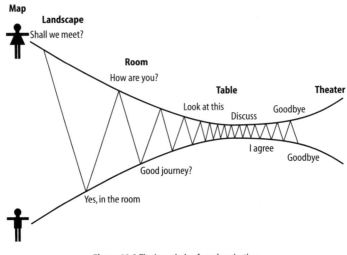

Figure 18.2 The hyperbola of synchronization.

intercepted by an assistant. As common ground is built up, the messages get shorter, more codified and more intense until sufficient rapport and trust has been established for the sharing of information, the distributed cognition of collaborative problem solving, and joint decision-making. Eventually the result of the combined contributions is captured in some way, perhaps as an agreed document or a diagram and the meeting can be said to have achieved its objective.

If this process takes place across the network then the relevant services need to offer appropriate bandwidth and latency characteristics at each stage and seamlessly transfer from one to another as the individuals move forward.

The hyperbola of synchronization is a way of looking at the dynamics of moving through the stages of the Cycle of Collaboration from the Map via the Landscape and Room to the Table until one member goes off to present results in the Theater. As such, it is closely related to the process of building trust.

18.5.4 Trust Time-Scales

Collaboration, and even civilized competition, requires trust. Trust is a surprisingly objective parameter. People are comfortable with weighing the degree of trust against the opportunity for gain when playing anything from a game of poker to the stockmarket. Trust is an ability to predict to a certain distance into the future. For a member of the family this trust time-scale is measured in decades, close friends in years – and insurance salespeople in minutes.

The quality of the technology is both a controlling and a controlled parameter for trust. The style of an email does not reveal much, but a home page gives away an immense amount. On the one hand the material can be checked, and on the other there is some expectation that, because the information is shared with a larger community, others can check it and therefore it is unlikely to be wrong. If the home page has only just been set up it would be viewed with caution; there may still be typing errors, the owner's definition of a success may not correspond with the views of others and so on.

A number of future Web enhancements will provide better support for building trust. These include an awareness of who is browsing a page now and in the recent past, where the master information is located, and meta-information such as the wear and tear of conventional documents.

18.6 The Cycle of Collaboration

The Cycle of Collaboration (Figure 18.3) is the temporal framework for transitions between the different communications modes. By focusing on the most likely transitions from one mode to another this cycle provides a way of relating the diversity of human communication activities to the variety of voice, data and video services.

The stages of the cycle – Territory, Map, Landscape, Room, Table and Theater – cover a typical route through different services and their real world predecessors. Each stage can be made up of any combination of digital and natural resources.

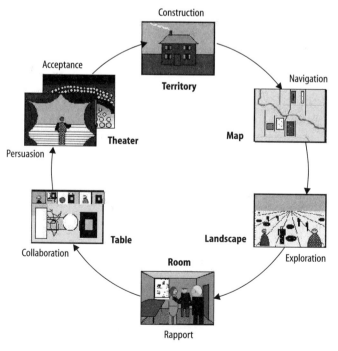

Figure 18.3 The Cycle of Collaboration.

18.6.1 Territory

The word "Territory" is used to indicate the non-communicating stage, when the individual is safely inside their personal fortress of home or workplace, working, relaxing or asleep. Every workplace has some area within which the individual's tasks are performed: the wall the bricklayer has been asked to build or the office where a paper is written. It is usual for others to respect this area and avoid interruption unless invited. At home this territory is that quiet corner where ideas are formulated and plans are made.

There is an equivalent mental territory: that part of the unconscious mind that reviews what we have recently learnt and adjusts the existing mental model of the world to fit in with new experiences. We rehearse the implications of new ideas, perhaps in dreams or in play, and start to formulate what to do next.

18.6.2 Map

The Map is any passive material that is effectively a signpost to the next stage, to a real place or to real information. When we start to venture out from the security of our own home we are not immediately ready to confront colleagues. The Map might be the morning paper, Yellow Pages, Web pages or database information – anything that provides an easy and reliable starting point for the tasks of the day. The map is usually familiar and not necessarily completely up-to-date, but that is an assurance of its stability. The stable reference points of the map prepares the mind for the more dynamic interactions in the landscape.

18.6.3 Landscape

As issues become clearer it becomes necessary to track down the most up-to-date information in a Landscape made up of people and the documents and databases that they are working with. The Landscape can be a real space, such as an open plan office or a building site where actions are visible and conversations overheard, or it can be a shared virtual environment in which remote people are represented as avatars and data as icons. When two or three members of a virtual team get into conversation video from cameras on their PCs can be shown in windows in the virtual landscape, thus simulating the casual multi-way conversations that are one of the main justifications for team offices.

18.6.4 Room

Contentious or unresolved issues need a more committed discussion than is possible in the rather public "open plan" Landscape. The Room supports the building of rapport and trust before starting a meeting. It is where the real or metaphoric handshake takes place. In real life it is often an impressive reception area, not the dull room where the meeting will take place. Similarly the virtual room requires different resources from the meeting itself – a high-quality video link rather than a shared whiteboard.

The walls of a real room are usually a complete security and privacy barrier that encourages occupants to share confidences. Similarly the walls of a shared virtual room that is displayed on each participant's screen remain dominant until the group have established mutual trust and respect. Then they feel confident enough to look down at the shared Table.

18.6.5 Table

The Table is the space where the common artifacts required for collaboration are displayed. In real life it obviously includes the workplace and the building site. Unlike real life the shared window of a virtual table can display identical material to all participants. However, each person still has their private area, their real life notebook or a private part of their own screen.

In trials the virtual table has occupied the lower part of the computer screen. Across the top are video windows of the other participants together with minia-ture copies of their own screens. These miniatures serve the same function as looking across a real table to see what the others are doing. As in real life, the miniatures are not clear enough to read what they are writing. The video windows indicate the extent to which the others are focusing on the shared task. These views maintain rapport and trust, even when their occupant is not contributing to the conversation.

18.6.6 Theater

The Theater is that place where the results of collaborative activities are conveyed to others. A meeting is only of value to others if the results are accepted by the rele-vant audience: customers, colleagues or students. A representative from the meeting has to take on a storytelling role to convey the conclusions as a narrative. In such a performance the narrative flow is usually decided in advance but the emotional emphasis can depend on the mood of the audience. Members of a live audience are prepared to accept the narrative if they know that the specialists have already reached agreement and, perhaps more significantly, if they sense that the rest of the audience is also accepting the message.

In project work the theater metaphor applies to any material that conveys results to a wider audience: minutes of meetings, a project database, multimedia presenta-tions, giving instructions to staff at the start of the day.

Any effective performance changes the way members of the audience will think in future. The performance can be said to have killed the previous personality and given birth to a slightly different one. This is one reason for the rituals of trust asso-ciated with becoming a member of an audience: checking reviews before buying a ticket, studying the mood of others in the foyer and being aware of their presence during the performance. It was the loss of these rituals on the early Internet that led to such scepticism about the quality of the information found on it.

TV has taken over many of the functions of the physical theater while adding the new element of a global shared experience. What it cannot do is re-create the atmosphere of excitement and the sense of togetherness experienced by an audience when they share the real physical space of an auditorium. There is hope that the interactive two-way feature of digital television will be used to convey this feeling of being part of a vast and responsive audience.

18.7 Narrative Continuity

By breaking collaborative activities down into a number of stages the CyColl follows a narrative and sequential model rather than a static and spatial one, and this narrative model includes both storytelling and logical argumentation. It shows the "left brain" function of sequential logic processes being grounded in and springing from the sensually rich panorama of the "right brain" and proceeding to a conclusion that is absorbed as some change to that panorama.

Such situated delta logic of short but convincing narrative threads avoids fundamental issues and thus is not troubled by the barber paradox (the barber cuts the hair of those who do not cut their own hair). The internal logic of each narrative thread stitches the objects and associations of memory into a better and better match with those parts of the outside world that are relevant to the survival and fulfillment of the individual.

18.8 Scope of the Cycle of Collaboration

The Cycle of Collaboration can be seen as reflecting daily life: waking at home, setting off using a map, actively browsing the office landscape in the morning, negotiating over the midday meal and collaborating in the hazy glow of the afternoon, then taking a seat in the theater as the Sun sets to surrender the mind to the persuasive powers of playwright and actor, finally going home with new ideas teeming inside the head, ideas that will have slightly altered us when we wake up next morning.

Similarly the cycle can be seen to reflect our journey through life: emerging from the home of the womb, spending a few months in a map of poorly understood sensations, then learning from the social landscape of other children and adults. Adolescence is spent working towards a rapport with the rest of society in a constantly changing meeting room of contrasting personalities. Then the individual settles down to more focused activities round the table of career and family. Finally the respect of the community is gained and cultural memes are passed on to the next generation in the theater of grandparents' stories.

18.9 Fractal Communications

Participants in a meeting room or round a table will individually go through a complete cycle in reacting to what someone else has said and then presenting a response. Thus the CyColl can be applied to an enormous range of time-scales from the formulation and presentation of a single statement to the life cycle of a civilization. The longer cycles include many levels of smaller cycles which are enmeshed with each other as the complementary components of each collaboration event.

18.10 What Is the Cycle of Collaboration for?

A bottom-up approach can identify some services, but is always trapped within its initial metaphor. The CyColl provides an opportunity to approach new services from the top down. As such it has proved to be very stimulating within the EC ACTS community.

18.10.1 Example: Shared Virtual Environments

Several years ago 3D shared virtual environments showed great promise as a way of supporting the affordances of collaboration in the real world. However, they have proved disappointing. Commercial services such as Blaxxun have confined the 3D world to just one of several windows. Looking at the CyColl diagram it can be seen that the 3D virtual environment is a suitable "Landscape" for meeting others casually but that it is not appropriate for later stages in a conversation.

18.10.2 Example: Video Conferences

The two-way high-quality video link is most relevant to the process of building trust and rapport. Work cannot start until trust is built, but real work requires a shared workspace, the Table, and an effective language channel (voice or text) – video is only required if there is a loss of rapport or a lack of trust. Thus the services that have blossomed have been shared whiteboards and video glances, whereas video conferencing has been confined to the boardroom, an environment where the subject of the discussion is often the trustworthiness of an individual and high-quality video is needed simply to pick up every nuance of body and face language.

In the real world setting of manufacturing and construction there are a vast number of different communications configurations: people in different places of different status, some on the shop floor and some on the construction site, and many engineers constantly driving from site to site. Thus planning a communications infrastructure requires the integration of a vast repertoire of different services, mobile, VR, Video, Webs and so on. It is not possible to draw on laboratory HCI for guidance on how they will work over the lifetime of a project. The CyColl provides a framework for relating new services and transitions between them to our natural behavior in the real world.

The CICC project has given us the opportunity to understand how the many different collaboration services are related to each other and when and where they should be used. As they come to occupy an increasing fraction of the working day, so the tools for switching from one type of services to another becomes as important as the services themselves.

The CyColl is a temporal framework for indicating which transitions are most relevant and the PIF supports these transitions. However, the CyColl might well be the swan song of the user interface metaphor. By completing the set of metaphors for collaborative processes it is creating an enhanced reality that is greater than the sum of its metaphoric parts. At the end of the day the CyColl may be more important as a hidden technical framework for coordinating the many function fragments that are delivered by future information appliances and wearables.

The charateristics of the stages of the Cycle of Collaboration are shown in Table 18.1.

18.11 Design Guidelines for Shared Virtual Environments

The Telepresence and Shared Virtual Environment projects are helping to identify a number of design guidelines, such as:

1. Treat the virtual environment as a window within the real world, not an alternative to the real world (immersive VR is most relevant to game and simulation applications).
2. Recognize that humans have a predator brain structure which uses stereo vision to focus on the prey, rather than 360° vision to detect other predators. We only feel secure enough to think constructively when the action is taking place in front of us. This is why any group, not just Arthur's Knights of the Round Table, tend to form a circle, and why bigger groups that have to sit in rows need a chairperson. This also indicates that the screen is better matched to our cognitive abilities than the immersive headset or CAVE.
3. Recognize the power of humans to establish rapport and trust across any sort of communication link provided it is two-way and has predictable performance. The handshake, the shared meal and the golf game are all real-world examples. A shared visualization is not required to establish rapport across the network. Latency is not a big issue providing it is predictable. It simply determines the rate at which trust builds: a few seconds in the case of a handshake, several days for email exchanges.
4. Recognize that collaboration, and even competition, requires that all parties see the subject from a shared point of view as well as from their private specialist points of view. Once this can be achieved, conflict of personalities and values usually dissipates into clarification of facts rather than arguments over principles. This may explain the difficulty of placing participants in primitive shared virtual environments: they would have to get intimately close to

Table 18.1 The Cycle of Collaboration – characteristics of each stage

Stage	Key feature	Typical time	Bandwidth	Topology	Number of people	User interface	Objective	Comments
Territory (mental workspace)	Private thought, typing and writing	Hours	Zero	None	One	None when thinking, otherwise pencil or keyboard	Consolidating and expressing a concept triggered by the theatre	Building new concepts or mental models in the private territory of the mind
Territory (physical workplace)	Embodied interaction with the surroundings	Hours	Zero	None	One	The workplace tools	Apply procedures learnt in the "theater" of instructions	Constructing something in the temporary territory of the workplace
Map	Static, validated, consolidated documents	Minutes	Low	One to one, one way, e.g. HTML	Historic information from 1000s of others	Static images and text	Navigate to the relevant area	
Landscape	Brief interactions with trusted others	Minutes for each interaction	Medium	Two way and multiway	150 trusted coleeagues to 1 user	Brief exchanges, Q & A, email, people at shouting distances	Explore the relevant area	
Room	Establishing rapport for creativity	10 min	High	Mesh, few to few	4 member group	High realism, people at whispering distances	Rapport with others with complementary potential	This negotiating is intended to equalize status in order to encourage collaboration
Table	Distributed creativity in private	1 hour	Medium	Mesh, few to few	4 Group	Common artifacts on table or whiteboard	Distributed cognition	
Theater								
Presenter	Narrative thread		High	One to many	1	Two way "proscenium arch" interface	Convey the results agreed at the meeting	
Member of audience		30 min	Low	Many to one	25	Plus panoramic awareness of the audience by each member of audience	Learn a new behaviour	The narrative interface

each other's virtual bodies in order to see the same view on the screen (people do not enjoy the experience of walking through other bodies, even when they are virtual). This also explains why the British House of Commons is a disastrous model for achieving consensus: participants are forced into a confrontational paradigm, seeing diametrically opposite views of their surroundings – and shared whiteboards are forbidden

5. Recognize that individuals need to share two distinct spaces, a "mind space" in which they interact with others, and a "problem space" in which they see the common artifacts. This problem space is often a 2D electronic whiteboard, but it might be a shared 3D visualization of a future building. A shared virtual environment that combines the two may raise more problems than it solves.

6. Recognize that the hands and body need to feel as comfortable as the eyes, ears and mouth. The touch environment of chairs, tables and evocative interfaces such as the virtual steering wheel and motorbike seat, need to be realistic and satisfying for the experience to be complete.

18.12 Sharing the Culture of Enhanced Reality

The telepresence and virtual presence services of today are comparable in quality to the car of 100 years ago. They need the full-time services of a "Windows Chauffeur" to hide their limitations and unreliability from the user. Telepresence and virtual presence are themselves immature metaphoric terms, comparable with the first name for a car: the horseless carriage. We have not yet made the conceptual leap to treating tele- and virtual experiences as the real thing and "Travel Presence" (the complete package of return travel and physical presence) as an inadequate substitute. Perhaps this is because the technology is not yet good enough to feel that the tele- and virtual fragments of daily life are seamless enhancements of local reality.

Eventually the process of physical travel could be regarded as vulgar and undesirable, in the same way as other aspects of Stone Age life that have now been hidden: the abattoir hides the killing of the lamb we eat, bodies are covered with clothes and the water closet hides human waste. However, not all travel is unpleasant and a small amount of leisure travel can be expected to outlast the Machine Age just as a small amount of leisure nudity outlasted the Stone Age!

18.12.1 Collaboration and Culture

Some level of shared culture is an essential prerequisite for effective collaboration. Each participant has to be able to anticipate the responses of the others. Such shared culture predated the network and has spread around the world with the common artifacts of global manufacturing, from the first mechanical clock to the most recent videogame. These artifacts are forcing all communities into similar social conventions, from "clockwise" to new types of hand–eye coordination.

It has been so difficult to achieve effective real time collaboration across the network that the complementary need for competition has hardly been addressed. In fact, it is difficult to think of a case where collaboration within the group is not driven by the desire to compete with other groups, the research team competing for funds, the business competing for survival and the neighborhood competing for honor.

The soccer World Cup and the Olympic Games force every community with television to accept a set of values that are becoming universal. Whereas there can be collaboration without local culture, there cannot be competition without local culture – it is very difficult to get a player to make the supreme sacrifice if they do not know which side they belong to. Thus the more global the competition the more each local culture tries to differentiate itself. This leads to increased interest in the local community at the expense of the nation state.

18.12.2 Geographic and Digital Cultures

CSCW researchers have usually had to stay away from social and cultural value systems, but over the last 40 years, others have taken the West on a rollercoaster ride from cultural arrogance to cultural relativism. Only now, after the worldwide diffusion of Western middle-class culture, are we trying to understand how the steamroller of the West can beneficially coexist with local indigenous cultures. Perhaps it is too late: just as European diseases wiped out most native Americans, so this steamroller is flattening many indigenous cultures. However, the situation may not be that serious. There are not as many dead bodies and there are plenty of examples of people being enriched by a stimulating mixture of the universal global culture and their own grounded local culture.

Our physical surroundings are now being enhanced by multimedia information streams that transcend barriers of time, space and culture. The traditional geographic cultures are not necessarily strong enough to provide a moral resilience that can stand up to intrusions from outside. They are being challenged by a complementary global culture that changes as rapidly from year to year as traditional cultures vary from country to country. The interaction between the two is a vast opportunity to create a fount of cultural richness that need never run dry.

The definition of culture that is being used here is that deep structure of individual behavior that is acquired in early childhood. This basic culture is absorbed in much the same way as a first language. Later cultural experiences do not become part of the personality in the same way. In the past this deep culture could only be acquired from immediate family, friends and community. Children in advanced countries now spend so much time in front of the television, listening to global music and logging on to the Web that a significant fraction of their early cultural experience is synchronized with other children of the same age worldwide. Figure 18.4 shows the different types of culture.

18.12.3 Global Sustainability

Global social stability, global environmental sustainability and a western quality of life to 10 billion people cannot be achieved with the western pattern of

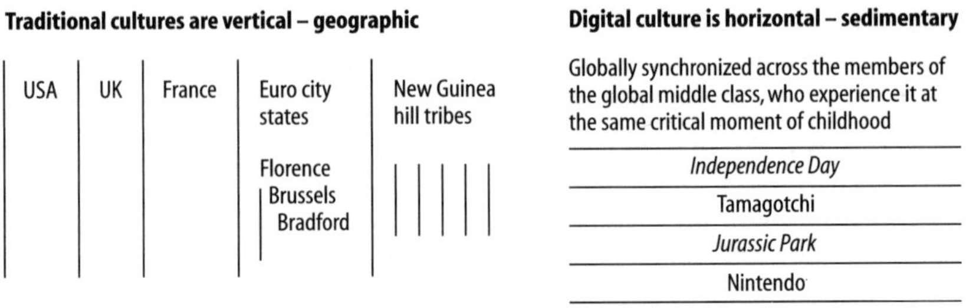

Traditional cultures are vertical – geographic					Digital culture is horizontal – sedimentary
USA	UK	France	Euro city states	New Guinea hill tribes	Globally synchronized across the members of the global middle class, who experience it at the same critical moment of childhood
			Florence Brussels Bradford		*Independence Day*
					Tamagotchi
					Jurassic Park
					Nintendo

Figure 18.4 Geographic and digital cultures.

material consumption. The most promising solution (apart from war, pestilence and plague) is to use Information Society Technologies (IST) to create virtual replacements for fractions of physical experiences. However, many of these experiences are so deeply embedded in the individual psyche and in community values that progress will be slow until the present network-literate children reach maturity.

Most of the consumer products of the West may be no more than clumsy physical prototypes of fractions of a future enhanced reality. We are a long way from understanding how to make this enhanced reality as challenging and fulfilling as the accoutrements of the Western lifestyle. However, the next generation is growing up with this technology embedded in their deep culture as social human beings. The compact disc has replaced the live orchestra. The videogame is more vivid and fulfilling than most board games and the multigym is more convenient than the sports field.

However, the IST approach is vulnerable in that it depends on as-yet unproved hypotheses about the humanity of Information Society Technologies and their ability to deliver experiences that are truly "better than being there". The track record of the ICT industry is not good. It has grown from nothing over the last 50 years, making many mistakes along the way and alienating many of the more mature members of the population. Credible demonstrations of the cultural richness of networked experiences are desperately needed in order to remove associations with the IT disasters of the past.

Manufacturing broke away from a stultifying framework of the assembly line only when a Post-Fordist vision was formulated. Perhaps now is the time to formulate a "Post-PC" vision of the Post-Information Society: the Global Networked Society, a human-centered culture supported by information appliances in the surroundings and wearable computers on the body.

We will always remain firmly attached to the sensory panorama of our immediate physical and social surroundings, but the new technology will add magic to these surroundings in the way that only the emperor could hope for in the past. Wizards and intelligent agents will be everywhere, supporting every co-emperor of the Global Networked Society.

18.13 Conclusions

Relative body positioning in the real world lies at the heart of effective collaboration. Thus Shared Virtual Environments were expected to be an important element in supporting collaboration across the network. This chapter has discussed a framework for analyzing collaborative processes that can be used to suggest when and where such virtual environments are most effective.

The CyColl, a comprehensive set of metaphors for the user interface, has been proposed. This has proved most useful in understanding the scope and limits of current communications services and in distinguishing different forms of collaborative activity. For instance, what may appear to be a fully effective meeting may have been preceded by travel experiences that have put some participants at a psychological disadvantage. The phrase "travel presence" may be an important reminder that virtually all physical meetings require some degree of travel.

The original opportunity for shared virtual environments was as a replacement for such travel presence. However, this statement of the problem takes us down the wrong path, trying to simulate presence at a single other place, whereas the fundamental requirement is to include the remote within our local reality. There is no point in bouncing around the world like a horizontal yo-yo, even virtually.

A complete parallel mental world may not be what we want. Because the mind is embodied, there is no way that we can, like Alice, step through the looking glass of the PC screen and take our complete identity into cyberspace.

Fortunately there is an alternative, enhancing the reality of the social and physical world within which humans evolved to survive. Perhaps the next HCI task is to build a greater understanding of how the embodied minds of humans find fulfillment in the real world so that the function fragments delivered by information appliances and wearables can be invisibly interleaved into our natural surroundings. This may be helped by a paradigm switch from network-centered shared virtual environments to human-centered enhanced reality.

Bibliography

Barkow, J, Cosmides, L and Toomby, J (1992) *The Adapted Mind – Evolutionary Psychology and the Generation of Culture*, New York, Oxford University Press.

CICC project, http://www.vers.co.uk/cicc/.

Cooley, M (1982) *Architect or Bee?: The Human/Technology Relationship*, Slough, Langley Technical Services.

Devlin, K and Rosenberg, D (1996) *Language at Work – Analysing Communication Breakdown in the Workplace to Inform Systems Design*, Stanford, CA, CSLI Publications.

Fox, R (1989) *The Search for Society – Quest for a Biosocial Science and Morality*, New Brunswick, NJ, Rutgers University Press.

Fukuyama, F (1995) *Trust – the Social Virtues and the Creation of Prosperity*, New York, The Free Press.

Harre, R and van Langenhove, L (1999) *Positioning Theory*, Malden, MA, Blackwell.

Hutchins, E (1995) *Cognition in the Wild*, Cambridge, MA, MIT Press.

Lakoff, G and Johnson, M (1999) *Philosophy in the Flesh*, New York, Basic Books.

Ridley, M (1997) *The Origins of Virtue*, London, Viking.

Shapiro, C and Varian, H (1999) *Information Rules, the Economics of the Global Networked Society*, Boston, MA, Harvard Business School Press.

Turkle, S (1995) *Life on the Screen*, New York, Simon & Schuster.

19

On the Need for Cultural Representation in Interactive Systems

Sudhir P. Mudur

Abstract

It is well recognized that a culture-like environment must be at the core of all developmental activities. Technology developments that are at cross-purposes with the culture and environment are not likely to result in the expected human development process of enlarging people's choices. Cultural sensitivity is thus of extreme importance in digital information technology, which is growing so rapidly as to encompass virtually all aspects of our living. The cultural composition of a digital information space will certainly define its ultimate impact, but more importantly, if not properly addressed it will also limit its audience.

Currently, the field of digital information systems design is dominated by engineers and their milieu, so-called technical wizards, largely from the USA. This is reflected in the way information representation standards are being evolved, or in the way systems and interaction frameworks are being architected. This chapter will address four issues:

1. The need for culture sensitive representation at core systems level
2. The necessity to integrate the indigenous knowledge and cultural heritage of developing countries
3. Design-level separation of interaction and function in interactive systems
4. The importance of truly interdisciplinary collaborative efforts in interactive systems design

In addressing these issues I will draw upon my past experience, and more specifically, my experience with localization of a widely used platform.

19.1 The Need for Cultural Localization of Interactive Systems

The Human development process must primarily result in enlarging people's choices for learning, working and, generally speaking, living in this world.

Information technology, particularly interactive digital technology, is growing at phenomenal rates to affect and encompass virtually all aspects of our lives. Clearly the manner in which this technology develops and gets deployed in our world is of extreme importance to us all. It is well recognized that a culture-like environment must be at the core of all developmental activities. Technology developments that are at cross-purposes with the culture and environment are not likely to result in the expected human development process of enlarging people's choices. Cultural sensitivity is thus of the utmost importance in digital information technology. The cultural composition of a digital information space will certainly define its ultimate impact. But even more importantly, if improperly addressed it could seriously limit its audience and hence the market.

Currently, the field of digital information systems design is dominated by engineers and their milieu, so-called technical wizards, largely from the USA. This is reflected in the way information representation standards are being evolved, or in the way systems and interaction frameworks are being architected. A basic assumption being made in systems development activities, even where there is some concern for internationalization, is that all culture-specific requirements can be built in the form of associative resource databases and software layers laid on top of the core systems engine. However, my own experience has been that, unless these core engines are built taking into account the cultural requirements, it is almost impossible to *slap on* culture specific needs in the form of culture-specific resource data tables or as software layers. Even in something as simple as character encoding and display, or font representation standards, this problem manifests itself in a glaringly noticeable manner. In the rest of this chapter four major issues will be addressed:

1. The need for culture-sensitive representation at core systems level
2. The necessity to integrate the indigenous knowledge and cultural heritage of developing countries
3. Design-level separation of interaction and function in interactive systems
4. The importance of truly interdisciplinary collaborative efforts in interactive systems design

In addressing these issues I will draw upon my past experience, and more specifically, my recent experience with localization of a widely used platform [1].

19.2 Major Issues in Cultural Localization

19.2.1 Technology Carries Culture

Cultural localization is the process by which an interactive system developed in one culture is adapted for use in another culture, in a manner indistinguishable from a system with the same functionality if developed within that culture [2,3]. Contrary to popular belief, although cultural localization presupposes proper addressing of linguistic requirements, it goes far beyond. Just like film, television, painting, literature etc., an interactive digital system developed in one culture inevitably carries embedded cultural assumptions that are alien to users from other cultures. Of particular significance is the common observation that most of the current systems are primarily designed to be used for real-world problem solving in an isolated individualistic manner, and not by a group in a collaborative fashion.

19.2.2 Culture Sensitivity Cannot Be Merely Added on

Localization or internationalization, as it is often referred to, is approached by most system builders as an "add-on" after the original system development work is complete and made fully functional. Thus it is common to hear of localization being carried out on a completed and released version of Windows or Lotus Notes. But it has become clear in many situations that such efforts are inadequate and often produce undesirable results, and may even require redevelopment of many parts of the software. It is essential to recognize the fact that cultural requirements must be addressed as part of the initial design of the system and that appropriate cultural representation mechanisms must be embedded in the core software engine itself. Many authors have also argued similarly [4].

Currently the best example of cultural representation in software systems is the notion of a *locale* database available as a resource file to be substituted and used for different cultures/environments. Typically the *locale* resource could include:

- fonts and keymaps to implement the writing system
- resource files containing translations of all the messages and other text indexed by message number
- resource files containing material like pictures and icons
- code-level implementation of specific formatting requirements, sorting etc.

Clearly the above is far from adequate to handle the cultural diversity that exists. More importantly, many of the truly culture-sensitive requirements are completely missed out, as we shall see next. And these must necessarily be embedded at the core level. Simple substitution of data and code resources is in no way adequate.

19.2.3 Building Culture-Sensitive Systems Is Not Merely Technological

Even if, as at present, the cultural localization of interactive systems is merely addressed through the use of *locale* add-ons, it is important to recognize that it is not a mere technology problem. It is difficult to imagine that engineers or even designers sitting in far-off countries will all of a sudden be in a position to build into their design the needs of another culture, having never even visited the other part of the world, let alone being part of it. Thus many different issues need to be addressed which are difficult to handle at the design stages without adequate knowledge and experience. The following is only a short list provided as a sampler.

- The special requirements of the scripts or writing system used [5].

- Specific translation needs of all text that needs to be translated (e.g. from English to Hindi) taking into account whether the text will fit into the space reserved.
- Language rules for spelling checks, hyphenation and similar.
- Number representations – particular problems are the use of *lakhs* and *crores* in India.
- Calendars and dates: most of the developed world has adopted the Gregorian calendar based on a solar year, but the Indian calendar is not the same.
- Time zones are not necessarily based on the 12 hour division of AM and PM.
- Measurement units and currency symbols: one or two special symbols may be used, placed either before or after the number involved.
- Colors and icons: these can be very culturally sensitive. For example red indicates danger and black may indicate sorrow in Europe, but not in India.
- Names and their processing: European tradition is for people to have family and one or more familiar names.
- Examples are usually chosen to be familiar to those in the location concerned, and for software of US origin this often involves the sport baseball, which is not widely known in India.
- Business, commercial practices and the laws within which these operate could be very different.
- Accountancy and tax rules: these differ widely.
- Most importantly, the interaction patterns that are culturally most acceptable can be very different; in current systems these are based on the "hacker" culture – individualism; risk-taking; rebelliousness; irreverence; no great respect for tradition, hierarchy and authority; emphasis on novelty; achievement-oriented rather than conforming to ascribed characteristics; etc.

The locale information of most software producers does include some of the above requirements. Although issues like color and icons are not presently addressed they could possibly be. What is truly challenging and difficult is the incorporation of culturally sensitive interaction modes and patterns. This can only be done by ensuring the integration of indigenous knowledge and cultural heritage at the systems design level.

Unfortunately, information systems are designed and standardized without any regard to this. A specific example is what is normally perceived as the *very simple* task of text encoding. Unicode [6] is the text encoding scheme standardized by a consortium of all major information technology vendors (from the developed countries). Unicode version 2 supports a number of Indic scripts. Yet the basis on which the Indic script encoding has been derived does not have any cultural foundation. I am not aware if Indian linguists were consulted when arriving at this coding scheme. But I do believe that had they been consulted, then perhaps the result would have been different. Now, because of the so-called standardization process, there is tremendous reluctance to change it to something that is ideally needed for dealing with the digital representation of textual information in Indian languages. This is like the repeat of the QWERTY phenomenon. The Appendix at the end of this chapter provides a detailed note on this

19.2.4 No Clear Separation of Concerns Between Interaction and Function

Much of interactive design is dominated by so-called technical wizards. For a variety of reasons, and an oft-repeated important reason is system performance, the software design tends to have no clear separation of concerns with respect to interaction and function. There is usually a very fuzzy separation between the parts that handle the interaction and the parts that handle the functionality. Often there is an absence of adequate parameterization of user interface determinants.

For example, when developing the display code for shell-level text in the standard user interface of a widely used operating system we were clearly told by the development team that our text cannot be displayed in more than 11 pixels height including all ascenders, descenders and inter-line gaps. Our font designers gasped at the constraint and showed me text which they said just could not be fitted into a height of 11 pixels (see Figure 19.1). After multiple rounds of message exchanges from both ends, we were finally able to get to the crux of the matter. The figure of 11 was hard coded in some dialog boxes deep in the kernel of the operating system. And it was impossible to change it!

A similar problem occurs in the handling of keyboard input and mouse-based cursor positioning in a given piece of text in Indian scripts. Most Western engineers find it very difficult to grasp the rather simple fact that a single keystroke could in principle result in the input of many characters, and conversely many keystrokes may result in the input of a single character. This requirement of a many-to-many mapping of keystrokes to character codes is virtually impossible to accommodate in current system architectures. There is no clear separation of key operations and text character encoding!

There are indeed many such examples that we have encountered in our work on localization of operating systems and application packages.

Figure 19.1 Some examples of Indian letter shapes.

19.2.5 Truly Interdisciplinary Collaborative Efforts Are Rare

In spite of all the emphasis on interdisciplinary teams, it is common to see technical wizards talk down to graphic designers and other professionals who do not understand everything about our technology. Examples of error messages like "Error Number 21: Abort, Retry or Ignore" which loop infinitely unless you *Abort* are ample reflections of this. A good interactive system can only be built by getting a good understanding of the user(s). Understanding the needs, feelings, tasks, environment and usage culture of people who will all form part of this interactive digital space is essential before interactive systems design is undertaken. In fact, not only should the final interactions be in the language of the users, even initial communication with potential users in the language of the user and within that cultural setup may be important. If more cultural modes are to be represented in human–machine interfaces, so that more people find these systems accessible, then truly interdisciplinary teams are the only solution.

19.3 Conclusions

1. Interactive digital technology is a covert carrier of cultural values. Sensitivity to the requirements of individual cultures is of utmost importance.
2. Culture sensitivity must be built in during the initial design stages itself. Even the design of hardware, peripherals and devices which are directly used by people must be designed with this in mind.
3. There is an urgent need to ensure that the technology producers understand the fact that building in culture sensitivity is not merely a problem of technology alone. It is important to ensure that people from different cultures are directly involved in the building of these systems.
4. Undoubtedly interactive system design is a truly multi-disciplinary activity. The involvement of technologists, designers, social scientists and other people from related disciplines on an equitable basis is essential.
5. Direct user involvement and user representation in design are important so that there exists a clear separation of concerns between interaction and function.
6. Even if culture sensitivity were to entail diverse demands in systems design, it is important to develop/search for a common framework that could form the basis for interactive systems development.
7. The framework should also enable the study and analysis of the interactive system from the point of view of embodying culture from the real world [7].

References

[1] SP Mudur, Niranjan Nayak, Shrinath Shanbhag and RK Joshi (1999) An architecture for the shaping of Indic scripts, *Computers and Graphics*, January.

[2] K Keniston (1998) Politics, culture and software, *Political and Economic Weekly*, Mumbai, 17 January.

[3] PAV Hall and J Clews (1998) Customisable internationalised software: a win–win strategy for the South Asian software industry, in *Proceedings of SAARC EMMIT'98*, Pune, India, pp. 26-1–26-8,

[4] K Nadine (1995) *Developing International Software for Windows 95 and Windows NT*, Redmond, WA, Microsoft Press.

[5] RK Joshi (1999) The Indian tradition of calligraphy and multilinguality in the new digital era, in *Proceedings ICVC99*, Goa, February.

[6] A Kerne (1998) Cultural representation in interface ecosystems, *Interactions*, Jan–Feb, 37–44.

[7] Unicode Consortium (1996) *The Unicode Standard – Version 2.0*, Reading, MA, Addison-Wesley.

About the Author

S.P. Mudur is Associate Director and Head of the Graphics and CAD Division at the National Centre for Software Technology in Bombay, India. He received his Ph.D. at the Tata Institute of Fundamental Research from the University in 1976. He has been actively working in the field of computer graphics and visual computing since 1970, has published a large number of papers on various topics in computer graphics and related subjects, and organized a number of high-quality national and international conferences.

Mudur is on the editorial board of the international journals *Computers & Graphics, Computer Graphics Forum* and *Journal of Visualization and Computer Animation*. For four years, from 1992–1996, he was the Chairman, Publications of the Computer Society of India, which has four different publications covering its entire computer-related activities. He is also on the editorial board of the *Computer Science and Informatics* journal of the Computer Society of India. Mudur is a fellow of the Computer Society of India.

Mudur is the Indian representative on Technical Committee 5 of the International Federation for Information Processing (IFIP) on Computer Applications in Technology, and Governor of the International Council for Computer Communication.

He is a member of the Computer Society of India, EUROGRAPHICS, and IFIP Working Groups 5.2 on Computer Aided Design and 5.10 on Computer Graphics. Mudur is also a member of a number of national and international level advisory/review committees concerning large-scale computer graphics and other Information Technology projects. Mudur has recently been appointed as Chairman for the newly constituted SRIG – MLC, South East Asia Regional Computer Confederation's (SEARCC) regional interest group on multilingual computing. Mudur's current research interests include geometric modeling, realistic image synthesis, physically based modeling and visualization, and multimedia virtual environment technology and interactive systems design.

Appendix: Unicode Text Encoding for Indian Languages: Recurrence of the QWERTY Phenomenon?

A.1 Digital Information – a Fundamental Shift in Recording and Communication

Unicode has the goal of providing a digital encoding for recording and communicating information in all the world languages. It has been a constant endeavor of humans to devise means and techniques that enable recording and communication of information in an unambiguous manner. Indians have a rich tradition in this. Let us consider for example India's ancient oral method used to record information and pass it down successive generations through the Guru-Shishya mechanism.

The "Gurus" (teachers) meticulously recited and their "Shishyas" (disciples) had to repeat the information perfectly with identical pronunciation, intonation etc. so as to be unambiguously interpretable by the listener. As a result the Indian alphabet enjoys phonetic richness, variety and subtlety rarely found in any other civilization – so many different vowel sounds, consonant groups, nasal sounds (four different forms of the "T" and "D" sounds, three forms of the "S" and so on).

The oral form gave way to the graphic form (written, scribed, etched and printed). The graphic form too has evolved over centuries so as to be unambiguously interpreted by the reader and also when converting to the oral form. This largely explains why letter shape (font) design is such a complex design activity. It is not merely the design of single letter forms but of visualizing all their combinations and ensuring their unambiguous interpretation by all readers.

Today, while we are in the throes of an information revolution, there is a fundamental shift in this process of recording and communicating information – from the graphic form to the digital form. This shift is not merely in the means and techniques that computer technology provides, but a shift in the primary user of the information itself. Increasingly computers and humans will be equal partners in the use of information encoded in the digital format. In fact, digitally encoded information is first "read" by the computer and then processed by it to provide visual or speech renderings in a form that is easily accessible to humans. But we also know today that visual or speech rendering (display/print or speech synthesis respectively) are not the only computer processes that will make use of the digital information. As the worldwide information base in the digital format increases and network-centric computer processing dominates, humans will look forward to digital agents doing much of the searching and sifting of this vast information space and providing us with specific information extracts, summaries recommendations etc. Should this not be possible in Indian languages as well?

What all this implies is the need for a coding scheme in which encoded strings result in unique and consistent interpretation by other computer processes – not just those computer processes that we can list today, but also those that will evolve in this digital information era. It would be totally lacking in vision if we merely think of the digital information format as one that must provide the transfer of words in books onto words on the screen.

It is in this context that the present Unicode scheme for Indic scripts has flaws.

A.2 Problems with Unicode for Indic Scripts

Ambiguous Encoding, Inconsistent Interpretation and Invalid Strings

The basic problems arise due to the fact that Unicode for Indic scripts is not minimal and encodes at a level higher than the atomic (metaphorically speaking) level. For brevity, henceforth, reference to Unicode is to be read as Unicode for Indic scripts. Three aspects of the present Unicode cause the problems:

1. Unicode does not encode the pure consonant. Rather, the consonant is encoded at a macro level, with a single code denoting a consonant along with the "A" vowel.

2. It then includes the special character, "halant" (\), to denote the operation of subtracting the "A" present in the immediately preceding consonant. Here it is important to note that our ancient grammarian Panini has clearly stated that the notional element of the "A" vowel in the consonants is only to facilitate pronunciation of the alphabet, just as the "I" vowel sound is used to pronounce consonants like B, C, D, G etc. of the English alphabet. The relevant page from Siddhanta-kaumudi is appended. Similarly, the use of the "halant" is meant *only* for graphically indicating the absence of a vowel in a word ending, and *not* as the subtractor of the "A" vowel.

3. The "matras" are merely different visual renderings of those vowels that immediately follow a sequence of consonants. They are basically vowels, to be pronounced identically. Unicode encodes matras as distinct from vowels. Not only does this result in redundant coding, but more importantly, coupled with the manner in which Unicode encodes consonants, it also necessitates that they be given the special interpretation of replacing the "A" present in the immediately preceding consonant with the corresponding vowel.

Keeping the above three aspects of Unicode in mind, let us consider three computer processes operating on the two Unicode strings shown in Figure 19.2. The three computer processes are:

1. The visual rendering process for displaying on screen, printing on paper, film etc.

2. The speech rendering process for digital synthesis of encoded text to speech.

3. The consonant–vowel separator process, so essential in all Indian language processing for finding root words, gender, plurality etc. (LadkA, Ladki and so on).

Clearly, the use of the "halant" with its special interpretation enables the encoding of multiple strings, resulting in inconsistent interpretation by the different

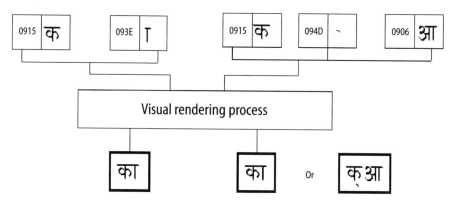

Figure 19.2

computer processes. In fact, the need to graphically disambiguate the two strings results in an orthographically inaccurate rendering. It is the orthographic rule for all Indic scripts that if a vowel immediately follows a consonant without any embedded vowel then it can *only* take the form of the matra.

Consider the process of speech input (Figure 19.3). The sound associated with the "Aa" matra is the same as the "Aa" vowel. Which of these two sounds should it produce? Phonetically both strings *must* produce the same sound "Kaa". Thus it is inconsistent with the interpretation of the visual rendering process, unless one forces the interpretation as being unpronounceable for the second string and "speaks out" the three Unicode character pronunciations independently.

Let's look at the dilemma of the consonant–vowel separator process. If its interpretation has to be consistent with the visual rendering process, then it has to interpret the code "Ka" followed by the "Aa" matra as the sequence "Ka", "halant" followed by the "Aa" vowel. *But* ironically it has to interpret the Unicode sequence "Ka", "halant" followed by "Aa" vowel as not the same.

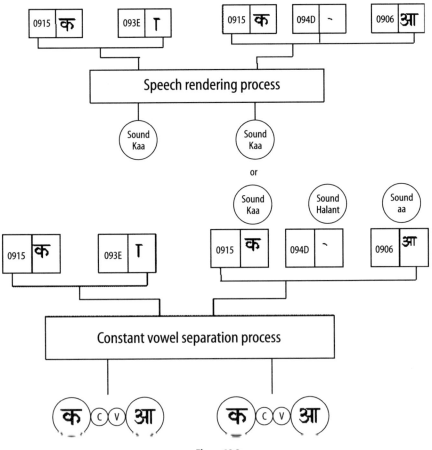

Figure 19.3

Because the "halant" and the "matras" are like special context-dependent operators with operands, they can be given interpretation only if the operands are proper. That is, the "halant" suppresses the "A" vowel only if the immediately preceding code is a Unicode consonant code. If it is the vowel "A" or the matra "A" then it does not have the same meaning. Similarly, for any other code that immediately precedes the "halant", it has no meaningful interpretation. Again, a matra has meaning only if it is immediately preceded by a Unicode consonant. As a result, Unicode rendering has to have the concept of invalid code sequences or strings. Consider the two Unicode strings in Devanagari and the computer rendering process (Figure 19.4).

This time we have strings which encode "so-called" invalid or illegal character sequences – not very natural. What should a speech rendering process do when it encounters such strings? Ignore them? Treat them as invalid and weed them out of the encoded text?

Indian language information encoded in the present Unicode code would always have to be pre-processed for disambiguation and validation to enable interpretations consistent with the computer process itself. There is no simple way of guaranteeing consistency in interpretation by different computer processes. Should we carry forward this burden eternally? In particular, when we have to visualize that computer processing programs can be developed anywhere in the world, and we would like newly developed applications to be directly applicable to Indian

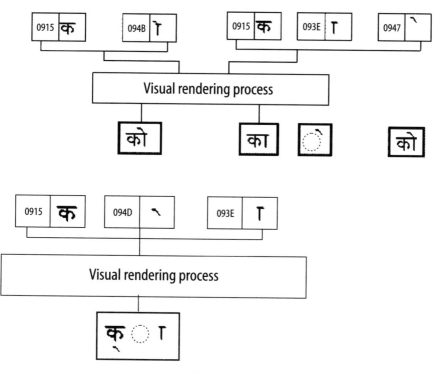

Figure 19.4

language information as well, it is imperative that one must consider suitably revising Unicode to eliminate such problems – *especially, when the alternative is inherently present and clearly stated by our ancient grammarians.*

The Solution: From Our Own Ancient Writings

Panini's classification of the Indian alphabet into pure consonants and vowels and his simple rendering rules for writing provide us with a beautiful encoding scheme which is devoid of all the above problems. In their simplest form the rendering rules are as follows:

1. In a sequence of consonants (pure) and vowels the vowel immediately following a consonant must always be rendered in its matra form. All other vowels will be rendered in their standalone form.
2. The sequence of consonants immediately preceding a vowel forms a conjunct.

Certainly, it was difficult for us to make imported mechanical machinery designed for linear graphic composition follow these rules. Hence we have had to accept distinct input of vowels, matras and many other graphic forms of the basic alphabet. In the name of technology-driven reforms, we have been forced to accept curbing and mutilation of our scripts. But today we have a highly flexible, versatile and programmable rendering process built into the digital computer. This is the period of the digital renaissance for our languages and our scripts, and for the recording and communicating of information in our languages. In a multilingual country like India, with its multiplicity of scripts and languages, it is truly unfortunate not to evolve a proper encoding scheme, one that has been very much our own tradition for possibly over 2000 years, and one that had already considered rendering as being external to the basic encoding – which incidentally is also the current international thinking regarding the encoding of language information.

20

Internet Security from Diverse Viewpoints

Christoph Busch

Abstract

This chapter elucidates security needs and concerns related to the use of the Internet in e-commerce applications. It reviews recent developments in information technology and analyzes their impact on information providers as well as their need for copyright protection. These technologies are analyzed from the vantages of both content providers and businesses as well as end-users, with particular attention paid to the often conflicting perspectives on privacy matters. Privacy issues in recent developments of major vendors in the e-commerce area are observed. From these observations general guidelines are formulated which might provide a helpful base for assessment of future technological developments.

20.1 Introduction

Electronic commerce in all its variations is one of the applications with the biggest potential that has been established over the last few years on the Internet infrastructure now available to more and more users worldwide. The pioneers of e-commerce, with their visions of a boundless global market have seen their high hopes daunted, and even today with tremendous participation by both Internet-only startups and divisions of well-established traditional merchants and content providers, the vast majority of e-commerce businesses are hard pressed to show a profit despite outlandish stock valuations. In addition, early efforts in e-commerce were often limited to mere advertising material carried over from the print versions, sometimes coupled with a limited shopping model. While these activities undoubtedly improved product advertisement and customer information, online trading was limited to some success stories, such as online book shopping [1].

Recent surveys of the development of e-commerce now present a different scenario. As Eco (Electronic Commerce Forum e.V. – an association of industrial enterprises representing the Internet economy) reported, the market volume of e-commerce in

Germany was more than [EURO]0.5 billion in 1998 and is estimated to reach more than [EURO]2.5 billion in 1999 [2]. International market surveys report an increase in the Internet-based market turnover to $47 billion worldwide [3]. According to the same source, 51% of the actors (*netizens*) will participate from outside the USA. Thus more than 150 million entities (consumers and companies) at the end of the year will be participating in e-commerce, an increase of 30% over the preceding year.

The development of e-commerce applications is closely related to the underlying technologies. Major efforts were mounted in research for online payment protocols (e.g. ecash, SET, ...) and even though one of the key players in that area (DigiCash) had to cease its activities, advanced solutions are now available and are currently in the integration and evaluation process (for example, at Deutsche Bank). Furthermore, it is essential to establish trust in the technology for all parties concerned – consumers and vendors alike – in the electronic market-place. Therefore the use and integration of well-known strong cryptographic protocols in e-commerce applications is a mandatory precondition. These protocols realize general and classical security requirements such as mutual authentication of communication/trading partners, confidentiality of the transaction and authenticity and integrity of the delivered digital good. These requirements [4] can be fulfilled with classical security mechanisms using strong symmetric and asymmetric ciphers [5]. Confidential communication among partners in a business-to-business scenario is one of the fundamental needs that must be satisfied. Email and voice-over-IP, along with other communication protocols, are used today for the exchange of confidential and valuable information. The intrinsic risk is that valuable business information (i.e. trade secrets, statistics etc.) are subject to eavesdropping without significant risk to perpetrators. Unfortunately it is not a myth that such eavesdropping is performed by bored hackers but also by intelligence services worldwide [6]. With the lines between intelligence and law enforcement blurring and fueled by advances in surveillance technology, an ever-increasing amount of information is being gathered and the fundamental right to privacy enshrined in most Western nations' constitutions is quickly headed for oblivion. Ironically, this development is perpetrated by the very governments tasked with the protection of these rights. While the interception of private communication by surveillance technologies must be accepted as a fundamental risk, the use of cryptographic protocols is a good starting point to establish security.

This chapter will investigate some complementary security aspects which have turned out to be crucial issues in the development of e-commerce applications. These are: protection of copyright holders on the one hand and protection of consumers on the other hand. By nature these requirements represent diverging viewpoints on the theme of security, and in fact any technology providing a solution for one side carries drawbacks for the other. This chapter will shed light on both conflicting positions. In Section 19.2 boundary conditions, which up to now have presented an obstructing factor for creators and content producers to place their products in the WWW, are discussed. Section 19.3 investigates privacy concerns and reviews recent examples where rudimentary privacy considerations have been neglected. Section 19.4 briefly discusses related legal regulations and sets up recommendations for the focus points of future research.

20.2 Security for Content Providers

Many artists, creators and content producers are open minded, if not enthusiastic, about the Internet and the opportunities presented by it. Many of them exploit the Web for announcements, advertisements or general customer information. While the intrinsic features of the WWW to immediately address an unlimited number of potential customers at practically zero cost[1] is exploited extensively for marketing activities one must state that the WWW as an Internet distribution channel has rarely been tapped for its potential. As outlined in the introduction to this chapter, we can now observe a trend showing growth of the electronic market. But still we have to investigate the reasons for the currently prevailing obstructionist attitude that remains. The crucial point is closely correlated with the intrinsic characteristics of the items exchanged on the digital market: digital goods such as software, images, videos, music or valuable business news can be ordered immediately and delivered online. Distribution costs are minimized or even eliminated and any delay due to trans-shipment ceases to apply. This improves the quality of service for the customer, since the order is fulfilled immediately in full quality. At the same time there is no technological limitation implying that the customer is the end of the distribution chain.

The copy is the original, with no decrease in quality.

The above statement, as simple and trivial as it sounds, has far-reaching implications. Data can be duplicated and redistributed by basically any customer. In other words, once the data is delivered the digital goods are outside the control of the merchant. Even worse, the creator does not even know whether or when misappropriated use of the goods occurs. A possible illegal market and loss of license revenues are the direct consequence. The reactions of content providers (i.e. immaterial goods such as music or movies) have been predictably sharp. As video data is still beyond the grasp of existing technology with regard to duplication and particularly transmission over data networks, the main focus so far has been on the future of the music industry, whose very existence is being threatened by the factors outlined below

With the evolution of MPEG standards, the audio file format MP3 (MPEG-1, Audio Layer 3) has become established as the *de facto* standard for music files alongside other contenders for certain specialized applications such as media streaming (Real Networks' G2). Its key feature is that the file size is relatively small, while the quality is perfectly sufficient for most applications, particularly popular music. Audio files in MP3 format are widely available for download on the Net and *audio on demand* servers have already adopted the new technology [7,8]. In addition, user-friendly search engines for MP3 are already provided, featuring intuitive user interfaces [9,10]. Search algorithms are explicitly designed for MP3 files. Once

---

1 This refers to passive marketing activity, such as WWW presentations, as opposed to the repugnant molestation of netizens by email spamming, which is a reprehensible activity burdening the time and financial resources of unwilling recipients and is not addressed here.

items of interest are downloaded, consumers can store MP3 files on their PCs or portable handheld devices[2], which might in the near future replace the classical portable audio device. While consumers welcome the technology, the issue is a vital threat to the music industry. Major vendors consider MP3 a major cause of piracy[3]. The International Federation of the Phonographic Industry (IFPI) has filed a suit against a Norwegian software company[4] which provided the MP3 search engine for Lycos. According to *Wired* [11], IFPI claims a contributory infringement under copyright law. It must be doubted that the development and use of a search engine can be considered an illegal act, since it simply provides links to consumers, abstracting from the fact whether these links refer to an item that is legally or illegally presented on the target of the link. Nevertheless one must concede that the concern of the music industry regarding a disappearing market and even its entire business model is substantial. According to the recently published year-end shipments statistics of the Recording Industry Association of America (RIAA) the most important consumer group for music records (ages 15–24) caused a drop-off in the proportion of purchases from 32.2% in 1996 down to 28% in 1998 [12]. This consumer group has previously formed the mainstay of the market. The same study reports that consumers over 30 were the only age demographic to show any growth in the last year. Do all the above numbers indicate that the young generation – presumably more familiar with the Internet – is consuming illegal copies of records downloaded from the net? Undoubtedly, the MP3 scare does have its merit, but then one should not lose sight of another threat, posed by the more pedestrian emergence of cheap CD recording equipment. The RIAA reports that the number of counterfeit or bootleg CD confiscated skyrocketed from 442 CDs in 1997 to 103 971 CDs in 1998 [13]. Alarmed by these numbers the recording industry has started to establish countermeasures. The Secure Digital Music Initiative (SDMI) is an association of 28 worldwide recording industry and technology companies formed to develop an open, interoperable architecture and specification for digital music security [14]. The goal of the initiative is to develop a viable and secure marketplace for the distribution of music online [15]. In order to establish adequate copyright protection for artists and their work, these companies are considering technology such as digital watermarks and multiple encryption methods. Digital watermarks are a promising technology to provide security for content contributors, since it allows an imperceptible (inaudible) mark to be embedded in the audio signal itself which bears the identity of the purchaser. As a consequence, if Internet users upload copyrighted material to a Web server, they leave their fingerprint to be traced by law enforcement.

Let us consider yet another example of copyright law violation: as TELEPOLIS reports, five photographers have filed suit against a major German publisher claiming that their creations have been used without regard to the contracted licensing conditions [16]. Photographers provided their work to a Berlin

---

2   The Diamond Rio PMP300 Portable Music Player is an example of an MP3-compatible handheld player.
3   For a definition of piracy see http://www.ipti.org/piracy-index.html
4   FAST Search & Transfer ASA.

newspaper for one-time print publication, while other newspapers belonging to the same publisher reprinted the material multiple times without payment of appropriate royalties. Licensing contracts for photographs usually have a fine granularity of well-specified licensing conditions [17], including exclusive vs. non-exclusive usage, territorial restrictions, temporal limitations for the usage, online/offline exploitation etc. The purchase of the least expensive option (i.e. non-exclusive one-time print in a local newspaper) and later reuse of the material in high-price categories such as international digital distribution on CD-ROM undoubtedly affects the rights of the content creators and infringes upon copyright laws. If we raise the question of how to provide security for copyright holders, we can state that there is a good chance of at least providing a certain measure of deterrence against potential misuse of the material by means of watermarking. Embedding the fingerprint of the purchaser and additional information about the licensing conditions in the image itself enables the creators to prove contract violations, possibly aided by automatic mechanisms instead of relying on chance via manual examination of copy material.

These two examples have illustrated the crucial security concerns for copyright holders that are associated with the distribution of digital goods. It should be clear that providing technical countermeasures against piracy is essential to establish trust in an electronic market-place from the vantage point of content providers and other merchants.

20.3 Security and Privacy for Netizens

Let us now change our viewpoint and consider security for consumers in the market-place – or in general, for the Internet user. Citizens nowadays enjoy more and more services on the Net. Handling everyday business online saves time and traveling costs, and offers a breadth of selection not found in the confines of the physical world. As an example, one can consider the interaction of citizens with public administration. The virtual civil hall is no longer science fiction. In Germany, for example, the German federal ministry of research currently sponsors three consortia for the establishment of online administrative services for their citizens. Communication with the local registration office and public libraries, and the handling of administrative procedures such as the approval of building permissions and many other services, which traditionally devour time, will become easier for all of us. The need to appear in person at times conflicting with normal working schedules might be avoided in most cases. The overall goal of that program is to operate services more efficiently and to transparently inform citizens on internal administrative decisions (the virtual and transparent civic hall). While all the above changes represent advantages, one must keep the associated risks in view. The privacy of the user interacting with the online administration may under no circumstances be compromised. The information transmitted must be kept confidential between the citizen and the administration: no one except the submitter and the administrative reviewer should know the details of an income tax filing. Another important issue is to prevent the creation of comprehensive profiles on citizens. While technically this has always been possible for governments, only the move away from paper has made it possible to routinely compile dossiers on each and every individual.

This may sound redundant, since the protection of privacy has a long tradition. It is defined as a fundamental, though not absolute, human right. The roots of legislative formulations of the right of privacy go back to the year 1361 and the Peace Act in England [18]. The major milestone in the definition of modern privacy was the Declaration of Human Rights in 1948. "No one shall be subjected to arbitrary interference with his privacy, family, home or correspondence, nor to attacks upon his honour and reputation. Everyone has the right to the protection of the law against such interference or attacks" states Article 12 of the Declaration [19]. The fundamental principle underlying this and other declarations and laws on privacy state that personal information must be obtained fairly and with full knowledge and approval, that the information may only be used for the specified purpose, any distribution of the information must be with the express prior consent of the individual, and that information must be destroyed after its purpose is completed [18]. Accordingly, the European Union has enacted two directives to guarantee citizens protection from abuse of their data [20,21].

The proper respect of privacy in e-commerce applications, despite the above-mentioned directives, is no certainty. Many commercial services generate a user profile, automatically logging users' interactions and preferences [1]. With this personal information e-commerce merchants can offer an optimized selection to the consumer as well as performing personally targeted advertisements. They can also offer such profiles to other companies as an interesting revenue stream on the side. Consumers can profit from individually selected content, but bear the risk that their personal data is stored or even forwarded. Undoubtedly such data records are of high interest to those setting up strategies for targeted advertising.

That major companies have a lax attitude to privacy became transparent in the discussion about the use of a Global Unique Identifier (GUID). This discussion was publicly launched with Intel's announcement at the RSA Data Security Conference in San Jose that the new Pentium III processor would be equipped with an electronic hardware serial number [22]. The number acts as a unique worldwide identifier, marking each PC. Whenever the computer is connected to the Internet, the serial number will be transparent to the outside and identify the user's computer, and the identity of the user could (possibly wrongly) be derived from this. Reportedly the initial idea behind the numbering system is to identify stolen PC hardware as soon as it goes online. In addition, the identification number was offered as a tool to provide more security for commerce and communication, although it should be immediately obvious that this mechanism is totally unsuitable, since it is not firmly associated with a user, is easily falsified, and can be observed by individuals subsequently committing illegal acts under the easily spoofed identity of an innocent victim.

Immediately after the announcement of the GUID, the American Civil Liberties Union raised its concerns: "The feature will force consumers to leave an identifying mark wherever they go in cyberspace" [23]. In fact, the new Intel feature would operate as a permanent hardware cookie[5]. Any interaction could be traceable, and privacy risks are inherent. Because of this risk privacy groups called for a boycott of Intel products until the chip vendor revises and drops the plan. Reacting to these voices, Intel stated that users still have the option to deactivate the transmission of the identification number. Nevertheless the mere fact that personal data is transmitted without the explicit affirmation of the user is a violation of privacy principles.

While the Intel hardware numbering system was still being intensively discussed, it turned out some weeks later that Microsoft Corporation is already one step ahead in establishing identification numbers [24]. With Windows 98 it followed a similar approach and assigned to its customers a Globally Unique Identifier when they performed online registration of the product. The number itself also includes the number derived from the MAC-address of the Ethernet network interface card where possible, using an already existing GUID that has been in use for more than a decade. Once the number is assigned it will be found in multiple places, such as Word or Excel documents, leaving a digital fingerprint of the user. Furthermore Microsoft has databases in place where unique numbers are stored [24]. Microsoft argued that the initial idea of the numbering and storage system was to improve the online diagnosis and support facilities for their customers. In addition they defended the numbering system in that transmitting the number is an option of the operating system which could be deactivated (again after explicit affirmation of the user). Later on it was discovered that numbers are assigned and transmitted regardless of whether users specified "deactivation" [24]. It is astonishing to note that the chairman of Sun Microsystems, Scott McNealy, was recently defending the use of the numbering system, claiming that any transmission of ID would help to chase senders of terrorizing anonymous mails [25]. Ironically, this "feature" was instrumental in apprehending the perpetrator of the now infamous "Melissa" macro virus – he was traced back using ISP records and a GUID found in the virus. While at the time of writing it is still not technically clear under what conditions mailer applications such as Microsoft Outlook propagate the GUID, one must reject the use of GUIDs as an appropriate approach to trace emails. Such identification mechanisms without cryptographic integrity protection are trivial to duplicate and are easily misused.

Following this discussion of GUIDs one must get the impression that the real driving force behind the concept is to detect, localize and prove unregistered software copies. The example outlines the conflict between the justified fight against unlicenced use of software on the one hand and fundamental privacy rights on the other hand. The latter should under no circumstances be affected or weakened by the use of information technology.

---

5   "Cookies" are stored on the client side by WWW browsers. They are used to recognize the users when they reconnect to a Web server and to maintain state information over an otherwise stateless protocol. Many servers log user interactions using cookies and can thus generate user profiles.

20.4 A Guideline for the Future

Sections 20.2 and 20.3 have shed some light on recent trends in information technology, causing substantial security risks for either content creators or content consumers. If we now come to an intermediate assessment of the situation, the consequences are twofold. On the one hand, one can analyze the situation and derive consequences for policy makers, defining the legal framework related to the Internet. On the other hand there are technical recommendations which can be sketched and which could operate as a guideline for future development both for scientific research and commercial applications. Both aspects will be covered below.

● *Reinforcement of privacy protection*
The fact that fundamental privacy rights are neglected by engineers or software developers has been a subject of intense debate for some time. An aggravating circumstance is that there is neither a commercial nor a political lobby controlling a proper defense of privacy rights. Of course, there is no commercial benefit associated with privacy protection. As a consequence, the protection of the individual relies on the complementary initiatives such as a recently started campaign against spamming in Germany [26]. Therefore it is essential to reinforce all activities protecting personal privacy by law, directives and other legal regulations. In this context one should again mention the European Data Protection Directive 95/46/EC, which strengthens protection against the use of sensitive personal data and defines that commercial or governmental use of such information requires explicit and unambiguous consent of the data object [20]. The definitions in the Directive must be transformed into national law. Even though the directive itself requests that each EU state must pass conferring laws and regulations implementing the directive by October 1998, there are still many national legislations which have not done so. One should emphasize that the view embraced by the current US administration, i.e. to rely solely on self-policing by industry, is supported neither by empirical evidence nor by plain common sense.

● *Abolition of grant-aided industrial espionage*
Many commercial entities that utilize the Internet for business-to-business communication are facing the omnipresent danger of confidential or valuable information being subject to electronic eavesdropping. Industrial espionage, whether by competitors or by the intelligence agencies of nations home to competing enterprises, is often subsidized and in several instances openly supported by national governments. One would hope that in an age in which the nationality of business entities is rapidly becoming an arbitrary constant, governments would cease such actions and commit themselves to a corresponding code of conduct. Similarly, intelligence agencies spying in the interest of theoretically allied nations would have to be dismantled. Nonetheless, business and individuals alike will always have to preserve their communications subject to interception. As such, precautions such as the use of strong cryptography are always advisable.

- *Abandon export regulations for cryptographic technology*

  The current regulations regarding export and commerce in cryptographic soft-ware and equipment are largely useless since the genre won the battle more than twenty years ago. Any rogue nation, criminal organization or individual can simply walk into a university bookstore and obtain all the necessary information for the implementation of reasonably strong cryptography. Even if one were to outlaw cryptography completely, it would be impossible to enforce such regula-tions, since any such data would drown in the sheer volume of data to be moni-tored. Beyond this, there would always be the option of steganography [27–29]. As it is, the regulations serve mainly as an impediment to privacy and electronic commerce.

- *Research for copyright protection*

  We have seen that the setup of a powerful scheme for copyright protection is a key issue for content creators and commercial content providers. Comprehensive solutions must be available to satisfy their need for technical means for the protection of IP rights. The discrepancy between the demands of copyright holders for fingerprinting methods using GUIDs on the one hand and the demand for privacy protection raised by users on the other could be resolved by using limited pseudonymity. This concept to uniquely identify users via a pseudonym is already in place with digital certificates under the German digital signature law and allows users to operate under a pseudonym which may be uncovered by law enforcement authorities with good cause. Sound solutions – accepted worldwide – will be an essential condition to encourage creators to position their content on the WWW and finally for a prospering electronic market. In this context research into digital watermarking technology must be strengthened. While research in this area during recent years has shown substantial progress, branching out into many different areas, there is still a high demand from the industry for more improvements. Research efforts should be continued with the goal of robust and high capacity algorithms for many multimedia formats.

- *Research into intuitive perception of the security environment*

  Current software systems do not give adequate feedback when security operations are concerned. Dialog boxes – which are usually disabled after a few uses, since they annoy users – and minuscule icons are insufficient. The notifying of users of unencrypted or encrypted traffic (without disrupting the normal workflow), and particularly notifying users of transactions in which their privacy is endangered and of acts with possible legal consequences (digital signatures) needs to be visu-alized. There is a fundamental need to develop intuitive methods for perception of the security environment. Humans have a natural perception of their environ-ment and the correspondent impact on their security. This perception must be addressed by machine–human interaction!

The idea behind this may be illustrated with the following comparison: a road repairer knows from experience that more self-protection mechanisms need to be set up when working on a crowded freeway than when working on a quiet road in the countryside. Naturally the worker will raise the level of protection mechanisms according to the indicators perceived, such as the number and speed of passing cars, visibility and so on.

Compared with the road repairer, who reacts intuitively to risk, a netizen working at an online computer generally has no chance to perceive the "traffic" or any danger that arises from intruders to his or her system[6]. The same holds true for the countermeasures that the user – or the user's system – decides to undertake to fighting against intrusion. In most cases the configuration of the level of security will be hidden in rarely visited Web browser dialogs. If alerts about security-critical situations are displayed at all, they contain rather dull and obscure wording.

People should be addressed at the perceptual level that they use to understand risk. Inverting the human–machine interaction concepts, the machine should notify the user about intrusions and other risks utilizing multimedia components, such as security avatars or security wizards which raise their "voices" according to the degree and urgency of the threat. To visualize and make people understand intuitively a potential risk in their environment is definitely a challenging and promising research field for the future.

20.5 Conclusion

This chapter has considered security concerns from several conflicting viewpoints. While the Internet provides almost unlimited possibilities to us, it carries significant risks at the same time. Nevertheless, we have tried to formulate recommendations to guide future developments to establish a prosperous electronic marketplace and respect the needs of the participants in the market.

Acknowledgments

I would like to thank my colleagues Stephan Hüttinger, Volker Roth and Stephen Wolthusen for fruitful discussions on the issues addressed in this chapter and also for proofreading of the manuscript.

References

[1] Amazon.com online shopping, "Earth's Biggest Selection", http://www.amazon.com/.
[2] Eco, Electronic Commerce Forum e.V., Press Release, 29 January 1999, http://www.eco.de/Presse/pm/366.htm.
[3] Eco, Electronic Commerce Forum e.V., Press Release, 5 February 1999, http://www.eco.de/Presse/pm/365.htm.
[4] K Ranneberg, A Pfitzmann and G Müller (1996) Sicherheit, insbesondere mehrseitige IT-Sicherheit, *Informationstechni und Technische Informatik*, 4/1996, p. 710.
[5] B Schneier (1994) *Applied Cryptography: protocols, algorithms, and source code in C*, New York, Wiley.

---

6   We are not considering for the moment those users who have the skills to analyse the traffic on an IP packet basis.

[6] European Parliament (1998) *Scientific and Technological Options Assessment – an Appraisal of Technologies of Political Control,* http://jya.com/stoa-atpc.htm.

[7] Deutsche Telekom (1999) Audio on Demand Server, http://www.audio-on-demand.de/.

[8] MP3.com homepage, http://www.mp3.com/.

[9] Lycos search engine, http://www.de.lycos.de.

[10] Altavista search engine, http://image.altavista.com/.

[11] Wired News (1999) MP3 search engine under fire, http://www.wired.com/news/news/politics/story/18688.html.

[12] A Welsh (1999) Recording industry releases 1998 consumer profile, http://www.riaa.com/stats/press/consumer98.htm.

[13] L Pelliccia, RIAA releases year end anti-piracy statistics, http://www.riaa.com/piracy/press/040699.htm.

[14] SDMI, Secure Digital Music Initiative, http://www.sdmi.org/.

[15] RIAA-FAQ, Is technology helping the recording industry keep up with all the changes?, http://www.ria.com/techn/techn_faq.htm.

[16] M Jansen (1999) Wer sind die größten Piraten im Land?, in *TELEPOLIS,* http://www.heise.de/tp/deutsch/inhalt/on/2662/1.html.

[17] BFF-Pilot, Image Server of the Bund Freischaffender Foto-Designer, http://bff-pilot.igd.fhg.de/.

[18] D Banisar and S Davies (1999) "Privacy and Human Rights", An International Survey of Privacy Laws and Practice, http://www.gilc.org/privacy/survey/intro.htm.

[19] United Nations (1948) Universal Declaration of Human Rights, http://www.hrweb.org/legal/udhr.html.

[20] European Union, Directive95/46/EC of the European Parliament, http://www.odpr.org/restofit/Legislation/Directive/Directive_Contents.html.

[21] European Union, Directive97/66/EC of the European Parliament, http://www2.echo.lu/leagl/en/dataprot/protection.html.

[22] F Rötzer (1999) ID-Nummer für Intel-Prozessoren, in *TELEPOLIS,* http://www.heise.de/tp/deutsch/inhalt/te/1774/1.html.

[23] B Steinhardt (1999) American Civil Liberties Union, "Privacy Downside to Intel Inside", http://www.aclu.org/news/1999/w012599a.html.

[24] C Persson and P Siering (1999) Big Brother Bill, in c't 6/99, http://www.heise.de/ct/99/06/016/.

[25] *Computer Zeitung* (1999) Vernünftige Menschen schätzen Identifikationsnummern, in *Computer Zeitung,* No. 12, p. 2.

[26] c't (1999) Vote against SPAM!, http://www.politik-digital.de/spam/.

[27] D Chaum (1985) Security without identification: transaction systems to make big brother obsolete, *Communications of the Association for Computing Machinery,* 28(10), 1030–1044.

[28] A Pfitzmann and M Waidner (1985) Networks without user observability – design options, in *Advances in Cryptology: Eurocrypt 85: Proceeding of a Workshop on the Theory and Application of Cryptographic Techniques,* Linz, Austria, April.

[29] S Moller and A Pfitzmann (1994) Rechnergestützte Steganographie: Wie sie funktioniert und warum folglich jede Reglementierung von Verschlüsselung unsinnig ist, *Datenschutz und Datensicherheit,* 18(6), 318–326.

Foundations for Interaction

21

Why Performance Always Comes Last in Interactive System Design, and What To Do About It

William Newman

Abstract

Interactive systems pay their way, ultimately, by enabling people to perform their work better and with less effort. A lot of design ingenuity goes into addressing the "better" requirement, often with the goal of radically changing work practice. Meanwhile, little attention is paid to the "less effort" side – to improving work performance. The main underlying reason is designers' lack of means to measure whether the performance of work has been improved. This chapter will explain how this has come about, why product usability testing is not the answer, and how the identification of application-specific critical parameters could be crucial, enabling designers to deliver real performance improvements to the user.

21.1 Introduction

Issues of performance and its measurement usually come fairly low down on the list of priorities in human-centered computing. After all, we can assume that performance problems will always be taken care of by steady improvements in processing speeds, memory capacities and network bandwidths. So we can relegate performance to the bottom of our list of concerns, to the last of the things we attend to in the design process (and the first thing we abandon when we slip our deadlines), and to the final topic on our list of issues to discuss.

But is performance a non-issue? Do improvements in the performance of technology automatically bring improvements for the user? It would be worrying to discover that they do not. It's even more worrying to realize that we hardly ever know. There are documented cases of system designs being "improved" in ways that led to a significant degradation in overall performance – outcomes that would normally be viewed as design failures (Newman, 1998). Yet these failed designs are being purchased as "upgrades" by customers who simply have no means of measuring whether they are getting any return on their investment. In this sense our design methodology shows signs of losing control over performance improvement. The issue of performance has been neglected for too long.

Far from being a non-issue, performance improvement should be our number one concern, for this is how computer systems pay their way. In our working lives there are a succession of things that have to get done in the workplace, within certain time-frames and to certain levels of quality. People and organizations look constantly for better ways to perform them, and if a computer system offers sufficient benefits they may decide to invest in it. So the designer's first imperative should be to make sure that the investment pays off – that the benefits delivered by the system outweigh the costs. The new system must be designed to deliver improved cost-performance relative to the system in current use.

Of course, performance is not ignored entirely in the design of interactive systems, but it does often get pushed down to a point where it's at risk of being forgotten or treated as a matter of detail. In particular, performance testing is often bundled in with the usability testing of prototypes and finished systems. However, usability testing is mostly – and sometimes entirely – about finding functional problems in the user interface. If serious performance problems are found at this late stage, it may be too late to do anything about them.

This chapter explores some of the main issues contributing to the current stance on interactive system performance. It argues that a central issue is the need for ways of measuring the overall performance of systems, and points out that this depends on knowledge of the *critical parameters* that measure the system's success in serving its purpose. It discusses how HCI could benefit from paying more attention to system performance, and concludes with questions about the readiness of the market-place, and of HCI itself, to take performance more seriously.

21.2 The Critical Issues

The overall issue here is the lack of prominence given to performance when interactive systems are designed. As a whole, developers and users seem relatively unconcerned, if not oblivious, about performance and the need to pay attention to it. But there are a number of further issues surrounding the topic of performance, and these are hard to ignore entirely:

- *Choosing between design options*
  When we face a choice between design options, how do we choose? Typically we assess the various options against design criteria and choose the one that comes out best. Now in many design situations (such as hardware design, for example) it is normal to include overall performance measures amongst the design criteria; but what about other situations where these measures are not known? The choice

then has to be made on some other basis. In other words, the final design may be arrived at without ever making a choice on the basis of overall performance. Is this how we would like to see interactive systems designed?

- *Selecting performance targets but getting them wrong*

   HCI textbooks teach us to set performance targets when drawing up requirements and when conducting usability tests, but are generally vague about how to select these targets. Thus Preece *et al.* (1994) conclude their coverage of performance metrics with the words, "Before choosing the specific measure, however, it is important to consider what you want to measure and why". But this is surely an inadequate basis for selecting performance metrics – it's all too easy to choose metrics arbitrarily and thus gain a misleading impression of overall performance.

- *The perils of piecewise evaluation*

   When we have designed the system and built a prototype, how do we evaluate it? The most effective method, the "gold standard" according to Landauer (1995), is usability testing. However, a complex system may involve a complex usability test. Consider the problem of testing a system designed for use by doctors during consultations: how should we evaluate its usability? Recommended practice here is to choose a representative set of tasks and ask a set of users to perform them. We might choose, for example, the tasks of entering patient information, searching for a record of a previous consultation, and preparing a prescription. But if we were to base our estimates of overall performance on these tasks we could get a very inaccurate impression, for we would be ignoring much of what goes on during a consultation – we would be evaluating *piecewise*. This is a common source of inaccurate performance testing (Newman, 1998).

- *Understanding the work that users do*

   To design for performance we need to understand the work that we are trying to support. Without this understanding it is unlikely that we will find it easy to achieve improvements in the work's performance. Unfortunately there exists a culture of designing systems on a basis of a very superficial understanding of the work that the systems are to support. At worst, designers focus on the work *they* do and design systems to support *themselves*. At best, they undertake workplace studies with a view to finding problems that technology can address. There is a notable absence of the concept of developing a *model* of how the work is performed, so that different solution strategies can be tested in order to choose the one that supports the work best.

- *Treating system design as engineering*

   The above issues combine to make it hard to treat interactive system design as an engineering exercise. In order for this situation to change, we have to find a way to organize design so as to achieve the result we want, rather than just achieving change for its own sake. The result we want must, for reasons already given, involve an improvement in performance for the user. The first step towards establishing an engineering approach to interactive computing is to develop ways of measuring performance improvements. This involves identifying *critical parameters* by which the success of the design in supporting users can be measured (Newman, 1997). If research effort were devoted to identifying these parameters, it could become easier to measure performance improvements, and to design to achieve specific performance targets.

- *Training designers to deal with performance targets*
  If and when we know what performance targets we must achieve in design, do we know *how* to achieve them? Suppose we're trying to design call-center software that increases the number of calls handled per hour by 5% – how do we go about achieving this performance improvement? Many designers will answer this question by saying, "we test the prototype and improve it if it doesn't meet the target". But it would be far better if designers could aim towards a specific performance target *while* they design. There are techniques for doing this, such as GOMS (Kieras, 1997), but few designers have been trained to use them.

In summary, we're a long way from being able to deal adequately with performance issues. It's not surprising, therefore, that performance usually comes last – there's little we can do about it, even if we tackle it early on. But by paying attention to these issues, and particularly to critical parameters, we could start to change this state of affairs.

21.3 Justification: Why Pay Attention to Critical Parameters?

This chapter has been arguing that more attention should be paid to performance issues, suggesting that particular attention should be paid to identifying critical performance parameters. In this way a basis could be created for achieving real performance improvements and thus providing payoff to those who invest in interactive systems. From the user's standpoint, this would surely be justification enough for the attention invested. Are there payoffs for the researcher too?

HCI research is about enabling progress in the design of interactive systems and techniques. Researchers need to know when they are generating progress and when they are not. If progress in system design cannot be measured – if one system cannot be shown to be an improvement on another – then research itself cannot move forward. This is, in all likelihood, one of the main reasons why serious HCI researchers have devoted so much attention to interaction techniques, where improvements *can* be measured. If performance of systems could be measured too, many new and exciting research avenues would open up.

HCI research generally makes faster progress when it builds incrementally on what is already known. Research into performance improvement has this incremental property. The simplest test of whether we are making progress here is: are designers meeting their performance targets more reliably? Given where we are now, there is room for a great deal of progress. Furthermore, progress in this direction need not clash with other methodological research. Performance measurement methods can readily be integrated with other human-centered methods.

HCI research is somewhat fragmented these days, with some people working on novel designs while others conduct experiments or user studies, and yet others develop design methodologies. There need to be stronger links between these activities. Performance could be one topic that provides a link, for performance targets can drive the search for improved designs while providing the basis for experimental measurement.

Overall, HCI needs to find a way to move towards center-stage in systems development. Too many systems are being developed in a non-human-centered way, with little or no attention being paid to the user. HCI practitioners can change this if they are invited to take part in design, but this happens only sporadically. One reason for this is the inability of HCI methods to provide system designers with criteria that they can work with. The vast majority of empirical HCI research aims to unearth new findings about the way people interact with computers (Newman, 1994). These join the vast collection of findings and guidelines already documented. The designer who wants to apply these findings in an effective way faces an impossible task – what if one finding contradicts another, or if no technical solution can be found that complies with a set of guidelines? In contrast, a target based on a critical performance parameter is something that the designer can get to grips with. If HCI could deliver such parameters to designers, it would probably be taken more seriously.

21.4 Questions for the Future

This discussion of performance, and of the potential role of critical parameters in making performance more tractable, leaves us with two main questions.

First, does the market-place want to be offered performance improvements when it is offered new systems? Or does it simply want more and more functionality? We cannot afford to ignore this question – our work, like everyone else's in the computer business, is market-driven. One plausible answer is that the market-place doesn't know that it could demand improved performance in the software systems it buys. It doesn't know how to specify the improvements it wants. Thus customers may need to know about critical parameters too, just as urgently as designers. Until both camps understand performance better, and one camp can demand what the other camp can deliver, the situation may not change.

Second, can we in HCI change our habits? At present, HCI research is dominated by explorations of novel technology and by empirical studies that generate yet more findings. These two domains of research hardly overlap each other, and have embarrassingly little impact on system design practice. It is rare, for example, to find that HCI research has influenced the design of commercial systems described in the literature – even in the HCI literature! Unfortunately, the two dominant fields of research, novel technologies and empirical studies, have a common attraction for the researcher – they are relatively easy fields in which to produce publishable results. Research into performance is likely to present much more of a challenge, but can generate enormous dividends if real progress is made.

References

Kieras DE (1997) A guide to GOMS model usability evaluation using NGOMSL, in *Handbook of Human–Computer Interaction*, 2nd edn (eds. MG Helander and TK Landauer), Amsterdam, Elsevier.

Landauer TK (1995) *The Trouble with Computers.* Cambridge, MA, MIT Press.

Newman WM (1994) A preliminary analysis of the products of HCI research, based on pro forma abstracts, in *Proceedings of CHI '94 Human Factors in Computing Systems*, 24–28 April, Boston, MA, ACM/SIGCHI, New York, pp. 278–284.

Newman WM (1997) Better or just different? On the benefits of designing interactive systems in terms of critical parameters, in *Proc. DIS '97, Designing Interactive Systems*, Amsterdam, 18–20 August, pp. 239–245.

Newman WM (1998) On simulation, measurement and piecewise usability evaluation, *Human Computer Interaction*, 13(3), 316–323.

Preece, J, Rogers, Y, Sharp, H, Benyon, D, Holland, S and Carey, T (1994) *Human Computer Interaction*, Wokingham, Addison-Wesley.

About the Author

William Newman is a Principal Scientist at the Cambridge laboratory of Xerox Research Centre Europe. He gained a PhD in Computer Science from Imperial College London in 1968. Between 1973 and 1979 he was a member of research staff at the Xerox Palo Alto Research Center, where he contributed to the development of raster graphics techniques, page description languages, laser printing software, illustration tools, integrated office systems and user interface design methodology. He joined XRCE (then Rank Xerox EuroPARC) in 1988. His current interests are in technologies for integrating paper and electronic documents, and in methods for designing systems so as to achieve performance improvements for the user. He is co-author, with Mik Lamming, of the recent textbook *Interactive System Design*; previously he co-authored a pioneering graphics text, *Principles of Interactive Computer Graphics*, with Robert Sproull. He was recently Papers Co-chair of the CHI 99 Conference, and is a member of the recently formed ACM SIGCHI Publications Board. Since 1980 he has been a Visiting Professor in the Computer Science Department, Queen Mary Westfield College, London.

22

Virtual Environments for Human-Centered Computing

Tosiyasu L. Kunii

Abstract

A novel model is presented that can provide drastically improved virtual environments for human-centered computing. The model links human cognition with virtual environments by providing a common space to identify objects in a shared space based on cellular spatial structures. The model covers both cognitive- and design- aspects of virtual environments in an integrated manner.

22.1 The Potential of Human-Centered Virtual Environments

When I coined the term "virtual worlds" in 1984, the term was not immediately popular [14,15]. There was almost nowhere to present and discuss virtual worlds. Now, it seems that people are becoming serious about virtual worlds and environments. Virtual environments actually offer potential for both the present and the future. For the future, virtual environments basically provide a basis for possible developments, including design testing and validation environments. For the present, they increase the functionality of existing systems by removing the physical constraints, macroscopically and microscopically. Macroscopically, for example, virtual financial trading environments and virtual university environments can span geographically widespread areas and locations. A microscopic example includes a group of micromachines that can function only with the support of virtual environments to go through extremely complex and hazardous real environments, by simulation and human cognition of the constantly changing situations. A decompositional assembly method is proven to decrease the assembly complexity from exponential to square [8,9].

What is commonly required in macroscopic and microscopic cases to realize such potential is a provision to identify objects in virtual environments and human cognitive spaces. By modeling virtual environments and cognitive spaces by cellular spatial structures [18], we can establish necessary identification by continuous and surjective mapping, called identification mapping. Identification mapping is also called quotient mapping.

The identification is mathematically based on equivalence relations [17,27]. The equivalence relations preserve invariants. Modern science is built on invariants. For example, classical physics is built on mass and energy as invariants, and the theory of relativity has broken the boundary between mass and energy. The process of identifying invariants is a type of abstraction. For any abstraction to be systematic, abstraction is performed based on an abstraction hierarchy. In virtual environments, presenting any objects in the environments requires an appropriate abstraction hierarchy in this sense. What is it then?

22.2 An Abstraction Hierarchy for Virtual Environments

Let us design an abstraction hierarchy. In terms of the abstraction of invariants hierarchically organized from general to specific to realize the modular and incremental design of objects, the following is a reasonable abstraction hierarchy:

1. A set level
2. An extension level
3. A homotopy level
4. A topology level
5. A geometry level
6. A visualization level

We outline the levels briefly as needed.

22.2.1 Set Theoretical Design

First of all, we start our design work by defining a collection of objects we are looking at. To be able to conduct automation on such a collection by using computers as intelligent machines, each collection must be a set because computers are built as set theoretical machines. Intuitively, a set X is a collection of all objects x having an identical property, say P(x). Symbolically $X = \{x|P(x)\}$. Any object in a set is called an element. A set without an element is named the empty set $\downarrow$. A set is said to be open if all of its elements are interior. Given sets X and Y, computers perform set theoretical operations such as the union $X \cup Y$, the intersection $X \cap Y$ and the difference $X - Y$ (also denoted as $x\downarrow y$). Suppose we begin our cyberspace architecture design to install virtual environments from a set X as the initial cyberspace. Given all elements u of an unknown cyberspace U, if they are confirmed to be the elements of our cyberspace X, the unknown cyberspace is called a subset or a subcyberspace and denoted as $U \subseteq X$. Thus, the subset check is automatically performed by processing $(\forall u) (u \in U \Rightarrow u \in X)$. The closure U of U is the intersection of all closed subsets of X containing U. In other words, the closure U is the elements of X that are not the exterior elements of U. The set of all the subsets of X, $\{U|U \subseteq X\}$, is called a power set 2^X. The power set is quite useful for designing a cyberspace consisting of sub-cyberspaces.

22.2.2 Topological Design

Now, we go into the business of designing the cyberspace as the union of the sub-cyberspaces and their overlaps. The cyberspace thus designed is generally called a topological space (X, T) where $T \subset 2^X$. Designing a topological space is automated by the following specification:

1. $X \in T$ and $\downarrow \in T$

2. For an arbitrary index set J,
   $\forall j \in J \, (U_j \in T) \to \cap_{j \in J} U_j \in T$

3. $U, V \in T \to U \cup V \in T$

T is said to be the topology of the topological space (X, T). Given two topologies T_1 and T_2 on X such that $T_1 \subset T_2$, we say T_1 is weaker than T_2 (or T_2 is stronger than T_1). For simplicity, we often use X instead of (X, T) to represent a topological space whenever no ambiguity arises. When we see two topological spaces (X, T) and (Y, T'), how we can tell that (X, T) and (Y, T') are equivalent? Here is a criterion for us to use computers to automatically validate that they are topologically equivalent. Two topological spaces (X, T) and (Y, T') are topologically equivalent (or homeomorphic) if there is a function $f:(X, T) \to (Y, T')$ that is continuous, and its inverse exists and is continuous. We write $(X, T) \cong (Y, T')$ for (X, T) to be homeomorphic to (Y, T'). Then how do we validate the continuity of a function? It amounts to checking $\forall B \in T', f^{\leftarrow} B \in T$, where $f^{\leftarrow} B$ means the inverse image of B by f. $f^{\leftarrow}$ is also denoted as f^{-1}.

22.2.3 Extension Theoretical and Homotopy Theoretical Design

The cyberspaces we are designing are actually dynamically changing, as seen in various cases shown previously. The change we specify in our design must be homotopic, meaning continuously deforming, if our design is to maintain generality as explained previously. Homotopy is a case of continuous extension by which we extend a given point, for example to a surface. In that sense, extension does not preserve space dimensions. Now we go back to homotopy. Let us consider the changes of a mapping function f relating a cyberspace X to another cyberspace Y. After the change, f becomes another mapping function g. In short, we are designing the continuous deformation of f into g where $f, g: X \to Y$. We consider the deformation during the normalized interval $I = [0, 1]$, which can be a time interval or a space interval. X and Y are topological spaces as designed earlier. Let us denote the unchanging part A of the cyberspace X as a subspace $A \subset X$. Then, what we are designing is a homotopy H, where $H:X \times I \to Y$ such that $(\forall x \in X) \, (H(x, 0) = f(x)$ and $H(x, 1) = g(x))$ and $(\forall a \in A, \forall t \in I) \, (H(a, t) = f(a) = g(a))$. F is said to be homotopic to g relative to A, and denoted as f > g (rel A). Now here is a new design problem. That is, how can we design two topological spaces X and Y to be homotopically equivalent X > Y, namely of the same homotopy type? It is done by designing f:X → Y and h:Y → X such that h ⌊ f > 1_X and f ⌊ h > 1_Y, where 1_X and 1_Y are identity maps 1_X:X → X and 1_Y:Y → Y.

Homotopy equivalence is more general than topology equivalence so that homotopy equivalence can identify a changing cyberspace that is topologically no longer equivalent after the change. As an example, let us look at the human body. (By the way, the human body is so complex that it is often called a microcosmos, and it itself is a cyberspace.) What we are looking at is a very simple case for illustration purposes only, but it is sufficient. Consider a silhouette of the human body of a person dancing. Figure 22.1 shows how we can identify it automatically while the silhouette shape is changing during the dance. In manufacturing automation, where a component goes through a manufacturing line, for example to be deformed into a desired shape by a group of automated press machines, the deformation process is specified by a homotopy and validated by homotopy equivalence.

In medical imagery, from a set of computed tomographical 2D sliced images, we can reconstruct 3D images homotopically in the following way: consider that a slice is homotopically deformed to the next slice, and then from the algorithm derived from the law of formation of the organ for which the images have been obtained tomographically we can record all the intermediate shapes between the two

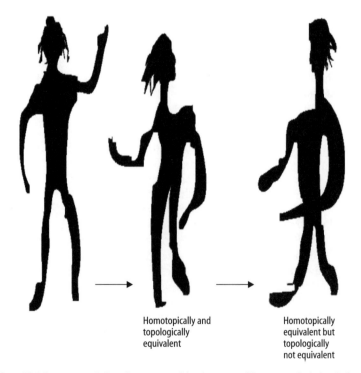

Homotopically and
topologically
equivalent

Homotopically
equivalent but
topologically
not equivalent

Figure 22.1 Homotopy equivalence is more general than homeomorphism as a topological equivalence.

neighboring slices faithfully without loss. The same applies to the topography case. Further applications are in financial trading areas, where from discrete financial data we can build the entire features automatically and then conduct automated financial trading in a cyberspace based on the expected financial value change shapes thus derived homotopically.

22.2.4 Cellular Structured Space Design

We first look into cellular structured spaces (or simply "cellular spaces") [2,5,20] formulated by J.H.C. Whitehead in 1949 [26]. First of all, a cell is designed as a topological space X that is topologically equivalent (homeomorphic) to an n-dimensional open ball Int B^n and called an n-cell e^n. From X, via attaching cells as explained later, we can inductively compose a finite or infinite sequence X^p of cells that are subspaces of X, indexed by integer $\wedge$, namely $\{X^p | p \in \wedge\}$ called a filtration [5], such that:

X^p covers X (or X^p is a covering of X)

That is:

$X = \cap_{p \in \wedge} X^p$ and

X^{p-1} is a subspace of X^p,

That is:

$X^0 \subseteq X^1 \subseteq X^2 \subseteq \ldots \subseteq X^{p-1} \subseteq X^p \subseteq \ldots \subseteq X$

We can thus inductively compose a quite general cellular space called a filtration space for a cellular space X as a space X with a filtration composed above, and denote it by $\{X; X^p | p \in \wedge\}$. We also say that $\{X; X^p | p \in \wedge\}$ is a cell decomposition of a topological space X, or a partition of topological space X into subspaces X^p which are cells. Cell composition and decomposition can be exploited to compute cellular spatial structures to create homotopically valid computational shape modeling. Cell composition and decomposition via cell attachment creates spaces of the same homotopy type and hence are homotopically equivalent, and the spaces thus created are not necessarily homeomorphic.

We can actually build a little bit more structured cellular space, and hence not as general as a filtration space. It is called a closure finite and weak topology space, abbreviated as a CW–space constructed by the open subspaces X^p of X [20,21]. It is sufficient for our space composition with finite numbers of cells. If we need to think about an infinite case some extra care is required. Further, as in most cases in natural sciences as seen in theoretical physics [4], smoothness, the existence of continuous derivatives of all orders, is assumed either implicitly or explicitly, and sometimes diffeomorphism (differentiability with a differential inverse) is further assumed to turn a CW-complex into a more special case named a manifold. There we can use differential topology to extract singularities [16,23–25] and critical points [12,13,24,25] as indexes to identify the characteristics of objects. However, in general cases, such as cyberworld modeling and applications [3], we do not usually have the luxury of enjoying such a limited space built on top of the assumptions.

22.3 Homotopically Composing Cellular Structured Spaces via Attaching Cells

We can homotopically compose a new cellular structured space Y by attaching an open n-cell e^n to the already composed topological space X, using a surjective and continuous map f called an attaching map (also called an adjoining map or an adjunction map). In handling geometrical invariants, surjective maps and open maps are of great value in producing a consistent theory of the inherited properties [17]. "A map f: X $\rightarrow$ Y is surjective" means $(\forall y \in Y)\,(\exists x \in X)\,[f(x) = y]$. "A map f: X $\rightarrow$ Y is continuous" means "a subset A $\subset$ Y is open in Y if and only if $\{f^{-1}(y)|y \in A\}$ is open in X". The new space Y thus obtained is called an adjunction space (or an adjoining space). Let us present a more precise definition.

Given two disjoint topological spaces X and Y,

$$Y +_f X = Y + X / \sim$$

is an attaching space (an adjunction space, or an adjoining space) obtained by attaching (gluing, adjuncting or adjoining) X to Y by an attaching map (adjunction map, or an adjoining map) f (or by identifying points $x \in X_0|X_0 \subset X$ with their images $f(x) \in Y$, namely by a surjective map f). The symbol + denotes a disjoint union and often a + symbol is used instead (sometimes it is called an "exclusive or"). $\sim$ is an equivalence relation. An equivalence relation is simply a relation that is reflexive, symmetric and transitive. It can be a set theoretical equivalence relation, a topological equivalence relation, a geometrical equivalence relation or a homotopic equivalence relation. The transitivity divides the space naturally into a disjoint union of subspaces called equivalence classes. If we denote an equivalence class by $x/\sim$, it is, then,

$$x / \sim = \{y \in X \mid x \sim y\}.$$

The set of all equivalence classes is denoted as $X/\sim$, and is called the quotient space or the identification space of X:

$$X / \sim = \{\, x / \sim \,\in 2^X \mid x \in X\} \subseteq 2^X.$$

An attaching map f is a surjective (onto) and continuous map

$$f: X_0 \rightarrow Y,$$

where $X_0 \subset X$.

$X + Y / \sim$ is a quotient space

$$X + Y / \sim = X + Y / (x \sim f(x) \mid \forall x \in X_0) = X +_f Y.$$

Here is a special case for later use in composing valid shape modeling. Let S^{n-1} be the boundary of a closed n-cell B^n, namely ∂B^n. That is,

$$S^{n-1} = \partial B^n = B^n - \text{Int } B^n = B^n - e^n$$

Let an attaching map f be a surjective (onto) and continuous map

$$f: S^{n-1} \rightarrow X$$

An adjunction space Y is defined as a quotient space

$$Y = X +_f B^n = X + B^n /\{f(u) \sim u \mid u \in S^{n-1}\}$$

Given two homotopic maps f and g

$$f, g: S^{n-1} \rightarrow X,$$

then $X +_f B^n$ and $X +_g B^n$ have the same homotopy type (or are homotopically equivalent):

$$X +_f B^n > X +_g B^n$$

22.4 A Case Study of Homotopically Composing Cellular Structured Spaces via Attaching Cells

As a case study of homotopically composing cellular structured spaces via attaching cells, let us look at frill composition via cell attachment.

There are many cases where geometrical representation cannot be used to specify graphics images properly. A frill consisting of tucks is a typical case. Tucks differ in the width of folds, they usually change shape during the manufacturing processes and use, and they wear where the tucks are attached. Hence geometrical definition is neither appropriate nor applicable. We have to find geometrical invariants to specify tucks. The geometrical invariants are preserved and inherited while geometrical shape changes take place homotopically. What then are the geometrical invariants? An example of real tucked objects, shirt sleeves, is shown in Figure 22.2, and the geometrical invariants are briefly sketched as follows and shown in Figure 22.3. Each tuck consists of a particular type of fold (actually a pair of folds). The tuck is then homotopically attached to the other part through a cell attaching (also called adjoining or adjunction) operation. Before the cell attachment, the tuck is decomposed into three 1-cells and one 2-cell. The cell attachment is a surjective operation that maps a line on the collar to the three 1-cells of the tuck. The three 1-cells are topologically equivalent and form an equivalence class. Hence, the

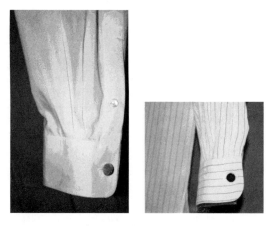

Figure 22.2 Shirt sleeve tucks.

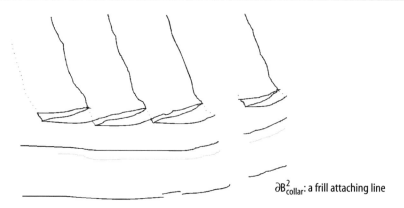

∂B^2_{collar}: a frill attaching line

Figure 22.3 Frill composition = collar attachment to tucks via the attaching map:f: $\partial B^2_{collar} B^2_{collar} \rightarrow +_i (B^1_i + B^1_i + B^1_i)_{tuck\ edge\ i}$

mapping is an identification map (also called a quotient map). To be more precise, frill composition is collar attachment to tucks via the attaching map

$$f: \partial B^2_{collar} \rightarrow +_i (B^1_i + B^1_i + B^1_i)_{tuck\ edge\ i}$$

to obtain a frill composed as

$$+_i (B^1_i + B^1_i + B^1_i)_{tuck\ edge\ i} +_f B^2_{collar} / \sim$$

$$= +_i (e^1_i + e^1_i + e^1_i)_{tuck\ edge\ i} + e^2_{collar}.$$

22.5 Conclusions

The proposed approach is valid in modeling varieties of problems of industrial products such as copiers and fax machines where paper sheets being processed inside the machines need to be properly characterized. Business structures such as corporate M&A structures, business relationships and global electronic financial trading such as practiced by George Soros [6,22] are also all properly modeled using the cellular space composition approach as explained so far. The world is shifting from linear to nonlinear structures [1–3]. What we need on the human side is to shift the world view drastically. A similar drastic change of world view was seen in the shift from the Ptolemaic theory of the cosmos to the Copernican theory in the 16th century [19]. The necessary virtual reality environments are being lined up as real business products [10,11]. Case studies for abstraction hierarchy applications in industrial and business structure modeling are in progress.

References

[1]   TL Kunii (1998) *Pax Japonica* (in Japanese), President Co. Ltd, Tokyo, October.
[2]   TL Kunii (1989) creating a new world inside computers – methods and implications, In *Proceedings of the Seventh Annual Conference of the Australian Society for Computers in Learning in Tertiary*

Education (ASCILITE 89) (eds. G Bishop and J Baker), pp. 28-51. Also available as Technical Report 89-034, Dept. of Information Science, The University of Tokyo.

[3]   TL Kunii (1998) The architecture of synthetic worlds, in *Cyberworlds* (eds. TL Kunii and A Luciani), pp. 19–30, Tokyo, Springer-Verlag.

[4]   S Hawking and R Penrose (1996) *The Nature of Space and Time*, New Jersey, Princeton University Press.

[5]   F Fritsch and RA Piccinini (1990) *Cellular Structures in Topology*, Cambridge, Cambridge University Press.

[6]   G Soros (1998) The crisis of global capitalism – open society endangered, *Public Affairs*, New York.

[7]   P Kennedy (1987) *The Rise and Fall of the Great Powers*, New York, Random House.

[8]   TL Kunii, T Noma and K-J Lee (1992) SYDEM: a new approach to computer-aided design of assemblies and assemblability testing, in *Visual Computing: Integrating Computer Graphics with Computer Vision (Proc. CG International 92)*, (ed. TL Kunii), Tokyo, Springer-Verlag, pp. 469–479.

[9]   TL Kunii, T Noma and K Lee (1991) Assemblability discriminating method and assembling sequence generating method, *United States Patent No. 5058026*, October.

[10] http://www.sun.com/.

[11] http://www.microsoft.com/.

[12] J Milner (1969) *Morse Theory*, New Jersey, Princeton University Press.

[13] T Ikeda, TL Kunii, Y Shinagawa and M Ueda (1992) A geographical database system based on the homotopy model, in *Modern Geometric Computing for Visualization* (eds. TL Kunii and Y Shinagawa), Tokyo, Springer-Verlag, pp. 193–206.

[14] TL Kunii and T Noma (1984) Computer graphics as a tool to visualize virtual worlds, in *Video Culture Canada's Second Annual International Festival "The New Media"*, Toronto, 2–6 November.

[15] TL Kunii (1985) Electronic Alice's Wonderland, in *Graphics Interface 85*, Montreal, 27–31 May.

[16] TL Kunii and H Gotoda (1990) Singularity theoretical modeling and animation of garment wrinkle formation processes, *The Visual Computer: An International Journal of Computer Graphics*, 6(6), 326–336.

[17] TL Kunii (1998) Graphics with shape property inheritance, in *Proceedings of Pacific Graphics '98 (PG98)*, Singapore, 26–29 October, Los Alamitos, CA, IEEE Computer Society Press, pp. 2–6.

[18] TL Kunii (1997) The 3rd industrial revolution through integrated intelligent processing systems, in *Proceedings of IEEE First International Conference on Intelligent Processing Systems*, Beijing, 28–31 October, New York, The Institute of Electrical and Electronics Engineers, pp. 1–6.

[19] DJ Boorstin (1983) *The Discoverers*, New York, Random House.

[20] H-J Baues (1996) *Homotopy Types and Homology*, Oxford, Oxford University Press.

[21] CTJ Dodson and PE Parker (1997) *User's Guide to Algebraic Topology*, Dordrecht, Kluwer Academic.

[22] http://www.foreignrelations.org/studies/transcripts/soros.html.

[23] H Whitney (1955) On singularities of mappings of Euclidean spaces. I. Mappings of the plane into the plane, *Annals of Math.*, 62, 373–410.

[24] Y Shinagawa, TL Kunii, Y Nomura, T Okuno and Y Young (1990) Automating view function generation for walk-through automation using a Reeb graph, in *Proceedings of Computer Animation '90*, Tokyo, Springer-Verlag, pp. 227–237.

[25] Y Kergosien (1992) Topology and visualization: from generic singularities to combinatorial shape modeling, in *Modern Geometric Computing for Visualization* (eds. TL Kunii and Y Shinagawa), Tokyo, Springer-Verlag, pp. 31–54.

[26] JHC Whitehead (1949) Combinatorial homotopy I, *Bulletin of the American Mathematical Society*, 55, 213–245.

[27] TL Kunii (1999) Computational shape modeling: valid and invalid, *Proceedings of the International Conference on Shape Modeling and Applications (Shape Modeling International '99)*, Aizu-Wakamatsu, Japan, 1–4 March, Los Alamitos, CA, IEEE Computer Society Press, pp. 2–7.

23

Some Aspects of the Human Communication Process: Preliminary Steps Towards a Conceptual Framework

Richard A. Guedj

It is better to try and risk an error than to be passive
Martinet in the Foreword to The Origins of Basque Language

23.1 The Question Addressed

Looking for the conditions to get a proper conceptual framework – to talk about information systems – to emerge within the community of scientists.

I would like to find out whether there are some preliminary conditions to be met in order to get a proper conceptual framework to emerge within our scientific community.

I refer to the conceptual framework that we should have in mind when dealing with (interacting with or through) our information systems, whether designing, producing, using or talking about those systems.

I feel that we are, at present, so far from any preliminary skeleton of a conceptual framework that we ought to be concerned more by the process of setting some conditions for the likely emergence of a candidate framework than with the nature of the framework itself. This should appear compelling from an examination of the global context of the information technology revolution.

23.2 The Motivation for Acting Now

The existence of some severe negative aspects of the global context of information technology revolution, such as the growing and diffuse sense of disorientation.

Interacting with our information systems – or through them with other people – leaves us with mixed feelings and with a growing and diffuse sense of anxiety more often than should be expected. I have tried to convey a feel for this situation in the following statements:

- Great expectations when catching a glimpse of the immense potential – witness the mushrooming of innovations and new applications which involve IT in almost every field.
- + Legitimate optimism when confronted with staggering achievements – witness the bewildering rate of growth of performance in some areas.
- − Frustration when facing stumbling blocks in trying to accomplish some simple actions – for example when one is getting far from relevant responses.
- − A growing sense of disorientation, of having to interact in a world of chaos, of not being able to discriminate easily between noise and information in this whirlpool of streams of bits, of not being able to notice whether there are any threats or malevolence in the current operating network environment – see [1] for a frightening account of searching the Web.
- − A puzzling feeling when watching so many human beings showing resignation or acceptance of sometime queer: non-human protocols and procedures.
- − Diffuse anxiety linked to such questions as:
  1. are we condemned to do our everyday activities with an ever-increasing mental (cognitive) load?
  2. are some of our essential human skills – such as establishing and maintaining alive a simple conversation between two persons who will get to know each other by holding that "conversation" – going to disappear just because we cannot formally specify those skills and embody them properly on the Web?

I am inclined to summarize this situation by saying that we do not have a proper conceptual framework to deal with our information systems. In fact, do we have any conceptual framework at all?

By a conceptual framework one usually understands "a theory or a scheme or system of ideas or statements held as an explanation or account of a group of facts or phenomena; a hypothesis that has been confirmed or established by observation or experiment and is accepted for the known facts; a statement of what are held to be the general laws, principles, or causes of something known or observed" [2].

23.3 The First Recommended Step

The Gonsethian three-pronged approach for conceptual framework emergence: experimentation, theorization, insight, or why it is necessary to start a process to get a conceptual framework to emerge rather than to try to build directly a framework.

The great thinker, mathematician and philosopher F. Gonseth has suggested [3] a three-pronged approach to building a common framework:

- providing data through intuition (hence the role of insight)
- confronting results from experiment (demos, feasibility studies, etc.)
- making efforts to provide a theoretical approach (rationalization, convincing arguments through predictive results from efforts of theorization)

Consistency in the three approaches must come by establishing schematic correspondences between the three approaches in specific situations.

What makes the Gonsethian simultaneous three-pronged approach for conceptual framework emergence compelling is that through the correspondences it tries to establish a common framework, and thus it takes a long-term view. What is at stake is too important to take a short-term view.

23.4 From Information Processing to the Search for Meaning

There are deeper reasons for taking a long-term view. Those reasons have to do with the concept of Information itself and with our relationship to technology.

Mathematicians have given us a clear definition of "information" that we can measure in bits and which is helpful for the design of our systems of communication.

However, for the recipient of a piece of information, the value of the information can be grasped only within a theory of knowledge and cognition. All I want to stress now, following Grize [4], is that if transmission of information is always linked to the presence of signals, of all kinds – electrical, chemical, acoustic, visual, tactile etc. – in all cases, what is important is that the signal carries a *meaning*, that it is *meaningful* at least to the recipient. The human recipient must understand the signal, and make sense of the signs that he or she perceives.

Let us see what some thinkers – historians of thought mostly – have said about the arts of understanding, about our capacity to "process" signs in the *search for meaning*.

> In the great developments of western culture emphasis has been shifting from *the search for meaning* to the *management of information*; there has been an overall move away from the elaboration of integrative goals towards the processing of discrete elements. [5]

What this move has led to? Not more "management of information" than "search for meaning" and more "digital" than "analog", but "management of information" instead of "search for meaning" and "digital" instead of "analog". We are deep into that situation now.

Let us look at another long-term appraisal.

> Once the ideas of computation, algorithms and commensurability permeate culture at large, a message is only "meaningful" if it reduces alternative choices and minimizes *polysemous, connotative or metaphoric* components. [6]

All the italicized words have become almost dirty words in our digital world.

Let us consider the challenge of understanding.

> The arts of understanding (hermeneutics) are as manifold as their objects. Signs are unbounded; both in combinatorial modes and in potentialities of significance. There is nothing more unnerving in the human condition than the fact that we can mean and/or say *anything*. [7].

Where are we now?

The contrasts between "digital" and "analog", and between "discrete" and " continuous" have taken on a definite negative connotation.

The connections between the corresponding processes, the reasoning process (seemingly of a digital nature) and the thinking process (of an analog nature) have disappeared. The balance, the play, the trade, the interaction between them are completely new to us.

Both have been studied by philosophers for some time, and they are quite relevant to our ambition of providing a satisfactory conceptual framework, as both processes seem basic and necessary. We seem quite ignorant of that work.

We are justly proud of our systems of transmission of information and of our ways of managing information (when we can manage it). But have we taken a scientific approach to our current problems? How come we are so ignorant of the foundations of cognition when cognition seems to play such a fundamental role in our interaction with our information systems?

Without dismissing any results from the theorization or experimentation approaches, I would like to suggest below something from the intuitive approach.

23.5 Two Potential Sources of Insight Arising from "Similar" Situations

23.5.1 A Revival of Interest in Conversation Theory

Let us take a common and not so simple example.

The situation is a visit to a museum, where the artist (or the curator or the guide) knows little about the visitors, but he or she is or may be eventually professionally open to an "encounter". In order for an interesting encounter between the two people - who may have completely different objectives – to have a chance to happen and to be somehow fruitful and positive for both, according to Marin [8] there are some conditions to be fulfilled. Basically, the two people are going to have a conversation about some objects, some artifacts, that have been designed or built or studied carefully by one of the people, and which are located around the place of the encounter.

The situation of a Web site designer, confronted with Web site visitors whose needs and abilities are not known, visitors who may come for a visit to become interested in objects placed on the Web, seems "similar" to the situation described by Marin.

It is interesting to note that Marin specifically makes reference to the work of Paul Grice on conversation theory [9]. One summary of Grice's Laws can be found in a recent report [10]. Below is reproduced another summary of Grice's Laws as expressed in [11]:

> A quick examination of that work reveals one Cooperative Principle:
>
> "make your conversational contribution such as is required, at the stage at which it occurs, by the accepted progress or direction of the talk exchange in which you are engaged."
>
> and two Conversational Maxims:
>
> Quantity
>
> 1. Make your contribution as informative as is required (for the current purpose of the exchange)
>
> 2. Do not make your contribution more informative than is required.
>
> and on Quality
>
> 1. Do not say what you believe to be false.

Could these rules and principles be expressed as guidelines for the design of Web sites?

I have the feeling that this whole field, called "computational implicature" (see [10] for an annotated bibliography), which has received a recent surge of attention (a recent workshop, for example, was held in Italy on this subject in May 1998) is likely to provide at least some of the guiding rules we are looking for to establish and maintain this "conversation" about the objects.

I believe that it might be worth trying, because we are addressing similar situations.

23.5.2 A Fresh Look at Styles and What We Can Learn from What Some Thinkers Have Said on What Is "Classic"

The recent evolution of Web tools from HTML to XML has shown a decisive step towards more abstraction with the introduction of so-called style sheets. But if style sheets are certainly attributes of styles, they do not define a particular style as we generally understand styles of expression.

An interesting comparison could be made between learning to write and learning to design a document for the Web. Learning to write cannot be reduced to acquiring writing skills, as learning to write inevitably involves learning styles of writing, and styles derive from conceptual stands.

In a similar way, learning to design a document for the Web cannot be reduced to acquiring programming skills. Styles of design for the Web are also likely to derive from conceptual stands.

A taxonomy of styles of design will probably soon exist to parallel the taxonomy of styles of writing: reflexive, practical, plain, romantic etc. – and classic.

In particular, what can be said about the classic conceptual stand for writing is likely to hold for the classic conceptual stand for designing for the Web.

Below, we will borrow from a recent book on classical style in writing a set of clear and precise statements that characterize classic style. Most of them should inspire a transposition into guidelines and criteria for designing documents for the Web.

> Classic Style is focused and assured.
> Its virtues are clarity and simplicity.
> It declines to acknowledge ambiguities, unessential qualifications, doubts.
> Classic Style is, above all, a style of presentation with claims to transparency.
> Every word counts.
> Clarity everywhere is not Accuracy everywhere.
> The model is one person speaking to another.
> Classic style is energetic but not anxious.
> Elite is not exclusive.
> Classic style is for everybody.
> The reader is competent.
> The writer is authentic, sufficient, competent, does all the work invisibly. [12]

23.6 The Deontological Level: Some Critical Issues

23.6.1 Being Part of a Community: What Obligations this Entails

I am talking about our community, the community of researchers, key actors in different institutions gathered to explore areas at the frontiers of human and information systems. What obligations – being part of this loose network – does this entail?

First, I believe that we have to strictly and always follow a scientific approach. The fact that there are many disciplines involved does not allow any of us to dispense this approach. We all have to check the observed data systematically, verify any theoretical assumptions in empirical reality, express as clearly as possible our hypotheses and communicate to others to obtain feedback.

Those are deontological obligations that are often forgotten at one stage or another. A slip in one of those obligations leads us to a world of chaos.

23.6.2 The Community of Scientists Who Research and Develop New Concepts: Are There Any Special Responsibilities?

I should like to stress a special responsibility, the one to name properly the concepts – the notions we are creating or using. An unsatisfactory name for a concept delays its full development. We should never be happy with something we know to be wrongly named. Even if we do not yet have a proper substitute, we should not stop trying to look for a better one.

23.7 Conclusions

I have attempted to express some preliminary conditions to get a proper conceptual framework to emerge within our scientific community when dealing with our information systems.

As a first step, I have suggested taking a Gonsethian three-pronged approach to the emergence of a conceptual framework: experimentation, theorization, intuition.

I feel that the two areas of interest mentioned – conversation theory and what constitutes a style, in particular a classic style – are capable of leading us to the preliminary skeleton of a conceptual framework.

On a deontological level, I have outlined some critical issues, namely obligations and special responsibilities for members of our community of researchers.

Those issues are as important for setting up the right conditions for the emergence of a conceptual framework as the framework itself.

Acknowledgments

This work was carried out while on sabbatical at the Fraunhofer Institute for Computer Graphics, IGD, Darmstadt. It has benefitted from a most stimulating and hospitable research environment. I would like to thank especially the Director, Professor Jose Luis Encarnaçao for extending the invitation and making the conditions of work so congenial.

References

[1] IS Nathenson (1998) Internet infoglut and invisible ink: spamdexing search engines with meta tags, *Harvard Journal of Law and Technology*, 12(1).
[2] *The Oxford English Dictionary*, 2nd edn, 1989 (see "theory").
[3] E Emery (1995) *Pour une Philosophie du dialogue – les combats singuliers de Ferdinand Gonseth*, Editions L'Age d'Homme (in French).
[4] J-B Grize (1993) Semiologie et langage, in *Approches semiologiques dans les Sciences Humaines*, publie sous la direction de Denis Mieville, Lausanne, Editions Payot, pp. 33–41 (in French).
[5] J Bruner (1990) *Acts of Meaning*, Princeton, NJ, Harvard University Press, p. 4.
[6] GC Fiumara (1995) *The Metaphoric Process*, London, Routledge.
[7] L Marin (1997) *De l'entretien*, editions de Minuit (in French).
[8] G Steiner (1997) *Errata: an Examined Life*, London, Weidenfeld & Nicolson.
[9] P Grice (1975) Logic and conversation, in *Syntax and Semantics III: Speech Acts* (eds. P Cole and JL Morgan), New York, Academic Press, pp. 41–58.
[10] R Guedj (1998), http://www-dienst.rl.ac.uk/library/1998/tr/ral-1998077/.
[11] Computational implicature, annotated bibliography, http://www.pitt.edu/implicature/.
[12] F-N Thomas and M Turner (1997) *Clear and Simple as the Truth*, New Jersey, Princeton University Press.

24
Natural Human–Human-System Interaction

Niels Ole Bernsen

Abstract

The importance of a vision can lie in providing a model within which we think and create. If the model is outdated, thinking becomes unduly constrained. The chapter proposes replacing the paradigm of human–computer interaction (HCI) with a more comprehensive model for thinking about future systems and interfaces. Recent progress in speech technologies has managed to establish a powerful application paradigm, i.e. that of natural task-oriented spoken language dialog systems. This application paradigm points towards the broader goal of natural human–human-system interaction (HHSI) in virtual, combined virtual and physical, and physical environments. Against the backdrop of the natural HHSI model and the rapidly changing environment of advanced systems research, the types of research that are likely to be needed in the future are discussed. The discussion deliberately de-emphasizes next-generation systems research in order to shift the focus to a range of equally important, existing or emerging research objectives which sometimes show a tendency to be overshadowed by the next generation challenges.

24.1 From Single Word to Spoken Dialog

During the past 40 years or so, the field of speech technology has moved its focus from research on single word recognition to research on natural spoken human-system dialog. The underlying tale of gradual progress in research is not the whole story, however. In those four decades, the environment in which research progress has been made has changed dramatically, leading to entirely new perspectives for speech technology research. Taking a closer look at these developments may be helpful in trying to understand the roles and objectives of research in today's Information Society as well as where we are, or should be, going into the 21st century.

In 1960, promising speech recognition rates were reported for very small vocabulary (10 words), speaker-dependent, real-time recognition of isolated words [1]. Today, academic research in speech recognition seems about to reach the end of the road, being replaced by steady progress through competitive industrial development [2].

Medium-sized vocabulary (~5000 words), speaker-independent, real-time recognition of continuous (or spontaneous) speech has become a commercial reality, and very large vocabulary (~60 000 words) spoken dictation systems which only need a minimum of speaker-dependent training can be purchased for less than US$100 from companies such as IBM, Dragon Systems and Philips. Today, unlimited vocabulary, real-time speaker-independent continuous speech recognition is within reach, and speech recognition technology has become a component technology which is finding its way into all sorts of interfaces to computer systems.

In itself, speech recognition is a transformation of the acoustic signal into an uninterpreted string of words which may or may not make sense to a human but does not make any sense to the machine. This enables applications such as the "phonetic typewriter" [1] as well as spoken command applications in which the system executes in response to a spoken word or phrase rather than in response to the push of a button on the keyboard, mouse or otherwise. Between humans, speech is much more than that, of course. Speech is the primary modality for the interactive exchange of information among people. While hardly visible – even as a long-term goal – in 1960, the past 10–15 years have seen the emergence of a powerful form of interactive speech systems, i.e. task-oriented spoken language dialog systems [3]. These systems not only recognize speech but understand, process what they have understood, and return spoken output to the user, who may then choose to continue the spoken interaction with the machine in order to complete the interactive task. In their most versatile form, today's spoken language dialog systems, or SLDSs, for short, incorporate speaker-independent, spontaneous speech recognition in close to real time.

It is the task orientation which has made SLDSs possible now. It is still much too early to build fully fledged conversational SLDSs which can undertake spoken interaction with humans in the same way that humans communicate with one another using speech only – about virtually any topic, in free order, through free negotiation of initiative, using unrestricted vocabulary and unrestricted grammar, and so on. However, a range of collaborative tasks are already being solved commercially through speech-only dialog with computer systems over the telephone or otherwise. One of the simplest possible examples is a system which asks if the user wants to receive a collect call. If the user accepts the call, the system connects the user, and if the user refuses the call, the system informs the caller that the call was rejected [4]. A more complex task for which commercial solutions already exist, is train timetable information [5]. The user phones the system to inquire, for instance, when there are trains from Zürich to Geneva on Thursday morning, and receives a (spoken) list of departures in return. As these examples show, task-oriented SLDSs constitute a potentially very powerful application paradigm for interactive speech technologies, which could be used for a virtually unlimited number of interactive user-system tasks in company switchboard services, banking, homes, cars etc. However, successful SLDSs remain difficult to build for reasons which go beyond the purely theoretical and technical issues involved and which illustrate the general state of speech technology research at this point.

Even if capable of working as standalone systems, speech recognizers are increasingly becoming components of larger and more complex systems. Likewise, speech generators which can also work as standalone technologies, i.e. as text-to-speech systems, are increasingly becoming system components as well. The SLDS is probably the most important technology which integrates speech-to-text, text-to-speech and other components, such as natural language understanding and generation and dialog management, but it is not the only one. Other integrated systems technologies incorporating some form of speech processing include speech translation systems [6] and multimodal systems having speech as one of their input-output modalities (see, for example, Chapter 9.3 in [3]). All of these integrated technologies represent a level of complexity which is comparatively new to the field of speech technology research. Together with the rapid increase in commercial exploitation of speech technology in general, those technologies have introduced an urgent need for system integration skills, human factors skills and general software engineering skills to be added to the skills of the groups which used to work in basic component technologies. The speech technology field, in other words, is now faced with the need to specialize software engineering best practice to speech technologies, and to do so swiftly and efficiently. This process of reorientation has only just begun. This is why, for instance, the development of task-oriented SLDSs remains fraught with home-grown solutions, lack of best practice methodologies and tools, ignorance about systems evaluation, lack of development platforms and standards, and so on. Only by solving problems such as these will it be possible to efficiently design and build task-oriented SLDSs which achieve their ultimate purpose: to conduct smooth and effortless natural dialog with their users during interactive task resolution.

To summarize, today's speech technology research has several general characteristics, including:

- from components research to integrated systems research
- one high-potential systems application paradigm (the SLDS)
- universality, speech components can be included in all sorts of systems and interfaces
- industry and research are increasingly working on "the same things"
- researchers are facing the entire spectrum of issues of field-specific software engineering best practice, including life cycle best practice, evaluation best practice, human factors, the need for dedicated development support tools, quality control standardization etc.

It is difficult to exaggerate the present significance of the above characteristics for the field of speech technology research. Together, those characteristics subsume most of the challenges facing researchers in the field. Comparison may be useful with a related technology field which also holds a strong potential for the future, i.e. that of natural language processing. While the "basic unit of research" in the speech field is the spoken dialog, the basic unit of research in the natural language processing field is the written text. In several ways, current research is at comparable stages in speech processing and natural language processing. For instance, just as the speech field has developed mature speech recognition, the natural language processing field has developed mature spelling checkers and parsers. At the moment, however, perhaps the main difference between the two fields is that the natural language processing field has not yet developed any system application paradigm corresponding to SLDSs. There are reasons for that, of course, the principal (and deepest) one being that there is no such thing as a task-oriented text, not to speak of a task-oriented interactive text. It continues to be difficult to identify an initial powerful systems application paradigm for text processing which does not require a solution to the massive research problem of processing texts in general. If such a paradigm could be found, we could expect rapid progress to be made in extremely important areas, such as task/domain-specific text translation, or task/domain-specific text summarization. The many failed attempts at doing these things suggest that those attempts may have been incompatible with the very nature of texts, which is to be unrestricted in principle, or to be unpredictably restricted, which amounts to the same thing. This is not to say, of course, that highly useful text translation or text summarization will not happen until we have mastered the processing of unrestricted text, only that one or more powerful application paradigms are still missing. The lack of a systems application paradigm for text processing means that the natural language processing field is a considerable distance behind the speech processing field with respect to having to address integrated systems research, field-specific software (systems) engineering best practice, human factors and so on.

24.2 From Spoken Dialog to Natural Human–Human-System Interaction

The challenges to current speech technology research described in the previous section can be viewed in a different perspective as well. In this latter perspective, those challenges serve to generate a much more long-term vision, the gradual realization of which will transform speech technology research even more, eventually absorbing it into the wider field of natural interactive systems. Moreover, this vision appears to be a necessary one in the rather precise sense that the vision seems to be the only possible projection from the present state of the art.

Task-oriented SLDSs are not task-independent conversational systems, of course, and it is straightforward from the existence of task-oriented SLDSs to project the ulterior goal of building unrestricted conversational systems. So the creation of unrestricted conversational systems is part of the long-term vision presented here. From the point of view of technological feasibility, however, this goal is of the same magnitude and complexity as the production of unlimited text processing (understanding, translation etc.) systems. In what follows, I shall focus on some other limitations that are inherent to task-oriented SLDSs as described above, limitations which might be surmounted without having to go all the way to unlimited conversation machines.

One such limitation is the tacitly assumed human–computer interaction (HCI) paradigm: typically, a person phones the computer and conducts a spoken dialog with it until the task has been completed (or abandoned). There is no reason why our thinking should be limited in this way. In human spoken communication, two-person-only dialog has no privileged position or overall advantage over dialog among three or more people. Moreover, the "computer" part of the phrase "human–computer interaction" has become highly misleading in the present world of networks, client–server architectures, call centers etc. A more adequate interactive paradigm for the future, then, is the human–human-system interaction (HHSI) paradigm in which two humans communicate with each other as well as with the system. An example of this setup is the Magic Lounge project, which belongs to the focused research program on computing for communities under the European Intelligent Information Interfaces (i3) initiative [7]. In the Magic Lounge, several humans meet to conduct virtual meetings among themselves with the system as note-taker, information seeker and meeting moderator [8,9]. It should be added here that, clearly, human–human-system interaction is not limited to communication in virtual space, but applies to physical (or local) communication and to mixed-reality communication as well. The one system/two people configuration is the basic model. One system/one person and one system/+2 people configurations are viewed as extensions of the basic model. The HHSI paradigm is perfectly compatible with task-oriented communication rather than unrestricted communication.

A third important limitation of task-oriented SLDS applications concerns the speech-only aspect. Humans tend to use speech-only when they communicate using, for example, ordinary telephones, mobile phones or MBone speech-only. When humans meet physically, however, their communication tends to become far richer. When interacting face-to-face through speech, humans communicate in many other ways in parallel, using a rich set of partly redundant, partly complementary modalities for the exchange of information, including lip movement, facial expression, gesture and bodily posture, and they frequently make use of, or create, objects which are present in the environment and which themselves may have communicative contents, such as texts, maps, images, data graphics, physical models etc. As humans, in other words, we are already implementations of the *natural interaction paradigm* within which spoken dialog is merely an (admittedly central) input–output modality among others. Researchers have begun to endow computer systems and interfaces with capabilities for natural interaction. Output lip movement synchronized with output speech has been achieved. Input lip movement recognition, output facial expression generation, and input facial expression comprehension by machine are topics for ongoing research [10]. Prototype systems exist which are capable of understanding task-oriented combinations of input speech and pointing gesture [11,12]. Gesture-only recognition by machines using cameras or other sensor systems has become a popular research topic with gesture-based music generation as an early application.

Combining the two paradigms that were projected from current task-oriented SLDSs above, we get the vision, or model, of *natural human–human-system interaction*. The task-orientation that is required today will probably go away in due course but this is not the main point. The main point is a new interaction paradigm which is capable of tremendous progress through generation of an unlimited number of increasingly sophisticated applications. In the natural HHSI paradigm, the system's role is twofold. First, the system increasingly communicates with humans in the same way in which humans communicate with each other. In virtual co-presence situations, for instance, humans will communicate primarily using speech, whether or not the communication is augmented with video, application sharing etc. The present chat technologies seem unnatural and are likely to largely disappear. Secondly, the system will become an increasingly all-knowing tool capable of quickly retrieving any information needed by the humans in the course of their interaction. Bottlenecks today include, among other things, bandwidth limitations on network access, software platform incompatibilities and the primitiveness of current agent technologies.

In brief, traditional human interaction for highly generic purposes, such as problem solving, is characterized by:

- X people physically together, documents, drawings, physical models, phone, fax, oral discussion, gesture, facial expression, emotion, sketching, demonstrating how to do etc.
- Natural human–human communication, in one place, with limited access to external knowledge.

Human problem solving in the future will be characterized by:

- X people together in physical and/or virtual space.
- The system is an (increasingly) all-knowing tool.
- The system is a natural communication partner.
- Natural human–human-machine communication, ubiquitous, unlimited knowledge access – for all users.

Obviously, joint problem solving is not the only broad family of tasks which will be "taken over" by the natural HHSI paradigm. Game-playing, for instance, will be so as well. The phrase "for all users" is important. Enabling natural communication with machines will serve to reduce the GUI to its proper role (graphical user interface) paradigm in which interaction is being done through mouse-like input devices, keyboard input and screen output. Instead, ubiquitous systems use will increase, the classical computer will increasingly fade from our environment, and computing will no more assume the literacy and dexterity that tends to be required by GUI interfaces.

24.3 Future Research Challenges

The natural HHSI paradigm is easy to comprehend, seems to follow by projection from current system and paradigm limitations and current development trends in an almost deterministic manner, and has tremendous potential. However, like the purely technical development from single word speech recognizers to task-oriented spoken dialog systems described at the start of Section 24.1, this method of presenting natural HHSI fails to consider the changing context of research, the surprises it may hold for traditional points of view, and the challenges it poses to the selection of research directions to undertake or fund. This wider context and the challenges it offers are discussed in the present section.

24.3.1 Mainstream Technology Research

It seems that research is moving away from focusing on basic components. There is still basic components research to do, of course, but even what remains of basic components research is increasingly being influenced by demands stemming from systems research and general software engineering requirements. Increasingly, the natural HHSI paradigm demands research into high-complexity systems, integration of several components, APIs development etc. Researchers who want to compete in the race to invent and build the next system generation(s), in other words, will need to work in the context of large and complex systems. The problem posed by this development is not so much that many researchers are not used to doing that. Rather, it means that it is no longer possible to "build what one needs from scratch". To do so is simply infeasible in terms of the resources needed, as well as, in most cases, extremely inefficient or even silly. Instead, researchers, just like industry, have to select the components they do not want, or need, to build from off the shelf. And the shelf itself is growing larger by the minute. Knowing what's on the big shelf is quickly becoming very difficult, the growing risk being that the research team might spend years of effort reinventing the wheel. Furthermore, selecting from the big shelf is not always free, which means rapidly increasing demands on financial resources.

Moreover, to be sensible, systems design and specification based on what is on the big shelf needs to take into account emerging platforms, standards and even market trends. If any one of these factors evolves differently from what was expected when the research system prototype work was launched, large amounts of effort may have been wasted. Similarly, if an expected, emerging platform or program version gets delayed, the research system prototype work may fail to reach its objectives.

These points suggest that research system prototype work following the natural HHSI paradigm involves high-risk opportunistic technology research. That the research is high-risk and potentially resource intensive has been made clear above. That the research is opportunistic is partly coincidental with the high risk of advanced systems development in research, partly due to the fact that failed expectations concerning how the underlying technologies will develop will not necessarily lead to research project failure. Sometimes, it will be possible to redirect efforts to follow leads that were discovered underway, thereby avoiding total failure. It is difficult to guess how often this will be the case, but clear that drastic project reorientation imposes strong demands on the inventiveness and flexibility of the research team(s) involved. It is much easier to continue to follow an effectively dead plan than to reorient in a flexible and opportunistic manner.

The natural HHSI paradigm, in other words, poses considerable challenges to systems research. The conditions under which this research is being carried out strongly resemble those faced by industry. The difference, however, is that innovative systems research takes place without most of the safeguarding infrastructure of sound industrial R&D laboratories, including specialization in one or a few ranges of products, substantial in-house platform resources created through past efforts, professional awareness of standards and market developments etc. It is hard to see how these challenges to research are likely to be met in the future, unless one assumes either (a) a few large non-industrial advanced research laboratories, (b) much more effective collaborative research than we are used to from the past, with real synergy among highly specialized teams covering all of the crucial aspects of the system technology to be built, or (c) that industry more or less takes over the entire research and development process, leaving non-industrial research teams to do something else. Some may continue the work that remains to be done in components research. Others may do work of the kinds described in Sections 24.3.2–24.3.6 below.

In Europe, there is no significant tradition for (a) above. (b), however, is currently being piloted in i3, the Intelligent Information Interfaces initiative [7]. i3 features groups (or research programs) of around 10 research projects in a focused research area. The research projects start simultaneously, run for 2–3 years in parallel and have strong incentives for cross-project collaboration. The two ongoing i3 research programs address computing for local and virtual communities, and computing in schools for 4–8-year-old, respectively. i3 will be followed, in the fall of 1999, by a third, related, research program called Universal Information Ecosystems [13]. As for (c), there are indications that some of the larger European IT/telecoms companies are turning skeptical about the development of advanced systems prototypes in non-industrial research laboratories.

24.3.2 Futuristic Scenarios of Use

In some advanced systems and interfaces research areas, the picture conveyed in Section 24.3.1 is already commonplace. This may be particularly true of core software (and hardware) research areas. However, it may be suspected that the picture may be less familiar to many of the research teams who are best placed to adopt the natural HHSI vision. If these groups are inclined to hesitate in joining the race for the next system generation(s), or at least inclined to diversify their research pursuits, the wider context of the natural HHSI paradigm would seem to offer plenty of novel opportunities. Many of these opportunities may appear to a traditional point of view to represent a stretching of the classical concept of research – but so much the worse for the classical concept! In fact, some of us always felt slightly uneasy about academic researchers who fell victim to the "see my beautiful system" condition. When asked for underlying theory or theoretical implications, those researchers had nothing to say except that it was interesting that their system could do what it did, wasn't it? Arguably, researchers should not, as a group, merely build advanced systems but also generalize what they discovered while doing so.

One way of facing the tough demands on development of next-generation complex systems following the natural HHSI paradigm, is to work several generations ahead, aiming at concept demonstrators rather than complete working systems. This raises other difficulties, to be sure, but at least it frees the researcher from having to face most of the hard issues described in Section 24.3.1. Rather, the starting point becomes one of designing the future lives of people. User needs and social trends come into focus, replacing the question of what might be an example of the next system generation given the state of the art in products, prototypes and standards. Viewed from a high level of abstraction, user needs do not change at all. People's needs for information, transportation, shelter, entertainment etc. remain constant throughout history. What changes are the ways in which new technologies could satisfy those needs in the context of the enormous complexity of technological and societal developments. Futuristic use scenario research seems likely to strongly increase in importance in the coming years. And, once a future scenario of use has been identified, questions arise as to how people will behave, what they will prefer and why they will do that. i3 research, which is probably some of the most long-term research done in Europe at the moment, clearly illustrates this trend towards invention of the future based on future scenarios of use and investigation of the lives of ordinary users of all kinds, from little kids to the elderly, and from all cultures.

In futuristic use scenario-based research, the technology demonstrators to be developed are likely to be, in terms of person-years of technology development, relatively modest concept demonstrators which show how something could be done in the future through innovative technical solutions, without worrying about available platforms, existing or emerging standards etc.

However, the demonstrators might also be something else entirely, namely innovative, carefully designed product illustrations which are uniquely based on today's technology. In other words, many companies could build and market those things right away from off-the-shelf components. The point of this research is not to innovate in technology *per se* but to innovate in design and in the technology's role in people's lives and/or the intended user population. Is this "research"? I don't know. Yet innovative product designs are certainly an important form of innovation to be expected from futuristic use scenario-based research, especially from the kind which integrates technology, design and people as in i3.

24.3.3 Specialized Best Practice

The need for specialized software engineering best practice methodologies for SLDSs that was noted in Section 24.1, can be straightforwardly generalized to systems for natural HHSI. Work on best practice for SLDSs is ongoing at the moment [14,15]. For natural HHSI systems more generally, nothing exists beyond general software engineering best practice, ISO standards and the like. There are no specialized software engineering best practice methodologies at all. This means that substantial research efforts are needed.

24.3.4 Efficient Data Handling

The task orientation of much natural HHSI research implies the need for huge amounts of data. The task orientation of such systems is due to the fact that general natural interaction systems are not likely to be built in the foreseeable future (cf. Section 24.1). Task orientation implies that systems must be carefully crafted to fit human behavior in the task domain in order to work at all. This requires deep understanding of human behavior in the task domain. If one looks to speech recognizer and spoken language dialog systems (SLDSs) development projects, the amounts of data needed to make these technologies succeed have been staggering. And when research is now beginning to address speech and gesture combinations for task resolution, or speech and gesture and facial expression combinations for task resolution, data capture will necessarily continue to be a major activity. This data deals with how humans actually behave when communicating in those ways and there are presently no short-cuts available for dispensing with data from experimentation, simulation, user testing, and the field where the corresponding systems are to be developed.

Data capture, of course, is only a first step. Upon capture, the data needs to be marked up electronically, analyzed, used for development and, whenever possible, reused. In the speech recognition field, there are now standards for the data which are needed, i.e. for the amount, structure and quality of the data needed for the automatic training of speech recognizers for new languages. However, in the far more complex field of SLDSs, data standards do not yet exist. Moreover, for many increasingly important types of data, such as data on the speech (or dialog) acts which people execute when interactively performing a task with the system through spoken language dialog, the underlying theories and theoretically motivated concepts needed for identifying the appropriate phenomena of interest in the data, are not yet in place. This implies a need for theory which will be discussed in Section 24.3.6.

Finally, to handle data efficiently, software tools are needed to electronically mark up, query, visualize, import and export the data. In the field of markup (or data annotation) tools, global standards barely exist at the moment. This means that each research team or group of industrial developers marks up its own data in inefficient ways, often lacking appropriate tools, and using idiosyncratic formalisms for their purposes. This situation is only now being addressed in the case of spoken language dialog data, for instance in the MATE project on Multilingual Annotation Tools Engineering [16]. When it comes to natural HHSI applications more generally, such as those requiring speech and video data conceptualization, annotation and analysis, for instance of the communicative gestures accompanying speech, there is even more virgin territory to be explored and cultivated.

There are several rather obvious reasons why progress has been severely lacking in the general field of the handling of data on human communication behavior. One is that the need for development efficiency is relatively recent, the first not-quite-simple SLDSs having been developed only recently. Another is that industry is not necessarily strongly motivated to develop tools and standardization for reuse in a field in which data used to be proprietary. A third reason is that the field used to be considered one of rather esoteric research. Today, the needs for reusable data, efficient data handling tools and global standards have finally become clear. This implies a need for very substantial research if the natural HHSI paradigm is to be realized without undue difficulty. In view of the number of languages and cultures to be mastered, an analogy with the current high-profile genome projects, human and otherwise, comes to mind.

24.3.5 Design Support Tools for Usability

The field addressed in this section, i.e. that of design support tools and, in particular, design support tools for usability, still remains more of a dream than a tangible reality in what used to be called human–computer interaction (HCI) research. Current natural HHSI systems must be carefully crafted to fit human behavior in order to work at all. The capture, markup and analysis of data on human behavior tends to be very costly, for several reasons. Some of these were noted in Section 24.3.4, i.e. the lack of theory, concepts, standards and markup tools. Another reason is equally important. Truly realistic data on user behavior can only be produced from field trials with the implemented system. The Wizard of Oz simulation method [3] is useful for data capture during early design and prior to system development, but this method is far from sufficient to ensure the generation of fully realistic data. And if the field trials demonstrate serious system flaws it may be necessary to start all over again. In other words, it would seem highly desirable to have design support tools for usability which, during early design and before implementation has begun, could ensure that the system to be built will not turn out to be fatally flawed when tested in the field towards the end of the project. In the early 1990s, I participated in the Esprit long-term research project AMODEUS [17]. AMODEUS was probably the largest-scale basic research project there ever was in what used to be called HCI. To me, at least, the main outcome of AMODEUS was that design support tools for usability are (a) difficult to do (AMODEUS never developed a single such tool for actual use by developers), and (b) probably the best that HCI or, rather, HHSI research could do for system developers. It appears correct to say that few tools of this kind have been developed in the 1990s.

Stubbornly adhering to the main outcome of AMODEUS, I have continued with colleagues to explore opportunities for developing design support tools for usability. Two such tools are now about to appear after several years of work, both having been built in the DISC project on spoken language dialog systems best practice in development and evaluation [15].

One tool supports the development of cooperative spoken system dialog for SLDSs [18]. The basic idea is a simple one. Task-oriented spoken dialog is undertaken to complete a particular task with a minimum of hassle. To do that, the interlocutors (human(s) and the system) should conduct a shared-goal dialog, the shared goal being that of completing the task. Such dialog demands full dialog cooperativity from the interlocutors. The user is not the problem. For one thing, human users implicitly know how to be cooperative in dialog. For another, if they refuse to cooperate, they will not get their interactive task done and there is nothing that we, as system developers, can or should do about that. However, if the system's dialog is consistently cooperative, following a more or less complete set of principles of cooperativity, there is every chance that the dialog will run as smoothly as possible, avoiding the need for clarification and repair sub-dialogs which are still rather difficult to handle by machine. The cooperativity tool, then, supports the identification, during early design, of flaws in the design of the system's dialog contributions.

The second tool supports modality choice in the early design of complex systems which include speech as one of their modalities. As systems and interfaces depart from the GUI paradigm, developers are faced with a growing diversity of implementable ways of exchanging information between systems and their users. A simple example is that of using output speech and output data graphics together. However, much too little is known about the (always limited) functionality of available input and output modalities. Even in the apparently simple case of speech-only, the developer runs an important risk of using speech for input to, and/or output from, a system for which speech is not appropriate at all, or is not appropriate in the form in which it is planned to be used. Speech functionality has turned out to be a very complex problem. However, based on Modality Theory [19] and analysis of large sets of claims about speech functionality derived from the literature, it has turned out that a small set of basic properties of speech is sufficient to provide guidance for developers in the large majority of cases they are likely to face. The speech functionality tool provides this guidance during early design [20]. Obviously, the proper understanding of speech functionality is but part of the much larger problem of understanding all possible modalities for the exchange of information between humans and machines. This is a problem for future research.

Both of the above tools are meant to be used by system developers during early design, and might help avoid early design decisions that might later prove fatal to the usability of the implemented system. It may be worth mentioning some reasons why design support tools for usability have not been developed to any greater extent so far. One reason is that much HCI research still tends to take place too far from actual systems development. It is very hard, if not impossible, to develop useful tools for systems developers if one is not deeply familiar with systems development oneself. Research in the natural HHSI paradigm, it is proposed, should not commit the same mistake of divorcing the study of usability from actual systems development practice. A second reason is that design support tools for usability need theory, and HCI has not been particularly effective in developing theory. Research within the natural HHSI paradigm, it is proposed, should do better than that (see below). A third reason is that, even with a useful theory in hand, developing design support tools for usability tends to be quite time-consuming to do, primarily because of the iterative tools testing involved, but also because it demands the capability for thinking in terms of educational systems design. The latter is a particular skill which is not necessarily present in someone with a useful theory for backing up an early design support tool.

24.3.6 Useful Theory

The scarcity of applicable theory pertaining to the natural HHSI paradigm has been noted above. However, before addressing the topic of missing and greatly needed natural HHSI theory, it may be appropriate to inquire about the status of theory in the world of advanced IT/telecoms research more generally. I recently asked a project officer working under the European Commission's huge 5th Framework Programme's US$4 billion Action Line on Information Society Technologies if the term "theory" was mentioned anywhere as something that might be funded in research projects supported by the program. He answered that he didn't think so. Ten years ago, the corresponding 2nd Framework Programme actually did fund theoretical work as part of its long-term research branch. For instance, funding was provided for core computer science topics, such as complexity theory and petri nets, and for HCI research. Meanwhile, core computer science has become somewhat marginalized, and general HCI research has been dropped largely because it failed to deliver to a satisfactory extent. Obviously, however, facts such as these do not imply that highly relevant theory is not needed, or feasible, any more.

I would like the following discussion to serve as a plea for basic theory. It is possible, of course, that nobody disagrees with the argument below and that basic theory was just forgotten in FP5. Or it may be that everybody agrees but does not view basic theory development as part of the long-term research to be funded by the European Commission's research programs. There are reasons for endorsing the latter view, to be sure. It can be easy, and hence tempting, to "over-sell" theory by stressing its application potential, but forgetting the time it takes to develop the theory itself as well as the time it takes to render it applicable. Furthermore, theory is often done by single individuals, which makes its development less amenable to funding through collaborative research programs. Whatever the prevailing thinking, here follows a plea for practically useful theory.

The 1980s, with their visions of unifying research programs in artificial intelligence, cognitive science, HCI etc., are long gone. In the practical and entrepreneurial 1990s, general software engineering has tended to form the only center of our work, the rest of which has been about creating innovative technical solutions. As argued above, the scene is rapidly changing once again, towards the union of technology, design and people, towards creative contents, cultural diversity and so on. From the point of view of practically useful theory, the focus on providing next-step technical solutions ignores the progress that has been made towards increasingly sophisticated interactive technologies.

Let us, once again, take speech technology as an example. Task-oriented spoken language dialog systems (SLDSs) research is now reaching into hitherto rather obscure research areas traditionally belonging to the arts and humanities, such as speech act theory, co-reference resolution theory, cooperativity theory, politeness theory, the theory of cultural differences in the way information is being exchanged etc. To quote just one example, the huge eight-year DM160 million German national project in task-oriented spoken translation by machine, Verbmobil [6], could not have proceeded without making machines able to identify and process the speech acts involved in the task chosen for the project (appointment scheduling between humans). In response, the Verbmobil researchers had to create a speech acts taxonomy from scratch, and this taxonomy remains one of the few major efforts in applicable speech acts analysis worldwide [21]. The interesting question is: why could the Verbmobil researchers not just fetch the theory they needed from the big shelf in the arts and humanities field? The answer is that, so far, the arts and humanities have not at all been geared to providing technologically applicable theory. The Verbmobil researchers could fetch the generic concept of speech acts (or dialog acts) from their shelf, but that was all.

Let us add to the above line of argument a more general observation. In developing tomorrow's SLDSs, we are actually facing the task of "reconstructing", from the bottom up, the entire field of human spoken communication. As the state of the art in arts and humanities research cannot deliver, except sporadically, we have to start doing this ourselves, thereby creating what is potentially a tremendously productive interface to entirely new disciplines as viewed from the world of IT/telecoms research. The work on cooperativity theory mentioned in Section 24.3.5 is a case in point. We found that by analyzing real data from human interaction with a spoken language dialog system, it became possible to significantly augment an existing "theoretical island" in arts and humanities research, i.e. that of Grice's cooperativity theory [22,23]. The results of this work have now been incorporated into an early design support tool for SLDSs developers. The general point just illustrated is that research into non-technological theory is strictly and provably needed for technological progress. Another example comes from the development of annotation tools for the markup of spoken language dialog data. To mark up some corpus of data, one needs concepts of the phenomena to be marked up. These concepts, such as "subject" and "object" in syntactical annotation or the concepts of different types of speech act, come from the corresponding theory, which has the task of providing some form of closure and a rationale for why the conceptualized phenomena are those and only those to expect in a certain segment of natural spoken dialog. Theory is needed for corpus markup for exactly the same reason that enabling the machine to recognize those phenomena is needed.

Now, generalizing in earnest, so to speak, beyond current research issues, the advent of natural HHSI systems including the full combinatorics of speech, lip movements, gesture, facial expressions, bodily posture, intentions communication, emotions communication and inherent reference to all sorts of environmental objects is not only likely, but certain to produce an increased need for theory about human behavior. Note, incidentally, that this is not about psychology, about what goes on in people's minds, but about objectively observable entities and regularities in data from natural human–human-system interaction. It is strictly necessary to be able to conceptualize those entities and regularities in order for machines to identify and use them, and in order to be able to mark them up in the data analysis in order to train the machines to identify them.

What the above argument suggests is that the building of tomorrow's natural HHSI machines requires what amounts to a complete rebuilding of the theory of human–human communication from the bottom up, with the system thrown into the loop. Without it, we shall not be making the progress which we can very easily envision through simple intuition, as demonstrated by the intuitive convincingness of the natural HHSI vision.

Shifting the topic to the virtual and/or physical co-presence of humans and machines, the same picture emerges. Social theory has technologically relevant "islands of theory" concerning human co-presence in meetings and otherwise. We are now actually building virtual co-presence systems. To do that, we need solid knowledge about the needs and behaviors of humans in group encounters aiming at the resolution of particular tasks. Existing social theory is far from being able to deliver everything we need because it has been developed with different, less technologically focused, objectives in mind. However, to plausibly specify a virtual meeting support system we need all the theoretical knowledge we can get. If we cannot find it on the shelf in the social sciences, we must begin developing that knowledge ourselves. The needs of technology are likely to enforce a reconstruction, from the bottom up, of social theory. Otherwise, we will not be able to make sense of the data we collect on human–human-machine interaction and, maybe even more strikingly, we cannot make the systems which we painstakingly build usable by their intended users.

In a final example, Modality Theory, which was used as a foundation for building the speech functionality tool mentioned in Section 24.3.5, was not imported from the arts and humanities but was developed from scratch in the context of anticipating the needs for applicable theory in the emerging world of multimodal systems and interfaces [24].

24.4 Conclusion

The natural HHSI vision has been proposed in this chapter as a model which might be useful for thinking about future research on systems and interfaces. However, instead of discussing at length which those families of systems and interfaces might be, the chapter has deliberately de-emphasized next-generation IT/telecoms demonstrators and applications. Instead, a broad look was taken at future lines of research which appear to be needed independently of the particular nature of the natural HHSI systems which will be developed in the coming years. The result was a number of research directions, including the exploration of the future lives of people, futuristic concept demonstrators, specialized software engineering best practice methodologies, data handling schemes and tools, design support tools for usability and, last but not least, a renewed emphasis on theory development. Underlying these directions of research is something else, i.e. the need for systems development to forge strong links with hitherto remote areas, such as design, arts and humanities, social theory, and prospective users of all kinds and from all cultures. This is not just a matter of speech technologists talking to natural language processing researchers or to machine vision researchers. I don't think that the term "interdisciplinarity" which has been around in our fields for more than 15 years, and which has begun to carry the same antiquarian connotations as, for example, the term "modern", adequately captures those contemporary and future needs. What we are looking towards is the *post-disciplinary* world of tomorrow's research for the Information Society, in which researchers work along lines such as those described above, and on the basis of knowledge and experience which is far from that represented by any known classical discipline.

References

[1] R Fatehchand (1990) Machine recognition of spoken words, in *Advances in Computers*, Vol. 1 (ed. FL Alt), New York, Academic Press, pp. 193–229.

[2] *Elsnews* (1999) The Newsletter of the European Network in Language and Speech, 8, 1.
[3] NO Bernsen, H Dybkjær and L Dybkjær (1998) *Designing Interactive Speech Systems. From First Ideas to User Testing*, Berlin, Springer-Verlag.
[4] RW Bossemeyer and EC Schwab (1991) Automated alternate billing services at Ameritech: speech recognition and the human interface, *Speech Technology Magazine*, 5(3), 24–30.
[5] H Aust (1995) The Philips automatic train timetable information system, *Speech Communication*, 17, 249–262.
[6] W Wahlster (1993) Verbmobil – translation of face to face dialogs, in *Machine Translation Summary IV*, Kobe, Japan.
[7] http://www.i3net.org/.
[8] http://www.dfki.de/imedia/mlounge/.
[9] NO Bernsen, T Rist, JC Martin, C Hauck, D Boullier, X Briffault, L Dybkjær, C Henry, M Masoodian, F Néel, HJ Profitlich, E André, J Schweitzer and J Vapillon (1998) Magic Lounge: a thematic inhabited information space with "intelligent" communication services, in *La Lettre de l'Intelligence Artificielle, Proceedings of the International Conference on Complex Systems, Intelligent Systems, & Interfaces (NIMES'98)* (ed. JC Rault), Nimes, France, pp. 188–192.
[10] RA Cole, J Mariani, H Uszkoreit, G Varile, A Zaenen, A Zampolli and VW Zue (eds.) (1996) *Survey of the State of the Art in Human Language Technology*, Chapter 9, http://www.cse.ogi.edu/CSLU/HLTsurvey/.
[11] D Goddeau, E Brill, J Glass, C Pao, M Phillips, J Polifroni, S Seneff and VW Zue (1994) Galaxy: a human-language interface to on-line travel information, in *Proceedings of the ICSLP94*, Yokohama, pp. 707–710.
[12] M Guyomard, D Le Meur, S Poignonnec and J Siroux (1995) Experimental work on the dual usage of voice and touch screen for a cartographic application, in *Proceedings of the ESCA Workshop on Spoken Dialog Systems*, Vigsø, Denmark, pp. 153–156.
[13] http://www.cordis.lu/ist/fetuie.htm.
[14] L Dybkjær, NO Bernsen, R Carlson, L Chase, N Dahlbäck, K Failenschmid, U Heid, P Heisterkamp, A Jönsson, H Kamp, I Karlsson, J van Kuppevelt, L Lamel, P Paroubek and D Williams (1998) The DISC approach to spoken language systems development and evaluation, in *Proceedings of the First International Conference on Language Resources and Evaluation, Granada* (ed. A Rubio, N Gallardo, R Castro and A Tejada), Paris, The European Language Resources Association, pp. 185–189.
[15] http://www.elsnet.org/disc/.
[16] http://mate.mip.ou.dk/.
[17] http://www.mrc-cbu.cam.ac.uk/amodeus/.
[18] NO Bernsen, H Dybkjær and L Dybkjær (1997) What should your speech system say to its users, and how? Guidelines for the design of spoken language dialog systems, *IEEE Computer*, 30(12), 25–31.
[19] NO Bernsen (1997) Defining a taxonomy of output modalities from an HCI perspective, *Computer Standards and Interfaces*, Special Double Issue, 18(6–7), 537–553.
[20] NO Bernsen (1997) Towards a tool for predicting speech functionality, *Speech Communication*, 23, 181–210.
[21] S Jekat, A Klein, E Maier, I Maleck, M Mast and J Quantz (1995) Dialogue acts in VERBMOBIL. *Verbmobil Report* 65, Universität Hamburg, DFKI Saarbrücken, Universität Erlangen, TU Berlin.
[22] P Grice (1975) Logic and conversation, in *Syntax and Semantics, Vol. 3, Speech Acts* (eds. P Cole and JL Morgan), New York, Academic Press, pp. 41–58.
[23] NO Bernsen, H Dybkjær and L Dybkjær (1996) Cooperativity in human–machine and human–human spoken dialogue, *Discourse Processes*, 21(2), 213–236.
[24] NO Bernsen (1994) Foundations of multimodal representations: a taxonomy of representational modalities, *Interacting with Computers*, 6(4), 347–371.

About the Author

Niels Ole Bernsen is director of the Natural Interactive Systems Laboratory at Odense University in Denmark. He was trained as a philosopher, took his PhD equivalent in epistemology and his dr. phil. degree in the theory of cognitive situations. He worked in Brussels 1986–89, first as a researcher investigating future perspectives of cognitive science and later assisting in launching the Esprit Basic Research Actions in microelectronics, computer science, artificial intelligence and cognitive science. He went back to Denmark as a State Budget research professor in cognitive science working in HCI and connectionism. Gradually, this work has changed into systems engineering and he is now a professor of engineering at Odense University working in natural interactive systems, design support tools, modality theory and systems evaluation.

The Business/Academia/Research/Government Axis

25

Challenges and Frontiers of Computer Graphics: a Vision for an Applied Research Agenda

José L. Encarnação

Abstract

Future Research directions for IT-based, visual applications are presented as visions developed from evolutionary, technological trends and presented based on observations from different views (system, application, user). These visions, for

- human media technology
- augmented Reality
- digital storytelling
- integrated, interactive broadcasting
- multimedia workspaces
- interactive appliances

are then discussed in some detail, together giving a rich picture of what we can expect to be reality in the market-place by 2010.

25.1 Motivation

In industrialized countries, computers can be found practically everywhere. But we are only at the beginning of a fundamental change. The current limitations of IT devices will vanish. In foreign cities, ticket machines are often difficult to operate. A lot of precious time is wasted every day in offices – time (and thus, money) can be saved by automating tedious routine work. Millions of dollars are wasted every year for physical prototypes of cars – again, time and money can be saved by means of virtual prototypes in the future.

In a few years, augmented reality will show workers and civil engineers on the construction site of a new building where to place pipes, walls or cables. Much more user-friendly systems will allow designers and media people to create high-quality interactive multimedia content without having to bother about the underlying software. Intelligent agent software will help people to gather important information for their job, to select the best TV (or interactive Internet broadcast) channel to relax with in the evening, or to find the best insurance at the best price.

Where are computers present today? In the office and in other working environments, at home in household appliances like microwave ovens, clocks, TV sets, VCRs, cameras, CD players and telephones, but also in public places like info terminals, bus ticket machines, automated teller machines, point of sale devices etc. Slowly but surely they are changing the way people communicate, the way people work, the way people relax – the way people live.

Of course, this development is driven by the availability of increasingly smaller, cheaper, yet more powerful hardware. But other fields are gaining influence within this development, including human media technology, the Internet and interactive broadcasting, agent technologies, digital storytelling, 3D graphics and augmented reality.

One main motivation for this is that people are faced with increasingly large amounts of information and increasingly more complicated systems to handle this information. This has resulted in a vast number of complex specialized solutions which are difficult to handle by users and difficult to configure and maintain by developers. Encapsulation and the use of standardized components – including, but not limited to, human–machine interfaces – are the way to deal with these challenges.

In some respects, this development will lead to the intermingling of private and professional life for most people. Many people already use word processors, spreadsheets, cellular phones, email and the Web both at home and at the office. In the future, all of the aspects which are described in this chapter will contribute to this process. So in the following, some of these important trends and their future impact on people's lives will be discussed in more detail.

25.2 Overview

This chapter describes the research agenda of the INI-GraphicsNet, a network of institutions which consists of eight institutes in four countries. The core institutes are located in Darmstadt: the Fraunhofer Institute for Computer Graphics (IGD), the Computer Graphics Centre (ZGDV) and the Graphics Interactive Systems group of the technical university. Branches are located in Rostock (Germany), Coimbra (Portugal), Providence (Rhode Island, USA) and Singapore.

The main activities of the INI-GraphicsNet are the development of products (hardware and software) and the realization of concepts, models and solutions for computer graphics and their adaptation to specific application requirements. The work is supplemented by object-oriented basic research projects and the realization of single devices and computer graphics systems as pilot projects.

The R&D projects are directly related to current problems in industry, trade, traffic and service. For the implementation of these projects the institutes have developed excellent competencies in computer graphics.

All the institutes cooperate synergetically and thus permit technology development in basic and applied research as well as application development up to product development and commercialization.

Each department carries out projects (applied research, industry) based on existing core competencies and market opportunities. In the context of these projects, prototypes and innovative applications have already been developed. At present, a significant aspect is the development of Intellectual Property Rights (IPRs – patents, copyrights, trademarks etc). These form the basis for the foundation of small enterprises (spin-offs) (Figure 25.1).

The subsequent sections address the following questions:

- What can we expect by the year 2010?
- What is the future of computer graphics, interaction and visualization over a time frame of 10–15 years?
- How will users and developers interact with the related technologies?
- Which new applications and technological opportunities will IT, telecommunication and microelectronics offer in combination with computer graphics?

Exact predictions are hard to make and therefore visions of future developments are the right way to go.

Those visions assume that no revolutions will occur, since these are almost impossible to predict, therefore extrapolations called "futuristic evolutions" must serve

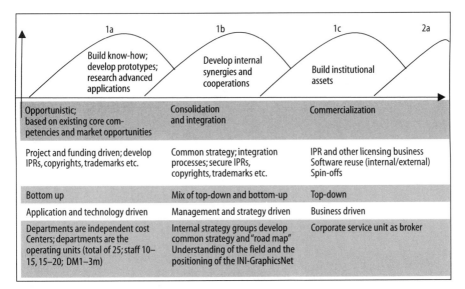

Figure 25.1 Strategic plan of the INI-GraphicsNet.

the purpose of this goal. In order to structure the broad field of our subject three different views considering new trends are discussed in detail:

- View 1: The System Level
- View 2: The Application Level
- View 3: The Anthropospheric Level

25.2.1 System-Level View

As already mentioned, the tidal wave of the Information Society with its demands and needs is emerging over the horizon. In recent decades technology has merely offered "boxes" for particular problems. Greater systematic challenges or, to be more specific, demands for an information infrastructure evolve out of this. At the system level, issues of new advanced basic tools and interfaces need to be discussed as well as the notion of bridging the gap between natural life and the technological benefits inside the system. The ubiquity of technology today is merely the presence of a lot of separated boxes – special little gadgets that do not blend well into the environment, that do not naturally sense, adapt and cooperate with it. Technology needs to get out of the box and has to be unified with the natural sphere. Two trends emerge from this.

First, bringing the system away from desktop and laptop computing and closer to the user and the physical phenomena offers new possibilities to also physically implement user-centered technology. "Human Media Technology" (Figure 25.2) as a new trend will become a strong alternative especially with the growing demand for mobile applications.

On the other hand, current "Virtual Environments" only allow access to completely computer-generated artificial worlds. In the future, they will be enhanced to use more real-world information like video data and by overlaying the computer-generated objects and scenes with the user's direct view of the physical world by means of see-through devices. This trend (called "Augmented Reality" – Figure 25.2) will help in making application environments more physical and real and will open new opportunities for online/real-time operation of new, advanced applications in industry, medicine, education/training etc.

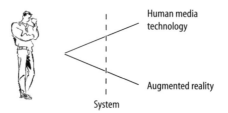

Figure 25.2 View 1 – the system trends.

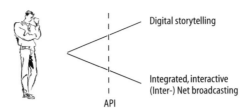

Figure 25.3 View 2 – the application and communication trends.

25.2.2 The Application-Level View

This view is concerned with the way developers and users will conduct what we nowadays call application programming and the ways in which communication interfaces will be used, and therefore how they have to be designed.

To come to terms with the designation "application" we need to take a look at the broad market: from scientific and purely numerical applications running on computers to the well-known office applications of the last decade and to multimedia presentation of information and context a clear trend can be seen. The communication of information as such becomes the application – be it locally or remote. On the generating part this means "composition"; on the consuming part it is "navigation" and "discovery".

In the near future not only will end-users demand easy-to-use tools for creating and using these kinds of application, but due to the growing complexity of professional applications developers too will have to leave the track of deterministic and algorithmic "programming" and move towards a more descriptive and implicit approach.

Based on multimedia, video and special interaction technologies a new kind of application programming will emerge. Will that turn up in a school of API (Figure 25.3)? New APIs for composing and orchestrating content will take advantage of experiences originating from movie production and will use multidisciplinary, multi-task-oriented programming interfaces. This development is called "Digital Storytelling" and will have a strong impact on the design and implementation of future multimedia applications.

No matter what the future Internet/intranet/extranet and related browsers will be, there will be an additional trend to integrate different types of broadcasting (for example Internet and DTV broadcasting of interactive, multimedia services). Integrated, Interactive (Inter-) Net Broadcasting is considered to be one of the megatrends for the future.

25.2.3 The Anthropospheric Level

The third important aspect of ongoing development covers the impact that the pictured changes in system and applications will have on the way humans live and

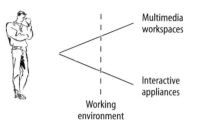

Figure 25.4 View 3 – the anthropospheric level.

work in their personal and professional environments. It will become obvious that these changes will affect the notion of "the environment" itself. The strong distinction between the professional and personal sphere will become more subtle or in some cases even melt down in total. This does not coercively mean that work and leisure time will become undistinguishable but there will be a strong demand and need for professional organizational and structural tools to satisfy today's requirements for living a comfortable yet efficient and well-organized life. In addition, the notion of "usability" will be extended into the large communities of the young and elderly populations as well as disabled and handicapped people.

To address this topic questions and solutions related to the "Multimedia Workspace" as well as "Interactive Appliances" will be discussed (Figure 25.4).

The world will experience significant improvements and an increase of productivity in the office. The office environment will be reorganized by means of intelligent assistant systems or agents in order to reduce time-consuming routine tasks and unnecessary interrupts. Progresses in the fields of delegation of tasks to intelligent assistant systems, human–machine communication, mobility and security will lead to new multimedia workspaces.

On the other hand, interactive appliances allow for the unified and simplified access to and control of items of everyday life. Having a single control with a customized user interface for interacting with appliances, not only at home (e.g. a washing machine) but in the streets (e.g. a ticket-vending machine), locally or remotely offers significant advantages in respect of efficiency of use, ease of operation and opportunities for assistance in multiple ways.

In the following, each of the areas bearing a main aspect of the views mentioned above will be described and discussed in detail. Specific developments and the opportunities for future research will be pointed out.

25.3 Human Media Technology

The information and technology flood is reaching a point where the next step of technological revolution is imperative. The increased speed of innovations in the information and communication technologies and systems makes it harder to integrate users with different skills, cultures and habits into a human-centered infrastructure environment. Technology is available, but acceptance and integration of the different users have not yet been considered. Easy and intuitive use of new technology is a key issue to reach this goal.

Users want to focus on the task, not on the technology for fulfilling the task. The technological developments in the 1990s led to a change in the pattern of education. Lifelong learning is the basic concept for being able to survive in the Information Society. But current solutions are based on existing technology developments. This is not sufficient. The learning and training concepts are focused on application functionality and facilities. This means that the user has to learn the different behavior and peculiarities of the application or technology. This is a time- and cost-intensive process which also can lead to demotivation instead of motivation of the user of new technologies. Discovering the inconvenience of handling applications and technologies for special user groups is already established by the development of usability labs. But this only leads to a change of the user interface, which itself is part of an application and its architecture [2].

For reaching the next level of innovation we have to change application and technology development [3]. Therefore human–machine interface development needs to get more detached from the application. Let us take a short retrospective look at program and technology development.

Initially, programs were based purely on algorithms. Only experts were able to handle the program. They needed to know the technology in detail. The computer improved the realization of a single task for one person or a small but highly specialized group. The next larger step has been in the development of graphical user interfaces for a program or application. Using the desktop and mouse metaphor led to an improvement for a larger user group, but there was still a platform and operating system dependence.

Users are still involved in data exchange, conversion and organization. They have to know the different functionality and features of the used applications and technologies. The user is still the bottleneck.

To take the next step of evolution the Web was born. Suddenly the Information Society exploded. No more platform and operating systems dependence – in theory. The installation procedure and access to information has become much easier. HTML and Java led to new frontiers.

Now everybody is running Web applications. But there is still a lack of data exchange, conversion and organization. The new Web generation will be based on XML applications. This guarantees a more complex structuring and separation of layout, interaction and content for improved media convergence and media exchange.

Here we start with a new technology development direction: human-centered [4]. An application will be separated into small kernels and agents fulfilling specific tasks and communicating and interacting with each other to achieve a common goal. Kernels will exist that are solely dedicated to learning users' preferences by interacting with them and studying their "mentality". Such a personal kernel will be developed "mentally" with the users' behavior and knowledge.

As an example, the kernel can be dedicated to modeling the activities of the user and thus be able to generate a workflow for these. Such a kernel controls and executes the applications according to the sequence of activities. Other kernels exist solely for to execute applications independently of an operating system to achieve higher transparency in the invocation of applications. Another one will be dedicated to the adaptive presentation of the information, according to the preferences of the user.

Such an architecture of kernels [5] provides a new way of developing applications and user interfaces based more on the communication of events than on the presentation of data which will be part of the communication.

In order to obtain the behavior and demands of the user, the adaptation process must be based not only on feedback reactions, but also on feedforward intensive design actions. The kernel assumes in advance certain criteria and parameters, using them for its adaptation, especially for multimodal interaction.

In this way, independence between the activities of users and the characteristics of the platform are achieved, obtaining higher transparency between the human workers and their interaction with the computer. It is no longer only the users themselves who are in a lifelong learning process – the kernels and agents are also within this lifelong learning process.

With such a concept we can bring humans outside the loop. They can use the technology based on their knowledge and attitude. They are no longer dependent on the architectural model of the application. Here we get economic evolution instead of ending in an innovative deadlock.

Another key technique in human media technology is the "focus and context" approach which can be used to visualize directory content and information spaces. The idea is to display as much content as possible as a context for the selected data which is in focus and visually emphasized. Examples are the hyperbolic tree [6], which is used for visualization and navigation, as well as the perspective wall [7], which is used to visualize directory content in chronological form.

So we need a new programming paradigm and a flexible infrastructure which takes the human–machine interface development to a more abstract level, away from the application and towards the user. This can be achieved by separating visualization and interaction from application and content, as well as by combining structured information which will be handled by small kernels via an application level on one side with human adaptable visualization and interaction techniques on the other side. Figure 25.5 illustrates this approach.

25.4 Augmented Reality: a New Generation of Human–Machine Interfaces?

Another aspect of the system view is that new visualization techniques lead to new interaction techniques. Today, 2D interaction is standardized with mouse, menus and windows, and can be found as state-of-the-art technology in every PC. However, the growing complexity of data sets and process interactions requires better visualization techniques. 3D visualization has proved its potential in many

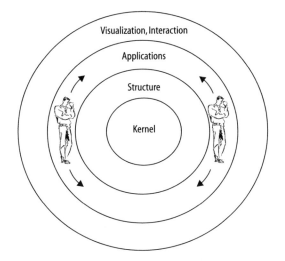

Figure 25.5 Kernel-based structure for human media technology.

application areas. Immersive 3D visualization is the high-end technology which is now established in a number of application areas, e.g. in the automotive industry. Very powerful 3D graphics hardware is available on the market and will be part of the standard configuration in every PC in the very near future. The question is: how will we interact with 3D environments and how will the new interaction paradigms look like? Augmented reality might be an answer to this question [9].

Augmented reality (AR) is a technology that integrates virtual objects into images of the real world. These images can be taken from the user's direct view on the

Figure 25.6 Augmented reality devices.

world and can be augmented with the use of a see-through head-mounted display (Figure 25.6) or handheld device. Augmented reality technology is still at an early stage, but its potential has been demonstrated for architectural construction [10,11], for manufacturing scenarios like the computer-guided repair of copier machines, for the installation of aluminum struts in diamond-shaped space frames, and for electric wire bundle assembly before their installation in airplanes [8].

The driving demands for AR solutions can be foreseen in the area of "Digital Prototyping" or "Digital Mock-Up (DMU)". In order to remain competitive in a worldwide market, the reduction of product development time (*time-to-market*) and development cost plays a very important role, especially in the manufacturing industry. A crucial step towards that direction is to avoid mock-ups during the whole development process by applying new and innovative digital prototyping technology. As a result, new product releases will be faster to market with more variations. Therefore service or maintenance will become a difficult issue. In order to close the loop of digital prototyping, AR seems to provide the right solution. In Figure 25.7a, the first results of maintenance with AR support are shown. The user is guided step by step through the assembly task, while the virtual information (objects and movements) is directly integrated from the VR assembly system [10].

Another important AR application area can be foreseen in the area of mixed mock-up solutions (Figure 25.7b). One major problem of DMU technology is the lack of force feedback or haptic devices. In some applications, this problem can be overcome by using a "coarse" physical prototype, which is augmented by the constructed data set of the actual product. Very good examples are cockpit layout, ergonomic analysis, verification of simulation results (e.g. crash tests) or optimization of assembly tasks.

To realize the vision of AR presented here, a number of technical challenges have to be overcome. First and foremost the problem of *tracking* the motion of the user has to be solved. This problem has been intensively studied in virtual reality, but AR adds higher complexity. In general, the see-through nature of AR output devices amplifies the problem of lag. Inconsistencies between virtual and real objects become immediately apparent and thus AR demands much faster updates. For

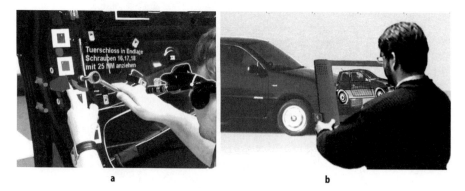

a   b

Figure 25.7 AR with see-through head-mounted display and handheld device for **a** maintenance and **b** mixed mock-up applications.

industrial applications the electromagnetic trackers often found in VR systems are inadequate, as they are sensitive to metal, which is ubiquitous in these environments. Optical and hybrid methods have been tried and are considered the best alternative right now, but a solution that is small enough to be worn on an HMD, precise enough for pixel-accurate augmentation and robust enough for an industrial environment is still to be found.

Other problems on the hardware side concerning *output devices* have to be faced. Only a small number of see-through devices, either HMDs or transparent flat-screen displays, are available. However, these displays often absorb a large part of the light and can only be used in bright environments. The usually small field of view that is bearable for VR is not useful for AR, as the non-augmented, peripheral area is still visible and distracts from the small augmented part.

Another open problem is the *interaction* with AR applications. One idea of AR is to make the computer disappear and let the users work in their natural environment. This also implies making the interaction devices disappear by developing interaction techniques that work by passively detecting the user's actions. For some applications, the user's hands are occupied by other tasks. Thus other interaction techniques need to be investigated. The first results using gesture and speech recognition have been obtained, but the area is wide open for new approaches. Computer vision will play an important role in achieving better human-centered interaction.

Last, but not least, the whole area of *wearable computers* and *mobile computing* needs further development. If computer-generated information and computer-rendered objects are to be integrated into the professional and private everyday life, then computers and input–output devices need to be at least portable, and in the best case not noticeable at all.

So the area of augmented reality offers great potential, but also presents challenges in many fields, mainly hardware development, computer graphics and computer vision.

25.5 Digital Storytelling

As already mentioned, the first interactive computer applications were software tools to be used only by specialists. Later, with the establishment of graphical user interfaces, and finally with the introduction of the Web, information systems have become more and more the majority of all computer applications. By including multimedia, video and VR in information systems, people can build upon the fundamentals for presenting content in an easy to comprehend and compelling way, in just the same way that they use television and film technology.

As a consequence, people tend to interact with a computer in a way that they would interact with other media. During this development media presentations have evolved from static and linear to dynamic and non-linear. In parallel, people's attitude towards media has changed, for example in the ways that people want to use media and the possibilities that they expect from them.

It took only a few years for new industries of multimedia developers to take over the field to make their business in developing content for interactive multimedia such as CD-ROMs and Web sites. In addition to software engineers, new job descriptions have been developed, such as "Multimedia Author" and "Screen Designer", and a network of service providers has grown up. But, at the end of the millennium, there are still several limitations to overcome. Currently, multimedia applications are not used by everybody, compared with other media, such as television or film, but by a rather small group of computer-literates. The question arises of whether today's multimedia systems are not useful enough, or not usable enough. Does the user's navigational attempt to access various multimedia fragments not provide the same impact and involvement as a linear video presentation can do?

Furthermore, today's multimedia applications often do not make use of a variety of technical possibilities, sticking with the known techniques of the WIMP interface (windows, icons, menus and pointers) with its point-and-click interaction. Current trends in human-centered interfaces including human-oriented communication channels such as speech and gesture, or the possibilities of immersion in high-end computer graphics, are currently not yet addressed by commercial applications in general.

"Digital Storytelling" (Figure 25.8), as a new field of research and application development will solve the mentioned problems and will consider human-centered interaction techniques.

The main goal is to achieve an integrated multimedia experience for the user by orchestration of all multimedia and multimodal possibilities rather than the well-known fragmented view of single media-object selection.

Digital storytelling will also integrate virtual reality (VR) technology. VR has been using metaphors since the beginning of its existence to resemble aspects of the real world inside the computer. Virtuality is used for tools as well as for information

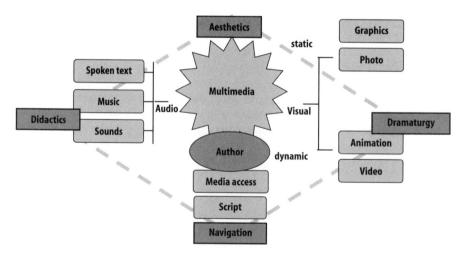

Figure 25.8 Digital storytelling is the programmed integration of multimedia building blocks to a wider experience, including didactics, esthetics and dramaturgy rather than only simple navigation possibilities.

Figure 25.9 The Virtual Oceanarium is a compelling VR edutainment application that was shown at the Expo'98 exhibit at Lisbon, Portugal. The show not only provides a photorealistic stereo experience of artificial life. In addition, it allows users to gain access to further information on request, such as the presentation of special behavior of the ocean's inhabitants. The VR application was realized by an interdisciplinary team of designer and computer scientists.

systems (see Figure 25.9). An information system of the future that will be used by everybody as a non-computer-specialist can have various shapes and can be realized in various situations: from totally immersive environments, e.g. a cave installation in a museum, up to ubiquitous and mobile appliances or even wearable computers (Figure 25.6).

Obviously the interaction technique of point-and-click has to be abandoned with those applications, and new techniques have to be developed. Depending on the type of application and metaphorical use, interaction paradigms can therefore resemble various actions from the real world:

- *navigating* through a rather static landscape of data
- *controlling* handles of objects and buttons of tools
- *pointing* at a menu of multiple choice
- *communicating* with an assistant that helps, informs and answers questions

The new metaphor for interaction with an information system is therefore to see a multimedia application as an interaction partner that is not only capable of *talking* to the user by displaying multimedia information, but which also *listens* to the user in multimodal ways and "thinks" first before generating an answer [12]. In the

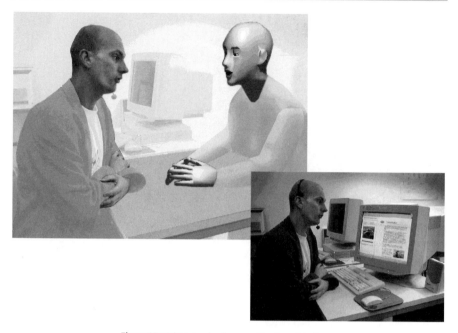

Figure 25.10 An example of conversational user interfaces.

future, rather than simply navigating through multimedia fragments, the user will be able to have a conversation with an intelligent application, and will not necessarily be aware of an interface any more. This communication can be supported by a visualized life-like character, e.g. an avatar as an anthropomorphic user interface agent (Figure 25.10).

Human-centered technology is the basis for human-oriented communication with the system. As in established media, such as film and television, this communication will not be designed by scientists or technicians. In the future, "communication designers" and "storytellers" will have to shape the field of interactive multimedia, since they are the professionals at communicating in the right way, defining the proper level of courtesy, and feeling responsible for the communication results achieved.

In the future, interaction designers will get a feeling for the new channels that are to be addressed with interactive applications, such as the appropriate amount of interaction and guidance that the human–media communication needs; this is analogous to aspects of timing, which had to be developed as a new channel when film was a new phenomenon. Also by analogy with current film production methods, interdisciplinary teams consisting of creative and technical people will build software and multimedia applications. To accomplish this, digital storytelling techniques will have to be developed. These will result in new high-level APIs that give non-programmers the ability to "write" and prototype interactive multimedia applications while using all of their creativity [13].

25.6 Internet Interactive Broadcasting

A further area of the application level focuses on the convergence of classical broadcast services, e.g. DVB or DAB and enhanced interactive network services, e.g. the Internet. This endeavor will be called "Internet Interactive Broadcasting (IIB)". Traditionally, the usage of today's media is mostly separated between private and business, broadcast and personalized, entertainment and serious information. In the private home area, TV sets have been used for consuming broadcast video; while in the office the computer offers personalized information, mostly text, graphics or images. This separation of all areas originates in the available technology. The reasons for these technological limitations can be seen on the one hand in the separation of the media channels, e.g. media, telecommunication or data with, on the other hand, fixed connections to different end-user appliances, e.g. TV set, telephone or computer terminal. Therefore, at present broadcast and cable networks for video are mostly applied to consume video information to be presented on a TV set.

However, progress in technology development opens the way to overcome and remove those limitations. Nowadays, strong convergence between all these different areas – the usage of media, networks and end devices etc. – can be clearly observed. These facts will influence and therefore change our future and the way we live, communicate and work.

A major part of this development will be *Internet Interactive Broadcasting* (Figure 25.11). All three areas are known from today's technology and will merge to allow wider use of media and delivery and presentation methods in the future. This also leads to an opportunity for enabling new business models and sophisticated value chains for broadcast and online services.

In the future, new kinds of devices will be used which will offer a broader range of interactivity and usability. The home, the train, the car, the office and we ourselves

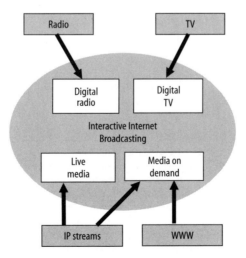

Figure 25.11 Internet Interactive Broadcasting.

will be equipped with or wear these devices, which can be used for different kinds of services in different contexts.

For example, at home in the morning people will use appliances which can present them their personalized newspaper, augmented with actual video clips. This information can be transmitted to the corresponding appliances during the night by using digital broadcasting technologies. Based on Internet and push technology it offers the ability on the one hand to be personalized and on the other hand to be interactive. People can specify and change the topics of interest, they can request more detailed information and can use the information offered for other tasks. On moving to the office other kinds of mobile appliances will help to prepare tasks for the job or give the information needed to get to the office. Mobile cellular networks will guarantee this connectivity. Again, broadcasting as well as the Internet will be used to give access to interactive media.

In the office, the appliances support the preparation of all business duties in different contexts. Mark Weiser [14] has presented prototypes of possible devices which can lead to ubiquitous computing in office environments. This allows increasing mobility and therefore there is no need to have fixed office rooms or to meet at dedicated places. By combining the different technologies no specific location will be needed to continue to have access to all the information, presented using all the possible but appropriate media. Broadcast, Internet and interactivity will play a major role for the realization of this vision, so video conferences and business TV will have interactive features. They will not just provide the delivery of the media audio and video, but there will also be interaction capabilities with *objects* inside these media. It will be possible to mark an object inside a video stream, e.g. using a gesture, and to get additional information provided by an online service provider. A prototypical implementation of an interactive video presentation component (MOVieGoer) is currently available and was presented in [15]. This component provides a linkage of the two media hypertext and video object, i.e. a user might select objects within a video stream to get further information (Figure 25.12).

Back to the example: in the area of the private home, the appliances used at leisure time will have the ability to combine different kind of services. These devices will be connected to the Internet to have access to TV channels. Today URLs are used to address documents, but in the future we will also apply them to address or select all media channels as well as all involved devices. Combining animation with broadcast and Internet will allow us to realize visions such as [16] have described:

Sports – live 3D stadium with instrumented players: Imagine that all of the ballplayers in a sports stadium wear a small device which senses location and transmits this information over a wireless network. Similar sensors are embedded in gloves, balls, bats and even shoes. A computer server in the stadium feeds telemetry inputs into a physical-based artificial model which extrapolates individual body and limb motions. The server also maintains a scene database for the stadium complete with textured images of the edifice, current weather and representative pictures of fans in the stands. Meanwhile, Internet users have browsers which can navigate and view the stadium from any perspective. Users can also tune to multicast channels providing updated player positions and postures along with live video and audio. Statistics, background information and Web home pages are available for each player. Online fan clubs and

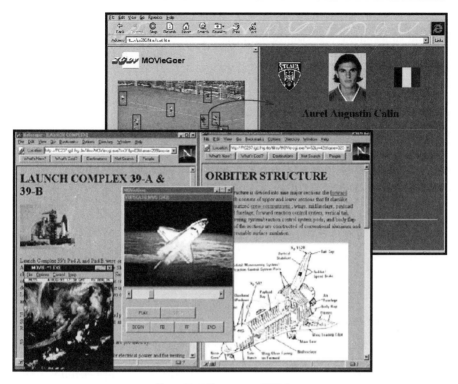

Figure 25.12 The prototype MOVieGoer.

electronic mail lists let fans trade opinions and even send messages to the players. Thus any number of remote fans might supplement traditional television coverage with a live interactive computer-generated view.

Internet Interactive Broadcasting will be a technological evolution in the future. The technology available in the present and in the future will allow the realization of the vision of *Internet Interactive Broadcasting*. However, this vision is not driven by technology, because technology is still not the limiting factor as it was with the development of different services in the past, e.g. television and telephony. But the development is driven by the requirements of the user who requests for interactivity together with appliances as well as user interfaces that provide and support this interactivity. As Mark Weiser wrote, "therefore we are trying to conceive a new way of thinking about computers in the world, one that takes into account the natural human environment and allows the computers themselves to vanish into the background".

25.7 The Multimedia Workspace of the Future

Turning from the system level across to the application level we have already illuminated the broad changes in technology and their impact of the particular interaction with and use of the specific systems. As a consequence the changes at the anthropospheric level will be immense. This level includes both the professional and private environments. In this chapter, two extremes of the anthropospheric level will be discussed. The technical and therefore structural changes in the working environment - the office of the future - at one extreme, and, at the opposite extreme, the opportunities that interactive appliances will offer for private life will be discussed, although the effects will not be limited to this.

Taking a look at the professional environment leads to new evolutionary visions for spontaneous and effective means of responding to the shortening periods for preparation and decision-making in modern markets. So far, the computer has mostly been used to emulate electronically the ancient tools, structures and cycles of offices as we know them from their beginning. But the fact that one can edit documents electronically with "copy and paste" on larger and faster machines and print them or send them electronically so far has not really made use of the great potential we foresee in the future. The main problems we are facing are "attention and interaction". Up to now the computer has needed the user's attention to keep on working. As the name "interactive" systems suggests, the users has to operate each single step of a composite operation. Writing and sending messages or information retrieval are tasks for which the user has to sit in front of the computer to interact and to control the application online.

One significant vision is to realize significant improvements related to this systematic problem and increase productivity in modern office environments, including real offices as much as mobile work-entities. The aim is to reorganize the office environment by introducing the following features:

- Time-consuming routine tasks are delegated to intelligent assistant systems called agents. The time gained by this delegation can then be spent on performing more demanding office tasks.
- System and application interrupts and events (like incoming mail or error messages) must be weighted, prioritized in more detail and presented to the user in a scalable manner to minimize or even prevent the user's distraction from the primary tasks.
- Parallel and concurrent work processes are organized and controlled efficiently by keeping the user optimally informed about their actual status.

These new systems should enable the user to formulate tasks or jobs to be delegated to the agent in a problem- and task-oriented manner [19]. Working with such an office system will be based on natural methods of interaction and communication. This can be achieved by improving the multimedia communication channels, their interchangeability and the automatic selection of a communication assistant so that users do not have to submit themselves to the paradigms of computer systems. The computer itself should be considered an assistant of the user and not a device or tool. The office system of the future (Figure 25.13) must adapt to the human working with it. Human-centered design will play a key role in the office environment of the future.

In order to develop and realize such an office system, five key aspects must be considered:

Figure 25.13 Office desk of the future?

- Delegation of tasks to intelligent assistant systems
- Device- and media-independent communication
- Natural human–machine communication
- Mobility of services
- Security

Besides the consideration of technologies common to all four areas, such as information visualization, information selection and ubiquitous computing, each of these key aspects involves the evaluation and development of these new technologies.

25.7.1 Delegation

To tempt users to make use of agents, they must be able to easily configure and instruct them. Single instructions and conditions should not be given, but instead a goal-oriented formulation must be found from which the agent implicitly derives the different strategies and steps he needs to accomplish in order to achieve the goal. To ensure the ability to perform a delegated task the user must not be left alone with trial and error. In software engineering's usual scheme this only works for very local concepts. But agents operate globally with a lot of responsibility, with which the user should not have to experiment. Adaptive and certified behaviors will become a major challenge for modern software quality assurance. Since the strategies of agent technology build upon collaboration and cooperation, the strategies for negotiation and information exchange need to be developed and customized for the specific application areas. The main technologies to be addressed for *delegation* are:

- Intelligent assistant systems
- Visual programming of tasks to be delegated to an agent
- Certification of benchmarked agent behaviors and performance
- Adaptive behaviors of agents (e.g. politeness)
- Negotiation strategies

25.7.2 Human–Machine Communication

The complex nature of delegation, reporting, monitoring and interception demand a broader bandwidth for the human–machine communication [18]. Development will go far beyond the desktop and windows and their mechanisms of direct response. The interaction needs to benefit from the well-established natural means of human communication which also include facial and body gestures and postures. The limitation of the assistant to the virtual components needs to be lifted by visually and conceptually merging the virtual and real components using the methods of virtual and augmented reality. For *human–machine communication,* the following technologies must be considered:

- Anthropomorphic user interface agents (Figure 25.14)
- Conversational user interfaces
- Non-verbal communication
- Situation- and context-dependent user interfaces
- Remote visualization for status and process information of highly distributed systems
- Avoidable break of media and change of paradigms
- Augmented reality
- Virtual reality

Figure 25.14 Anthropomorphic avatars.

25.7.3 Mobility

The location of work is changing: people work in fast-changing environments, dynamic virtual companies and off-site workplaces. As a consequence, in the last five years turmoil has been seen in the availability of information resources. The Internet, and especially the World Wide Web, have given us a glimpse at where and how end users and developers will store and access information in the near future. While actual developments concentrate on building an infrastructure of resident but loosely linked servers and contents, which are used by mobile clients, modern agent technology supports mobility of both the information sources and the information consumers. Information exchange will no longer be limited to static services, but providers can supply services at several locations (Figure 25.15 offers an example). The benefit will be enhanced availability of information and services independent of the momentary quality of network services between two fixed points.

Whether the user is online or offline will not matter, since systems will be able to handle requests and delegation either locally or remotely by making optimized use of the currently available resources. After an agent has been instructed it can "sit and wait" on a mobile device until it gets connected to the Net; it can then roam the Net independently of the home-base's location and execute the tasks. After finishing the tasks the agent will be waiting on a remote location for the user and the mobile device to reconnect to the Net and return. It is important that on every device the user is communicating with "his" (or her) well-known system. It is perceived by the user as a perceptual whole, making optimal use of the user's communication channels. This kind of *mobility* will consequently benefit from:

Figure 25.15 Calendar management agent.

- Support for location independence of users
- Integration of mobile devices
- Support of user localization
- Transparent usage of different communication channels

25.7.4 Security

When talking about mobility and interconnection of devices and applications the issue of security must be considered. With mobile agents technology it is not only the "imported" or downloaded application that can corrupt the user's host by violating or circumventing security boundaries and spying on or corrupting the data stored on the host. Beyond this, the agents themselves are exposed to unknown environments and are vulnerable to different security attacks. Two possibilities are hostile "partner" agents or even hostile hosts. The interdependencies of security mechanisms are hard to solve, but solutions are on their way. The important technologies for *security* we foresee being crucial for the success of the exposed visions are:

- Intrusion detection
- Media specific encryption
- Security of mobile agents
- Authentication and authorization
- Non-repudiation
- Confidentiality
- Integrity

An agent-supported group scheduling tool briefly exemplifies the problem. Private or otherwise confidential information is carried over an unknown network and exchanged with unknown partners based on an unknown independent host. Without security this kind of agent technology is more of a risk than a benefit.

Based on the technologies described, the multimedia workspaces of the future will lead to better office environments with improved productivity, since users can concentrate on their creative process of generating information and communicating it efficiently.

25.8 Interactive Appliances – an Intelligent Assistance System

Another facet of the anthropospheric level is the so-called "Interactive Appliance". Due to the growing complexity of appliances in everyday, life the notions of "interactivity" and "interaction design", which has its own forum at conferences like the ACM's CHI, need to be extended to systems that are not "computers" at first sight. VCRs, microwaves, dishwashers or ticket-vending machines are boldly pushed forward into the realm of unusable complexity through functionality.

People working professionally with computers or other complex systems are used to the "non-human" type of interaction, but easy human–machine interaction should be for everyone. Considering three areas that everyone deals with every day:

- home entertainment, communications and appliances
- cars
- point of interest and point of sales terminal systems in public and private places

By "easy" we denote the minimization of the cognitive and physical load that use of the appliance places on the user. The following specific goals are identified:

- assistance for human centered, anthropomorphic, individualized interaction with appliances
- assistance for ubiquitous access to telecommunications and IT services, considering user preferences
- added value in ease of operation through network-connected appliances

To avoid the most common mistake, i.e. doing only what technology allows, the first focus lies on the question of what kind of support and assistance certain user groups need (e.g. ordinary people, experts, children, elderly people, handicapped people). This question must be solved by a generalized procedure model for assistance systems. The model itself must finally be implemented as a guidance tool by a group of industrial psychologists, human engineers and software engineers. This group must also provide the evaluation methods against which the results of the project are measured.

The second point of interest is technology itself. In the field of computer graphics in particular, plenty of basic technologies for interaction, networking and utilization of services are available which must be tailored to fit the needs identified in the first focus area.

As already mentioned, anthropomorphic interaction is what we should aim at. Humans usually use all their senses to communicate with their environment. Their sensors and activators are not fitted to deal with keyboards and mouse devices. Multimodal interfaces lead the way with the following specific features:

- speech input (command phrase and natural dialog) and output
- video-based interaction (e.g. gesture and position recognition)
- "magic wand" for menu navigation
- avatars as a graphical output metaphor,
- haptic feedback for buttons and knobs (e.g. in a car environment)
- tactile "graphics" output device for blind people

These technologies are implemented as a modular system from which different user interfaces depending on the requirements of certain appliances can be build.

With mobile assistants, similar to a mixture of PDA and cellular phone, the user will then be able to operate virtually any compatible machine (see Figure 25.16) [20].

As a fundamental change the envisioned system for the first time separates the functionality and the user interface for appliances. Therefore customization of the user

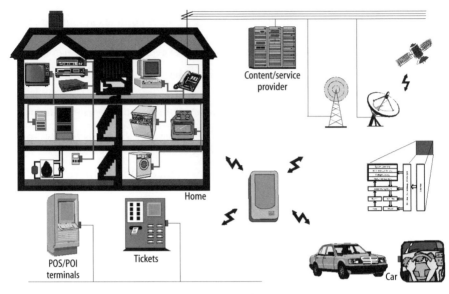

Figure 25.16 Interactive appliance scenario.

interface and the human–machine communication will be highly user-centric and context-sensitive. This will not only include language preferences, but also the favorite and most often used items of functionality and preferred methods of interaction [21].

The built-in agent software of the mobile device, for example will negotiate with the ticket machine in Greek, if necessary, through services on the Net and pay with electronic money. Monitoring the status of the cake in the oven will be possible on a TV screen while concurrently watching a program. All the clocks will adjust themselves, for example, to change from winter to summer time. Car appliances will be voice-controlled. In the event of a critical traffic situation, the assistant will not allow unnecessary interaction (e.g. surfing for a new route) all will even interrupt ongoing diversions to help the user to stay on the road.

25.9 Conclusions

We took three different views to develop some visions based on existing technological trends. These views (system, application and user) resulted in the discussion of several technologies, tools, APIs, interfaces and working environments which can be expected to be in place and have a strong impact on IT-based applications in our Information Society.

The result is a software-based human-centered system architecture, shown in Figure 25.17. Future applications on top of this architecture will be "real" tools, which means that they will really solve problems instead of generating new ones. The system will operate online and in real time to enhance efficiency and produc tivity at work and at home.

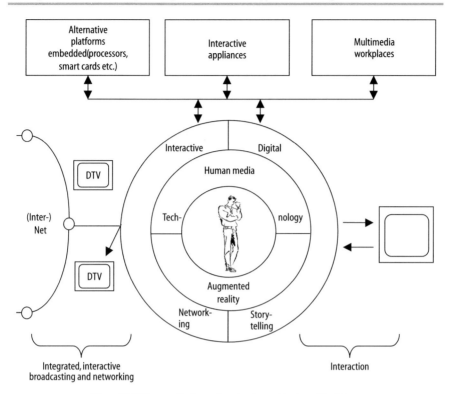

Figure 25.17 The overall software-based system architecture of the future.

25.10 Research Agenda of the INI-GraphicsNet

The technology trends described here form the basis of the research agenda and the current and future activities of the INI GraphicsNet (see Figure 25.18).

To date, prototype developments for systems and applications have already been implemented in all areas. The existing core competencies are used and further developed. New competencies will be acquired by carrying out projects within new research areas. The basis for this is formed by the current strategic projects and new technology laboratories.

The results of these developments are commercialized by spin-off enterprises. As already mentioned, the implementation of IPRs (patents, copyrights, trademarks etc.) to protect the acquired core competencies and their resulting products plays an important role. Furthermore it is important to build an intelligent platform for software reuse among all institutions.

The combination of applied research and development and commercialization by the spin-off enterprises within the INI-GraphicsNet is so far unique in the international R&D landscape.

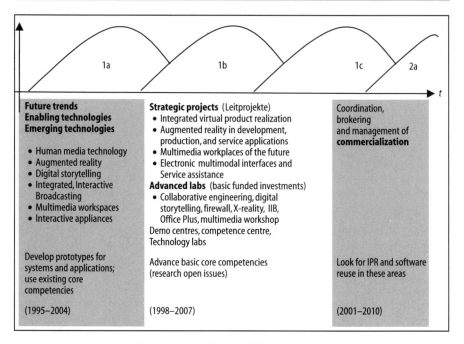

Figure 25.18 Research agenda of the INI-GraphicsNet.

Acknowledgments

This chapter and the visions presented are based on the research agenda 2010 of the INI-GraphicsNet (Fraunhofer IGD, CRCG and CAMTech; Computer Graphics Center and CCG; in Darmstadt and Rostock, Germany, in Coimbra, Portugal, in Providence, RI, USA and in Singapore; for further information see http:// www.igd.fhg.de/). Contributions to the text were prepared by H.-J. Ackermann, N. Gerfelder, D. Krömker, F. Loseries, S. Müller and U. Spierling. The editing was done by C. Dohrmann, H. Haase, H. Jung, B. Merten and R. Ziegler. The author very much appreciates this support and thanks for all the efforts.

References

[1] D Tennenhouse (1998) *DARPA Workshop: New Agency Directions*, July.
[2] B Shneiderman (1998) *Designing the User Interface*, 3rd edn, Reading, MA, Addison-Wesley Longman.
[3] T Salker (1996) New paradigms for using computers, *Communications of the ACM*, 39(8), 60–69.
[4] JL Encarnação, F Loseries and Chr Sifaqui (1998) Human media technology – the human-centered, sustainable technology development, in *Proceedings of Computer Graphics International*.
[5] DR Cheriton and KJ Duda (1994) A caching model of operating system kernel functionality, in *Proceedings of the First Symposium on Operating System Design and Implementation, USENIX*, November.
[6] http://www.inxight.com/.

[7]   JD Mackinlay, GG Robertson and SK Card (1991) The perspective wall: detail and context smoothly integrated, in *Proceedings of CHI'91*, pp. 173–179.

[8]   D Curtis, D Mizell, P Gruenbaum and A Janin (1998) Several devils in the details: making an AR app work in the airplane factory, in *First IEEE International Workshop on Augmented Reality*, San Francisco, CA, November.

[9]   S Feiner, B MacIntyre and D Seligmann (1993) Knowledge-based augmented reality, in *Communications of the ACM*, Special Issue on Augmented Reality, 39(7), 53–62.

[10] D Reiners, D Stricker, G Klinker and S Müller (1998) Augmented reality for construction tasks: doorlock assembly, in *First IEEE International Workshop on Augmented Reality*, San Francisco, CA, November.

[11] A Webster, S Feiner, B MacIntyre, W Massie and T Krueger (1996) Augmented reality in architectural construction, inspection and renovation, in *Proc. ASCE Third Congress on Computing in Civil Engineering*, Anaheim, CA, 17–19 June, pp. 913–919.

[12] K Perlin and A Goldberg (1996) Improv: a system for scripting interactive actors in virtual worlds, *Computer Graphics*, 29(3).

[13] R Pausch, J Snoddy, R Taylor, S Watson and E Haseltine (1996) Disney's Aladdin: first steps toward storytelling in virtual reality, in *Proceedings of ACM SIGGRAPH 96*, August.

[14] M Weiser (1991) The computer for the 21st century, *Scientific American*, 265(3), 94–104.

[15] N Gerfelder and L Neumann (1998) Internet Interactive Broadcasting – convergence of the World Wide Web and digital TV, in *European SMPTE Conference '98*, Cologne, September.

[16] DP Brutzman, MR Macedonia and MJ Zyda (1995) Internetwork infrastructure requirements for virtual environments, in *Proceedings of the Virtual Reality Modeling Language (VRML) Symposium*, San Diego Supercomputing Center (SDSC), San Diego, CA, December.

[17] T Mandel (1997) *The Elements of User Interface Design*, New York, John Wiley & Sons.

[18] C Nass, J Steuer and E Tauber (1994) Computers are social actors, in *Proceedings of ACM CHI '94*, Boston, MA.

[19] P Maes (1994) Agents that reduce work and information overload, in *Communications of the ACM*, 37(7), 31–40.

[20] SH Wildstrom (1998) The last days of the home PC?, *Business Week*, 9 November.

[21] M Hall and R Barker (1998) The death of the desktop, in *Performance Computing*, August.

[22] K Kelly and S Reiss (1998) One huge computer, *Wired*, August.

26

Society and Human Action: Technology Revisited

Véronique Havelange

Abstract

The question of mind, long the preserve of philosophy, was claimed as a legitimate object of study by the human and social sciences in the 18th century. Two contrasting approaches have structured this field: the *naturalist explanation of the mental* and the *hermeneutical understanding of meaning*. This debate has been renewed in the second part of the 20th century by the advent of cognitive science, which openly declares as its aim the naturalization of the mind.

The aim of this chapter is to present the current state of the art, emphasizing not only the contrasting premises and implications, but also the hidden affinities which are now, little by little, leading to a reconciliation of these two paradigms. Cognitive science, initially physicalist or functionalist, is progressively integrating a hermeneutic dimension; conversely, an intense reflection on the question of action is leading the hermeneutic human and social sciences to elaborate a renewed concept of cognition.

Finally, the concepts of a double hermeneutics and the relational nature of the social will call for completion by a *material* hermeneutics, taking into account the fact that human action in society is both enabled and constrained by technical artifacts.

26.1 The Question of a Science of Mind

26.1.1 The Paradigms of Explanation and Understanding

What does it mean to "know"? What is meant by "mind"?

To a first approximation, to know is to go out of oneself, to be born to oneself (*conoscere* : "to be born with"). These have been basic questions for philosophy ever since Socrates and Plato, and for the human/social sciences which have endeavored, since the 18th century, to build up a scientific approach to the act of knowing and the mind. However, a preliminary remark is necessary to emphasize the divergent conceptual orientations of the words we use in different languages, often without realizing the implications they involve. The English "mind" is very distinct from the German "Geist".

To put this distinction in historical perspective, we need to go back to the 18th century when Vico (1725) first introduced a definite demarcation between the natural sciences and the human sciences (Pompa, 1990). At the end of the 19th century, in the context of the German "Conflict of Methods" (*Methodenstreite*), this demarcation was raised to the level of a systematic opposition by a number of authors, among whom the most important was Dilthey (1883, 1900).

This demarcation can be spelled out in the following terms. On the one hand, the *naturalist* paradigm adopts an external third-person point of view, with the aim of providing explanations (*Erklären*). It considers that there is only one sort of science, which in principle will ultimately be unified; it follows, on this view, that the human sciences should adopt the same methods as the natural sciences based on mathematics, the prototype being *explanation by causal laws*, as in physics.

On the other hand, the *hermeneutical* paradigm is based on the interpretation of meaning, on a method of qualitative understanding and making sense. It adopts either a psychological point of view, with the aim of understanding (*Verstehen*) the mental states and intentions of the author through empathy, or a linguistic and grammatical standpoint seeking to interpret texts and other symbolic expressions as objective and public traces (*Deuten*). The *hermeneutical* paradigm, first elaborated in terms of a general doctrine of interpretation by Schleiermacher at the turn of the 19th century (Schleiermacher, 1959), underlies the project of the *Geisteswissenschaften*, so named in the 19th century (Dilthey 1883, 1900, 1907–10), and still strongly present up to this day in the continental human and social sciences. This paradigm clearly asserts the epistemological autonomy of the *Geisteswissenschaften* with respect to the natural sciences (von Wright, 1971; Havelange, 1998).

The frontier which separates these two categories of science does not stem from a difference in their objects of study, but from a difference in the point of view that they adopt: "explanation" versus "understanding". There are thus two distinct approaches to a science of mind. The word *Geist* comes from the German idealistic philosophy – it could be translated by "spirit" – and underlies the project of the hermeneutical *Geisteswissenschaften*. On the other side, the word "mind" goes back to the Anglo-Saxon empiricist philosophy that supports the scientific enterprise aiming at a naturalist explanation of cognitive behavior: from this rises cognitive science, which is the contemporary version of the naturalist paradigm. What is at stake in this perspective is to account for the cognitive behavior by means of causal laws, in principle reducible to physics. It is not by accident that cognitive science exhibits and defines itself as the project of "naturalizing the mind".

26.1.2 Beyond the Opposition Between Naturalization and Interpretation

It is essential to recognize the clear distinction between natural explanations of the mind and the hermeneutical approach to understanding and meaning. However, these two paradigms are also inhabited by unrecognized relationships and, recently there have been some signs that they may be tending towards a convergence. Thus, partly due to the decline of classical cognitivism, and partly due to the renewed vitality of the hermeneutical paradigm in the latter part of the 20th century, contemporary cognitive science is shifting from its initial strictly naturalist origins towards an integration of the hermeneutical perspective. From within cognitive science, the problem of the interpretation of its mental states by the cognitive system itself has become increasingly acute, and has led to a conception of cognition as a dynamic loop between perception and action, so that the organism is engaged in a permanent process of materially producing both itself and its *Umwelt* (i.e. its own lived world). At the same time, the range of hermeneutics has been extended from the methodological constitution of the human and social sciences to include the practical everyday activity of ordinary members of human society.

In this process of convergence between the naturalist and hermeneutical paradigms, the conceptualization of *action* plays a recurrent and preponderant part. Indeed, in seeking to articulate the dimensions of explanation and understanding, and those of the individual and the social, action is a key theme. And while cognitive science is being renewed by this conceptualization of the close links between cognition and action, the recognition that action has a cognitive dimension is leading to a renewal of the hermeneutical social and human sciences (Havelange, 1998).

26.1.3 The Project of Naturalizing the Mind and Classical Cognitive Science

Kant (1786) had decreed the impossibility of a natural science of mind. Mental processes, indeed, are given in an internal perception that deploys itself in time. Since scientific explanation requires its objects to be given in space and apprehended by an external perception, mental processes, reputed to be subjective, were for a long time excluded from its scope.

Two original factors allowed for the bringing forth of cognitive science:

• The notion of mind was extended from the epistemology of scientific knowledge to the ordinary everyday knowledge of humans and animals (hence the neologism "cognition").
• the notion of mind was identified with a machine, first logical (the Turing machine), then material (the computer). This is quite crucial, since a computer algorithm effectively spatializes the temporal process of computation.

Classical cognitive science rests upon two main postulates: the theses of *computation* and *representation*.

• Cognition consists in a computation on the sole formal aspect of symbols that are physically implemented (computation).
• These symbols, however, possess a semantic dimension: they refer to objects in the world (representation).

It is a direct consequence of these theses that the computer is considered to be the prototypical model of human cognition, and thus a "machine that thinks". It also follows directly that human cognition takes place in a "language of thought" (Fodor, 1975), or "mentalese" (Pylyshyn, 1984) which is essentially identical in nature to the formal programming languages of computer science.

Whatever the material substrate of the computation may be, the laws of its functioning are supposed to remain identical and to define an independent mental level: this is the thesis of *functionalism*, central to computo-representationalist cognitive science. There is thus an important sense in which classical cognitivism, in spite of its clear identity as a natural science, is not reductionist in the strong sense of physicalism, since it claims that there are certain entities – mental states – which are not strictly reducible to physical states. Different mental states always correspond to different physical states, but the converse is not true: a mental state can be achieved by many different physical states, and the basis for this categorical gathering of physical states is not accessible to physics as such.

Mind is thus conceived of as a formal language spatialized in the computer, and as we have mentioned, this makes it possible to surmount Kant's negative verdict on the possibility of a natural science of mind. Intentionality, the property by which the mind is about something (whatever it be), is then analyzed into two elements:

- The propositional attitude consists of a generic belief (not only to believe, but to fear, to want, to hope...). It relates the cognitive system to its representations.
- The propositional content is the description of a state of affairs in the world.

A mental state is thus analysed in the following terms: "S believes that (P)". For example, in the utterance "Peter believes that Russell is a great mathematician", "Peter" is the cognitive system, "believes that" is the propositional attitude, and "Russell is a great mathematician" is the propositional content. Propositional attitudes are particularly important, because they ensure the cognitive status and the rationality of the system. A system could not rightly be called "cognitive" if it did not relate itself to its representations (Andler, 1986, 1987).

Classical cognitive science therefore installs itself in a non-eliminativist standpoint in respect to folk (i.e. common sense) psychology. Its attractive quality precisely resides in the fact that it proposes a scientific explanation of mental states and processes – thanks to the identification of the mind with the computer – that does not require us to dispense with our common beliefs. For example, in the perspective of classical cognitve science, a scientific account can be given of the fact that I do such or such action because I believe in the existence of Father Christmas. Classical cognitive science also allows for strong interdisciplinary articulations between logic, psychology, linguistics, artificial intelligence and neuroscience, to name only these.

26.1.4 The Limitations of Classical Cognitive Science

In spite of its strength of proposal, the computo-representational theory of mind meets internal problems which are by now clearly identified and elicited by an abundant literature. I call them internal because they rise from within the paradigm of classical cognitive science and are phrased by its own representatives. The case of Putnam, for example, is quite evocative: starting as an orthodox cognitivist, he subsequently became one of the sharpest exponents of its limitations and aporias.

The major problems, which I shall not examine in detail here, are the symbol grounding problem (how does meaning come to symbols?) (Dreyfus, 1972; Lakoff, 1987); the indeterminacy of the referent (Putnam 1975, 1988); the problem of context (Shanon, 1993; Rastier 1994); and last but not least, the problem of intentionality, which is reduced to linguistic intensionality (Pacherie, 1993; Dupuy, 1994), with all the difficulties that entails.

It must be noticed that, in spite of these difficulties, cognitivism is far from dead. The main form it adopts at the present time consists in juxtaposing computo-representationalism and neo-Darwinian sociobiology. Hence the notion of a natural selection of representations, whose variants are generically identified in the literature as "biological functionalisms" or "biosemantics" (Dretske, 1988; Millikan, 1984, 1989, 1991). However, whereas these authors think they are solving the problem, they actually aggravate it (Lenay, 1993).

26.1.5 The Socio-Historical Dimension of Cognition

Beyond the internal problems mentioned above, these latest adjustments do not solve some broader problems which are intrinsic to functionalist cognitive science as a whole. Cognitivism, based on the notion of mental state and functionalism, entails an intrinsically a-historical conception of cognition.

By contrast, it is now necessary and possible to reintroduce the social and historical dimensions into cognitive research. This puts into question its alignment with the natural sciences in the latter's endeavor to "naturalize the mind", and brings back to the foreground the hermeneutical tradition in the human/social sciences. Furthermore, it sheds new light on the relationships between psychology, sociology and history: whereas these disciplines were classically dissociated (and even rival to one another), they are now acknowledged in their intertwining – an idea that both the naturalist-positivist trend (Mauss, 1924) and the phenomenological approach (Merleau-Ponty, 1951–52) in the human/social sciences had acknowledged as early as the first half of this century.

26.2 The Conceptualization of Action and Society in Cognitive Science

The limitations of cognitivism mentioned above have special implications regarding the conceptualization of human action and society. Since this is the theme of this chapter it is appropriate to spell them out in more detail.

26.2.1 Action

In classical cognitivism, cognition is identified as a linear system of information processing: the sense-data are considered as an input; perception, reasoning and decision are considered as purely formal computational processes; and the instructions for action come at the end as an output. Thus action is defined as follows: a *rational* agent is a system that executes certain *actions* in order to achieve *aims* as a function of determined *beliefs*. To take a simple example, if I am hungry and I believe that there is some food in the refrigerator, I will move towards it and open it.

This definition calls for a certain number of comments. Firstly, it links actions to the intentions of the agent, who must have them in mind explicitly, or at least in a form that can be made explicit. Thus, a human agent who is questioned about his or her actions is supposed to be able to account for them rationally. This point establishes a tight correlation between cognitivism and *Rational Choice Theory* in the social sciences. At the same time, as we have seen, cognitivism expressly stipulates that representations owe their causal efficacy in cognitive behavior solely to their formal dimension. The result of this double postulate is that in functionalist cognitivism the actual action is supplanted by a change in the intentional status of a representation. Consider for example the following sequence, which is cast in the style of analytical philosophy:

1. X wishes to please his wife
2. X believes that, if he offers her flowers, she will be pleased
3. Therefore X offers some flowers to his wife

It looks at first sight as though the action is present in the statement formulating the mental state (3). However, closer examination reveals that this sequence implies two additional statements:

2'. X therefore decides to offer some flowers to his wife
3. X offers some flowers to his wife
4. X now believes that he has pleased his wife

The complete sequence can thus be analyzed as follows. A goal is defined as the representation of a factual state of affairs which is not yet manifest (i.e. it can be doubted, denied, hoped for...) – this is statement (1). A belief consists of a representation of a manifest state of affairs (i.e. a belief held to be true) – this is statement (4). The "action" thus consists of a change in propositional attitude: passing from statement (1) to statement (4), the representation of a manifest fact replaces the representation of a non-manifest fact. But this reveals that the actual action itself is sidelined, put into parentheses, since it is purely abstract, formal and empty. In his famous critique, Searle (1981) remarks that "action" conceptualized in this way is not really carried out, but is only represented. In other words, there is a prescription for action, but no action as such; the effectiveness of the action does not enter into account. It is indeed a direct consequence of the premises of functionalism that actual material events only count as cognitive because they are the substrate for formal operations on symbols.

These limitations of classical cognitivism come even more clearly into focus if they are compared with more recent perspectives in cognitive science which are inspired by the hermeneutical approach. Rather than considering a linear sequence of information processing in which perception precedes a decision to act, in this alternative approach perception itself is constituted by the feedback effects which actions have on sensations. From this point of view, action and perception form an ongoing dynamic loop and are therefore inseparable. This is indeed closely related to the phenomenology of Husserl (1901), for whom intentionality is to be understood as a *relational act* and not as a static mental *state*. The notion of "Being-in-the-World" developed by Heidegger (1927) and Merleau-Ponty (1945) eventually conferred an *ontological* status to hermeneutics (by contrast with the purely methodological and epistemological status of Diltheyan *Geisteswissenschaften*).

Inherited from these phenomenological anlayses, the concept of the *sensory-motor loop* introduced by von Uexküll (1934) and Piaget (1945) has given rise to a number of relevant developments in biology, ethology and psychology. Firstly, this concept has made it possible to root an alternative theory of cognition in a biology of living organisms. In this perspective, cognition appears as a process of interpretation of its environment whereby an organism gives rise to an *Umwelt* – i.e. its own lived world (von Uexküll, 1934) – by means of its embodied actions and perceptions. This constructivist version of cognitive science, which stems from the work of Maturana and Varela (Maturana and Varela, 1980; Varela 1989), places the notions of enaction (Varela *et al.*, 1991) and interpretation (Clément *et al.*, 1997; Stewart *et al.*, 1997) at the heart of an alternative project of the "naturalization" of mind. "Cognition" is no longer the "representation" of a pre-given, referential "state of affairs"; it is rather the ongoing "bringing into being" of a world that is inseparable from the situated action of the subject himself. Secondly, this rooting of cognition in the particularities of embodied sensori-motor loops leads on to the effects of the *externalization* of sensori-motor organs in the form of human technical devices (Leroi-Gourhan, 1964, 1965). This shows that technical artifacts are not just instrumental means to a predefined end; since they mediate the perception–action loop, they are actually *constitutive* of anthropological cognition (Bach-y-Rita, 1972; Lenay *et al.*, 1997) and of social memory as such (Havelange *et al.*, 1999).

26.2.2 Society

In order to address the social dimension of cognition, classical cognitivism takes as its basis the postulate of methodological individualism, which originated in the moral philosophy and political economics of the Enlightenment (Smith, 1759; Ferguson, 1767) and became one of the most predominant features of modern interpretative sociology. Methodological individualism is composed of three axioms: (1) the individual is considered as the elementary or atomic unit of sociology; (2) social order is the result of the aggregation or composition of individual actions and behaviors; and (3) mental states can be properly attributed only to individuals, and *not* to collective entities such as the State, the Church, social classes and so on (Boudon, 1984; Havelange, 1994).

The cognitivist approach to the social sciences thus consists in postulating that culture is determined by universal cognitive capacities, and not the reverse. Thus the "language of thought" (Fodor, 1975) or "mentalese" (Pylyshyn, 1984) are essentially innate, private and universal. This is in accordance with Chomsky's insistence that the "deep structures" of grammar are likewise universal (Chomsky, 1968). The strong form of this postulate is the following: the cognitive capacities of human beings *a priori* determine the form and the content of all real or possible cultures. The research program which follows from this consists in explaining the diverse social forms on the basis of their cognitive origin, but excludes an understanding of cognitive forms on the basis of their social origin. Two sorts of question are then addressed: how, on the basis of individual cognitive capacities, do representations spread? And how do these processes of diffusion generate collective conventions, norms and rules? In the framework of functionalist cognitivism, Sperber (1987) has put forward the notion of an "epidemiology of representations" in order to build a scientific theory of society. He invokes an alternating causal nexus between private representations and public representations in order to explain the formation of society both at the level of myths and rituals (which he considers as linguistic acts) and at the level of institutions.

However, whenever this sort of theory encounters the *circular* relation between the individual agent and the social, it runs into difficulty. For this reason, the strictly formal cognitivist approach is currently giving way to alternative responses to the question of the formation of human society. These alternatives can be gathered in three theoretical families. All three belong to systems theory or, as von Foerster would have said, "second-order cybernetics".

The first sort of theory is based on the concept of *self-organization*. It considers the social as a sort of *natural automaton* capable of engendering forms of spontaneous order that no one has specified and that no one, least of all the social order itself, is able to command. This spontaneous collective order arises on the basis of the "disorder" of the individual agents. However, unlike the properties of a gas or a liquid predicted by statistical mechanics, these theories postulate a recursive feedback between the collective level and the level of individual agents who are "cognitive", i.e. endowed with representations and intentions. This sort of theory has given rise to what Dupuy (1991, 1992), following Smith's (1759, 1774) and Hayek's (1973, 1976, 1979) insight, has termed "complex methodological individualism", which aims at grasping the "non-intentional configurations and regularities which arise in human society and which it is the task of social theory to explain" (Hayek, 1967). However, although these theories introduce the notions of "limited rationality", "undecidability" (Livet, 1991) and "contagion" (Sperber, 1996), supported by those of symapthy (Smith, 1759) or specularity (Girard, 1982), they continue to elude the effectiveness of action in favour of purely representational processes. Consequently, all mental processes – be they individual or collective – are apprehended from a strictly nominalist point of view: while the mind is conceived of as a "process without a subject" (Dupuy, 1994), society is viewed as a "virtual community" (Livet, 1994) or "a communication between elements of a totality considered as transcendent" by an external observer (Dupuy, 1991, 1992). The result is that the ontological constitution of society is absorbed into the epistemic constitution of the social sciences (Havelange, 1995).

The second sort of theory goes under the name of "distributed intelligence". These systems are composed of "reactive" agents who have neither representations nor goals and whose behavior is simply determined by their reaction to material traces left in the environment by other agents. These models have been remarkably successful in explaining the emergent "swarm intelligence" of social insects in constructing trails and nests and in organizing their collective division of labor (Theraulaz and Spitz, 1997; Theraulaz *et al.*, 1999); and their computer simulations interestingly illustrate the importance of external material traces (Lenay, 1994a,b). However, these "reactive" multi-agent systems are not able to take into account the specifically symbolic level of language, and they cannot therefore be taken as models of human society.

A third type of cognitive approach to social phenomena is based on the biological theory of *autopoiesis* (Maturana and Varela, 1980), as transposed to the social realm by Maturana (1980a,b) and, more fully, by Luhmann (1982, 1984, 1990) and Hejl (1982). According to Luhmann, in order to mobilize the central notion of organizational closure, social systems should be considered as being composed not of agents but of recursively closed networks of *communications*. The elementary components of the legal (or economic, political etc.) system are not conscious individuals and their actions, but occurrences of legal (economic, political, ...) communications. The idea is that individual occurrences of communication are ephemeral, but the system functions in such a way as to continually regenerate new occurrences. Each of these systems is closed, in the sense that events external to the specific network of communications can perturb, but not *inform* its functioning. Thus the legal system has to do purely with legal communications and does not in any way communicate with the economic system (and vice versa); the legal system will interpret economic events (e.g. financial profits and costs) *as* legal events (e.g. the distinction between what is lawful and what is not). In this way the various systems co-evolve without being subordinated to each other. This autopoietic theory of society thus radically rejects the notions of representation and methodological individualism. Habermas, the major critic of Luhmann, emphasizes that the process of socialization, as a process of integration, involves subjects actively engaged in lived worlds that are symbolically structured; a satisfactory theory of society must therefore take into account *both* the individual and the holistic dimensions (Habermas, 1981).

26.3 Technics Revisited: the Constitutive Status of Technics in Social Processes

26.3.1 The Reappraisal and Renewal of Hermeneutics in the 1950s

In the second half of the 20th century, the notion of *Verstehen* was revitalized by hermeneutical phenomenology and post-Wittgensteinian social theory. In Germany, Gadamer (1960) extended Heidegger's "hermeneutical phenomenology". In England, Winch (1972) considered sociology as a form of philosophy, influenced in that direction by the second Wittgenstein. In France, Ricoeur (1965) wrote a hermeneutical essay on Freud; a few years later, he renewed hermeneutics in a work which emphasized the "conflict of interpretations" (Ricoeur, 1969), and elaborated an ongoing production on hermeneutics up to this day (Ricoeur, 1986). The influence of Wittgenstein also reached the USA, where Garfinkel (1967) introduced the idea of an "ethnomethodology" (Palmer, 1969; Outhwaite, 1975, 1998; for a study of the current expansion of hermeneutics, cf. Salankis *et al.*, 1997).

This renewal of hermeneutics differs in one very important way from the classical hermeneutics of Dilthey and Weber. The latter considered the *Verstehen* as a *method*; in other words, they attributed it a purely epistemological status. By contrast, the 20th century authors we have mentioned place the *Verstehen* at the very heart of the ontological constitution of society. The activity of understanding is not the sole prerogative of social scientists; it is first and foremost performed daily by ordinary lay members of society. In fact, it is by their routine everyday activities of understanding and interpreting that human beings actually *constitute* society. This ontological apprehension of the *Verstehen*, which derives from Heidegger (1927) and which clearly represents a "cognitive turn", leads to an emphasis on five distinctive themes:

- The importance of human action in sociological theory.
- Reflexivity, in the sense that human agents exert a rational control over their behaviour (cf. metacommunication in ethnomethodology).
- The temporal and contextual localization of action (situated action and indexicality in ethnomethodology).
- Language, considered as the medium of practical activity. Ordinary language cannot therefore be ignored; nor can it be replaced by a separate technical meta-language which would supposedly "purify" ordinary language of its confusions and ambiguities.
- Understanding which is tacit or "taken for granted".

These themes have been notably elaborated by ethnomethodology (Garfinkel, 1967; Goffman, 1959, 1963, 1972; Turner, 1974; Centre d'Etudes des Mouvements Sociaux, 1985), and they have nourished current research in "cognitive sociology" (Cicourel, 1972) and "situated cognition" (Suchman, 1987; Lave, 1988; Norman, 1988; Conein and Jacopin, 1994; Hutchins, 1995). The movement of "situated cognition" seeks in addition to enlarge the notion of interaction, and attributes an important role to the relations of agents with space and the manipulation of objects. Together, these new movements present themselves as a "hermeneutical correction" of classical cognitive science.

It is clear that this renewed form of hermeneutics represents a radical break with methodological individualism. In the second Wittgenstein, in particular, language is considered as essentially social and public (in contrast to Fodor's "private language"). It also represents a break with the subjectivism which characterized the previous "transcendental" phase of phenomenology. It does, however, possess its own limitations, to which we now turn.

26.3.2 The Limitations of Hermeneutics

The limits of the hermeneutical paradigm, even in its renewed forms, derive from the fact that it considers social rules, norms, values etc. as *given*. Three main points are to be noted.

Firstly, the hermeneutical paradigm is unable to account for the diversification of interests and for the historical transformation of norms and institutionalized values. This limitation stems directly from the fact that this paradigm takes norms and values as given.

Secondly, since action is considered as deriving logically from intentions and motivations, this paradigm is unable to distinguish between norms as constitutive of a social space of interaction (for example, the fact that it is forbidden to sell rotten meat and vegetables), and norms as morality (which can run against the agent's rational interests). Thus, Winch (1972) considers that meaningful conduct can be taken as rule-governed behavior. This fails to recognize that norms or social rules are open to different interpretations, and that a differential interpretation of the "same" systems of ideas is at the heart of conflicts based on a division of interests (for example, the conflicts between Catholics and Protestants which have so widely fashioned modern Christianity).

Finally, this paradigm remains attached to a form of empirical realism. Dilthey himself considered that the mental contents and psychological states of other human beings were empirically given. In the 20th century authors we have mentioned there is an analogous attachment to actions that are dictated by "forms of life". The result is an idealistic conception of the notions of social structure and society. The insistence on the production of society by its members leads to the idea of the "social construction of reality" (Berger and Luckmann, 1966). For Touraine (1973), "actionalism" means nothing other than "the production of society" by historical agents. For Cicourel (1972) also, the only sound basis for sociology is the purely local interaction of situated actors; he considers that the concepts of structure, role and so on should be eschewed as misleadingly facile shortcuts.

26.3.3 Ontological Constitution: the Relational Nature of the Social

The limitations identified in the preceding section converge on a single point: it is necessary to thematize not only *cognitive or interpretative action*, but also *social structures*. The work of Giddens (1976, 1984, 1990) is especially worthy of note here, since he has addressed the question of social structures in a way quite consonant with the "ontological turn" of the hermeneutical renewal itself. The central idea is that social structures are both constituted by human action, and at the same time are the medium within which cognitive action takes place. Indeed, social structures condition the very possibility of most forms of human action, while they themselves have no origin other than the action they have made possible. In other words, society has a *relational* nature, because social structures and cognitive action mutually determine each other in a form of circular causality.

This is a form of complexity quite different from that in the systemic social sciences mentioned in Section 26.2.2. In particular, "complex methodological individualism", as put forward by Dupuy (1991), mobilizes the formalisms of self-organization; but since the "complexity" there is purely epistemological, it results in eliminating all reference to the actual constitution of subjective *and* social reality. By contrast, the complexity in Giddens' work is as much ontological as epistemological. It is to be noted that for Giddens, action does not necessarily or even usually derive logically from intentions as it does in the classical theories. Thus, action is primarily a pre-reflexive flow, which nevertheless involves knowledge and power. The key point is that this knowledge is not necessarily formulated (or formulatable) by the agent in propositional terms (cf. the tacit knowledge of ethnomethodology); it is a practical sort of knowledge in action. This sort of action can still be reflexively monitored, but this control is plastic: motivation is not always conscious in the actor, and she often does not know the structural conditions of her action. The ongoing process by which the actor rationalizes her conduct entails new meaningful developments of her self-understanding and her understanding of the social world. This double articulation of the psychic and the social makes it possible to overcome the twin pitfalls of holism and individualism, by directing the attention of the social scientist towards the actual constitution of the social bond.

26.3.4 Epistemological Constitution: the Double Hermeneutics of the Social Sciences

The relational nature of the social also entails epistemological consequences: it implies a double hermeneutics (Giddens, 1976, 1984). The point here is that the social sciences deal with a world which is *already* interpreted by the actors themselves; indeed, the meanings, understandings and interpretations of the active human subjects enter into the effective production of this world itself. Social actors are not "cultural dopes", blindly obeying forces that only the social scientist could perceive; they are fully competent practical theoreticians. There is therefore a reciprocal relation between the concepts used by social actors and those employed or coined by the social scientists. Concepts which were initially elaborated by social scientists in order to analyze the behavior of certain actors can be appropriated by those actors themselves, and therefore can easily become a part of that behavior. This meets the theme of "self-fulfilling prophecies", which is a special case of the central problem in social science of the non-intended results of an action: if the actors are aware of a prediction concerning their own behavior, this awareness can contribute to fulfill (or to defeat) the prediction. The fact that it is always possible for social actors to incorporate knowledge which concerns them gives the epistemology of the social sciences a dimension of indeterminacy which is specific and quite different from that in physics.

26.4 The Technical Constitution of Action and Society

26.4.1 Technics Revisited: the Constitutive Status of Technics in Social Processes

The concepts of the relational nature of society and double hermeneutics, which we have just addressed, have so far been elaborated principally in a linguistic perspective. In order to fully avoid the twin pitfalls of considering that social structures are idealistic or pre-given, and to achieve a full grasp of this relational nature of the social, it is necessary to thematize interpretation not only as linguistic and practical, but material and technical. Until recently indeed (apart from the notable exception of Marx's works), technics has been largely ignored by the human and social sciences, by cognitive science, and by philosophy; but since in human society the double articulation between action and structures is massively mediated by technical artifacts, the thematization of technics offers a great opportunity to address the material inscription of both action and social structures (Leroi-Gourhan, 1964, 1965; Simondon, 1958, 1989; Castoriadis, 1975, 1978; Derrida, 1990; Stiegler, 1994a,b, 1996; Havelange, 1999).

From an anthropological point of view, the process of hominization closely associates the tool, the gesture and speech (Leroi-Gourhan, 1964, 1965). Leroi-Gourhan proposes a reading of vertebrate evolution, from fishes to humans, as the gradual constitution of an "anterior field of relation", and "the division of this into two complementary territories, one delimited by the action of the facial organs, the other by the action of the extremity of the anterior limb". In other words, "ever since their origins, the spinal column, the face and the hand have been inseparably linked". In this way "man began with his feet", since "the upright stance (...) renders the development of the human brain something more and other than a simple increase in volume. The relation between the face and the hand remains quite as close as it was previously throughout evolution; tools for the hand and language for the face are two poles of the same entity". The specificity of humans is thus related to the "externalization" of the bodily motor and sensory organs (Leroi-Gourhan, 1964). But this specificity consists less of the externalization as such than in what the latter makes possible, i.e. technical invention. In fact, it is more precise to speak of a dual movement of externalization/internalization. A new technical object – be it a means of action, an instrument of perception or measurement, or a device for inscribing or manipulating speech – only becomes really effective when it is so intimately integrated in the dynamic loop of action and perception that it disappears from consciousness and becomes, effectively, an extension of the body. For example, experience shows that when driving a car, I perceive the surface of the road with "my" wheels, just as if they were indeed a part of my body.

26.4.2 Towards a Material Hermeneutics

It is therefore not correct to consider that a technical object is simply a lump of inert matter which has been shaped from the outside by a designer, nor that it is simply an instrumental means to a predefined end (Stiegler, 1994b). This classical utilitarian view is consonant with methodological individualism and a conception of the social as a mere aggregate of predefined individuals; we have already examined the limitations and defects of such a view. The concept of a clear and distinct goal formed by an isolated and self-sufficient individual is quite misleading. For one thing, goals emerge during a social process which is distributed over many actors and which no single individual is able to control completely. For another, technical objects quite systematically outrun their preconceived ends, because social actors quite irrepressibly divert technical devices and reappropriate them for quite unforeseen (and indeed unforeseeable) ends. In other words, the goal of a technical object barely exists prior to its manufacture and use.

Far from being reducible to a series of objects circumscribed in time and place and subordinated to an instrumental scheme of means to predefined ends, technics is actually *constitutive* of hominization, sociality and history. The invention and/or the appropriation of a technique conjointly bring into play both the historical heritage of what is already there, and the dynamic fashioning of a psyche. It is clear, in particular, that the appropriation of a collective past that the individual has not himself experienced – a central element in every process of individuation (Simondon 1989) – entirely depends on the *technical* possibilities of gaining access to the past in question (a prime example being the technique of writing). Consequently, it appears that the formation of the social bond is a process of individuation which is indissolubly psychical and collective... and which is mediated by technics.

As Stiegler (1994a) has pointed out, this thematization of technics confirms and enriches the whole field of hermeneutical potentialities. Technics not only places limits on interpretation, because of its material finiteness and facticity; it also provides positive possibilities for constitution by a process of individuation. A technical device both proposes and imposes a gesture; in other words, it has both an enabling and a constraining dimension. As we have said, it is thus a form of collective memory which continually calls for new reappropriations, and which contributes to the joint fashioning of society and psyches (Havelange, 1999). Since technics is anthropologically constitutive, it enlarges the domain of hermeneutics beyond the purely linguistic to include, now, the perspective of a *material* hermeneutics. This is quite decisive for the conception of new technical devices. Bachimont (1992, 1996) has argued how it is possible, by fully and explicitly taking into account the digital basis for knowledge-based computer systems, to restore the interpretative and authorial dimension for users of these systems.

26.5 Conclusion and Perspectives: Alienation and Emancipation

Finally, it will also be noted that this thematization of technics consolidates and enriches the duality that Giddens identified as being an essential feature of social structures. A technical device or artifact of a certain type is always the materially inscribed memory of the operational chains which were involved in its production; in other words, it is not only the result of its own production, it is also the *condition* of that production. This is, of course, even more true of technical systems composed of a network of interrelated technologies (for example, coal and iron mining, railways and so on): such a system is necessary for its own production, which is why the first industrial revolution in Britain was spread over centuries but, once it had occurred, could be exported and rapidly reproduced all over the world. Now this rooting of the duality of social structures in material technologies confers a new density to the indeterminacy and the double hermeneutics characteristic of the human sciences. The knowledge and concepts forged by social scientists that social actors can incorporate into their practice is not limited to knowledge of social structures; it also includes awareness of the fact that technical mediation is both enabling and constraining. Henceforth, the classical questions of alienation and emancipation must be enlarged. It is no longer sufficient to say that alienation is the process whereby social actors are ignorant of the social structures that are the true causes of their actions, and ignorant of their own role in reproducing these structures; nor that emancipation is the process whereby social actors become explicitly conscious of the social structures in which they are involved, and act quite deliberately to maintain or to change them. As Marx had already seen so clearly in his critique of commodity fetishism and reification, a technical object (such as a car or a computer) is not just a "material object", it is an incarnate set of social relations. Alienation involves being blind to the social and psychical significance of every technical artefact; emancipation, if it is not to be frustratingly limited, must include a reflexive reappropriation of the way in which the technological systems we create exert an influence which permeates to every corner of our lives.

References

Andler, D (1986) Le cognitivisme orthodoxe en question, in *Cahiers du CREA*, 9, 7–106.
Andler, D (1987) Progrès en situation d'incertitude, in *Une nouvelle science de l'esprit: Intelligence artificielle, sciences cognitives, nature du cerveau, Le débat*, 47, 5–25.
Bach-Y-Rita, P (1972) *Brain mechanisms in sensory substitution*, New York, Academic Press.
Bachimont, B (1992) *Le contrôle dans les systèmes à base de connaissances*, Paris, Editions Hermès.
Bachimont, B (1996) *Herméneutique matérielle et artéfacture: des machines qui pensent aux machines qui donnent à penser*, Thèse de doctorat de l'Ecole Polytechnique en épistémologie.
Berger, P and Luckmann, T (1966) *The Social Construction of Reality*, Garden City, NY, Doubleday (translated as *La Construction Sociale De La Réalité*, Paris, Méridiens-Klienksieck, 1986).
Boudon, R (1984) *La Place du Désordre*, Paris, PUF.
Castoriadis, C (1975) *L'Institution Imaginaire de la Société*, Paris, Editions du Seuil.
Castoriadis, C (1978) Technique, in *Les Carrefours du Labyrinthe*, Vol. 1, Paris, Editions du Seuil, pp. 221–248.
Centre d'Etude des Mouvements Sociaux (ed.) (1985) *Arguments Ethnométhodologiques*, Vol. III, Paris, EHESS.
Cicourel, AV (1972) *Cognitive Sociology*, Harmondsworth, Penguin Education (translated by J and M Olson as *La Sociologie Cognitive*, Paris, PUF, 1979).
Chomsky, N (1968) *Language and Mind*, New York, Harcourt Brace (translated by L-J Calvet as *Le Langage et la Pensée*, Paris, Payot, 1970).
Clement P, Scheps, R and Stewart, J (1997) *Umwelt* et interprétation, in *Herméneutique: Textes, Sciences* (eds. J-M Salankis, F Rastier and R Scheps), Paris, PUF, pp. 209–232.
Conein, E and Jacopin, E (1994) Action située et cognition: le savoir en place, *Sociologie du Travail*, 44, 475–500.
Derrida, J (1990) *Le Problème de la Genèse dans la Philosophie de Husserl*, Paris, Presses Universitaires de France

Dilthey, W (1883) *Einleitung in die Geisteswissenschaften, Gesammelte Schriften*, Vol. I, Stuttgart, Teubner (translated by L Sauzin as *Introduction à L'Étude des Sciences Humaines*, Paris, PUF, 1942; a new translation, with the more accurate title *Introduction aux Sciences de L'Esprit*, which also includes other works, appears in Dilthey, W (1992) *Oeuvres*, Vol. 1, *Critique de la raison historique*, translated by S. Mesure, Paris, Editions du Cerf).

Dilthey, W (1900) Die Entstehung der Hermeneutik, in *Der Geistige Welt. Einleitung in die Philosophie des Lebens. I. Abhandlungen zur Grundlegung des Geisteswissenschaften*, Vol. V of *Gesammelte Shriften*, Stuttgart, B.G. Teubner (translated by M Remy as La naissance de l'herméneutique, in *Le Monde de L'Esprit*, Vol. 1, Paris, Aubier-Montaigne, 1947, pp. 319–340; a new translation by D Cohn and E Lafon appears in Dilthey, *Oeuvres*, Vol. 7, Paris, Editions du Cerf, 1995, pp. 289–307).

Dilthey, W (1907–10) *Der Aufbau der geschichtlichen Welt in den Geisteswissenschaften*, Vol. VII of *Gesammelte Schriften*, Stuttgart, B.G. Teubner, 1958 (translated by S Mesure as *L'Édification du Monde Historique dans les Sciences de L'Esprit, Oeuvres*, Vol. 3, Paris, Editions du Cerf, 1988).

Dretske, F (1988) *Explaining Behavior*, Cambridge, MA, MIT Press.

Dreyfus, HL (1972) *What Computers Can't Do: The Limits of Artificial Intelligence*, New York, Harper & Row (2nd edn 1979) (translated by R-M Vassallo-Villaneau as *Intelligence Artificielle: Mythes et Limites*, Paris, Flammarion, 1984).

Dupuy, J-P (1991) Sur la complexité du social, in *Les Théories de la Complexité. Autour de L'Oeuvre d'Henri Atlan* (ed. F Fogelman Soulie in collaboration with V Havelange and M Milgram), Paris, Editions du Seuil, pp. 394–409.

Dupuy, J-P (1992) *Introduction aux Sciences Sociales. Logique des Phénomènes Collectifs*, Paris, Editions Ellipses.

Dupuy J-P (1994) *Aux Origines des Sciences Cognitives*, Paris, La Découverte.

Ferguson, A (1767) *An Essay on the History of Civil Society*, London.

Fodor, JA (1975) *The Language of Thought*, New York, Crowell.

Gadamer, H-G (1960) *Wahrheit und Methode* (translated by E Sacre and P Ricoeur as *Vérité et Méthode*, Paris, Editions du Seuil, 1976).

Garfinkel, H (1967) *Studies in Ethnomethodology*, Englewood Cliffs, NJ, Prentice Hall; republished Cambridge, Polity Press, 1984, 1996.

Giddens, A (1976) *New Rules of Sociological Method*, London, Hutchinson/New York, Basic Books.

Giddens, A (1984) *The Constitution of Society*, Cambridge, Polity Press/Oxford, Basil Blackwell (translated by M Audet as *La Constitution de la Société*, Paris, PUF, 1987).

Giddens, A (1990) *The Consequences of Modernity*, Cambridge, Polity Press (translated by O Meyer as *Les Conséquences de la Modernité*, Paris, L'Harmattan, 1994).

Girard, R (1982) *Le Bouc Émissaire*, Paris, Grasset.

Goffman, E (1959) *The Presentation of Self in Everyday Life*, New York, Doubleday (translated as *La Mise en Scène de la Vie Quotidienne*, Paris, Editions de Minuit, 1973, Vol. 1, *La Présentation de Soi*.

Goffman, E (1963) *Behaviour in Public Places*, New York, Free Press (translated as *La Mise en Scène de la Vie Quotidienne*, Paris, Editions de Minuit, 1973; Vol. 2, *Les Relations en Public*.

Goffman, E (1972) *Interaction Ritual*, London, Allen Lane (translated as *Les Rites D'Interaction*, Paris, Editions de Minuit, 1974).

Goffman, E (1974) *Frame Analysis. An Essay on the Organization of Experience*, New York, Harper (translated by I Joseph, with M Dartevelle and P Joseph, as *Les Cadres de L'Espérience*, Paris, Editions de Minuit, 1991).

Habermas, J (1981) *Theorie des Kommunikativen Handelns*, Frankfurt, Suhrkamp.

Havelange, V (1994) Sciences cognitives et tradition sociologique, *Revue Internationale de Systémique*, 8(1), 79–89.

Havelange, V (1995) Article critique: Jean-Pierre Dupuy, *Aux origines des sciences cognitives*, Paris, La Découverte, 1994, *Intellectica*, 1(20), 247–261.

Havelange, V (1998) Le social en débat: cognition ou interprétation?, *Sciences Sociales et Cognition, Intellectica*, Special Issue, 1–2(26–27), 9–55.

Havelange, V (1999) Mémoire collective: la constitution technique de la cognition, Introduction to *Mémoire de la Technique, Techniques de la Mémoire* (eds. C Lenay and V Havelange), Special Issue of *Technologies, Idéologies, Pratiques. Revue d'anthropologie des connaissances*.

Havelange, V, Lenay, C and Stewart, J (1999) Les représentations: mémoire externe et objets techniques, in *Les Modèles de Représentation: Quelles Alternatives?* (ed. J-P Müller), Paris, Editions Hermès.

Hayek, FA (1967) *Studies in Philosophy, Politics and Economy*, London, Chicago.

Hayek, FA (1973, 1976, 1979) *Law, Legislation and Liberty*, London, Routledge & Kegan Paul (translated by R Audouin as *Droit, Législation et Liberté*, Paris, PUF: Vol. 1, 1980; Vol. 2, 1981; Vol. 3, 1983.

Heidegger, M (1927) *Sein und Zeit* (translated by A Martineau as *Etre et Temps*, Paris, Authentica, 1985; translated by F Fédier as *Etre et Temps*, Paris, Gallimard, 1986).

Hejl, PM (1982) *Sozialwissenschaft als Theorie selbstreferentieller Systeme*, Frankfurt.

Husserl, E (1901) *Logische Untersuchungen. Zweiter Band: Untersuchungen zur Phänomenologie und Theorie der Erkenntnis*, Halle, Niemeyer, 2ème éd. 1913; éd. Panzer, *Husserliana XIX* et *Husserliana XX*, Den Haag, Martinus Nijhoff, 1984 (translated by H Elie, A Kelkel and R Schérer as *des Recherches I et II, Recherches Logiques. Tome 2: Recherches pour la phénoménologie et la théorie de la connaissance*, Paris, Presses Universitaires de France, 1961, 1991; this translation is of the 1913 edition).

Hutchins, E (1995) *Cognition in the Wild*, Boston, MA, MIT Press.

Kant, I (1786) *Metaphysische Anfangsgründe der Naturwissenschaft, Immanuel Kants Werke* (ed. B Cassirer), 1910–1922, Berlin, Bruno Cassirer, Vol. IV(translated by J. Gibelin as *Premiers Principes Métaphysiques de la Science de la Nature*, Paris, Vrin, 1952, 1990).

Lakoff, G (1987), *Women, Fire and Dangerous Things*, Chicago, IL, Chicago University Press.

Lave, J (1988) *Cognition in Practice*, Cambridge, MA, Cambridge University Press.

Lenay, C (1993) Caractères adaptatifs et représentations symboliques, *Intellectica*, 16, 209–257.

Lenay, C (1994a) Organization émergente dans les populations: biologie, éthologie, systèmes artificiels, *Intellectica*, 2(19), 9–17.

Lenay, C (1994b) Introduction, *Intelligence artificielle Distribuée: Modèle ou Métaphore des Phénomènes Sociaux, Revue Internationale de Systémique*, 8(1), 1–11.

Lenay, C, Canu, S and Villon, P (1997) Technology and perception: the contribution of sensory substitution systems, in *Proceedings of the Conference Humanizing the Information Age, Cognitive Technology*, University of Aizu, 24–27 August.

Lenay, C and Havelange V (eds.) (in press) *Mémoire de la Technique, Techniques de la Mémoire*, Special issue of *Technologies, Idéologies, Pratiques. Revue d'anthropologie des connaissances*.

Leroi-Gourhan, A (1964, 1965) *Le Geste et la Parole*, Paris, Albin Michel (translated as *Gesture and Speech*, Boston, MA, MIT Press, 1993).

Livet, P (1991) Un facteur de complexité: le jeu de l'indétermination dans les relations humaines, in *Les Théories de la Complexité. Autour de L'Oeuvre d'Henri Atlan* (ed. F Fogelman Soulie in collaboration with V Havelange and M Milgram), Paris, Editions du Seuil, pp. 436-452.

Livet, P (1994) *La Communauté Virtuelle. Action et communication*, Combas, Editions de l'Eclat.

Luhmann, N (1982) *The Differentiation of Society*, New York, Columbia University Press.

Luhmann, N (1984) *Soziale Systeme: Grundriss einer allgemeinen Theorie*, Frankfurt, Suhrkamp.

Luhmann, N (1990) *Essays on Self-Reference*, New York, Columbia University Press.

Maturana, HR (1980a) Introduction, in *Autopoiesis and Cognition: The Realization of the Living* (eds. HR Maturana and FJ Varela), Dordrecht, Reidel, pp. XI–XXX; section "Society and Ethics", pp. XXIV–XXX.

Maturana, HR (1980b) Man and Society, in *Autopoiesis, Communication and Society; The Theory of Autpoietic Systems in the Social Sciences* (eds. F Benseler, PM Hejl and W KÖCK), Frankfurt, 1980, pp. 11–31.

Maturana, HR and Varela, FJ (1980) *Autopoiesis and Cognition: The Realization of the Living*, Dordrecht, Reidel.

Mauss, M (1924) Rapport réels et pratiques de la psychologie et de la sociologie, reissued in *Sociologie et Anthropologie*, Paris, PUF, 1950; collected in "Quadrige", 1985, pp. 281–310.

Merleau-Ponty, M (1945) *Phénoménologie de la Perception*, Paris, Gallimard; reissued in "Tel", 1976 (translation by C Smith as *Phenomenology of Perception*, London, Routledge & Kegan Paul, 1962).

Merleau-Ponty, M (1951-1952) *Les Sciences de L'Homme et la Phénoménologie*, Paris, Centre de Documentation Universitaire.

Millikan, RG (1984) *Language, Thought and Other Biological Categories: New Foundations for Realism*, Cambridge, MA, MIT Press.

Millikan, RG (1989) Biosemantics, *The Journal of Philosophy*, LXXXVI(6), 281–297.

Millikan, RG (1991) Speaking up for Darwin, in *Meaning and Mind: Fodor and his Critics* (eds. G Rey and B Loewer), Cambridge, MA, Basic Blackwell, pp. 151–163.

Norman, DA (1988) *The Psychology of Everyday Things*, New York, Basic Books.

Outhwaite, W (1975) *Understanding Social Life. The Method Called Verstehen*, London, George Allen & Unwin; 2nd edn Jean Stroud, 1986.

Outhwaite, W (1998) L'actualité du paradigme herméneutique, in *Sciences Sociales et Cognition, Intellectica*, Special Issue, 1–2(26–27), 135–148.
Pacherie, E (1993) *Naturaliser L'Intentionnalité*, Paris, Presses Universitaires de France.
Palmer, RE (1969) *Hermeneutics. Interpretation Theory in Schleiermacher, Dilthey, Heidegger, and Gadamer*, Evanston, IL, Northwestern University Press.
Piaget, J (1945) *La Formation du Symbole chez L'Enfant*, Neuchâtel-Paris, Delachaux et Niestlé; reissued 1976.
Pompa, L (1990) *Vico. A Study of the "New Science"*, Cambridge, Cambridge University Press.
Putnam, H (1975) The Meaning of 'Meaning', *Mind, Language and Reality: Philosophical Papers*, Vol. 2, Cambridge, Cambridge University Press, pp. 215–271.
Putnam, H (1988) *Representation and Reality*, Cambridge, MA, MIT Press.
Pylyshyn, ZW (1984) *Computation and Cognition*, Cambridge, MA, MIT Press.
Rastier, F (1994) *Sémantique pour L'Analyse* (in collaboration with M Cavazza and A Abeille), Paris, Masson.
Ricoeur, P (1965) *De l'interprétation. Essai sur Freud*, Paris, Editions du Seuil.
Ricoeur, P (1969) *Le Conflit des Interprétations. Essais d'herméneutique*, Paris, Editions du Seuil.
Ricoeur, P (1986) *Du Texte à L'Action. Essais D'Herméneutique II*, Paris, Editions du Seuil.
Salankis, J-M, Rastier, F and Scheps, R (eds.) (1997) *Herméneutique: Textes, Sciences*, Paris, PUF.
Schleiermacher, F (1959) *Hermeneutik* (ed H. Kimmerle), Heidelberg (translated by C Berner as *Herméneutique*, Paris, Cerf, 1989).
Searle, J (1981) Minds, brains and programs, in *Mind Design* (ed. J Haugeland), Cambridge, MA, MIT Press.
Shanon, B (1993) *The Representational and the Presentational. An Essay on Cognition and the Study of the Mind*, New York/London, Harvester Wheatsheaf.
Simondon, G (1958) *Du Mode D'Existence des Objets Techniques*, Paris, Aubier; reissued 1989.
Simondon, G (1989) *L'Individuation Psychique et Collective*, Paris, Editions Aubier (posthumous edition).
Smith, A (1759) *The Theory of Moral Sentiments*, Indianapolis, IN, Liberty Classics, 1969, 1976 (translated by la Marquise de Condorcet as *Théorie des sentiments moraux*, 1798; reissued by Editions d'aujourd'hui in "Les introuvables").
Smith, A (1774) *An Inquiry into the Nature and Causes of the Wealth of Nations*, London, 1904 (translated as *La Richesse des Nations*).
Sperber, D (1987) Les sciences cognitives, les sciences sociales et le matérialisme, in *Une Nouvelle Science de L'Esprit: Intelligence Artificielle, Sciences Cognitives, Nature du Cerveau, Le Débat*, No. 47, pp. 103–115.
Sperber, D (1996) *La Contagion des Idées*, Paris, Odile Jacob.
Stewart J, Scheps, R and Clement, P (1997) Phylogenèse de l'interprétation, in *Herméneutique: Textes, Sciences* (eds. J-M Salankis, F Rastier and R Scheps), Paris, PUF, pp. 233–252.
Stiegler, B (1994a) Temps et individuations technique, psychique et collective dans l'oeuvre de Simondon, *Futur antérieur*; reprinted in *Sciences Sociales et Cognition, Intellectica*, Special Issue, 1998, 1–2(26–27), 241–256.
Stiegler, B (1994b) *La Technique et le Temps*, tome 1: *La faute d'Epiméthée*, Paris, Editions Galilée (translation by R Beardsworth and G Collins as *Technics and Time*, Vol. 1, Stanford University Press).
Stiegler, B (1996), *La Technique et le Temps*, tome 2: *La Désorientation*, Paris, Editions Galilée.
Suchman, L (1987) *Plans and Situated Actions*, Cambridge, MA, Cambridge University Press.
Theraulaz, G and Spitz, F (eds.) (1997) *Auto-Organization et Comportement*, Paris, Hermè, Part 2 "Auto-organization et comportements collectifs dans les sociétés animales", pp. 77–200.
Theraulaz, G, Bonabeau, E and Deneubourg, J-L (1999) Mémoire collective et coordination des activités chez les insectes sociaux, in *Mémoire de la Technique, Techniques de la Mémoire* (eds. C Lenay and V Havelange), Special issue of *Technologies, Idéologies, Pratiques. Revue d'anthropologie des connaissances*.
Touraine, A (1973) *Production de la Société*, Paris, Editions du Seuil.
Turner, R (ed.) (1974) *Ethnomethodology*, London, Penguin.
Varela, FJ (1989) *Connaître les Sciences Cognitives*, Paris, Editions du Seuil.
Varela, FJ, Thompson, E and Rosch E (1991) *The Embodied Mind. Cognitive Science and Human Experience*, Cambridge, MA, MIT Press (translated by V Havelange as *L'Inscription Corporelle de L'Esprit*, Paris, Seuil, 1993).

Vico, G (1725) *La scienza nuova*, reissued by P Rossi, Rizzoli Editore, Milan, 1963 (translated by C Trivulzio, princesse de Belgiojoso, as *La Science Nouvelle*, Paris, Gallimard, in "Tel", 1993).

von Uexküll, J (1934) *Streifzüge durch die Umwelten von Tieren und Menschen – Bedeutungslehre* (1940) (translated as *Mondes Animaux et Monde Humain*, followed by *Théorie de la Signification*, Paris, Denoël, 1965).

von Wright, GH (1971) *Explanation and Understanding*, London, Routledge & Kegan Paul.

Winch, P (1972) *The Idea of a Social Science*, London, Routledge & Kegan Paul.

27

Business, Academia, Government: Toward Symbiotic Collaboration in a Networked Society

Kozo Akiyoshi, Nobuo Akiyoshi, Tosiyasu L. Kunii and Sakaki Morishita

Abstract

In the past, the worlds of business, academia and government rarely mixed, but recently economic and other factors have been driving these strange bedfellows together in new and interesting ways. A number of new models for how these sectors can interact have been developing, but the end result is far from settled. In this chapter, we examine some of these developing models and propose a new model of interaction that is founded on the interests of each societal sector so that cross-sector interactions are optimized to create symbiotic relationships among all sectors. The new model factors in the economic and other interests of each sector and takes advantage of the enhanced speed of communication and other benefits provided by a networked society. We believe that this new network model is more open and will produce more fundamental breakthroughs than today's common models. The chapter concludes with a brief review of the results of our experiences operating under the network model and some thoughts for the future.

27.1 Background

Not too long ago, the world was a place in which business, academia, and government all worked in separate areas. Business was concerned with the practical aspects of making things that could be sold to the public. Academia was concerned with the pursuit of knowledge in its most fundamental form. Government was focused on public service and was only peripherally involved in academia through hands-off funding arrangements and in business through regulation and taxation.

Times have changed! Business has taken to investing larger sums into research and development and has even taken an interest in basic research. Academia has been hit with funding crises and by an ever-increasing number of public and private researchers and research labs that are all after a slice of the pie. Government has moved into the field of funding research and developing technology in order to "kick start" the economy by encouraging new technologies that will create jobs and consumer demand.

Simultaneous with these changes, advances in computer and communications technology have resulted in the development of the world as a networked society. In this chapter, it is important to note that "networked society" is used in its broadest sense. A networked society is not just a world where a significant proportion of the populace is connected through information networks such as the Internet, but also a world in which new *human* networks are formed because of the access that people have to these information networks.

Which of these changes came first, which ones may be driving the others, the causes of these changes, and other issues that might be raised by the above statements are perhaps less important at this point that the question of how business, academia, and government can interact in the most beneficial way.

In this chapter, we address this question by first considering some of the driving forces of each of the sectors in pursuing interaction. Next, we examine some of the developing models of interaction. We then introduce our proposal for a new network model. Lastly, we provide some early results from our ongoing experiment with this model and conclude with some thoughts for the future.

27.2 Driving Forces

In order to understand the factors affecting these changing interactions and to predict where the future of interaction may go, it is quite important to understand the various driving forces behind each of the sectors, including the prime motivator: money. In the following, we discuss only the base or general motivations, but of course there will be many others and also some exceptions to every rule.

27.2.1 Business

Over the last few decades we have seen a series of changes occur in society that have been unprecedented in their speed of upheaval. We have seen big companies fall and small companies rise. One of the main factors in these changes has been technological research and development. It has not just been development within companies that has made the change; developments that have occurred in a garage or in an academic lab have made some of the biggest leaps.

Business has seen this and wants to be a part of it. It wants to get these technologies and make use of them to make money. Thus business has tried to enter the traditional field of academia and has tried to attract researchers by cultivating the "garage" or "academic" feeling with casual clothing and business parks that are called "campuses".

However, the end result must generally be the same: somewhere down the road there has to be a "product", and then that product must be maintained and improved upon. Thus business's main goal remains getting a monetary return on its investment.

27.2.2 Academia

Academia seems to be moving into a situation where more time must be spent looking for funding than is spent on the fundamental research that most academic workers would much rather be doing. The battle to find funding has made for a world where those most proficient at fundraising are getting more attention than those most proficient at research.

Academia has been responding to the funding issue by seeking out many alternative sources of funding. This search covers the whole spectrum from business to government, even going so far as to have corporate sponsors of entire universities!

Unfortunately, some researchers are finding that these sponsorships and funding arrangements can sometimes affect academic freedom, and researchers are losing access to a major motivating factor: the freedom to set the course of their own academic research.

27.2.3 Government

Governments throughout much of the world have gone through some tough times over the last few years trying to keep economies moving and to keep their countries involved in the economic shift from production to information. Many governments have chosen to initiate projects in technological development to tackle these issues.

Governments undertaking these projects have had a difficult time understanding how to make these projects stand out in the public interest. It is much harder to showcase technological developments than it is a new bridge or a highway. It is also more difficult to determine how new technological developments can best be applied for the public good in order to satisfy government's main role.

27.3 Models

There are many different models for interaction among business, academia, and government that have been developed and are continuing to be developed. In this section, we look at a few of the recent models and analyze them briefly, keeping in mind the driving forces described above and the increasing impact of the networked society.

27.3.1 Technology Transfer Model

Many universities have set up Technology Transfer Offices in an attempt to provide a means of interacting with business in order to transfer technology (often patents) developed within the university to business for use in developing commercial technology.

Typically, business will receive a license to use certain technology in retain for a payment of a royalty or the like to the university. In some cases, a new entity may be created in which the researchers will have a role or a stake.

This model suffers from the problem that quite often the level of technology coming out of academia will be quite fundamental and not ideally suited for commercial application. It may take additional investment on behalf of business before there are any returns on the investment.

Further, the researcher may not be available after the initial deal to provide assistance and may be prevented from adding new information that could in fact be the subject of a subsequent patent.

This model also does not fully benefit from modern networks and communities in the networked society, since typically each university may have advances in only certain key areas or may only have technology patents or rights covering a small area of a larger technology field.

27.3.2 Venture Capital Model

In this model, academia approaches business with a new idea and receives funding in order to create a company that will exploit the new technology. This model has been incredibly successful in the world of Internet technology in the USA.

Typically, the researcher receives funding and may occasionally receive some business advice and assistance in the creation and operation of company.

While this model can provide enormous financial reward for the right ideas, it has the problem of placing the researcher in the role of businessperson. More often than not this can cause many problems due to lack of experience and/or lack of interest in business.

Recently, some venture capital (VC) firms have been expanding their roles in the companies that they fund, providing more and more business advice and input. However, for the researcher this result ends up much like the Corporate Research Center model described below.

Another development in this area is that some VC firms have been specializing in particular areas of technology, for example, e-commerce or Web content. This is interesting in that they are using the effect of networking to produce a larger synergy between a number of entities all working in the same area

27.3.3 Government-Funded Research Model

In this model, the government either sets up a research institution or provides funding to targeted "centers" in a university or the like.

This model results in some similar problems to those of the technology transfer model. For example, there is only a weak link to business and issues of protectionism make it difficult to consolidate technologies from a number of centers.

There are also problems with determining how innovations will be protected and who will have ownership and control.

27.3.4 Corporate Research Facility Model

This model is one in which a corporation sets up a research facility and attempts to lure academia to work for business.

While this model may present academia with an attractive financial package, there is usually some friction between the goals of an academic in pursuing fundamental research and the goals of business in (eventually) producing a finished product. This tendency of business to focus inward on the development of only its own or similar products can also cause further problems. If a new development is found, it is unlikely that applications in other areas or potential synergies with the work of others will be examined. In this way, it is difficult to flow upstream to fundamental research from a downstream position.

This model may also suffer from a lack of interaction with outside sources, owing to the fact that business will generally want to protect and own the results of research.

27.3.5 Open Source Development Model

In this model, researchers release their new technologies (or at least portions of them) on the Internet and allow them to permeate the networked society in the hope that the developments will provide some benefit to society and will spur further development.

While very altruistic and perhaps closer to what government may be trying to achieve, this model encounters the problem that there is no direct benefit in terms of receiving funding to allow the continued development of the technological area or in terms of keeping business happy.

This model may be effective in setting a base *de facto* standard, but in many cases it will be hampered by a lack of any central focus that can coordinate the integration and dissemination of new developments.

Also, similar to the corporate research model, it will be difficult to flow upstream from the narrow requirements of a growing development to a more general or fundamental position.

27.4 Factors Leading to the Development of the Network Model

There are a number of factors that have led to the development of our new model for interaction among business, academia, and government. These factors are discussed in more detail in each of the following sections.

27.4.1 Development Stream

The process of development generally flows in a stream from an original, most fundamental (or "upstream") idea; it is then incorporated into or added to other technologies, and continues flowing downstream until it may end up producing a large number of "products". This same kind of flow is sometimes reflected in the flow of fundamental new technologies through various levels in society.

Generally, fundamental development begins with the public sector, quite often in universities or through government-funded programs. Also, one of the first users of fundamental new technology is often the government, particularly in areas in which it has provided the initial funding. The government wants to be able to show that there is some "direct" benefit from its expenditure.

Next, technology enters the industrial sector and is applied in the processes that keep industry running. Acceptance of a new technology in the governmental and academic sectors generally leads to demand for the technology in the industrial sector.

Lastly, technology enters the commercial sector. Historically, a commercial market has developed for all tools that have been accepted by industry professionals. Professional word processors created a demand for home PCs, professional graphic tools led to an explosion in desktop publishing, and computer-assisted video editing tools, only a short while ago the purview of professionals, are now commonly pre-installed on new PCs for the home.

Here, the key is realizing that many downstream technologies can flow out of one fundamental or upstream technology.

27.4.2 Networked Society

As described briefly above, the advent of a networked society is a part of the current upheaval in interactions between business, academia and government.

Just as the Industrial Revolution was only possible when technical and social evolution provided an environment that allowed for the construction of factories and the collection of human and natural resources, our proposed new model of technology development has only now become possible with the debut of the communication and legal infrastructures needed to support such a business.

The networked society creates subworlds, or communities, of networked individuals who connect through data networks to discuss areas of mutual interest. The existence of these online communities is overwhelmingly evident in the large number of newsgroups, mailing lists and bulletin boards devoted to topical discussions. Mirroring other communities, the topicality of discussion varies greatly.

It is now very common for a researcher to first learn of new developments over a network, to begin a project by searching for information published electronically, and to regularly communicate and collaborate with other individuals in that field through a network.

One of the most powerful examples of the effect of these networks is the current idea of open source software. The idea that open source software may have the ability to challenge some of the largest companies in the world is phenomenal.

27.4.3 Intellectual Property

Equally important for the proposed model is the development of methods of international intellectual property (IP) protection.

In the IP area, there are two main tools for international patent protection: the Paris Convention [1] and the Patent Cooperation Treaty (PCT) [2]. The Paris Convention generally states that a patent application filed in one convention country has worldwide priority in any Paris Convention country, which is almost every country in the world. The PCT allows for something very close to a "global patent" in that PCT applications can be filed in one country and then later be converted into domestic applications in more than 90 countries.

Although these systems are far from perfect, the combined effect of these treaties is that it is possible for researchers to retain worldwide rights over their technology based on a limited initial investment.

Interestingly, a look at records of patent filings clearly shows that examples of downstream collaboration, cooperation designed to produce a specific product, are common, but there is actually very little focused upstream collaboration at the cusp where raw science meets applied technology.

The world is moving further and further to an Information Society – perhaps even moving to a "post-capital" world in which the most important commodity will be intellectual property rather than capital.

27.5 Network Model

The proposed model has been developed based on ideas of symbiosis and of networks, both systems in which two or more entities mix their strength, abilities, and goals to their mutual benefit and to produce something that none of them could produce alone.

The network model is one in which all entities, business, academia and government, benefit. In fact, the model represents a system where each entity *prospers* because it has joined the collaboration.

27.5.1 Framework

The proposed model consists of the formation of a separate entity, called a Hub Group, that will not be entirely business, or academia, or government. This Hub Group will be a neutral interface that maintains its ties to each of business, academia and government through the formation of a human network and facilitated by the technology networks that are still developing around us.

The Hub Group will focus on fundamental upstream technology or on areas in which a new breakthrough is approaching. These areas will be identified by consultations with leading researchers in the relevant fields, not just at one institution, but at many locations around the world. The Hub Group will then develop a plan to pursue the new technologies on a very fundamental level, seeking fundamental patent protection at each stage. The Hub Group may then approach governments in order to further develop the fundamental technology for specialized government uses and in order to bring the technology to a level at which it will fuel the economy by being of interest to business. At any stage, the Hub Group may also approach business in order to license the technology to businesses in a wide number of areas so that downstream commercial products can be produced.

27.5.2 Foundation

The foundation of the proposed model is that the word "benefit" has different meanings to different entities. It is very important to understand the various goals, strengths and abilities of the entities involved and determine where goals, strengths and abilities differ.

For example, while all parties are likely to desire financial gain, the importance of other factors will vary and affect their approach towards money. A businessperson may be very highly motivated to realize profit for stockholders. On the other hand, the lifestyles of most academicians are evidence that they value other factors, perhaps peer recognition or the thrill of exploration, highly enough to sacrifice some immediate financial advantages. Lastly, governments clearly have goals that put benefit to the general public at the forefront.

Further, though downplayed in many economic models, by focusing on fundamental breakthroughs the proposed model takes account of the importance of altruism and the human desire to take part in work viewed as meaningful. A great deal of empirical evidence shows that human beings are generally eager to participate in a project when they believe it will have broad significance or have a large effect. The success of the US Apollo space program is a good example of how dedicated, involved humans of all levels will produce exceptional results for average financial gain when they have a reasonable belief in the significance of the overall project.

The development of the network model also requires the ability to collect widespread efforts on a worldwide basis. This has only been made possible by the development of the Internet as a tool for information exchange and advances in communications and travel that allow worldwide human networks to flourish.

Intellectual property is both a tool and an asset in the proposed model. Because a Hub Group will focus on the filing of the most fundamental applications, it can use its rights as a tool and have some control of the downstream or practical applications of its technology. The Hub Group will not market final products, but by using its IP rights will facilitate the creation of applications using the technology it has developed into a practical form. IP rights are also an asset as these are the means by which the Hub Group will survive. In the proposed model, the Hub Group will set licensing fees so as to balance the ability of industry to produce final products with the need to provide income for new research and development. Again, an underlying premise is that wide, liberal licensing will provide not only the widest benefits, but will maximize the rewards for the developers of the technology and for the Hub Group.

Also, because the patent filings will focus on only the most fundamental upstream developments, the patents can be prepared and managed by a small group of people.

27.5.3 Illustrative Scenarios

Scenario A: Government, Academia, Hub Group

A group of academicians, possibly working at a number of facilities around the world, have developed their science to the point where breakthroughs to basic practical technology are possible. In order to obtain funding they approach the Hub Group because of the Hub Group's focus in a related area and because the Hub Group will allow the academicians to control the direction of their research.

The Hub Group approaches government and requests funding in return for agreements to make the results broadly available within that country. The government agency has a need for the technology, a mission that includes promoting that technological area, or perhaps considers that the project will promote the general welfare, and thus provides the funds the Hub Group has requested.

The academicians obtain ongoing funding for conducting basic research and enhance the prestige of their institution. The government obtains new technologies, keeps its country involved in the technology at a relatively low cost, and enhances the status of the government. The Hub Group receives new IP resources that will eventually increase the flow of funding through the hub to fund further research and development.

Scenario B: Business, Academia, Hub Group

A Hub Group has developed a human network related to a key technology and, through development, possesses intellectual property in that technology. The Hub Group approaches or is approached by a business that is interested in developing a new product. The Hub Group assembles a research team that knows the technology and quickly develops the technology to a prototype level. The business then develops, packages and markets a finished product.

The business benefits from the development of the prototype by acknowledged experts and financially from the sale of its new product. The academicians benefit from receiving funding to be able to explore the boundaries of their field further. The Hub Group benefits from the flow through the hub of upfront or license fees paid by the business.

Scenario C: Government, Business, Hub Group

Government may, due to its interest in a certain technology for its own use, encourage business to meet with a Hub Group that has developed that technology. After reviewing the technology, business signs licenses to use the technology and develops a number of products that exploit the advantages of the new technology. In this case, the first customer may be the government.

The business benefits financially from the sale of technology to government and others. The Hub Group benefits from the flow of license fees to recover its investment in the technology, and, as society benefits from a number of new products, the government receives recognition for its support of the technology.

27.5.4 Benefits

By maintaining a separate role from business, academia, and government, a Hub Group provides all entities with advantages and avoids direct competition with any of its client entities. This structure ensures that the Hub Group remains focused on IP creation (i.e. research) and licensing and will give the Hub Group the flexibility to form effective working relationships and realize successful cross-sector collaboration.

Since the Hub Group focuses on the development and patenting of fundamental technology across a broad range of science, there is a broader range of coverage than if individual universities or researchers were to file individual patents. This avoids the problem of each university or group having its own narrow interest that will not be worth as much as an integrated package of fully thought out and integrated technologies.

A Hub Group will be in a better position to receive public funding than a traditional large corporation because the Hub Group will be able to provide a coordinated effort that will provide maximum benefit to all downstream entities, including all large corporations and the public. There is no benefit to the Hub Group in keeping its developments secret and tightly held. The inclusive nature of the model more readily complies with the ideals of most public entities, the development of the common good and the promotion of general prosperity.

27.5.5 Issues

It is important for the Hub Group to maintain a small enough size that operating costs do not rise, as is occasionally the case in government or government institutions that grow too large and bureaucratic. By staying small and efficient, the Hub Group can provide maximum benefit to all entities by providing an efficient hub through which information, ideas and money flow with little resistance.

While focusing on fundamental development, the pace of change and development may require that Hub Groups also consider relationships regarding the development of consumer products and the co-development of applications. However, this may cause problems because, as indicated, the proposed model holds that this commercial market is best managed by focusing upstream. This caution is also important in light of the short lifespan of commercial products and the general, and understandable, lack of interest among pure researchers in pursuing downstream products.

27.6 Ongoing Experiment

In order to prove the concept of the new network model we have invested a large amount of time and money in an ongoing experiment. We have been working hard to create a Hub Group that embodies the ideals listed above. It is our hope that if our experiment proves successful, others will also use the model.

Our experiment has gone through some difficult growing pains as we have refined the details and presented the model to different entities, but, on the whole, the model has been very successful to date.

We have focused on the emerging technology of homotopy [3–5] and have been successful in developing an international network of interested parties in all sectors: business, academia and government.

Initial applications for fundamental IP rights have been made. Although we work with a very small staff, we have already filed more than 50 fundamental applications. Of those applications, several have been allowed covering very broad patent rights.

We have also been able to effectively link international researchers in Italy with government funding (as an eventual end-user) from Japan to develop some aspects of the homotopy technology to prototype level.

Our next challenge is to use our business contacts to complete the integration and produce groundbreaking new technology for the general public.

27.7 Conclusions

In this chapter we have proposed a new network model for interaction among business, academia and government. Although the proposed model is still in its development stage we feel that it has a very good chance of success. We have already had some very favorable results in our ongoing test of the model. It is our hope that once we can prove the benefits of the network model, other Hub Groups will appear and help lead to further advances in fundamental science and their application in daily life.

In the future, we envisage a further point of convergence in which these Hub Groups also connect, creating an even larger network and thereby increasing the flow and development of fundamental science and eventually leading to vast improvements in the human condition.

References

[1] *Paris Convention For The Protection Of Industrial Property* of March 20, 1883, as revised at Brussels on December 14, 1900, at Washington on June 2, 1911, at the Hague on November 6, 1925, at London on June 2, 1934, at Lisbon on October 31, 1958, and at Stockholm on July 14, 1967 (gopher://gopher.law.cornell.edu:70/00/foreign/fletcher/UNTS11851.txt).
[2] *Patent Cooperation Treaty* (PCT) Done at Washington on June 19, 1970, amended on September 28, 1979, and modified on February 3, 1984 (http://www.wipo.org/eng/pct/treaty/pct.htm).
[3] TL Kunii (1997) The 3rd industrial revolution through integrated intelligent processing systems, in *Proceedings of IEEE First International Conference on Intelligent Processing Systems*, 28-31 October, Beijing, New York, The Institute of Electrical and Electronics Engineers, pp. 1–6.
[4] TL Kunii (1998) Graphics with shape property inheritance, in *Proceedings of Pacific Graphics '98 (PG98)*, 26–29 October, Singapore, Los Alamitos, CA, IEEE Computer Society Press, pp. 2–6.
[5] Y Shinagawa and TL Kunii (1991) The Homotopy Model: a generalized model for smooth surface generation from cross sectional data, *The Visual Computer*, 7(2–3), 72–86.

28

A Research Agenda for Visualization and Human Interfaces: a Position Paper

Charles Koelbel

28.1 Introduction

Computer Science research in the USA has recently been energized by the final report of the President's Information Technology Advisory Committee (PITAC). The full report is available at `http://www.hpcc.gov/ac/report/`. In its executive summary, the committee stated:

> Information Technology will be one of the key factors driving progress in the 21st century – it will transform the way we live, learn, work, and play. Advances in computing and communications technology will create a new infrastructure for business, scientific research, and social interaction. This expanding infrastructure will provide us with new tools for communicating throughout the world and for acquiring knowledge and insight from information. Information technology will help us understand how we affect the natural environment and how best to protect it. It will provide a vehicle for economic growth. Information technology will make the workplace more rewarding, improve the quality of health care, and make government more responsive and accessible to the needs of our citizens...

> The Nation needs significant new research on computing and communication systems. This research will help sustain the economic boom in information technology, address important societal problems such as education and crisis management, and protect us from catastrophic failures of the complex systems that now underpin our transportation, defense, business, finance, and healthcare infrastructures. If the results are to be available when needed, we must act now to reinvigorate the long-term IT research endeavor and to revitalize the computing infrastructure at university campuses and other civilian research facilities, which are rapidly falling behind the state of the art. If we do not take these steps, the flow of ideas that have fueled the information revolution over the past decades may slow to a trickle in the next.

Regarding human–computer interfaces, PITAC recommended:

Recommendation: Support fundamental research in human–computer interfaces and interaction.

The purpose of many computer applications is to inform people. Moreover, most computer applications require information and guidance from us. Yet the interaction between people and computers is still primarily limited to very rudimentary actions and outputs, such as keyboard strokes, simple gestures using pointing devices such as a mouse or touch-sensitive screen, and textual and simple graphical output on displays. People are capable of far richer interaction. More to the point, humans are perceptual creatures, using all their varied sensory systems in concert to form a harmonious interpretation of the environment. The sensory-motor systems of the human brain are tightly integrated, yet in our computer programs, computer inputs (from human motor systems) and computer output (which go to human sensory systems) are treated as independent and somewhat unrelated activities.

People and computers both deserve better. Fundamental research in human sensory-motor systems, perception, attention, pattern recognition, and decision-making has the potential to make dramatic improvements in the interaction of people and machines...

Recommendation: Fund more fundamental research in information management techniques to (1) capture, organize, process, analyze and explain information and (2) make information available for its myriad uses.

We already have on-line access to vast quantities of information. Now the challenge is finding the right information quickly and easily, and using it effectively. Ideally, the information will come to us in anticipation of our needs. The Committee recommends increased funding for basic research on capturing, organizing, processing, and using information. Information management is based on the classic computer science disciplines of new and better data structures and algorithms, but also includes theories and new approaches to digital libraries, databases, knowledge discovery, data visualization, and information-intensive applications. Software tools that augment our intelligence and increase our productivity will be key components of the Nation's prosperity in the future.

This chapter suggests how some of these recommendations might be realized. We address two sides of this question:

- *Visualizing large and remote data.* Every interface is a presentation of *something* (presumably of interest to the user). These presentations cannot be uncoupled from the data driving them, nor from the computation that prepared that data. We therefore consider the needs and research opportunities for dealing with demanding data-driven applications.
- *The human–computer interface.* Carefully prepared data is worthless if users have difficulty accessing and comprehending it. The presentation of the same data may differ depending on the audience; for example, high-quality graphics are useless to a blind person. We therefore consider the needs and research opportunities for developing the interfaces themselves.

28.2 Visualizing Large and Remote Data

As the memory, secondary storage and computational capacity of computers have increased, so has the amount of data available for study. This is perhaps most notable in the scientific arena, where simulations of realistic three-dimensional physical phenomena are now possible. The Advanced Scientific Computing Initiative (ASCI), for example, has performed computations on billion-zone fluid dynamics problems that generate terabyte data sets (see `http://www.lanl.gov/ASCI/`, `http://www.llnl.gov/asci/` and `http://www.sandia.gov/ASCI/` for more detailed examples). Physical experiments and observations are also creating a flood of data; the NASA Earth Observing System (EOS) will soon generate 1 Tbyte of data per day (see `http://eospso.gsfc.nasa.gov/` for more information on that project). In addition, companies are collecting huge data warehouses of transactions for analysis. Although the details of the sizes are proprietary, some indication of their size (and importance to the company) can be gleaned from the fact that the Wal-Mart discount store chain now owns the largest non-classified supercomputer in the USA. Finally, there is increasing interest in combining networked collections of data. The NSF-sponsored Digital Libraries Initiative, for example, is sponsoring consortia to build interlinked networks of national libraries and scientific data banks. Indeed, another recommendation of the PITAC report was to develop a "National Digital Library [to] integrate all electronic knowledge sources, including books, journals, music, films, and informal 'documents.'".

Endless reams of data, however, are not necessarily directly useful. Anybody who has used the current generation of World Wide Web search engines knows the frustrations of sorting through too much information. Even well-organized data sets, such as regularly indexed time-step data from a CFD calculation, are too large for humans to comprehend directly. This problem becomes much worse when the user must access data across a network; not only is the data difficult to comprehend, but the response time is too long to keep users interested. The solution is to find ways to organize, summarize, reduce and transform the data in order to bring out its essence. Accomplishing this task, in turn, requires developments in the algorithms, applications software, systems software and hardware that will process the data.

For historical reasons, we tie all of these activities together with the word "visualization". Unfortunately, the word is a misnomer – vision is not the only sense that we can engage to present the information to people. Nor is the information necessarily presented to any human – data reduction techniques also provide compression for faster reading and writing, and the reduced data structures often provide the basis for more efficient algorithms in further processing. However, we will continue to use "visualization" until a better term comes along.

The characteristics of the new data sources and new uses we are finding for them drive many of the challenges for data visualization. Areas with the most need for new development include:

1. *Large data storage and processing.* Electrons in semiconductors move at the speed of light, while disks rotate at the speed of sound. This simple fact explains much of the growing IO bottleneck for large computations. New hardware technologies such as holographic storage may improve access speeds, but they will not be able to keep up with CPU improvements as long as Moore's Law holds. Parallelism ("disk farms") is an obvious way to increase capacity, but without intricate system software this does not solve latency and

bandwidth limitations. In addition, redundant design is necessary for reliability as systems scale to thousands of devices. We need research in fundamental algorithms for parallel IO, including contributions from database techniques, out-of-core algorithms and scheduling methods.

2. *Remote data access.* There are hundreds of research universities and institutes in the world, many with unique data collections. Collaborations require either moving some researchers to this data, or moving the data to all the researchers; most researchers prefer the latter. The technical problems in doing so, however, are substantial. Faster network hardware is part of the answer, but more efficient data access is equally important. Data subsetting and compression reduce the demands on any network. Progressive rendering, multi-resolution data structures and quality of service guarantees can improve the interactive performance for users. We need research in all of these areas.

3. Hierarchical and heterogeneous data representations. A large data set is used for many purposes: qualitative exploration, quantitative analysis and visualizations for technical talks and for non-technical public presentations. Satisfying all these uses using a single data representation is challenging at best. Moreover, many large data sets are actually combinations of data from various sources, such as a merging of satellite observations with mapping data. Format mismatches make this a difficult process, even when there are no questions about the mathematics of corresponding data. Recent work in hierarchical methods, such as level sets and tree structures, gives some hope that unified methods are possible. Much more research is needed, however, to develop a theory of creating structures to represent many levels of detail, possibly to different users.

In addition, new visualization techniques need wide exposure, testing and (if successful) adoption. One way to accomplish this is by providing common interfaces, including standard application programming interfaces (APIs). Setting true standards in a fast-moving field is a tricky business, and is often counter-productive. However, researchers need to collaborate with each other and industry to agree on common frameworks and, to the extent possible, make their work interoperable.

28.3 The Human–Computer Interface

Although computers are ever more powerful, we cannot seem to make better use of them. For the past three decades, Moore's Law has given us a growth rate of 60% per year in computer power. Over the same period, the increase in human productivity using those computers has been below 5% per year, at least as measured by economic statistics. Explanations for these phenomenons vary: slow adoption of computer technology, inaccurate productivity measurement and feedback in the economy have all been suggested. Everyday experience, however, suggests that at least part of the explanation is the prevalence of poor interface design. From personal computers to the latest teraflop machine, users complain about difficulty of use. At the societal level, we need to spend more time working with information and less time working with our machines' quirks. Nor is economic productivity the only concern with interfaces. Interfaces to safety-critical systems, such as aircraft controls, must be understood quickly to reduce operator error. Equally important, such systems must respond interactively to user input to control the situation. Interfaces for universal access are both a technical issue and a political one (in the USA). PITAC recommends working toward "easy access for all people, regardless of economic circumstances, physical impairment, or intellectual limitations", particularly by depending less on manual dexterity, visual or auditory acuity, or specialized languages. Advocates of universal access point out that these steps will improve the interface for both handicapped and non-handicapped users.

Solving the above problems requires research in interface fundamentals. Before all else, we need cognitive science studies to understand the principles of human perception and its relation to computer displays. We can hardly hope to present data intuitively without a basic model of how the user will handle the information. We also need models for translation from machine representations to human perceptions; these will provide the algorithms for the displays, and possibly inspire new displays to present. Even as those studies are under way, we must start new research in implementing and extending interfaces. Some of the most fruitful areas for research include:

1. *Natural language processing.* It is a truism of interface design that "The best interface is no interface". Speech is an obvious means of achieving this goal, since most people use it from an early age. Unfortunately, progress in incorporating human language has been slow. Unlike most computer inputs, natural language is rife with context-sensitive references, ambiguous expressions and imprecise meaning. In addition, audio input tends to be "noisy" and difficult to decipher. We need more research to increase both the reliability and speed of natural language understanding; this will require both improved heuristics for existing algorithms and entire new methods to recognize new structures.

2. *Multimodal displays.* Confucius said, "A good picture is worth a thousand words". The ancient sages never quantified a good sculpture, but adding a third dimension is clearly worth a healthy premium. All this goes to show that natural language is not the only, or even most desirable, interface. Visual, audio and haptic feedback is necessary to draw users into a virtual environment. (Smell and taste may also be required in some applications, such as medical simulators.) As these technologies come online, future users will think that today's GUIs are as impoverished as today's users think that 1970s text interfaces were. We need more research in good algorithms to drive these advanced displays, as well as innovative metaphors using these displays. In short, we need the haptic equivalent of an icon.

3. *Sensors and actuators.* Returning to the theme of "the best interface is no interface", we might want the machine to accept input without the user's (explicit) guidance. For example, knowing where the user is looking would allow the system to increase screen resolution in that area. Tracking such details unobtrusively requires much-improved sensors for light, position, speed, sound and other measurements. Fortunately, such sensors are becoming more common and affordable. We still need more input, however, in integrating

their information with the rest of the system. Similarly, MEMS devices provide very small actuators; applications today include adapting the shape of skis to snow conditions. We need research to integrate these small-scale motions into large-scale physical systems.

Acknowledgments

Thanks first go to the participants in the NSF Computer Graphics and Scientific Visualization Science and Technology Center, who provided much background on the needs of visualization and interfaces. I would also like to thank Michael Lesk of the National Science Foundation for many helpful comments on research on human–computer interfaces, as well as presentation materials that formed the basis of the HCI section. The views and opinions expressed in this chapter are the author's own and do not imply the endorsement of the government of the United States of America or any agency thereof.

29

Publishing Technologies: Towards a Wider Concept of Documents and Related Issues

Jürgen Schönhut

Abstract

Our concept of a document is perhaps modeled and certainly highly dependent on our previous experience. This experience is mainly derived from dealing with printed documents. However, in the past decade, "electronic documents" have become a predominant focus of attention. But even with electronic documents, the "resemblance" to paper is still evident. In this chapter I want to express some of the critical issues that are related to this. Before going into more depth with some of those issues, I would like to explain my concept of a document.

29.1 The Fundamentals of Documents

Documents are a *structured collection of information*. We will not define "information" but accept a general meaning like that in "information processing" etc., which implies content. In their representation both structure and content are indispensable and significant components.

In addition, each document may have one or more presentations. Each presentation of a document is governed by some *layout* mechanism, for paper documents as well as for electronic documents.

Access to documents is characterized by its ease of use; *accessibility of information* provides the availability of up-to-date information for personal use. This access must be *structured access* which allows multiple concurrent access structures to the same information.

Documents offer the possibility of *interaction with information*. Documents are no longer passive pieces of information only. Documents may contain active components. Active documents may contain or may even be programs in our common terminology. They are still documents.

29.2 Information Components of a Document

The information components which constitute a document can be of a variety of types. Here is a non-exhaustive list of *information types in documents*:

- *Text, graphics* and *images* are items well known already from classical paper documents.
- *Sound* is a medium that has been available for a long time; advances in compression techniques have made the integration of sound straightforward.
- *Speech* is an alternate presentation for text, which has sound as a low-level representation.
- *Music* may be seen as already covered by sound, but here not only a digitized acoustical representation of music has to be taken into consideration; musical scores and notes of music are another important incarnation of music.
- *Animation*, both as sequences of images played in time, as well as the scene descriptions and scripts that making the scenes move, is required.
- *Links*, or references, are a convenient concept for distributing different pieces of information and loading components only when they are needed.
- *Synchronization* is a critical aspect for integration of different media, and especially for media integration.
- *Models* of scenes or processes can be used for representations of complex 3D applications; a typical representative in the context of the internet is VRML, the Virtual Reality Modeling Language.
- *Video* is of course a necessary data type; in contrast to animation, video already contains integrated sound. A generalized concept of "generalized video" may contain other objects, such as sequences of regions of interest or links to related animation.
- *Algorithms*, or *programs*, are important components in multimedia documents today. Different scripts and the technologies around Java (e.g. applets for WWW applications), are typical representatives of this group.
- *Forms* are a common means of allowing a certain degree of interactivity in multimedia applications.
- In a world of more and more network connections and firewalls to protect information, *security* becomes a critical issue. *Authentication* is one aspect to be considered. *Encryption* methods are another means of protecting information from unauthorized access. In addition to encryption, different types of *watermarking*, allowing the distribution of information to be traced, have come into use.
- *Intellectual Property Rights (IPR)* must be embedded and protected in order for electronic markets with electronic documents to flourish.
- *Annotations* are also becoming common; an annotation can be just for personal use, or it can be open to public access.

29.3 Active Documents

In the past documents used to be data only. There existed a strong dichotomy between data and programs. This has changed over the past few years. We have come a long way from training manuals to simulators for training, with material from training handbooks included. Documents may have integrated active components.

Active electronic documents often imply an object-oriented view on data which are associated with the respective methods that allow access and manipulation of those data. On media integration this leads to media data associated with media-specific methods. Modern Web technologies support this concept.

29.4 Some Problems To Be Solved

Here we will consider a list of critical issues which can lead to research problems related to documents as explained before.

- Some problems are related to the reuse of information, an area often associated with *cross-media publishing.*

  There is a strong need for *meta-data, data about data,* and for new formats encompassing all information required to make these data useful for publication on different media. This ranges from specific meta-data describing the valid range of parameters, e.g. for a color management system, to information describing rules for *mapping preferences to specific environments.* Especially critical with regard to different presentation media is layout. A critical data type in this regard is text. It is not sufficient to lay out text on screen in an identical way to paper – nobody really wants to scroll large portions of text on the display in order to read it. One can think of alternative presentation styles, e.g. *speech output for text,* under certain circumstances. For some applications the *concept of an intentional layout* is required, where not the layout but the layout intention is specified. As an example we can consider emergency room documentation, where many vital parameters are measured and displayed for observation. In such an emergency room environment it may be necessary for safety reasons to present all vital parameters as curves using an identical time axis.

- *Quality of document presentation* is another critical issue that still requires much research. It is not always possible to measure quality, but it may be compared, and there may be more dimensions of quality that the ones discussed here.

  Much has been done with regard to *device-independent color* by specifying ICC profiles, but still a lot of work remains to provide solutions that are really practical for printing (here I mean high-quality printing, e.g. on an offset press). The solutions provided today can improve desktop quality, but are absolutely insufficient for offset printing. A quick look at press shops that have tried to implement ICC and color management proves the correctness of this statement. The presentation quality should only be limited by device, not by insufficiencies in the information process.

- Issues linked with the emergence of new *display technologies* need consideration here.
  - Recent developments have surfaced that may lead to new media for display output. Especially promising is the work around *organic light-emitting diodes (OLED)* displays. This may revolutionize display and projection techniques, and it may be able to remove the restrictions of displays which have led to the problems of lack of display space and resolution.
  - Another technology needing attention is *digital holography* and its application to displays. 3D displays using digital holography may have the advantage that they can provide the appropriate movement parallax and natural convergence and accommodation of the eyes. I believe digital holography will probably need another five to ten years of R&D in order to compete in a meaningful way with other technologies for 3D display. Much research is still needed in this area to be ready when the technology is ready. Among others, parallelization and high-speed numeric computation, as well as possible hybrid solutions, are the key research topics here.
  - Research into the combination of conventional laser projection technology with *holographic screens* may also lead to a landmark in computer projection technologies used for display.
- *Speech output* can highly enrich human–computer communication.
  - With regard to speech output, the generation of *synthetic voice* needs improvement. In order for the human to be satisfied, speech presentation should be done with a human-like voice for which one can define preferences, e.g. should this be a male or a female voice, pleasing or alarming? A rule-based system together with a thesaurus for pronunciation can be utilized to generate a method similar to spell-checking for written text: a speech-checker tool.
  - Together with improved voice input this can make up a much more *natural interface* to the computer for humans. Such new interactive interfaces should, not surprisingly, include agents like talking heads transferring an expression of emotion when talking to the user, an approach that is also included in *digital storytelling*. In this area a cross-disciplinary look at productive systems in communities of illiterates may give a good starting point for progress. With the application of production rules in oral tradition, which are built upon a plot and an exposition of "tales", can give insight to digital storytelling issues. Such rules are needed (and they may prove similar to the way in which MPEG-4 works). They may well provide a model for digital story telling.
- *Paper document identification* is a necessary complement to the electronic equivalent of links.

  The *intelligent paper* approach from Xerox is a solution to uniquely referencing printed documents (and parts thereof). However, it requires a special paper with identification invisible to the human eye. Allowing each document to contain its identification, even in a visible form, can allow more efficient handling of paper documents. So 2D bar codes, for example, could be used for document identification. This requires a unique referencing scheme that is either a *universal document resource locator*, or at least unique in a certain application environment, e.g. in the context of a document management system.

- The *document creation process* will also need drastic improvement.

In the document creation process we observe a combination of design and content creation. Many documents, especially company documents, are formed according to special corporate design (CD) rules. These rules should not be violated, and the content creator should not bother about these rules. Instead of having each document designed by a designer, one can imagine providing a *design-rule driven document creation environment* allowing the designer to produce the generic design, with a software system providing the implementation of the document design for a specific content.

29.5 Perspectives

Documents are an interesting field of *interdisciplinary* research. This implies a richer and wider concept of documents, as explained above. With advances in technology many solutions can be worked out that were possible in the past. Sometimes we tend to believe that we are witnessing completely new ideas, ingenious new inventions; all seems to be new – doesn't it? On the other hand it is quite clear that we sometimes regard solutions as new because we don't know any better – they are not new at all. I am not saying that those inventors or developers were plagiarists, but many ideas have come around several times before finally being realized in practice. Let me present here a small example that allows a reflection on early visions. It not only shows a vision that pre-dates the technology (the Web), but also contains allusions to possible new meanings for our previous experience.

H.G. Wells, in an essay entitled "The brain organization of the modern world" (Wells, 1938) had foreseen many of these new inventions, and the following is just a list of quotes from his essay to give an idea of how advanced his thinking was.

He talks about the evolution of a "World's Knowledge Apparatus" that contains a "wealth of knowledge dispersed, unorganized"; doesn't this remind us of some of the information chaotically unorganized in the Web? Wells eventually talks about a "world encyclopaedia", a "World Brain" that "need not be concentrated in one place", but "might have the form of a network". A "world brain" can be understood as active, as outlined earlier. This "Standard Encyclopaedia" is "published for individual use", and forms a "perpetual digest and conference"; he also refers to it as a "system of publication and distribution".

When I first read this it really struck me, and I have since found many other examples of ideas that could not be realized at the time, but which came about as fantastic new inventions of later times.

Sometimes we need to be reminded of the fact that ideas come here and there, often independently of each other, and sometimes ideas are too new and advanced, so they get forgotten again – and at some time later, when common thinking has adopted, they reappear and lead to a real breakthrough. I hope that at least some ideas may be taken up and lead to an advancement of the document community.

Reference

Wells, HG (1938) The brain organization of the modern world, in *World Brain*, Doubleday, New York, pp. 40–57; reprinted in Cawkell, AE (ed.) (1987) *Evolution of an Information Society*, London, Aslib, pp. 155–164.

About the Author

Jürgen Schönhut obtained his PhD (Dr. phil.) in 1972 with a thesis in Computational Linguistics. After that he worked as scientist at the Regional Computer Center of the University of Erlangen-Nürnberg from mid-1972 to the end of 1985 (responsible for non-numerics, computer graphics and image processing). Since January 1986 he has been head of department at the Fraunhofer-Institut für Graphische Datenverarbeitung (IGD), Darmstadt.

He had various teaching obligations at the universities of Erlangen-Nürnberg, Tübingen, Frankfurt/Main and Darmstadt. From 1979 to 1990 he was active in standardization, and from 1983 to 1990 he was chairman of ISO JTC1/SC24 Computer Graphics. From 1991 to 1992 he was elected Chairman of the Eurographics Association. Since the end of 1993 he has directed the scientific work of the CIP3 consortiums (International Cooperation for Integration of Prepress, Press, and Postpress) to allow computer-integrated manufacturing of print products.

Since his study at the university he has been dealing with interdisciplinary projects.

He has published a textbook on document imaging with Springer-Verlag: *Document Imaging – Computer Meets Press* (1997).

30
The Future and Its Enemies

Bertram Herzog

30.1 Introduction

It is generally accepted that the current state of information technology, especially as epitomized by its most widely distributed products, is less than optimal, if not downright bad. This chapter seeks to offer a proposal for altering the situation and hopes that colleagues will add their insights either to reject the initial assumption (unlikely) or, more likely, to refine or replace the proposal.

Today we have enormous computing power at our fingertips and at consumer and disposable prices. This book's contributors provide their visions, inventions, and points of view that will extol a glorious vision of the future and even greater advances to come. Nevertheless, I feel it is necessary to examine the current situation lest we build the next generation of products on the shaky foundation of current products.

At this point, I want to mention the "Principle of Least Astonishment". Simply put, it states that one should not be astonished by the results obtained from a computer. This statement, originally offered in the good old batch processing days, surely applies more urgently in today's highly interactive computing world. The principle needs to be applied, in my opinion, as a test for all computer applications and innovations.[1] On that basis alone, I believe current products are shaky. This conclusion is emphatically supported by Norman in his book *The Invisible Computer* (Norman, 1998), wherein he identifies the folly of ever more technopower, more megabytes and more megahertz, rather than attending to users' needs or requirements. Norman identifies a solution that favors the notion of limited and specific task-oriented information appliances. I want to propose another, though complementary, solution. The solution will specify architectural considerations and design and manufacturing process matters.

---

1   Need one mention the blinking interface of VCRs?

437

30.2 The Complaint or Problem

So what is the complaint? What we deliver as information products are of alarmingly low quality. I use many of the so-called productivity tools on a regular daily basis. I hardly ever write with pen or pencil any more. My laptop computer and its word processor, the spreadsheet program, several database products and the slide maker might just as well be attached via an umbilical cord. I can more easily do without my automobile than without my laptop or desktop computer. However, violations of the Principle of Least Astonishment alone descend upon me with astonishingly high frequency. The surprises are never-ending. Worse, however, are the occasions when what should be conceptually and easily satisfied eludes the user trying to ferret out the "how to" from the user interface, from the manual if it exists or is incomplete, or from the help file.

Like so many others I use these products because they help me do my daily work. Like so many others I can use trial and error to solve problems. Electronic spreadsheets are the liberators from green eyeshades and paper spreadsheets. The improved productivity is real. To dampen this enthusiasm, however, we can point out that all too often it takes dedicated persistence to climb the learning curve when easy and intuitive methods should be available. The marketers can demonstrate that millions of happy users are using these tools. My conjecture is that these millions are each using less than 5% of what is provided. Do they need more? Would they use more if it were made readily available? Good questions. We can invoke the 80–20 rule. Eighty per cent of people probably don't need more. The other 20% would like to use more if they could discover what is available or, if known to be available, if they could find out how to use it. When I claim that most people use less than, say, 5% of the potential, I must hasten to add that it is not the same 5% for each individual.

Early instantiations of word processors were simple and the interface presented itself accordingly. For example, the taxonomy of a document could be: a document consists of sections or chapters; sections consist of paragraphs; paragraphs could be styled and each style could be named and have its attributes specified. Documents could be presented on pages whose margins were specifiable. Each element of this taxonomy could be clearly and reasonably independently described and specified. Interaction between these elements could be specified so that widows and orphans could behave in a specified manner – if not always in the expected manner in the execution! A good taxonomy would be implemented using object-oriented principles. Paragraphs would be a member of an object class that would include tables and graphical objects. We need not mention the concept of pointers to embrace the advantages of hypertext. So much for simple principles upon which to build more complex and specialized (for the local knowledge pool and needs) custom applications.

Instead, we now have feature bloat. Word processors, for example, have evolved into feature-laden applications (see Figure 30.1). Norton states that Microsoft Word, by 1992, had 311 commands, but five years later, the count had reached 1033 commands. That is a lot of commands to explore for their possible utility. Each feature useful for some specialized purpose is used to enlarge the pool of non-overlapping five-per-centers. However, if one of these initially satisfied users wants to

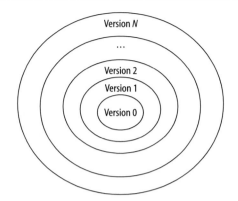

Figure 30.1 Structure of current application demonstrating feature bloat.

venture toward another use then these unprincipled features refuse to bend, intuitively or via documentation, to meet that need. I want to be able to extend a particular use in a smooth and incremental way.

Those that disagree with this complaint dismiss it by stating "Of course, I turn off
all those features before I even use the word processor". Unwittingly, they under-
score my position on this matter. Further, it should be noted that "turning off"
these features is not such an obvious alternative for most users. Why not reverse the
situation? Start out with a concise but capable core, which can be extended to
provide features, built upon the core, and able to be invoked by those needing the
specialized feature. It used to be possible to instruct novices easily in the use of
word processors using a simple taxonomy and its associated structure. Now it is
necessary to remember where to find each feature distributed over menus in an
unpredictable manner.

The Luddites refuse to use newer versions of the feature-bloated applications. A
typical comment is: "I continue to use my older Mac and MacWrite, thank you".
This is just fine for the isolated user who is totally content with the increased
productivity of an older, less capable, but sufficiently productive application. That
same Luddite, however, also reported recently that when seeking help with an older
version of a slide-making program he was told by the original supplier: "We no
longer support that version, but you can obtain help from Company X specializing
in support for the unsupported version" – at $37/hour, of course.

Apart from isolation, the ultimate result of not keeping up with the latest versions
eventually leads to inoperability when the computer fails and a newer model needs to
be purchased. The cherished old friendly application will not run and the Luddite
must catch up with the latest and greatest after all. The vendor is the apparent victor.

30.3 The Architectural Solution

What I seek is a conceptually clear and compact architecture for the application,
and its application core, that is able to perform the fundamental operations. Such a

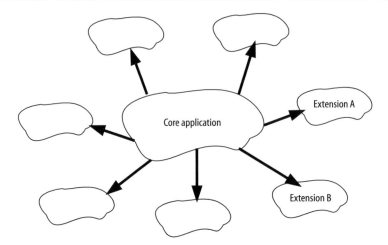

Figure 30.2 Architecture allowing user-specialized extensions.

core application can then be extended and provided with specialized user features and interfaces to match a particular market segment (Figure 30.2). Developing such an application tempts one to classify it as a good engineering accomplishment – a successful software engineering accomplishment. Clearly, we have not yet reached this ideal.

30.4 The Process Solution

That the process of creating information technology products is faulty is not subject to argument. To put it more civilly, the process can be improved. But how? Norton and others argue that technologists dominate the industry. Engineers fiddle with a product without considering what a user wants. These critics propose, as an antidote, that marketing should and must control the products. They assert that to find out what a user wants we need marketing people. Only they can find out what users want, and thus the marketing people must specify what engineers should produce. At a recent meeting of a software consortium this credo of distinction between engineers (read programmers) and marketing people was religiously upheld.

The implied lesson is that users can describe what they want and engineers can produce the consequent application to achieve the desired result. However, a good dose of technical analysis and knowledge can be and must be used to obtain a far more reasonable and efficient result. Technical efforts in the absence of user input (market studies) are as foolish as using market studies alone to specify technical requirements. I blame the feature bloat, mentioned above, on an excess of real or perceived market-driven demands with insufficient technical analysis to define the core technical application capable of meeting those demands in a coherent technical manner. This is a faulty overreaction which can be construed to be the source of the feature bloat mentioned above. The dichotomy of technologists and marke-teers is too simplistic. Therefore it is appropriate to make a proposal.

30.5 A Proposal

As a starting point, I borrow freely from the automobile industry. The products deliv-ered by all car makers appear to satisfy market demands. Further, the product is deliv-ered on time: when new car models are to appear in the showroom they are there.

The software production and delivery process can be modeled with four essential elements:

- Marketing
- Product planning
- Engineering (or engineering product design)
- Manufacturing (including especially quality assurance)

Here neither marketeers nor technologists are ignored. One of the roles of marketing is to measure what customers want. Ultimately, marketing must define market niches and sales strategies to help the sales force deliver the product.

There are two distinctive features I want to emphasize: product planning and product design. Product planning is a separate function in the quartet of marketing, product planning, design and manufacturing. The role of product plan-ning is to specify the product intended to meet the market demand but with full consideration of the advantages and constraints of design and manufacturing. In software applications the manufacturing process is relatively simple but does include quality assurance and testing – one wonders at times to what degree these two elements are neglected. Engineering design, for automobiles, involves disci-plines such as machine design, electronics and other disciplines, just as analysis and algorithms should in software design. But it does not end there. Drawings are made either by hand or, now, via CAD. These drawings are checked by one or more levels of checkers or supervisors who acknowledge compliance with product plans and engineering practice. It is not news that software engineering generally fails to omit these critical steps of checks and balances. My experience, grounded in such practices, leads me to be cynically suspicious of our software production methods.

As in the automobile industry, the combined roles of engineering and manufac-turing also require special attention in software production. One could argue that in the software industry manufacturing is merely making CDs and manuals and that software development and production are engineering functions. No matter how that is resolved, one can agree that technological innovations originate from engineering/manufacturing. Production of software is similarly a combined responsibility. Structured programming, style recommendations and object-oriented design are recognized as helpful, but are all too often ignored in practice, with designers being the testers and judges of quality. The dismissal of well-estab-lished practices is, in my opinion, a major cause of the malady. Practicing software engineers need to be persuaded about the merits of such practices. These practices are particularly needed in an industry where change and innovation proceed with greater speed than in any other field of engineering.

30.6   A Matter of Attitude or Practice

There is another troublesome behavior or attitude held by information technologists, and especially programmers. How often have you heard the statement: "We are researchers. We do not produce code of production quality. We just cobble up an implementation of our ideas to demonstrate their feasibility. We just barely make a demonstrable prototype".

A sense of double outrage engulfs me when I hear that statement – and I hear it all too often. I value my research efforts too much to endanger them by implementing them with sloppily developed code. How many times have research efforts prompted new and cleverer discoveries? Therefore, I must write well-structured and easily revisable code to meet the demands of new research results. Sloppily written programs will most likely produce erroneous results in the first place. A prototype may not be ready for prime time because it is incomplete for full production use. However, it should never be implemented with other than first-class code. Unfortunately believers in the above quotation not only eschew good programming practice but also almost deliberately hack code that must inevitably be thrown away – seemingly by design! The concept of cobbled code is unprofessional, at least, and possibly evil. The practice of cobbled code can only be deplored and then stamped out.

30.7   Conclusion

An immediate conversion from the present bloated and ill-behaved application to a conceptually concise and compact core application may ultimately be economically necessary, but may not be a marketable idea. Still, avoiding collapse under the sheer weight of bloat demands a strategy of replacement. Before such a replacement can be undertaken we need to recognize the folly of our current practices and move to a more deliberate application-building approach. In other words we have identified the enemy of the future and the enemy is "us". Ending on a note of optimism: if we throw out the old bloats and replace them with the trim and fit replacements, we know that our children will easily adopt our new products.

I hope this chapter will foster some discussion to refine the proposal and to elicit suggestions and directions for the future. If we carry on as we have so far the future is doomed. Let us convert ourselves from enemies to liberators.

References

Norman, DA (1998) *The Invisible Computer*, Cambridge, MA, MIT Press.
Postrel, V (1998) *The Future and its Enemies, The Growing Conflict Over Creativity, Enterprise and Progress*, New York, The Free Press.

Invited Authors

31
New Industrial Temporal Objects

Bernard Stiegler

31.1 Total Digitization

I would like to begin with an affirmation which at first glance may seem shocking, if not iconoclastic: I include television in cinema. For quite some time it has been said that television killed cinema. Today this is heard less often because the interactions between the two media now appear more complex – and cinema is now enjoying better days, luckily. French cinema is dynamic today, owing to the support it gets from TV broadcasters, and to the harmonious interaction over the last decade between television and cinema, regardless of the problems posed by this interaction. For example, one might object that their economic interaction increases the influence of television advertisers and their needs with respect to cinematographic production. And then there is the classic objection: the difference between a cinema screen and the television screen (and now the computer's), with the resulting difference in "spectatorial attitudes".

Given that cinema is that which allows the recording and transmission/distribution of moving images, enabling them to be given back to a public (seated in a movie theater or not), I nevertheless consider television as an epoch of cinema. Moreover, on a more general plane, cinema and television produce audiovisual objects which are also temporal objects. Phonography, cinema, radio and television constitute a sector of the production of industrial temporal objects.

Broadcasting in general is considered to be an industry of program fluxes. Now, if broadcasting can be an industry of flux, this is mainly because an *audiovisual program is itself a temporal flux*. I am using the word here in the sense in which Husserl, the founder of phenomenology, used it. In 1905 Husserl underscored the fact that consciousness is essentially a flux, a passage, a flowing away. Consciousness is first and foremost, and immediately, consciousness of the time of consciousness, consciousness of its own duration. To understand what consciousness is thus requires the understanding of what time is – the same question taken up by Saint Augustine in the fourth century.

In an attempt to answer this question, Husserl begins an analysis of the singular structure of what he calls temporal objects. Such objects, in this context, have nothing to do with objects in time: all real sensate objects are in time. In question here are objects characterized by the conditions whereby they flow away with time and whereby they constitute themselves in this process (in the course of their flowing away) – as for example in the case of a melody.

Since temporal objects are, like consciousness, essentially flowing, then they are the objects of that consciousness they *intertwine* with it, since it too is a flux flowing away. The flowing away of consciousness thus precisely *coincides* – in a certain fashion point by point – with the flowing away of the temporal object.

Audiovisual programs are themselves such temporal objects; the force with which they are able to capture audience attention and in the same stroke to facilitate the process of adoption is in fact a direct result of this characteristic of temporal objects in general.

During the 90 or 52 minute duration of a program, the time of our consciousness passes into the time of these moving images: 90 or 52 minutes of our life pass outside our real life and pass into the life or lives of real or fictitious characters, whose time we make our own by adopting the events happening to us as they are happening to them. The time of the audiovisual program intertwines with our time; the former becomes the temporal woof of these 90 or 52 minutes of the film viewer's unconscious consciousness immobilized by the image movement.

This is because cinema – and in its wake television – combines two fundamental principles.

The first is that cinematographic recording is an extension of photography, which is a technology of analog recording that produces what Roland Barthes called the "effect of the real" or what André Bazin named "the objectivity of the lens".

Cinema is a succession of photographs whose time of pose and projection must not exceed 1/24 per second: under these conditions, movement in the image can be reproduced due to the effects of retinal persistence. This succession constitutes a temporal image flux, wherein lies the second principle of cinema, which can now be examined. To more easily understand this second principle, we shall direct our attention to the talking movie.

With the advent of sound in cinema, phonographic recording is incorporated as well. Like the photograph, the phonogram stems from a technique of artificial analog memorization. This is why what holds for the photograph holds also, but only up to a certain point, for the phonogram: as I listen to a recording of a Toscanini concert or to the voice of Sarah Bernhard, I insert into my listening the fact that the concert actually took place, or that Bernhard's voice was actually the one I now hear. I do not feel as though I am listening to a simple voice or concert reconstruction, but to the voice itself, the concert as it actually took place, coming to me from out of a past at once both irremediably lost and nevertheless conserved in the resin of the recording.

The truth of the photograph, however, is that of the phonogram only up to a certain point. In the case of the phonogram, I am dealing with a fluid object, with a flowing away that modifies the very terms of the analysis: the sound-object is a flux in which it would be impossible to cut out a fixed instant. The sound object cannot be turned into a pose, for even silence lasts and flows away with the consciousness for which there is this silence. It is a temporal object in the Husserlian sense.

If cinema can take on sound, it is because film, as a technique of photographic recording capable of representing movement, is itself a temporal object. A film, like a melody, is essentially a flux, constituting itself in its flowing away. Now this temporal object, as flux, coincides with the flux of consciousness of which it is the object – the consciousness of the spectator, which itself is a flowing away. That is why the spectator can so staunchly adhere to what he or she sees on the screen, to the point of identifying with what happens to the film's heros, whose life stories the spectator adopts during the 90 or 52 minutes it takes the film to flow away.

The singularity of the cinematographic recording technique[1] therefore results from the combination of two coincidences, engendering a double phenomenon of belief and adoption:

- On the one hand, there is the photo-phonographic coincidence between the past time of the cinematographed object, in the form in which in which let out light and sound frequencies, and the time of the present reality of reproduction, which once again emits the same light and sound frequencies. This is the coincidence that induces the effect of the real and the spontaneous belief effect in which the spectator is in advance set by this technique itself.

- On the other hand, we have the coincidence between the flux of the film and the flux of the film's spectator's consciousness, a coincidence which, by the play of fluid movement created between the photographic poses, themselves bonded together by the phonographic flux, sets off the mechanism of total adoption of the film's time by the time of the spectator's consciousness, which in turn, in so far as it is itself a flux, ends up captured and "channeled" by the movement of the images. This is the movement that sets off the movements of consciousness typical of cinematographic emotion.

Televisual channels constitute a programming system of diverse temporal objects set into a grid schedule organized around "rendezvous". This grid constitutes for each broadcast channel a kind of arch-flux which is called, precisely, a channel or station. As a program industry broadcasting temporal objects, this broadcasting organizes a worldwide calendarity controllable second by second based on the time-code. Imparting its rhythm to the time of society, the televisual arch-flux is organized in time segments distinguished by their audiences and their prices for advertisers, and which in the final analysis must measure up to audience ratings.

What's more, if the animated cartoon can be considered a part of cinema (as animated cinema, with the animation of volumes), and if the production of

---

1 Characterized, as Jean-Michel Frodon shows in his *La Projection Nationale, Cinema et Nation*, by "a double mechanism with respect to time: 1) the present recording not only of 'things' as in photography but of duration itself" and 2) "deferred representation". Editions Odile Jacob, 1998, p. 27.

computer-generated images can become a part of cinematographic and televisual production, this is due to the fact that these are all temporal objects.

Thus if one is to apprehend the contemporary stakes of cinema, stakes linked especially to the technological evolution of the digital, television must be included in the question of cinema. You will immediately understand why I have had to maintain this inclusive status for television. I believe that at the present time, due to what can only be a major evolution in broadcasting, which previously has consisted in the mass broadcasting of the same program to hundreds of thousands, millions, and even hundreds of millions of television viewers at the same moment – the digital revolution is bringing about major transformations which will profoundly affect, as a counter-reaction, the world of cinema in the usual sense of the term.

The digital world made its appearance in the audiovisual world in the 1980s, coming on stage from the narrowest of its wings: special effects. This is still the way in which its effects are most generally felt, as the film *Titanic* shows. Following *Tron* and *Blade Runner*, this use of the digital has developed and become widespread while remaining essentially limited to the field of special effects. Today, still, a film producer or director can totally ignore digital techniques or synthesis. No one needs computer-generated images to make a good film. On the other hand, however, these techniques are now omnipresent in the domain of editing and there the question is one of a much more central evolution.

If, then, over the last 15 years the digital has been limited to the field of special effects, the second half of the 1990s has ushered in the first virtual editing centers. Now, most audiovisual productions are edited virtually. This is extremely important: editing is a central function in the process. It is indeed the function *par excellence* of cinema. Virtual editing brings about something radically new, to which I shall return in a moment.

In 1997 something occurred which will mark the history of mass media. The American government, specifically one of its regulating agencies, the FCC (Federal Commission of Communications) which combines if you will the roles of our CSA and ART (which is the state organism is charge of the regulation of all forms of telecommunications, and the broadcasting industry), announced the end of all analog broadcasting by the year 2006. The aim was for the group of 3800 American radio and television stations to be ready for to switch over to total digitization by the year 2003. This means that since 3 April 1997, American broadcasting executives have known that investment in analog techniques is worthless. This is an essential turning point. If, in fact, until 1997 one could still say that digital technology applied to broadcasting and cinema remained marginal, there is no longer any doubt that such technology will become central in the next few years, and that it will have an effect on everything: production, post-production, control room activity and technology and broadcasting. Moreover, a convergence in transmission techniques is taking place in the world of cinema. In California, the possibility of liking up movie theaters by fiber-optic networks is being studied, and the television set is evolving toward the concept of home theater. The process of integration of cinema and broadcasting is intensifying at the level of materials and techniques, well beyond the capitalistic mergers responsible for cinema having been financed mainly by television.

1997 was the beginning of a second era in the development of the digital. Not only have the tools of post-production, editing and special effects now become digital, but so have video cameras, control room apparatus and broadcast/distribution networks. Television stations – for the moment this concerns only news teams – have been equipped with servers capable of storing several hundred hours of programs, which allows the entire PAD to be brought on line. For the moment, this "going on line" is being carried out mainly by station professionals. But soon (I shall come back to this) everything online will be available to the public. Now, owing to the techniques of image compression, digital communication networks now permit the distribution of animated images, which means that the access modes to broadcast programs will be forced to diversify to a considerable extent.

Whereas formerly television broadcasting required just a single network (directed in France by the TDF Hertzien relays), soon all kinds of operators will be offering access to television programs stored in image data banks. There has been, therefore, a complete transformation of a system which for 50 years functioned by combining two analog techniques, that of film production (followed by video) and Hertzien transmission. These two techniques are disappearing and recombining in a totally digital cinema that I call total digitization.

Of course things remain different for cinema in the usual sense of the term – a film still has to be shot. And it is still too early to envisage video cameras with image quality capacity equal to that of cinema. But that day will come. Cinema, for the time being, remains an analog technique. But to the extent that now the duplication of film into digital form is largely done at the editor's level, even here a total integration is on the way.

31.2 The Delinearization of the Audiovisual Flux

The primary consequence of the above is that the mode of television and radio broadcasting will be forced to evolve in upcoming years. Flux broadcasting will progressively yield to stock broadcasting. The access modes of programs by analog–Hertzien broadcasting, now 50 years old, necessarily implies, because of its technical characteristics, a type of television consumerism overdetermined by horo-broadcasting, that is, with the grid of scheduled hour by hour programs. That which governs modes of productions – especially the documentary formats broadcast over stations today – means that for a film, being an analog document, its access can be made available only in sequential form: a producer or broadcaster, in an analog–Hertzien system, has no other choice than to align his or her audiovisual objects on the grid of scheduled programs. This scheduled program is itself built around the "rendezvous". These rendezvous exist as constitutive elements of time segments, which in turn serve as audience targets for advertisers. It is well known, moreover, what effect this has on cinema in those countries in which television advertising is totally uncontrolled by the state: it takes on the form of interruptions in the scenario to allow adverts to be inserted. Today this constraint – horo-broadcasting – brought on by the analog–Hertzien system, is being relaxed due to two major technological innovations which have appeared in the last two years. The first is the MPEG standard, allowing images to be compressed and stored in broadcast format and quality on digital servers without requiring an exorbitant amount of memory space.

Channel 5, in France, has inaugurated a digital server for its main control room. Sylvain Anichini, Channel 5's former technical director, in fact first installed a digital control room to meet the need of the station's professionals, but then realized that the teaching profession, which the station has always prioritized, was not satisfied with the offer of educational, pedagogical programs offered on scheduled grids. These programs correspond in no way to their needs and situations: it is indeed inconceivable that a program of work or classes in a grade or high school be inserted into the scheduled broadcasts of the station – whatever the quality of such programs. Now, the existence of a control room image bank created the initial condition required for an offer of a stock of programs accessible outside the sequential flux of scheduled broadcasts. This was how the first French image bank linked to a TV station was born, and would soon become the showcase of all others of its kind. This is why, to my mind, the total digitization of the audiovisual technical system obeys a logic which will ineluctably lead to the transformation of flux broadcasting into stock broadcasting. The flux will not disappear, but will become an access mode to stocked programs, a showcase that can be contemplated for itself, just as Christmas shoppers admire store windows in big cities before making final decisions for their loved ones.

When you go to the movies, the movie theater proprietor/distributor shows you previews of upcoming films on its network. In fact, the system set up by Channel 5 prefigures a new organization of broadcasting which will use the programming of flux as an enticement to refer viewers to the programming of stock, which is no longer scheduled programming but a program bank accessible through specific instruments; and I believe these instruments will themselves become objects to be produced. This will lead broadcasting industries to commence multiformat and multisupport programming and production.

Let us consider an example. Suppose I teach contemporary history, and that I am watching an interesting programmed television subject (this is the flux) on Channel 5 dealing in 13 minutes with the problem of European construction. I see how, in 13 minutes, I will be able to handle the subject of De Gaulle's relations with Britain in the construction of the ECC, but I would like to explore the subject in more detail and I say to myself: "13 minutes is just fine: they've given me a general idea on how to present my topic. But it's too short. I need more, I need to go deeper into the subject. By consulting the program bank, I gain delinearized access to a two-hour long program". I consider the possibility of delinearizing access modes, for both professionals and the general public, to be the great revolution engendered by image digitization.

What is *delinearization*? To gain access to some specific element of a program, you must scroll through the entire tape or film. This is a time-consuming process. If you are in an archive, and if you are lucky, a slip of paper tells you, using time-code, that your subject is dealt with 45 minutes into the program. Whatever the case, you will have to scroll through the whole program. In other words, you don't have direct access to that part of the document which interests you. With the digital, you do.

This is extremely important. This is delinearization. It is taking effect at two distinct levels. The first is the delinearization of the television grid schedule itself. Passing from flux to stock simply means that hitherto, when you wanted to access a TV program, you had to wait for it to be programmed on the grid of linear time. In an industry of stock, you will be able to directly access a program and thus to escape the constraints of linear broadcast schedules.

In France, programs are called *émissions* because the broadcast model is the broadcast transmitter station broadcasting to the greater viewing/listening public. Now this is precisely the model which will disappear in a few years. A server is not a transmitter, but rather an apparatus giving access to that person who has formulated a request for access. The question thus becomes: what can produce or entice such a request? And what will become of the grid program schedule in such a context? In fact, I don't think the program schedule will disappear. Rather, it will progressively become that which produces and induces requests.

The second important aspect to delinearization is that it will allow users of broadcast program banks to access program elements rather than entire programs. Why? With delinearization, the program becomes a document which can be browsed and to which access to a particular page is possible. Saying "to a particular page" is an obvious reference to the book. The problems were similar, five or six centuries ago: the book used to be in scroll form, and to access particular content you had to unroll the whole book. There was no table of contents, no pagination – access in a certain respect was also sequential. Then the printing press came on the scene, with folioing, the table of contents and navigation tools allowing non-linear access to the material, for example a thesaurus or word-list. When a book is used as a manual, it is not used cursively: you read it discretely, looking for specific elements and consulting the thesaurus or table of contents in order to go directly to the place you want. In the audiovisual world, navigation tools of this kind are being brought into use to delinearize the temporal flux of images. What makes this delinearization possible? On the one hand, the sheer fact of digitally stocking an image allows direct access to it, as on a CD record for example, where you can choose the track you prefer. Before, this had to be done by hand: the stylus had to be placed on the record groove, which could always end up scratched. Now it is all neater: a table of contents is given on the CD player screen.

31.3 Image Analysis

Today we see the development of techniques of automatic or semi-automatic image analysis which permit the identification of the discreet regularities constitutive of the document. To better understand what is at stake here, I will go back through the history of techniques for image compression developed for the world of telecommunications so that audiovisual programs may actually travel over telephone networks.

Compression allows one to greatly diminish the amount of information necessary to digitally copy an animated sequence. A photographic or videographic image is made up of grains or pixels. Digitizing an image consists in the transformation of the value of these points into binary digits. It is, however, more economical to locate homogeneous zones defined by coordinates and to give a value to the whole rather than giving one to each pixel: this cuts the quantity of information to be encoded, and consequently the size of the digital file engendered from the analogy source. What holds for the fixed image is even more interesting for the animated image. A video sequence is composed of shots. A shot is a temporal flux of 25 images per second: a one minute shot is composed of 1500 images. Compression here consists in the encoding only of differences between the shot's images. Between the first and second image of the shot, 1/25th of a second has elapsed, and the differences between the two images are so minute they are invisible to the naked eye. Algorithms of geometrical analysis allow pertinent differences between the two images to be detected, and only those differences are recorded; that is, these algorithms "compress" the shot and then reconstitute the movement during "decompression" through the reconstitution of complete images based solely on differences.

The MPEG standard allows bits of information relevant to the program content to be inserted into the "binary train" of the flux of digitized images, and as soon as the broadcast technologies used by telecommunications networks are sufficiently developed, the television viewer will be able to access stored programs in central digital servers via audiovisual research engines.

Over the next five years, the main question will be access to programs, navigational aids and research into image banks. Documentary skills and technologies will be a key element in the implementation of these audiovisual and hypermedia research engines. The worldwide industry of information technologies is getting ready for this mutation.

Algorithms of digital analysis, developed for the telecommunication requirements of images, now allow for the realization of tools for the automatic or semi-automatic indexing of audiovisual contents. Compression techniques immediately pose the problem of automatic recognition of certain constitutive forms of audiovisual documents. In the first place, an algorithm can only carry out the compression of a shot when it can automatically pick up a change in the shot. But on the other hand, the same algorithm is not used to compress a fixed shot, a panorama or a zoom. The morphogenesis of differences between successive images is each and every time specific. For example, the process of transforming the images that comprise a zoom is controlled by the laws of perspective. Optimizing compression techniques thus leads to the identification of camera movements.

Photograms and videograms can thus be analyzed and manipulated by algorithms recognizing forms, syntax and elements of content. The stakes for the standardization of description formats are so high already that they have become the object of international negotiations which are defining a veritable worldwide grammar of animated and sound images.

In the final analysis, the techniques of digital analysis will allow for the discretization and finally the delinearization of content.

Discretization will be possible to the extent to which contents will be able to be categorized by algorithmic systems capable of distinguishing discrete regularities, that is, lists of elements in finite, combinable digits submitted to compositional rules constitutive of the basic grains of indexation.

We have the delinearization of the flux of an audiovisual temporal object in the sense that the process consists in the description of the structure and contents of the program by referral to the time-code of the videotape, just as in the case of the book, where the summary and index refer back to the corresponding pages. From this point, non-sequential access to vast stocks of programs and audiovisual archives becomes conceivable, and the first video-digital "libraries" will appear.

This is why the documentary unit of the banks of programs to come will no longer be the program itself: these services will allow extracts to be called up, which will themselves be located and described by combining classical documentary analysis and indexing with the new possibilities of form recognition and algorithmic analysis of images and sound (automatic or semi-automatic).

Image digitization will first of all upset existing professional documentary habits in the field of broadcasting (in the reuse of news extracts in news programs as well as in the use of archive images)[2]. But these systems, allowing professionals to navigate among the programs stocked in the control room, will also upset the access modes of the greater viewing public when these control rooms become digital server centers for program stocks for the public itself.

For example, for a program such as a live televised debate, a machine could be used which could automatically recognize that on stage there are eight different people taking part in the debate. Thanks to a series of algorithms, the vocal signal can be separated from the music track or from the background noise. Once the various vocal signatures of the participants have been localized, one can determine where a voice is now, and where it will be three minutes later, and since the vocal cords of the participants have been analyzed, I can say that in a particular sequence eight different people are talking at the same time. From here, I can make automatic annotations and indexations by asking the machine to match the eight participants, to give them variable values: H talks for 4 min 32 s in this document during such and such a segment of the time code. H is present at $T = 1$ min 30 s to 1 min 34 s etc. If I then sample out the vocal values of each recognized participant (here we here Mister de Virieu, here Fabius, here Le Pen) all such formats can be named and I can thus navigate in the document by saying "I only want to see those images and sequences in which Fabius is participating". But how to recognize Fabius when he is speaking and when he is in the image, simultaneously? The solution to this kind of problem combines several different kinds of procedure. To begin with, one uses techniques both of image signature and sampling. Thanks to algorithms of form recognition, I can pick up a silhouette – with varying degrees of accuracy, but which

---

2 The simple face that the flux of the audiovisual temporal object is digitized already permits the indexing of an audiovisual document to be done: no longer in a textual note separate from the physical support of the image itself (as is still the case in the major systems of analog audiovisual archiving) but within the flux of images itself, through the insertion of a "documentary track" along with the shots, in the way that a sound track accompanies its images.

are getting better by day. In this silhouette, I can identify the person speaking; then with samples I will be able to assign parameters to it. I recognize, for example, everything related to the glare of glasses, the texture of a hairdo or suit of clothes, and by combining that with voice, I can, with a high degree of probability, conclude that I have Fabius in the image. In addition to this, techniques of vocal recognition are being developed. Algorithms of the analysis of vocal content are already able to recognize not only that such and such a person is speaking, but that the person is saying this or that. L'INA is cooperating in this research with LIMSI (Laboratory of Computer Science for Mechanics and the Engineering Sciences – CNRS): this is the OLIVE program. Of course, if we succeed in coupling this recognition capacity with a finite list of key words, we will be able to obtain extremely precise tools of navigation throughout the images. All such instruments, which in the end are those of digital documentary techniques, allow for the implementation of detection and normalization of the discrete regularities composing audiovisual contents – both syntactic elements (shots, shot values, camera movements, sequences – thanks to image signatures, sequences can now be reconstituted from shots) and content elements (objects, what is said, etc.).

31.4 A Universal Grammar of Images

To recap, digital broadcasting will undergo a double delinearization: firstly, the delinearization of the arch-flux as scheduled program, which implies the end of the constraint of mass horo-broadcasting, and secondly, the delinearization of the temporal flux of the programs themselves, which means the possibility of navigation among these temporal objects by means of criteria made possible by audiovisual research engines.

The algorithmic analysis of audiovisual contents will profoundly revamp image practices, and this constitutes the determining element in the social appropriation of the new system: the languages of program description and the discretization of fluxes will end up engendering new forms of intelligence of animated images, based on a veritable audiovisual education.

There will inevitably result a *general theory of animated images*, bringing back to the fore, but on a new basis, the old questions of semiology – *on bases issuing from technology and its normative effects.*

These techniques will need years of research and development before they begin to yield precise and intricate results. But already languages of description of audiovisual contents are being developed, to such a point that the worldwide group for the standardization of compression image techniques, MPEG – which developed the MPEG-1 and MPEG-2 standards, allowing images to be passed into telecommunication networks (and recently into computers) – has named a new commission to define MPEG-7. Its vocation is not the invention of algorithmic analysis of contents but a universal grammar of image contents, and to see to it that designers all over the world agree on the ways of describing an audiovisual document: what is to be called a close shot, a sequence etc.? These are not only questions. But engineers are handling them now. Simple or not, engineers do not ask themselves questions for long: they must make decisions. They do not look to have completely non-contradictory theories, theories entirely uncriticized by the academic community: they are looking for systems that work. Even if their theories are theoretically questionable, they will be implemented if they work and if they satisfy the demands of the market. This is a crucial approach, for right now, at the industrial level and the digital level, a phenomenon of standardization in the description of audiovisual content will eventually have a performative effect on the world of production. I consider it essential for this world of production – the directors, authors, producers, critics etc. to study these questions and problems. Ten years from now will be too late to criticize the telecommunications and computer science engineers for having made decisions of description that do not correspond in quality or coherence with respect to a semiological theory of images as well as with respect to what is known of technical and esthetic practices, and to the history of cinema and television.

These engineers are faced with worldwide competition. They have to solve problems of compatibility between machines. It is thus crucial that a universal language of image content description should exist, so that, in order to switch from one system to another, one network to another, I have in my possession a universal language that will enable me to make the different description systems compatible. In the universe of the written word, word processors were developed all over the world, by Microsoft and other software manufacturers, but there came a time when a serious problem arose: phototypesetters were no longer able to decode the floppy disks of their authors. Thus exchange formats, as they are called, had to be devised. SGML (Standard Generalized Markup Language) became standard. This is a metalanguage for the description of structured textual contents capable of deciding: that is such and such a character, such and such an attribute; that is a paragraph, a footnote, a chapter heading, a table of contents; etc. An entire language came into being, allowing, in an absolutely universal fashion, for software to communicate in the description of the contents of a work. Today, the typo-dispositional structure, that is, the typography, of a dictionary or a book published by Gallimard, whatever the software used, can be analyzed. SGML next led to the development of HTML (Hypertext Markup Language) on the Internet, which appeared on the Web. This is the SGML of hypertext. In the wake of HTML, the Hy-Time standard is developing. This is hypertext with a capacity for the management of time, that is, of temporal objects – the time of a musical document as well as a cinema or television one. Parallel to these developments, two new worldwide standards are being produced: MPEG-7, which we have already mentioned, and SMPTE.

31.5 Towards House Video

The consequences of these techniques of discretization will be numerous in the world of cinema and notably in television broadcasting as an epoch of cinema. The most immediate and massive consequence, at the level of access modes, is that the implementation of content analysis algorithms will urge users of image banks on digital networks to actually look for programs outside the schedule grid: this is the delinearization of the arch-flux which is the television program schedule: from the inside of the flux of temporal objects, tomorrow's viewer will have access to discrete elements on the inside of the temporal object that is the program. In other words, he or she will be able to search inside the program for the element of his or her interest, independently of the program itself. I will be able to say: I want shots of such and such length, concerning a subject at one particular moment, with such and such a shot value, in this or that audiovisual genre, and regardless of the programs they all come from. This means that, little by little, viewing audiences are going to realize that audiovisual documents are composed of discrete elements. This is, moreover, an essential problematic of this universal language of document description: they must be able to distinguish everything generic in every audiovisual document. For example, one can say that every audiovisual document is constituted by the time-code. First of all, it is a temporal document. Secondly, the temporal flux strings shots one after another. Thirdly, these shots combine to form sequences. Fourthly, in a sequence, there are some elements to be taken into account: shot values, camera movements, depth of field, criteria of lighting – here the same criteria as those used in technical cut-ups will be used: interior daytime, exterior night, etc. An entire language of production will be invested with a value no longer that of production professionals having produced the document, but one of analysis *a posteriori* for the public, which should generalize a quite professional language, an analytic language which will become the language of navigation for the public. This will spread professional skills throughout the greater viewing public. This is a crucial aspect of the question. A culture of the image will be enabled in society, providing there is the political will to stimulate it, of course.

People will be learning new access forms. Not only will they be manipulating discrete regularities, but documents they will have chosen by formulating requests through these discrete regularities. They will be screened on television screens which will have become computers. Avid Technology has decided to create a $70 piece of software for today's computers and tomorrow's mass market combination TV-computers. Avid is the worldwide leader in the creation of professional virtual editing software. Professional Avid software equipment can cost up to several hundred thousand francs. Such an initiative – aiming at the greater viewing public – means that the manipulation of images by that public is already here, and that what I call house video will inevitably develop, just as in the 1980s, with house music. The day that Atari launched its 6000 franc computer equipped with a sound compression card and virtual sound editing software was the day sampling was born in the nightclubs, before giving birth to house music, techno and rap. These techniques are today widely used by musicians, and this has radically transformed the very nature of music broadcasting. I would wager that in the years to come, house video as a savage technique of image manipulation, will develop along the same lines: I do not make images, I sample among existing images. I do video will the images of others. Of course there will be legal problems. But for the moment let us leave them aside. I believe that publishing rights societies should now be studying the question without opposing these practices, for, one way or the other, according to law or outside of legal frameworks, all the technical conditions required for these practices will exist.

Discretization will thus transform the relation of the public to the program, by allowing access to content elements and not to the programs themselves. This will also profoundly transform production techniques, first of all because in the main control rooms documentary techniques will suddenly appear, being used by those working in the control rooms to navigate in the image banks. Thanks to these search engines, journalists will be able to locate just those shots they need for a particular event, either in their own archive or in those of the AFP, Euronews or INA. Also, the control room will have to implement documentary techniques to manage its own productions. If I am an editor, for example, I am faced with a delicate problem since, when working in analog, whether cinema or video, I have a physical apprehension or grasp of the documents I must edit: cassettes or rushes. When I edit the film, I pin the rushes to their board, and all I need is an intuitive glance to measure the parameters. I visualize the quantity and geography of documents – the geography of my immediate work space. With virtual editing, all the rushes are in digital form. Here, they are on the server; I can no longer see them. I no longer have the physical apprehension of their size or localization. I have a navigation problem. And a major film can involve dozens of hours of shots, even hundreds, and that represents tens of thousands of documentary units. The editors themselves have access problems with these shots: documentation problems. Moreover, digitization is offering professionals the possibility of working in a home studio, the professional version of house video. The home studio lets directors completely free themselves from the techno-industrial infrastructure. Likewise, more and more journalists edit their own interviews; they are beginning to forego editors – creating an employment problem. They edit directly from their own digital equipment, having incorporated that function into their instrument. Today, directors have 200 000 franc equipment capable of doing almost everything. The autonomy of directors will in some ways give them unheard of creative leeway. The consequences in industry and trade will be huge, and what happened in the world of music 10 years ago will no doubt occur in the world of image production: a lot of technicians in the studios disappeared or had to be recycled or retrained. Whatever happens, the access mode to images has greatly evolved. At a workstation, pre-editing will be able to be accomplished; a great deal of work will be done without relying on labs – editing tables, post-production studios etc. And this will have consequences for the very esthetics of the documents. Will this lead to a development of the clip? I am not so sure. If in the world of music it is true that house music did lead to techno, to sampling and to generalized audio clips, it also permitted musicians from other fields, especially from the field of jazz (listen for example to Eddy Louis) to continue making their music through the use of the computer, the sampler and the synthesizer. All music has thereby been transformed. And today, few indeed are the musicians who are not using these technologies, even when they are making acoustic music. I believe this process will develop in the world of cinema and television. It is a great challenge for all those working in the audiovisual field.

31.6 Multi-Support and Multi-Format

Another extraordinary challenge comes in the form of what has been called multi-support – and also multi-format – production. Format is essential in the world of industrial temporal objects, in the world, that is, of audiovisual programs.

It sometimes happens that we are able to see, either in a movie theater or a television channel, a film by a major Hollywood director in a 125 minute version rather than the 90 minute version seen before. The director had intended a film of 125 minutes, but the producer who, in the USA, can always impose his or her point of view, decided that the format would be 90 minutes. This 90 minute standard from cinema first imposed itself in the world of broadcasting; then other standards developed from it – standards defined by compromise with the management of advertising space: 13, 26, 52, 60 minutes etc. This corresponds to a set of format definitions which developed in the context of competition between TV stations for advertising. If, for example, I wish to wrench the French viewer from channel one (TF1), and if I know that 40% of the viewers watch the news program, before going to channel two, three, arte, then I must concentrate on channel one's news program format. This is how these formats were defined in the first place, overdetermined by imperatives imposed by advertising control rooms. This has resulted in a set of extremely constraining standards. I am today a producer, and for each production the first element to be defined is the format. A contract is signed with such and such a broadcaster, producer, director or author for a serial lasting 6 times 52 minutes, and with another for 10 times 13 minutes etc. This format has been totally interiorized by the people working in broadcast industries and even in cinema. The travail of every director is to find the right compromise: one subject in 13, 26, 52 or 90 minutes. The art consists in managing this kind of time increment.

In the 1930s, German refugee cinema directors came to Hollywood, where they were welcomed with a warning: welcome to Hollywood, but you will have to submit to some rules. You have left the cinema of authorship to discover industrial cinema. This is how it can happen than on Arte, Paris Première, or ciné-cinéfil, a film can be discovered in a new format, a film already seen 10 times over in another format. Obviously, this is to discover another film, because it is perfectly obvious that doing away with 15 shots has transformed the film object. Now, the digital world will allow engagement with multi-format production. The esthetic stakes are complex and absolutely enthralling. The audiovisual world will soon be in the middle of a period of exercises in style – in the Raymond Queneau or Oulipo sense of the term. Let us consider the example of a production where my objective is not to achieved a standard format of 52 or 60 minutes. I will, on the contrary, propose to my staff a budget for the realization of some 20 hours of shooting out of which will come five different formats. A scheme of this type can easily be imagined for tomorrow: not a pre-ordained format, but a conjugation of a number of hours of shooting into an ensemble of documents in various forms of interrelationship with one another. One of them could be broadcast on TV in the format required by the schedule, then be developed with another two-hour or five-hour format. Accessing all the shots can even be envisaged. The same starting point could very well be used by different directors to obtain many different programs. Whatever the scenario, I am convinced that delinearization and discretization (which make possible different products from the same database) are opening up new esthetic perspectives. I really believe that the possibilities now offered by the digital will enhance the chances of a new art of the audiovisual emerging (which was previously impossible due to production cost considerations). L'INA would become the school of such developments through its studio of multi-support production, designed to facilitate work by young creators alongside experienced artists, in these perspectives.

Tomorrow's producer should not be producing a single source format for scheduled broadcasting, from which derived products can be extracted, but rather a generic concept of contents centered around an intention, which can then be developed in diverse channels and supports, the scheduled broadcast being one element among others. Up until now, products were derivative products in that they were produced after the source product, *a posteriori*, the source being the scheduled broadcast. Now the producer will have to learn to produce and conceive not a derivation from a source but the conjugation of a concept issuing from an initial database, which will become the source from which a set of programs will be developed, with variable formats, with services and resources complementary to one another allowing the viewer to be sent from one channel to another, where online services await, or to media such as the DVD.

Will the DVD be the first school of interactive television ? I am not so sure. I believe rather that this will develop essentially around program fluxes. The DVD arrived first, but the progression in transmission techniques leads me to believe that the articulation between scheduled programs and the image banks will be the foremost consideration in the near future. This said, it is true that the USA has invested much in DVD technology and related multilingual productions. The USA sees in this optical medium a production vector with immediate worldwide impact, evidently to be connected to digital broadcasting, for digital television will be global, and that is an unprecedented issue at stake today.

I prefer to speak of activity rather than of interactivity. I do not put much stock in programs in which the user will intervene from raw image banks, without being guided by linear and clickable programs. I should specify this point. In multi-support production, the source from which the conjugations will grow will be the server on which will be installed the data bank collecting all the relevant documents, several hours long or longer, on which "views" and access modes are found, with the TV viewer accessing the same sources as the professional. The documentary tools of control rooms thus become those of production, editing, broadcasting and access. But on the other hand, the linear scheduled formats become "clicable", that is, dynamic: noticed on a TV schedule, these are programs just like any other programs, but noticed on a server, they allow for navigation, not only in content, but by content.

For example, a 13 minute format is composed of x sequences of 1 to 3 minutes: the program is represented by a vector on which the sequences following each other in the flux of the program are proportionally depicted, where the viewer plays the program and an arrow moves along the time vector representing the program. This allows the viewer to view the program with an eye to the entire succession of sequences, which have as attributes, subtitles and key words, but also source lists, that is, the list of all the documents used to constitute the sequence by editing etc. In this group, each sequence is clickable, which means, on the one hand, that it can be replayed as a sequence, and on the other hand, that it allows the viewing of sources from which the editing was done, sources which can be themselves edited into a longer sequence, or even composed into several other sequences.

In a word, from the source, which has become the total amount of documents necessary for production, products are conjugated to be consultable in themselves, but which also allow access, in clickable video and in navigation by content, to other longer or more granular products.

One of the tasks of tomorrow's directors will be to be capable of offering views on the contents of image banks. This will remain a linear activity allowing for first access (through the flux of the scheduled programs on TV) to the image banks on the server (the stock), but it will be delinearizable by the user who, himself or herself, will do an exercise in style and will come to an esthetic compromise with his or her addressee. This may come as a shock to many directors, who sometimes say to me that each work has its own unique format, and that variations are not possible. I understand well this point of view: it is a legitimate and coherent esthetic choice. But other choices are possible. It will be up to the authors. Everything is open and, depending on whether we are dealing with fiction, magazine, news or new types of documents still unknown to us (which will be audiovisual documents for professional use), the situation will be variable to the extreme. A virgin continent is here to be conquered, in which all trades and professions – people from fiction, magazine, news and documentalists in the sense of documentary art – will have their heyday. They will have to incorporate a fundamental element if they are to embark on this adventure: their addressee's attitude will be completely different from what it is today. And it will be precisely their job to provoke this attitude, to make sure that it is as rich as possible, and to open it up to the greatest possible image intelligence and the greatest possible intelligence in images.

Acknowledgment

Translated into American English by George Collins.

About the Author

Bernard Stiegler is a philosopher and teacher at the Université de technologie de Compiègne, having previously been Executive Manager of the Institut National de l'Audiovisuel of France from 1996 to 1999. He has written three books, *Technics and Time 1, The Fault of Epimetheus*, translated and published by Stanford University Press 1998 (and Paris 1994), *Technics and Time 2, "La Desorientation"*, Paris 1996, and *Echographies*, 1996.

32

Cognition and Computers: The Context of the Matter, the Matter of Context

Daniel Andler

Abstract

There is an age-old and very general problem regarding techniques and technology in their relation to science. Can good technology do without good science? Yes: the Iron Age had no metallurgy, and No: eventually optimal iron-making required a true science of metals. The case of cognitive technology raises the same problems, but it has a number of special features, such as the existence of a well-developed folk theory, on which cognitive technologists rely, and the ethical issue of launching cognitive and perceptual prostheses which may be unfit for long-term consumption or sound human development. Thus both cognitive science and philosophy, it will be argued on general grounds, are natural partners in the pursuit of adaptive computer-based information technologies. As a case in point, the issue of context will be examined. It is well known that mental processes tend to be highly context-sensitive. In particular, communication, linguistic and otherwise, relies crucially on contextual clues. There are a number of theoretical proposals, prominently Relevance Theory, which purport to account for such effects. However, some quite basic issues remain untouched; in particular, it can be argued that context is to some extent a normative, rather than factual, notion, so that context-sensitivity must be understood, and if needs be engineered, with consideration for the norm to be attained.

32.1 Introduction

This chapter will argue that cognitive science and philosophy are natural partners of computer-based technology. In some respects, this is an uncontroversial claim, in as much as any technology is by definition intimately connected to basic science, and in as much as philosophy's business is invariably to try to help people grasp how the various dimensions of a human enterprise hang together. And there is no claim that computer technologists are unaware or unsympathetic to the partnership. However, there are some special features of their field which make the need for interactions more pressing perhaps than is usually realized. At any rate, reviewing those features and putting up for discussion the reasons for and modes of the interaction may be of interest. I will attempt to provide an illustration by considering the issue of context, as it is both taken up, and, I will argue, somehow missed, by cognitive science.

In order to keep my main goal in focus, I will make simplifying assumptions (SA), and rather than fudge or apologize about them, I will try to make them explicit as I go along.

32.2 Science, Technology, Common Sense and Folk Theories

I assume that the field or fields represented in book conference are essentially techno-logical, i.e. have as their main goal to invent, promote and improve advanced computer-based tools designed to assist and expand the cognitive capacities of human agents and groups (SA1). I also assume that at present the main knowledge source that is called upon to provide concepts and principles is computer science, although doubt-less some ideas from ergonomics and neighboring fields are also used (SA2).

This scientific input is what makes the field or fields under discussion technologies as opposed to mere techniques: they could not have arisen were it not for the exis-tence of at least one major scientific development. However, this does not imply that all relevant scientific sources have been tapped. Just like techniques, technolo-gies can go a very long way without all the help which some branch of science or other could provide. A case in point is provided by pharmaceutical drugs: at least until recently, this all-important technology, although made possible only by the existence of the well-developed sciences of human physiology and organic chem-istry, was almost completely lacking in foundations – there simply was no theory of why and how drugs work. This severely limited – and to a large extent still does – its potential in terms of therapeutic success, limitation of side effects and heuristic efficiency. This is not just saying that the drug industry is imperfect, like not a few other human enterprises. To say that the potential of a technology to limit its side effects has not been reached by a wide margin is a complicated and polite way of saying that it presents major risks and drawbacks which may not be ethically justi-fied. The fact that its heuristics are so-so implies that people may be paying more than they could and therefore perhaps should for the goods. And finally, to say that the therapeutic potential of drugs is not fully attained means that people are sick and sometimes dying of illnesses which could be cured by drugs if we had a better grasp of how drugs work.

So far so good: advanced computer technologies of concern to this audience are in the same ballpark as other technologies. But there are features that are special to the field under consideration, and which give the issue of the proper scientific context for its development a character as well as an urgency which may be lacking in other cases.

The features I have in mind are the following:

1. The computer is in important respects human-like.
2. The computer-based technologies help themselves not only to common sense knowledge in the usual sense, but to well-developed folk theories.

3. These technologies have the potential not simply, like all successful technologies, to change certain well-defined aspects of human existence, but to reshape fundamental dimensions of humanness. Let us review them in order.

1. When Alan Turing, in order to solve the Enscheidungsproblem (the decision problem), looked for a general mathematical theory of computability, he took as his model, in the classical sense of a natural object after which the sought-after artificial object is manufactured, an idealized human calculator. So from its very inception, the computer is quite literally shaped after the human mind under a certain circumscribed description. As computer science developed and the means to turn the computer into a versatile cognitive tool were sought, programming languages were developed which, as their name indicates, were fashioned upon that most human of all faculties: language (the important differences between natural and formal languages notwithstanding). Thus, quite independently of the claims, achievements and limitations of artificial intelligence, the fully equipped computer as we know it today is heavily imprinted with human-like characteristics. This makes it an artifact of a very different sort than penicillin, the printing machine, the automobile, the cellular phone, the transistor, the electricity network or the good old book (hardly a technology, as a matter of fact). And the human–computer interface is an infinitely more intimate affair than the human–drug, or human–car, or human–print interfaces, however crucial these interfaces may be to modern humans. By labeling the computer a cognitive prosthesis one emphasizes this proximity, contrasting it with most other machines and tools, as well as books, pictures and recordings, which do serve the function of aiding the human mind, but not by resembling it in any way, rather simply by being adapted to fit some of its needs.

The important consequence is that just as our fellow human beings not only fill some of our needs by fulfilling certain functions (as bosses, work partners, tennis partners, sexual partners, offspring, food suppliers, military opponents etc.), but also interact with us and change our lives due to a general similarity which underwrites many processes above and beyond their official roles, computers are not simply word processors and flight simulators and Internet channels and virtual reality providers, they are connected to us by means of interactive processes, not all of which are explicitly recruited in the execution of their official functions. To put it starkly and misleadingly, a computer is not simply a rational partner, it is also an intuitive one.

2. All techniques, and all technologies, help themselves to commonsense knowledge. What is special about computer technology is that it also taps a largely hidden form of knowledge, that which is contained in so-called folk theories. I use the term in the meaning given it by contemporary cognitive science (naïve theory is also used in this context), not the more anthropological sense of pre-scientific knowledge, accumulated by generations through experience and transmission, about certain orders of phenomena. Cognitive scientists believe that human beings deal with certain ecologically essential dimensions of the world by means of highly specialized, encapsulated, developmentally semi-autonomous bodies of largely implicit knowledge. Examples are naïve physics (which enables us to deal with medium-sized objects, fluids etc., manipulated under normal circumstances), naïve biology (allowing us to identify, classify and make predictions about living

beings), naïve sociology (allowing us to identify, classify and make predictions about human groups and individuals as belonging to groups), and, most importantly, naïve psychology (allowing us to attribute to others psychological states of believing and of knowing, and to track the specific contents and dynamics of these states, by identifying perceptual sources and attentional trajectories, and hypothesizing mnemonic and inferential capacities).

I conjecture that computer technologies make essential use of such folk-theoretical resources, during two (interdependent) phases of the design process. The computer is designed, on the one hand, so as to accomplish certain pre-specified cognitive functions; folk knowledge is brought to bear, I contend, to solve the problem of how to endow the computer with the prescribed capacity, on the basis of more elementary ones which are, rightly or wrongly, taken for granted. On the other hand, the computer is designed to interact in certain ways with an agent whose expectations, beliefs and behavior conform to certain patterns, and again those patterns and their probable dynamics are conjectured on the basis of folk knowledge.

Now, because folk knowledge is for the most part implicit, the manner in which it is deployed in the design process remains largely beyond control. No doubt the fact that folk theories have plausibly evolved under the pressure of natural selection explains both their cognitive value in ecologically valid situations and, to a lesser extent, their usefulness in the process of designing cognitive prostheses. However, clearly, the more advanced the technology, the less permissible the reliance on implicit knowledge. Car manufacturers may content themselves with implicit understanding of the perceptual and motor abilities of the average human being, supersonic bomber manufacturers had better get their psychophysics straight.

Finally, although we have not stressed it here, explicit knowledge of the ordinary commonsense sort is also presumably extensively used in design – simple and purportedly obvious facts regarding memory, for example – and this must also be submitted to a thorough checking procedure, which only basic science will conduct with the proper care.

3. Mankind, like all living species, is unavoidably ecologically determined. It could be argued that it is less so than any other species because of its extraordinary adaptability: human groups, through space and time, have inhabited a stupendous variety of niches. But the argument cuts both ways: mankind has survived and prospered only by virtue of paying extraordinary attention to its environment. In other words, it is open to the environment in a way in which no other species is. In addition, it can shape its environment like no other species can. This dual capacity – identification with and modification of the environment – is due to the enormous development of mankind's cognitive abilities. This in turn results in the fact that mankind's environment comprises a large cognitive dimension. Major modifications in the cognitive environment profoundly change the human condition, which some philosophers have called the destiny of man. Now, despite being immersed in the natural order, mankind in a sense moves about within that order by choosing, at least as far as it can judge by its own lights, its proper place.

How do these platitudes relate to the issue at hand? First step: computer-based technologies, possibly due to the closeness of computers to humans, modify the cognitive environment in ways unequalled by any other technology. For example, virtually unlimited access to information and virtually immediate sorting of information change the human condition at least as much as virtually unlimited access to food and to nearly perfectly fresh food. In fact, the change is greater, I would argue, both in magnitude and in the number of dimensions or levels affected. This is only one obvious example; we may also consider far more exotic and possibly deeper ones. Now for the second step: we are responsible for these changes, and we must put ourselves in a position to understand as well as we can what these changes consist of, before we can decide whether we want to become the avatar of mankind which these changes would give rise to if we chose to bring them about. We should also bear in mind a rather simpler fact: not only could it turn out that we do not particularly care to become a certain sort of human beast despite the apparent benefits brought about by the expansion of some computer-based abilities, but the technology itself could have directly deleterious effects on our physical and mental health as we view them in the present state of our development.

(Compare: Not only could we question the desirability of becoming (or having become) the sort of human beast that has unlimited access to non-poisonous food; but the means deployed to bring this situation about may have (had) adverse effects, such as the spread of obesity and diabetes, or the pollution of soil and water by pesticides, or the destruction of the countryside or of the traditional town based on small shops, etc. But again, tampering with our cognitive environment may make such changes seem trifles by comparison.)

The upshot of all this is that, possibly more than any other technology, computer-based technology has a duty to develop the means to tap all the resources which could conceivably be brought to bear on its scientific foundations and anthropological and ethical import. These resources are at present located mostly in cognitive science and in philosophy.

It is not within the means of the present writer to spell out the specific areas with which fruitful exchange can be relied on. Besides, it is not a novel idea, and clearly some commerce is already going on – in fact always has gone on – whether explicitly in interdisciplinary programs and workgroups, or, more often, in the minds of multiply trained professionals. Rather, I would press the issue as a matter for discussion. The pressure towards competitive edge on the technological front tends to push it rather lower on the agenda than it deserves.

What I propose to do in the remainder of this chapter is to take a look back at the case of artificial intelligence, and illustrate some of my points by a consideration of the issue of context.

32.3 The Lessons from Classical AI

I assume that the present historical verdict on classical AI is negative [SA3]. By this I do not mean to imply that classical AI (what the philosopher John Haugeland has dubbed GOFAI, Good Old-Fashioned Artificial Intelligence) has borne no intellectual or practical fruit whatever. Rather, it has failed to deliver significant results in the area it had set out to explore, viz. human cognitive abilities and their replication, at whatever fineness of granularity, in the form of computer programs.

I can see three ways to account for this failure. Two have been extensively aired, the third has to my mind been given inadequate attention.

In a famous paper written in 1976, Allen Newell and Herbert Simon proposed as a theoretical basis for (classical) AI a structural hypothesis about the nature of intelligence. Any physical symbol system, they wrote, has the necessary and sufficient means for general intelligent behavior. Many people have argued that the reason why AI failed (in its major ambition) is that this hypothesis is simply false. Despite my sympathy for this criticism, I will have nothing to say about it here, as I do not think there is much to draw from it for our present purpose.

The second explanation has more to tell us: AI failed, we were told, in particular by Hubert Dreyfus, and later by Hubert and Stuart Dreyfus, because it did not, and in fact could not, give any attention to certain crucial features of human intelligence. Two of these features (there were others) were commonsense implicit knowledge and context-sensitivity. The first relates to what I pointed out earlier, namely that the design of cognitive prostheses draws upon the intuitive grasp or deployment, by the designer, of some uncodified, implicit knowledge of a certain kind. What the Dreyfuses had in mind was commonsense knowledge, whereas what I was calling attention to was folk or naïve knowledge, but the two have something important in common: they are not part of the knowledge which the designer thinks of herself as coding into the artifact which she is designing. And while the Dreyfuses were content with pointing out that AI could not succeed if it were true that people use commonsense knowledge to go about intelligently doing their thing, I suggested earlier that naïve theories must be unpacked and made explicit as far as possible. This will hook up with the third reason for the failure of AI, to which I will come presently.

Before I come to it, I should say a word about the second feature which AI purportedly missed, i.e. context-sensitivity. This, I think, relates directly to our concern, also in a way not foreseen by the Dreyfuses, and I will come back to it in the sections following this one.

Now for my third attempt at explaining the problems of AI. It may be too simple to be noticed, or appear to some to be too obvious to be worth mentioning, but I see it differently. I believe that the basic reason why AI did not succeed is that it tried to bypass fundamental science and move on directly to technology. In other words, detailed theories of parts of human cognition were needed before one could hope to simulate them. Cognitive science was, and still is, the proper framework for AI, and my claim is, as should by now be boringly clear, that it is the proper framework for any ambitious computer-based technology. Admittedly, an important feature of AI does not generalize: the research programs we are concerned with in this workshop do not generally aim (I believe) for simulation or replication of human cognition or behavior. However, because they are at bottom cognitive prostheses, they require, just as much as AI, the best available theories of human cognition.

(Compare: In order to build an artificial eye, we have to know a great deal about human vision; but equally, if we want to build visual prostheses based on tactile perception, which is precisely what Bach-y-Rita does, we need to know a lot about the visual system and about the tactile system, and cortical plasticity besides.)

32.4 The Technical Problem of Context

Just like AI, all computer-based technologies encounter the context issue in one form or another. One series of problems is raised by the desirability of devising artifacts which are sensitive to the context of their use, so as to reduce the need for the human agent to adjust the device on the spot or foresee and compensate for the contextual factors. Another series of problems are raised not by the desire for the devices themselves to be context-sensitive, but by the need to view their deployment in their entire human and social context, and to tune their integration in the overarching system accordingly.

Context has, over the years, become a central concern in cognitive science. It originates, as the word's etymology makes clear, from the study of language, and more specifically, of written texts and oral communication. But it extends to other cognitive abilities, from pattern recognition to problem solving, from word pronunciation to decision making. What I call the technical problem of context consists in isolating a naturally defined set of tasks or abilities, together with a naturally defined set of contextual factors and effects, and providing a theory which accounts for the context sensitivity of the human ability in question. In some cases, designing artifacts which exhibit a similar context-sensitivity, if possible for the reasons which explain this property in human cognition, is an important goal.

Solutions to the technical context problem are many, and I will give a flavor of some of them. I will say something about linguistic communication, and the account provided by Dan Sperber's and Deirdre Wilson's Relevance Theory. My conclusion will be twofold. I will first stress that if designers of advanced computer applications wish to deal with the context issue head-on, they may well gain from a careful study of the theories of context made available by some branches of cognitive science. But I will also argue that there is something important which these theories miss that is of interest to computer technologies. There is a dimension of context which raises what some philosophers of science call a conceptual problem, one not apparently amenable to the methods of established science.

32.5 The Conceptual Problem of Context

First there is the intriguing fact that context is hardly ever defined, and that what different theorists refer to under that name varies widely. The deflationary view here consists in taking context to be a loose, everyday kind of word with no technical counterpart in science. But this view is not at all satisfactory, for it does not account for the intuition of a deep commonality between the various kinds of situation where context comes in. Is context nothing but the residue which remains after idealization and formalization or modelization have been achieved? Or is it a more significant feature of human cognition?

I will briefly argue for the second answer, and will base my argument on the conjecture that context is essentially normative, by which I mean that context-sensitivity, and context choice for that matter, is no mere fact, but that it is the bearer of a norm, a value. Perceiving and understanding, reasoning and evaluating, judging and deciding, doing and not doing, as accomplished by humans, invariably occur within a context. The context dictates, or at least constrains, the proper accomplishment of the act. This can be understood in a naturalistic way: one can think of the context as a positive given, and of the constraints it creates as constituting a natural fact. Whether the act is carried out in conformity with these constraints is then a mere matter of correct functioning of the cognitive system. However, I contend that this is not the only, nor even the more plausible, way of considering the matter. The context is not a given, nor are the constraints it generates: context choice and contextual constraints are irreducibly normative. The norm they carry is *sui generis*, and goes under the (disreputable) name of intelligence.

I said earlier that computer technologies meet the context problem under two guises. One is the design of context-sensitive artifacts. The other is the understanding of the human and social context in which the artifacts will be used, and which they will in fact contribute to shape. For the second of these two problems, the intelligence which we need to deploy is concerned specifically with the anthropological issue of the sort of human mind which we want to result from the extended deployment of the devices and systems which we should strive to make available. And that intelligence is essentially philosophical in nature.

About the Author

Prof Daniel Andler was trained in mathematical logic, and to a lesser extent in philosophy, in Paris and Berkeley. He specialized in model theory and taught mathematics for over twenty years in various universities. In 1989 he took up a position in philosophy at Université de Lille III, then at Nanterre (Université Paris X), where he was in charge of the Center For the History and Philosophy of science for several years. He helped set up CREA (Centre de recherche en épistémologie appliquée), an interdisciplinary center affiliated with Ecole Polytechnique and CNRS, focusing on anaytic philosophy, economics and the modeling of complex systems. He was co-director of CREA for many years, and has recently been appointed Director. He is also in charge of a graduate program in cognitive science. For nearly ten years, he co-headed (with A. Berthoz) CogniSeine, a federation of laboratories involved in one or several fields related to cognitive science. As a philosopher of science and a logician working on the foundations of cognitive science, he is interested in a number of areas, among which the status of models in cognitive science, the nature and function of context in mental life and specifically in reasoning, and the broader issue of the nature of mental representations. He has published numerous papers and edited several collections. He is working on a book on the foundations of cognitive science, co-authoring an essay in the philosophy of science, and finishing a textbook in logic.

33

Supporting Creativity with Advanced Information-Abundant User Interfaces

Ben Shneiderman

Abstract

A challenge for human–computer interaction researchers and user interface designers is to construct information technologies that support creativity. This ambitious goal can be attained if designers build on an adequate understanding of creative processes. This chapter describes a model of creativity, the four-phase genex framework for generating excellence:

- Collect: learn from previous works stored in digital libraries, the Web etc.
- Relate: consult with peers and mentors at early, middle and late stages
- Create: explore, compose, discover and evaluate possible solutions
- Donate: disseminate the results and contribute to the digital libraries, the Web etc.

Within this integrated framework, there are eight activities that require human–computer interaction research and advanced user interface design. This chapter concentrates on techniques of information visualization that support creative work by enabling users to find relevant information resources, identify desired items in a set, or discover patterns in a collection. It describes information visualization methods and proposes five questions for the future: generality, integration, perceptual foundations, cognitive principles and collaboration.

33.1 Introduction

Ambitious visions can be helpful in shaping more concrete research agendas. Vannevar Bush's (1945) vision of a system to support memory expansion (memex) inspired researchers for a half century in the development of what has become the World Wide Web. Engelbart's goal of augmenting human intellect (Engelbart and English, 1968) led to innovations such as the mouse and windows. Later, Brooks's belief in the importance of toolmaking (Brooks, 1996) led to innovations such as haptic feedback in 3D graphical environments. Hiltz's recognition of the power of online communities (Hiltz, 1984), inspired early software development (Hiltz and Turoff, 1993) and the emergence of ideas such as the collaboratory (National Research Council, 1993). These inspirational visions were important predecessors for genex (generator of excellence), an integrated framework for creativity support tools (Shneiderman, 1998b, 1999).

33.1.1 Creativity Support

Supporting creativity is a bold ambition, but it is becoming feasible because of refined understandings of the creative processes (Rosner and Abt, 1970; De Bono, 1973; Boden, 1990; Mayer, 1992; Czikszentmihalyi, 1996; Couger, 1996) and the emergence of advanced user interfaces to support creativity (Massetti, 1996; Massetti *et al.*, 1999). While theories of creativity vary widely, common features describe a preparatory phase that deals with the need to find information, understand the problem and explore alternatives privately, followed by discussion with peers and mentors. These steps lay the basis for an incubation phase, and moments of inspiration to break a too rigid mind set. Then come the hours of perspiration to evaluate possibilities, refine potential solutions, implement the chosen solution and disseminate it.

The diverse theories contributed to the four phases in an integrated user interface framework, called genex:

- Collect: learn from previous works stored in digital libraries, the Web etc.
- Relate: consult with peers and mentors at early, middle and late stages
- Create: explore, compose, discover and evaluate possible solutions
- Donate: disseminate the results and contribute to the digital libraries, the Web etc.

Across these four phases, at least eight activities are opportunities for research in user interface design and human–computer interaction (Shneiderman, 1999) (Figure 33.1):

- Searching and browsing digital libraries
- Consulting with peers and mentors
- Visualizing data and processes
- Thinking by free associations
- Exploring solutions – "what if?" tools
- Composing artifacts and performances
- Reviewing and replaying session histories
- Disseminating results

These activities are richly interwoven, for example, visualizing supports searching, exploring, reviewing etc. Each activity deserves consideration as part of a research agenda, but this chapter focuses on the third item – visualizing data and processes and discusses its place in the broad array of genex activities.

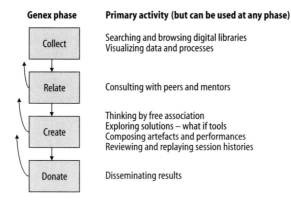

Genex phase	Primary activity (but can be used at any phase)
Collect	Searching and browsing digital libraries Visualizing data and processes
Relate	Consulting with peers and mentors
Create	Thinking by free association Exploring solutions – what if tools Composing artefacts and performances Reviewing and replaying session histories
Donate	Disseminating results

Figure 33.1 Genex phases and their related primary activities.

33.1.2 Visualizing as a Support for Creativity

Visualizing is one of the eight activities that support the genex framework because visual information processing is central to many problem-solving tasks and creative explorations. Information visualization can contribute to early stages of collecting information from vast digital resources, to exploring alternative solutions and to identifying appropriate people for consultations or dissemination.

Evolutionary needs have made the human visual system extremely well adapted to recognizing patterns, extracting features and detecting unexpected items. Humans can rapidly process enormous amounts of visual information and take action rapidly. The human perceptual apparatus integrates interpretation so that people can rapidly identify familiar faces or recognize threats.

Linear or tabular presentations of text, numbers and music extend human memory, enable transmission of information across time and space, and support creativity. The process of recording an idea facilitates innovation and discovery by compelling an author to produce a coherent presentation, develop a consistent notation and present a logical argument. The linear or tabular formats enable the author and others to review, edit, refine, compare and search presentations rapidly.

The goal for visual designers is to match the task to the presentation (Tufte, 1983, 1990, 1997). Bertin (1983) dramatically portrays the possibilities by showing one hundred different presentations of information about French provinces, each suited to a specific task.

Two-dimensional visual presentations such as drawings, tree structures, flowcharts and maps have additional advantages. They can present affinities among multiple items, enabling users to see relationships that might be difficult to discover in linear textual presentations. Proximity or links in two-dimensional presentations can show rich structural relationships. Coding by size and color are easily perceived and further coding by shape, texture, rotation or markings can highlight additional relationships.

World maps are especially rich information sources that enable designers to show complex relationships while allowing users to plan trips and make further discoveries. Mental maps of information spaces and special designs such as the periodic table of elements, monthly calendars or the Linnaean taxonomy of animal phyla also support creativity. By placing known information in an orderly compact structure they support users in solving problems, planning activities and making further discoveries.

33.1.3 Information Visualization

Human perceptual abilities are remarkable and still largely underutilized by the current graphical user interfaces. Computer-based visual presentations bring additional opportunities and dangers. Adding animations such as blinking, color shifts and movements enriches the possibilities for presentations but risks overwhelming readers. However, a great benefit of computing environments is the opportunity for users to rapidly revise the presentation to suit their tasks. Users can quickly change the rules governing proximity, linking, color, size, shape, texture, rotation, marking, blinking, color shifts and movements. In addition, zooming in or clicking on specific items to get greater detail increases the possibilities for designers and users (Bederson and Hollan, 1994). The simple process of viewing a year-long display and clicking on the month and then the day enables users to get an overview and quickly move to details. A picture is often said to be worth a thousand words. Similarly, an interface is worth a thousand pictures.

A reasonable expectation of the future of user interfaces is for the growth of larger, information-abundant displays. While small portable personal devices will proliferate, the attraction of large desk-mounted or projected displays will be great. Human perceptual skills are remarkable and largely underutilized in current information and computing systems. Based on this insight, designers at several leading research centers have developed advanced prototypes and a variety of widgets to present, search, browse, filter and explore rich information spaces (Card *et al.*, 1999).

We can define information visualization as: a compact graphical presentation and user interface for rapidly manipulating large numbers of items (10^2–10^6), possibly extracted from far larger datasets. Effective information visualizations enable users to make discoveries, decisions or explanations about patterns (correlations, clusters, gaps, outliers,...), groups of items or individual items. This definition emphasizes the user interface for control of the presentation (location, color, size, rotation, shape, texture, blinking, movement, animation and other variables).

For the purposes of this discussion, information visualization deals with abstract multidimensional and multi-variate data and is quite different from scientific visualization or 3D modeling. Scientific visualization typically deals with three-dimensional real-world phenomena such as storms, crystal growth or human anatomy, and 3D modeling typically deals with mechanical parts, architectural walkthroughs or aircraft design.

33.2 Examples of Information Visualization Supporting Creativity

One of our early visualizations was based on dynamic queries, which are animated user-controlled displays. These update immediately (no "run" button) in response to movements of sliders, buttons, maps or other widgets (Shneiderman, 1994). For example, in the HomeFinder the users see points of light on a map representing homes for sale (Ahlberg et al., 1992; Williamson and Shneiderman, 1993). As they shift sliders for the price, number of bedrooms etc. the points of light come and go within 100 milliseconds, offering a quick understanding of how many and where suitable homes are being sold. Clicking on a point of light produces a full description and, potentially, a picture of the house. A controlled experiment with 18 subjects confirmed the performance and preference advantages of dynamic queries over a natural language interface and a paper database.

A next step was the starfield display, which was created for the FilmFinder to provide visual access to a film database (Ahlberg and Shneiderman, 1994). The films were arranged as color-coded rectangles along the x-axis by production year and along the y-axis by popularity. Recent popular films were in the upper right-hand corner. Zoombars (a variant of scroll bars) enabled users to zoom in on a single axis in milliseconds to view the desired region. When fewer than 25 films were on the screen, the film titles appeared, and when the users clicked on a film's rectangle, a dialog box would appear giving full information and an image from the film. The commercial version of starfield displays became available late in 1996 (Figure 33.2) (http://www.spotfire.com/).

In our LifeLines prototype, we applied multiple timeline representations to personal histories such as medical records (Plaisant et al., 1996). Horizontal and vertical zooming, focusing, and filtering enabled us to represent complex histories and support exploration by clicking on timelines to get detailed information.

Information visualization supports creative work by enabling users to:

- find relevant information resources in digital libraries
- identify desired items in a set
- discover patterns in a collection

Figure 33.2 demonstrates how a digital library of films could be viewed in a way that presents large amounts of information in an orderly way. Users can understand the distribution of films in this library and find specific films to satisfy their needs. Similarly, in a legal information library, users may be seeking the relevant precedents to support their arguments. The West key number system organizes information in a hierarchy whose first three levels have 470 items, which then expands into a tree with 85 000 nodes. Figure 33.3 shows how the results of a search might be displayed to reveal where the cases fall within the key number hierarchy (Shneiderman et al., 1999). Additional information is supplied on the x-axis, currently organizing the cases by year, and by color coding, currently showing the region the case came from. This visualization makes it clear that the major topic is Criminal Law. This visualization enables users to find the relevant

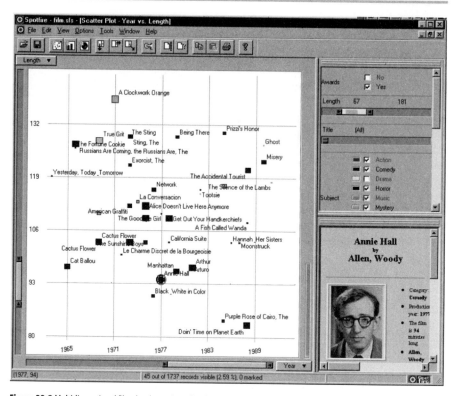

Figure 33.2 Multidimensional film database viewed with a two-dimensional starfield display in Spotfire. The x-axis contains the years and the y-axis is the popularity of the film. Color coding is film type (action, drama, mystery etc.), and larger dots indicate longer movies.

resources that would be very difficult to discover in a typical paged list with 20 cases per page.

A second form of creativity support is to identify items in a set. The legal information library is an example of this as well, but the drug discovery task is more typical. In this example, 379 compounds are viewed at once, organized by the amount of carbon and oxygen, color coded by dipole moment and size coded by polarizability (Figure 33.4). The unusual compound (the selected square at the upper right) is clearly visible by its distinct color coding.

Important patterns can also be seen in visual displays. The familiar chemical periodic table of elements becomes more informative when color and size coding are added, and when users can make selections by moving the double box sliders. Figure 33.5 shows the usual layout, but the high electronegativity is immediately visible from the color coding. Figure 33.6 shows a strong correlation between electronegativity and ionization energy, with two dramatic outliers: helium and radon.

The three ways that information visualization interfaces support creativity are not a complete set, but they give designers some specific goals to work towards.

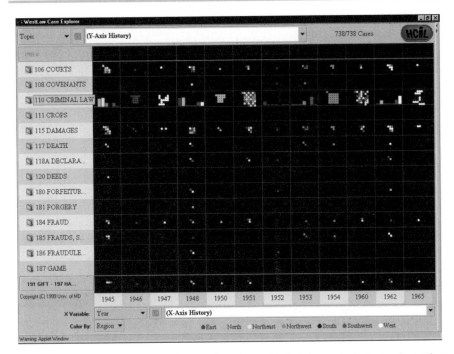

Figure 33.3 The results of a search in a legal information library. The *x*-axis is the topic, organized by the West key numbers, and the *y*-axis is the year. Color coding is by region.

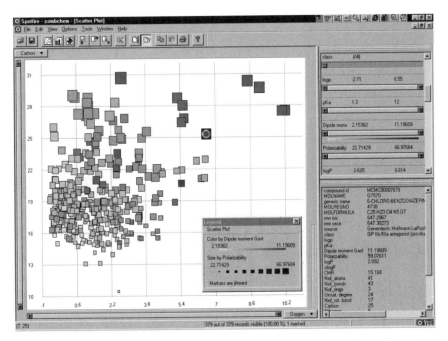

Figure 33.4 Information visualization of 379 chemical compounds. The *x*-axis is the amount of carbon and the *y*-axis is the amount of oxygen. Color coding is by dipole moment and size coding is by polarizability.

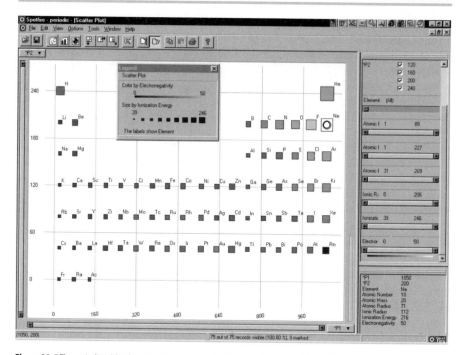

Figure 33.5 The periodic table of elements with color coding to show electronegativity and size coding by ionization energy.

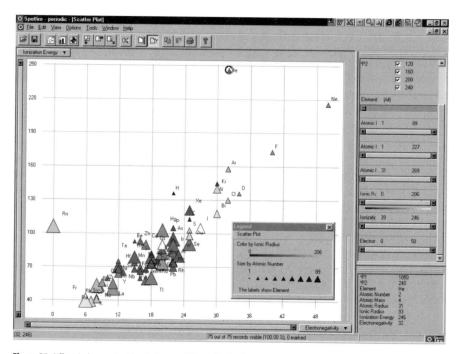

Figure 33.6 Chemicals organized by electronegativity and ionization energy, revealing a strong correlation and two outliers: helium and radon.

33.3 Questions for the Future

The computing industry and the research community are moving ahead with a new generation of systems. In addition to our work, research on information visualization is emerging at key sites such as Georgia Tech's Graphics Visualization and Usability Center, Xerox's Palo Alto Research Center and Lucent Technologies (formerly AT&T Bell Labs) in Naperville, IL. Commercial activity ranges from expansion of existing statistical, spreadsheet, or database packages to include visualization capabilities, for example SPSS and SAS. Specialized visualization tools have emerged from new companies such as Inxight, Visual Insight, Visible Decisions and Spotfire. However, numerous questions remain that are the basis for this research agenda.

Generality: Many creativity support and information visualization tools are designed for a specific type of data and task, so generalization is an important issue. Since the range of information visualization situations includes at least 1D, 2D, 3D, multidimensional, temporal, hierarchical and network data types, it is not clear that a single tool can be useful to a wide range of users (Robertson *et al.*, 1993; Becker *et al.*, 1995; Shneiderman, 1998a). Tasks include presenting meaningful overviews, zooming in on desired items, filtering out undesired items, obtaining details-on-demand, showing relationships among items, extracting information for use in other programs and keeping a history of user actions to allow review and replay. Developing general purpose tools that support the range of data and tasks would be a major step forward.

Integration: Successful support for creativity and practical application of information visualization requires a smooth integration with other tools. The results of a Web or database search should be easily imported (for example by cut and paste) into a visual presentation. Then users should be able to filter the data appropriately and adjust the visualization features, such as x,y axes, color, size or other codings. When an interesting group of items is found, users should be able to select them and paste them into a spreadsheet or statistics package for further processing. At the next stage, the visualization and processed items should be embeddable in a written report, slide presentation, or email note. Email recipients should be able to manipulate the visualization or report still further (Roth *et al.*, 1996).

Perceptual foundations: A necessary foundation is an understanding of the perceptual principles concerning location, color, size, shape, animation and other codings (Rohrer *et al.*, 1999). While much is known about static displays, the dynamic environment of user interfaces is in need of extensive human factors analysis. Preconscious recognition of small numbers of items, simple patterns or outliers from a large group occurs very rapidly (less than 400 milliseconds), but recognition of more complex relationships involving multiple colors or shapes can take much longer. Strategies for rapid panning or zooming are beginning to be understood, but comparisons between these animated approaches, distortion-oriented (fisheye) and dual views would be very helpful (Plaisant *et al.*, 1995; Schaffer *et al.*, 1996). Another key comparison that deserves extensive study is between 2D and 3D visual presentations (Sutcliffe and Patel, 1996). Advocates of each style claim superiority, but the empirical evidence is still shallow.

Cognitive principles: A solid theory for creativity support by way of information visualization would rest on a thorough understanding of cognitive principles to guide design (Card, 1996). Existing design principles such as direct manipulation have been demonstrated to be successful by empirical studies, and they have been widely applied in word processors, spreadsheets, drawing tools and many other environments:

- Visual representation of the "world of action"
  - Objects and actions are shown
  - Tap analogical reasoning by appropriate metaphors and icons
- Rapid, incremental and reversible actions
- Replace typing with pointing/selecting
- Continuous feedback

These principles are helpful to designers but need to be more rigorous if they are to provide predictive power. Another basic principle that has been applied for browsing and searching, might be summarized as the Visual Information Seeking Mantra:

Overview first, zoom and filter, then details-on-demand
Overview first, zoom and filter, then details-on-demand
Overview first, zoom and filter, then details-on-demand
Overview first, zoom and filter, then details-on-demand
Overview first, zoom and filter, then details-on-demand
Overview first, zoom and filter, then details-on-demand
Overview first, zoom and filter, then details-on-demand
Overview first, zoom and filter, then details-on-demand
Overview first, zoom and filter, then details-on-demand

Each line represents a project in which we struggled with a design only to rediscover this principle, and therefore I wrote it down as a continuing reminder. If we can design systems with effective visual displays, direct manipulation interfaces and dynamic queries, then users may be able to responsibly and confidently take on more ambitious tasks. However, empirical studies would be helpful in assessing the benefits.

Collaboration: A key phase of genex, and many creativity models, is the process of consultation with peers and mentors (Olson and Olson, 1997). Such consultations may occur at early, middle or late stages of a creative problem solving process. Users need to conference over some materials using an appropriate communications medium such as a face-to-face meeting, videoconference, telephone, email exchange or printed documents. Therefore creativity support and information visualization tools need to make it easy for users to save, extract, replay and annotate their activities.

33.4 Conclusions

Creativity support is a risky term because it may sound vague and difficult to evaluate. However, it can become a vigorous research topic if work focuses on more identifiable user activities, such as the list of eight offered in Section 33.1.1. This chapter concentrates on the activity of visualizing and explores how information visualization techniques can support creativity. Researchers will have to deal with at least five key questions in order to develop useful software: generality, integration, perceptual foundations, cognitive principles and collaboration.

However, implementation of novel tools is not a sufficient goal. New visualizations and their use must be subjected to rigorous empirical studies to get past the developer's bias and wishful thinking. Evaluations, ranging from controlled experiments to field trials with ethnographic observations, will validate or overturn hypotheses, refine theories, and sharpen our understanding of what to measure. Such studies are likely to be the rapid route to development of advanced information-abundant user interfaces.

Acknowledgments

I greatly appreciate my partners at IBM, NASA and WestGroup for partial support of this research. Thanks to Benjamin Bederson, David Ebert and Jenny Preece for their thoughtful comments on earlier drafts.

References

Ahlberg, C and Shneiderman, B (1994) Visual information seeking: tight coupling of dynamic query filters with starfield displays, in *Proc. ACM CHI'94 Conference: Human Factors in Computing Systems*, ACM, New York, pp. 313–321 and color plates.

Ahlberg, C, Williamson, C and Shneiderman, B (1992) Dynamic queries for information exploration: an implementation and evaluation, in *Proc. ACM CHI'92: Human Factors in Computing Systems*, ACM, New York, pp. 619–626.

Becker, RA, Eick, SG and Wilks, AR (1995) Visualizing network data, *IEEE Transactions on Visualization and Computer Graphics* 1(1), 16–28.

Bederson, BB and Hollan, JD (1994) PAD++: a zooming graphical user interface for exploring alternate interface physics, in *Proc. User Interfaces Software and Technology '94*, ACM, New York, pp. 17–27.

Bertin, J (1983) *Semiology of Graphics*, Madison, WI, University of Wisconsin Press.

Boden, M (1990) *The Creative Mind: Myths & Mechanisms*, New York, Basic Books.

Brooks, F, Jr (1996) The computer scientist as toolsmith II, *Communications of the ACM* 39(3), 61–68.

Bush, V (1945) As we may think, *Atlantic Monthly*, 76(1), 101–108. Also at http://www.theatlantic.com/unbound/flashbks/computer/bushf.htm.

Candy, L (1997) Computers and creativity support: knowledge, visualization and collaboration, *Knowledge-Based Systems* 10, 3–13.

Card, SC (1996) Visualizing retrieved information: a survey, *IEEE Computer Graphics and Applications* 16(2), 63–67.

Card, S, Mackinlay, J and Shneiderman, B (1999) *Readings in Information Visualization: Using Vision to Think*, San Francisco, CA, Morgan Kaufmann.

Couger, D (1996) *Creativity & Innovation in Information Systems Organizations*, Danvers, MA, Boyd & Fraser.

Csikszentmihalyi, M (1996) *Creativity: Flow and the Psychology of Discovery and Invention*, New York, HarperCollins.

De Bono, E (1973) *Lateral Thinking: Creativity Step by Step*, New York, Harper Colophon Books.

Engelbart, DC and English, WK (1968) A research center for augmenting human intellect, *AFIPS Proc. Fall Joint Computer Conference* 33, 395–410.

Hiltz, RS (1984) *Online Communities: A Case Study of the Office of the Future*, Norwood, NJ, Ablex.

Hiltz, RS and Turoff, M (1993) *The Network Nation: Human Communication via Computer*, rev. edn, Cambridge, MA, MIT Press.

Massetti, B (1996) An empirical examination of the value of creativity support systems on idea generation, *MIS Quarterly*, 20(1), 83–97.

Massetti, B, White, NH and Spitler, VK (1999) The impact of the World Wide Web on idea generation, in *Proc. 32nd Hawaii International Conference on System Sciences*, IEEE Press.

Mayer, RE (1992) *Thinking, Problem Solving, Cognition*, 2nd edn, New York, W. H. Freeman.

National Research Council – Committee on a National Collaboratory (1993) *National Collaboratories: Applying Information Technology for Scientific Research*, Washington, DC, National Academy Press.

Olson, GM and Olson, JS (1997) Research on computer supported cooperative work, in *Handbook of Human–Computer Interaction*, 2nd edn (eds. MG Helander, TK Landauer and PV Prabhu), Amsterdam, Elsevier, pp. 1433–1456.

Plaisant, C, Carr, D and Shneiderman, B (1995) Image-browser taxonomy and guidelines for designers, *IEEE Software* 12(2), 21–32.

Plaisant, C, Rose, A, Milash, B, Widoff, S and Shneiderman, B (1996) LifeLines: visualizing personal histories, in *Proc. of ACM CHI'96 Conference: Human Factors in Computing Systems*, New York, ACM, pp. 221–227, 518.

Robertson, GG, Card, SK and Mackinlay, JD (1993) Information visualization using 3D interactive animation, *Communications of the ACM*, 36(4), 56–71.

Rohrer, R, Ebert, D and Sibert, J (1999) A shape-based visual interface for text retrieval, *IEEE Computer Graphics and Applications*, 19.

Rose, A, Eckard, D and Rubloff, G (1998) An application framework for creating simulation-based learning environments, *Univrsity of Maryland Department of Computer Science Technical Report CS-TR-3907.*

Rosner, S and Abt, LE (eds.) (1970) *The Creative Experience*, New York, Dell Publishing.

Roth, SF, Lucas, P, Senn, JA, Gomberg, CC, Burks, MB, Stroffolino, PJ, Kolojejchick, JA and Dunmire, C (1996) Visage: a user interface environment for exploring information, in *Proc. Information Visualization '96*, Los Alamitos, CA, IEEE, pp. 3–12.

Schaffer, D, Zuo, Z, Greenberg, S, Bartram, L, Dill, J, Dubs, S and Roseman, M (1996) Navigating hierarchically clustered networks through fisheye and full-zoom methods, *ACM Transactions on Computer-Human Interaction*, 3(2), 162–188.

Shneiderman, B (1994) Dynamic queries for visual information seeking, *IEEE Software*, 11(6), 70–77.

Shneiderman, B (1998a) *Designing the User Interface: Strategies for Effective Human–computer Interaction*, 3rd edn, Reading, MA, Addison-Wesley.

Shneiderman, B (1998b) Codex, memex, genex: the pursuit of transformational technologies, *International Journal of Human–Computer Interaction*, 10(2), 87–106.

Shneiderman, B (1999) Creating creativity for everyone: User interfaces for supporting innovation, *Univ. of Maryland Dept of Computer Science Technical Report.*

Shneiderman, B, Feldman, D and Rose, A (1999) Visualizing digital library search results with categorical and hierarchical axes, *University of Maryland Department of Computer Science Technical Report CS-TR-3992.*

Sutcliffe, A and Patel, U (1996) 3D or not 3D: is it nobler in the mind?, in *Proc. British HCI Conference*, pp. 79–94.

Tufte, E (1983) *The Visual Display of Quantitative Information*, Cheshire, CT, Graphics Press.

Tufte, E (1990) *Envisioning Information*, Cheshire, CT, Graphics Press.

Tufte, E (1997) *Visual Explanations: Images and Quantities, Evidence and Narrative*, Cheshire, CT, Graphics Press.

Williamson, C and Shneiderman, B (1992) The Dynamic HomeFinder: evaluating dynamic queries in a real-estate information exploration system, in *Proc. ACM SIGIR'92 Conference*, Copenhagen, Denmark, June, pp. 338–346. Reprinted in Shneiderman, B (ed.) (1993) *Sparks of Innovation in Human–Computer Interaction*, Norwood, NJ, Ablex, pp. 295–307.

Author Index